Society in India

Society in India

Concepts, Theories and Recent Trends

RAM AHUJA

RAWAT PUBLICATIONS
Jaipur • New Delhi • Bangalore • Guwahati • Kolkata

ISBN 978-81-7033-544-3 (hardback)

Reprinted, 2026

Published by
Prem Rawat for **Rawat Publications**
Satyam Apts, Sector 3, Jawahar Nagar, Jaipur 302 004 (India)
Phone: 0141 265 1748 / 7006
E-mail: info@rawatbooks.com
Website: www.rawatbooks.com

New Delhi Office
4858/24, Ansari Road, Daryaganj, New Delhi 110 002
Phone: 011 2326 3290

Printed and bound in India

Contents

Preface

This book marks a deviation from my previous books. It presents a traditional-modern framework of different systems—social, economic, political, religious, educational, rural, urban and tribal—and discusses some crucial problems and issues. The traditional approach establishes relationship amongst sociology, history and other social sciences and focuses on established values and ideologies while the modern framework takes interest in contemporary changes, social developments, and 'march of progress'—all of which raise a whole range of new questions. The sociological framework focuses on 'what was', 'what is', and 'what is likely to be'. Each chapter presents the contemporary variants, the emerging components and the future perspective. Such an approach is functional in examining issues of transition from past to present. The functioning of various systems in a society requires in-depth analysis as also theoretical evaluation.

The present Indian society is no longer perceived as a traditional society. It is now viewed as a modern society. But changes in systems in modern society brought about by various planned measures have also to focus on the negative consequences of the measures adopted. If reservation policy is functional today and if it proves to be dysfunctional after two-three decades, will the power elite manage to change it? If various movements by youth, women, peasants and the weaker sections of society are not contained, how will these accentuate social unrest? Evaluation of social issues like these requires to be presented both in the existing and the emerging societies. While an attempt has been made in this book to analyse and review all important aspects of the various systems, it does not aim at providing large-scale and ambitious analysis. The intention has not been to present any new theory but to explain as to what has been happening in the Indian society from time to time.

Over the years, I have written several books—both in English and Hindi—focusing on different aspects of crime, women and social problems, etc. This book recognises the importance of stimulus materials for competitive examinations. As such, the analysis of various topics attempts to give a sense of development of the subject and provides access to different sources. The emerging sociology has to lay emphasis on a constant interrogation of constantly changing society. Frankly, it is not being claimed that there would be no omissions and no weak chapters. However, an honest effort has been made to cover extensively all the major aspects of the systems. I have discussed different viewpoints, analysed typologies developed by eminent scholars, examined various theoretical explanations, and drawn from the contributions of some of the most important and well-known scholars in their fields to make the book more comprehensive in scope. I am confident that students will find the book a welcome contribution. Keeping in view the perceptions of different categories of students, including those studying sociology at the masters level, I have tried to discuss even those components of the topics prescribed in various competitive examinations which students generally avoid for the want of available literature. The object is to create a wider understanding of the subject in its broadest sense.

The chapters have been arranged in sequential clusters as presented in the prescribed courses of the Indian Civil Services and State Civil Services competitive examinations. Discussion of some aspects not prescribed in the syllabus is intended to be student friendly. I hope and trust, the book will be of some use to the students for whom it is meant as it provides the required data and a scientific analysis of various systems and issues in a readable and comprehensive manner.

Ram Ahuja

Author's Note

Since long I had been thinking of working on a book in which students offering sociology in competitive examinations for the Indian Civil Services, State Civil Services, Banking Services and NET, etc. find adequate and detailed discussion and analysis of various topics generally prescribed for these examinations. Though my two earlier books—Indian Social System and Social Problems in India—did cover many topics prescribed for the competitive examinations, yet there were quite a few topics which were not specifically covered in these books, e.g., economic system, political system, religious system, rural system, urban system, tribal system, educational system, and the host of others. The present book aims at bridging this gap by expanding the coverage of topics. The topics discussed in the earlier books have been revised and updated with fresh data and new facts. Efforts have also been made to rectify the shortcomings that had inadvertently crept into. I hope, students appearing in career examinations would find this book quite useful—at least, for one of the two prescribed papers in sociology. Postgraduate students in sociology in the Indian Universities, would surely find the book equally helpful and full of enlightenment.

I would like to express my sincere thanks to my colleague Dr. G.S. Kewalramani, and to my son Dr. Mukesh Ahuja for assisting me in various ways in the preparation of this book, especially with regard to locating the necessary books and journals from different sources. I am also grateful to my son Sanjay Ahuja for typing the manuscript on a computer. Last but not least, my grateful thanks to my wife for her constant encouragement and support. I look forward to receiving comments from students, teachers and other readers to enable me to further improve this book.

Ram Ahuja

1 Historical Moorings of the Indian Society

TRADITIONAL HINDU SOCIAL ORGANISATION

Traditional, Modern and Post-Modern Societies

A society may be classified as traditional, modern, or post-modern. *Traditional* society lays emphasis on religion (and magic) in behavioural norms and values, implying continuity (deep links) with a real or imagined past. It widely accepts rituals, sacrifices and holy feasts. Broadly speaking, traditional society is described as one in which: (1) individual's status is determined by his birth and he does not strive for social mobility; (2) individual's behaviour is governed by customs, traditions, norms and values having deep links with the past. The social practices of people vary only slightly from generation to generation; (3) social organisation (stable pattern of social relationships of individuals and sub-groups within a society that provides regularity and predictability in social interaction) is based on hierarchy; (4) kinship relations predominate in interaction and individual identifies himself with primary groups; (5) individual is given more importance in social relations than what his position actually warrants; (6) people are conservative; (7) economy is simple, i.e., tool economy (and not machine economy) prevails and is conspicuous and economic productivity above subsistence level is relatively low; and (8) mythical thought (and not logical reasoning) predominates in society.

Modernity is substantial break with traditional society. *Modern* society focuses on science and reason. According to Stuart Hall (Hall and

Gay, 1996; also see O' Donnell, Mike, 1977:40), the six distinctive characteristics of modern society (which also distinguish it from traditional society) are: (1) The decline of religion and rise of a secular materialistic culture (religious characteristic). (2) The replacing of feudal economy (getting services by the owner of land) by an economy in which money system provides the medium for exchange (in trade) based on large-scale production and consumption of commodities for the market, extensive ownership of private property, and accumulation of capital on a long-term basis (economic characteristic). (3)The dominance of secular political authority over state and marginalisation of religious influence from state/political matters (political characteristic). (4) The decline of social order based on simple division of labour and the development of new division of labour based on specialisation, the emergence of new classes, and changed relations between men and women (social characteristic). (5) The forming of new nations (communities-ethnic or national) having their own identities and traditions to suit their own purposes, e.g., rejection of aristocracy and monarchy by France, Britain accepting monarchy only as a symbol, Egypt rejecting monarchy and accepting democracy, and so on (cultural characteristic). (6) The rise of scientific, rationalist way of looking at the world (intellectual characteristic). Thus, while the traditional society is characterised by ritual, custom, collectivity, community ownership, status quo and continuity and simple division of labour, the modern society is characterised by rise of science, emphasis on reason and rationality, belief in progress, viewing government and the state as essential in bringing about progress, emphasis on economic development and complex division of labour, perceiving human-beings as capable of acquiring great control over nature and environment and seeing world in terms of dualisms or opposites. *Post-modern* society, or late modernity, concentrates on critical awareness and is concerned about the damaging effects of applied science on nature, environment and humanity. It points out risks and unintended negative consequences of the pursuit of progress. From nationalism (emphasised in modern society), it moves to the process of globalisation. Instead of giving importance to economic development (as in modern society), it gives importance to culture. Unlike modern society (which sees world in terms of opposites or dualisms), post-modern society views unities, similarities and connections as important.

Traditional Indian Society: Three Perspectives

With the above concept and characteristics of traditional society, how can

Indian society be sociologically perceived as traditional society? Three perspectives may be used in sociologically understanding the traditional Indian society: functionalist, Marxist, and social action. Durkheim's functionalist perspective is based on the approach that major social institutions and sub-systems (e.g., family, kinship, economic, etc.) exist to meet fundamental human needs (like procreation, social support, production, consumption). The Marxist perspective is based on the approach that class conflict is a fundamental social force and functioning of society is affected by classes with conflicting interests. Weber's social action perspective holds that individuals affect and create society rather than society affects and makes individuals, or that it is not society that forms and structures the 'self's' experience but the 'self' helps to create its own social experience.

The first two perspectives are structural in nature, i.e., they are primarily concerned with how society affects individual and group behaviour rather than with how individuals and groups create society. (In fact, the third perspective is also viewed as structural). Thus, the sort of issue a structural sociologist would be interested in is: how religious beliefs and values, or science and reasoning, or caste and class, or family and kinship group, or tool and industrial economies, or individual's social-structural position affect his/her chances of performing roles expected of him by the society. While functionalism stresses consensus in social behaviour, Marxism and social action perspectives stress conflict in society. Following O' Donnell (1997:6), the questions which can be constructed and answered about traditional Indian society with structural perspective are: (1) how is society constructed; (2) how does it operate; (3) how are some groups in society more powerful than others; (4) what causes social change; (5) is society based on consensus or conflict; and (6) what is the relationship of an individual to society? We will analyse traditional Indian society in terms of these six bases.

TRADITIONAL HINDU SOCIETY: BASIC TENETS AND DOCTRINES

Hindu View of Life: *Karma* and *Dharma*

Before answering the above-mentioned questions pertaining to the traditional Indian society, let us examine what was the Hindu view of life in the Vedic thought? This view was that man is altogether composed of desires (*kama*). As are his desires, so is his discretion/insight (*kratu*); as is his discretion, so are his deeds, as are his deeds, so is his destiny. Hence, if a man has left any desires in him while he lives, he takes birth again, but if no desires are left in him, he becomes one with *Brahma* (God). Under the circumstances, one must eradicate discretion (*kratu*) in order to destroy his desires. It is desire that binds a man to this world and makes him liable to birth and death. *Karma* (deed) is, thus, only a connecting link between desires and rebirth. Hence, on getting rid of desires, the mortal becomes immortal and attains salvation (*moksha*).

It will be wrong to hold that this is the only view of the Hindu philosophy. In fact, the Hindu literature presents varied approaches to ultimate reality. One approach was made at a later stage in the *Gita* to the problem of dispensing with desires. The *Gita* presents a new philosophy of life—the philosophy of *karma*. The *Gita* insisted on sublimation rather than on eradication of desires and that was to be done by knowing the true nature of *karma* (Kapadia, 1972:13-14).

The Hindu philosophy believes in the continuity of the present with the past in which it is rooted, and its projection into the future. The Hindu respect for tradition has a purpose. It seeks to achieve homogeneity and harmony of thought. The different phases merely represent differences in emphasis in different historical periods. For example, truth is *dharma* in *Satyayuga*, *yajna* (sacrifice) in *Tratayuga*, *jnana* (knowledge) in *Dvaparayuga*, and *dana* (alms) in *Kaliyuga*. The Hindu philosophy also believes in certain theological ideas such as *papa*, *punya*, *dharma*, etc. We will discuss these ideas as basic tenets of Hinduism.

Basic Tenets of Hinduism

Focusing on the basic tenets and the normative principles of Hinduism, it may be said that Hinduism believes in equality, *karma* and *rebirth* ideas, *moksha* (salvation) as the ultimate goal of life, toleration as individual character, non-violence as important feature of social life, and the merger of individual soul into the ultimate soul? Singh (1973:31) is of the opinion that the normative principles of Hinduism are based on beliefs, ideals and logic of permissiveness (permission that it shall be done), liberalism (generous and free views, opinions and principles), being and becoming, creation and destruction, hedonism (belief that pleasure is the chief goal), utilitarianism, and spiritual transcendence (outside the range of human experience, reason and description, etc.) Broadly speaking, the basic tenets of Hinduism may be described as below:

Theological Ideas

Hinduism believes in certain theological ideas (a series of theories about the nature of God and of the foundations of religious belief) such as *punarjanma* (rebirth), immortality of *atma* (soul), *papa* (sin), *punya* (merit), *karma* (deeds), *dharma* (morality), and *moksha* (salvation). The idea of *karma* teaches a Hindu that he is born into a particular social group (caste/family) because of his deeds he performed in his previous life (*purva janma*). The idea of *dharma* tells him that if he follows good deeds in the present birth, he will be born in a high social group in the next birth. The idea of *moksha* reminds him that his *papa* and *punya* will determine the release of his soul from the chain of birth and death.

Pollution and Purity

The ideas of pollution and purity are equally important in Hinduism. Though the rules of pollution and purity vary from region to region, yet they cover a large sector of life everywhere. They are important in commensal relations, in touching or maintaining physical distance from the members of other group, in inter-caste marriages, and in personal life of an individual on occasions like birth, marriage, menstruation, death, offering prayers, etc. The concept of pollution is related to birth and not to cleanliness. A person has to undergo a purificatory rite, simple or elaborate, according to the seriousness of the violation of rules of purity. In such matters, it is the caste council that takes the necessary disciplinary action.

Hierarchy

Hierarchy in Hinduism exists in terms of: (a) a division in *varnas* and castes; (b) in charismatic qualities (*guna*) of individuals (the highest and most virtuous being *sattva*, that is, virtues associated with sages and the Brahmins, followed by *rajas*, that is, commitment to action and power as attributed to kings and Kshatriyas, and *tamas*, the lowest in hierarchy, associated with dullness and profane inclinations); and (c) in values regarding life-goals, like *kama* (that is, pursuit of sex and material goals of sensory enjoyments), *artha* (that is, achieving wealth), *dharma* (that is, moral obligations in social, religious and cultural realms), and *moksha* (that is, pursuit of salvation from the chain of birth and rebirth).

Idol-Worship

The most noticeable common feature of Hindu religion is its belief in idol-worship. The worshipped idol is not uniform but it varies according to the sect. Each sect keeps its idol (Krishna, Rama, Shiva, Ganesh, Hanuman, etc.), in a separate temple and worships it on specific occasions. The idea of not allowing *Malecchas* (including Muslims and untouchables) in these temples was more in the nature of protecting the temple from pollution rather than confrontation with another religion.

Monolithic Character

The major characteristic of Hinduism is that it is not a uniform monolithic (single God) religion, but a juxtaposition (placing side by side) of flexible religious sects. This flexibility is its strength, allowing the existence even of non-caste, anti-Vedic groups, denying approval of the injunctions of the *Dharmashastras*.

Tolerance

Tolerating opinions, beliefs, customs, behaviour, etc. of other religions, castes is an important feature of Hindu religion. But is Hinduism really tolerant? One view is that Hinduism is a secular and tolerant philosophy as it embraces within its fold different cults and sects, even as all Hindus swear by the common (Hindu) divinities. The segregation of communities and the relatively distinct religious identity of these led to the possibility of each group leading a comparatively separate existence. The clash could only come in the competition for patronage. This explains the notion of tolerance in Hindu religion.

But there is also a group of scholars which refers to religious intolerance of Hinduism. It refers to sectarian rivalries and conflicts. Initially, the Shaiva sect persecuted Buddhists and Jains. Buddhist monasteries were destroyed and monks were killed by Mihirakula and Shashanka in the northern India in mid-first millennium A.D. The rewriting of texts from Vaisnava perspective was another form of religious intolerance because it was done only to correct the Jaina perspective. Even among the ascetic groups, hostility was known to exist between the Dasnamis and Bairagis over the question of precedence at the Kumbh Mela. Such antagonism was not that of the 'Hindu' against another religion but that of a particular sect towards other sects.

Segregation

Yet another characteristic of Hindu religion is that it supports the segregation of castes in social relations, worship and religious beliefs. The nature of segregation depends on the status of varnas/castes which were created from the body of *purusha* (Brahmins from his mouth, Kshatriyas from his arms, Vaishyas from his thighs, and Sudras from his feet). The argument given against this is that it was only certain sects and certain prominent Brahmins, the most prominent being Shankaracharya, which believed in such segregation. But this argument is not correct because all Hindus believe that membership in a particular group is determined by birth and not merit. However, it is said that various sects in Hinduism could not have flourished and would have decayed if intellectual positions had been entirely determined by birth in a particular group.

Non-violence
Hinduism is characterised by non-violence. However, a question is raised: Does Hinduism really believe in non-violence? One school accepts that Hindus are non-violent people, but other school maintains that religious violence is not alien to Hinduism. The message given in the *Gita* is surely not non-violent. The emphasis on sacrifices is surely not based on the ideal of non-violence. But then Bhakti cult, predominant through the subcontinent by the seventeenth century, surely was against the use of violence.

It may be said that non-violence was characterised in Hinduism only after devotional and ritual aspect of Hinduism was emphasised, or *Vaisnavism* and *Saivism* cults emerged after the twelfth century A.D., or devotional-liberal traditions grew in the fifteenth and sixteenth centuries A.D. with the emergence of saints (*bhaktas*) like Kabir and Tulsidas in Uttar Pradesh, Guru Nanak in Punjab, Chaitanya in Bengal, Meera Bai in Rajasthan, and Tukaram and Ramdas in Maharashtra. These saints not only carried religious beliefs to the people in their own languages but they also changed the ritual-ridden religious beliefs into simple humanistic values, criticising orthodoxy.

***Purushartha*: Values of Hindu Culture**
Hindu culture centres round four values: *kama*, *artha*, *dharma* and *moksha*. This four-fold value order is based on the understanding that the human personality has many needs (see, Kanal, 1955:8). Man needs food and sex, power and property, and human society and relations with the universe, i.e., human society. The satisfaction of bodily needs is *kama*. The satisfaction of needs of power and property is *artha*. The satisfaction of needs of social order is *dharma*. The satisfaction of needs of oneness with the universe is *moksha*.

Kama, in its general sense, means the desire for pleasurable experiences through the five senses of sight, hearing, touch, taste and smell under the guidance of the mind. The question may be raised: Is seeking the pleasures of body good? The answer is that pain and suffering is in itself bad. Today, just as we are all agreed that misery and poverty of the masses be removed by preventing and treating their diseases, improving their economic lot, providing them housing and recreational etc., facilities, similarly body pleasures also reduce man's sufferings. For example, tasty food gives pleasure but if it causes indigestion and becomes injurious to health, we have pain of ill-health. To achieve pleasure of health, we stop taking spicy food. Thus, pain caused by one pleasure is removed by another pleasure through the principle of selection between competing pleasures. Where the sense satisfactions are not guided by the mind, it is not *kama* at human level. Human society has developed the objects of sense satisfaction. We have developed cookery, fashions, picnic sites, gardens, music, art, and so forth. All these developments are progress in the satisfaction of *kama. Kama* includes sex pleasure too since it is a bodily pleasure. Freud has also held that all bodily pleasures mature into sex pleasures. Thus, *kama* is a value which refers to satisfactions through the senses.

Artha is the need of human personality to acquire power over nature and man. The conquest of Everest and control on floods, famines and epidemics is an expression of a desire for power over nature. Science is an expression of a desire for power over nature while wealth is a form of power over nature and men. Today we speak of power politics. The ideals of dictators like Mussolini and Hitler were not sense pleasures but power over the globe. The declaration of five nuclear powers (America, Russia, Britain, China, and France) in 1998 that they will not destroy their nuclear weapons and asking India (which had conducted Pokhran tests in May 1998 purely for national security reasons) to sign the CTBT was the expression of a desire of power over the globe. Indian culture views such desires as *artha*.

Artha is both a desire for power over nature and man and also a desire for wealth. Is this desire valuable? If yes, why do we condemn capitalism and power politics? *Artha* becomes evil when it spurns all other demands of human nature, when it is not controlled by righteousness, i.e., by consideration of others' rights, or others' needs of personality. The modern progress of America, Russia, Europe, etc. in science and industry is due to *artha*. We call their civilisations materialistic because they are engrossed in conquest over nature and man. If *artha* is allowed unrestricted play, it may destroy its own achievements and lead mankind to final extinction. The ethical principles of *dharma* must control the sensuous, economic and political cravings of man.

Dharma stands for the principle of integration that works through the entire gamut of life in the individual, in the community, and in the world at large. Anything that breaks up the integrity of the individual and society is *adharma. Dharma*, thus, refers to duties which individuals must fulfill if society is not to disorganise. Just as a college/university has rules for teachers (taking classes, completing courses within a specific period, etc.) for students (attending classes, paying fees, taking examinations, etc.), and for administrative and ministerial staff (maintaining records, conducting examinations, and so on), and, adherence to rules by all the elements keeps the system stable and any deviation leads to collapse of the entire system, in the same way all individuals in society have duties to perform. What guide these duties are customs, conventions and laws. Thinkers like Manu, Ramanuja, etc., have talked of these duties in *Dharmshastras* to regulate human relations and have considered them valuable for our existence, enjoyment and evolution.

In Indian culture, what underlines these duties, according to Kanal (1955) are: (a) *varnashram dharmas* or *vishesha dharmas* (b) *sadharan dharmas* or *samanya dharmas*. The *varnashram* duties are divided in four stages of life: student life, family life, retired life, and life of renunciation. These are also related to professional roles. *Sadharan dharma* refers to common duties not attached to one stage of life or professional role, e.g., refraining from theft (*asteya*), restraint of anger (*akrodha*), forgiveness (*kshama*), refraining from injury to living-beings (*ahimsa*), cleanliness (*shoucha*), and truth (*satya*). These (*samanya*) duties are duties of man to man.

Dharma also includes *virtues* (duties and virtues are different). 'Duty' refers to action and 'virtue' refers to inner disposition of mind. For example, preventing a person from indulging in illicit sexual acts is a duty and being free from sexual thoughts is a virtue. Since virtue is purity of mind, virtuous life is higher than performance of duty. To *be* good is better than to *do* good. Duties are performed without much thought about what makes them good. Virtue leads to *reflection* over right and wrong. Duties represent *conventional* morality and virtues represent *reflective* morality. There is a difference between a son who loves his parents and a son who just provides economic support to his parents. The latter does what the society prescribes as his duties towards his parents while the former performs many acts of kindness which are not prescribed by the society. Virtues are dynamic whereas duties are static. But duties lead to virtues. Dharma helps to keep society together, virtues create integrity in our minds.

Moksha refers to a state of liberation or freedom. Shankara distinguishes between *Mukhya Proyojanas* or ultimate ends and *Gouna Proyojanas* or secondary ends. Desiring anything for itself is called *Mukhya Proyojana* but achieving some for *Mukhya Proyojana* is *Gouna Proyojana*. Pleasure is a case of *Mukhya Proyojana* while training for a job, and earning of money are *Gouna Proyojana*. Shankara holds that pleasure is of two kinds: empirical pleasure and transcendental pleasure. The former comes through the medium of our body while the latter is spiritual pleasure. *Moksha* consists in the realisation of the *identity* of the soul with the *Brahma* or total reality.

Hindu culture prescribes two stages in attaining *moksha* (liberation):

Pravrtti Marg and *Nivrtti Marg*. The former is a stage of regularised satisfaction of bodily needs and consists in the enjoyment of desirable objects of the world, while the latter consists in developing *vairagya* or detachment from things of the world. The two stages are continuous, one leading to the other. (see, Kanal, 1955).

Ashramas: Stages of Life in Realising the Ideal of Life

Ashramas are the stages of life which provide training and environment for realising the ideal of our life. There are four *ashramas* in all: *Brahmacharya* (student life), *Garhasthya* (family life), *Vanaprastha* (retired life), and *Sannyasa* (life of renunciation). The first two provide the training and environment for the *Pravrtti Marg* and the last two for the *Nivrtti Marg* of development. Each stage has its own specific duties (*Vishesha* Dharmas). We will discuss the duties of a *garhasthi* (householder), a student (*Brahmacharin*), a retired person, and a renunciated person separately. Just as *ashramas* refer to specific duties in life, *varnas* refer to duties related to the four professional roles in life: the profession of scholarship, of defence and administration, of production and distribution, and of unskilled labour. Thus, along with *ashramas*, we will analyse the *varnas* too.

Brahmacharya Ashram: It is a specific period of education for all young persons before they can grow independent to work for life. At home, a child gets education in how to eat, walk, talk, dress, meet other people, and behave in their presence. In some castes and communities, a child also learns how to plough land, make shoes, do pottery work, ironsmith's work, goldsmith's work, carpentry work, and so on. But he does not get education in reading and writing or skilled and professional training. He gets this education from teachers (*gurus*). During this period of education, he has to follow some ideals and live in a specific environment. In the ancient past, schools were boarding schools where a child was admitted at the age of 8-12 years, after following certain ceremonies and imparted knowledge, skills and crafts, general and physical education, and training in logic. What was important was 'comradeship' between the teacher and the taught, skills, knowledge and dedication of the teacher, and commitment of students to certain values and ideals. The students were taught discipline of life during this stage and were asked to take four vows of sexual purity (to check sex indulgence), simplicity in food and dress (to generate a sense of equality, fraternity and independence), respect for and obedience to the teacher (to create discipline) and enjoying self-exertion in acquiring knowledge and offering prayer (reciting hymns and meditation) for the cooperation of the divine powers. Thus, chastity, simplicity, hard work, devotion to knowledge, and spiritual reality were the ideals of student life.

Garhasthya Ashram: This period of life covers an active period of effective membership of society and covers 25 years of life after the first 25 years of education. This is householder's life, a married life. The ideal marriage was considered one which was performed for *moksha* or final liberation and intellectual companionship through the performance of household duties, including upbringing of children and offering reverence (*shradha*) to ancestors. Thus, by developing virtues of purity of heart, fidelity, chastity and mutual love, marriage is raised from being merely a biological association. Indian culture considers marriage not merely as an association but as absolute oneness. The marriage ceremony binds a man and a woman into a single complete being of which one half is the man and the other half is the woman. The oneness is not to last for a lifetime but it is to be continuous birth after birth. Thus, since marriage is for spiritual ends of oneness (as different from union motivated by biological and social ends), it is regarded as a *sacrament* and not as a contract.

Vanaprastha Ashram: After the responsibilities to children are over, the parents are expected to take to social welfare work, so that they do not remain entrapped in *moha* (attachment). The idea is not to retire to forests and live in a place away from human habitation but to live in villages, away from thickly populated cities. Thus, the idea of third stage is to develop a new level of interest and action and not merely a retirement into a particular place. The idea also is that people in far off places (villages) will get an opportunity to consult for their problems those who have spent their best years in that field. Even kings and rulers visited retired people for similar purposes. Thus, *vanaprastha* people were superior guides on social problems. The retirement of the old people (after 50 years of age, which is not a fixed age but is an average age which permits variations) also gives an opportunity to the youth to make experiments and contribute to the variety and richness of life. Very late retirement of the 'old' denies the opportunity to the young of initiation into new fields of activity. *Vanaprastha* stage does not expect husband and wife to break up their relationship. It is left to the option of the couple. But they are expected to lead an austere and ascetic life. The cultural importance of this third stage is that after enjoying physical pleasures when the body ages, a person experiences a sense of frustration and a sense of degeneracy. One wishes to return to bodily pleasures by artificial stimulation. By retiring, one is saved from frustrations. The decline in biological urges (sex, self-assertion, etc.) is compensated by interest in human welfare.

Sanyasa Ashram: *Sanyasa* is the final stage in life's growth. It differs from the *vanaprastha* stage in two respects—in the development of *inter-*

ests and in the development of *motivation*. While the dominant interest in *grahasthya* stage is the family, in *vanaprastha* stage it is human society as a whole, in *sanyasa* stage, the interest is the Universe with its universal consciousness. Interest in the *universal consciousness* is identification with total existence in its deepest being. As regards motivation in *grahasthya* stage, the individual is motivated to seek the interest of members of family, while in the *vanaprastha* stage, he is motivated to work for the interest of a particular group or community or human society. In both cases, if interests are achieved, the *grahasthi* and the *vanaprasthi* feel happy and experience pleasure; if not, they feel unhappy and experience pain. When motivation is related to an end, success or failure in them leads to pleasure or pain respectively. Such actions are called *interested actions*, i.e., actions inspired by fruit of action. Contrary to these, action in *sanyasa* is disinterested action. Let us take the example of speaking truth. A person may speak truth when it pays him, another person may do so even if he has to lose by it. One does it (speaks truth) viewing it as a duty or a command that comes from conscience without the calculation of gains or losses, or even at the cost of his life. Only a *sanyasi* will be motivated to perform a disinterested action which is not desirous of any fruits here or hereafter. The simple dress of a *sanyasi* symbolises the ideal of life for which he stands and lives. A *sanyasi* surrenders home and possessions because he perceives the whole Universe as his home. He is above fears, passions and hatred. Thus, *sanyasa* is not a life of inaction but a life of action risen to the highest level of motivation and widest interest.

It may, however, be noted that these stages of life are meant for average persons. These are not necessary for a genius or for an extraordinarily gifted person. Persons like Tagore, (and Charles Dickens) never went to school. Persons like Shelley and Wordsworth did not have much college education and yet they were master poets. A genius can by-pass any stage(s) and reach the highest stage.

Varnas: Four-fold Order of Society

Varna order is different from the caste system. While the latter is believed to be the greatest blot on Indian culture, since it has divided the society into conflicting camps, perpetrated harsh sufferings on a large section of the Indian people, and has made social justice difficult, or has proved socially monstrous, politically suicidal, morally obnoxious and economically disastrous, the former is the division of people into groups on the basis of aptitudes and abilities and vocations. The aptitudes and abilities are classified as those (a) for scholarship, (b) for administration and defence, (c) for production and distribution, and (d) for unskilled labour. The first group of people came to be called *brahmins* who were engaged in priestly function, teaching, medicine etc.; the second group *kshatriyas*, who were engaged in fighting, ruling and administration; the third group *vaishyas* who were engaged in agriculture, trade and commerce; and the last group *sudras* who were engaged in unskilled work under the direction of the members of other three groups.

The Brahmins have the qualities of self restraint, austerity, purity, serenity, forgiveness, simplicity, wisdom and philosophic insight into truth and reality. The Kshatriyas have the qualities of courage, strength, firmness, skillfulness, charitableness, and administrative ability. The Vaishyas have the qualities of hard work, intelligence, and quick decision-making. The Sudras lack abilities and aptitudes; hence they have to work under others' direction and accept their authority and dominance.

The duties (*dharmas*) of Brahmins are: offering prayers, performing ceremonies and sacrifices, and teaching. The duties of Kshatriyas are: protecting people from external aggression and internal disturbances as well as governing them, punishing the wicked and contributing liberally for nation-building institutions. The duties of Vaishyas are: engaging in agriculture, procuring commodities from others and selling them, rearing cattle and rendering help to the poor and the needy. The duties of Sudras are to do those things which others want them to do. Sudras are not permitted to read *Vedas* or observe Vedic rites or recite *mantras* (incantations).

Since a person or a group was entitled to a *varna* membership by satisfying the qualifications, any individual or a group could find a place in any of the *varnas*, if he/it satisfied the qualifications. Thus, membership of a *varna* was not determined by birth but by qualifications. A Sudra became a Brahmin in his life by sheer merit; a Brahmin became a Sudra if he did not study the *Vedas*; and so also a Kshatriya or a Vaishya. The *Bhagwad Gita* also states that the four varnas are constituted on the principle of *guna*, i.e., natural and acquired qualities and character, and *karma*, i.e., calling and profession.

Some scholars have, however, maintained that varna system was as rigid as caste system today. A few examples of upgrading of individuals mentioned in some early religious books (say, of Vasistha who was born of a prostitute, Vyasa of a fisher-woman, Parasara of a low-born girl) were exceptions rather than a rule.

Castes

Castes in principle refer to division of people into *groups* on the basis of *birth* and giving particular privileges to some groups and denying similar privileges to others. These groups (i.e. castes) have their own *ethos*, i.e., their own way of life, their ideas of right and wrong and their customs and manners. The motive underlying the caste system was racial and ethnic. India was subjected to racial invasion one after another. Even at the beginning of history, India consisted of people/tribes of different races—Dravidians, Mongols, Mediterraneans. Later on, people of other races—the Persians, the Greeks and the Scythians—settled down in India. When other countries (like Britain, America) faced the racial problem by extermination, conversion (including converting the way of life) and denying all human rights (e.g., denying the protection of the law), India faced it by adjustment process, i.e., mutual adjustment in a manner that each racial group was able to develop its own pattern of life. To start with, the migrant racial groups were not rigid in terms of commensal, social and marital, etc. relations, in beliefs and customs, and were elastic to shelter most of the indigenous populations of India but gradually they became rigid. Initially, the number of these groups was small but gradually, many groups changed their callings as well as way of life and assumed new names. These groups came to be known as castes (*jatis*) and their number went on increasing. Each caste, motivated to preserve its characteristic ways of life, imposed various social and economic restrictions on interaction with others. Thus emerged new and new castes, as well as the division of castes into sub-castes. By the Gupta period (300 A.D. to 500 A.D), the caste system became very rigid and the ascendancy of Brahmins over all other castes came to be established. It was this rigidity, Brahmins' superiority and various restrictions imposed on the low caste Hindus, that came to be attacked, starting with Buddha and later on by various *Bhagtas* after the initiation of Bhakti movement. But the (caste) system remained rigid till the Britishers started, in the last quarter of the 19th century and first quarter of the 20th century, the process of industrialisation and with it urbanisation, and spread of education, and the social ideologies preached by great scholars like Ramakrishna, Vivekananda, Gandhi, etc., attacked the caste system. Today, the caste system has lost much of its hold on its members, though it cannot be said that the caste system has disappeared or will disappear in future. Now that the caste system has come to play a crucial role in politics and the scheduled castes and the backward castes, which form a good percentage of the total population of our country have come to enjoy certain privileges (like reservation of seats in jobs, educational institutions, legislatures, etc., and getting scholarships, age concessions and so on), and new vested interests have arisen, it appears that caste system will continue to exist in our society.

INDIAN SOCIETY THROUGH THE AGES

Impact of Cultural Renaissance and Buddhism

The Vedic philosophy of early Hinduism was influenced by Buddhism and Jainism. Though both developed as separate religions yet they had deep roots in the Hindu tradition. Jainism had the patronage of urban-mercantile community while Buddhism had princely patronage. Both emphasised the value of continuity (predestination, rebirth and transmigration) and criticised hierarchy (belief in *varna* and caste system). Both rejected the rituals of sacrifice in temples and talked of non-violence. The membership of Buddhism was open to all castes and both the sexes. Buddhism focused on soul liberation through *nirwan* (salvation), while Jainism referred to soul liberation through inculcation of a spirit of moral virtues through self-restraints. In short, it may be said that Buddhism and Jainism have an atheistic world-view whereas Hinduism is based on theistic beliefs. In a way, Buddhism and Jainism protested against some important characteristics of Hinduism like its rigid formalism, tyrannical ritualism, value system based on hierarchy, supremacy of Brahmins, and religious orthodoxy.

Hindu beliefs and values were further affected by the preachings of Shankaracharya (ninth century), Ramanujacharya (1017-1137 A.D. that is, eleventh and twelfth centuries), and Madhavacharya (fourteenth century), who established monasteries in different corners of the country for propagating monotheism. Ramanuja founded Vaishnava sect and got followers from Jains, Shaivities and low castes. The Lingayat sect in South India converted many non-Brahmins to the exclusive worship of Shiva.

The devotional schools emerged between the fifteenth and the sixteenth centuries which attempted to popularise some new values in the Hindu religion. Saints like Kabir (1440-1518), Guru Nanak (1469-1538), Ramananda (fourteenth and fifteenth centuries), Chaitanya (1485-1535), Mira (1504-1550), Tulsidas (1532-1623), Tukaram and Ramdas, etc., emphasised equalitarian and non-hierarchical value system in Hinduism. They also made efforts towards liberalisation of the Hindu tradition and its synthesis with Islam.

Impact of Islam

Islam influenced Hindu ideals in the medieval period. Though attacks by Muslims on India had started in the tenth century but it was more from the fifteenth century onwards that the impact of Islamic culture on Hindu great tradition was observed. Islam does not believe in idol-worship. It is monotheistic and non-hierarchical, that is, it believes in equality. Though both Islam and Hinduism are oriented to the principle of holism (collectivism), yet in Hinduism, holism is linked with hierarchy while in Islam, holism is differentiated from hierarchy.

Singh (1973:67) has discussed the impact of Islam on Hindu traditions in three stages: during the Islamic rule (1206-1818), during the British rule (of eighteenth, nineteenth and the first quarter of the twentieth centuries), and during the Indian freedom movement (from 1930s onwards up to the country's partition). During the Islamic rule, some Muslim rulers had adopted the policy of destroying Hindu temples, spreading Islam (Islamisation) and converting Hindus into Muslims (proselytisation). This period was marked not only by conflicts and tensions between the two religions (Hinduism and Islam) but it also led to adaptations, cultural synthesis of traditions and cultural co-existence of Hindus and Muslims. Sufism influenced Hindus. It emphasised ascetic personal morality, material phenomena lasting for a short time, and mystical self-denial or self-sacrifice. Non-ritualism and abstract monotheism, as preached by the Sufi saints and philosophers, also appealed to Hindu masses. Singh has pointed out that some Muslim rulers and scholars tried to reconcile some aspects of the Hindu tradition with Islam. For example, Akbar introduced a new synthetic cult called *Din-e-Illahi* (Divine Faith) which was a mixture of Islam, Hinduism, Jainism and Zoroastrianism. Dara Singh pleaded for a synthesis of Upanishadic monotheism with that of Islam. Famous scholar Amir Khusro interpreted Hindu traditions to the Muslim world. Many Muslim poets and writers even wrote in Hindi in the sixteenth and seventeenth centuries. However, religious and political elite of Islam not only occupied important administrative, judicial and political posts but they also believed in perpetuation and expansion of Islam. During the British regime, the position changed and the Muslim elite began to lose their status and power.

The Great Islamic tradition, therefore, could not maintain itself with the earlier vigour and confidence. In the eighteenth century, Islam lost its earlier liberal tendencies and in its place orthodoxy and revivalism became its chief pre-occupations. The Hindu tradition became more reactive than adaptive in ethos and lagged behind in cultural change. Islamic tradition, on the other hand, got highly politicised. But in the nineteenth century, liberal and orthodox Islamic traditions began to polarise. The politico-cultural phenomenon generated by the tussle between these two cultural forces culminated in the creation of a separate Islamic nation (Pakistan).

During the British rule in India, two types of reform movements in Hinduism emerged according to Singh (1973:43). First, reforms which called for changes in the cultural practices and values of Hinduism on the pattern of the primordial tradition of the Vedas; and second, which postulated synthesis of new cultural norms and values with the traditional norms and values. Among the reformers of the first category were Swami Dayananda Saraswati, Ramakrishna (1836-1886), Vivekananda (1863-1902), and Mahatma Gandhi; while among the reformers of the second category were Raja Ram Mohan Roy and Jawaharlal Nehru. Swami Dayananda, Vivekananda and Gandhi did not reject the basic ideal-typical cultural themes of Hinduism. All of them accepted the *varna* system, the principle of hierarchy, and the *karma-yoga* or detached social action. All of them considered the ritualistic disabilities of caste as being based on misunderstanding of the Hindu tradition and called for their rejection. While, Swami Dayananda pleaded for the rejection of non-Hindu cultural values and religious beliefs, Vivekananda and Gandhi did not emphasise such rejection.

All this shows how Hinduism and Hindu beliefs and values have undergone changes from time to time and low religio-cultural transformation has taken place in Indian culture.

Impact of the West and Modernisation

The impact of the West on India, following Alatas (1972:121), can be discussed in five phases. The first phase is that of hostile contact with the conquest of Alexander, etc., followed by contact of peaceful interchange as the result of trade and commerce of successive centuries. The second phase began by the end of the fifteenth century when Vasco de Gama arrived with his ships at Calicut in 1498 A.D. Within a few years, the Portuguese occupied Goa. But the effect of these westerners was relatively restricted. The third phase began when East India Company established its rule in the beginning of the eighteenth century and later on the British rule was established in the country by the middle of the eighteenth century. This was the first step in the expansion of western culture in India. The fourth phase commenced with the beginning of the nineteenth century following the industrial revolution. With the economic exploitation of India by the British as source of raw materials, began the spread and dominance of western culture in social and cultural fields too. The fifth and the last phase began after the political independence of the country in 1947.

What has been the impact of the western culture on our society in terms of effect on our culture and our social systems? The impact may be briefly described as follows:

(1) Western institutions like banking system, public administration,

military organisation, modern medicine, law, etc., were introduced in our country.

(2) Western education broadened the outlook of the people who started talking of their rights and freedom. The introduction of the new values, the rational and secular spirit, and the ideologies of individualism, equality and justice assumed great importance.

(3) Acceptance of scientific innovations hightened the aspirations for raising the standard of living and providing material welfare for the people.

(4) Many reform movements came into being. Several traditional beliefs and practices dysfunctional to society were discarded and many new customs, institutions and social practices were adopted.

(5) Our technology, agriculture, entrepreneurship and industry were modernised leading to the economic well-being of our country.

(6) The hierarchy of political values has been restructured. Accepting the democratic form of government, all native states, which had been under a monarchic form of government, have been merged into the Indian State and the authority and domination of feudals and *zamindars* has been demolished. There have been structural changes in social institutions like marriage, family and caste, creating new forms of relations in social life, religion, etc.

(7) The introduction of the modern means of communication, such as railway and bus travel, postal service, air and sea travel, press, and radio and television have affected man's life in varied respects.

(8) There is rise in the feeling of nationalism.

(9) The emergence of the middle class has changed the dominant values of society.

The impact of western culture has also been described by Alatas in terms of four types of changes in our culture and social system: eliminative changes, additive changes, supportive changes and synthetic changes. The *eliminative* changes are those which cause the disappearance of culture traits, behaviour patterns, values, beliefs, institutions, etc. As an illustration, we can cite the example of total change in weapons used in fighting wars, abolition of *sati*, and so forth. The *additive* changes refer to the adoption of new culture traits, institutions, behaviour patterns and belief systems covering diverse aspects of life. These additions were not present earlier in the culture of people. Introducing divorce in the Hindu society, giving share to daughters in father's property, introducing election system in panchayats, etc., are a few examples of this type of change. The *supportive* changes are those which strengthen the values, beliefs or behaviour patterns present in society before contact with the West. A simple example of this change is the use of *Hundi* system in loan transactions. The *synthetic* changes result in the creation of new form from existing elements plus adopted ones. The most simple instance is the creation of residentially nuclear but functionally joint family which continues to fulfill social obligations to parents and siblings. Continuing dowry system but putting restrictions on amount to be given or taken, and associating children along with parents in mate selection are two other examples of synthetic change.

This categorisation of changes due to western impact is only for analytical purposes. In practice, it is not possible to isolate them from each other. Within one type of change, we may find elements of other types of changes too. For example, the introduction of the textile industry contains supportive element in the sense that it facilitates the production of cloth. But at the same time, since it pushed back the traditional handloom and weaving industry, it may be said to have the element of eliminative change. Opening of the wall-less prisons in the prison system is another example of change having elements of three different types. So are the changes in the education system, banking system, family system, marriage system, and so forth.

The main question now is: Where has India reached after contact with the West? Has India progressed? Has it contributed to the welfare of the people? Is it possible to answer this question objectively? Can subjectivism and philosophical partiality be avoided in such analysis? Some intellectuals feel that India faced a number of problems at the end of the Second World War, like the problems of economic backwardness and a large number of people living below the poverty line, unemployment, predominance of religion in all walks of life, rural indebtedness, caste conflicts, communal disharmony, shortage of capital, lack of trained personnel with technical skills, imperfect means for mobilising human and material resources, and so forth. The western impact has provided alternative solutions to handle these problems. But other scholars hold that western impact has not helped India much in facing the problems. If some problems have been solved, many new problems have been created. And India is not trying to meet them through western models. It is using its indigenous elements in its approach. It was only after the independence of the country that there was a rise in industrial development, dissemination of education, rural development, control over population, and so on. It was, thus, independence from western rule rather than contact with the West that made modernisation possible.

The fact is that in certain areas of life, we may be justified in acclaiming the positive impact of the West. Modern medical science, modern technology, modern methods of combating natural catostrophies, modern methods of providing security from external dangers to the country, etc., will go down in Indian history as incontestable contributions of the West. But India is using at the same time its traditional institutions, beliefs and practices for the uplift of the masses. Thus, even after the impact of the West, and after the modernisation of various systems, India will remain India. Indian culture will subsist and survive in decades to come.

The Hindu philosophy of today is different from the early Hindu philosophy. The new Hinduism, also called 'syndicated Hinduism', is different from the indigeneous one both in scale and scope. It is not the creation of a new sect but it is new religious form seeking to encapsulate all the earlier sects. The creation of this syndicated Hinduism is more for political purposes than the religious ones; hence it is called political Hinduism too. The Muslims and the Christains regarded Hindus as 'the other' as the Hindus regarded them as *Malecchas*. Inevitably, a new Hinduism was unavoidable in the nineteenth and the twentieth centuries. The neo-Hindu movements in the twentieth century, particularly after independence, were given a political edge which remains recognisable even today. According to Thapar (1985:21), this development was responsible for the emergence of the present-day syndicated Hinduism, which is being pushed forward as the sole claimant to the inheritance of indigenous Indian religion.

The religious expressions of this syndicated Hinduism are directed more to the rural rich and the urban middle-class to bring into politics a uniform monolithic Hinduism to serve its new requirements. Under the guise of a new reformed Hinduism, an effort is being made to draw a large clientele and to speak with the voice of numbers. The appeal of this syndicated Hinduism has always a political purpose.

Following are the basic postulates of this new Hinduism as given by Thapar (1985:21-22) and some other scholars:

1. The syndicated Hinduism though draws largely on Brahmanical texts—the *Gita* and the Vedantic thought, yet it attempts to present a modern reformed religion. It may be said that the ideology of *Hindutva* is based on the combination of received tradition and active refashioning of this tradition. Or, it may be pointed out that *Hindutva* is a newly structured belief system involving the interpretation of the past, an analysis of the present, and a set of precepts for future conduct.
2. It holds that the non-caste religious sects would have to accept the *dharma* of the powerful and remain subordinate. The lower-down in

the society can try for upward mobility through a new religious movement.

3. It believes in proselytisation because it claims that Hindus were persecuted for thousands of years and were converted to other religions by the Greeks, the Turks, the Mughals and the Britishers. In this context, they refer to proselytisation, destroying of temples, breaking of idols, seizing the wealth of temples, etc. They, therefore, justify the creation of *mathas, ashramas*, temples, *rath-yatras*, and so forth, and also rationalise the reconversion of Muslims and Christians as Hindus. The organisation of conversion camps in Meenakshipuram (1982), Madhya Pradesh, Rajasthan, Gujarat (1998), South India (1998) etc., has been defended by the Hindu fundamentalists. In the last twenty years, the Vishwa Hindu Parishad claims to have converted about 47,000 Muslims belonging to about 8,000 families (mainly of Mehrat and Rawat communities practising traditional customs like burying the dead, performing the *Nikah* ceremony, eating *halal*, abjuring idol-worship, and celeberating festivals like Id and Shab-e-Barat) and about 2,000 Christians.
4. It does not support egalitarianism. It approves social and economic inequality and accepts hierarchial structure. Against this, religions like Islam are egalitarian in theory. Others like Buddhism restrict equality to the moral and ethical spheres of life. Hinduism arose and evolved in a period when inequality was a fact of life and the social function of religion was not to change this but to try and ameliorate the reality for those who found it harsh and abrasive.
5. It does not accept multiplicity of religious manifestations as being equally important. It regards some selected beliefs, rituals and practices as essential and therefore more significant. This is a major departure from the traditional position. Who does the selecting and from what sources and to what purpose also becomes a matter of considerable significance.
6. A factor of increasing importance to the syndicated Hinduism is the dispersion of Hindus to other countries. The Hindus settled outside India experience a sense of cultural insecurity since they are a minority community in a largely Islamic or Christian societies as in Europe (United Kingdom, France, Germany, Russian Federation), North America (Canada, USA), South America (Brazil, Argentina), Africa (Ghana, Kenya, Nigeria, South Africa, Uganda, Zambia), etc. This minority community (the Hindus) is often for a form of Hinduism which they can teach their children through Hindu schools and which will support their new enterprise. These minority communi-

ties settled in other countries and their financial support will provide a basis for the institutions and the ecclesia of syndicated Hinduism. The importance of this 'dispersion' is clearly reflected not only in the social links between those in India and those abroad supporting the new Hinduism, but also in the growing frequency with which the *Sanghas, Parishads* and *Samajs* hold their meetings abroad and seek support and 'conversion' of the affluent.

7. The syndicated Hinduism or *Hindutva* has presented a new concept of Indian nationalism, what is called 'Hindu nationalism'. According to this concept, the Hindus being the majority and being the heirs and continuers of all that was exalted and heroic in the past, are entitled to excercise authority, precedence and domination over others. We are told that anyone, including a non-Hindu, can be Indian provided he accepts Hindu gods and denounces non-Hindus as foreigners. Hindus are more patriotic than non-Hindus. The latter, in order to prove their nationalistic bonafides, must profess their loyalty to the majority community and join the Hindus in the patriotic duty of demolishing those places of worship which were set up by the non-Hindu over the Hindu temples. Hindu nationalism threatens those non-Hindus of facing the wrath of Hindus who refuse to follow the above line. Those fundamentalist religious leaders who talk of *Hindutva* and 'Hindu nationalism' have no faith in the judiciary and have no reverence for the established institutions. They maintain that the *Lok-Shakti* (people's power) is greater than the *Rashtra-Shakti* (nation's power).
8. The proponents of new Hinduism or *Hindutva* talk of 'positive secularism'. They consider the pampering and protection of Muslims and granting rights and special privileges to the minorities by the state as 'pseudo-secularism'. Positive secularism, according to them, envisages the coming together of all religious communities bound by a uniform code of conduct, rights and responsibilities. They, thus, want that a 'civil code' be enacted by the government which may be uniformly applicable to all people in India, irrespective of their religion and caste. They do not want separate marriage and property laws to be made applicable only to Hindus or only to Muslims or Christains or Parsis, etc. They believe that this will be an ideal democratic solution to communal conflicts. They do not believe that this will submerge the distinct religious and the cultural identity of the minorities in the larger majority community. Rather, they believe that such policy (of having a common civil code) will do away with religious superstitions and obscurantist customs and irrational and regressive practices

among all the communities and develop a scientific temper which should be the cornerstone of secular states.

The feeling that is emerging is that syndicated Hinduism, which claims to be re-establishing the indigenous Hinduism, is in fact only establishing itself. Time alone will tell, how far the new Hinduism or Hindutva or re-interpretation of Hinduism, that is, the ideology of 'Hindu nationalism' will affect the secular credentials of the Indian polity. Similarly, time alone will determine whether the hold which religious ideologues will gain over masses of people will achieve the interests and aspirations of people in India or will create the sociopathological conditions that provoke sudden outburst of ill-will in the society.

FACTORS IN CONTINUITY AND CHANGE IN INDIAN SOCIETY

There are a number of factors which are responsible for continuity and change in Indian society. Change may occur through adaptation or integration. Adaptation occurs when existing institutions readjust to meet new needs. Integration occurs when a society adopts a new element and makes it part of itself. Of the various factors which have enabled our society to adapt/integrate or fail to adapt/integrate, the most important ones are: political independence and introduction of democratic values, industrialisation, urbanisation, increase in education, legislative measures, social change in caste system, and social movements and social awareness (like feminism, globalisation and anti-casteism). We will analyse all these factors separately.

Political Independence and Introduction of Democratic Values

Political independence has provided opportunity to all individuals to develop self around conscious and unconscious orientation towards vital interests and values involving identity, status, commitment and desires. Today, individuals are more concerned with 'individuality'. The groups which were wholly or largely excluded from free social interaction for generations together, also now insist on getting discriminatory privileges to rise in social scale. The regions which had remained economically backward because of British rulers' policies want a share in developmental schemes. Some ethnic groups want political independence to preserve their cultural identity. Religious groups want freedom to teach certain values and sub-cultural norms to their members. All these desires and demands have affected the nature of social change and the process of modernisation in our country in the last five decades.

The political independence has also led to major changes in social structure of our society and its system of authority by abolishing the feudal systems of zamindari, jagirdari, and the princely states. It has revolutionised the social and economic base of our rural society, whose results can now be seen everywhere in India's villages. The liberated tenantry has now emerged as the powerful rural middle class. It commands a major voice in the political domain. The green revolution in the country has largely been a contribution of this class. The social and cultural resilience (or quality of quickly recovering the original condition after being pressed or crushed), tolerant indifference towards Brahmanical tradition, continual involvement in cultural and agrarian movements, and a pugnacious utilitarianism provide this class today with a major role in the country's social and economic development. This group today leads the powerful backward class movement.

Political independence has made possible for the nation to achieve credible development and establish a sound foundation of industrial, technological, scientific and managerial growth. A very substantial technological manpower has been created. Singh (1994:22) has also said that a new middle class, quite different in character from the middle class of pre-independence period, has emerged. This class has a much broader social base, coming as it does from the middle and lower caste and social strata of society. The new entrepreneurs and professional classes in urban areas and the rich peasantry in villages constitute a middle class in India estimated to be around one-fourth of its total population. There has been a progressive increase in the percentage of service sector in gross domestic product (GDP) of the country, which indicates the extent of changes in the economic structure and the composition of society. Colonialism had totally made the industrial foundation of Indian society lean, and following independence, the country today ranks about thirteenth in terms of industrial advancement. These achievements have resulted from the planned development of society in basic sectors of its life.

Urbanisation

Urbanisation is another factor that has affected the society. Urban population has grown at a faster rate in our country in the last few decades. In the mid-eighteenth century, approximately 10 per cent of the population in India were town-dwellers. During the nineteenth century, the number of inhabitants of India's towns grew ten-fold over a hundred years. In the twentieth century, while the country's entire population grew from 238 million in 1901 to 846.30 million in 1991, the number of town-dwellers grew by 520 per cent. In 1951, the urban population constituted 17.29 per cent of the total population which increased to 17.97 per cent in 1961, 19.9 per cent in 1971, 23.34 per cent in 1981 and 25.73 per cent in 1991.

The decennial growth rate of urban population in 1961 was 26.41 per cent which increased to 38.23 per cent in 1971, 46.14 per cent in 1981 and 36.19 per cent in 1991. In exact terms, the urban population of India in 1961 was 78 million which increased to 109 million in 1971, 159 million in 1981 and 217 million in 1991(*Manpower Profile, India*, 1998:24).

The family, kinship, caste and marriage etc., systems in the urban areas differ from those in the rural areas not only in composition but in ideology and functioning too. It has already been stated that the nuclear family in urban areas in somewhat smaller than the non-urban nuclear family, and that the urban-dweller is more likely to choose the nuclear family than the rural-dweller. Gore (1968) has maintained that the urban families show a shift away from joint family norms in their attitudes, role perceptions, and in their behaviour. For example, in the area of decision-making in the urban families, unlike the rural families, parents rather than the eldest males take decisions about their children. Similarly, urban people who favour the idea of brothers living together after the death of parents are fewer than the rural people with the same attitude.

Desai (1964), however, did not share this belief that urbanisation as such leads to the break-up of the joint family system. In his analysis of the effect of urbanisation on jointness, he observed significant relationship between the duration of the stay of the family in the urban area and traditional jointness. His presumption was that longer the duration of the stay of family in an urban area, lower will be the degree of jointness. However, he found that the jointness tends to exist more among the 'very old' (living in the town for fifty years or more) and 'old' families (living in the town for twenty-five to fifty years) than in the 'new' ones (living since twenty-five years or less).

Louis Wirth (1938) also believed that city is not conducive to the traditional type of family life. According to him, family as a unit of social life is emancipated from the larger kinship group characteristic of the village, and individual members pursue their own diverging interests in vocational, educational, religious, recreational, and political life.

Changes in cities are also reflected in many other social systems. The kinship relations in the urban areas are not so close as in the rural areas. Whereas in cities, only primary and secondary kin have intimate contacts, in villages, the relations are extensively extended to tertiary and distant kin too. The caste system in the urban areas is not as rigid as in the rural areas. In cities, caste no longer is dominant social identity through which people articulate their social intercourse. But in villages, people still mediate their social, political and cultural goals through caste. In cities, the caste panchayats have increasingly been transformed into caste associations. These associations no longer perform the traditional role of enforcing norms of endogamy, pollution and purity, or settlement of caste disputes, etc., but these caste associations have extended their functional and federative scope. About 3,000 castes are reported to be active in this functioning.

Our view is that role of urbanisation in changing various social systems has been very significant. The urban living has weakened joint family pattern and strengthened nuclear families. Cities provide increasing opportunities for new occupations and higher education. Those who deviate from the traditional family occupation and take to new professions show a greater shift in their attitudes than those who follow traditional occupations. Similarly, educated persons in urban areas are less in favour of, if not less conforming to, joint family norms. It may, however, be maintained that change in attitudes has direct relationship with length of stay in the city. Cities provide opportunities to females also for gainful employment and when woman starts earning, she seeks freedom in many spheres. She tries to breakaway more and more from her husband's family of orientation. Urban residence, thus, seems to introduce a certain measure of variation in family pattern in our society.

Industrialisation

Industrialisation got under way in India in the last quarter of the nineteenth and first half of the twentieth century. Cities grew around the new industries. Before industrialisation, we had (i) agrarian non-monetised economy, (ii) a level of technology where the domestic unit was also the unit of economic exchange, (iii) a non-differentiation of occupations between father and son and between brothers and brothers, and (iv) a value system where authority of the elders and the sanctity of tradition were both supported as against the criterion of 'rationality'. But industrialisation has brought about economic and socio-cultural changes in our society. In the economic field, it has resulted in specialisation in work, occupational mobility, monetisation of economy, and a breakdown of link between kinship and occupational structures; in the social field, it has resulted in the migration of people from rural to urban areas, spread of education, and a strong centralised political structure; in the cultural field, it has brought secularisation of beliefs.

There have been three important effects of industrialisation on family organisation: *First*, family which was a principal unit of production has been transformed into a consumption unit. Instead of all family members working together in an integrated economic enterprise, a few male members go out of the home to earn the family's living. This has affected not only the traditional structure of the joint family but also the relations among its members. *Secondly*, factory employment has freed young adults from direct dependence upon their families. As their wages have made them financially independent, the authority of the head of the household has weakened further. In the city, in many cases, along with men, their wives also have started working and earning. This has affected intra-family relations to some extent. *Finally*, children have ceased to be economic assets and have become liabilities. Although in a few cases, the use and abuse of child labour has also increased, law does not permit children to work. At the same time, educational requirements have increased, lengthening dependence upon parental support. Accommodation in the cities is expensive and child-care is demanding. Thus, work and home have become separated due to industrialisation.

Some sociologists have, however, recently challenged the theory of emergence of nuclear families due to industrialisation. This challenge is based on the results of empirical studies and the documentation of the variety of family systems in different parts of the world. Studies by scholars like M.S.A Rao, M.S. Gore, and Milton Singer have shown that jointness is more preferred and prevalent in business communities, and many nuclear families maintain widespread kin ties. Several recent researchers in the industrialised West have also emphasised the supportive role of kin and their function of acting as a buffer between the family and the impersonal wider world (Abbi, 1970). Social historians too have shown that the nuclear family was prevalent as a cultural norm in Europe and the United States even before industrialisation. However, it has to be noted that the supportive role of the kin does not have the compulsory character which is found in the family obligations of the Indian nuclear family. The youngsters in the nuclear family still willingly follow the normal responsibility towards the primary kin (such as parents and siblings), solidarity of the close kin, and some sense of unity of the family, even though living in separate households (Dube, 1974:311).

All these changes have modified our family system. While the population movement from the rural to the urban areas has led to decline in authoritarian power, growth of secularism has developed a value system which emphasises individual initiative and responsibility. Individual now functions without any restrictive familial controls. Formerly, when man worked in the family and all family members helped him in his work, there was more intimacy among the family members but now since he works in the industry away from the family, the intimacy in relations has been adversely affected. The effect of industrialisation on the pattern of family relationship is also evident from the decline in self-sufficiency of the family, and attitudinal changes toward family. Industrialisation has, thus, contributed markedly to the creation of a new social and psychological setting in which the survival of the early joint family with its authoritarian organisation has become very difficult.

The social profile of communities under the impact of industrialisation is indicative of many dimensions of linkages and interactions among segments of region, culture, social categories and communities. It is reflected in migration of people from one region to another which has contributed to increase of bilingualism. The Census of India, 1991 placed bilinguilism to about 15 per cent, which in reality has been estimated to be as high as 60 per cent in survey of communities. Interaction and commonality among cultural regions too is reflected in shared cultural traits, which is also true for large number of communities across regions and territories. Such cultural traits belong not only to rituals and institutional practices but also to technologies of occupation, skills and division of labour. Most communities have also moved away from their traditional occupations and show keen awareness of developmental programmes sponsored by the government. This awareness, together with high aspirations, introduces in the social system a measure of tension and conflict now manifest in various dimensions of our social life (see, Singh in Murty and Dasgupta, 1995:22-23).

Increase in Education

In the modern age, Indian society has tried to expand its educational system because it requires a more literate and numerate population. Though the literacy percentage has increased from 36 in 1951 to about 60 in 1997, yet there are about 330 million illiterate people to be made literate. The male literacy rate has now reached to about 70 per cent and female rate to about 50 per cent (by end of 1997). In states, the literacy rate has gone beyond 75 per cent in states like Kerala, Mizoram, Goa, and Delhi, and beyond 70 per cent in five out of six union territories. In 16 states, the literacy percentage varies between 50 and 65. Amongst the SCs, the literary percentage has increased to 37 per cent and among STs to 30 per cent (in 1991). The number of students studying in schools and colleges (up to graduation level only) has increased from 548 million in 1971 to 846 million in 1991 (*Manpower Profile, India*, 1998: 42-47).

Education has not only brought about changes in the attitudes, beliefs, values and ideologies of the people but has also created and aroused individualistic feelings. The increasing education not only brings changes in the philosophy of life of men and women but also provides new avenues of employment to the latter. After becoming economically independent, women demand more voice in family affairs and also refuse to accept anybody's dominance over them. This shows how education brings changes in relations in the family, ultimately leading to the structural changes too.

Deasi (1964), and Ross (1961) have also referred to the reciprocal influence of educational system and family system on each other. The former has referred to the working of education against the joint family in two ways: one, by emphasising individualism, it puts before people the concept of the type of the family which is contrary to the prevailing concept of joint family, and two, it prepares people for occupations which cannot be found in their native places, as a result of which they separate from the ancestral family and live in areas which provide them the occupations suited to their educational equipment. In course of time, these people lose contact with the parental family and imbibe new ways of living and thinking which are inimical to the joint family sentiment and conducive to the nuclear family. But in his own study in Mahuva, surprisingly Desai found that with the increase in the educational level, jointness increased and nuclearity decreased. Desai's opinion is that only a few people subscribe to newspapers or purchase general and popular books, and the views and the beliefs of the people are not directly affected by the general reading of the newspapers, periodicals or English books in particular or by the western educational system in general. Whatever effect education might have on the people can be through the influence of what we might call the new elite, and the home and the school environment. Thus, it is not the level of education of the head of family or the whole household that may be the proper indication of the effect of the new or different views and beliefs as the position of persons with new ideas and patterns of communication in a place.

We, however, do not find much logic in Desai's argument. It is true that the type of contacts of an individual outside the family do affect his attitudes and beliefs but the educational level of his own and his family members also is an important factor that changes his beliefs and ideologies. It, therefore, cannot be maintained, as Desai does, that the level of education of family members is not a very significant factor in change in the structure and the organisation of the family.

Similarly, Desai's finding that with the increase in the educational level, jointness increases and nuclearity decreases also does not appear to be true. Probably, his finding is the result of wrong methodology used in his research for finding out the educational level of the family. He had taken the average education of the family on the basis of the average number of years of schooling put in by the 'non-educant' members (that is, those adults and grown-up children who are not likely to take any further education). Thus, the total years of schooling put in by all these members divided by the number of members was taken as the average education of the family. This method of assessing the educational level of family is definitely questionable. Had he used the method generally used by other scholars, he might have got different results. And even just for the sake of argument, assuming that his above method of finding out the educational level of family was correct, why did the group of families with graduate members show all the families nuclear and not a single family as joint? If more education leads to preferences for jointness, the 'graduate families' must have shown higher number of joint families than the matriculate or non-matriculate families. On the basis of these arguments, therefore, we do not feel like agreeing with Desai about the type of relationship he has shown between education and family structure. We believe, education increases the choice for nuclearity and not for jointness.

Ross (1961) has said that the present occupations are such that they require special education, skill and training. Therefore, to raise the living standard of their children as compared to their own, parents are always anxious to give better education to their sons, particularly in middle and upper class families in the urban areas. Some of the poorer parents are so keen that they try to give the highest possible education to their sons even at the cost of their sufferings, sacrifice, and trials and tribulations. Sometimes, they deprive themselves of comforts and even food and clothes. In such cases, however, if by chance their sons fail in examinations or do not come up to the mark, they bring disappointment to their parents. In a few such cases, parents start nagging their children and this becomes so extreme that sons' ability to succeed is crippled and they break off from their parents. On the other hand, there are some parents who, because of their poverty, are not very keen about their children's education, but their children are extremely ambitious. They (children), therefore, leave their parents and go to different towns and cities for education. To support themselves economically, they take up tutions or jobs. These children, thus, gradually are cut off from family ties. After marriage also, they continue to live in cities. This is how their education affects their families. In the case of females also, educated girls develop new attitudes towards husband, children and family, and clash with their convention-minded mother-in-law and insist on separate households. All this shows the impact of education on family pattern. As the level of education rises, the percentage of those in favour of the nuclear family increases and the percentage of people who conform to the pattern of joint family living (in behaviour) decreases.

Legislative Measures

Legislative measures too have their impact on society. Prohibition of early marriage and fixing the minimum age of marriage under the Child Marriage Restraint Act, 1929, and the Hindu Marriage Act, 1955, have lengthened the period of education and functionally contributed to the adjustment of couples in new environment after marriage. The freedom of mate selection and marriage in any caste and religion without parents' consent after certain age permitted through the Special Marriage Act, 1954, sanctioning of widow remarriage by the Hindu Widow Remarriage Act, 1856, the freedom of breaking marriage by the Hindu Marriage Act, 1955, and giving share to daughters in paternal property by the Hindu Succession Act, 1956, have not only modified the interpersonal relations and the composition of family but also the stability of joint family.

The Succession Act, 1956, Hindu Widow Remarriage Act, 1856, the Commission of Sati (Prevention) Act, 1987, Dowry Prohibition Act, 1961, Immoral Traffic (Prevention) Act, 1956 (SIT Act renamed) and Indecent Representation of Women (Prohibition) Act, 1986, have all contributed to preventing exploitation of and violence against women and raising their status in society. The Protection of Civil Rights Act, 1955, the Untouchability Act, 1955 and the Scheduled Castes and the Scheduled Tribes (Prevention of Atrocities) Act, 1989 have checked the exploitation of weaker sections of society. Besides these Acts, the Bonded Labour System (Abolition) Act, 1976, Child Labour (Prohibition and Regulation) Act, 1986, Protection of Human Rights Act, 1993, Equal Remuneration Act, 1976, Muslim Women (Protection of Right of Divorce) Act, 1986 have provided relief to many suffering sectors of the society.

Changes in Caste System

The changes in the caste system have been discussed in Chapter 2 on "Social Stratification".

Social Movements and Social Awareness

Different types of movements have created awareness for rights among different groups. Social movements of tribals, peasants, women and backward castes have been discussed in Chapter 12 on "Social Change and

Modernisation". Here, we will specifically discuss three movements: feminism, globalisation and anti-casteism.

Feminism

Till the 1950s, women in our society were subjugated to men in all respects. They had secondary and subordinate position in the society. Today, women have become aware of their rights. They want opportunities of equality as well as an identity of their own. Though there is a greater increase in the proportion of women in higher status positions yet rate of violence against women is increasing. The feminist movements want women to be empowered and given opportunities to perform roles of their choice. No wonder, social scientists, intellectuals and journalists have started talking in gender-neutral language. The issue of patriarchy and priorities of women have become part of all socio-political discussions. The feminist movement has developed the sentiment that mainstream political and public life has become remote from the experience and values of the majority. The feminist slogan "the personal is political" is not only an ideological expression but also a programme for social change.

Globalisation

Globalisation is a social process in which the constraints of geography on social and cultural arrangements recede and in which people become increasingly aware that they are receding (Malcolm Waters, 1995:3). Thus, in the process of globalisation, physical distance and obstacle have become less important in communication and exchange in social (which includes political and economic) and cultural matters. Fifty years ago, mobility was more from villages to cities, then it increased from cities to cities, from region to region, and now it has extended from country to country. Everybody now knows that people and objects are conveyed round the world more swiftly than in the past and that the words and messages can cross the world in minutes and seconds. Fifty years ago, a message pertaining to trade and commerce or a social, cultural and even a political message took several weeks and considerable physical effort to deliver, now it takes only minutes. Thus, global dimension to contemporary life in economics, politics and culture is apparent. With increase in the various levels of interaction, reactions and responses occur at all levels quickly. The interplay at local, state, national and international levels has affected action and identity. The consequences of globalisation among people in India are perceived now in economic, political and cultural fields. The *economic* effects are perceived in the development of trade routes, in the growth of trade, in economic independency, in the massive flow of capital around the world, and so on. The *political* consequence is that block-wise inter-governmental institutions have developed a global power and presence. 'Nation-state' has now come to be viewed as 'too small for the big problems of life'. Nation-states have ceded some sovereignty to larger entities so that a range of 'big' problems may be dealt with more effectively. In short, the power of the modern nation-state has declined, global political institutions have developed and a supra-national state has emerged. The *cultural* consequence is that "a common culture has developed across the globe. Culture here is used in more general terms. It refers to a 'way of life'. This includes not only political, economic and social norms but also leisure and consumption. Featherstone gives as an example of cultural globalisation, the development of global financial markets in which the main actors share many business and lifestyle norms and values, e.g., an international frame of reference in leisure as well as work. Some other areas of consumption like fast food, 'world' cars, etc., have also become globalised. However, cultural globalisation does not mean that cultural differentiation does not exist" (see, O' Donnell, 1997:596-97).

Anti-Casteism

There have been movements of opposition to caste exploitation and casteism and in favour of caste equality and giving special privileges to depressed caste people. These movements have had both a cultural and structural dimension. Culturally, they have opposed caste-prejudices by attacking caste restrictions and asserting the reality of social achievements and social mobility. The structural dimension of anti-casteism focuses on lack of power within institutions: business, services, education, legislations, etc.

It may be concluded that the forces of change which India encounters today have not only the functional aspect but they also have the dysfunctional aspect. Cultural, social and political tensions based on caste, ethnicity and politics of interest groups rampant today have been a part of this process ever since independence. The cultural dimension of change today is reflected not only in the search for new identities by the Dalits, religious minorities and women but also in the exposure given to their problems by the media. As development programmes gain momentum, the social inequalities are bound to sharpen further. With media reporting these issues, the perception of inequalities undergoes a dangerous metamorphosis resulting into extremisms of various sorts.

Further Readings

Ahuja, Ram, *Indian Social System*, Rawat Publications, Jaipur, 1993.

Dasgupta, S.N., *History of Indian Philosophy*, Kitab Mahal, Allahabad, 1969.

Frontline, Article on "Hindu Nationalism", February 14, 1992.

Gore, M.S., *Urbanisation and Family Change*, Popular, Bombay, 1968.

Hall, Stuart and Gay, *Question of Cultural Identity*, Sage, 1996.

Desai, I.P., *Some Aspects of Family in Mahuva*, Asia, Bombay, 1964.

Kanal, S.P., *Dialogues on Indian Culture*, Panchal, Delhi, 1955.

Kapadia, K.M., *Marriage and Family in India*, Oxford, Bombay, 1972.

Manpower Profile, India, 1998.

Muller, Max, *Vedanta Philosophy*, Calcutta, 1955.

O'Donnell, Mike, *Sociology*, Thomas Nelson & Sons, U.K., 1997.

Pande, Raj Bali, *The Hindu Sanskaras*, Bombay, 1949.

Radhakrishnan, S., *The Hindu View of Life*, George Allen and Unwin, 1949.

Ross, Aileen D., *Hindu Family in Urban Setting*, Oxford, Bombay, 1961.

Singh, Yogendra, *Modernisation of Indian Tradition*, Thompson Press, Delhi, 1973.

Singh, Yogendra, "Present Social Situation in India" in K. Sachidananda Murty and Amit Dasgupta (eds.), *The Divine Peacock*, Wiley Eastern, New Delhi, 1995.

Thapar, Romila, *Seminar*, No. 313, Delhi, September, 1985.

2 Social Stratification

CASTE SYSTEM AND SOCIAL STRATIFICATION

Societies are divided into hierarchical groups in a way that though various groups are considered inequal in relation to each other but within one group, members are viewed as equals. Two main criteria of social stratification are caste and class, but some other recognised units of stratification are age, gender and race/ethnicity too. Social stratification is different from social differentiation. The term 'differentiation' has broader application as it makes individuals and groups separate and distinct from each other for purposes of comparison. For example, within class strata, income, occupation, and education provide basis for differentiation and comparison. Stratification occurs where differences are ranked hierarchically.

Caste as a Unit and a System

In India, both caste and class are used as basis of hierarchical ranking and exist side by side. However, caste, which is rooted in religious belief, is considered a more important basis of social stratification for social, economic, and religious purposes. 'Caste' is a hereditary social group which does not permit social mobility to its members. It involves ranking according to birth which affects one's occupation, marriage, and social relationships.

Caste is used both as a unit and as a system. As a unit, caste is defined as 'a closed-rank status group', i.e., a group in which the status of members, their occupations, the field of mate-selection, and interaction with others is fixed. As a system, it refers to collectivity of restrictions, namely, restrictions on change of membership, occupation, marriage, and commensal and social relations. In this context, there is a presupposition that no caste can exist in isolation and that each caste is closely involved with other castes in the network of economic, political, and ritual relationships. The 'closed-rank group' feature of caste also explains its structure.

Caste: Structural and Cultural Concepts

Caste is looked upon as a structural as well as a cultural phenomenon. As a structural phenomenon, it refers to interrelated statuses, patterned interaction among castes on the basis of different restrictions, and a stable set of social relations. As a cultural phenomenon, it is viewed as 'a set of values, beliefs and practices'. Most scholars have viewed caste as a solidarity and not as a set of values and attitudes. The structure of the caste system is such that it has an organised pattern of interrelated rights and obligations of members of each caste and individual castes as groups, in terms of statuses, roles and social norms.

In structural terms, Bougle (1958:9) has explained castes as "hereditarily specialised and hierarchically arranged groups", while as a system, he has referred to its three characteristics: hierarchy, hereditary specialisation, and repulsion. Explaining the last characteristic, he claims that different castes *repel* rather than *attract* each other. Repulsion is manifested in endogamy, commensal restriction, and social contact. This interpretation is, however, not true. We do not and cannot find repulsion among castes because they need each other. Gough (cf. Leach, 1960:11) views castes as "ranked birth-status groups which are usually endogamous and tend to be associated with an occupation". Senart (1930) has described caste as "a closed corporation, rigorously hereditary, bound with others (castes) by common occupation, and equipped with a council that rules its members by the sanction of certain penalties". In this definition, the words 'closed corporation' have been questioned. Besides, all castes do not have councils. Bailey and Srinivas have viewed castes as structures and have avoided the definition of caste. Dutt (1931:3-4), describing caste system has referred to restrictions on marriage, eating and drinking, occupation, change in hereditary membership, and the hierarchical gradation of castes. Morris (1950:284) also believes that a short definition of caste is not satisfactory; so it is more illuminating to talk in terms of the characteristics of caste. He describes caste system as "characterised by hereditary membership and endogamy and prescribing specific norms which regulate social interaction". Ghurye (1957:2-19) too has given similar features of the caste system. Besides, referring to hereditary membership, caste councils, hierarchy and endogamy as important features of the caste system, he also refers to the restrictions on feeding and social intercourse, lack of unrestricted choice of occupation, and civil and religious disabilities. D'Souza (1969:72) has referred to the definition of caste system as "the integration of the interacting and heterogeneous but internally homogeneous hereditary groups into a structure of status hierarchy". This concept not only describes the caste system as a superior or subordinate relationship among hereditary groups in a society, but also explains the conditions under which such a relationship takes place.

Singh (1974:319) holds that structurally, the caste system simultaneously manifests two tendencies: one, segmental and other, organic. As a segmental reality, each caste or a sub-caste tends to articulate mutual repulsion, social distance and social inequality, but as an organic system, the caste segments are mutually interlinked by a principle of reciprocity through the *jajmani* system. Bailey (1960) has referred to caste stratification as a 'closed organic stratification' in contra-distinction with the class principle which is based on 'segmentary stratification'. In the former, the social segments (castes or sub-castes) interact through cooperation and in the latter through competition.

Caste: Three Perspectives of the Study

The caste system in India has been studied with three perspectives: indological, socio-anthropological and sociological. The indologists have viewed caste from the scriptural point of view, social anthropologists from the cultural point of view, and sociologists from the social stratification point of view.

The *indological perspective* takes its cue from the scriptures about the origin, purpose and future of the caste system. Those who have used this perspective maintain that *varnas* have originated from Brahma's body and castes or *jatis* are fissioned units within the *varna* system, developed as the result of hypergamy and hypogamy practices. Though the customs and the rituals, etc., to be followed by different castes are prescribed in the *Smrits* written in about 200-100 B.C. but the regional, linguistic, ethnic, and sectarian variations have gradually come to affect the ordering of *jati* relationships. The object of the origin of castes, according to the indologists, was the division of labour. Gradually, castes became more and more rigid and membership and occupation became hereditary. The rigidity in the caste system is the result of the beliefs in *karma* (deeds) and *dharma* (duties and obligations) which means that the motive force for the caste dogmas was religious. The indologists further maintain that since castes are divine, they will continue to exist in future (Verma, 1972: 159).

The *cultural perspective* of the social anthropologists (Hutton, Risley, Kroeber) ramifies itself in three directions: structural, institutional and relational. The structural view focuses its attention on the origin of the caste system, its development, and the processes of change in the structure. The institutional approach (John Rex) views caste system not only as a unique phenomenon found in India but also in ancient Egypt, medieval Europe and present southern United States, etc. The relational approach finds caste situations in army, business, factory management, politics, and so forth. Caste system in these organisations is weak if mobility is normal and strong if it is barred.

The *sociological perspective* views caste system as a phenomenon of social inequality. Society has certain structural aspects which distribute members in different social positions.

The reference to three different perspectives does not mean that sociologists do not take interest in the origin and development of the caste system like indologists and social anthropologists or that the social anthropologists do not accept caste system as resultant of social stratification as the sociologists do.

CASTE AND VARNA, SUB-CASTE AND CLASS

Caste and Varna

Caste and *varna* are two separate concepts. The Hindu theory of social organisation has referred to *varnashram* organisation, where *varna* and the *ashram* organisations are perceived as two separate organisations. *Ashram* organisation refers to the conduct of individual in the world (i.e., nurture) in different stages of his life, while the *varna* organisation refers to the work that an individual would undertake in society according to his position in relation to group and with reference to his innate nature and his tendencies and dispositions. Though in *Rig Veda*, there is mention of two *varnas*—Arya and Dasa—and the division of society into three orders—*Brahma* (priests), *Kshatra* (warriors) and *Vis* (common people) but there is no mention of the fourth order, i.e., *Sudras*. However, there is a reference to groups despised by the Aryans, like *Ayogya*, *Chandal*, and *Nishad*, etc. These four orders ultimately became four *varnas*. There was nothing like lower or higher *varna* in the vedic period. The division of society in four *varnas*—Brahmin, Kshatriya, Vaishya and Sudra—was based on the division of labour. Members of each *varna* performed different functions (of priests, rulers and fighters, traders and serviles respectivelv), worshipped different dieties and followed different rituals but there were no restrictions on the commensal or social relations or even on the change of membership from one to other *varna*. Later on, however, as we pass from the vedic period (4000-1000 B.C) to the Brahmanic period (230 B.C. to 700 A.D), the four *varnas* came to be arranged hierarchically, with Brahmins at the top. According to one view, *varna* means colour and, therefore, perhaps the division of society was based on fair and dark colours respectively. Hutton (1963:66) believes that it is possible that this colour distinction is in some way associated with race. According to Hocart (1950:46), however, the colour has a ritual and not a racial significance.

Like the origin of *varnas*, the origin of castes is also explained by scholars like Risley, Ghurye, Majumdar, etc., in terms of racial factors but it can not be said that castes are the sub-divisions of *varnas*. The origin of castes has nothing to do with *varnas*, though in the process of development of castes, they came to be associated with *varnas*. The hierarchy of castes and the mobility of a caste came to be stated in *varna* terms. *Varna*, thus, provided a framework which conditioned all Indian thinking about and reaction to caste (Hsu, 1963:96). Srinivas (1962:69) also suggests that *varna* has provided a common social language which holds good for India as a whole, i.e., it has enabled ordinary men and women to grasp the caste system by providing them with a simple and a clear scheme which is applicable to all parts of India. He further holds that the importance of the varna system consists in that it furnishes an all India frame into which the *jatis* occupying the lower rungs have throughout tried to raise their status by taking over the customs and rituals of the top *jatis*. This has helped the spread of a uniform culture throughout the Hindu society.

Caste and Sub-Caste

Difference between caste and sub-caste is not clear-cut. Both have similar attributes. However, a subcaste is a sub-division of a caste. Brahmin is designated both as a varna and a caste. Kanyakubja, Suryupari and Gaur Brahmins are examples of castes, and Shrimali, Purohit and Pushkarna Brahmins are examples of sub-castes, while Bhardwaj, Gautam and Kashyap Brahmins are examples of *gotras*. Castes and sub-castes are endogenous groups but *gotra* is an exogamous group.

For the origin of sub-castes, there are two different views: one, that they have arisen out of a fission from a parent group, and two, they have emerged as independent groups (A.C. Mayer, 1960; Yogesh Atal, 1968; Irawati Karve, 1958; B.R. Chauhan, 1966:44). According to Ghurye (1957:34), the sub-castes came to be distinguished from castes due to territorial separateness, mixed origin, occupational distinction, difference in technique of occupation, dissimilarity of customs, and due to nicknames. Risley (1915), Hutton (1961:55) and Majumdar (1958:357) have referred to sub-castes breaking away from the main castes/tribes to raise their status. Chauhan (1966:45) has maintained that the origin of sub-castes, due to the process of fission, may be explained in terms of factors like, migration, change of customs, political decisions, etc. Krickpatrick (1912) has explained that sub-castes, which are fissioned groups of caste, were earlier formed as the result of migration and political and social factors but today, they are the results of attempts by the well-to-do persons in a despised caste to cut adrift from their humbler caste brethern and raise themselves in the social scale by finding a new name and a dubious origin and associating themselves with some higher caste. Andre Beteille (1965) has highlighted the subsuming of many sub-castes by a caste and the multi-polarity in the functioning of caste.

Castes and sub-castes today are assigned different functions and activities. The three functions performed by sub-castes are: controlling marriages, restricting commensal relations, and regulating behaviour or communal life in terms of subsisting within the larger society. The three functions performed by castes are: assigning status, delimiting civil and religious rights and determining the occupation. Referring to these characteristics, Ghurye (1957:19) has asserted: "We should recognise sub-castes as real castes." A.C. Mayer (1960:151) has also talked of recognising the need to distinguish caste from sub-caste. He found Ghurye's reference to caste as meaningful for the society at large and reference to sub-caste as meaningful for the individual. Referring to members within a caste, he maintained that sub-caste is more meaningful to them, while referring to members of other castes, he thought that caste is the key-point of cognition. He, thus, has opined that caste and sub-caste can co-exist, neither being more real than the other.

What is the unit of caste system? Is it caste or sub-caste? Srinivas (1952:24) believes that sub-caste is the 'real' unit of the caste system. However, in his own study (of Rampura village in Mysore in Karnataka), he had confined himself to the study of caste. According to Mayer (1960:8), at regional level a sub-caste may be the unit of inter-caste as well as intra-caste relations but within the village, inter-caste relations are viewed in terms of castes rather than sub-castes. Irawati Karve (1938:33) considers sub-castes as 'ultimate units' of analysis. Ghurye (1950:20) maintains that stated generally, though it is the caste that is recognised by the society at large, it is the sub-caste that is regarded important by the particular caste and individuals. We should, therefore, recognise sub-castes as real castes to get a sociologically correct idea of the institution of caste. According to Stevenson (1954), however, because of the confusion between the concepts of caste and sub-caste, the best thing is to ignore the difference between the two. But this cannot be done because of different functions performed by the two.

Caste and Class

Caste and class are both 'status groups' in Max Weber's phraseology. A 'status group' is a collection of persons who share a distinctive style of life and a certain consciousness of kind. While caste is perceived as a hereditary group with a fixed ritual status, a social class is a category of people who have a similar socio-economic status in relation to other segments of their community or society. The individuals and families who compose a social class are relatively similar in educational, economic and prestige status. Those who are classified as part of the same social class have similar life chances. Some sociologists regard social classes as being primarily economic in nature whereas others tend to stress factors such as prestige, style of life, attitudes, etc. Caste system is characterised by 'cumulative inequality' but class system is characterised by 'dispersed inequality'. The members of a class have a similar socio-economic status in relation to other classes in the society, while the members of a caste have either a high or low ritual status in relation to other castes. Caste is a unique phenomenon (Leach and Dumont) found in India but class is a universal phenomenon found all over the world. Caste works as an active political force in a village but not the class. Andre Beteille (1965), on the basis of his study of caste and class in Sripuram in South India found that classes do not constitute a basis for communal and political action. Referring to this, Leach (1960) has said that while caste assumes economic and political functions and competes with other castes, it defies caste principles. Gough and Richard Fox also hold the same position. M.N. Srinivas (1962:7), however, does not agree with Leach on this. He maintains that competition between caste groups cannot be described as defiance of caste principles. It is true that castes depend on each other (*jajmani* system) but besides interdependence, castes also compete with each other for acquiring political and economic power and high ritual position. Yet another difference between caste and class is that caste has an organic character but class has a segmentary character. In caste system, upper castes compete with each other for the services of the lower castes but in the class system, lower classes compete with each other for the favour of the upper classes (Leach,1960:5-6). Further, in the caste system, status of a caste is determined not by the economic and the political privileges but by the ritualistic legitimation of authority, i.e., in the caste system, ritual norms encompass the norms of power and wealth (Dumont). For example, even though Brahmins have no economic and political power, yet they are placed at the top in the caste hierarchy. In the class system, ritual norms have no importance at all but power and wealth alone determine one's status. Bailey, however, does not accept Dumont's statement that religious ideas rather than the economic values establish the rank of each caste. He says that if we accept this statement, it would mean that changes in control over economic resources can take place without causing changes in rank. This is only partially true. It may be true for Brahmins and untouchables but not for the intermediate castes. In his own study in Bisipara, he found that change in wealth is followed by change in rank (1957:264-65). Lastly, social mobility is not possible in caste system but in the class system, change in status is possible. D.N. Majumdar (1958) in this context explained caste as a closed class. This view is not accepted by M.N. Srinivas. He thinks that movement is always possible through the processes of sanskritisation and westernisation (1962:42). Beteille (1965) has also said that no social system is absolutely closed. There is always some scope, however limited, for alternative combinations.

Caste Among Non-Hindus

Is caste a particularistic or a universalistic phenomenon? Is it a unique system found only in India or it is found in other countries too? The main view is that caste when viewed as a cultural phenomenon (i.e., as a matter of ideology or value system) is found only in India while when it is viewed as a structural phenomenon, it is found in other societies too.

Before independence, the Census Commissioners had reported the existence of caste-like endogamous strata and occupational specialisation among non-Hindus in India (including present Pakistan). According to N.K. Bose (1949, 1951), why Muslims, converted from Hinduism, adhered to caste-patterned endogamy and hereditary traditional occupation was because they found in it economic security. Several studies conducted between 1956 and 1965 by R. Gupta (on 'Muslims of a village in North-Western Uttar Pradesh' in 1956), G. Ansari (on 'Muslim Castes in Uttar Pradesh' in 1960), Z. Ahmed (on 'Muslims Castes in Uttar Pradesh' in 1962), U. Guha (on 'Rural Bengali Muslims' in 1965), M.K. Siddiqui (on Caste among Muslims of Calcutta in 1970), Sangare (on Jains in 1959), I.P. Singh (on the Sikhs in 1958), Schifra Strizower (on Jews in 1959) and by McKim Marriott in 1960s have pointed out the prevalance of caste system among non-Hindus (see Sinha, 1974:243). Dumont, Leach, Pocock and

Madan studied people outside Indian civilisation and found social structural features of caste amongst them. Leach in his study (1960) found castes among Buddhists in Ceylon and Muslims of Swat in Pakistan. Knight (1967) and Berreman (1966) also have referred to some characteristics of caste system in racial stratification in Europe and America and pariah castes in Japan. In spite of this comparison of caste and race systems of stratification, it will be more correct to say that both structurally and culturally, the caste system is confined to those regions where some elements of Indian civilisation are traced. The population in these regions is segmented into numerous endogamous social units which interact hierarchically, following roughly the regional version of the *varna* model.

Singh (1974:316) has referred to four approaches to caste by distinguishing between the two levels of theoretical formulation, i.e., cultural and structural, and universalistic and particularistic. These four approaches are: cultural-universalistic, cultural-particularistic, structural-universalistic and structural-particularistic. While Leach (1960) using structural-particularistic view of caste has maintained that caste system is restricted to the Indian society, others who view caste as a structural-universalistic category hold that caste in India is a general phenomenon of a closed form of social stratification. The third position of sociologists like Ghurye (1957, 1961) who treat caste as a cultural universalistic phenomenon, particularly in terms of *hierarchy* which forms the basis for ranking of persons or groups, maintains that caste-like cultural bases of stratification are found in most traditional societies. Caste in India, as a basis of social ranking, is a special form of the general system of status-based social stratification. This viewpoint, early formulated by Max Weber, has continued in contemporary sociology. The fourth view on caste, that of cultural-particularistic, is held by Louis Dumont (1966, 1961) who holds that caste is found only in India.

Singh (1974:317), using structural-particularistic view of caste, has said that institutionalised inequality and its cultural and economic coordinates are indeed the factors which render caste in India as a unique system of social stratification. Structurally, four issues are crucial in caste system, (i) relating to the unit components in caste ranking (e.g., *varna*, caste, sub-caste), (ii) relating to the modes of caste fusion and fission, formation of caste associations, caste federations or formation of new sub-castes by sanskritisation, (iii) relating to caste dominance and conflict in the process of social mobility, and (iv) relating to the extent of social mobility in the caste system. In these contexts, caste is found in India alone.

TRANSFORMATION OF CASTE SYSTEM FROM EARLY TO MEDIEVAL AND BRITISH PERIODS: ITS RITUAL, ECONOMIC AND SOCIAL ASPECTS

The caste system, as it exists today, has developed through many centuries. Its structure and functioning in ancient period (from 4000 B.C to 700 A.D., i.e., Vedic, Brahmanical, Maurya and post-Maurya (or Sanga, Kushan and Gupta) periods was much different from the medieval (Rajput and Muslim, i.e., 700 A.D. to 1757 A.D.) and the British periods (i.e., 1757-1947 A.D.).

In the *Vedic Period* (1500-322 B.C.), there are two views pertaining to the prevalence of the caste system. One school (Haug, 1863; Kern, Dutt and Apte, 1940; Kamble, 1979) holds that the caste system had existed and Brahmins, Kshatriyas and Vaisyas were the three caste divisions that the society of *Rig Veda* period clearly recognised. However, Sudra caste did not exist. The other school (Weber, 1882; Ghurye, 1932) maintains that these three were not castes but *varnas* which were not hereditary but flexible. In the Brahmanical period that followed the *Brahmanas* and *Upnishads*, the hierarchical system of four *varnas* had firmly established itself and remained enduring for all times to come. The privileges enjoyed by the Brahmins through the instrumentality of religion enabled them to impose several restrictions. Though Brahmins and Kshatriyas remained in conflict with each other trying to assert their superiority over the other, but Kshatriyas increased their power over Vaisyas and Sudras. On the issue of social relations among various social groups, caste distinctions became clearer in *Samhitas* and the *Brahmanas*. In the latter part of the Epic period, priesthood became hereditary and inevitably the Brahmins began to pay attention to the purity of the blood and attaining a position of superiority over others. They prescribed codes of social behaviour and relationships through *Grihsutras* (700-300 B.C.) and *Dharmasutras* (600-300 B.C.). It may, therefore, be said that the starting point of the caste system was the later Vedic Age (800-500 B.C.) and the Epic Age (500-200 B.C.). Since the basis of social stratification was division of labour, in its original form, it was a class system rather than a caste system. The racial factor, the occupational bias, the philosophy of action, and the religious concept of purity and pollution—all contributed to the formation of the caste system.

In the *Maurya period* (i.e., from 322-184 B.C.), whole of India was politically united for the first time under one head and rule. Political unity led to cultural unity of the country. Kautilya's writings give some idea about the social organisation and the functioning of the caste system in this period. Kautilya (a Brahmin minister of a Sudra ruler Chandragupta Maurya) tried to remove various restrictions imposed by the Brahmins on the Sudras by declaring that the royal law would supersede the *dharma* law. The rights and the privileges of Brahmins received a further blow in the days of Ashoka, grandson of Chandragupta Maurya. Ashoka's religious policy was broadly based on toleration and universal brotherhood which did not recognise the caste barriers. The caste system, because of all these measures could not develop as a rigid institution in this period.

In *post-Maurya period*, a fresh stimulus was provided to the revival of the Brahmanical religion and the development of the caste system. Brahmins gave themselves special privileges in *Manu Smriti* (185 B.C.) and imposed various restrictions on the Sudras. The *Smriti* prescribed severe punishment to Sudras for insulting Brahmins (cutting out tongue, thrusting iron-nail in mouth, pouring hot oil into ears). Thus, equality in law was completely destroyed by such prescriptions and the caste system developed on rigid lines and assumed a new structure. The Gupta period (that followed the Sanga period from 300-500 A.D) was the period of Hindu renaissance. Brahminism became the ethnic religion of India in this period and caste system got a further incentive. However, it did not become very rigid. Marriage rules were elastic and examples of inter-marriages and inter-dining were not unknown. Sudras were permitted to become traders, artisans and agriculturists. But untouchability existed in this period more or less in its present form. The untouchables lived outside the main settlements. In post-Gupta period (Harsh Vardhana and others: 606-700 A.D.) also, the caste system continued to have the same structure as it had in the Gupta period. An elaborate account of social, religious and economic conditions of India of this period is available in Chinese scholar Hieun Tsang's writings who visited India in 630 A.D. and remained here for 13 years. He writes that caste ruled the social structure, Brahminism dominated, and persons following unclean occupations (scavengers, butchers, etc.) had to live outside the four walls of the city.

The *Medieval period* includes the Rajput period (700-1200 A.D.) and the Muslim period (1200-1757 A.D.). In the *Rajput period*, the cultural life of the Hindus was not very different from the one found in earlier periods. The Indian social system did not change due to political security. Brahmins gave themselves more privileges. The *mathas*, established by

Shankaracharya, became the centres of luxurious life. The system of *devdasi* fostered the growth of temple prostitution which led to the growth of the loosening of moral codes. Rajputs' loyalty to their own clans made them indifferent to the larger patriotism of the whole country. New castes and sub-castes came into being which were so circumscribed by vested interests that they had evil repercussions on the social and political life of the country. Consequently, foreign Muslims started attacking India. The foundation of the Muslim empire in India was laid down by Mohamood Ghori in 1175 A.D. which was followed by Mughal attacks. The caste system in the Muslim period (1206-1857 A.D.) became still more rigid because Muslims were not absorbed in the elastic Hindu-fold. Their religion (Islam), being fiercely monotheistic, could not allow any compromise with polytheism. Since Muslims led a religious crusade against India and tried to convert people to Islam, Brahmins assuming upon themselves the responsibility of protecting the Hindus from being proselytised, imposed severe restrictions on Hindus, making caste system a very rigid system. Though some *Bhaktas* (saints) like Ramanuj, Kabir, Guru Nanak, Chaitanya, Tukaram, Tulsidas, Namdev, etc. preached *Bhakti* cult in this period which denounced idolatory and caste, and preached equality of all people, protested against excessive ritualism and domination of the priestly class, yet this cult could not disintegrate the caste system. Brahmins could retain their leadership of Hindus because temples were used not only for religious purposes but also for social, political and cultural activities. Brahmins made caste distinctions more rigorous by declaring that all those Hindus who worked with or for Muslims would be treated as *Malechha*, like Muslims. Thus, castes like *Sunar* (goldsmiths), *Luhar* (blacksmiths), *Nai* (barbers), *Dhobi* (washermen), *Khati* (carpenters) and the like came to be treated as castes of low status. *Puranas* were rewritten and new commandments were prescribed, making the caste system very rigid.

In *early British* (or pre-industrial) *period*, the material development of the country, contact with the outer world, socio-economic policies of the government, and some legislative measures taken, brought about a change in our religious doctrines, social practices, and also in the caste structure of the society. The judicial powers of the caste councils were transferred to the civil and the criminal courts. The Caste Disabilities Removal Act of 1850, the Widow Remarriage Act of 1856, and the Special Marriage Act of 1872 also attacked the caste system. The integrity of the caste system got a further blow when through some social measures, some of the disabilities of untouchables were removed. However, the British government had taken these measures purely for administrative reasons and not because it wanted to abolish the caste system. Ghurye (1961:190) also has expressed a similar opinion. Some social movements of social reformers also attacked the caste system. The Brahmo Samaj movement led by Raja Ram Mohan Roy rejected the barriers of caste divisions and stood for universalisation and brotherhood of man. The Prarthana Sabha movement supported by Justice Ranade also devoted its attention to social reform such as inter-caste marriage, interdining and remarriage of widows, etc. The Arya Samaj movement founded by Swami Dayanand Saraswati and Ramakrishna Mission movement raised voice against caste and preached its abolition. The Lingayat movement in South India also preached the giving up of the caste system. However, all these attacks did not remove the rigidity of the caste system in this period (i.e., in the first quarter of the twentieth century) though some structural features of caste were definitely affected.

The *industrial phase* in the *British period* started from 1920-25 onwards after the First World War. The processes of industrialisation and urbanisation (migration of people from villages to cities) affected caste structure to a great extent. Industrial growth provided new sources of livelihood to people and made occupational mobility possible. New transportation facilities also made frequent communication possible, which threw together millions of people of all castes. Taboos against food-sharing started weakening when industrial workers belonging to different castes started living together in the same house, leaving their families behind in villages.

Urbanisation and growth of cities also considerably changed the functioning of the caste system. Not only were commensal inhibitions relaxed but the authority of the Brahmins also came to be questioned. Kingsley Davis (1951) has held that the anonymity, congestion, mobility, secularism and changeability of the city makes the operation of the caste virtually impossible. Ghurye (1961:202) also holds that changes in the rigidities of the caste system were due to the growth of city life. M.N. Srinivas too (1962:85-86) holds that due to the migration of Brahmins to the towns, the non-Brahmins refused to show same respect to them which they showed before, and inter-caste eating and drinking taboos were also weakened. It may, thus, be said that the structure and the functioning of the caste system and its ritual economic and social aspects were greatly changed in the industrial phase of the British period.

CASTE SYSTEM IN PRESENT INDIA

After the political independence of the country in 1947, besides industrialisation and urbanisation, other factors which affected the caste system are: merger of various states, enactment of several laws, spread of education, socio-religious reform measures and movements, westernisation, growth of modern professions, spatial mobility and the growth of the market economy. Broadly speaking, the following changes in caste functioning may be pointed out in the present times.

- Caste system is not in the process of abolition but is making adequate adjustment with modern changes.
- The religious basis of caste has cramped. Old social practices of imposing restrictions of varied types have dwindled. Caste no longer restricts newly valued individual freedom.
- Caste no longer determines the occupational career of an individual, though his social status continues to be dependent on his caste membership.
- Serious efforts are being made to grant equality to the backward castes/dalits.
- Inter-caste conflicts are increasing. However, these are more for achieving power than on grounds of ritual status.
- Casteism has increased.
- The *jajmani* system in the villages has weakened, affecting inter-caste relations.
- The dominance of a caste in a village no longer depends upon its ritual status.
- Caste and politics have come to affect each other.
- On the one hand, some caste organisations have strengthened while on the other hand, a large number of castes have lost their group solidarity and a sense of responsibility.
- Caste no longer acts as a barrier to social progress and to nation's development. India is on the move in spite of the caste system.

IS CASTE SYSTEM CHANGING, WEAKENING OR DISINTEGRATING?

There are two views regarding the present and the future of the caste system. One view is that caste system is fast changing and is weakening though it is not being disintegrated or abolished. To this school belonged early scholars of the 1950s, 1960s, and 1970s like D.N. Majumdar, Kuppuswami, Kali Prasad, Gardner Murphy, Pauline Kolenda, and Max Weber, and scholars of the 1980s and 1990s like R.K.Mukerjee, E.J. Miller and M.N. Srinivas. The other view is that caste system is not transforming itself fast and changes are gradual. To this school belonged early scholars like G.S. Ghurye, I.P.Desai, Narmadeshwar Prasad and K.M. Kapadia and present scholars like Y.B. Damle, Louis Dumont, Andre

Beteille, Harold Gould, Yogendra Singh, S.C. Dube and T.N. Madan.

D.N. Majumdar, while explaining how the caste system has fast changed, has referred to fusion and fission of castes and assimilation of tribes. Kuppuswami (see, *Sociological Bulletin*, September 1962) and Kali Prasad (1954:3) also pointed out some basic changes in the caste system. Kali Prasad's empirical conclusion that 90 per cent of the upper caste people accepted the lower-caste people as their fellow-diners enabled him to give a statement that caste cleavages are being levelled up fast. Murphy (1953:65) (who conducted study on social tensions in India during 1950-52) concluded that caste system has come to be challenged. Weber's (1952) view was that all caste relations have been shaken and the intellectuals are the bearers of specific nationalism. Ram Krishna Mukerjee (1958) stated that both the economic aspect (change in occupational specialisation) and the social aspect (adoption of higher caste customs, giving up polluting professions, etc.) of the caste system have vastly changed. He said that change is more specific in urban areas where rules on social intercourse and caste commensalities have greatly relaxed and civil and religious disabilities of lower castes have been lifted. E.J. Miller (1958), talking of change in the caste system, pointed out that while in the past, inter-caste relations involved traditionally ordained and clear-cut rights and obligations and authority and subordination, at present the pattern of inter-caste relations has vastly changed. Along with Miller, several other scholars like Bryce Ryan, M.N. Srinivas and S.C. Dube have also suggested the changing pattern of the caste system. M.N. Srinivas (1952, reprinted 1985) has maintained that the mutual rights and obligations among the castes are crumbling down. Change of loyalty of an individual from his village to his caste is noted. Change has also come through sanskritisation and westernisation. Brahmins were preceded by the British even though they ate pork and beaf, drank whisky and smoked a pipe. But because they had the economic power, they were feared, admired and respected. The result was that new and secular caste system got superimposed on the traditional system in which the British, the new Kshatriyas, stood at the top.

But the scholars of the other viewpoint (who describe changes in the caste system taking place slowly and gradually and in some cases even superficially) do not consider these changes as being disintegrative of the caste system as a whole. These scholars, though they do not imply the dissolution of caste, yet have made it clear that caste today is not the same as it was half a century or a century ago. For example, A.R. Desai and Y.B.

Damle (1981:66) said: "The magnitude of changes in parts of the caste system is not as great as it is believed to be. These changes have not affected the essential aspects of the caste system as a whole." Ghurye (1961:209-210) was of the opinion that caste system has shed some of its features. He said: "Caste no longer rigidly determines an individual's occupation but continues to prescribe almost in its old vigour the circle into which one has to marry. One has still to depend very largely on one's caste for help at critical periods of one's life, like marriage and death." He further said: "Though caste has ceased to be a unit administering justice, yet it has not lost its hold on its individual members who still continue to be controlled by the opinion of the caste" (*Ibid*:190). He believed that vitality of the (caste) system in social life is as strong today as it ever was *(Ibid*:211).

Narmadeshwar Prasad (1956:240) analysed caste functions at two levels: ritual (marriage, dining, etc.) and ideology (attitude to Brahmins uniting to fight elections, etc.). He found that changes were taking place on both the levels of ritual and ideology. In spite of these changes, he maintained that the caste system as such remains very much the same. Changes within the system do take place but not beyond the system.

Kapadia (1962:75) tried to study the transitional nature of the different characteristics of the caste system by focusing on four characteristics: caste councils, commensal taboos, ceremonial purity, and endogamy. Analysing the functioning of caste councils, he found that while caste councils were very powerful in the 1860s and in 1910s, in the 1960s, though they were legally deprived of their authority to enforce their traditional norms upon their members by ex-communication, yet they continued to regulate the conduct and minds of their members. Talking of the change in the commensal taboo, he found that though it was true that even in the rural areas inter-dining, where members of all castes (including the Harijans) sat together in a row, was not uncommon in the 1960s, yet there was evidence to indicate that these inhibitions were not completely uprooted psychologically even in the urban areas (*Ibid*:74). Referring to the change in ceremonial purity, Kapadia (*Ibid*:77) stated that the Hindu concept of pollution was very extensive in its scope and mandatory in its observance till the twenties of this century. These rules are still observed in some high caste families—more often in moffusil and rural areas. But on the whole, they may be said to have been almost dispensed with. Lastly, pointing to endogamy (*Ibid*:77) he said that "the change in the endogamy characteristic of caste is not clearly intelligible. We do find the number of inter-caste marriages is on the increase, particularly during the last twenty years. At the same time, we have clear evidence of the persistence of caste endogamy". He, thus, concluded (*Ibid*:87) that whatever people may say about caste, there is yet acceptance of caste inhibitions. There is an unmistakable evidence that caste is not on its last leg though it has undergone a significant change.

Dumont taking up the question of "what is the caste system becoming nowadays" in his book *Homo Hierarchicus* (1971:217-18) holds that contemporary literature 'exaggerates' change. What is certain is that the caste system, as an overall framework, has not changed. The only change that seems to have taken place is that the traditional interdependence of castes has been replaced by a universe of impenetrable blocks, self-sufficient and in competition with one another. Dumont calls this "the substantialisation of caste' (cf. T.N. Madan's article in Dipankar Gupta, 1992:82).

Andre Beteille (1976:61-65) too has referred to some changes in the caste system; for example, in structural distance, in style of life, in commensal relations, and in endogamy, etc. In the past, structural distance among castes was maintained not only through the pursuit of different styles of life but by interdictions or prohibitions of various kinds—on marriage, commensality and social interchange in general. Today, the structural distance between two sub-divisions of the same subcaste is smaller than that between any one of these and a sub-division of a different caste. Changes have also taken place in styles of life distinctive of particular castes in the traditional system. In the traditional system, the unit of commensality was defined fairly rigidly in terms of caste affiliation. In recent decades, there has been a gradual expansion of this unit. Today, Brahmins may interdine with 'clean' Sudras but not generally with members of the polluting castes. The unit of endogamy has also expanded, though to a far smaller extent. All these changes in the caste system, according to Beteille, are the result of geographical mobility, western education, creation of new occupation to which recruitment is at least in principle based on factors other than caste, process of modernisation and political factors. However, it is evident that internal differentiation has proceeded much further among some castes than others. Those castes which have been most open to westernisation are probably the ones which have changed most. Such castes, for example, are Brahmins, Kayasths, Nairs, etc. and in general castes which have taken to western education and middle-class occupations and are predominantly urban in their distribution. Peasant castes in the rural areas have perhaps retained a greater measure of homogeneity and appear on the whole to have undergone less change.

Harold Gould (1988:158) concludes that the truth lies somewhere between these two positions. The effect of industrialisation on caste system has gone further than Weber seems to have believed possible. But there has been no dissolution of caste on the scale Marx foresaw. Parsons (1952:185) has characterised this reality through what he calls 'adaptive structures', which have mitigated the structural strains inherent in the exposure of people to competitive pressure where detailed universalistic discriminations are impracticable. Gould holds that this feature (of adaptive structure) of caste in India is evident not only in cities but in the villages too where the caste system continues to perform functions of security, solidarity and preferential treatment to groupings of people.

According to Gould (1988:162-164), castes functioning as adaptive structures in a modernising Indian society (which make their future stable and secure) can be examined at three levels—political, economic and social. At the political level, both in cities and villages, caste, communalism and political factionalism are inextricably interwoven. Parliamentary democracy, linked to the secret ballot, has meant that the manipulation of numbers, resources and favours which successful election to office confers, now occupy an important place. Since democratic politics is a competition among interest groups for the positions and spoils of power, it seems but natural that in India the formation of interest groups would reflect the deepest lines of cleavage and solidarity in the society—those dividing castes and ethnic communities. Casteism affects political issues and political decisions. Caste appeals are followed by religious appeals. This is vindicated by political functioning of both Hindus and Muslims in India. No wonder, caste will continue to be exploited at all political levels.

At the economic level, though it is true that role recruitment, reward distribution, and economic mobility of workers and wage earners are determined on the basis of their performance qualities, and people of different castes take to modern occupations, but it is equally true that in villages particularly, their position depends on pervasive caste structures and on inter-caste relations. In India today, the economic problem for individuals is scarcity—of wealth, jobs and opportunities—to participate in the new economic system that is slowly being built and is obviously the prime source of wealth and power. Thus, the aspects of caste that are most useful to the potential striver for position and power in the modern occupational order are nepotism and casteism.

At the social level, castes continue to be important in terms of determining the style of living as well as the rank positions of castes in which marriages are to be settled. Though the old ritual and occupational functions of castes are rapidly disappearing, yet caste endogamy is still preserved and the idea of the structure's sanctity has been retained and adapted to the needs of modern social indexing. It is also to be noted that the elite of India are overwhelmingly of high caste whereas the lower and menial castes display a precisely opposite placing of castes.

Singh (1974:324-327) has talked of three hypotheses pertaining to the future of the caste system in India: (i) mode of production hypothesis (ii) caste resilience hypothesis and (iii) structural adaptation hypothesis.

According to the 'mode of production' hypothesis, supported both by the Marxist (A.R.Desai) and non-Marxist (Kingsley Davis) sociologists, caste is declining. According to Kingsley Davis, the evidences of the decline of caste are: (1) noticeable loosening of commensal restrictions and toleration of violation of food taboos; (2) increasing tendency to ignore inter-marriage barriers or increasing number of inter-caste marriages; (3) increase in occupational mobility; (4) total weakening of caste councils; (5) weakening of *jajmani* system; (6) decreasing influence and dominance of upper castes on lower castes; (7) gradual removal of untouchability; and (8) growth of social mobility.

Kingsley Davis foresees the possibility of transformation of caste into class through adaptive changes under the impact of industrialisation though he does not employ the Marxist conceptual scheme for explaining such changes. On the other hand, A.R.Desai though holds the same view yet he bases his argument on the Marxist thesis. According to him, caste is social manifestation of forces of production and ownership of property based on agrarian feudal complex. The caste ranking contains an explosive class character. He holds (1969:111-112) that a couple of dozens of castes hold the monopoly of economic resources, political power and available educational and cultural facilities. It will not be possible to abolish caste hierarchy and caste system without adopting basic changes in the economic structure.

According to 'caste resilience' (recovering the original condition) hypothesis, industriaisation, growth of technology, westernisation and other democratic institutional spreads tend to activate and enlarge rather than restrict the process of caste functions. These also contribute to its (caste's) organisational mobilisation, rationalisation and fusion of ranks. M.N. Srinivas (1964) states that whereas caste mobility in medieval India was based on fission, in modern India it takes the form of fusion of caste segments. In this process, the nature of caste no doubt undergoes some transformation but it would not be true to assume, as Bailey does, that castes change their character. Caste system as such is not altered. Andre Beteille has also supported the thesis of caste resilience. He has referred to evidence for emergence of new caste-like structural forms (professional and occupational groups) which are rigid in structure. He has maintained (1965) "The changes in political and economic systems are not likely to lead to disappearance of castes. The castes of the future will no doubt carry the marks of the caste system".

Opposed to 'caste resilience' hypothesis is the 'structural adaptation' hypothesis. This hypothesis (Leach, 1960; Bailey, 1963; Singh, 1969; Kothari, 1970) holds that through formation of caste associations, caste federations and caste clusters, castes lose their original character and assume class-like forms. The proponents of this view do not link these changes with inevitable stages of transformation. They also do not talk about the disappearance of the caste system or its replacement by the class system.

Future of Caste System in India

There is no sign of caste system losing its grip. The only visible change is in the attitude of different castes to rise in caste hierarchy and gain social prestige. While changes in the caste system are continuous and regular, the (caste) system remains intact for all practical purposes. It must be held that change is not in the direction of dissolving the caste system. Some sort of class consciousness has crept into different castes. Electrified by the in-group feeling, they want to hold on to the caste system all the more tenaciously. Nowadays, a caste tries to organise itself for social, economic, and political purposes. Elections are being fought on caste basis. There are caste organisations like All India Kshatriya Mahasabha, All India Mathur Sangh, All India Bhargava Organisation, etc.

Progressive Hindus take three distinct stands about the future of the caste system:

(i) that caste is something evil and it should be abolished;
(ii) that the caste system has degenerated and efforts should be made to reinstate the traditional four orders. The greatest exponent of this thought was Mahatma Gandhi (*Young India*, 1919:479-88); and
(iii) that the caste system should be continued but it should be reinstated under totally different conditions. These people want to amalgamate various sub-castes having cultural unity and economic similarity. Gradually, the castes which will approximately be on a footing of equality will consolidate and ultimately a casteless society

will be established. These people want the process to be slow because it would afford sufficient time for education and the formation of informed opinion with the require adjustment of those castes/classes which are not yet prepared for a wholesale change in their age-old customs (see Ghurye, 1961:305-307.).

Scholars like A.J. Toynbee, T.H. Marshall, P. Kodanda Rao, etc., have evaluated these three schools of thought. Discussing the first school led by Gandhi, they contend that: first, it is impractical because the only basis of assigning a particular order (out of four orders) to persons is the occupation they follow. In the present society, occupations are so specialised and varied and people of the same family are engaged in so many different occupations that it would be impossible to assign them membership of one or the other order. *Secondly*, even if this settlement (of including castes in one or the other of the first three orders) were possible, what about the untouchable castes? Gandhiji being against untouchability naturally proposed some respectable status for these castes. But where are they to be provided for? In whatever order they may be included, there is bound to be tremendous protest from that order. *Thirdly*, assuming that the classification of castes in four orders would be possible, are we going to permit or prohibit marriages between these four orders? Are we going to continue restrictions in the matter of marriage, food, etc.? Both would create their own problems. It may, therefore, be concluded that a return to the four-fold division of society is impractical and even if accomplished, it would serve no useful purpose.

Taking the other point of view that castes should be slowly abolished by consolidation of the sub-castes into larger castes, scholars have said that to propose this point is to miss the real problem. This method, they claim, was tried in Bombay for a number of decades but the results were disastrous. The sub-castes that joined together to create a big group retained their internal feelings of exclusiveness with undiminishing vigour. The new group took up rather a militant attitude against other castes, especially those which were popularly regarded as immediately higher or lower than the caste which it represented. Thus, scholars claimed that the spirit of caste patriotism or casteism is created and if we followed the second viewpoint, diminishing of casteism would be very difficult and it would create an unhealthy atmosphere for the full growth of national consciousness.

Some scholars have supported the third view that the caste system should be immediately abolished. They are of the opinion that we have to fight against and totally uproot casteism. Ghurye was one scholar who favoured this viewpoint. But this opinion of Ghurye was expressed in about 1931. Since then about seven decades have passed and lot of changes have taken place in Indian society, including independence of the country and the promalgamation of many laws against the caste system. For example, the Constitution of India (implemented from January 26, 1950) says that: (i) the State shall not discriminate against any citizen on the ground of caste, (equal opportunity to all castes), (ii) no citizen shall, on the ground of caste, be subject to restriction regarding access to or use of shops, restuarants and public wells and tanks (removal of civil disabilities), and (iii) the practice of untouchability is forbidden. Similarly, there are no restrictions on the following of any occupation. Feelings of equality, liberty and fraternity have been promoted which have cut the very roots of caste. A special officer (Commissioner) was appointed in 1951 for looking after the scheduled castes and the backward classes. No more individual's caste is recorded in census. In spite of these changes in the last several decades, and particularly in the last two decades, casteism and the evils of caste have not been rooted out. Asirvatham (1957) was of the opinion that "whatever uses caste might have had in the past, it is a hinderance to progress today and, therefore, we should oppose it tooth and nail". D.N. Majumdar also maintained in the 1950s and 1960s that just as a broken or a poisoned finger is amputated and not the whole hand, similarly untouchability, exploitation of one caste by another, and such other harmful concomitants of the caste system should be done away with and not the whole system.

More than one and a quarter century ago (in 1869), Max Muller had opined that caste cannot be abolished in India and to attempt it would be one of the most hazardous operations that was ever performed in a political body. As a religious institution, caste will die; as a social institution, it will live and improve. Kolenda (1997:4-5) is of the opinion that the traditional caste system as a set of occupationally specialised, interdependent castes, ranked by purity and pollution customs, shows signs of disappearing. With decline in occupational specialisation and in the system of purity and pollution which ranked castes relative to each other and kept them separate from one another, the key question now is whether there will be a new integration into a new caste system. Her opinion is that it is indeed unlikely that a social structure organising the political, economic and ritual life of a people for over one thousand years could be totally expunged within a few decades. Social scientists working in the field, all report that the caste system is alive.

It is true that the caste system is a stumbling block in attaining the material and spiritual prosperity or in the social and national development. So long this cankerous system holds sway, we cannot achieve our social ideas. Hence, the sooner its death-knell is sounded, the higher our prospects of progress. Yet it is a fact that it is not easy to abolish this system.

Narmadeshwar Prasad in his study of three areas—industrial, non-industrial and rural—was given a few remedies by his respondents (1,225) to weaken the caste system. These were: education and proper opportunity to all (39.1%), inter-caste marriages (35.3%), removal of untouchability (12.2%), and treating people on the basis of equality (13.4%). But will these measures really help in abolishing or even weakening the caste system? Perhaps not. Even the Supreme Court in giving its verdict on the implementation of Mandal Commission's report in November 1992 had virtually implied that caste alone would be the basis of reservation.

What are the properties and functions of caste which account for its continuance in the contemporary society? Two functions appear to be crucial today: (i) it provides opportunity for power, and (ii) it makes social mobility feasible (if we accept Srinivas's view of the possibility of sanskritisation of a caste). Mobility—occupational, economic and social—in modern societies depends on education, training, material resources, nepotic networks available, personal influence, social refinement, as well as caste rank. It may, thus, be concluded that the caste system will continue to be a reality in the years and decades to come.

MOBILITY IN CASTE

Indian social reality has been analysed by social scientists in terms of social categories like caste, class, tribe and religious and linguistic groups. The same categories have been used for getting an insight into the process of change in the society. While earlier it was maintained that caste system keeps Indian society as a closed system, now it is said that the triangle of endogamy, hierarchy and pollution is breaking down (K.S. Singh, 1992:23). The problem of social mobility is directly linked with the system of social stratification. Yogendra Singh (1974:403) is of the opinion that the tradition-modernity dichotomy in the studies of social mobility has often led to a confusion of perspectives. Such confusion was found among western scholars. It led them to contend that mobility was absent in the social system of traditional India which was said to have a closed system (ascriptive-oriented) of social stratification. This only shows the ideological bias of the scholars. M.N. Srinivas (1968:18-35) too has said that while traditional Indian society was stationary in character, it did not preclude the mobility, upward as well as downward, of individual castes in the local hierarchy. Surajit Sinha (1957) has also pointed out that many tribals ascended to the position of royalty in India by establishing claim to Kshatriyahood by conquest and accumulation of power.

Silverberg (1968:128) has talked of social mobility in India through renunciation. In the scheme of *ashramas*, renunciation was prescribed for the twice-born castes. In practice, however, members from the lower castes also used to become *sanyasins* (mendicants/monks) to escape the deprivations of their own place in the social hierarchy.

In recent times, social mobility as a process has become more active. M.N. Srinivas has explained it through the processes of sanskritisation and westernisation. McKim Marriott, Louis Dumont and Rajni Kothari have also found social mobility prevalent at different levels. On the one hand, the members of lower castes attempt to raise their social status in the caste hierarchy, on the other hand, caste as a group attempts mobility by gaining political power or through the process of politicisation of castes. We will, thus, study caste mobility at different levels: (i) through warfare, (ii) through serving rulers, (iii) through census commissioners at different levels, (iv) through social processes of sanskritisation and westernisation, and (v) by use of politics.

Mobility Through Warfare

M.N. Srinivas and Pauline Kolenda have referred to caste mobility through resort to warfare in Mughal period. Kolenda has said that until the British unification in the first half of the nineteenth century, the most effective way to rise in the caste system was by the acquisition of territory either through conquest or by peaceful occupancy of sparsely populated or empty land. K. M. Panikkar (the historian) has said that "since the fifth century B.C., every known royal family has come from a non-Kshatriya caste". Kolenda (1998:97) has said that in ancient India, rulers were Kshatriyas. There were however, some rulers of peasant *jati* who after capturing territory had established a kingdom. The peasant conquerors after becoming rulers made claims to being Kshatriyas. Thus, the peasant conquerors rose to Kshatriya rank.

M. N. Srinivas has given the example of Shivaji in Moghul period. Shivaji's father was Jagirdar or vassal to the Muslim ruler of Bijapur (in present Maharashtra). Shivaji overthrew the Moghul rule and established his own empire from the Arabian sea to the Bay of Bengal. His caste, the Maratha, was considered to be of Sudra varna. So Shivaji went through a religious rite of transition into Kshtriyahood. Along with Shivaji's rise in varna status, his caste, the Marathas, also came to have Kshatriya rank (Srinivas, 1968:189, Marriott 1968: 112-113, Kolenda, 1968:97).

Mobility Through Serving Rulers

Jatis whose members served either Hindu or non-Hindu rulers attained higher varna rank. For example, the Patidars of Gujarat, a peasant group of Sudra *varna*, supported the Maratha descendants of Shivaji, the Gaekwads, who ruled Central Gujarat. Gradually, claiming to be Kshatriyas, they established their own small regimes (Shah, 1964). Another example of rise in caste through service to rulers is that of Kayasthas, a caste of scribes (who, before the invention of printing, were professional letter-writers, or who made copies of writing, or who kept records). The Kayasthas made themselves useful first to the Moghuls, then to the British rulers. While they were a low caste in the twelfth century, by the nineteenth century, the Kayasthas in Northern India had risen to the 'twice-born' category, although the Kayastha caste further to the East in Bengal remained Sudras (Cohn in Silverberg, 1968: 122-123). Burton Stein 1968), a historian, has also said that in medieval South India, families rose through association with Muslim rulers. The unit of mobility was not the caste (jati) but the family or a group of families. Srinivas suggests that such familial upward mobility resulted in the formation of a new *jati* out of an established larger one.

Assigning Higher Status (to Castes) by the Census Commissioners in the British Period

Recording *jati* identities in census enumerations from 1891 to 1931, many middle and low castes made efforts to get themselves registered as members of the twice-born *varnas*. These claims reached a peak in 1901 census when Herbert Risley, the Census Commissioner, tried to rank all castes. Hundreds of *jatis* tried to ensure a higher rank by claiming high *varna* titles. For example, the Kurmi cultivators of Bengal wanted to be Kurmi Kshatriyas; the Teli (oil-pressers) wanted to be called Vaishyas. Evidence was offered from myths and history for each claim. District committees were set up to evaluate the claims, some of which were sustained but most were rejected.

Caste Mobility Through Social Processes of Sanskritisation and Westernisation

Caste system had become so rigid in Brahmancial, Muslim, and the British periods that through several restrictions like hereditary membership, endogamy, denial of occupational mobility, and commensal and social restrictions, etc. members enjoyed a fixed status for all times. However, from the third decade of the twentieth century onwards, caste system could not remain rigid because of the processes of industrialisation, urbanisation, spread of education, enactment of some legislative measures, and social movements of several social reformers. M.N. Srinivas explained status mobility in caste in 1952 through the process of sanskritisation and westernisation. He maintained that a low caste was able to rise in a generation or two to a higher position in the hierarchy by adopting vegetarianism and teetotalism. It took over rituals, customs, rites and beliefs of the Brahmins and gave up some of their own considered to be impure.

Initially, Srinivas talked of emulating the Brahmin style of life by the lower castes but later on he talked of emulation of life style of dominant castes of any high varna. Lynch (1969:218) has called this 'elite emulation'. Barnett has referred to emulating the style of life of Brahmins and Kshatriyas as 'kingly model' of emulation. Thus, an upwardly mobile *jati* tried to improve its status through sanskritisation or 'elite emulation' or 'kingly emulation'. However, M.N. Srinivas (1962:58) has claimed that untouchables are never able to cross the line of Sudra and move to 'higher' caste.

A few facts worth noting in the process of sanskritisation are: (1) The process of sanskritisation has been integrated with economic and political domination, i.e., role of local dominant caste in the process of cultural domination has been stressed. Thus, though initially the lower castes imitated Brahmins but soon the local dominant caste, i.e., a non-Brahmin caste, came to be imitated. (2) Sanskritisation occurred in those castes which enjoyed political and economic power but were not rated high in ritual ranking, i.e., there was a gap between their ritual and politico-economic positions. (3) Economic betterment is not a necessary precondition to sanskritisation. (4) Sanskritisation is a two-way process. Not only a caste 'took' from the caste higher to it but in turn it 'gave' some thing to the caste. (5) Unit of mobility is group and not individual or family. (6) After independence, the process of sanskritisation has been weakened. The emphasis is now on vertical mobility and not on horizontal mobility. (7) Sanskritisation explains social change primarily in cultural and not in structural terms. (8) Sanskritisation does not automatically result in the achievement of a higher status for the group. The group has to wait for an indefinite period to get higher status. (9) Changing polluting occupation, stopping the use of alcohol and beef and adopting sanskritic customs, beliefs and deities by the lower castes does not necessarily lead to mobility. Mobility may not be a goal for these activities.

Factors that have made sanskritisation possible are industrialisation, occupational mobility, developed means of communication, spread of literacy, western technology, and awakening among the lower castes to give up polluting occupations and evil customs and social practices. According to Srinivas himself, one factor which has helped the spread of sanskritisation is the separation of ritual acts from the accompanying *mantras* (citations) which facilitated the spread of Brahmanical rituals.

Along with sanskritisation, the process of *westernisation* has also made social mobility possible. Westernisation is a process of change in ideology, values, institutions and technology of a non-western society as a result of cultural contact with the western society for a long period (Srinivas, 1962:55). The important feature of Westernisation is emphasis on technology and rationalism. Scholars like Daniel Lerner, Harold Gould, Milton Singer and Yogendra Singh prefer 'modernisation' to 'westernisation'. But Srinivas considers this term (modernisation) as 'subjective' (*Seminar*, 88, 1986:2). Criticisms against using the process of sanskritisation for explaining social mobility are: (1) In some parts of the country (like Punjab and former Sind) what was imitated by castes was not sanskritic tradition but the Islamic tradition. Sikhism emerged as synthesis of the Hindu tradition with the Islamic movements of Sufism and mysticism. (2) Sanskritisation fails to account for the adoption of non-sanskritic tradition (Yogendra Singh, 1973:11). (3) Srinivas' process (of sanskritisation) explains social mobility (and also social change) only in Indian society (where caste system exists). It is not useful for other societies.

Caste Mobility Through Politicisation

Several castes have used politics in their attempt to better their condition or to achieve their goals. Use of politics, according to Eleanor Zelliot, covers securing governmental benefits and representation on legislative and political bodies. Some examples which may be given in this connection are: Mahars of Maharashtra, Kshatriyas of Gujarat, Nadars of Tamil Nadu, and Reddys and Kammas of Andhra Pradesh.

The Mahars of Maharashtra, constituting about 10 per cent of the population of the state (out of the total 13 per cent scheduled caste population), initially operated under conditions of social degradation but ultimately used politics for ameliorating their social condition. Ambedkar organised them into a political force and formed a Scheduled Caste Federation which was ultimately used as a political tool for achieving the goals of social equality and social mobility. Mahars, who were regarded as untouchable, worked as watchmen, messengers, sweeping roads, carrying death notices to other villages and so forth. Temples, schools, and wells were all closed to them. Later on (from the 1860s onwards), they started working in factories, railways, docks, ammunition factories, etc. Even those who lived in villages discarded traditional low occupations. A good number joined the military too. The military service helped them not only to climb in the social hierarchy but also exposed them to western culture. In World War II, a Mahar regiment was also raised. Some Mahars were converted to Christianity while some joined the Kabir and Ramadi *panths* (sects) which stressed equality. In 1936, under the leadership of Ambedkar, their temple-entry attempt turned into political movement, rejecting Hinduism altogether. In 1937, Ambedkar established Independent Labour Party which gave majority of tickets to Mahars. Since then, through the Republic Party as well as through Parliament and Vidhan Sabha elections of 1946, 1951 and 1956, the Mahars have established themselves as an important political force in Maharashtra politics.

Rajni Kothari and Rushikesh Maru (1973: 70-101) have given examples of some middle and lower castes and economically depressed communities of cultivators in Gujarat who federated together into a common organisation in the late 1940s and the 1950s for achieving political power. After winning elections against the Congress, they were 'accepted' into the Kshatriya fold. Thus, politics worked as a cementing force for them.

Robert Hardgrave Jr. (1973:102-126) examined the solidarity and cohesion among Nadars in Tamil Nadu and its integrated political culture. The breakdown of economic dependence on other castes and the extension of caste ties over a wide geographic area gave this caste (Nadars) a new solidarity, which uplifted them socially, economically and politically. After improving their status economically, they claimed the Kshatriya status. In 1921 census, all Nadars declared themselves as 'Nadar Kshatriyas'. Today, the Nadars have become one of the most economically and politically successful community in the south. All these examples show how lower castes used politics, achieved political power and caste solidarity, and ultimately high social position in society.

K.L. Sharma (1997:158-173) has pointed out three approaches to social mobility: structural-historical, Marxist, and culturological or indological. A.R. Kamat has used first approach in explaining caste mobility in Maharashtra by referring to the displacement of the old urban-dominated political leadership by a new set of leaders drawn from the advanced rural elements, widespread political consciousness and democratisation of politics. The marxist approach has been used by Arvind Das (1984: 1616-19) and Pradhan H. Prasad (1979:481) in their analysis of class-caste situation of inter-caste conflicts in Bihar. Social mobility has also been explained in terms of decline of *jajmani* system, emergence of modern occupations (Sharma, 1974), decline of untouchability and the pollution-purity principle (Kolenda, 1986), and education, state policy of protective discrimination, and social movements.

CASTEISM

The rising trends of casteism and communalism and the accompanying violence have created a feeling of suspicion and insecurity among various castes. People in high positions in a caste give preference to members of their own castes and sub-castes in appointments and promotions. This creates the caste solidarity to the extent that: (i) one caste attempts to dominate over others, (ii) higher castes exploit the lower castes, (iii) elections are contested and won on caste basis, and (iv) inter-caste conflicts increase in society. Though casteism, inter-caste conflicts and incidents of caste violence are more prevalent in rural areas yet they occur in the urban areas as well. In independent India, competition among different castes seems to be the normal situation. With the passing of political power to the people, castes have become pressure groups and are competing for power and using power to benefit caste fellows. Many examples are cited in this regard. A few years ago, in one state, a very large number of Yadavas were recruited in the police department because a Yadav enjoyed the highest political power in the state. In the 1950s, there was a case of a state in which a Reddy Chief Minister appointed a large number of Reddys as ministers. In one state, a Jain officer gave preference to Jains and a Rajput officer to Rajputs in all appointments. This tendency increases not only hatred for other castes but also leads to caste conflicts in the country. Such conflicts abound in Bihar, Uttar Pradesh, Rajasthan, Tamil Nadu, Karnataka, Gujarat and Maharashtra. When one caste numerically preponderates over other castes in one geographical area, it seeks the position of a 'dominant' caste by attempting to secure economic and political power. When a caste enjoys one form of dominance, it is frequently able to acquire the other forms as well in course of time.

Casteism creates such solidarity among members that they use their unity to assert themselves or exploit the deprived caste(s). The best examples of this nature are found in Bihar among Bhumihars, Yadavs, Kurmis, Dalits, etc.

In politics, since last few decades casteism factor has been playing an important role even in the selection of candidates for contesting elections. In seeking votes also, this factor is played upon heavily.

The National Integration Council, set up in June 1962, has been striving to deal with problems of casteism, regionalism and communalism. The Council set up in 1968 separate committees to deal with these problems. All these committees produced worthy recommendations focusing on guidelines, legislation and administrative action. By 1970, all this lapsed into inaction. In 1980, the second incarnation of the National Integration Council met in 1980 and again in 1984. This time also, three subcommittees were set up but they too failed to do anything substantial. The September 1986 meeting set up a sub-group of five persons to foster national integration. In February 1990, and again in 1991 and in July 1993 came yet other incarnation of the NIC but no solution has been evolved till date on the burning problem of containing casteism and communalism and creating national harmony.

ISSUES OF EQUALITY AND SOCIAL JUSTICE

The issue of social inequality is a crucial problem of Indian society. The study of social stratification of a society, based either on caste or on class, is concerned largely with the understanding of inequality.

Louis Dumont, a French sociologist, has explained 'inequality' in caste system on a different basis. He holds that 'hierarchy' and not 'inequality' is the opposite of 'equality'. He explains 'hierarchy' in caste system in terms of 'purity and pollution', which according to him, is the basic principle of caste system. Hierarchy, according to him, involves the superiority of the pure to the impure, separation of the pure from the impure, and separation of pure occupations from the impure ones in the division of labour. He, thus, talks of (a) the hierarchical co-existence of the two opposites, (b) hierarchy being quite independent of natural inequalities or the distribution of power, (c) the ranking of castes is religious in nature, and (d) hierarchy is the relationship between the encompasser and the encompassed. Dumont's ideology of caste and perception of hierarchy in the caste system is thus totally different from that of other western scholars (Risley, Mayer, Marriott, etc.) who have explained it in terms of western concepts like individualism, egalitarianism, etc. He (Dumont) relates hierarchy with the theory of varna which involves gradation but is distinct from both power and authority. The subordination of the king to the priest in Hindu society involves religious (ritual) ranking. Thus, Dumont holds that hierarchy encompasses both the *varna* divisions and the caste system. He, thus, gives importance to *ideological orientation* in interaction and behaviour within and between castes. He also maintains that traditional division of labour (the *jajmani* system), regulation of marriage and social contacts are based on hierarchy or religious values rather than on economic or social logic.

T.N. Madan (1971; also see Gupta, Dipankar, 1998) has raised question against Dumont's notion of disjunction between status and power. He says that subordination of power (say king) to the status (say Brahmin) creates difficulties in understanding. The approach is ingenious but the understanding is not satisfactory.

In the analysis of inequality, our contention is that inequality caused by centuries of economic stagnation resulting into differences in life chances between classes and inequality caused by traditional values, social practices, and social restrictions imposed by the caste system, require an exercise in sociological analysis. Historically, the first step towards a sociological understanding of inequality was taken when attention came to be paid to inequalities among men in their conditions of existence. The Hindu view of life explained it in terms of different orders of men born into different castes and endowed with unequal abilities, aptitudes and aspirations. Rousseau talked of political inequalities such as those of wealth, honour and power based on the basis of convention and authorised by the consent of men. Though men are free to discard conventions and institute new ones, yet it is not clear how inequalities, which make men suffer, have been sustained since long. It is only when we started comparing inequalities among men in our society with other societies that a sociological approach was used to compare patterns of stratification and rates of mobility first in the industrial societies and later in the agrarian societies.

In traditional Indian society, the basis of hierarchy and existence of social inequalities was the idea of purity and pollution. In modern industrial society, the basis of inequalities is 'achievement' which is the result of 'open and fair' competition. Hindu religious texts tell us that our society is divided into four *varnas* and into numerous *jatis* arranged into certain types of mutual relations. People accepted status hierarchies so long they linked caste with religion. And this linkage continued up to the 1920s and the 1930s of the twentieth century. The contacts with western culture, spread of education and the processes of industrialisation and urbanisation changed people's ideas. They started questioning man-made inequalities. The political independence of the country provided them further opportunity to raise the question of inequalities and demand social justice. The recommendations of commissions like Kelkar, Mandal, etc. and political deeds of seeking votes on caste and community basis provided them further impetus to demand equality of opportunity and removal of social injustice. No wonder, the depressed castes and classes got reservations in jobs, legislative bodies and educational institutions, etc. in the name of social justice. Women partially succeeded in getting this justice when in some states, 20 per cent seats came to be reserved for women in panchayats and in middle of December 1998, a bill was introduced in the parliament for reserving one-third (33%) seats for women. But attempts to remove social inequalities on caste, class and community basis have created frustrations among some castes and communities, which have resulted into various agitations and violent actions. Somewhat more worrying are the extreme reactions from educated persons and views of politicians with vested interests. There is no doubt that social and cultural life has changed a great deal in the course of development. Many suggestions are also being forwarded as remedies for these evils. It is only the common framework of ideas and values on reducing social gradations that can reduce social inequalities and provide justice to varied categories of people.

Andre Beteille (*Inequality Among Men*, 1977:49) has talked of relationship between power and inequality. Power maintains inequality and it also transforms inequality. In the caste system, the inequalities among men were accepted not only because of the belief that people were endowed with different qualities but also because castes were viewed as instruments of power. Once the new instruments of power introduced by the British withdrew their support from the hierarchy and power of caste (say, taking away the powers of caste councils by the courts), the hierarchy itself began to crumble. In the class system, those who possess land or property dominate over the landless and the propertyless. The sociological analysis of power inequalities takes into account two features: one, the power of some over other, and two, their power to interpret, alter and create the rules by which all, including themselves, are bound. At the same time, scope of power is also significant in analysis. The same individual or group does not hold power equally in all spheres of society. We also ask, how far different individuals who hold and exercise power in one sphere or several, constitute a cohesive group, clearly marked out from the rest of society. In Bihar, the inequality of power has led to the origin of caste *senas* and caste massacres.

After referring to inequalities of status and inequalities of power, it is also important to refer to inequalities in general conditions of social existence. A very large number of people perceive inequality in terms of division of society into classes and the unequal distribution of wealth. The division of the industrial societies into two categories—the capitalist and the socialist—has its origin in social class. The capitalist societies are organised through private ownership of property and presence of classes in these societies is freely acknowledged, while in socialist societies, it is conditionally acknowledged. Has the abolition of private property in socialist societies led to the disappearance of classes ? Andre Beteille holds (*Ibid*:75) that since inequalities in Russia and other socialist countries continue to exist, it confirms that inequality is a much broader concept than class.

Talking of social inequalities in terms of status, power and income, a question may be raised: Is egalitarian society possible? Did it exist in the past? Can it emerge in future? Even though all our modern societies are built on the promise of equality, yet the prospect of an egalitarian society does not appear to be feasible. Beteille has also contended (*Ibid*:153) that so long as evaluation and organisation remain as inherent features of social life, the problem of inequality will continue to exist. We may conceive egalitarian society at two levels: one, in which different positions may enjoy same prestige and power, and two in which all members enjoy equal access to positions of power and prestige. It is now conceded by almost all people that envisaging such societies in the future will be illusory.

CASTE AND POLITICS

The relationship between caste and politics has been analysed at two levels: one, how caste affects politics, and two, how politics affects caste. We will first take up the relationship in terms of awareness of castes in politics.

The Awareness

The interest and awareness of various castes in politics may be studied in terms of four factors: interest of castes in politics, political knowledge and political awareness of castes, identification of castes with political parties, and influence of castes on political affairs. These four aspects were studied by Anil Bhatt in the 1970s by studying 1,713 persons of high, middle, and low castes with different backgrounds in four states (Uttar Pradesh, Gujarat, West Bengal and Andhra Pradesh). Analysing the political interest by taking all castes together, he found that about 25 per cent castes had high interest in politics, 45 per cent had moderate interest, and 30 per cent had no interest at all. With regard to the awareness of political changes and major political problems in the country, he found that higher castes had more interest than the middle and the lower castes. He did not find any relationship between caste status and identification with political parties. Lastly, he found that some high castes are politically influential while middle and low castes dominate only in few villages.

The Relationship

Rajni Kothari (1970) examined the relationship between caste and politics by analysing the issue as to what happens to political system because of the vote of castes. He found that three factors—education, government patronage, and slowly expanding franchise (including 18-21 year old young persons in electorate)—have penetrated the caste system because of which it (caste system) has come to affect democratic politics in the country. Economic opportunity, administrative patronage, and positions of power offered by the new institutions and the new leadership drew castes into politics. This involvement (of castes in politics) resulted in two things: the caste system made available to the leadership the structural and the ideological basis for political mobilisation, and two, leadership was forced to make concessions to local opinion and organise castes for economic and political purposes.

The use of caste in politics was analysed by Rajni Kothari (1970) in two different stages. The first stage involved intellectuals, and antagonism and resentment between high entrenched castes (like Reddi in Andhra Pradesh, Pattidars in Gujarat, Lingayats in Karnataka, Bhumihars in Bihar, and Rajputs in Rajasthan) and high ascendant castes (like Kayastha in Bihar, Jats in Rajasthan). The second stage involved factionalism and fragmentation within the competing (entrenched and ascendant) castes as a result of which multi-caste and multi-factional alignments develop. The lower castes also are brought in to support high caste leaders and to strengthen a faction. In the first stage, only three components of caste are involved—the power structure of caste, distribution of economic benefits, and caste consciousness. But in the second stage, other components of castes like caste consciousness, client loyalties etc. also come to be involved. Further, three sub-stages are pointed out by Kothari in the first stage. In the first sub-stage, the struggle for power and benefits is at first limited to the entrenched castes, i.e., those which exercised preponderant influence economically and politically but not necessarily numerically. In the second sub-stage, ascendant castes (i.e., unsatisfied castes wanting higher roles) also start competing for power. In the third sub-stage, there is not only competition between entrenched and ascendant castes (for power and benefits) but also within these castes. In the second stage, called as the stage of caste fragmentation or factionalism, the leadership cleavages are created and multi-caste and multi-factional alignments come into being. This also creates the problem of rival caste leaders in politics. These leaders come to involve masses too because they (leaders) want to appeal to wider identities. There is also change in leadership in this stage.

Kothari has talked of the third stage also in relationship between caste and politics. While in the first stage, 'entrenched' high castes are first politicised and 'ascendant' high castes respond with resentment and feelings of relative deprivation (e.g., entrenched caste of Brahmins and ascendant caste of Marathas in Maharashtra) and in the second stage factions emerge within the competing (entrenched and ascendant) castes and lower castes are also brought in for support, in the third stage, identifications other than those of caste are likely to become more important with advancing education, urbanisation and adoption of modern achievement orientation. There, thus, emerge cross-cutting alliances.

The process of fusion of castes is illustrated by the DMK in Tamil Nadu and Republican Party (consisting of Mahars and other untouchable castes) in Maharashtra. The former party is politically powerful but the latter party has not yet wielded much political power.

In panchayats at the village level these days, elections are often contested on cross-cutting votes. Large landless castes now have the power of voting strength; so they challenge the traditionally dominant caste which has power derived from land control. Dominant castes as well as ascendant (higher) castes are usually tied in with the important political parties of the region and upward mobility through the political party organisation takes place. Thus, today on the one side caste ceases to be an exclusive political support-base and on the other it greatly affects politics.

Kothari draws four conclusions from the present relationship between caste and politics:

(1) New elite structure has emerged in politics which is drawn from different castes but shares a common secular outlook and is homogeneous in terms of some values.
(2) Castes have assumed new organisational form Thus (i) caste associations are now functioning at various levels (universities, hostels, clubs, government offices, and so forth; (ii) caste conferences have become broad-based; and (iii) caste federations have emerged.
(3) Castes have started functioning on factional basis. These factions divide not only political groups but also social groups.
(4) The caste identifications have given a new relevance to the electorate system. It is not only the large castes which affect politics but also the smaller castes which have become important in seeking votes.

Caste and Voting Behaviour

Voting provides an opportunity to castes to assert their influence. Scholars like Rajni Kothari (1970), Lindzey Gardner, Miller (1950), Key (1955), Campbell (1960), and Norman Palmer (1976) have referred to caste as a voting determinant. Just as in Britain, voting is class-determinant, in United States, it is race-determinant, in India it is caste-determinant. For those castes which are at the bottom of the hierarchy, voting right serves as a powerful activity. The lower the social and economic status of a caste, the higher the importance of the vote. Several studies like those of Kothari, Mayer, Verma and Bhambhri, Ramashray Roy, Cohn, etc., have shown that castes exert influence and have gained a bargaining power because of their voting strength. Andre Beteille (see Kothari, 1970:291) has also said that loyalties of caste are exploited in voting. New alliances cutting across caste are also formed. Rudolph is of the opinion that caste association has given caste a new vitality and democracy has enabled caste to play an important political role in India. D.L. Seth (*Economic and Political Weekly*, January 1970:147) conducted a study in 1967 in which he interviewed 2,287 persons from different constituencies of India and found that among various factors, voting behaviour was determined on the advice of caste leaders only in 1 per cent cases, by family in 46 per cent cases and by voters' own decision in 49 per cent cases. In 4 per cent cases, the determinant could not be traced. Another study conducted among 1,000 voters in Puna in the same year (1967) revealed that caste affected voting in 58 per cent cases. In the last three Lok Sabha elections (1996, 1998 and September 1999) as well as in the Vidhan Sabha elections in four states in December 1998, caste was found to be an important factor in voting. Harold Gould (*Economic and Political Weekly*, August 1977), however, is of the opinion that caste has ceased to be a determinant of politics in India.

Political Elite, Political Parties and Caste Mobilisation

Caste has become a determinant factor of 'political elite' status. Studies conducted on political elite by scholars like Sirsikar, Sachchidananda, Ram Ahuja, S.K. Lal, etc., have all pointed out that in the emergence of elite, higher castes have an extraordinary advantage over the middle and the lower castes. Before independence, generally the upper caste groups occupied the centre of the political stage in the Congress party engaged in the freedom struggle but after independence, individuals from the middle and the lower castes also entered political power field. The reservation policy enabled individuals from the lower castes to emerge as leaders, while elite from the middle castes emerged due to their improved educational and socio-economic status. Thus, caste system which had only ritualistic function (including determining occupation and social status) assumed the new role of regulating political behaviour of the people. In villages also, caste has assumed great significance in emerging power structure. In offices, universities, secretariats, etc. we hear of Jain lobby, Rajput lobby, Brahmin lobby, Yadav lobby, Kayasth lobby, Reddy lobby, etc. If activists operate as casteist in social and occupational life, how can they think in terms of operating as non-casteist in political life? Our political elite, thus, may talk of secularism and denounce caste and casteist politics but in practice they function under the pressure of caste, since their own emergence as leaders has a caste background.

Political parties also mobilise caste support. In fact, the problems of mobilisation of masses today (1999) are the same as they were four decades ago. Just as in the 1930s and the 1940s social reformers believed that without the enlightment of masses, their organisation for political activity was not possible, similarly today also politicians try to get support from the caste leaders and at the same time drive home to them the utility of political means in achieveing their goals. Some scholars have studied mobilisation of castes by the political parties in different states in the last three or four decades. For example, Richard Sission analysed (see Kothari, 1973: 175-227) the development of Congress party in one district (Nagaur) in Rajasthan in the 1960s in terms of the caste support; Ramashray Roy (see Kothari, 1973: 228-255) studied recruitment to a political party on caste basis in Bihar in the 1960s; Andre Beteille (see Kothari, 1973: 259-297) studied shift in the power of political parties through the caste system in Tamil Nadu in the 1970s; Anil Bhatt (see Kothari, 1973: 299-339) studied political mobilisation of castes in Gujarat, Donald Rosenthal in two cities (Agra in Uttar Pradesh and Poona in Maharashtra in 1963-64), and Harold Gould in Uttar Pradesh in 1990. All these studies showed that political parties mobilise castes for their functioning and seek their support in winning elections.

People's Perception of the Use of Caste in Politics

How do people perceive the use of caste in politics? We can classify people in three groups on the basis of their perceptions: one, who lament this role and think that politics should be free of caste and casteism; second, who think that political relationships have no independent capacity to influence social relationships; lastly, who claim the autonomy of either caste or politics or both. As regards the first view, Rajni Kothari (1973: 4-7) does not agree with it. He says that politics is the acquisition of power for the realisation of certain goals and power is acquired by consolidating positions through mobilising the group (caste) support. Since in India social system is organised around caste structure, therefore, caste and politics can never be separated. Thus, casteism in politics is nothing but politicisation of caste. As regards the second view, politics is seen as an instrument to consolidate or raise its position. As such, politics does not affect the structure of society. Kothari has criticised this view also. He says, there is always mutual effect of caste and politics on each other. As regards the third view, this includes progressive economists, indologists and political and social anthropologists. They want to protect caste and free caste from politics and politics from caste. Kothari has criticised this view too, holding that all these scholars have failed to see that there never was a complete polarisation between the caste system and the political system. A.R. Desai, K.M. Kapadia, G.S. Ghurye also held the same view. Politics has used caste and will continue to use it for socio-political purposes.

Further Readings

Bailey, F.G., *Caste, Tribe and Nation*, Manchester University Press, Manchester, England, 1960.

Berreman, Gerald D., *Caste in the Modern World*, General Learning Press, Morristown, N.J. 1973.

Beteille, Andre, *Inequality Among Men*, 1977.

Dumont, Louis, *Homo Hierarchicus*, Chicago University Press, Chicago, 1970.

Ghurye, G.S, *Caste, Class and Occupation*, Popular Book Depot, Bombay, 1961.

Gupta, Dipankar, *Social Stratification*, The Oxford University Press, Delhi, 1998 (5th impression).

Imtiaz, Ahmad (ed.), *Caste and Social Stratification among the Muslims*, Manohar Book Service, Delhi, 1973.

Kapadia, K.M., "Caste in Transition", *Sociological Bulletin*, September 1962.

Kolenda, Pauline, *Caste in Contemporary* India, Rawat Publications, Jaipur, 1997 (originally published in 1968).

Kothari, Rajni (ed.), *Caste in Indian Politics*, Orient Longman Ltd, New Delhi, 1970 (reprinted 1973).

Leach, E.R. (ed.), *Aspects of Caste in South India, Ceylon and North-West Pakistan*, Cambridge University Press, Cambridge, 1955.

Madan, T.N., "On the Nature of Caste in India", *Contribution to Indian Sociology*, 5, 1971.

Mandelbaum, David G., *Society in India*, University of California Press, Berkeley, 1970.

Mukerjee, Ram Krishna, *The Rise and Fall of the East India Company*, 1958.

Murphy, Gardner, *In the Minds of Man*, 1953.

Parsons, Talcott, *The Social System*, 1952.

Prasad, Kali, *Social Integration Research: A Study of Inter-Caste Relationship*, Lucknow University, 1954.

Sharma, K.L., *Social Stratification in India*, Sage Publications, New Delhi, 1997.

Silverberg, James (ed.), *Social Mobility in the Caste System in India*, Monton, Hague, 1968.

Singer, Milton and Bernard S. Cohn (eds.), *Structure and Change in Indian Society*, Aldine Publishers, Chicago, 1968.

Sinha, Surajit, "Caste in India", *A Survey of Research in Sociology and Anthropology*, ICSSR, New Delhi, 1974.

Singh, Yogendra, "Sociology of Social Stratification", *A Survey of Research in Sociology and Anthropology*, ICSSR, New Delhi, 1974.

—, *Modernisation of Indian Tradition*, Rawat Publications, Jaipur, 1983.

Weber, Max, *Essays on Sociology*, 1952.

3 Scheduled Castes, Untouchability and Backward Classes

THE SCHEDULED CASTES

The institutionalised inequality in the caste system manifests its extreme form in the growth of completely segregated set of castes called 'untouchable castes'. The scheduled castes (SCs) who comprise the bulk of 'untouchables' are technically outside the four-fold *varna* scheme. These castes were imputed with maximum degree of ritual and social impurity, while their occupations were held to be the lowest in normative hierarchy. This led to their residential segregation in villages and towns. The SCs did not constitute a homogeneous stratum. Before being 'scheduled' in 1935, these castes were classified as exterior castes, depressed castes, broken men and outcastes. Gandhiji designated them as 'Harijans' or the children of God. In 1931 census, some social criteria were used for identifying the caste as 'exterior'. On the same basis, the castes were listed as 'scheduled castes' in 1935. Some of these criteria were: whether they are served by Brahmins as *purohits*, whether served by barbers, tailors, etc., whether they can serve water to caste Hindus, whether they can enter Hindu temples, whether they can use public conveniences such as roads, wells, schools, etc., whether their touch or proximity pollutes high castes, whether in ordinary social intercourse, they are treated as equals by high caste men, whether they are engaged in despised occupations and so forth. In 1935, in all 227 castes with a total population of 50.1 million, were listed as SCs. In 1991, this population increased to 138.22 million, which comprised 16.3 per cent of the country's total population. In 1999, SC population is estimated to be about 140 million.

Prohibitions Against Scheduled Castes

Severe restrictions were imposed on the scheduled castes, also called dalits today, since early periods, like not allowing them to wear shirts or vests, not to use ornaments, sandals and umbrellas, to use only earthen-ware vessels in homes, not to enter cities after sun-set and before sunrise, and keep a prescribed distance of steps from upper-caste Hindus. They were, thus, totally ostracised. The excesses committed against them under the garb of untouchability, continue to exist even today. In spite of the welfare programmes and ameliorative measures taken by the State, there has been social sabotage side by side by the dark forces of society. For example, cases are reported where though dalits are admitted to schools yet they are segregated on separate benches in one corner of the same class. If common lunches for high caste and SC staff in an office are arranged, the high caste people first serve the low caste people in the name of 'special occasion' and then ask them to take rest, when they take food separately. Cases are also reported where the utensils/plates of caste Hindus after use, are washed by the menials of the hostel but the SC students are required to wash their own plates. About five years ago, there was a strike in Jawahar Lal Nehru University, Delhi, on the issue of food being served to the SC students in the common mess. In 1998, a dalit youth (named Sanwle) was killed in Maharashtra (Pipra Parwan village) for taking refuge in a temple during rains. In villages, the scheduled castes face humiliation and exploitation of their wives in many states. In one study conducted about three decades ago by Sinha and Sinha of 200 students of Patna University on the attitudes towards Harijans (*Social Forces*, 1967), 69 per cent respondents had described Harijans as backward, 56 per cent as crooked, 55 per cent as uncultured, 54 per cent as dull, 52 per cent as dirty, 52 per cent as drunkards, and 48 per cent as ugly. This only points out the stereotyped image about SCs.

Atrocities Against Scheduled Castes

Atrocities against SCs are increasing. Every two hours, one dalit is assaulted, every day three dalit women are raped, two dalits are murdered and two dalit houses burnt (*Crime in India*, 1995:260). The increase in the number of crimes against the SCs is evident from the fact that as against 180 cases registered with the police in 1955, the number of cases increased to 18,336 in 1991 and to 32,990 in 1995 (*Ibid*:260). The SC men are exploited by usurping their lands, giving them low wages and using them as bonded labour.

Exploitation of SCs has led to caste conflicts and the formation of caste senas in several states, particularly in Bihar. There exist Bhoomi Sena of the Kurmis, Lorik Sena of the Yadavs, Brahmarishi and Ranvir Sena of the Bhumihars, Ganga Sena of the Brahmins, and the Kunwar Sena of the Rajputs. Then there are Naxal groups of Maoist Communist Centre (MCC) and CPI-ML which dominate in several districts. The MCC cadre is mostly drawn from the Yadavs, Koeris and Paswans. In one incident in December 1998, 300 armed men of the Ranvir Sena massacred 61 dalits at Lakshmanpur Bathe village in Jahanabad district. The MCC group had butchered a large number of upper caste people in different villages in Gaya, Aurangabad and Jahanabad districts between 1987 and 1999. Similarly, Ranvir Sena and PWG (People's War Group) had killed many persons in six different attacks between January 1999 and June 1999. The reason of massacres was a long-standing tussle between upper caste landowners and landless dalit farmers of the area. The total lack of political will to tackle the menace has been the bane of Bihar.

The reports of the National Commission on SCs and STs have also been regularly reporting an increase in the number of crimes against the SCs. The central government has issued detailed directions to all the state governments for checking this exploitation. Some of the measures taken by the states in this connection are:

- Gearing up machinery for solving disputes of low wages, etc. concerning the SCs.
- Helping the SCs in getting possession of lands belonging or allotted to them.
- Specially instructing police authorities to intervene in instances of criminal tresspass into lands belonging to SCs and treat cases of crimes against the SCs as special cases and arrange for quick trial and prosecution.
- Helping the SC agricultural labourers in getting statutory minimum wages.
- Setting up special courts (in some states) for ensuring quick disposal of cases pertaining to the SCs.
- Setting up special SC cells under the DIG Police to ensure that crimes against SCs are properly registered, investigated and expeditiously prosecuted.
- Setting up state-level committees to look after various aspects concerning the welfare of the SCs.

The long-standing exploitation made the SCs conscious of their separate identity, raised their self-consciousness, led to the emergence of SC movements, and activated the process of sanskritisation as noted by Srinivas. The consequences of all this awareness and movements were: (i) emergence of some SCs in different parts of the country as political groups, (ii) putting pressure on the national leadership for taking measures to do away with the social disabilities of the dalits, (iii) demand for constitutional safeguards, (iv) starting various alienative (by Ambedkar) and integrative (by Gandhiji) movements, and (v) conscious attempts of dalits for status mobility. The alienative movements led to the horizontal-level caste consolidation of SCs by fusion of a number of sub-castes into one caste group, e.g., Vannya Kula Kshatriya Sangham in Tamil Nadu, and 52 sub-castes of Mahars forming one community in Maharashtra, Chamars and Jatavs in Uttar Pradesh, Pans in Orissa and so forth (see, Rudolph and Rudolph, 1965; Sunanda Patwardhan, 1968, Lynch, 1968; Bailey, 1963).

Ameliorative Measures

Being dissatisfied with the social status of the SCs, Ambedkar launched a drive in 1956 for their mass conversion to Buddhism. In 1957, he organised the political wing of the SCs, known as Republican Party. There have been many instances of conversion of the SCs to Christianity too. Since after the conversion, the SCs ceased to be entitled for benefits offered by the government, the Republican Party launched an agitation in 1964 for the restoration of these privileges to neo-Buddhist SCs. Gandhiji had taken up the cause of Harijan welfare in 1924. The uplift of the Harijans was an important item in the Bardoli programme of constructive work drawn up in 1922. The Harijan Sevak Sangh was organised in 1932 to work for the removal of the social disabilities of the Harijans.

After independence, the Constitution of India prescribed protection and safeguards for the SCs (and STs). The important measures taken are: (i) abolition of untouchability, (ii) protection from social injustice and various forms of exploitation, (iii) throwing open to them religious institutions of public character, (iv) removal of restrictions on their access to wells, tanks, shops, restaurants and roads, etc., (v) giving them the right to move freely and acquire property, (vi) giving them the right of admission to educational institutions and receiving grants out of state funds, (vii) permitting the state governments to make reservation for them in services, (viii) giving them special representation in the Lok Sabha and the

Vidhan Sabhas, (ix) setting up separate departments and advisory councils to promote their welfare and safeguard their interests, (x) prohibiting forced labour, and (xi) making special provision for the administration and control of the scheduled areas.

The Scheduled Caste and the Scheduled Tribe (Prevention of Atrocities) Act, 1989 has described the following acts as punishable crimes: (1) Forcing an SC/ST person to eat or drink some disgusting substance. (2) Throwing in the house or the neighbourhood of an SC/ST person refuse, rubbish or dead animal, etc. which may humiliate, harm or anger him. (3) Taking away clothes forcibly from the body of an SC/ST person and making him naked; or blackening his face and taking him round the public places. (4) Forcibly occupying and cultivating the land of an SC/ST person owned by him or allotted to him. (5) Usurping the land/property of any SC/ST person. (6) Compelling an SC/ST person for forced labour (*begar*) or using him as a bonded labourer. (7) Preventing an SC/ST person from voting, or forcing him to vote for a particular person. (8) Committing any act against an SC/ST person which may be distressive or punishable. (9) Humiliating a SC/ST person. (10) Molesting an SC/ST woman. (11) Sexual harassment of an SC/ST woman. (12) Polluting the drinking water used by an SC/ST person. (13) Forcing an SC/ST person to leave his house, neighbourhood or his village.

The machinery for safeguarding the interests of the SCs (and STs) has been created in the form of setting up a Commissioner for SCs and STs and recently a National Commission for SCs and STs. This Commission functions as an advisory body on issues/policies related to the development of the SCs (and STs). The State governments have separate departments to look after the welfare of the SCs (and STs and OBCs). A number of voluntary organisations is also engaged in promoting the welfare of these people. The important organisations of an all-India character include: The Harijan Sevak Sangh, Delhi, the Hindu Sweepers Sevak Samaj, New Delhi, and the Bhartiya Adimjati Sevak Sangh, New Delhi. The expenditure on the welfare of SCs (and STs) is given special attention in the Five Year Plans. The size of investment on the special programmes has increased from First Plan to Ninth Plan.

Have all these measures contributed to the uplift of the SCs? It appears that socially, economically and politically, their status has improved very little. Socially, they have not changed their many evil customs and their status remains the same; economically, more than 30 per cent SCs live below the poverty line and their occupational mobility does not lead them to social mobility; educationally, they are very backward; politically they are not organised and remain weak in the local power structure for asserting their rights.

Their discontent is evident from the fact that they launched a national campaign for the dalit human rights in December 1998 to coincide with the World Human Rights Day. The campaign focused on three areas: right to touch and be touched, 'no' to untouchability in the new millennium, and cast out caste. The campaign also demanded effective implementation of the SC/ST (Prevention of Atrocities) Act and Rules, handing over the responsibility of monitoring the implementation of the Act to the National SC/ST Commission, and providing full protection to all dalits participating in Panchayati Raj and other institutions, restoration of all lands taken away from the dalits, and considering them SCs irrespective of their faith and religion (i.e., including convert neo-buddhists, Christians, etc.).

Present Status

How far has the lot of the SCs improved within the caste system of stratification or independently? It is said that though there are some trends of upward social mobility among the SC families and some SC individuals are enjoying high administrative positions, yet broadly speaking the SCs have registered little progress in the last five decades. There is a ritualistic formalism about many welfare schemes formulated for these people. The financial incentives and educational reservations have bestowed little real benefit to these castes. With the strength of 16.48 per cent in the total population of the country in 1991 and with 15 per cent of reservation, the SCs have not been able to take full advantage of the reserved seats allotted to them in government jobs. If we depend on the data collected from the Reports of the Commissioner for SCs and STs and recently the National Commission for SCs and STs which monitors implementation of the policy by government offices and public sector undertakings, we find that representation in central government departments, public sector undertakings, and the nationalised banks in 1993 was 7 to 10 per cent in 'A' group posts, 9 to 14 per cent in 'B' group posts, 13 to 19 per cent in 'C' group posts, and 21 to 23 per cent in 'D' group posts. (see, Bhargava and Samal, 1998: 513). No doubt, there has been some improvement in the intake of positions for SCs in all categories of posts from 1965 onwards but the progress has not been satisfactory in group 'A' and 'B' posts, while in group 'D', the total posts have surpassed the quota and in group 'C', they come close to the quota (of 15%). Why full quota of positions in 'A' and 'B' groups is not filled is because eligible candidates are not available. To be eligible for applying for different positions under the union and the state governments, one needs to have some basic educational qualifications. The literacy percentage among the SC males (in 1991) was 49.9, among females was 23.76, and the total was 37.41 (against 40.65, 18.19 and 29.6 respectively amongst the STs and 64.13, 39.29 and 52.21 respectively among the general population). When the SC candidates do not have basic qualifications and are not even eligible for availing themselves of the facility of reservation, it is illogical to expect them to have a higher rate of representation in groups 'A' and 'B'. Complaining of class bias of the members of various selection boards is rather ludicrous. It seems easier to fill the non-technical and lower positions in services from amongst the SCs than the higher ones. Social legislation also has little impact on removing their disability.

The questions now raised are: Are SCs still being ignored or are they being pampered? Should we continue reservation for them? Let us take the example of their education. The enrolment of SCs at primary, secondary and high school levels is about 15 per cent and at higher secondary, graduate and postgraduate levels is about 8 per cent. Their performance in education is poor. Against the general pass average of 65 per cent at the high school level, the pass percentage of the SCs is 53, at graduate level is 35 (against general pass percentage of 57) and at the postgraduate level is 60 (against general pass percentage of 76). In professional courses, their percentage is about 35 (against general percentage of 60) (Prasad, L.M., "Educational Policy for SCs and STs and its Implementation", *The Indian Journal of Public Administration*, Delhi, October-December, 1996: 908-932). The poor quality of their education is evident in their performance at the entrance tests for professional courses. In some of the states, so few SC candidates qualify that even the minimum eligibility marks are lowered. In Madhya Pradesh, SC students even with 15 per cent (against prescribed 35 per cent marks) had to be admitted. In 1995, in the SC (freedom fighter) quota, a candidate who secured 33 out of 900 marks (i.e., 3.66%) found his name in the merit list of pre-engineering students (*The Hindustan Times*, June 16, 1995). In medicine, while in the SC category list, the lowest marks were 48.16 per cent, in the general category those scoring 73 per cent marks were either on the waiting list or were rejected (*The Hindustan Times*, June, 29, 1995).

UNTOUCHABILITY: ITS ERADICATION AND DALIT CONSCIOUSNESS

Dalits

Untouchability in India goes back to hoary past, though its origin and practice remain vague or unknown. Till the early 1930s, the *de jure* definition of the depressed classes, as they were then known, was in terms of the religious concept of pollution. The depressed classes were defined as "Hindu castes, contacts with whom entail purification on the part of high-caste Hindus" (Dushkin in Michael, 1998:171). In 1931 census, the Census Commissioner (J.H. Hutton) adopted several criteria to be employed for identifying the depressed classes. These criteria did not work well. Therefore, some adjustments were made before the promulgation of the schedule in 1935.

Today, the number of scheduled caste persons has gone up very high. One out of every six Indians belongs to this category—ex-untouchables by law but still untouchables in practice. The important ex-untouchable castes are Chamar, Dusadh, Musahar, Bhuiya, Dhobi, Pasi, Regar, Dom, Bhogta and Halalkhor in north India and Paraiyans, Pallans and Chakkilis in Tamil Nadu and Mehar, Balshi, Bauri Meghwal, Rajbans, Mazhabhi Siks, etc., in other states. The highest number of these people is found in Uttar Pradesh (21%) followed by West Bengal (12%), Bihar (9%), Tamil Nadu (8%), Andhra Pradesh (8%), Madhya Pradesh (7%), Maharashtra (6%), Rajasthan (5.5%) and so on. (*Manpower Profile, India*, 1998:35). Thus, about two-third of these people are concentrated in six states. About 84 per cent of them live in villages and are working as cultivators, sharecroppers, marginal farmers, and agricultural labourers. About 42 per cent of these people fall in the category of workers. Of the total workers, only 4 per cent work as scavengers while, the rest work as weavers (12%), fishermen (8%), toddy-tappers (7%) basket and rope-makers (5%), washermen (5%), artisans (1%), shoe-makers (1%), and so forth.

Though our Constitution outlawed the practice of untouchability and the Untouchability (Offences) Act of 1955 declared it as a legal offence, yet since Hindus are still deeply steeped in their concern for purity and pollution, the practice of untouchability has not been completely uprooted in the social and religious life of the country. Thus, untouchability may be understood from two angles: (i) the stigma attached to certain people because of ceremonial pollution they allegedly convey, and (ii) the set-practice engaged in by the rest of the society to protect itself from the pollution conveyed by the untouchables.

Degradation of Dalits

The social stigma of the untouchables manifests itself in all walks of life. They are denied access to temples and to the services of the Brahmins and are shunned by the higher castes. They are born as impure and live as impure. The rest of the society is so much concerned about purity that they permanently keep untouchables in a state of economic, social and political subordination. The stigma, congenital according to one's caste, lasts a lifetime and cannot be eliminated by rite or deed. Defined in relation to behaviour, untouchability refers to the set of practices followed by the rest of society to protect itself from the pollution conveyed by the untouchables. However, this concern with ritual pollution is not limited to the role of untouchables; it also served to keep the untouchables in an inferior economic and political position through physical separation. It is generally believed that the untouchable groups have come to realise that their problem can be solved only through effective political action. In recent times, due to reservation of posts in parliament, Vidhan Sabhas, jobs, educational institutions, etc. and other privileges granted by the government, a low ritual-status man has a better chance to achieve high economic and political status while high social status becomes an individual matter. Sociologists (like L.P. Vidyarthi, Sachchidananda, etc.) have attempted to study social transformation of dalits with reference to their caste disabilities, their educational efforts, acceptance of innovations, political consciousness, integration with the larger society, level of aspiration, internalisation of modern values, position of women, their leadership, dalit movements, and so on.

Though many dalits have given up their traditional caste-based occupations yet a good number is still engaged in polluting occupations. The change and diversification from polluting occupations has not only removed the stigma of their untouchability but has also enabled many to rise in class mobility. Some of them are owners of landed and household properties. They have been beneficiaries of various economic benefits offered to the scheduled castes by the government. The status disabilities are now largely confined to the village. Discriminations in the matter of using the public wells or the temples are not so widespread as before. High public servants and those who occupy higher positions are less subjected to disabilities in social intercourse. There now exists a direct correlation between the politico-economic status of an individual and his social status. In some cases, however, their ascriptive status scores over their achieved status, for example, in the field of marriage. The entry of a Harijan in modern professions like medicine, engineering, administration, management, higher education, judiciary and law is secretly resented by their colleagues. This is partly because of the stereotyped hatred and partly because of competition and jealousy on account of protective discrimination in their favour. Even the (Harijan) elite studied by Sachichidananda in Bihar in 1976 pointed out such jealousy.

A large number of Harijans suffer from an inbred inferiority complex which makes them sensitive to any treatment which they think smacks of discrimination. This does not mean that such alleged discrimination is always made and accusation is true. The immobility of the Harijans has also given place to mobility. This has been made possible by migration from rural to urban areas, education and entry in public services and in politics. All this points out how the structural distance between the dalits and others has considerably narrowed.

Ameliorative Measures

The changes among dalits have come through three avenues: (1) state policy in regard to untouchable groups, (2) reform movements at various periods of time, and (3) process of sanskritisation and westernisation. Amelioration of conditions of these underprivileged groups engaged the attention of the framers of the Constitution after independence.

Protective discrimination is one of the three ways in which government attempts to deal with the problems confronting the dalits. *First*, there are several constitutional and other legal provisions which remove discrimination against untouchables and grant them the same rights as other citizens. *Secondly*, some benefits make only scheduled castes eligible for them and make other persons ineligible, e.g., scholarships, loans, and grants, etc. Presenting certain certificates that the applicant belongs to one of the castes on the schedule enables him to get the benefit but makes non-members ineligible. Because of this protective character, the practice is called 'protective discrimination'.

Some constitutional provisions relating to the welfare and uplift of the Harijans (SCs) were: removal of disabilities with regard to access to public places (shops, restaurants, wells, bathing ghats, roads, etc.), forbidding denial of admission to educational institutions, throwing open Hindu religious institutions to them, setting up of advisory councils to promote their welfare, special representation in parliament and sate legislatures, and reservation in public services. The 1955 Untouchability Act provided penalties for violating these (constitutional) provisions.

Some other important centrally sponsored schemes launched for the welfare of the dalits are: coaching and training for various competitive examinations (IAS, IPS, etc.), financial assistance for higher education, financial assistance to institutions for research in the problems of dalits, including special programmes of development in Five Year Plans and providing reservation in public services and educational institutions. A committee was appointed by the Government of India in 1965 on untouchability evaluation. Studies made by Bernard Cohn (1955), Mrs. Epstein (1962), Harold Issacs (1964), Andre Beteille (1966), Harper (1968), Parvathamma (1968), Saberwal (1972), Michael Mahar (1972), Lynch (1976), L.P. Vidyarthi (1977), and Sachchidananda (1976) show some change in favour of the untouchables. Though the situation of social inequality characterised by social and economic exploitation of the untouchables does not exist to the same extent as before independence yet untouchability has not been abolished. Even the study of the Harijan elite made by Sachchidananda in Bihar in 1971-72 showed that while their status in economic field has improved, it has not changed in ritual, social or political fields. Interest in removing the disabilities of Harijans may be traced back to early thirties through some saints and reformers also like Mahatma Phule, Narsimha Mehta, etc. who had focused attention on their sad plight. Gandhiji took keen interest in the amelioration of their condition and abolition of untouchability in the thirtees. In 1932, he opposed B.R. Ambedkar on his demand for separate electorate for the untouchables and undertook fast on the issue, arguing that separate electorates would perpetuate the category of untouchables instead of encouraging them to merge with the Sudra population. He feared conflicts between caste Hindus and untouchables. Ambedkar bowed to Gandhiji's pressure, giving up his demand for separate electorates in return for a much higher number of seats (12.5% of the total population) in Parliament reserved for untouchables. He, thus, forced the British government to drop the idea by signing the Poona Pact. He then undertook a tour of the whole country and exhorted people to give up untouchability.

In addition to changes emanating from government policies and programmes, a major effort to ameliorate the lot of the untouchables has originated from these people themselves. Religion served as a major vehicle for the dissemination of revolutionary ideas among them and also provided a model for the organisation and support of such change. The most widespread and influential movement of this kind was their conversion to Buddhism, a phenomenon whose proportions were reflected in the census of India which recorded 1,81,000 Buddhists in 1951, 3.2 million in 1961, and 4.7 million in 1981. In Maharashtra alone, it is said that about 3.5 million Harijans were converted to Buddhism in 1956 under the leadership of B.R. Ambedkar, who himself adopted the *diksha* (conversion) in Nagpur on October 14, 1956. Ambedkar was of the opinion that only by leaving Hinduism, the Harijans would be able to free themselves from the burden of pollution and untouchability.

Some Harijans were converted to Christianity also, particularly in South India, in the second half of the 19th century. PutuChristians in Kerela are the low-caste Christians. Syrian Christians, converts from the higher castes, avoid interaction with them. However, converts from one untouchable caste—the Pulayas—have been integrated into the Syrian Christian church of Kerala. Satnami movement in Madhya Pradesh was a religious-cum-social-cum-political movement. Many Harijans joined the Satnami sect in Chhatisgarh region, which believed in quality of all men irrespective of caste and in 'Satnam'. This sect forbade the worship of Hindu deities, proscribed the use of liquor and tobacco and consumption of meat.

Dalits in Rural India

Dalits are a marginal group in rural India, both in economic sense and in view of low-status members of Hindu society. The two features observed about dalits in rural society are: (i) most dalits do not own land nor are they tenants, and (ii) most dalits earn an important part of their income by working on the land of others and/or by attaching themselves to land-holding cultivators. The employment of the dalit labour is determined by agricultural product and wages paid. The higher demand is at the time of harvest. The demand for the labour increases when there is more cultivable land, more irrigation, more fertilisers, and more capital. Modern agricultural implements like tractors, etc., increase the demand for skilled labourers but decrease the number of persons needed. The employer (landlord) gets labour from dalits as well as non-dalits. The labour, thus, is not homogeneous. Preference is always given to non-dalits as they are considered more hardworking. It is for this reason that the dalit in rural areas is referred to as 'marginal'.

Dalit Consciousness

The big question is: will dalits ever be integrated in the main stream of the society? The age-long bondage shackles may be shaken off when the dalits equip themselves with education and skills and effectively compete in modern society. Legislation alone will not do away with their disabilities. Along with dalits' own efforts for achieving resources, change in the attitudes of the caste Hindus is equally important for banishing untouchability. We agree with Sachchidananda (1976:172) who holds that the combination of factors like ameliorative efforts of the government, the growing consciousness of the dalits and the liberal attitudes of caste Hindus will diminish the disabilities and discriminations with the passage of time.

Politically, dalits are becomming conscious of the fact that they have to take advantage of their vast numbers in political terms. They may not be united to form a separate political party but by supporting the dominant national political parties like Congress or the Janata Dal or the BSP, etc., they may extract the price of their support. But the problem is that though the educated dalits show evidence of politicisation, the masses are not very much touched by this process. The elite have moved from the politics of compliance and affirmation to the politics of pressure and protest but they are still not able to present a common front and adopt a radical posture.

OTHER BACKWARD CASTES AND CLASSES (OBCs)

The 3,742 other backward castes and classes (not untouchables) comprised about 51 per cent of the total population of the country in 1981 and also in 1991. The 27 per cent reservation for these OBCs was announced by the Janata government led by V.P. Singh in August 1990. This was done by implementing the Mandal Commission report which was submitted to the government in December 1980, and after discussing it in both houses of parliament in 1982 was referred to a Committee of Secretaries for examination. The sudden announcement of accepting its recommendations by Prime Minister V.P.Singh was described by many as a political decision, taken without verifying the correctness and veracity of the selection of castes and its three indicators—social and economic and educational. In the social and economic indicators, there were four criteria each, while in the educational indicators, there were three criteria. Thus, in all there were eleven indicators. The weight that was given to each indicator was arbitrary and illogical. The social indicators were given weight of 3 points, the educational indicators 2 points, and the economic indicators 1 point. Thus, the total value was 22 points. Castes which secured 50 per cent scores (i.e., 11 points or above) were listed as 'backward'.

The National Front government's decision to implement Mandal Commission's report provoked widespread resentment among students. Spontaneous agitations erupted all over the country. During mid-September and mid-October 1990, 160 youth attempted to commit suicide against the government's decision. No political party had, however, openly opposed reservations.

When Narasimha Rao's Congress government came to power in 1991, it issued a notification in September 1991, stating that within 27 per cent of the union government's civilian jobs reserved for socially and educationally backward classes (SEBC), preference would be given to 'poorer sections' of such classes. Further, 10 per cent jobs would be reserved for other economically backward sections of the people who were not covered by any of the existing schemes of reservation.

The case of implementing Mandal Commission's report was taken to the Supreme Court which, in its judgement in November, 1992, endorsed job reservation formula and upheld the decision to reserve 27 per cent government jobs for the backward castes but struck down the Narasimha Rao government's decision to reserve 10 per cent vacancies for other economically backward sections. The salient features of the Supreme Court's verdict were: (1) Caste was accepted as basis for identifying the beneficiaries of reservations. (2) The upper limit of reservations was fixed at 50 per cent. (3) Creamy layer was to be excluded from reservations. (4) Reservation in certain technical posts was not advised. (5) There were to be no reservations in promotions. (6) The union government was to specify the socio-economic criteria to exclude socially advanced persons among the backward classes. (7) Permanent commission was to be set up by the Union and state governments to examine complaints of over-inclusion and under-inclusion and requests for inclusion in the list of backward castes.

Both types of arguments in favour and against the Mandal Commission's recommendations are given below: Arguments *in favour* of the recommendations are: (1) These will satisfy and uplift those backward sections of the society which were discontended and had suffered injustice for decades. (2) The reservation in the central government services was to affect only 1 per cent of the country's population. The reservations, therefore, will not adversely affect the general population. (3) The reservations are not based only on 'caste' as is wrongly believed, e.g., Rajputs in Bihar are not included in the list but Rajputs in Gujarat are included; the Yadavs of Bihar and Uttar Pradesh are included but not Yadavs of

Haryana; Patels of Gujarat are not included but Patels of Bihar are in the list. Thus, the basis is the situation of a particular caste in different states. (4) Nation's population of backward castes with 52 per cent strength has a mere 4 per cent representation in class 1 government and public sector employment. This is purely injustice with weaker sections and needed to be corrected. (5) The argument that handing over administrative jobs to these people will bring inefficiency is fallacious. The Britishers had also refused to give political freedom to Indians on the basis of similar argument and we had turned down this argument at that time. How can we accept the same argument now? The concrete opportunities to the 'backward' groups will give them experience and enable them to acquire 'merit'. Denying 'equal opportunity' to depressed castes and classes to acquire merit is nothing but continuing dominance of the oppressed.

The arguments *against* the Mandal Commission Report are: (1) The 'backwardness' has been defined only on 'caste' basis. This will perpetuate caste prejudices and discriminations endemic to the (caste) system. The provision should be meant for all the poor irrespective of their caste, and based only on economic criterion. (2) Though 'caste' has been defined but 'class' has not been defined, when sociologically speaking caste and class are two distinct categories. The Mandal Commission at best located 'backward castes' and not 'backward classes'. (3) The criterion used for identifying backward castes was erratic,, whimsical, and politically motivated. It was not based on a rigorous scientific basis. For example, the social indicator of early marriage is not wedded to any particular caste or class. It is an age-old social evil prevalent in all castes and classes in general. Hence, taking it as one indicator was totally wrong. The same thing can be said about many other indicators like women's work, father's education, parental income, source of drinking water, etc. (4) In identifying 'backward castes', state governments were not consulted. When Mandal Commission had identified 3,742 castes as backward, Kalelkar Committee earlier had identified around 2,000 castes as backward. Was Kalelkar Committee's identification incorrect? Similarly, Kerala government had identified 70 castes as backward but Mandal Commission recommended 208 castes as backward. Orissa did not specify even one caste as backward but Mandal Commission identified 224 backward castes in the state. (5) The population projection of castes was based on 1931 census data. Thus, changes between 1931 and 1980 were not taken into account. The land reforms after Independence have appreciably altered the social, economic and educational status of various castes. The Yadavs and the Kurmis in Bihar and Uttar Pradesh are the best examples. The percentage of the urban population, the occupational distribution of population, and the number of highly educated people had greatly changed between 1931 and 1980 and 1980 and 1990. Thus, the basis of population figures was unrealistic. (6) The assumption of the Mandal Commission that the proportion of the OBCs among the non-Hindus was of the same order as among the Hindus was wrong. (7) The sampling procedure used for the socio-educational field survey was defective as it involved the selection of two villages and one urban block from each district. This is unscientific and biased sampling. (8) In determining backwardness, the importance given to economic criteria was very inadequate as out of 22 points, only 4 points were given to economic criteria. (9) The chairman of the Mandal Commission himself was a member of a backward caste and was famous for his biased statements during his political career. He had played a biased role in identifying the indicators and assigning scores to them. Even the Commission had confessed that the listing of castes as socially and educationally backward was 'somewhat arbitrary'. (10) The Constitution lays down that a caste or a class cannot be categorised as backward when it is adequately represented in the state services. (11) Since the Mandal Commission did not divide the reservation of 27 per cent into quotas for each of the backward castes, the bulk of the 27 per cent reservations will be hogged by a few castes that are more dominant among the backward castes. Even among the dominant castes, it will be a few families which will prosper at the cost of their unfortunate brethern.

It may, thus, be said that the manner of implementation of Mandal Commission's recommendation was too hasty, meant only to defuse the then prevalent political crisis. No economic cut-off point was fixed, nor the period of continuing reservation was announced. No wonder, the assumptions, fallacies, paucity of relevant data, loopholes in information, arbitrariness, subjectivity, anomalies, and a high degree of irrational generalisation aroused the youth to fight against the reservation policy and the self-centred political elite.

The Reservation Policy

Our Constitution guarantees/stipulates justice and equality of opportunity to all its citizens. It also recognises that equal opportunity implies competition between equals, and not 'unequals'. Recognising the inequality in our social structure, the makers of the Constitution argued that weaker sections have to be dealt with on a preferential footing by the state. A special responsibility was, thus, placed upon the state to provide protection to the weaker sections of society. Accordingly, the Constitution provided for protective discrimination under various articles to accelerate the process of building an egalitarian social order. Thus, preferential treatment for the depressed classes (SCs and STs), including reservation of seats, should not be understood as an act of magnanimity on the part of the political elite at the national level but rather a strategy to give them a share in power in politics and administration and to uplift them socially and economically. Initially, the percentage of reservation (in 1950 Constitution) provided reservation of 12.5 per cent for the SCs and 5 per cent for the STs but these percentages were subsequently enhanced in 1970 to 15 per cent and 7.5 per cent for SCs and STs respectively. The reservation was provided in jobs, admission to colleges and universities, and the central and state legislative assemblies. Later, it was provided in public undertakings and nationalised banks, etc. All state governments also enacted laws providing for reservation for the SCs (and STs) in the services under their control. Further, other concessions like reservation in promotions, etc. were also provided by the governments.

In January 1999, the President of India's noting in a confidential file pertaining to judicial appointments to the effect that special quota should be considered for the weaker sections of society like SCs, STs and women in the appointment of judges in High Courts and the Supreme Court, led to a furore in legal circles and a debate on meritocracy versus protective discrimination. The controversy is not about whether the President has constitutional power to suggest changes in the selection process. The issue is: if Chief Justice of India's argument that merit alone is important in judicial appointments is logical, why can not it be applied to other areas like educational institutions, science laboratories, etc., and if President's view has logic, why can't reservations be extended to armed forces, formation of cabinets, etc. The President's notings are never casual. They are not personal opinions. They carry an official stamp. If judges and senior advocates believe in the primacy of merit in judiciary, will the Supreme Court review its earlier judgement given in November 1992 with regard to accepting 27 per cent reservation for the OBCs? The failure of the policy of reservation to uplift the SCs (and STs) over a period of around five decades on the one hand and the politics of reservation, i.e., the rat race among the political parties to net specific groups like OBCs, Dalit Christians and the Muslims, and recent demands of some castes (like Jats, etc. in Rajasthan) to include them in OBC category, on the other, have posed serious challenges for the society and economy. The Supreme Court ruling on the ceiling of the reservation limit at 50 per cent and subsequently, the passing of Tamil Nadu Reservation Act (1993) raising the reservation to 69 per cent and including this Act in the constitution by 85th amendment to take it beyond judicial review have opened the door with one state government after another rushing through similar kind of legislations. It is in this context that the issue of reservation assumes great importance.

The question now raised by many people is: Should we continue reservations for SCs and STs in educational institutions, services, Lok Sabha and Vidhan Sabhas? One argument is that these should have been discontinued ten years from the coming into force of the Constitution. By extending the term every decade, we are going against the wishes of the Constitution-makers. It is in fact derecognising merit and depriving the more qualified. The SCs and STs in India together constitute 24.56 per cent (16.48% and 8.08% respectively) of the total population, OBCs 51 per cent, economically weaker sections (destitutes) 10 per cent, and Muslims 12 per cent. All this adds up to 97.56 per cent. When nearly the whole country is backward, where is the justification for special measures for any particular section of the backwards?

Second argument is that we have tried out the reservation idea to improve the lot of the weaker sections for 50 years. If the reservations have really made no difference in their conditions so far, why persist with such an ineffectual arrangement? The reservation benefits are cornered by the creamy layer.

Third argument is that this (reservation) policy is being bartered for vote. There will be no objections if the reservations are provided for under the very concept of the equality of opportunity.

On the other hand, one view is that since the object of reservation (for SCs) has not been achieved, it should be continued for a few more decades. The other view is that it is time to phase out reservations slowly. This can be done either by removing the creamy layers or by letting the reservation percentages taper off to a vanishing point. In fact, this process should have been initiated much earlier. It would have indeed been a wonderful idea for our nation to enter the twenty-first century as a casteless society.

Our contention is that theoretically, it is inadmissible and practically difficult to scrap the policy of reservation. We agree with Roy Burman's view that for some more years, reservation should be extended to SCs, STs and OBCs. However, the policy of reservation has to be scientific and rational. In the given economic and political structure, caste (or birth or family) should not determine one's life chances. It is assumed that SCs (and for that matter STs and OBCs also) represent a homogeneous group but actually they are a heterogeneous group. Therefore, following B.S. Bhargava and Avinash Samal (1998: 518), it may be suggested that: (i) not caste but income should be given importance in determining backwardness; (ii) the concept of creamy layer should be applied to SCs (and STs) also; (iii) reservation should be restricted only to the first generation beneficiaries. The candidates whose parents have already availed reservation facilities in securing a job should not be given the facility again; (iv) concession of scholarship may be provided to SC (and ST and OBC) students securing more than the specified percentage of marks (say, 48%) in high school and graduate courses for getting quality education in good institutions. All these measures will benefit those who really deserve help.

AGRARIAN AND INDUSTRIAL CLASS STRUCTURE

Though caste and class are distinct from each other but class stratification is organically connected with caste stratification. Class is viewed as a universalistic phenomenon. While in industrial societies, the distinction is made between bourgeoisie and proletariat classes, in agrarian societies, it is made between landowners and landless classes. Using the attributed approach of Marx, it may be said that the bourgeoisie enjoy higher income, higher level of education and higher prestige. The proletariat have low income, low level of education and low prestige. In between these two classes, the petite-bourgeoisie have an intermediate income, enjoy medium prestige and their level of education is higher than that of the workers but lower than that of the bourgeoisie. In India, compared to the studies on caste, the literature on class is not substantial. The analysis of class stratification has been made by sociologists, both of the Marxist and the non-Marxist disposition. The census agencies in their analyses of class categories generally refer to agricultural or non-agricultural mode of earning livelihood. Some sociologists have used the terms 'maliks' and 'ryots' in their analysis of class structure.

Agrarian Class Structure

Caste stratification, according to some scholars, is associated with the rural and class stratification with the urban situation. Yogendra Singh (1974:358) has held that this statement is based on fallacy; it is not based on socio-historical evidence. Some western scholars held the view that early India was a static society, where not change but continuity was a dominant feature. But this fallacy of 'static India' hypothesis has been criticised by scholars like P.C. Joshi (1970), Yogendra Singh (1973), B. Cohn (1968) and Romila Thapar (1972). Many classes like priests, feudal chiefs, merchants, artisans, peasants, labourers, etc., existed in early India. Merchants did not occupy low position in social hierarchy. The base for their mobility was their economic relationship. Their caste status did not clash with the class status. Yogendra Singh (op. cit., 1974:334) holds that the position of many castes altered over time, and wealth and property played an important role in achieving an improved status, particularly among the merchant class.

The period after 1000 A.D saw the growth of classes of traders, artisans, etc., in cities. In the Mughal period too, since a large share of village produce was taken to the urban market, the dynamism of the class structure of both the cities and villages continued. This implied not only the existence of agrarian classes in villages but also a stable class of merchants, middlemen and bankers in towns and cities.

In the British period, the policy of trade and commerce affected the artisan classes and led to their large-scale migration to rural areas. Further, the British policy of favoured treatment to the port towns, neglect of vast number of other towns, policy of taxation and many other socio-economic policies led to the decline of the traditional Indian economic structure as well as the class structure. The class structure in the rural areas was also affected due to land settlement policy. At the same time, the British policies created new foundations for the emergence of a feudal-agrarian class structure. In cities, a new industrial and mercantile middle class came into being. There also emerged a new bureaucratic-administrative class.

The agrarian system that evolved in the rural areas during the British regime was based either on the *zamindari* or the *ryotwari* type of land systems. The zamindari system had three main agrarian classes: zamindars, tenants, and agricultural labourers. The ryotwari system had two main classes: ryot-landlords and the ryot-peasants. The agrarian class structure every where in India had a feudal character. The zamindars (i.e. non-cultivating owners of land) were tax-gatherers, the tenants were real cultivators (often without security of land tenure), and the agricultural labourers had the status of bonded labour. With the support of the rulers' power, this highly exploitative system continued to persist till the political independence of the country, despite peasant unrest and peasant movements. The nationalist movement also affected the feudal class structure. The national leadership raised voice against the exploitation of the peasants and led various *kisan* movements in various parts of the country.

After independence, land reforms were introduced and agrarian class structure was transformed. The abolition of the zamindari system took away the powers of the zamindars. Daniel Thorner (1973) referring to agrarian classes after independence has talked of three main classes: *malik*, *kisan*, and *mazdoor*, while Kotovsky (1964) has referred to classes like landowners, rich peasants, landless peasantry, and agricultural labourers. In the last two decades, some economists have referred to classes of big landholders (with 10+ hectare land), small landholders (with 2-10 hectare land), marginal landholders (with less than 2 hectares land), and agricultural labourers. Ram Krishna Mukherjee has referred to three classes in agrarian structure: landholders and supervisory farmers, self-sufficient peasantry and share-croppers, and agricultural labourers.

Yogendra Singh (1974: 343-344) has referred to several trends in agrarian class structure after independence. These are: (1) There is a wide gap between land-reform ideology projected during the freedom struggle and even thereafter and the actual measures introduced for land reforms. (2) This gap is the result of the class character of politicians and administrative elite. (3) The economic prosperity of the rich peasantry has increased but the economic condition of the small peasants has deteriorated. (4) The feudalistic type of tenancy has been replaced by the capitalistic type of lease-labour or wage labour agrarian system. (5) The inequalities between the top and the bottom levels of classes have increased rather than decreased. (6) Agricultural workers have not receieved the benefits of land reforms. (7) The sociological process dominant in the current class transformations in the villages involves 'embourgeoisiement' of some and 'proletarianisation' of many social strata. P.C. Joshi (1971) referring to the trend in agrarian class structure has pointed out: (1) The decline of feudalistic type of tenancy and its replacement by more exploitative lease arrangements. (2) The rise of commercially-oriented landlords. Andre Beteille has referred to change from 'cumulative' to 'dispersed' inequalities due to changing social stratification.

Industrial Class Structure

The effects of industrialisation have been: (1) The percentage of workers engaged in agriculture has come down while that of workers engaged in individual activities has gone up. (2) The process of social mobility has accelerated. (3) Trade unions have organised industrial workers to fight for their rights. (4) Since industrial workers maintain continued and close relationship with their kin-groups and castes, caste stratification has not affected class character. (5) The traditional and charismatic elite have been replaced by the professional elite.

Morris D. Morris (1991: 231-247) has referred to two viewpoints regarding the behaviour pattern of the industrial labour. One view is that labour being short in industry, employers had to scramble for their workforce and make all sorts of concessions which weakened their hold on the workers. The workers frequently returned to their villages to which they were very much attached. The other view talks of surplus of labour available in villages for urban employment. Because of easy availability, the employers abused workers unmercifully. Since working conditions in the factories were intolerable, the labour was forced to go back to their villages. Thus, in both views, it was held that workers retained their rural links which limited the supply of labour for industrial development. As a consequence, proletarian type of behaviour did not develop. It also resulted in high rates of absenteeism and labour turnover and the slow growth of trade unions.

Besides the above features, four other features were also visible: *First*, the employment of women and children in industries was very limited. About 20 to 25 per cent of labour force consisted of women and about 5 per cent of children. This was because employment of women in night shifts was prohibited and children below 14 years could not be legally employed. *Secondly*, though it is argued that industry is casteblind because no single caste can provide an adequate supply of labour and because employees are uninterested in caste affiliation, yet workers did not permit the employers to employ workers of untouchable castes. *Thirdly*, large number of workers in the industries were those who had no significant claim to land. *Fourthly*, workers employed were not necessarily from the same district in which the industry was located but were recruited from different districts as well as neighbouring states. There were, thus, no geographical barriers inhibiting the flow of labour into the industry. The rural social structure (joint family system, etc.) was also not a barrier to the flow of population needed for urban economic expansion. According to one estimate, of the total workers in any industry, about 25 per cent are local, 10 per cent come from within 100 kms of industry's location, 50 per cent from 100 to 750 kms and 15 per cent from more than 750 kms. This shows a tendency for industry hands to be drawn from increasingly distant areas. All these features explain the class aspect of industrial labour force in India.

Analysing the 'working class', Holmstrom (see, Dipankar Gupta, 1991: 248-260) has said that all workers do not share all interests; rather they share a few interests only. He has also said that it is necessary to draw a class line between the organised and the unorganised sector industrial workers. Joshi (1976) also has said that organised and unorganised sector industrial workers are two classes with different and conflicting interests. This can be explained on the basis of difference in four factors: wages, working conditions, security, and social worlds.

The *wages* depend upon whether the industry is big (more than 1,000 workers), small (250-1,000 workers) or very small (less than 50 workers). In 1973, West Bengal laid down different minimum wages for above three types of industries. The big industries pay much more than the small industries because of the economics of scale, unions and workers' strong bargaining position. Naturally, the interests of workers depend upon the type of industry they work in.

The *working conditions* also affect the interests of workers. Workers in industries with more pleasant conditions, having safety measures and fewer accidents and less noise and monotony and fatigue, shorter hours, more space, freedom from close control or harassment, a chance of learning something more, canteens and creches and washing rooms, have different interests from those which do not provide all these amenities. As such, they work as two different classes of workers.

Security and *career chances* also demarcate two classes of workers. A permanent worker has not only a job but also a career while the temporary worker is bothered more about the security of the job. The permanent worker's career extends into the future but the temporary one remains bogged down into the present. The former may plan to improve his job by learning a skill and getting promotion; the latter is terrified of losing his job if he joins a union.

Lastly, the *social worlds* also divide workers in two different classes. The 'social world' refers to differences in economic conditions, life chances, mutual aid and dependence, etc. The factory workers in the organised sector have more solidarity, fewer hostility and less tensions. Their interests and ideology keep them separate from the 'outsiders'. Thus, the organised sector workers form a privileged upper class.

Further Readings

Bhargava, B.S. and Avinash Samal, "Protective Discrimination and Development of SCs", *Indian Journal of Public Administration*, Vol. XLIV, No. 3, July-September, 1998.

Burman, Roy, *Beyond Mandal and After: Backward Classes Perspective*, Mittal Publications, New Delhi, 1992.

Mahar, J.Michael, *The Untouchables in Contemporary India*, Rawat Publications, Jaipur, 1998.

Morris, D. Morris, "The Emergence of an Industrial Labour Force in India" in Dipankar Gupta, *Social Stratification*, 1991.

Isaacs, Harold R., *India's Ex-Untouchables*, John Day, New York, 1965.

Parvathamma, C., *The Case for Untouchables*, United Asia, 1968.

Sachchidananda, *The Harijan Elite*, Thompson Press, Faridabad, 1977.

—, "Studies of Scheduled Castes with Special Reference to Change" in *Survey of Research in Sociology and Social Anthropology*, ICSSR, Vol. 1, Popular Prakashan, Bombay, 1974.

Singh, Yogendra, *A Survey of Research in Sociology and Social Anthropology*, ICSSR, Volume 1, 1974.

4 Family, Marriage and Kinship

FAMILY SYSTEM

Family: Concept and Forms

Family, as a reproductive or a biological unit, consists of a man and a woman having a socially approved sexual relationship and whatever offspring (natural or adopted) they might have. As a social unit, a family is referred to as "a group of persons of both sexes, related by marriage, blood or adoption, performing roles based on age, sex and relationship, and socially distinguished as making up a single household or a subhousehold". Aileen Ross' definition of family includes physical, social and psychological elements of family life. According to her (1961:31), family is "a group of people usually related as some particular type of kindred, who may live in one household and whose unity resides in patterning of rights and duties, sentiments and authority". She, thus, makes distinction between four sub-structures of family: (i) ecological sub-structure, i.e., spatial arrangement of family members and their households, or how relatives live geographically close to each other. In simple words, this refers to the size of the household and type of the family; (ii) sub-structure of rights and duties, i.e., division of labour within the household; (iii) substructure of power and authority, i.e., control over the action of members; and (iv) sub-structure of sentiments, i.e., relationship between different sets of members, say, between husband and wife, parents and children, and siblings and siblings, etc.

Different scholars have given different forms of family. K.P. Chattopadhyay (1961:75) has given three types of family: *simple* (man, wife, and unmarried children), *compound* (two simple families, say, ego, his wife and unmarried children, and ego's parents and unmarried brothers and sisters), and *composite* (i.e., lineal and collateral joint families). On the basis of *authority*, families have been classified as husband-dominant, wife-dominant, equalitarian, and autonomic families. Burgess and Locke (1963:26) have classified them as *institutional* and *companionship* families on the basis of the behaviour of the individual members. In the former family, the behaviour of the members is controlled by mores and public opinion, while in the latter family, behaviour arises from mutual affection and consensus. On the basis of kinship ties, families are classified as *conjugal* (priority given to marital ties) and *consanguine* (priority given to blood ties). Zimmerman (1947:20) has classified them as *trustee* (where members have to conform to family norms and they have no individual rights), *atomistic* (in which conventional mores lose their significance and each member can make his own choice) and *domestic* (which is an intermediate type between trustee and atomistic). I have introduced the concept of *fissioned* family which in structure and functioning is a nuclear family, separated from the parental family.

Joint Family: Nature, Types and Characteristics

The concept of joint family has varied with different scholars. While Irawati Karve regards '*co-residentiality*' as important in jointness, Harold Gould, I.P. Desai, S.C. Dube, B.S. Cohn, and Pauline Kolenda do not regard *coresidentiality and commensality* as essential ingredients of jointness. F.G. Bailey and T.N. Madan give importance to *joint ownership of property*, irrespective of the type of residence and commensality. I.P. Desai gives importance to fulfilment of obligations towards kin, even if residence is separate and there is no common ownership of property. According to Irawati Karve (1953:21), the traditional ancient Indian family (Vedic and Epic periods) was joint in terms of residence, property, and functions. She has given five characteristics of joint family: common residence, common kitchen, common property, common family worship, and some kinship relationship. On this basis, she defines joint family as "a group of people who generally live under one roof, eat food cooked at one hearth, hold property in common, participate in common family worship, and are related to each other as some particular type of kindred". The word 'common' or 'joint property' here (according to the Hindu Succession Act, 1956) means that all the living male and female members up to three generations have a share in the paternal property.

According to I.P. Desai (1956:140), co-residence and common kitchen are not as important dimensions of joint family as intra-family relationships are. He thinks that when two families having kinship relationship are living separately but function under one common authority, it will be a joint family. He calls it *functional joint family*. He calls a *traditional joint family* as one which consists of three or more generations. He calls two-generation family as a *marginal joint family*. Ramakrishna Mukherjee (1962:352-98) while giving five types of relations—conjugal, parental-filial, inter-sibling, lineal and affinal—has maintained that a joint family is a co-resident and commensal kin-group which consists of one or more of the first three types of relations and either lineal and/or affinal relations among the members.

While I.P. Desai has given five types of family—nuclear, functionally joint, functionally and substantially (in terms of property) joint, marginally joint, and traditional joint, K.M. Kapadia (1959:74) has given five types of family: nuclear (husband, wife and unmarried children), nuclear with married sons (what I.P. Desai calls Marginal Joint and Aileen Ross calls small joint family), lineal joint, collateral joint, and nuclear family with a dependant (widowed sister, etc.) Aileen Ross (1966:34) has given four types of families: large joint, small joint, nuclear, and nuclear with dependants.

Taking all these types of families together as given by different scholars, a joint family may be defined as 'a multiplicity of geneologically related nuclear families, joint in residence and commensal relations and functioning under one authority'. M.S. Gore (1968:6-7) has said that a joint family should be viewed as "a family of co-parceners and their dependants" instead of viewing it as a multiplicity of nuclear families. He holds that in a nuclear family, the emphasis is on conjugal relationship while in a joint family, emphasis is on filial and fraternal relationships. According to Gore, joint family is of three types: *filial* joint family (parents and their married sons with their offspring), *fraternal* joint family (two married brothers and their children) and filial and fraternal (combined) joint family.

I consider a nuclear family which has separated from father's or married brother's family, as a *fissioned* family. This fissioned family can be totally independent or dependent on some other nuclear family related through some type of kinship. On the other hand, I classify the joint families in terms of types of kin (primary, secondary, tertiary and distant) involved. Thus, I propose five family types as given in Diagram 1.

The *characteristics* of joint family may be described as below:

1. *It has an authoritarian structure*, i.e., power to make decisions lies in

Diagram 1

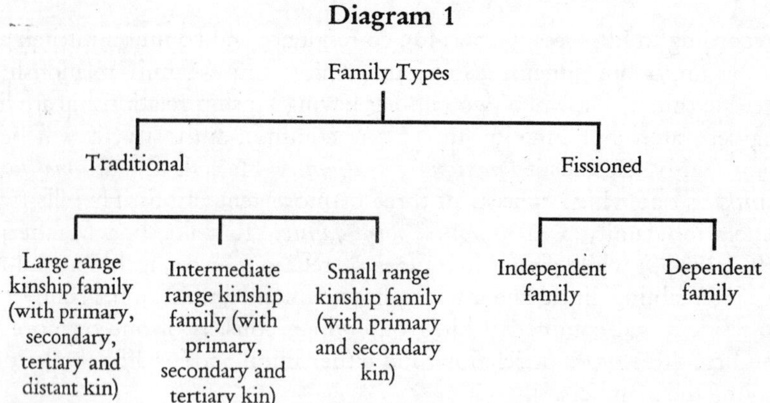

the hands of the head of the family (patriarch). Contrary to the *authoritarian* family, in a *democratic* family, the authority is vested in one or more individuals on the basis of competence and ability.

2. *It has familistic organisation*, i.e., individual's interests are subordinated to the interests of the family as a whole, or the goals of the family are the goals of the individual members.
3. *Status of members is determined by their age and relationship*. The status of a man is higher than his wife; in two generations, the status of a person in the higher generation is higher than the status of a person in the lower generation; in the same generation, the status of a person of higher age is higher than the status of a person of lower age; and the status of a woman is determined by the status of her husband in the family.
4. *The filial and fraternal relationship gets preference over conjugal relationship*, i.e., husband-wife relationship is subordinated to father-son or brother-brother relationship.
5. *The family functions on the ideal of joint responsibility*. If a father takes loan to marry his daughter, it is also the responsibility of his sons to repay the loan.
6. *All members get equal attention*. A poor brother's son will be admitted to the same school (even if costly) as rich brother's son.
7. *The authority in the family (between men and men, men and women, and women and women) is determined on the principle of seniority*. Though the eldest male (or female) may delegate the authority to someone else yet even this delegation is based on the principle of seniority, which limits the scope for the emergence of individualism.

Changing Pattern of Family

Is joint family structure being nuclearised? My contention is that "jointness of family in India is not disappearing and that stage can never be envisaged when the joint family will be lost in the mental horizon of the people; only the 'cutting off' point of jointness is changing. Instead of large joint families, we will have only locally functioning effective small joint families of two generations or so. At the same time, a nuclear fissioned family (of husband, wife and unmarried children) will not be totally independent but will be functionally dependent on (i.e., remain joint with) some primary kin like father or brother, etc. This is evident from various empirical studies conducted by various scholars in different parts of the country. We will analyse change in jointness at two levels: structural and interactional.

Structural Changes

We cite six empirical studies conducted in last four decades by scholars like I.P. Desai, K.M. Kapadia, Aileen Ross, M.S. Gore, A.M. Shah and Sachchidananda.

Desai (1964:41) studied urban families (in Mahuwa in Gujarat) in 1955 and found that: (i) nuclearity is increasing and jointness is decreasing; (ii) spirit of individualism is not growing, as about half of the households are joint with other households; and (iii) the radius of kinship relations within the circle of jointness is becoming smaller. The joint relations are mostly confined to parents-children, siblings, and uncles-nephews, i.e., lineal relationship is found between father, son and grandson, and the collateral relationship is found between a man and his brothers and uncles.

Kapadia (1956:112) studied rural and urban families (18% urban and 82% rural) in Gujarat (Navasari town and its 15 surrounding villages) in 1955. His main conclusions were: (1) In the rural community, the proportion of joint families is almost the same as that of the nuclear families. (2) Viewed in terms of castes, in villages, higher castes have predominantly joint family while lower castes show a greater incidence of nuclear family. (3) In the urban community, there are more joint families than nuclear families. (4) In the 'impact' villages (i.e., villages within the radius of 7 to 8 km from a town), the family pattern closely resembles the rural pattern and has no correspondence with the urban pattern. (5) Taking all areas (rural, urban and impact) together, it may be held that joint family structure is not being nuclearised. (6) The difference in the rural and the urban family patterns is the result of modification of the caste pattern by economic factors.

Ross (1961:303) studied only Hindu families in an urban setting (Bangalore in Karnataka state) in 1957. She found that: (1) The trend of family form is towards a breakaway from the traditional joint family form into nuclear family units. (2) The small joint family is now the most typical form of family life. (3) A growing number of people now spend at least part of their lives in single family units. (4) Living in several types of family during life-time seems so widespread that we can talk of a cycle of family types as being the normal sequence for city-dwellers. (5) Distant relatives are less important to the present generation than they were to their parents and grand-parents. (6) City-dweller son has become more spatially separated from all relatives.

Shah studied families in one village in Gujarat between 1955 and 1958. Classifying families as *simple* (consisting of whole or part of the *parental* family) and *complex* (consisting of two or more parental families), he found that one-third families were complex and two-third were simple, indicating the breakdown of joint family system in rural India.

Gore studied families in an urban (Delhi), rural, and fringe areas (of Rohtak and Hissar districts in Haryaṇa) in 1960 and found that two types of families: one, husband, wife and unmarried children, and two, husband, wife, unmarried and married sons-dominated over all others.

Sachchidananda (1977) studied families in 30 villages in one district (Shahabad) in Bihar and found that: (1) One-fourth families were nuclear and three-fourth were joint, indicating predominance of traditional families. (2) There were more nuclear families in upper castes than in middle and lower castes. (3) Nuclearity tends to rise with the level of education.

Kolenda (1968) used data from 26 studies conducted between the 1950s and 1970s and found that: (1) Majority of the families are nuclear. (2) There are regional differences in the proportions of joint families. There are higher proportions of joint families in Gangetic plain than in Central India or Eastern India (including West Bengal). (3) The joint family is more characteristic of upper and landowning castes than of lower and landless castes. (4) Caste is more closely related to the size and the proportion of joint families.

Ram Ahuja studied families in 1976 in an urban area and in 1988 in rural areas during his two research projects (on 'Drug Abuse Among College Students' and 'Rights of Women') in Rajasthan. Both studies pointed out that though the number of nuclear families is growing yet it does not indicate the disappearance of joint family system.

Ramakrishna Mukherjee studied family in West Bengal in 1960-61. He found (1975: 5-50) that: (1) Size is not an indicator of nuclear or joint structure of family. His own survey of 4,120 family units gave 4.50 and

4.83 as the average size of a nuclear and a joint family respectively. (2) Size of joint family is not large because the 'root couple' does not remain alive beyond 75 years or so. The husband and wife become 'parents' for the first time when the man is in the age group of 25-29 and the woman in that of 20-24. They become 'grandparents' for the first time when the man is in the age group of 45-49 and his wife in that of 40-44. They become 'great grandparents' for the first time when man in the 'root couple' is in the age group of 75-79 and his wife in that of 70-74, and their first son in the age group of 25-29 becomes a 'parent' for the first time with his wife in the age group of 20-24. The expansion of collateral relationship in a family is between two 'distant' cousins. Subsequently, the joint families expand within a limited generational extension. (3) In his analysis of studies on families (44,657) made in 30 villages and towns in 15 states in India by 18 scholars (like S.C. Dube, M.S.A. Rao, Kolenda, I.P.Desai, Kapadia, Irawati Karve, Kulkarni, T.N.Madan, Driver, Sovani, Mukherjee, Bose, Srivastava, etc.) Mukherjee found that the percentage of nuclear to total families ranged from 35 to 63 (*Ibid*:38). This points out the central tendency in Indian society to pursue the joint family organisation (*Ibid*:46). (4) The joint family is successively shaking off the collateral relations beyond grandparents' generation.

Taking all studies on structural changes in family together, we conclude:

(1) The number of fissioned families is increasing but even living separately, they fulfil their traditional obligations towards their parental families.
(2) There is more jointness in traditional (rural) communities and more nuclearity in communities exposed to forces of industrialisation, urbanisation and westernisation.
(3) The size of the (traditional) joint family has become smaller.
(4) So long the old cultural values persist among people, the functional type of joint family will be sustained in our society.
(5) Changes from 'traditional' to 'transitional' family include trends toward new-local residence, functional jointness, equality of individuals, equal status for women, increasing opportunity to individual members to achieve their aspirations and the weakening of family norms.

What are the set of values which nurtured, stabilised and sustained the joint family organisation and the values which are now breaking the joint family in India? The important values which sustained joint family structure are: (1) Filial devotion of sons. (2) Lack of economic viability of some brothers, i.e., their inability to support their children economically.

(3) Lack of a state-organised system of social security for the old-age men and women. (4) A material incentive for organising the size of labour unit since it constituted the major share of the capital required for production of goods and services and people had to depend on family labour.

The factors which are now breaking the joint family are: (1) Differential earnings of brothers generating tensions in the family, as unit of production and service today is predominantly an individual. Up to a point, the values the members inculcate may enable them to subside tension by mutual adjustment and compromise but brothers separate when they focus on the conjugal units. (2) The death of the 'root couple' who holds economic power, and inability, incompetence and self-interest of sons and their wives to take up the role of 'parental couple'. (3) Incentive of depending on family labour is disappearing with the emergence of a cash nexus. (4) System of social security, savings and extended earning opportunities of the people are leading to nuclearisation of joint family structures.

Interactional Changes

The changes in intra-family relations may be examined at three levels: husband-wife relations, parental-filial relations, and relations between daughter-in-law and parents-in-law.

The relations between *husband and wife* in Indian family have been reviewed by Goode (1963), Kapadia (1966), Gore (1968) and Murray Straus (1969). These studies indicate change in (a) power allocation in decision-making, (b) emancipation of wife, and (c) closeness.

In traditional family, wife had no voice in family decision-making. But in contemporary family, in budgeting the family expenditure, in disciplining the children, in purchasing goods and giving gifts, the wife now credits herself as equal in power role. Though husband continues to play the *instrumental* role and wife the *expressive* role, yet both often talk things over and consult each other in the process of arriving at a decision. This also does not mean that husband-dominant family is changing into wife-dominant or equalitarian family. The assumption of economic role and the education of wife have made wives potential equals. The source of power has shifted from 'culture' to 'resource', where 'resource' is 'anything that one partner may make available to the other helping the latter satisfy his/her needs or attain his/her goals'. As such, the balance of power will be on the side of that partner who contributes greater resources to the marriage. Murray Straus' study (1975:141) on 'husband to wife power score' also supported the hypothesis based on 'resource theory' rather than the 'cultural values theory'. He found that the middle-class husbands have a higher 'effective power' (+) score than the working class husbands. It indicated that compared to middle-class families, working class families are more role-segregated or 'autonomic', i.e., working class families have less joint husband-wife activity of all types. It also means that in middle class families, both husband and wife take more active part than do working class families in attempting to direct the behaviour of the family group toward solution of the problem. Straus's study thus indicated that both nuclearity and low socio-economic status are associated with reduction in the husband's power.

Emphasising 'resources' factor does not mean that 'culture' (what Max Weber has called 'traditional authority') has lost its importance. In fact, both factors are important today in 'conjugal bonds'. It may thus be averred that though an average Indian family is husband-dominant yet the *ideological* source of power of women is giving place to a *pragmatic* one.

The change in conjugal bonds is also evident from the increasing emancipation of wife. In urban areas, wife going with husband for social visits, taking food with husband or even before he does, going together to restaurants and movies, etc.—indicate increasing 'companion' role of wife. Husband no longer regards his wife as inferior to him or devoid of reasoning but consults her and trusts her with serious matters. As regards *closeness* of man to his wife and mother, man, particularly the educated one, is now equally close to both (Gore, 1968:180).

The relations between *parents and children* may be assessed in terms of holding authority, freedom of discussing problems, opposition of parents by children, and modes of imposing penalty. In traditional family, while power and authority was totally vested in the patriarch and he was virtually all powerful who decided everything about education, occupation, marriage and the career of children in the family (Kathleen Gough, Cf: McKim Marriott, 1955:44 and Ruth Anshen, 1949:94), in contemporary family—not only in nuclear but also in joint family—the grandfather has lost his authority. The authority has shifted from patriarch to parents who consult their children on all important issues before taking any decisions about them. Ross (1961:93) also maintains that grand-parents are no longer as influential as they were earlier. Gore (1968:138) also found that it is now parents who take decisions about schooling, occupation and marriage of their children. Children have also started discussing their problems with parents. They even oppose their parents. Kapadia (1966:323) and Margaret Cormack (1969) also found that children today enjoy more freedom. Some legislative measures have also given powers to children to demand their rights. Perhaps, it is because of all this that parents do not use old methods of punishing their children.

They use economic and psychological methods (denying money, scolding, restricting freedom, reasoning) more than the physical methods (beating). In spite of these changes in relations between parents and children, the children do not think only of their rights and privileges but also of the welfare of parents and siblings. They respect and fear their elders.

The relations between *daughter-in-law and parents-in-law* have also undergone change. However, this change is not so significant in daughter-in-law and mother-in-law (DIL-MIL) relations as in daughter-in-law and father-in-law (DIL-FIL) relations. The educated DIL does not observe *purdah* from her FIL and discusses not only the family problems but also the social and even the political issues.

Taking all three types of relations (husband-wife, parents-children, and DIL-PIL) together, it may be said: (1) Younger generation now claims more individuality. (2) Consanguineous relationship does not have primacy over conjugal relationship. (3) Along with 'culture' and 'ideological' factor, the 'resource' factor also affects relations.

Future of Indian Family

Stresses and Adoption

Are the arguments against the joint family system appropriate and relevant? Are the values of people really changing? Is there any evidence of a qualitative change in the value system of the people which will lead to complete nuclearisation of the joint family structures? If no, why are earlier values losing their influence in the contemporary period? What is the future of the Indian family?

The perspective on family in India is usually developed on the conceptual scale of 'tradition to modernity' by undertaking either opinion-surveys of youths or general public belonging to different forms of family structure, or making socio-economic surveys of people of different castes and classes in the rural and the urban areas. Do the studies that have been made so far on Indian family indicate some direction of change in future?

The question of future of family in India is concerned with two aspects: one, what is the future of joint family, and two, what is the future of family as an institution? As regards the first question, it has already been pointed out (in earlier pages) that joint family will never be completely nuclearised in our society. The two structures (joint and nuclear) will continue to survive. Only the nature of jointness will change from residential to functional one and the size of joint family will shrink to two or three generations. As regards the future of family (as an institution), it may be discussed in terms of four factors (which are not mutually exclusive) affecting the family: (a) *technological revolution*: access to such conveniences as electricity, piped water in homes, intricate home appliances like gas and fridge, telephone, buses and other vehicles have all changed common man's living and raised his standard of life. Effects of the industrial-technological changes on family are quite evident, like those of productive function, abandonment of self-sufficiency in family economy, occupational and population mobility, weakening of kinship ties, and so forth; (b) *population revolution*: shift from agriculture to manufacturing and service, migration from rural to urban areas, decrease in birth and death rates, increase in average expectation of life and availability of elderly persons in family, replacement of early marriages by post-puberty and late marriages, etc., have created problems of readjustment, changes in power structure, desire for smaller families and so on; (c) *democratic revolution*: ideals of democracy have filtered down to the level of family living. Demand of rights by women, emancipation of children from patriarch's authority, willingness to approach decision-making through democratic process, and change from familisim to individualism may be described as important trends in family; and (d) *secular revolution:* there is a shift away from religious values to rational values. Change in wife's attitude towards husband, demand for divorce on maladjustment, children's reluctance to support parents in old age, elimination of family worship—are all the result of rational thinking and deviation from moral and religious norms.

Succinctly stated, we find several dominant trends in Indian family in the last few decades. These are: (1) Increasing importance of nuclear family. (2) Transference of some functions (e.g., educational, recreational, protective, etc.) to some other institutions. (3) Fundamental change in family age structure, i.e., proportionately fewer children to care for and proportionately more elderly persons surviving. This has created the necessity of transferring support function from the family to the state and to private insurance companies. This has affected the family power structure too. (4) Freedom to women due to their education and increasing economic independence. (5) Declining reliance of children upon family controls. (6) Changing values of youth. Though they have respect for and fear of parents yet they want parental 'support' for achieving their individual interests. (7) Liberalisation of attitudes and practices towards sex (8) Change from pre-puberty to post-puberty marriages. (9) Decreasing family size. These characteristics of the present-day Indian family point out change in structure and family ties.

These family trends are ongoing processes. They have not come to a stop. Nevertheless, it is possible to get a fair idea of what the family will be like in the future, say in the next 25 to 30 years. Following Harold Christensen (1975:410), we envisage the following possible changes in Indian family in the first quarter of the twenty-first century:

(1) The family will continue to exist. It will not be replaced by state-controlled systems of reproduction and child bearing.
(2) Its stability will depend more on interpersonal bonds than on social pressures from outside or upon kinship loyalty.
(3) It will more depend upon community support and services.
(4) With medical advances, the family will have greater control over its biological processes (of separating sexual from reproductive function, controlling sickness and death, and determining sex of the offspring).
(5) Remarriage and divorce rates will be high.
(6) Parents and grand parents will continue to support their children and grandchildren even after their retirement.
(7) Woman's position of power within the family will further improve with increase in gainful employment.
(8) Viewed generally, the family will not be equalitarian but will remain husband-dominant family.

Functionalist and Marxist Perspectives

The future of family can be perceived with two perspectives: functionalist and Marxist. Functionalists perceive family as an important 'organ' in the 'body' of society. They are concerned with the functions that the family performs—sexual, reproductive, socialising or educational, and economic. The first two functions indicate that family is useful biologically while other functions point out that it is useful socially and culturally too. Can other institutions take over the functions of the family? It is argued that even when other institutions perform the functions of the family, they only 'help' the family in these functions and not that they 'deprive or relieve' family from performing them. Family's functions have been modified in recent years. The family gives 'something' to and gets 'something' from other sub-systems. Family's role is primary.

Other perspective on family is Marxist. The Marxists adopt a structural perspective on the family and gender relations. They explain male dominance in family in a historical context. Their hypothesis is that in the nomadic stage of man's social development, men performed only the 'launching' function; there was no exclusive sexual possessiveness nor did any private property exist. Gradually, the male sphere of activity became more specialised and along with hunting they also took up cattle-breeding, mining and trade. As men acquired greater control over wealth and property, they sought means to ensure that it stayed with them and passed on to their children. For this, they wanted to be sure who their offspring were. Thus, free sexual relations had to be replaced by monogamy. Family became male-dominated and patriarchal. The division of labour was gendered and females were subordinated. Women's oppression is thus a problem of history rather than of biology. Marxists, in this way, talk of the influence of class on family life, specially on socialisation. They see gendered division of labour as *socially constructed*, which is contrary to functionalists' *naturalistic* approach. Feminist Marxists thus recognise that sex, reproduction, socialisation and economic function 'need' to occur but not necessary in ways that 'exploit' female labour and leave them powerless. They (pluralist-feminist Marxists) thus believe that family will continue to survive in future but there will be changes (including individual freedom, political voice to women, etc.). This approach is political and has the emancipation of women at its heart. In other words, family will not break up; it will only adapt itself.

Inter-Generational Conflict and Youth Unrest

Youth, as a distinct social category, is largely a modern phenomenon. This stage in life is the outcome of the long and ever expanding period between childhood/adolescence, and work. Earlier, the child took to his family work at an early stage but now with work specialisation and required skill, he has to wait for several years before he finds work. The early modern industrial economy first required a literate and a disciplined labour supply but now it requires a skilled worker. Specialised education was, thus, imparted to meet this demand and modern youth is largely a by-product of it. Just as proletariat is the product of the factory system, so modern youth is partly the product of the education system. At first, education was mainly an upper and middle class privilege but now even the lower class (including SC, ST, OBC) person has a universal and a legal right to get education. All youths thus have now developed a shared interest. S.N. Eisenstadt observes that it is in the informal peer groups that intra-generational interaction is most free to flourish. In much the same way as universal education, though to a lesser extent, work in industry and service in office have also provided a basis of collective experience and identity to young men. Sometimes, the young people turn against dominant norms and adopt culturally deviant lifestyles. The young group, generated largely within the educational context, reflects the influence of class, gender and individuality. Thus emerged the youth culture (and subculture) after the 1950s. The political independence and democratic values further gave youth the opportunity to ask for more rights. They developed new values and started opposing those persons whom they considered barriers in achieveing their goals and aspirations. All this led to inter-generational conflicts, like conflicts between parents and children in family, between students and teachers in educational institutions, and between young and old employees in offices. Between the 1950s and 1990s, the media and the general public also seemed obsessed with youth.

What motivated the youth to come in conflict with and oppose older generation people were factors like influence of western culture, values picked up from commercial means of entertainment, increased leisure, greater affluence, and power of parents. Western culture changed their values based on individualism and equality; commercial recreation made them realise the importance of violence and threat of violence in achieving their goals, 'part-time' education provided them increased leisure and time to do things which busy life would not have permitted them to do; and parental affluence and power provided them power to influence. All this created a distinct culture leading to unrest and inter-generation conflict.

But could we say that youth in India oppose their parents and elders in the same way as in other societies? Has Indian culture lost its moorings? While it is true that surveys point out change in relations between parents and children in India, these studies also show that children respect their parents, are generally fairly satisfied with life, and want important decisions about their education, marriage, etc., to be taken by the parents. In traditional family, the patriarch was all powerful. It was considered bad manners for the youngsters to argue with or talk back to their seniors. They were not to question the orders or deeds of the elders. Even those children who moved away to distant cities were theoretically still members of the family and, therefore, under the control of the patriarch, although he could not supervise their day-to-day affairs.

In 1961, M.S. Gore in his study on family, asked his respondents as to who made major decisions regarding schooling, occupation, and the choice of bride/groom for children in the family? He found (1968:138) that in a very large number of cases, the children were not free to take their own decisions. He maintained that only a small number of children took the matter into their own hands. Margaret Cormack (1969) found in her study that more than half (55%) of her total respondents (500) from colleges *sometimes* opposed their parents, a few (6%) *often* opposed them, and one-third (33%) *never* opposed them. I.P. Desai (1953) in his study of high school students in Poone found severe strain on parent-ward relationship. As many as 168 respondents in his survey reported that they had wished at times to leave home. Of these, 117 students also gave reasons for it. About 64 per cent wanted to separate because of the authoritarian, humiliating, unfair, and unjust behaviour of their parents, 19 per cent because of the uncongenial atmosphere in the family and strain arising from it, 10 per cent due to quarrels in the family, and remaining 7 per cent for some other reasons. The causes of conflicts between the younger and the older generations were: (1) Feeling among the youngsters that elders try to impose their authoritarian, unfair and unjust behaviour upon them. (2) Growing belief among young children that they are more culturally advanced than their parents. (3) Children's feeling that their individualism is curbed due to temperamental strictness on the part of the elders. (4) Expectations of the younger members as to the way in which their needs should be served are not fulfilled. (5) Difference in attitudes to social customs and religious beliefs.

B.V. Shah's study (1964) of 200 students of Baroda university showed that children did not want complete freedom of selecting their partners but wanted selection jointly by parents and children. About two-third students (66.5%) wanted to select their brides in consultation with their parents, one-third (32.5%) wanted to give more importance to their own choice, and only 1 per cent wanted selection exclusively by parents' choice. Margaret Cormack also found that 65 per cent of her respondents (students from different universities) wanted that marriages should be arranged by parents with the consent of their children, in 3 per cent by parents without children's consent and in 32 per cent cases by their own choice. Vimal Shah (1975) in his study of 281 Hindu graduate students (boys and girls) of different castes of Gujarat University found that 92 per cent girls and 66 per cent boys believed in arranged marriage. This points out young persons' adherence to and slight deviation from the traditional norms.

Some legislative measures have also created disruptive relations between parents and children. Parents no longer can deprive their children of a share in the paternal property. The Hindu Succession Act, 1956 enjoins that the property of a male Hindu dying intestate shall devolve upon his specified heirs. On the other hand, there are cases where children file legal cases against their parents on property issues, criticise them (parents) for neglecting them because of which they take to alcoholism, drug abuse, etc. and suffer from feeling of insecurity. Decline in parental authority is also reported. The charge is that family is failing to act as effective agency of social control. But the same charge is also made against the schools and the police. The causes of juvenile delinquency, youth crime, drug abuse, etc., must, therefore, be sought in wider society rather than in integration conflicts or in the failure of family. Here, we can only hold that the more permissive and democratic ideals of the last few decades reduce the credibility of physical punishment as means of maintaining control both within the family and within society. It is difficult to imagine a widespread reversion to more traditional forms of discipline within the family without some comparable broader change in society.

MARRIAGE SYSTEM

Hindu Marriage: Concept, Types and Mate Selection

Marriage is perceived by sociologists as a system of roles of a man and a woman whose union has been given social sanction as husband and wife. The equilibrium of the system requires adjustment between the two partners so that the role enactment of one (partner) corresponds to the role expectations of the other (Robert O' Blood, 1960:189).

Indologists look upon Hindu marriage as a *sanskara*, having three objects of *dharma* (fulfilment of religious duties), *rati* (sex gratification), and *praja* (procreation). Marriage performed for *dharma* was called *dharmik* marriage, while one performed for sexual pleasure was regarded as *adharmik* marriage. Marriage was considered sacred because of several reasons· (i) *dharma* was the highest aim of marriage; (ii) performance of marriage ceremony included certain rites (like *havan*, *kanyadan*, *panigrahana*, *saptapadi*, etc.) which were considered sacred; (iii) rites were performed before sacred god *Agni* by reciting *mantras* from sacred scriptures *Vedas* by a sacred Brahmin; (iv) union (between man and woman) was considered indissoluble and irrevocable; and (v) emphasis was on chastity of the woman and faithfulness of the man. Even today, the sanctity of the marriage is recognised by Hindus in spite of the fact that marriage is performed for companionship and not for performing duties, and whenever found a failure, it is dissolved by divorce. Mutual fidelity and devotion to partner are still considered to be the essence of marriage. Kapadia (1966) has said: "Hindu marriage continues to be a sacrament; only it is raised to an ethical plane."

In simple words, marriage in Hindu culture is a spiritual union between a man and a woman for spiritual realisation. Hindu culture also recognises (besides the above-mentioned *Brahma* marriage) seven other forms of marriage with lesser and lower ideals. The four of these marriages—*Gandharva* (entering into sex before getting the social sanction of society), *Asura* (eloping with a woman), *Rakshasya* (forcibly abducting a woman from her home) and *Paisacha* (man molesting a girl when she is asleep or intoxicated or in a state of unbalanced mind)—had such a low ideal that they were termed as *Adharmik* marriages. The remaining three

—*Daiva* (woman is married to a priest, a man of intellect and money, belonging to an aristocratic class), *Prajapatiya* (entering wedlock for biological function of sex satisfaction and having children) and *Arsha* (woman marrying a man of intellect and character (sage) who is reluctant to enter marriage, so that she may get intelligent progeny and good home environment)—were given the label of *Dharmik* marriages. The main reason for recognising the four *Adharmik* marriages as marriages was to confer the respectful status of a wife on the 'injured' woman.

The regulation of *mate selection* in Hindu society is subsumed under the concepts of endogamy, exogamy and hypergamy. *Endogamy* is a social rule that requires a person to select the spouse from within the caste and sub-caste; *exogamy* forbids selection from the same *gotra* and *sapindas* (i.e., cousins like *chachera, mamera, phuphera* and *mausera*); and according to hypergamy, a boy from the upper caste can marry a girl from the lower caste and vice-versa. In early society, caste endogamy was functional because it preserved the occupational secrets of the caste, maintained the solidarity of the caste and checked decrease in the membership or strength of the caste. In the present society, though it makes marital adjustment easier, yet it has proved to be dysfunctional in some ways since it creates inter-caste tensions which adversely affect the political unity of the country, makes field of mate-selection limited and circumscribed, and creates problems of dowry, child marriage, etc. The exogamous taboos, according to Valvalkar, were designed for restricting free marital relations between parents and offspring and between siblings. Kane (*History of Dharamashastras*, 1930) has maintained that exogamous restrictions were imposed for preventing transmission of family defects through heredity and for the fear that there may be clandestine love affairs and consequent loss of morals. However, these arguments are not accepted today for the reasons that decay of lineage is not reported among non-Hindu communities (say, Muslims) who practise cousin marriages. Kapadia (1966:127) has said that the rule of *sapinda* exogamy was of the nature of a pious recommendation and remained so till the end of the eighth century. Today, though this rule is followed by and large by all Hindus, yet cases of cousin marriages are not unknown.

The mate selection today involves three important issues: party to selection, criteria of selection, and field of selection. While earlier mates for children were selected by parents, now children believe in joint selection by parents and children, though cases of individual selection (i.e., selection by children themselves) are not rare. The *criteria* of selecting mates by parents are quite different from those of children. While parents give importance to family status, *sanskaras*, caste, dowry and so forth, children give importance to education, character, physical appearance, equipment and skills, etc. The joint selection today keeps in mind the needs of the family as well as the interests of the person acquiring a spouse. No wonder, studies of scholars like B.V. Shah, Margaret Cormack, Vimal Shah, etc. showed that a very large number of young boys and girls wanted to select their mates in consultation with their parents.

Changes in Hindu Marriage System

Changes in marriage system among Hindus may be analysed in seven areas: object of marriage, process of mate selection, form of marriage, age of marriage, economic aspect of marriage (dowry), stability of marriage (divorce), and widow remarriage. Of these, we have already discussed change in two areas in earlier pages, viz., change in the object of marriage (from *dharma* to companionship), and change in mate selection (party, criteria, and field of selection). Change in the form of marriage refers to change from polygyny to monogamy and change in age of marriage points out change from pre-puberty marriages to post-puberty marriages. The remaining three changes may be examined by analysing marriage legislation.

Marriage Legislation

The laws enacted in India relate to (i) age at marriage, (ii) field of mate selection, (iii) number of spouses in marriage, (iv) dissolving marriage, (v) dowry, and (vi) remarriage. The important legislations relating to these aspects are: The Child Marriage Restraint Act, 1929 (amended in 1978, dealing with age at marriage), the Special Marriage Act, 1954 (dealing with age at marriage, freedom to children to marry without parental consent, bigamy, and dissolving marriage), the Hindu Marriage Act, 1955 (amended in 1986, and dealing with age at marriage with parents' consent, bigamy, and annulment of marriage), Anti Dowry Act, 1961, and the Widow Remarriage Act, 1856.

The first three Acts (of 1929, 1954 and 1955) pertaining to the age of marriage prescribe the marriage age of girls as 18 years and for boys as 21 years. The difference in the Acts is that the 1929 Act (amended in 1978) does not invalidate the marriage for violating the provisions in the Act. It only prescribes punishment for the bridegroom, parents, guardians and the priest (but not for women). The 1955 Act makes invalidation of the marriage possible for violation of the age provision. This (1955) Act covers marriages performed *with* the consent of parents but the 1954 Act covers marriages performed through courts, *with or without* the parental consent. Both these Acts (1954 and 1955) prohibit bigamy and permit divorce also on various grounds and put restrictions on marriage within the degrees of prohibited relationships, unless custom permits such marriages. The Anti-Dowry Act, 1961, has made giving and taking dowry as a legal offence. The Widow Remarriage Act, 1856 permits widows to remarry but forfeits them the right of maintenance from the property of the first husband. The Hindu Succession Act, 1956, has given share to wife and daughters in man's properly equal to that of sons and brothers.

But will social legislation remove the problems of marriage and family like abolishing dowry and child marriages? Will it contain the exploitation of women and raise their status? We agree that social legislation is necessary for providing new direction to culture and society and permitting change and removing evils by filling up the gap between social opinion and social needs of the people. Dr. Radhakrishnan, at the time of introducing the bills related to marriage in 1952, said: "The ancient history cannot solve the problems of modern society." The function of the social legislation is to adjust the legal system continually to a society which is constantly outgrowing that system. But is the government serious about implementing these Acts? Who does not know the loopholes in all the Acts? Who does not know the indifference and the callousness of the police in taking action against the law-violators? While social legislation is essential, the will to implement it is more crucial.

Marriage Among Muslims

Muslim society is stratified not only among Shias and Sunnis but also among Ashraf (Saiyed, Sheikh, Pathan, etc.), Azlab (Momins, Mansooris, Ibrahims, etc.) and Arzal (Halalkhor, etc.). The Ashrafs are the noble-born, the Azlabs are low-born, and the Arzals are the lowest of all. All these groups are endogamous and inter-marriages among them are condemned and discouraged.

Muslim marriage, called *nikah*, unlike the sacramental marriage of the Hindus, is considered to be a civil contract. Its important objectives are: control over sex, procreation of children and perpetuation of family, upbringing of children, and ordering of domestic life. S.C. Sarkar also maintains that marriage among Muslims is a civil contract. But it will be wrong to say that Muslim marriage has no religious duty. It is a devotion and an act of *ibaddat*. Jang (1953) is, therefore, more correct in maintaining that *nikah*, though essentially a contract, is also a devotional act. But it is surely not a sacrament like Hindus.

The Muslim marriage has five features: (i) proposal and its acceptance, (ii) capacity to contract marriage, (iii) doctrine of equality, (iv) preference system, and (v) *mahar*. The proposal is made by the bridegroom to the bride just before the wedding ceremony in the presence of two witnesses and a *Maulvi* (priest). For recognising marriage as *sahi* (regular), it is necessary that both the proposal and its acceptance must be at the same meeting. Not doing so makes marriage 'fasid' (irregular) but not *batil* (invalid). Further, female testimony has been rejected in Muslim marriage. *Fasid* marriage can be converted into *sahi* marriage but not the *batil* one. Examples of *fasid* marriages are: absence of witnesses at the time of making and accepting the proposal, fifth marriage of a man, marriage of a woman during the period when she is undergoing *iddat* (period of seclusion for three menstrual periods after husband's death or divorce), and difference of religion between husband and wife. Examples of *batil* marriages are: marriage with a person who worships idol or fire, polyandry, and marriage with some consanguineous kin (say, father's sister, mother's sister, own sister or brother, sister's daughter, son's wife and so on). The feature of *capacity to contract marriage* refers to not recognising child marriage or marriage of a person of an unsound mind. The Shia law gives the right to the guardian of a minor to contract his/her marriage. The marriage contracted by the *fazuli* relative of a minor gives the right to the minor to ratify the marriage on attaining puberty. The practice of ratification and option of repudiation is called *khairulbalig*. The *doctrine of equality* refers to marriage with a person of low status. Such marriages are looked down upon. Similarly, runaway marriages (called *kifa*) are also not recognised. The *preferential system* refers to giving preference first to parallel (*chachera* and *mausera*) cousin and then to cross-cousin (only *mamera* but not *phuphera*). But these days, cousin marriages are discouraged. *Mahr* (dower) custom in marriage refers to money which a wife is entitled to get from her husband in consideration of marriage. *Mahr* can be *specified* (fixed) or *proper* (considered reasonable). It can also be *prompt* (payable on husband's death or divorce) or *deferred*. At one time, the Muslims had a practice of *muta* (temporary) marriage but that practice has been abolished now.

Divorce (*talaq*) in Muslim society can be given with or without the intervention of the court. A woman can divorce her husband only through the court but a man can divorce his wife without approaching the court and by making a single pronouncement during one *tuhr* (one menstruation period, i.e., one month) (called *Talaq-e-Ahasan)* or three pronouncements in three *tuhrs* (called *Talaq-e-Hasan*) or three pronouncements in a single *tuhr* (called *Talaq-e-Ulbidat*). In addition to these three types of divorce, there are three other kinds of divorce too: *illa*, *zihar*, and *lian*. In *illa*, the husband swears by *Allah* (God) to abstain from sexual relations with his wife for a period of four or more months or for a specified period. After making *illa*, if he really abstains from sexual intercourse, the marriage is considered to be dissolved. In *zihar*, the husband declares in the presence of two witnesses that his wife is like a mother to him. *Zihar* does not dissolve the marriage but it provides a ground to the wife to sue her husband for divorce. In *lian*, the husband accuses his wife of adultery. This provides ground to wife to approach the court for divorce. Divorce given by mutual consent of husband and wife is called *khula* (initiated at the instance of the wife) or *mubarat* (initiative coming from wife or husband). After divorce, the wife is not entitled to get maintenance allowance from her husband. However, about fifteen years ago, the Supreme Court allowed maintenance allowance to one Shah Bano. Since this decision was questioned by the Muslim leaders, describing it as interference the Muslim Personal Law, the government had to amend the legislation. In February 1993, the Uttar Pradesh High Court also ordered the payment of maintenance allowance to one Hameedan and her two children. The All India Muslim Personal Law Board then filed a review petition in the High Court.

All these features point out the difference between the Hindu and the Muslim marriages in terms of aims and ideals of marriage, nature of marriage, characteristics of marriage, and dissolving marriage.

It is now contended that the belief that Muslims practise polygyny and easy divorce in large numbers is a misconception. The number of Muslims who have more than one wife is negligible now. There are more cases of bigamy amongst Hindus. Likewise, there are more divorces among Hindus and Sikhs than among Muslims. The statistics compiled by the Indian Statistical Institute reveal that 72 out of 1,000 non-Muslims have more than one wife while only 15 out of 1,000 Muslim males have more than one wife (*Hindustan Times*, June 27, 1998). Earlier, the report compiled by the Committee on the Status of Women, published in 1975 had also revealed that the incidence of polygamy was the highest among tribals (15.25%), followed by Buddhists (7.97%), Jains (6.75%), Hindus (5.8%), and Muslims (5.7%) (Shaukat Ali, 1995).

Uniform Civil Code (UCC)

The unilateral divorce and polygyny among Muslims is so much criticised that many people clamour for uniform civil code regarding marriage. The Muslims oppose it because they not only consider it interference in Muslim personal laws but also because the content of the UCC will be mainly drawn from the Hindu Act. A survey was conducted among 395 persons (187 Hindu and 208 Muslims) in Aligarh in 1995 by the Institute for Development Studies (*The Hindustan Times*, January 1, 1996). About 60 per cent of the total respondents expressed undesirability of the UCC irrespective of their religious background. On the other hand, on religious background basis, 74 per cent Hindus and 9 per cent Muslims expressed the desirability of the UCC. The arguments in favour of the UCC were: (1) national integration and secularism will be promoted; (2) growing communal and caste violence will be contained; (3) the process of civil justice will be strengthened; and (4) the gender biases will be mitigated and feelings of equality amongst women will be perpetuated. The 34 Muslims who supported the UCC were professional and white-collared persons (doctors, lawyers, engineers, college teachers, office workers and students). The arguments against the UCC were: (1) Muslims themselves do not feel any necessity for the change. (2) The political groups are exploiting the religious sentiments of the people for creating their vote bank. (3) Muslims hold that Hindus are trying to impose their cultural values on Muslims as the provisions in the UCC are mainly taken from the Hindu law. (4) The UCC will generate heat, discontent and intolerance among different religious groups, particularly amongst minorities. (5) Most Muslims hold that the UCC will tantamount to a denial of the fundamental right of freedom to religion and will hamper the development of the concept 'unity in diversity'. The Hindus, however, do not share this opinion. It may be averred that if the UCC is not perceived from the 'religious' perspective but is viewed as a measure to check evils of polygyny and easy verbal divorce, a detailed discussion with non-orthodox religious leaders of different communities can help in the formulation of legislation.

Marriage Among Christians

As among Hindus and Muslims, we find stratification among Christians too. The two groups in which Christians are divided are: Protestants and Catholics. The latter are further subdivided as Latin and Syrian Christians. All these groups and sub groups are endogamous.

The main object of marriage among Christians, as among Hindus and Muslims, is to get social sanction for sex relations and procreation. Further, religion also has great significance in Christian marriage. Christians believe that marriage takes place because of the will of God, and after marriage man and woman submerge themselves in each other. The three objects of Christian marriage are believed to be: procreation, escape from fornication (sex relations without marriage), and mutual help and comfort.

The marriage partners are selected either by parents, or by children, or jointly by parents and children. However, in 9 out of 10 cases, selection is made and marriage is settled by parents. While selecting partners, the focus is on avoiding blood relations, and giving importance to social status of family, character, education, physical fitness, etc. Restrictions on consanguinity and affinity among Christians and Hindus are almost the same. Christians have no practice of 'preferred persons' like the Muslims. After the engagement ceremony, the formalities to be fulfilled before the marriage are: producing a certificate of character, and submitting an application for marriage in the church three weeks before the due date. The church priest then invites objections against the proposed marriage and when no objection is received, marriage date is fixed. The marriage is solemnised in the church and the couple declares that they take each other as wedded partner in the presence of two witnesses and in the name of Lord Christ.

Christians do not permit polygyny and polyandry. The Indian Christian Marriage Act, 1872, amended six or seven times since then, covers all aspects of marriage. Christians practise divorce too, though the church does not appreciate it. The Indian Divorce Act, 1869 refers to the conditions under which divorce may be obtained. The Act covers dissolution of marriage, declaring marriage null and void, decree of judicial separation and restitution of conjugal rights. There is no practice of dowry or dower among Christians. Remarriage of widows is not only accepted but also encouraged. Thus, Christian marriage is not a sacrament like Hindu marriage but is a contract between a man and a woman like Muslim marriage in which there is greater stress on companionship. It is necessary that till a uniform civil code is enacted, the Divorce Act of Christians, which is a century and a quarter old, be amended and certain new laws passed. For example, the grounds for divorce are too limited and harsh. Even as between husband and wife, there is discrimination in asmuchas the husband has simply to prove adultery whereas the wife has to prove another matrimonial offence along with adultery for getting relief. Even when both parties wish on mutual consent basis to separate and the courts are convinced that living together is an impossibility, no relief can be given. The wife is considered to be a property of the husband as the provision in the Divorce Act entitles a husband to claim damages from the wife's adulteror. The Divorce Act was first challenged in the Madras High Court in 1953 and again in the Supreme Court in 1995 for being gender discriminative but the petitions were turned down. The Christian law as it exists today encourages perjury, collusion, and manoeuvring. Christians need a law which should cater to the changing needs of time. The Law Commission had formulated in 1960 the Christian Marriage and Matrimonial clauses Bill but the Bill was allowed to lapse after the government promised to introduce it in the parliament. In 1983, the Commission again recommended changes in 1869 Act but in vain. In 1994, the Joint Women's Programmes (JWP) drafted Christian Marriage and Matrimonial Classes Bill and Christian Maintenance Bill but no measures were taken to get them passed.

KINSHIP SYSTEM

Regional Variations in Kinship System: Its Socio-Cultural Correlates

Marriage is a link between the family of orientation and the family of procreation. This fact of individual membership in two nuclear families gives rise to kinship system. Kinship is defined as "a social relationship based upon family relatedness" (Theodorson, 1969:221). The relationship which may be consanguineal (based on blood) or affinal (based on marriage), determines the rights and obligations of related persons. As such, kinship system is referred to as "a structured system of statuses and roles and of relationship in which the kin (primary, secondary, tertiary and distant) are bound to one-another by complex interlocking ties". Part of the reciprocal behaviour, characterising every relationship between kin, consists of the terms by which each addresses the other, i.e., by personal name or by kinship term (*pitaji*, *dadaji*, *bahenji*) or by the combination of personal and kinship terms (Ram's father, Rita's mother, etc.). The kinship terms (of address and reference) which could be *elementary* (which cannot be reduced to any other term, e.g., *mata, pita, kaka, chacha, bhai, bahen,* etc.) or *derivative* (which is compounded from an elementary term, e.g., *bahnoi, mausa,* etc.) or *descriptive* (which combines two or more elementary terms, e.g., *mauseri bahen, phuphera bhai,* etc.) are differentiated as *isolative* (applied only to one kin as defined by generation, sex and geneological connection, e.g., *bhai, bahen, pati, patni,* etc.) or *classificatory* terms (applied to persons of two or more kinship categories (e.g., cousin, used for father's brother's son as well as mother's sister's son). Since the classificatory terms ignore one or more fundamental criteria (e.g., sex, age, generation, affinity, collaterality, bifurcation, etc.) they reduce the number of kinship categories from thousands to a very modest number.

After family, kinship group plays a very crucial role in daily life, rituals and social ceremonies of Hindus. People turn to their kin not only for help in exigencies of life but also on regular occasions. The important kinship groups, after the family, are *vansh* (lineage) and *gotra* (clan). *Vansh* is a consanguineous unilateral descent group whose members trace themselves from a known and real common ancestor. It may be either patrilineal or matrilineal and is an exogamous unit. The members of a *vansh* are treated as brothers and sisters. Lineage ties remain up to few generations only. The main linkage among the families of a lineage is common participation in ritual functions like birth, death etc. The *vansh* passes into *gotra* which though is a unilateral kin group but is larger than the lineage. It is an exogamous group.

The *feminal* kin (related through mother) are as important in an individual's life as patrilineal kin (related through father).

Features of Kinship in Different Zones

Northern Zone

The kinship features in North and Central India differ from those in South India. The socio-cultural correlates of kinship system are *language*, *caste* and (plain and hilly) *region*. In spite of the effect of these three factors on the kinship relations, it is possible to talk of kinship organisation on some collective bases, e.g., on caste and zonal basis. Though kinship behaviour in the northern zone changes slightly from region to region and within each region from caste to caste, yet comparative study shows that it is possible to talk of an 'ideal' northern pattern referring to practices and attitudes generally found to be common among a majority of the castes. Referring to the kinship organisation of the *northern zone*, Irawati Karve (1953:115) has given some important features. Some of these are: (1) Kin junior to ego are addressed by their personal names and senior to ego by the kinship term. (2) All children in ascending and descending generations are equated with one's own sibling group (brothers and sisters) and all children of one's sibling group are again equated with one's own children. (3) The principle of unity of generations is observed (for example, great-grandfather and grandfather are given same respect as father). (4) Within the same generation, the older and the younger kin are kept distinct. (5) The duties and behaviour patterns of the members of three generations are strictly regulated. (6) Some of the ancient kinship terms having Sanskrit origin have been replaced by new terms; for example, *pitamaha* is replaced by *pita*. Suffix 'ji' is added to kinship terms used for kin older than the speaker (for example, *chachaji, tauji,* etc.) In Bengal, instead of 'ji' suffix 'moshai' is added. (7) Marriage among close kin is not permitted. (8) After marriage, a girl is not expected to be free with her parents-in-law, but when she becomes a mother, she achieves position of respect and power and restrictions on her are lessened. (9) The family is so structured that children, parents and grand-parents either live together or social kinship obligations towards them are clearly met. (10) Apart from the joint family which represents a person's intimate and nearest circle of relations, there is always a larger circle of kin who play a part in his life. This kindred represents the circle of his *patri*-kin or *matri*-kin who may stand by him and help him when the immediate family no longer suffices.

Central Zone

The salient features of kinship organisation of the Central India are not much different from those of the North India. The important features of kinship in Central India are: (1) Every region follows northern India practices of marriage, that is, consanguinity is the main consideration which rules marriage. (2) Many castes are divided into exogamous clans. Among some castes, the exogamous clans are arranged in hypergamous hierarchy. (3) The kinship terminology shows intimacy and closeness between various kin. The relations between kin are governed by the custom of '*neota*-gifts' according to which cash-gift is given equivalent to cash-gift received. The *neota*-registers are maintained and preserved for generations. (4) In Gujarat, *mamera*-type of cousin marriage (with mother's brother) and levirate (marriage with husband's brother) are practised by some castes. (5) The custom of periodic marriages in Gujarat has led to child marriages as well as unequal marriages. Such marriages are practised even today. (6) In Maharashtra, there is impact of both modern and southern zones in kinship relations. For example, the clan organisation of the Marathas is similar to that of the Rajputs which is arranged in a ladder manner. Clans are grouped into divisions and each division in named according to the number of clans it comprises; for example *panch-kuli*, *sat-kuli*, etc. The clans are arranged in hypergamous order, the highest being the panch-kuli, followed by the *sat-kuli*, etc. The *panch-kuli* can marry among themselves or can take a girl from the *sat-kuli*, etc. but do not give their daughters outside the *panch-kuli*. (7) Some castes like Marathas and Kunbis in the central zone practice bride-price too, though dowry custom also exists among them. (8) Though the family system in Maharashtra is patrilineal and patrilocal, yet unlike in the north, where a wife permanently stays with her husband after *gauna* and rarely goes to her father's house, in castes like Marathas, she moves to and from her father's house very frequently. Once she goes to her father's house, it is difficult to get her back to her husband's house. This shows the impact of the south on relations with kin. (9) Though the kinship terms are mostly northern yet some terms are borrowed from the Dravidians in the south; for example, use of the term *anna* and *nana* for brother along with the term *dada*. Similarly, use of term *akka*, *tai* and *mai* for sister. (10) The kinship system of the tribals in Rajasthan and Madhya Pradesh is somewhat different from that of the caste Hindus. The difference exists in terms of kinship terminology, marriage rules, inheritance system, and clan obligations.

Thus, it may be stated that though the kinship organisation in the northern and central zones is almost similar, yet it can be described as a region of transition from the north to the south. A state like Maharashtra is a region of cultural borrowings and cultural synthesis (Karve, 1953:174).

Southern Zone

The *southern zone* presents a complicated pattern of kinship system. Though patrilineal and patrilocal family is the dominant family type for the greater number of castes and communities (for example, Namboodris), there are important sections of population which are matrilineal and matrilocal (for example, Nayars); also there are quite a few castes whose systems possess features of both patrilineal and matrilineal organisations (for example, Todas). Similarly, there are some castes/tribes who practise only polygyny (for example, Asari, Nayars) and yet others, who practise both polygyny and polyandry (for example, Todas). Then there are polyandrous patrilineal groups (for example, Asari) and also polyandrous matrilineal groups (for example, Tiyan, Nayars) and polygynous patritineal groups (for example, Namboodris) but no polygynous matrilineal groups. Similarly, there are patrilineal joint families and also matrilineal joint families. All this shows varied patterns in kinship organisation in southern zone. Let us examine some of these organisations/ patterns.

In the matrilineal family, the kinship relationship of women to one another is that of a daughter, mother, sister, mother's mother, mother's sister, and sister's daughter. In the kinship relationship of women with men, males are related to women as brother, son, daughter's son, and sister's son. The kinship relationship of males to one another is that of brother, mother's brother and sister's son. All these kinship relations are based on blood. There are no relations by marriage. This is because husband visits the family occasionally. We, therefore, find: (i) absence of companionship between husband and wife and absence of closeness between father and children; and (ii) there is complete independence of women as regards their livelihood; they do not partake of the earnings of their husband. This is how some southern families differ from the northern families.

Matrilineal joint family, called *Tarwad*, is found amongst the Nairs of Malabar in Travancore and a few other groups. The important characteristics of *Tarwad* are: (1) The property of *Tarwad* is the property of all males and females belonging to it. (2) Unmarried sons belong to mother's *tarward* but married sons belong to their wife's *Tarwad*. (3) Manager of *Tarwad* property is oldest male member in the family, called *Karnavan* (his wife is called *Ammayi*). (4) *Karnavan* is an absolute ruler in the family. On his death, the next senior male member becomes *Karnavan*. He can invest money in his own name, can mortgage property, can give money on loan, can give land as gift, and is not accountable to any member in respect of income and expenditure. (5) When *Tarwad* becomes too large and unwieldy, it is divided into *Tavazhis*. A *Tavazhi* in relation to a woman is 'a group of persons consisting of a female, her children, and all her descendants in the female line'.

Tarwad before 1912 Act and after 1912 are two different things: (a) Earlier, *Tarwad* property was indivisible, but now it can be divided. (b) Earlier, *Karnavan* was an absolute ruler of *Tarwad*, but now his authority has become limited. (c) Earlier, members of *Tarwad* were not entitled to maintenance unless they lived in the family house, but now members have become entitled to maintenance outside the ancestral house. (d) Earlier, ancestor worship of *Karnavan* was common, but now it is no longer common. (e) Earlier, relations between husband and wife were formal, but now the relations have become informal and personal and more close and intimate. (f) Earlier, the self-acquired property of a member of a *Tarward* went to *Tarward* after his death, but now it goes to his widow and children, and in their absence to mother and mother's mother.

Thus, *Tarwad* of Nairs has now disintegrated after the enactments of 1912 Act (Travancore), 1920 Act (Cochin), 1933 Act (Madras), and 1958 Act (Kerala). Woman's property now goes to her sons and daughters and then to her father and husband. Kapadia (1947:348) has drawn attention to the fact that more than 90 per cent of *veedus* (houses) have only one *Tavazhi;* this shows the extent of atomisation of *Tarwads* in the last few decades.

Let us now analyse the clan organisation and marriage rules in the South. A caste is divided into five exogamous clans. The important characteristics of clan organisation are:

(1) Each clan (composed of a number of families) possesses a name of some animal or a plant or some other object.
(2) A person from one clan can seek a spouse from any other clan except his own. However, this choice is theoretical because of the rule of exchange of daughters.
(3) In marriage, there is not only the rule of clan exogamy but also of family exchange of daughters.
(4) Because of the marriage rule of exchange of daughters, many kinship

terms are common. For example, the term used for *nanad* (HuSi) is also used for *bhabhi* (BrWi); the term used for *sala* (WiBr) is also used for *bahnoi* (SiHu); the term used for *sasur* (HuFa) is also used for *bhabhi*'s father (BrWiFa).

(5) Marriage between maternal parallel cousins, that is, between children of two sisters, is not permissible.

(6) Sororate marriage (that is, marriage with wife's younger sister) is practised. Also, two sisters can marry two brothers in one family).

(7) There is a system of preferential mating in the south. In a large number of castes, the first preference is given to elder sister's daughter, second preference to father's sister's daughter, and third preference to mother's brother's daughter. However, today cross-cousin marriage and especially the uncle-niece marriage is beginning to be considered as outmoded and a thing to be ashamed of among those groups which have come in contact with the northern Indians or with western culture.

(8) The taboos prescribed for marriage are: a man cannot marry his younger sister's daughter; a widow cannot marry her husband's elder or younger brother (that is, levirate is a toboo); and a man cannot marry his mother's sister's daughter.

(9) Marriage is dependent on the chronological age differences rather than the principle of generational divisions as in the north. One example is that the marriage of grandfather and granddaughter is possible in south.

(10) Yet, another feature of marriage and kinship in the south is that marriage is not arranged with a view to widening a kin group but each marriage strengthens already existing bonds and makes doubly near those people who were already very near kin.

(11) A girl has to marry a person who belongs to the groups older than her, that is, *tam-mum*, and also to the group younger than her parents, that is, she can marry any of her older cross-cousins. A boy must marry in a *tan-pin* group and to one who is a child of a group of *tam-mum*.

(12) The dichotomy of status and sentiments expressed in such northern terms like *kanya* (unmarried girl), *bahu* (married girl), *pihar* (mother's house) and *sasural* (husband's house) are absent in south. This is because in south, a girl after marriage does not enter the house of strangers as in north. One's husband is one's mother's brother's son and so on. Marriage in the south, thus, does not symbolise separation from father's house for a girl. A girl moves freely in her father-in-law's house.

Comparison of Kinship System of North and South India

(1) In a southern family, there is no clear-cut distinction between the family of birth (that is, family of orientation) and family of marriage (that is, family of procreation) as found in the northern family. In the north, no member from Ego's family of orientation (that is, of father, mother, brother and sister) can also become a member of his family of marriage; but this is possible in the south).

(2) In the north, every kinship term clearly indicates whether the person referred to is a blood relation or an affinal kin but this is not so in the south.

(3) In the south, an Ego (person under reference/study) has some kin who are his blood relatives only and others who are his blood relatives and affinal kin at the same time.

(4) In the south, organisation of kin is arranged according to age categories in the two groups, that is, older than Ego (*tam-mum*) and younger than Ego (*tam-pin*) (*tam* is 'self', *nun* is 'before' and pin is 'after').

(5) In the south, kinship organisation is dependent on the chronological age differences while in the north, it is dependent on the principle of generational divisions.

(6) No special norms of behaviour are evolved for married girls in the south whereas in the north, many restrictions are imposed on them.

(7) Marriage does not symbolise woman's separation from her father's house in the south but in the north, a woman becomes a casual visitor to her parents' family.

(8) In the north, marriage is to widen the kinship group while in the south it is to strengthen already existing bonds.

Eastern Zone

In *Eastern India*, kinship organisation is different. There are more tribes than caste Hindus in eastern India (consisting of parts of Bengal, Bihar, Assam and Orissa). The more important tribes are: Khasi, Birhor, Hos, Mundas and Uraon. The kinship organisation here has no one pattern. People speaking Mundari languages have patrilineal patrilocal families. However, joint families are rare in this zone. Cross-cousin marriages are rarely practised though bride-price is common. Woman is addressed as *dual* (you two), referred to as *dual* (she, the two and speaks as *dual* (1, two). Kinship terminology is borrowed both from Sanskrit and Dravidian languages. Khasis and Garos have matrilineal joint family system (like Nairs in the south). After marriage, a man rarely lives with his parents and establishes a separate house.

It may be concluded that the kinship organisation in India is influenced by caste and language. In this age of sharp competition for status and livelihood, a man and his family must have kin as allies. Caste and linguistic groups may help an individual from time to time but his most staunch, trustworthy and loyal supporters could only be his nearest kin. It is, therefore, necessary that a person must not only strengthen his bonds with kin but should also try to enlarge his circle of kin. Cousin marriages, preferential mating, exchange rules and the marriage norms which circumvent the field of mate selection are now so changing that kinship relations through marriage are being extended and a person is able to get their help in seeking power and the status-lift that power can bring.

CHANGING STATUS OF WOMEN

Changing Status

The status of women—social, economic, political, and general—in India today is much higher than in ancient and medieval periods. Women today enjoy many more rights—social and legal—and have greater freedom and voice, and participate more freely in public affairs. But it is also true that they are still discriminated, harassed, humiliated, dominated and even exploited.

In ancient India (Vedic and Epic periods), women by and large were treated 'equal to men'. They were treated and honoured and considered to be 'embodiment of all divine virtues on earth'. They were considered not only as pivots of domestic life but also of entire social organisation. Of course, there are scholars who refer to several passages from religious scriptures to point out that they enjoyed 'low status'. These passages refer to women as 'unworthy of being trusted', as 'only means of satisfying the physical desires of men and secure them progeny', as 'root of all evils', as 'things of possession', and so on. But all these references were 'contextual' i.e., given in some context. In the social field, they never observed purdah, had freedom of mate selection, were not denied education, and enjoyed freedom in the household as well as outside it. In the economic field, they had limited rights of property succession as wives and mothers. However, they did not serve and earn wages because it was not necessary for them to do so. In the political field, their status depended upon the then-existing political system. Since there were no elected governments, they had no voting rights or the opportunity of holding political posts. They were not permitted entry in the *sabhas* (assemblies) because these were used for gambling, drinking and such other purposes too. Kautilya has referred (in *Arthashastra*) to women soldiers armed with bows and arrows. In the religious field, they enjoyed full rights and regularly participated in religious ceremonies.

In the Pauranic, Brahmanical, and medieval periods, the status of women was lowered by imposition of several restrictions. Pre-puberty marriages came to be practised, widow remarriage was prohibited, husband was given the status of god for a woman, education was totally denied to her, custom of *sati* was introduced, *purdah* system came into vogue, polygyny came to be tolerated and women were forbidden to offer sacrifices and prayers and read religious books. In the Muslim period, more restrictions were imposed on them due to the rigidity of the caste system and imposition of Brahmanical austerities on the entire society.

However, situation did undergo some change owing to Bhakti movement which permitted some social and religious freedom to women. In the British period, the status of women improved a little because of spread of education, Christian missionaries' interest in girls' education, abolition of social customs like *sati*, enacting of some legal measures (like Widow Remarriage Act, 1856, Special Marriage Act, 1872, Child Marriage Restraint Act, 1929) and a few social movements initiated by enlightened leaders like Raja Ram Mohan Roy, Justice Ranade, Ishwar Chandra Vidyasagar, Maharishi Karve, Swami Dayanand Saraswati, Annie Beasant, Mahatma Gandhi, etc., and the growth of women's organisations like Banga Mahila Samaj, Bharat Mahila Parishad (1904), Womens' Indian Association (1917), National Council of Women in India (1925), and All India Women's Conference (1927).

The change in the status of women got further impetus after independence because of the enactment of new laws (Special Marriage Act, 1954, Hindu Marriage Act, 1955, Hindus Succession Act 1956 and Anti Dowry Act 1961). The laws pertaining to women's employment are: Factory Act, 1948, Employees State Insurance Act, 1948 and Maternity Benefit Acts. Other factors which affected women's status were: effect of education, leadership provided by educated elite women, increasing opportunities of employment, change in the rigidity of the caste system, and so on. The need for linkage between programmes oriented to women and national policy towards weaker sections has come to be increasingly realised. Several commissions have been appointed by the central and the state governments to suggest measures for protecting women's rights in various fields. Two such commissions were appointed by the Central government in 1971 and 1992. The National Commission for Women (NCW), set up in January 1992, was directed to look into women-related issues, probe the status of women, examine various legislations and point out loopholes and gaps and assess the causes of discrimination and violence against women and suggest possible remedies.

How do we assess the present status of women? What are the indicators of higher status of women? Some observers associate changing status of women with factors like increase in divorce and female share of divorce petitions outnumbering that of men, increase in intercaste marriages, decrease in number of crimes against women, and so forth. But factors which really point out the high status of women are: involvement of women in paid-work and acquiring economic independence, increase in the number of higher and better-paid positions in different departments occupied by women, increase in the number of female enterpreneurs and managers, etc., increase in the number of women in legislative bodies, increase in the number of girls studying in universities, colleges and professional institutions, and so forth.

Women's status can be analysed at two levels: women in the rural areas and women in the urban areas. In the urban areas, their status may further be examined at three sub-levels: rich women, middle-class women, and poor women. In the rural areas, there is little difference in the status of women who are non-working and those who are working. But in the urban areas, middle-class women are at the crossroads. The rich and the poor have always had a lifestyle of their own but the middle-class women have different perceptions and values. This class distinction is like three parallel streams with well-defined boundaries which are sacrosanct.

Not many decades ago (say, up to the 1950s), the urban middle-class women had their role clearly defined. They knew what was expected of them and responded accordingly. It was a predictable lifestyle with known challenges and solutions and with a little effort, they could adopt to their roles with reasonable ease and grace. Today, a large number of women with more education and with work to do for earning livelihood, find adjustment difficult. While earlier the priority for most girls was marriage at the right time and leading a life based on roles of wife, mother and daughter-in-law, parents remained more concerned about the family background of the prospective son in-law before fixing the marriage of their daughters. The demands of dowry were high. Walking out of marriage i.e., separation or divorce did not have social or legal sanction. Women after marriage had, therefore, no option but to try and make their marriage work. The relations between husband and wife were based on mutual trust where he appreciated and helped her in her efforts of adjustment based on patience, humility and understanding and she trusted him. Family hierarchy was well defined. The father-in-law was the boss and his word was law. It had to be obeyed. A woman had respect for social norms.

But today, housekeeping and bringing up children are no longer a full-time job for a middle-class woman. She is desperately trying to ape the rich class. Today, the main criteria for selecting a girl as life-partner are her education and her employability. This is an age of earning couples. The girls have taken up the challenge. Professionally, they have practically left no field where boys could claim exclusivity. Working couples leave their kids behind in creches and pick them up in the evening. Marriages have become late by choice because couples tend to give due weight to their career graphs. 'Live-in' relationships are being tolerated and divorce is no longer a social stigma. The traditional institution of marriage seems to be slowly losing its sanctity. The old joint family system is also breaking. This has also affected the bringing up of children. A child in a nuclear family is a loner and tends to be self-centered. Old values are being replaced with modern values of equality, individualism and rationality. Though males have yet to be domesticated to share the daily chores but they have been made to realise that they do not hold dominating position in the family. Thus, modern middle-class women have greater privacy, more opportunities, freedom of action and equal rights. They have broken away from many shackles and unfairly restrictive practices. Women have indeed arrived and got their place in society.

Thus, if we were to describe the woman of contemporary times, we could give her following characteristics (see, *New Woman*, December 1998:16-19): (1) She has struck a perfect balance between tradition and modernity. (2) She seems to be determined to try and prove to man that she is equal to him. (3) While earlier, a woman has had an identity always through a male (either she was known as somebody's daughter or wife or mother) and her plight was like a satellite that kept orbiting around one planet—the man, today she has an opportunity to shine independently and reflect an identity of her own. (4) She is no longer confined to orthodox beliefs, capitalises on her own potentials and merits, and has carved a nitch for herself that was once forbidden by society. (5) She has begun to take responsibility and decisions for her life rather than just playing wife's and mother's roles. Her aptitudes and skills are slowly breaking down all chauvinistic barriers. (6) There has been metamorphosis in a woman. From the conservative woman of the 1940s and 1950s, she became the feminist reactionary of the 1960s and the 1970s, the super woman mother-wife-career woman of the 1980s, and the empowered woman of the 1990s, who demands and enjoys her rights and is not afraid to stand alone. She accepts that this is what I am, this is what I am not, and this is what I have to be. (7) She makes her own decisions, and is not a doormat. She doesn't take any kind of injustice meted out to her. She can think for herself, she makes a life for herself, and she instils important values in her children too. (8) The new woman is part of the old woman. (9) She is not afraid to be tough, aggressive and assertive. At the same time, she is not afraid to be feminine, sensual, gentle, caring, and considerate. She can be a career woman as well as a house-mother. She loves the people around her—family, friends, work-folk, etc., but she also loves herself as a person. (10) She is full of aspirations, expectations and desires. But if she fails, she does not act like a weak woman.

We can give the example of Fatima Bi as a new woman of today. An ordinary illiterate wife and a mother of three children coming from Kalva village in the Karnaol district of Andhra Pradesh, she contested and won the post of sarpanch. A chance attendance of a UNDP project meeting inspired her to work for women and the development of her village. She built a school, constructed roads, grappled with illiteracy, sold various products which fetched nearly a lakh of rupees to her panchayat. She got international recognition and travelled to New York to receive award from the United Nations' General Secretary.

Taking the general status of women in contemporary society, it may be averred that: (1) There is more representation of women in parliament, vidhan sabhas, panchayats and Nagar Nigams (municipal corporations). There are more women enterpreneurs, more bureaucrats, more professionals, more managers and more administrative officers. (2) Rural women are still traditional, deeply ritualistic, and fiercely conservative in their behaviour, but urban women are fighting the real battles of life. Of course, in the urban areas, there are women who belong to lower middle class and work as housewives, teachers, nurses, clerks, stenographers, telephone operators and also women of lower classes who work as labourers, domestic maids, sweepers and rag-pickers, etc. for whom life hasn't changed much. They are still subdued in our society. They are still not economically emancipated from men. In social, psychological and moral dimensions also, their situation is not identical to that of men. When they start their career as adults, they are evaluated by the society with a different perspective. Since only a few women escape from the traditional feminine world and since they do not get from society nor from family the assistance they need to become in concrete fact the equals of men, they fail to get recognition as successful role-performers.

Feminism and Rights of Women

The feminist movement focuses on rights and roles of women. Three ideological propositions on feminism are: liberal feminism, Marxist feminism, and radical feminism. The *liberal* feminism believes in gender equality and rejects subordination of one sex by the other or treating women as sex objects instead of human beings. However, it does not challenge the division of labour on sex basis. It holds that woman is best suited for family roles and man for outside roles. *Marxist* feminism explains women's subordination as the result of emergence of private property and ownership of means of production. Unlike men, women's work has a 'use' value but not 'exchange' value. Men, therefore, hold more power than women and oppression of women is due to the unpaid home work. *Radical* feminism though believes in sexual equality yet rejects traditional division of labour. It holds that gender roles are not only the result of biological factors but also the product of culture. It believes in free sex and collective childcare. Thus, when Marxist feminism gave a deterministic orientation to women's oppression, radical feminism gave a humanistic orientation.

In a society where about half of the total population of about 100 crore (1999) and about half of the females are illiterate (at the beginning of 1998), according to the latest data based on National Sample Survey organisation, (the female literacy figure having gone up from 39% in 1991 to more than 49% by the end of 1997) (*The Hindustan Times*, December 26, 1998), what rights have been assured to women through various social laws?

The Indian Constitution provides to women the right to equality, freedom, property, education, constitutional remedies, and protection from exploitation. The state has also been enacting special laws for safegaurding the interests of women. In the *social* field, these laws relate to various aspects of marriage (like, mate selection, age at marriage, plurality of partners, divorce, alimony, dowry, restitution of conjugal rights, and remarriage), adoption of children and abortion. The *economic* laws pertain to: right to property or inheritance, equal wages, working conditions, maternity benefits, and job security. The *political* rights provided to women are: female enfranchisement and eligibility for the legislature.

Are women conscious of these rights? Do they actually enjoy these rights? My empirical study conducted among 753 women of 18-50 years age group in eight villages of one district in Rajasthan about a decade ago revealed that though the level of awareness depends upon four factors—woman's individual background, her social environment, her subjective perception, and her economic base—yet by and large, the level of awareness is very low (Ahuja, 1992). Though we do not hold that the awareness of rights *ipso facto* raises women's status yet we do raise a question that if males deny due rights to women because either women tolerate it and do not revolt, or because no punishment is given to the violators of the social laws, or because the advantages of denying rights out-weigh the costs, how do we break this cycle of injustice on the part of males? How do we protect the interests of women? What programmes and policies will make males liberal and just? The remedies appear to be legal, social, and economic.

Women's movements and some measures taken by the government give us a feeling that some structural and cultural changes have been brought about as a result of which women have been provided equality of opportunities in education, employment, and political participation. Further, these changes have reduced their exploitation, and oriented them to develop organisations which take keen interest in their problems. But the fact of the matter is that these changes are only cosmetic and superficial, and in actual practice, due rights are denied to women and they continue to be victims of male domination.

The reasons for the denial of rights may be related to individual, economic and demographic factors. The *individual* factors refer to the personality characteristics of those males who possess low intellectual ability (IQ), who suffer from immaturity, depression and frustrations, who are alcoholics, or who have unrealistically high expectations from women and expect them to remain docile and passive. As regards the *economic* factors, non-earning women are more frequently denied rights than earning women; women in the low and middle-income families are more generally denied rights than the upper-income families; and among earning women, those engaged in non-professional or low status jobs enjoy fewer rights than those engaged in professions or high status jobs. Lastly, as regards the *demographic* factors, women in the upper castes are not so frequently denied rights as compared to women in the intermediate or the lower castes; the older males deny rights to women more generally than the younger males; and rights denied by women to women are more common than the rights denied by men to women.

We can also identify males who deny rights to women. These men are those who have depressions, inferiority complex and low esteem; lack resources, that is, have personality disorders; have possessive, suspicious and domineering nature; were victims of violence in their own childhood; and face stressful situations in their families. Further, women who are denied rights most may be identified as those who have feelings of helplessness., suffer from inferiority complex, have poor self-image, lack social maturity, and are economically dependent. We may also identify six types of denials of rights: money-oriented, pleasure-oriented, power-oriented, victim-precipitated, denier's pathology-resulted, and stressful family situations-resulted.

Three Models for Women's Liberation

Three models have been suggested for women as a minority group for raising their position in society (Rossi, quoted by Michael Haralambos, 1981:399). These are: pluralism model, assimilation model, and hybrid model. According to the *pluralism* model, women should maintain and develop many of their distinctive characteristics while removing those circumstances which result in their inequality. This model forsees a future in which men and women will retain their differences. These differences would be welcomed and respected by both men and women in the context of equality and status between them. This means that men and women would be different but equal. However, some scholars have not accepted this model as they think that the idea of 'separate and equal' in practice will result in 'separate and unequal' which will result in women's oppression and exploitation. The *assimilation* model argues that women should join the mainstream of society. This would mean unisex society in which women will perform roles like men, i.e., women will lose their distinguishing characteristic of performing specific roles. Scholars argue that 'assimilation' is impossible because men's lifestyle is based on housewife in the background, ministering to their needs. If women have to adopt male roles, a functional equivalent for the housewife will have to be found, which will be impossible. The *hybrid* model rejects both pluralism and assimilation. It rejects the idea that women adopt traditional male roles and holds that traditional roles of both men and women should be changed. The change in the women's roles will remove their social inequality. The above models focus on the roles of men and women, particularly on change in women's roles for women's liberation. We consider the idea of women performing roles similar to those of men as practical but contend that the ideas of abolishing housewife's role by women or payment for housework to women are not feasible. Family cannot be abolished and sexual division of labour cannot be eradicated in all areas of social life. We need revolution in the ideology of gender roles current in our culture. We want that men and women should be viewed as individuals and not as gender. This does not indicate that change will tolerate homosexual and lesbian relationships. We only want cultural freedom to women to develop their personality and behaviour along lines best suited to themselves, rather than being cramped and confined by the culturally defined label of 'a woman'.

Women's liberation movements have led to the emergence of a separate branch of discipline in sociology called 'Sociology of Women'. This branch of sociology is basically concerned with two issues: (i) the assessment of women as people who are just as important as men, and (ii) women's subjugated position in society as a social problem. Both female and male sociologists committed to feminist ideals have turned their attention to the study of women in India. Some of them have proposed some stimulating ideas, like need of women giving up traditional values and imbibing modern values, discarding their 'helplessness' attitude, taking for their career worker's role as seriously as housewife's role, and giving priority to different values and concerns, and so on. Unless woman gives as much importance to her "worker's role in the labour market" as to her "expressive female role", discrimination against women will not be easy to end.

Violence Against Women

Violence against women refers to 'force, whether overt or convert, used to wrest from a woman something that she does not want to give of her own free will and which causes her either physical injury or emotional trauma or both'. Violence against women may be categorised as: criminal violence (rape, abduction, murder, molestation), *domestic* violence (dowry death, wife battering, sexual abuse by kin, maltreatment of widows and elderly women, torture of daughter-in-law), and *social* violence (forcing wife/daughter-in-law to go for female foeticide, eve-teasing, forcing a young widow to commit sati, refusing to give share to a woman in property).

Who are the victims of violence? On the basis of an empirical study conducted on crimes against women in 1985 and 1993 (see, Ahuja, 1998) I identify four types of women who are mostly the victims of violence: (1) who feel helpless, depressed, have a poor self-image and suffer from self-devaluation, or those who are 'emotionally consumed' by the perpetrators of violence or who suffer from 'altruistic powerlessness', (2) who live in stressful family situations or in families which cannot be called 'normal', i.e., which are structurally incomplete, economically insecure, morally deviant, and functionally inadequate, (3) who lack social maturity or social interpersonal skills and suffer from behavioural problems, (4) whose husbands have either pathological personalities or are alcoholics.

Who are the perpetrators of violence? Generally women are abused and attacked by men they know. One study conducted by the University of Warwick in England pointed out that about 60 per cent of women are abused by their own family members and about 40 per cent by strangers. In India also, the cases of violence reported to police in different states indicate that home (family of procreation) is not always a safe place for a woman (which also does not mean that a woman is safer outside her home than in it). Males argue that today a woman does not adhere to the conventional parameters expected of a wife. Does this reflect that a woman refusing to conform and asking for some freedom and independence needs violence—whether physical, psychological or emotional—to ensure that conformity? Can we accept this type of 'patriarchal consensus' in this age?

Seven types of victimisers of women may be identified. They are those:

- who have depressions, inferiority complex and low self-esteem;
- who have personality disorders and are psychopaths;
- who lack resources, skills, and talents and have sociopathic personality;
- who have possessive, suspicious and dominant nature;
- who face stressful situations in family life;
- who are victims of violence in childhood; and
- who are frequent users of alcohol.

If we were to develop a typology of violence against women, we may give six types of violence:

- violence which is money-oriented;
- violence which seeks power over the weak;
- violence which aims at pleasure-seeking;
- violence which is the result of the perpetrator's pathology;
- violence which is the result of stressful family situations; and
- violence which is victim-precipitated.

What are the motivating factors in violence against women? This may be explained on the basis of three factors: (i) situations which bring about violent behaviour, (ii) characteristics of victims, and (iii) characteristics of victimisers. Four causes may be identified in violence against women: (a) victim's provocation, (b) intoxication, (c) hostility towards women, and (d) situational urge.

Sometimes, the victim *provokes* a person to use violence against her by her behaviour, which is often unconscious, i.e., she creates the situation of her own victimisation. The victim either generates or triggers off the violent behaviour of the offender. Her actions transform him into an assaulter/aggressor making him direct his criminal intentions against her. In my own survey of rape, wife-battering, abduction, ill-treatment of widows, and murders, the focus was on victims, yet some offenders/assaulters/aggressors were also interviewed. Surprisingly, only a few seemed to suffer from any feelings of shame or anxiety. A large number did not suffer from any emotional turmoil or from what psychologists call the problem of 'troubled masculinity'. The assaulters in wife battering cases instead accused their wives of back-biting, talking to person(s) they disliked, ill-treating their sisters or parents or brothers, neglecting their home, talking rudely to relatives, having illicit relations with some person, refusing to obey their in-laws, irritating them with their quarrelsome or nagging nature, or interfering too much in their affairs. Similarly, in criminal assault (rape) cases, there were assaulters who described the behaviour of the victim as a direct invitation to sexual relations or a sign that she would be available if he persisted. It is significant to determine whether the victim actually intended to invite such behaviour or not, or whether it was merely the victimiser's own interpretation/perception that led him to exploit her. This may be called an 'act of omission' (failing to react strongly) on the part of the victim, if not an 'act of commission'.

Thus, the 'passive' victim contributes to the commission of violent act to the same extent as the 'active' victim. In murder cases too, we came across a few cases where, according to the assaulters, the homicide situation started when in arguments and altercations, the victims precipitated such circumstances which motivated them to attack them. In abduction cases too, some abductors pointed out that their 'victims' had willingly agreed to run away with them and get married but when they were arrested on the complaint of parents, the 'victim' on being coerced by their parents accused them of abduction. On an average, 39 per cent cases were found to be *willing* abductions, 24 per cent were *forced* abductions, 17 per cent were *accessory* abductions (in which victims neither gave their consent of going with the 'accused person' nor did they oppose it but succumbed to the relationship of 'power' of the accused over her) and 20 per cent were *stress* abductions (in which the victim initially agreed to leave her home willingly but later on repented when the 'offender' raped her or sold her ornaments or left her in the hotel).

This analysis enables us to classify victims as active, passive, and accidental. At least two kinds of victims create a situation in which the 'offender' becomes 'victim' of the situation and/or compulsion and behaves with the 'victim' (female) in such a way that he comes to be labelled as the 'assaulter' or 'victimiser'.

Intoxication too leads to violence, i.e., some cases of violence occur when the aggressors are intoxicated and are in a wildly excited and belligerent state of mind, scarcely comprehending the likely fallout of their actions. For example, in a few cases of rape, the offenders assaulted the victims when they had taken so much alcohol that they were in a state of inebriation and emotional excitement. Their normal restraints had disappeared and their aggressive fantasies were intimately intermingled with sexual lust which then took the shape of irresponsible actions. Alcohol-related sex crimes illustrate a reckless disregard of time, space and circumstances.

A similar relationship between alcoholism and violence was demonstrated in a few cases of wife-battering and murder. While in my own study, I found that wife-battering was accompanied by the use of alcohol in 32 per cent of cases (Ahuja, 1987:130), Hilberman and Munson (1978:460-71) had found it in 93 per cent of cases, Wolfgang (1978) in 67 per cent cases, and Tinklenberg (1973) in 71 per cent cases.

It is not clear whether alcohol induces violent behaviour directly or whether it acts primarily as a disinhibitor of pre-existing aggressive tendencies. The latter hypothesis is perhaps supported by the notion (Blumer, 1973:73-87) that some perpetrators of violence drink to gather courage prior to using violence against a person. But not a single case was reported in my study in which the assaulter became intoxicated for the specific purpose of assaulting his victim. However, we cannot provide any proof that the ingest of alcohol alone elicits violent behaviour. There are many people who take alcohol yet they hardly ever become violent. The use of alcohol in violence against women may, therefore, be accepted as a 'cooperative' factor rather than the 'chief' factor.

Violence is also motivated by a person's *hostility towards women*. Some of the reported cases of violence against women are of a nature that no amount of rationalisation could convert the aggressors into doing anything other than hostile acts of a cruel kind. A few of them had deeply entrenched feelings of hate and hostility for women that their violent act could be said to be primarily directed towards the humiliation of the victim. If the mere situation had been the motivating factor, it is hard to see why a violent act should have been necessary, considering the fact that most of the 'offenders' are described as 'normal' persons. Perhaps a desire to gloat over the victim's humiliation was far stronger.

Situational urge sometimes provokes a person to use violence. In this category, those cases may be included where violence is used neither because of the victim's behaviour nor because of the offender's psycho-pathological personality but rather because of the chance factors which create such situations which lead to violence. For example, in a wife-battering case, it may be that conflict over money matters or on the ill-treatment of husband's parent(s) may provoke the husband to assault his wife; or in a rape case, a man accidentally meets a female acquaintance from his neighbouring village in a field and begins conversation, ultimately attempting to have his way with her; or the male employer taking advantage of his young female employee finding her alone in his office/factory in the late hours of the evening; or a young girl runs away from her father's house and accepts a lift in a truck and the truck driver takes advantage of the situation and criminally assaults her. In all these cases, the 'offenders' had not planned the violent acts but when they found the situation conducive or provocative, they used violence. Apart from these violent acts, these offenders had not been living a life of deviant behaviour.

Lastly, *personality traits* also compel a person to indulge in violence. Some identifying traits of the violence-prone personalities are: extremely suspicious, passionate, dominant, irrational, immoral, easily emotionally upset, jealous, possessive and unjust. Traits developed in early life affect the aggressive behaviour of a person in adulthood. The aggressor being abused as a child, and/or his exposure to violence during childhood, therefore, must be examined to delve into his violent behaviour. For example, in the case of some wife-batterers, their childhood, adolescence and early adulthood experiences reveal that they learnt to respond to all emotionally distressing cues with angry and violent behaviour. Unhappy family life amounting to exposure to physical brutality or severe emotional rejection has been found to be the rule in the case of most of the aggressors. Some adult aggressors have faced such situations in their family in their childhood/adolescence where they always found their parents screaming and getting at each other, and their father beating them (children) on the slightest pretext. Often, their fathers would come home drunk and would charge around the house shouting and breaking things. Growing up in violent home inevitably leads to violent behaviour in individuals, who become aggressive persons in their adult life. Alfaro (1978), Potts, Henberger and Holland (1979), and Fagon, Stewart and Ilansen (1981) have also pointed out a similar correlation in their empirical studies on violent men and their children. Thus, we can say that a good number of aggressors are victims of child abuse and familial violence, and exposure to violence as a child strongly influences the probability of one being generally violent as an adult.

Theoretical Explanation of Violent Behaviour

Violence against a person is necessarily 'violence by somebody' and 'violence against somebody'. As such, violence against women has to be understood as 'violence by an individual against an individual' in contrast to 'violence by a group against an individual' or 'violence by a group against a group'. In violence by an individual, its origin or form must be determined in the individual himself and the situation around him. In this approach, not only individual's innate behaviour but also his acquired behaviour has to be taken into account. Our Social Bond Approach takes into consideration both types of behaviour as well as the social structural conditions.

My contention is that causes of violence against women are found to be related mainly to five factors: (1) structure of the situation in which violence is committed, (2) situational facilities which enable the use of violence, (3) precipitating factor(s) that lead to violence, (4) strains experienced by the perpetrator of violence, i.e., his individual problems, and (5) victim's behaviour with the user of violence much before violence is used against her. A holistic approach to the combination of these factors alone will give us the correct causes of use of violence against women.

Specifically, three factors seem to play a major role in prompting a man to use violence against a woman: (1) perpetrator's history of abuse as a child (like unhappy upbringing, physical beating by parents, and emotional rejection); (2) stressful situations in the family; and (3) status frustrations. The first factor points out that the perpetrator's violent behaviour is mostly learnt from childhood and adolescence experiences of emotional distresses. This posits the thesis of the Generational Theory that growing up in violent home increases the likelihood of an individual becoming violent as an adult. The fact that a very large number of offenders (78%) in my study on 'Violence Against Women' (1998:224) were the victims of violence in childhood shows that my data supports this theory. The data also supports the Social Learning Theory according to which indulging in violent (deviant) behaviour as a method of conflict resolution or as a coping mechanism is a learnt behaviour. Women's tolerance of violence is explained in terms of Learned Helplessness Theory and Traditional Socialisation Theory. The latter theory refers to woman's imbibing traditional values and sex role ideology through socialisation process that man is superior to woman and that woman has no right to protest. The former theory maintains that some events occur in a woman's life with sufficient regularity because of which she acquires feelings of depression, helplessness and poor self-image and comes to believe that she cannot escape abuse.

Using the integrated model, I have proposed a new theoretical model (see Ahuja: 193-195) for understanding violence against women or women's exploitation. My model focuses on the linkage between a woman's (victim's) personality traits and social environment in which she lives and functions. It assumes that woman's exploitation (rape, molestation, beating, harassment for dowry, kidnapping for leading the life of a prostitute) is the result of interaction between a woman's personality (including imbibed feelings of helplessness, timidity, etc.) and her environment. Each woman lives in a social environment composed of different persons with varied perceptions and expectations. A woman's exploitation will depend on her subjective perception of her status and role and her will, ability, and efforts to challenge it (exploitation) with courage and also on man's structural conditions of living and his personaility traits. In other words, taking the victim first, a woman's exploitation is dependent on five things: (i) social background (which refers to her age, education and training), (ii) level of support (which depends on the support of her parents, in-laws, peers and others), (iii) expectations of others (including her husband, parents, in-laws, children, kin, working colleagues, peers, etc.), (iv) economic base (i.e., whether she belongs to low, middle or upper income group), and (v) self-image (whether she considers herself timid, bold, helpless, weak, strong, etc.).

Taking the victimiser, my thesis is that the structural conditions of a person (family crises, role frustrations, unfortunate incidents in life, inappropriate upbringing) create anxieties and stresses in him because of which he fails to adjust himself according to his social status (maladjustment), fails to attach himself strongly to other persons and groups (non-attachment), and also fails to commit himself to roles and obligations (non-commitment) to follow a particular course of action. The resultant frustrations determine his attitude towards others, including the weaker sex or women. Depending on his personality traits and the resistance potential of the victim, a man will use violence against a woman. My theory is, thus, based on a conjunctive approach which takes into account social factors like stressful situations endogenous and exogeneous to family, personality traits of perpetrators of violence and victims, and cultural milieu like normative pressures and ambiguities.

Following Mukesh Ahuja's empirical study (1996: 137-138), the following important sociological facts may be pointed out about the female victims of violence and exploitation:

(1) *Structure as source of problems*: The problems of females who are victims of violence arise from the functioning of social structures in which they live and work, and the stresses caused by family interac-

tions and support systems.

(2) *Tradition of barriers to assertion*: The involvement of victims in social roles and relationships after being victimised is dependent less on their own initiative and self-confidence and more on the will of heads of families (of procreation and orientation) and social pressures, i.e., traditional culture discourages female victims from taking up assertive social engagements outside the home.

(3) *Resource deprivation and suffering of self*: Resources like higher education and work with wages enhance victim's self-image and self-esteem which considerably change her relations with others, and also enable her to face the strain of transition to life and 'recovery' and adjust herself in family and society.

(4) *Attachment*: A large number of victims of violence overcome their feelings of being isolated and condemned by attaching themselves to some love object, social service, religious commitments, etc.

(5) *Structural suffocation*: Factors which prevent victims of violence from renewing, redeeming, restoring, reviving, and revitalising their lives lie more in social structures than in their personalities.

(6) *Negation of revolt*: A few young and independent victims have a secret desire of rebelling and adopting modern methods of adjustment but they fail to rebel for the fear that their husbands, in-laws and parents might sever ties with them. They are also scared of being shunned and ostracised by their kin and friends.

(7) *Self-esteem situation*: Victims with soppy emotions lead a suppressed life but victims with courage of conviction, character and consciousness chart their own course in their (working) life.

The Depersonalisation Trauma and Humanistic Approach

The important question is: What measures should be adopted to prevent women's abuse?

First, we take up the issue that is already receiving attention from many women's organisations as well as government and private/public institutions. This is to meet the needs of protection, support and advice to the victims. What some, if not all, women need most is shelter. Women living with authoritarian in-laws and alcoholic husbands would leave their homes, temporarily or permanently, if some shelter is available to them. Voluntary organisations providing such accommodation to women have to publicise their schemes. It has to be borne in mind that even the existing Homes for Women—single and/or married—are not able to meet the required demands. They are often overcrowded, lack financial support, and fail to meet safety regulations. Providing short-term accom modation to women, particularly married women who are in distress, or victims of violence like rape, abduction, attempt to murder, and ultimately helping them find a permanent place by the women's organisations will contribute to the alleviation of the distress suffered by many women. There is an urgent need to evaluate and compare the different types of short-term accommodation that could be provided to the victimised women, including widows.

Secondly, assistance in finding employment and childcare facilities and immediate financial support is also the need of the suffering women. Advisory centres for this purpose could be located centrally but away from the existing Women Homes so that they can be well advertised without affecting the safety of the residents in the Homes.

Thirdly, establishment of cheaper and less formal courts could also be a measure to help women who are victims of exploitation. It is not being suggested that these courts will handle only female cases. Their scope has to be wider. We have at present the system of Family Courts in some states in our country. But these courts are mainly concerned with preventing break-up of marriages. The scope of these courts could be extended to deal with all types of domestic and non-domestic problems of women. The establishment of courts with judges, magistrates and lawyers chosen for their knowledge and interest in female matters would be an improvement and it will increase the number of women entering the legal profession. To many women, the courts and the laws would seem less frightening and more sympathetic and approachable, if they are less dominated by men. Female judges and lawyers may not differ significantly from their male counterparts in their attitudes and beliefs and in their interpretation of laws, but female victims might be happier to appear before other females in the expectation that there would be more understanding of the problems faced by them.

Fourthly, strengthening and increasing voluntary organisations which could take up individual women's problems with their in-laws or the police or the courts or the concerned individuals is equally necessary. This is because the voice of an individual woman carries no weight. In fact, she is accused of being unduly outspoken if she demands her rights or holds radical views or expresses her views and releases her frustrations. But if number of women join together and raise their voice against women's suffering, they can assert their views and make an impact.

Fifthly, publicity has to be given to those organisations which provide free legal aid to women so that the needy women could approach them and seek their help.

Lastly, a change in parents' attitudes is also necessary in women's cases. Why do parents force their daughters—married or widowed—who are frequently beaten by their husbands or ill-treated by their in-laws to live in their husbands' house against their own wishes? When parents come to know of their daughter's harassment, why should they not permit daughters to live with them for a short time till they are able to fend for themselves? Why should they remain so concerned about the social stigma and sacrifice their daughters for the sake of their family?

Why should women submit to oppression? Why do they not realise that they have the potential to look after themselves and their children? Why do they not understand that their torture creates an emotional trauma for their children also? Women have to learn to be assertive and accept new roles for themselves. They have to develop an optimistic and hopeful approach to life.

The Reservation Policy

The demands for special concessions and privileges to women are matters of right and not of charity or philanthropy. When reservation for women in panchayats was announced, some people supported it but some others said that it would generate a spirit of denigration. At the panchayat level, one-third seats were reserved for women by making an amendment (73rd) in the Constitution. Later on, a separate clause was added reserving one-third of seats for the SC and ST women within the SC and ST quotas. This means that if there are 100 seats in a local body, of which 23 seats are reserved for the SCs/STs, then 7 or 8 of these (23) seats would be reserved for SC/ST women. The 33 seats reserved for women would be adjusted to include the 7 SC/ST women seats so that the general category of women reserved seats would come down from 33 to 26. Some states (like U.P) have reserved seats for OBC women at the panchayat level. This means that out of 33 seats for women, 7 will be for SCs/STs, 9 will be for OBC and 17 will be for general women.

Before the Bill on 33 per cent reservation of seats for women in the Lok Sabha was introduced in December 1998; it had been prevented from being introduced on three different occasions: once, during Prime Minister Deve Gowda's time (1996), again during Prime Minister Gujral's time (1997), and once again, during Prime Minister Atal Bihari Vajpayee's time (1998). At one stage (during I.K.Gujral's regime), the Bill was submitted to Gita Mukherjee Committee which in its report, submitted in November 1996, recommended one-third reservation for women.

The Women's Bill pending in the parliament (84th amendment to Constitution) at the time of Vajpayee's losing Vote of Confidence provided for: (a) 33 per cent seats for women in legislatures; (b) it did *not* suggest reservation on caste basis (i.e., it did not permit reservation for SC/ST/OBC women; and (c) it suggested rotational system.

The question to be discussed today, therefore, is: Is reservation policy or protective discrimination for women a logical and a useful strategy for ensuring justice and equal opportunity to women?

The argument in favour of the Bill is that Women's representation in politics will be a first step towards women empowerment. About two years ago, a leading national daily published an urban opinion poll which showed wide support for the women's reservation bill. But then a number of articles were published against the Bill in a 10:1 ratio. These articles had started appearing after one OBC member of the parliament (president of a political party) had given a 'parkatti' (the bobbed-hair brigade) statement in the Lok Sabha against the members of women's organisations in a contemptuous way.

Several arguments are given against the Women's Bill. The *first* argument is that the political parties are talking in favour of the Women's Bill only to appease and entice their voters. Their non-seriousness in women's empowerment is indicated by the fact that within their own organisations they have not introduced the quota system, except the Congress Party which introduced 33 per cent women's reservation in the party only in December 1998. Even the BJP (which succeeded in introducing the Bill in the Parliament in December 1998) had allotted only 23 out of 477 seats it had contested in 1995 general elections to women, out of which 13 women were elected. In the BJP Working Committee, out of 75 members there are only eight women. In its 650-member National Council, there are only 150 women. The Congress Party has only three women in its 20-member Working Committee. The Communist Party has 12 women in its 150-member National Council, and three members in its 21-member National Executive. In September 1999 general elections for the Lok Sabha, no political party has given tickets to women in more them 10 per cent cases. In some parties the percentage of women candidates is not even 2 to 3.

The *second* argument is that reservation cannot achieve much. In fact, it can be counter-productive. At best, reservation is 'palliative' and no decisive transformation can take place unless such a measure is accompanied by structural changes in the nation's productive relations.

The *third* argument is that our country is already divided in various groups. Women's reservation will further divide the population artificially. Reservation for the backward castes and tribes were accepted under social conditions for a period of ten years only, and since then they have been continued for vested interest of catching political votes.

The *fourth* argument is that it will affect the efficiency and working of the parliament, as even now all women members in parliament are not active. There are cases of women MPs who have never spoken in their term of five years or spoken only once or twice in five years. If a large number of such women enter parliament, what will be the 'nature' and quality of debates? Even in panchayats,a large number of cases of women sarpanchas have been reported where decisions are taken by their husbands and other male members of their families. What can thus be expected of women in parliament?

The *fifth* argument is that just as because of the reservation policy, the SC, ST and OBC officers on higher administrative posts are working on the basis of caste and creed, women in parliament too will take interest in women's problems only. We want legislators who actively participate in national and international issues which requires vast knowledge and high education.

The *sixth* argument is that our experience in the last five decades has shown that the reservation policy has not delivered the desired results. The candidates selected against reserved seats have not been able to adequately articulate the grievances and needs of the people of their constituencies.

The *last* argument is that reservations will generate conflicts and tensions.

The main demand of some leaders and political parties opposing the Women's Bill is to include a built-in quota for the OBCs and minorities within the women's quota, i.e., they want caste-based reservation along with gender-based reservation. Surprisingly, these leaders and political parties have never demanded OBC reservation for men in the Lok Sabha, knowing well that if they did, the number of OBC men in the Lok Sabha will sharply *decline*, which will lead to their disempowerment.

Thus, what the members who want an amendment to the women's Bill favour in not only gender discrimination but also caste discrimination. The demand for representation for Muslims will further contribute to discrimination on religious basis. Will all these discriminations (gender, caste and religion) protect the secular fabric of the country?

Categorising women on the basis of caste and religion will be a step towards their further segregation in society because Muslim and OBC women representatives will have nothing to do with the general problems and issues concerning women. They will be 'sectoral' leaders than leaders of women in India.

Major political parties are taking vague positions on the issue of 'quota within quota' because they are only concentrating on electoral benefits. They appear to be least bothered about in the casteisation of political contests becoming institutionalised. What they want is an opportunity to send their wives, daughters and sisters to parliament. The present and past experiences cannot be forgotten. Two former chief ministers of two states got their own wives nominated as candidates for elections and one of them even became the Chief Minister in place of her husband. One Congress MP in one state had to quit his Lok Sabha seat and his wife was nominated to contest elections from the same constituency. The famous family consisting of mother, son and daughter are occupying seats in the Lok Sabha since many years. In November 1998 Assembly elections in three states and again in September 1999 general elections for the parliament, many MPs manipulated to get their wives and other female family members nominated for contesting elections. The opponents of the so-called concept of/'dynasty politics' are themselves practising 'family managed' politics.

The institution of democracy was expected to serve as instrument for building a new India. But has it produced the intended results? For its failure, it is not the institution itself which is to be blamed, it is the way it has worked, or the way its working has been distorted by those in power. It is because of the vested interests of the middle classes and upper castes that our country has a dualistic pattern of growth in which those with access to the holders of power flourish and the population at the lower level (socially and economically) is denied all the tangible gains from the development process. Will the reservation of seats for women and women's increasing entry in parliament remove the dissatisfaction of these people and give a new hope to poor, uneducated and the backward communities of our country?

The disadvantaged people do need protection and opportunity to rise but opportunities cannot be extended *en masse* and for all time to come. A watchdog body should keep an eye on the progress of the introduced scheme and as soon as it is found that certain disadvantaged group no longer needs the crutches of reservations, the scheme should be withdrawn.

The Women's Bill has opened up the debate about the future direction of Indian politics and society. Should male politicians and female activists look at the issue of seats in the legislatures from purely limited political point of view? It appears that the goal of entering the corridors of political power is becoming pre-eminent and the larger issues of social philosophy regarding emancipation of women are being abandoned by everyone. It will not be empowerment of women *per se* if they are segregated first on the basis of gender and then on the basis of religion and caste. One suggestion is that what we should be aiming at is not the reservation of 33 per cent of seats for women but ensuring their participation in the political system.

Whatever may be the theoretical arguments against the reservation policy, in practice this policy will continue to be supported by all political parties because of the electoral advantage the political parties derive from this issue. As such, the people, instead of raising the issue of reservation, should raise the issue of vested interests of the political parties and political leaders versus the logical interests of the common people in society. Secondly, there should be no compromise on quality and efficiency. The eligibility conditions should be such that women may think of political participation not for gaining status but for serving the community at large.

Further Readings

Abbi, B.L., "Urban Family in India", *Contributions to Indian Sociology*, No. 3, 1969.

Ahuja, Mukesh, *Widows: Role Adjustment and Violence*, Vishwa Prakashan, New Delhi, 1996.

Ahuja, Ram, *Indian Social System*, Rawat Publications, Jaipur, 1993.

—, *Social Problems in India*, Rawat Publications, Jaipur, 1997 edition.

—, *Rights of Women: A Feminist Perspective*, Rawat Publications, Jaipur, 1992.

—, Sociological Criminology, 1966.

—, *Crimes Against Women*, 1987.

—, *Violence Against Women*, Rawat Publications, Jaipur, 1998.

Cormack, Margaret, *She Who Rides a Peacock*, 1969.

Desai, Neera, *Women in Modern India*, Vora and Co., Bombay, 1957.

Desai, I.P., *Some Aspects of Family in Mahuva*, Asia Publishing House, Bombay, 1964.

Desai, Neera and Vibhuti Patel, *Indian Women*: Change and Challenge in the International Decade, 1975-85, Popular Prakashan, Bombay, 1985.

Gore, M.S., *Urbanisation and Family Change*, Popular Prakashan, Bombay, 1968.

Haralambos, Michael, Sociology: Themes and Perspectives, 1981.

Kapadia, K.M, *Marriage and Family in India*, Oxford University Press, Bombay, 1966.

Karve, Irawati, *Kinship Organisation in India*, Deccan College Monograph, Pune, 1953.

Madan, T.N., "The Hindu Joint Family", *Man*, 62(145), 1962.

Mandlebaum, David G, *Society in India*, (2 Vols), University of California Press, Berkley, 1970.

Murty, K. Sachchidananda (ed), *The Divine Peacock: Understanding Contemporary India*, Wiley Eastern Ltd (New Age International Publishers), New Delhi, 1995.

Narain, D. (ed.), *Explorations in the Family and other Essays*, Thacker and Co., Bombay, 1975.

Ross, Aileen D., *The Hindu Family in its Urban Setting*, Oxford University Press, Toronto, 1961.

Sachchidananda, "Rural Family in West Bihar", *Journal of Social and Economic Studies*, Patna, September, 1977.

Shaukat Ali, Zeenat, *The Empowerment of Women in Islam with Special Reference to Marriage and Divorce*, 1995.

Singer, Milton (eds.), *Structure and Change in Indian Society*, Aldine Publishing Co., Chicago, 1968.

Singh, Yogendra, *Modernisation of Indian Tradition*, Thomson Press, New Delhi, 1973.

5 Economic System

INDIAN ECONOMY: POVERTY AND INFLATION

The issues of poverty and inflation are of the first rank importance in Indian economy. That 320 million persons or 35.97 per cent of the total population in 1993-94 (37.27% in the rural areas and 32.36% in the urban areas) were living below the poverty line (*Manpower Profile, India*, 1998:343), that today about 5 per cent people are unemployed, that 24 paise of every rupee that the government earns goes into paying interest on debt, and that 10.7 per cent of our GDP is being spent by the central and the state governments on non-merit subsidies on items like water supply, higher education, irrigation, electricity, etc., all these facts present a shocking image of poverty, income and wealth in our country. Much debate and discussion have taken place on issues like how much of the nation's wealth and income should be spent on poverty and unemployment alleviation programmes? How can economic development be accelerated? How can economic inequalities be removed? How much should be spent on public services and welfare schemes? What is the role of welfare schemes? Should it be minimal safety-net for the poor or a comprehensive system of security for all? Are the social inequalities in our country the result of economic inequalities or differential income distribution? We will analyse, in this chapter, a few of these issues.

Poverty and *inequality* are not the same. A person with an income of Rs. 15,000 per annum and having a wife and a child to support is not as poor as a person with Rs. 25,000 per year and having a large family of 5-6 children to support. *Income* and *wealth* are also two distinct terms. 'Income' refers to the *flow* of economic resources while 'wealth' is the total *stock* of economic resources. While salary, wages, rent, interest, pension, income from self-employment and dividends from company shares, etc., are regarded as 'income', immovable property, gold, share bonds, etc., constitute 'wealth'. For understanding inequality and poverty, it is necessary to consider the concepts of poverty, income, wealth and inequality.

Concept of Poverty

What is poverty? Poverty may be defined either as *absolute* or *relative*. 'Absolute' poverty is "insufficiency in basic necessities of existence". In practical terms, this usually means "being without adequate food, clothing or shelter". The notion of 'poverty line' describes poverty in subsistence terms, i.e., the 'minimal' necessary for the maintenance of physical health. Berstein Henry (1992) has identified four dimensions of poverty: (1) lack of livelihood strategies, (2) inaccessibility to resources (money, land, credit), (3) feeling of insecurity and frustrations, and (4) inability to maintain and develop social relations with others as a consequence of lack of resources.

Three precepts are often used to define poverty: (i) the amount of money required by a person to subsist, (ii) the life below a 'minimum subsistence level' and 'living standard' prevalent at a given time in a given place, and (iii) the comparative state of well-being of a few and the deprivation and destitution of the majority in society. The last approach explains poverty in terms of relativity and inequality. Whereas the first two definitions refer to the economic concept of absolute poverty, the third one views it as a social concept, that is, in terms of the share of the total national income received by those at the bottom. We will explain each of the three views separately.

According to the *first* view, in terms of a minimum income required for subsistence, poverty has been defined as "an inability to gratify the physiological needs, that is, need for survival, safety and security". These physiological needs are different from the social needs (ego-satisfaction and self-esteem), the need for autonomy, the need for independence, and the need for self-actualisation. The minimum requirements for fulfilling the physiological needs are food and nutrition, shelter, and preventive and protective health care. This requires 'minimum' income (varying from society to society) to buy necessities and avail oneself of basic facilities.

Here, 'poverty' is perceived in terms of 'poverty line' which is determined by the prevailing standards of what is needed for health, efficiency, nurturing of children, social participation, and maintenance of self-respect (Becker, 1966:436). In practice, however, poverty line is drawn on the basis of the barest minimum desirable nutritional standard of calories intake. In India, poverty line is drawn on the basis of per capita (adult) daily intake of 2,400 calories for the rural and 2,100 calories for the urban areas. On the basis of this, the monthly per capita consumption expenditure can be worked out.

The minimum consumption expenditure in our country, as recommended in 1962 by the Perspective Planning Division of the Planning Commission and calculated on the basis of 1961 prices, was Rs. 100 for a household of five persons in the rural areas and Rs. 125 in the urban areas. This came to Rs. 20 per capita per month in the rural areas and Rs. 25 in the urban areas. In 1978-79, this was worked out as Rs. 76 for the rural and Rs. 88 for the urban areas, while in 1984-85, the revised poverty line was drawn at a per capita monthly expenditure of Rs. 107 for the rural and Rs. 122 for the urban areas (*India*, 1990:404). At 1993-94 price level, a person in a rural area required an income of Rs. 229 and in an urban area Rs. 264 per month to fulfil his food and other basic requirements (*Outlook*, February 14, 1996:26). Here, the focus is on a 'minimum subsistence' level which is different from a 'minimum adequacy' level and a 'minimum comfort' level. In 1963, in the United States, a family of four members with an annual income of $2,500 was described as living below 'minimum subsistence level', with an income of $3,500 as living below 'minimum adequacy level', and with an income of $5,500 as living below 'minimum comfort level' (Ornati, 1964:440). On this basis (in 1963), 10 per cent of the families in the United States were below the minimum subsistence level, 25 per cent were below the minimum adequacy level, and 38 per cent were below the minimum comfort level. The poverty level in the United States for a family of four in 1982 was $8,450 a year (Malgavkar, 1983:3), during 1986 it was $10,989 a year, and during 1990 it was $14,200 a year. The per capita income in the United States in 1998 was $29,080 (*India Today*, May 10, 1999:46). An average American earns eight times the income of an average Indian. In India, the number of poor people (that is, people below minimum subsistence level) in 1993-94 was estimated at 18.1 per cent of the total population by the Planning Commission. After accepting Lakdawala Committee's report in March 1997, the Planning Commission's estimate of the percentage of BPL people at present is 35.97 or 320 million, with a per capita monthly income as low as Rs. 264 (*The Hindustan Times*, April 16, 1997). It should, however, be noted that the 'poor' are not a homogeneous group. They can be classified into four sub-groups: (i) the destitutes (who spent less than Rs. 137 a month at 1993-94 prices), (ii) extremely poor (who spent less than Rs. 161 a month), (iii) very poor (who spent less than Rs. 201 a month), and (iv) the poor (who spent less than Rs. 246 a month).

The *second* view on poverty maintains that poverty has three main aspects of want of material goods or materialistic possessions: (i) those necessary to avoid physical suffering and needed to fulfil the requirements of hunger and shelter, that is, those needed to survive; (ii) those essential to meet human needs of health, that is, to get nutrition and to avoid disease; and (iii) those needed to maintain a minimum subsistence level. In simple terms, this refers to a minimum amount of food intake, adequate housing, clothing, and health care. At the 1993-94 price level, this refers to the ability to spend Rs. 259 a month (per person) in the rural areas and Rs. 294 a month in the urban areas.

Gross and Miller (1946:83) attempted to explain poverty in terms of three factors: income (covert and manifest), assets or material possessions, and availability of services (educational, medical, recreational). But others have considered the concept of poverty with this perspective elusive. For example, in the United States, out of those families living 'below the poverty level' in 1960, 57.6 per cent had a telephone, 79.2 per cent owned a TV set and 72.6 per cent possessed a washing machine (Becker, 1966:435). The assets or the material possessions, therefore, cannot be the basis of specifying poverty. Likewise, poverty cannot be related to the 'income' factor. If there is an increase in the price level, people may not be able to provide the necessities of life for their family members. Obviously then, poverty has to be related to time and place.

The *third* view defines poverty as a condition of falling below the minimum standards of subsistence appropriate to each society, or "the absence of enough money to secure life's necessities", or "a condition of acute physical want—starvation, malnutrition, disease, and want of clothing, shelter and medical care". The latter is measured by comparing the condition of those at the bottom of the society with the other segments of the population. It is, thus, a matter of subjective definition rather than of objective conditions. Poverty is determined by the standards that exist within a society. Miller and Roby (1970:34-37) have said that in this approach, poverty is sharply regarded as 'inequality'. From a sociological point of view, this definition is more important in terms of the impact which inequality of income has on the life situation and life chances of the poor. Absolute poverty can be reduced/eliminated by putting money into the hands of the poor but 'inequality' cannot be contained by moving people above a certain relative line. As long as there are people at the bottom of the income scale, they are in some way poor. Such a condition will continue to exist as long as we have social stratification.

Harrington (1958:83) defined poverty with reference to 'deprivation'. According to him, poverty is the deprivation of those minimal levels of food, health, housing, education and recreation which are compatible with the contemporary technology, beliefs and values of a particular society. Rein (1968:116) identifies three elements in poverty: subsistence, inequality and externality. *Subsistence* emphasises provision of sufficient resources to maintain health and working capacity in the sense of survival, and capacity to maintain physical efficiency. *Inequality* compares the lot of individuals at the bottom layer of stratified income levels with that of the more privileged people in the same society. Their deprivation is relative. *Externality* focuses on the social consequences of poverty for the rest of society, apart from the impact on the poor themselves. Sociologically speaking, the poor are caught up in vicious circles. Being poor means living in poor neighbourhood, unable to send children to schools, low-paying jobs or no jobs at all, and doomed to remain poor for ever. Also, being poor means eating poor food, having poor health, accepting low-paid work, and remaining poor for ever. Thus, each circle begins and ends with being poor. No wonder, sociologists like Thomas Gladwin (1967:76-77) give more importance to 'inequality' or the social concept of poverty.

Manifestation of Measurement of Poverty

The important measurements of poverty are: malnutrition (below a limit of 2,100 to 2,400 calories per day), low consumption expenditure (below Rs. 259 per person per month at 1993-94 price level), low income (below Rs. 520 per person per month at 1993-94 price level), chronic illness or poor health, illiteracy, unemployment and/or underemployment, and unsanitary housing conditions. Broadly, the poverty of a given society is expressed in terms of poor resources, low national income, low per capita income, high disparity in income distribution, weak defence, and the like.

Some scholars have referred to poverty-linked characteristics of households to point out that individuals from these households run a greater risk of being poor. The chances increase as the households exhibit more of these characteristics. The more important among these characteristics are: absence of a full-time wage-earner in the household, households where men are above 60 years age, households headed by a female, households with more than six children of less than 18 years of age, households whose heads are living on daily wages, households whose members have less than primary education, households with members without work experience, and households having members only with part-time employment.

Incidence and Magnitude of Poverty in India

India represents a dichotomy in development. It ranks 19th in world industrial production and twelfth in total gross national production (GNP); yet it has a large population that is extremely poor. The United Nations Human Development Index based on three indicators, viz., life expectancy, educational attainment and real GDP in purchasing power parity terms, ranks India 134th among 174 countries. In terms of real GDP per capita, it is ranked 141st, while Pakistan is 100th and China is 123rd (*Outlook*, February 14, 1996). Since independence, the country has registered a significant overall growth rate, and there has been a progressive increase in the per capita income—from Rs. 1,630 in 1980-81 to Rs. 3,269 in 1987-88, Rs. 4,974 in 1990-91, Rs. 6,234 in 1993-94 and Rs. 15,550 (or $370) in 1998-99. The per capita income at constant prices (1980-81) was estimated to be Rs. 2,226 in 1992-93, Rs. 2,282 in 1993-94 and Rs. 2,362 in 1994-95 (*The Hindustan Times*, August 22, 1995). If we calculate India's per capita income (of $ 370) in 1998-99, in terms of purchasing power parity (PPP) of the nation's currency, (i.e., with PPP correction) it will be $1,660 per annum. Even then, the US per capita income would be 18 times more than that of India (*India Today*, May 10, 1998:46).

The estimates of the Planning Commission held (before accepting Lakdawala Committee recommendations in March 1997) that the percentage of the population living below the poverty line decreased from 51.5 per cent in 1972-73 to 37.4 per cent in 1983-84, 29.9 per cent in 1987-88, and 18.1 per cent in 1993-94 (*The Hindustan Times*, August 22, 1995 and April 5, 1997). However, according to the Expert Group (National Institute of Public Finance and Policy) estimates, it was much higher. While in 1977-78, it was 51.8 per cent, in 1983-84 it was 44.8 per cent, in 1987-88 it was 39.3 per cent, and in 1993-94 it was 33.4 per cent (*Outlook*, February 14, 1996:26).

According to the UNDP, the number of poor persons in India in 1990 was 410 million (*The Hindustan Times*, August 4, 1993). Economists and the World Bank, however, claim the number of people below the poverty line to be near 400 million. This means that the poor in India total the population of Pakistan and Bangladesh put together.

The Planning Commission decided in March 1997 to adopt the Lakdawala methodology in measuring the present incidence of poverty in the country. Lakdawala Committee was appointed in September 1989, which submitted its report in July 1993. No action was taken on the report for more than three years till all of a sudden the Planning Commission invoked the authority of this report in 1996. At one stroke, the Lakdawala method revised upwards the estimate of the people below the poverty line to 35.97 per cent as against the 1993-94 estimate of 18.1 per cent. This decision had wide ramifications not only for the formulation of the development strategy for the Ninth Five Year Plan but also for all time to come.

Of about 320 million poor persons in India (according to new estimates of the Planning Commission), the absolute destitutes—which are the bottom 10 per cent of the society—are around 50-60 million. These are old, sick and disabled people, to whom it is not employment and the opportunity of earning of income that has to be provided, but some kind of social security, involving regular monthly payment. This leaves some 260 million (according to official figures) to 350 million (according to economists) people living at various levels of poverty for whom employment opportunities have to be provided. In the rural areas, these poor include landless agricultural labourers, casual non-agricultural labourers, marginal farmers, and displaced village artisans, such as blacksmiths, carpenters and leather-workers; while in the urban areas, these poor people comprise non-unionised industrial workers, vegetable, fruit and flower vendors, servants in tea-shops, domestic servants and daily wage earners.

As a result of economic growth over the past few years, the number of people in the upper, upper-middle and middle-middle income segments have been increasing according to various surveys. The number of households earning less than Rs. 30,000 a year at today's (1997-98) prices is about 50 per cent, with income above Rs. 3 lakh a year (i.e., upper class) is 0.7 per cent, and with income between Rs. 30,000 and Rs. 3 lakh (i.e., middle class) is 40 per cent of the total households. In the next ten years, the relative size of these income groups is expected to undergo a dramatic change. The number of households earning less than Rs. 30,000 per annum will constitute only about 14 per cent, the rich with income over Rs. 3 lakh per household will constitute about 3.5 per cent, while the middle-class people with income between Rs. 30,000 and Rs. 3 lakh will be more than 80 per cent of the total households (*The Hindustan Times*, August 24, 1998). Unless inequality in income distribution is reduced, the chances of reducing the number of people below the poverty line will be low.

While prices in India have soared, incomes have shrunk; and inflation has increased. In the first week of August 1999, inflation was reported to be 1.7 per cent. While in 1996-97, it was about 7 per cent, it was 2.7 per cent in Britain, 1.8 per cent in Canada, 0.8 per cent in Australia, 2 per cent in Spain, and 0.2 per cent in Sweden (*Economic and Political Weekly*, January 16-22/23-29, 1999:116). The important factors which contribute to inflation are: (1) Excessive increase in demand, with supply remaining the same, falling or stagnating. This is known as 'demand-pull' inflation. (2) Independent increase in costs which may be the result of increase in the wages of labourers under union pressures or due to the desire of industrialists to earn higher profits. This increase in higher prices or inflation is known as 'cost-push' inflation. (3) Inflation is also caused, particularly in a developing country like India, by developmental efforts and structural rigidities. The infrastructural, institutional or other bottlenecks restrict production activities and cause scarcities. This causes price increase or inflation. (4) Deficit financing causes excessive money supply with no corresponding increase in the supply of goods. This creates inflationary situation. (5) Sometimes, the developing countries have to import capital goods to generate growth. These goods are paid for in expensive foreign exchange. The project costs are higher and inflation gets built in. (6) People prefer investments in property, gold and other such non-productive uses. This fritters away a sizeable part of investable funds. It acts as a check on growth and prepares the ground for inflationary forces to operate. India has faced and continues to face all these problems which have increased inflation in the country.

MARKET ECONOMY AND LIBERALISATION POLICY: ITS SOCIAL CONSEQUENCES

Policy of Mixed Economy

After independence, India decided to follow the policy of mixed economy, that is, partially state control and partially free competition among private enterprises. But, the experience of forty years (from 1950 to 1990) prompted the central government in early 1990s to adopt structural change in their economic dealings, change from socialism to privatisation and make nationalisation limited. Consequently, state domination started diminishing and liberalisation became central point. The outbreak of hostilities in the West in 1990 and the consequent spiralling of oil prices and very low foreign exchange reserves created a serious economic crisis in India. The Janata government in power had even to mortgage gold to the Bank of England for solving the crisis temporarily. This made it necessary to liberalise licensing policy. Liberlisation was also necessary under pressures of the conditions attached to the International Monetary Fund (IMF) loan taken in the year 1990-91. It gave greater opportunity to private capital market to play a vital role in the country's economy.

What are the main economic reforms introduced in our country after 1990, that is, after accepting liberalisation policy. Some of these are (see, Shome and Mukhopadhyay, 1998: 25-31):

1. Quantitative import controls through licensing have been slashed, and almost all capital goods and raw materials have been made free to be imported.
2. The tax structure has been transformed which includes excise tax rebate for raw materials against excise on final products, reducing excise rates, custom duties, as well as income tax rates, and abolishing wealth tax on all productive assets.
3. The financial sector has been restructured by measures like introducing new norms related to income recognition and making provisions of 15 per cent advances in non-performing assets.
4. The industrial policy has been reformed which includes dismantling of many irrational regulations in the industrial sector.
5. The foreign exchange policy has been revised which has opened up foreign investment in many areas.

Liberalisation Policy: Its Achievements

The opening of economy to market as well as global forces reflects a decisive break with the past. What have we achieved in the last eight or nine years after introducing the liberalisation policy? We can analyse it at following five levels (see, Shome and Mukhopadhyay, op.cit., 1917-29):

Rate of Growth

The rate of growth of GDP has increased. In 1991-92, it had fallen to below 1 per cent whereas in the 1970s, it was about 3 per cent and in the 1980s, it was 4-5 per cent. In 1994-95, it rose to over 7 per cent, in 1995-96 and 1996-97 to 7.8 per cent but came down to 5 per cent in 1997-98 and again increased to 5.8 per cent in 1998-99 (*India Today*, March 1999: 43 and *Hindustan Times*, February 25, 1999).

Inflation

Inflation in the general price level has been controlled. While in the 1960s, it was 11 per cent, it increased to 18.5 per cent between 1972 and 1975, 15.5 per cent between 1979 and 1982, 11.36 per cent between 1990 and 1993, and then started decreasing to 10.9 per cent in 1994-95, 8.8 per cent in September 1998, 3.9 per cent in April 1999 and only 1.7 per cent in the first week of August 1999. Inflation in the early 1990s and its quick control in 1995-96 could be explained to some extent by the increase in the international petroleum prices and later easing out the supply constraint. But inflation after that could not be checked for two to three years because there were no strong structural improvements.

Revenue and Expenditure

After rationalising the structure of various taxes, neither the revenue has increased nor the expenditure and fiscal deficits have been reduced. In fact, there was a decline in the tax revenue to GDP ratio from about 11 per cent in 1990-91 (prior to reforms) to about 10 per cent in 1995-96, and around that range in 1998-99. This revenue loss has not been made up.

Industrial Performance

There has been no increase in industrial production due to the impact of liberalisation of economic forces of the 1990s. The fact is that the upward shift in the growth of production is lacking. A shadow of industrial recession emerged in 1996-97. The industrial production which had increased in 1994-95 to 13 per cent fell down to 6.7 per cent in 1996-97 (*India Today*, March 1, 1999:42) and 3.5 per cent in 1998-99 (*The Hindustan Times* February, 25, 1999).

Exports and Foreign Capital Inflows

There has been decline in exports from 1995-96 onwards. While the export growth rate had increased to 18 to 21 per cent between 1993-94 and 1995-96, it declined to 12.1 per cent in 1996-97 and 4.4 per cent in 1997-98 (*The Hindustan Times*, February 25, 1997; *India Today*, March 1, 1991:42). Of course, the foreign exchange reserves have increased greatly from 1990 to 1997-98, indicating investment flows.

It was expected that the liberlisation policy would introduce openness to external finance and trade, expose the country to international competition and bring such benefits as technology transfer, management know-how, export marketing access and a diversified investor base. Economic experts are of the opinion that these hopes are being fulfilled only to a limited degree. It is true that the external financing choices open to the country have increased but for a country with market access, the renewal of private flows has to be sustainable and volatile. India has yet to learn to meet the new challenges presented by a new pattern of external finance and growing integration with global capital market. It may be said that today, on the one hand, the revenue collections are low, fiscal deficit is high, the inflation rate has risen, and the capital outflow from other countries has not increased much; on the other hand, many schemes like the streamlining of incentives to broaden the revenue base, rationalisation of the subsidy structure to reduce tax expenditure, improving marginal cost pricing of public utilities such as electricity and water, removal of infrastructural bottlenecks, privatisation of loss-making public enterprises, and insurance sector reform, have unfortunately got bogged down. All this causes genuine concern to the more serious economists and to sociologists regarding some important aspects of the Indian economy, such as high poverty, unemployment, subsidy policies, indebtedness, impact of factional politics and political uncertainties. Some persons have even challenged the merits of liberalisation and interpreted it as undiluted globalisation. It is, therefore, necessary to evaluate critically the overall economic performance of the 1990 decade and examine the impact of the liberalisation policy.

JAJMANI SYSTEM

The Concept

Jajmani system is a system of traditional occupational obligations. Castes in early India were economically interdependent on one another. The traditional specialised occupation of a villager followed the specialisation assigned to his caste. The specialisation of occupation led to exchange of services in village society. This relationship between the 'servicing' and the 'served' castes was not contractual, individual, impersonal, temporary or limited but it was caste-oriented, long-termed and broadly supportive. This system with the durable relation between a landowning family and the landless families that supply them with goods and services is called the *jajmani* system.

Harold Gould (1987: 138-39) has described the *jajmani* system as inter-familial, inter-caste relationship pertaining to the patterning of superordinate-subordinate relations between patrons and suppliers of services. The patrons are the families of 'clean' castes while the suppliers of services are the families of lower and 'unclean' castes. It could be said that the *jajmani* system is a system of distribution whereby landowning families of high castes are provided services and products by various lower castes such as carpenters (Khati), barbers (Nai), potters (Kumhar), blacksmiths (Lohar), washermen (Dhobi), sweepers (Chuhra), etc. The servicing castes are called *kamins* while the castes served are called *jajmans*. For the services rendered, the servicing castes are paid in cash or in kind (grains, fodder, clothes, and animal products like milk, butter, etc.).

Yogendra Singh (1973:186) describes *jajmani* system as a system governed by relationship based on reciprocity in inter-caste relations in villages. Ishwaran (1966:41), referring to *jajmani* system (called '*aya*' in Mysore in South India), has said that it is a system in which each caste has a role to play in a community life as a whole. This role consists of economic, social and moral functions.

The term '*jajman*' originally referred to the client for whom a Brahmin priest performed rituals, but later on it came to be referred to the patron or recipient of specialised services. Beidelman (1959:6-7) has pointed out that for the providers of goods and services, besides the term *kamin*, other terms like *purjan*, *pardhan*, etc., are also used in different regions.

Jajmani Relations

Sometimes, the relations between two or more castes based on supplying a few things may only be contractual but not *jajmani*. For example, the weaver who is paid in cash for what he makes and sells is not entitled to customary share of the harvest. He is not a *kamin* and the purchaser is not his *jajman*. Further, even in *jajmani* relations, there may be some products or services that may be contracted and paid for separately. For example, the rope-makers in a village may supply farmers, under *jajmani* arrangements, all necessary ropes except the rope used in wells which is especially long and thick and for which special payment has to be made.

The *jajmani* relations entail ritual matters and social support as well as economic exchanges. The servicing castes perform the ritual and ceremonial duties at the *jajman's* house on occasions like birth, marriage and death. D.N. Majumdar (1958) has given the example of a Thakur family (of Rajput caste) in a village in Lucknow district in Uttar Pradesh which is served by as many as families of ten castes for the lifecycle rites. For example, at the birth-feast of a child, Brahmin presides over the ceremony of 'Nam-Sanskaran' (giving a name), Sunar (goldsmith) provides the gold ornament for the new born, Dhobi (washerman) washes soiled clothes, Nai (barber) carries messages, Khati (carpenter) provides a wooden stool (*patta*) on which the child is seated for the ceremony, Lohar (blacksmith) provides *kara* (iron bangle), Kumhar (potter) provides *kulhar* (jugs) for keeping cooked vegetables and drinking water, Pasi provides *patal* (leaf-plates) for taking food, and Bhangi (scavenger) cleans the place after the feast. All people who help, receive gifts of food, money and clothes depending partly on custom, partly on *jajman's* affluence, and partly on the recipient's entreaty.

The *kamins* (lower castes) who provide specialised skills and services to their *jajmans* (higher castes) themselves need goods and services of others. According to Harold Gould (1987:169-170), these lower castes make their own *jajmani* arrangements either through direct exchange of labour or by paying in cash or kind. The middle castes also, like the lower castes, either subscribe to each other's services in return for compensations and payments or exchange services with one another.

The *kamins* not only provide goods to their *jajmans* but also perform those tasks for them which pollute them (*jajmans*); for example, washing of soiled clothes (by Dhobis), cutting of hair (by Nais), delivery of the new-born (by Nain), cleaning toilets (by Bhangis), and so on. Though Dhobis, Nais, Lohars, etc., are themselves ranked as lower castes, yet they do not serve as *kamins* to Harijans, nor the Brahmins take these lower castes as their *jajmans*. However, when the lower caste families prosper, they discard their polluting occupations and try to get (and succeed also) ritual specialists to serve them.

The *jajmani* links are between families rather than castes. Thus, a family of Rajputs gets its metal tools from a particular family of the Lohar (blacksmith) caste and not from all Lohar families in the village. It is this particular family of Lohars which will get a share of the Rajput family's crop at harvest and not other Lohar families. This *jajmani* relationship between the two families (of Lohar and Rajput) is durable because the Lohar serves the same Rajput family that his father and grandfather served. The Rajput family also gets its tools (and repairs) from the descendants of the same Lohar family whose men made tools for their forefathers. If one of the associated families dies out, another of its lineage may take its place in the relationship. As an example, in the above case, if the Lohar's family has more sons than its clientele (Rajput family) can support, some seek other associates in places where there is shortage of Lohars.

Orenstein (1962:310-14) has held that the families of village officials or village servants (for example, watchmen) maintain *jajmani* relations with the whole village rather than with particular families. Thus, a watchman's family gets a contribution at harvest time from every landowner farmer's family in the village. The village servants may also have tax-free use of village land. Some service families maintain *jajmani* relations with a segment of the village rather than individual families. Such families have rights to serve all those who live in a particular section of the village.

Referring to the *jajmani* system, Kolenda (1963:11-31) has said: "Hindu *jajmani* system may be approached as an institution or social system within Indian villages made up of a network of roles and of norms integrated into the system as a whole and legitimised and supported by general cultural values." The important questions which need to be analysed in the context of *jajmani* system are: What is the function of the system? What are the roles involved? What are its norms and values?

How is the power and authority distributed in the system? How is the (*jajmani*) system related to other systems? What is the motivation in maintaining the (*jajmani*) system? What changes have this system undergone?

Functions and Roles

Analysing the functions of the *jajmani* system, Leach (1960) has said that the *jajmani* system maintains and regulates division of labour and economic interdependence of castes. According to Wiser (1967:35), the *jajmani* system serves to maintain the Indian village as a self-sufficing community. Gould (1987) has said that it (*jajmani* system) distributes agricultural produce in exchange for menial and craft services. Beidelman (1959) is of the opinion that it (*jajmani* system) maintains higher castes' prestige.

The roles involved in the *jajmani* system are those of *jajmans* and *kamins*. The *kamin* castes render certain occupational, economic and social services to the *jajman* castes for which the latter pay them at fixed intervals or on specified occasions. However, all castes do not necessarily participate in this reciprocal exchange. For example, Teli is one caste which is normally not involved in the exchange of services system. *Kamins'* clientele may include members of his own village as well as other villages. *Kamin* may sell his rights to a client to another *kamin*. The important thing in the role-relationship is that free food, free clothes, free residence, rent-free land, casual aid, aid in litigation, and protection are provided to *kamins* by *jajmans* during various exigencies of life.

However, the *jajmani* system is not reciprocal in all villages. Kolenda (1963:11-32) has maintained that dominant castes swing the balance of power in their favour in such relationships in many villages in India. Yogendra Singh (1973:187) also believes that villages in India are changing today in respect of economic institutions, power structure and inter-caste relationships. A major source of economic change is land reform which has been introduced through abolition of intermediaries, tenancy reforms, ceiling of landholdings, redistribution of land, development of co-operative farming and religio-economic movement for gift of surplus land by the rich to the poor as *bhoodan*. These measures have affected interaction among castes, *jajmani* system, and the social system of the villages.

Norms and Values

The traditional method of payment, almost in all regions in the country, is that it is made at harvest time when each landowning farmer family handsover some newly produced foodgrain to various *kamins*. However, these harvest payments are only part of what the *kamin* family receives. The *kamin* may be dependent on the *jajman* for his house-site, for places where his animals may graze, for wood and cow-dung fuel, for loan of tools, and so forth. In addition, the *jajman* may give him clothes and gifts on ceremonial occasions and may also help him with loan of money in emergencies.

Wiser (1956) has referred to seventeen considerations which *kamins* get from the *jajmans*. Gould (1985:140-141) also found all these considerations important in *jajmani* ties in his study of *jajmani* system in Sherupur village in Faizabad district (Uttar Pradesh) in 1954-55. Some of these considerations are: free residence site, free food for family, free clothing, free food for animals, free timber, free cow-dung, rent-free land, credit facilities, opportunity for supplementary employment, free use of tools, implements and animals, free hides, aid in litigation, free funeral pyre lot and free use of raw materials. Gould (1987) also studied the formal rate at which *jajmans* paid *purjans* for the services rendered. For example, in 1954-55, a Brahmin got 15 kilograms (28 pounds) of grain per family at the harvest time: Kori (weaver) got 15 kilograms of grain per harvest plus Rs. 20 per month per *jajman*; Kumhar (potter), Nai (barber) and Lohar (blacksmith) got 8 kilograms of grain per family per harvest; and Dhobi (washerman) got 4 kilograms of grain per woman in the household per harvest.

Giving the example of grain income of one *kamin* family from all the *jajmans* in the 'serving villages', Gould (1987) says that in his village he found that a Nai (barber) got about 312 kilograms of grains in a year (1954-55) from fifteen joint families consisting of twenty-five nuclear units. Taking the *jajmani* relations with different castes, Gould found that all *jajmans* in the village (Sherupur) gave 2,039 kilograms of grains in one year to all the *purjan* families. The village consisted of forty-three families with a total population of 228 people. Of these, only nineteen families functioned as *jajmans* (who received services and disbursed grains). This suggests the magnitude of the economic interaction involved.

During a lean year, the farmer *jajman* does not give much foodgrain to his *kamins* but when he gets a good produce, he does not mind giving some extra foodgrains to those *kamins* who have rendered good services to him. However, if the *kamin* dodges work for his *jajman*, say in repairing farmer's instruments or if the Dhobi (washerman) loses or tears many clothes, the *jajman* does not give him much. Similarly, the *kamin* renders services to *jajman* according to the payment he receives. According to M.N. Srinivas (1955:11-13) also, those *jajmans* who pay in grains are preferred to those who pay in cash.

In the allocation of power between the *jajmans* and the *kamins*, according to Beidelman (1959), ritual purity and pollution are not significant. Low caste person, even if he is a *jajman*, is considered subordinate to *kamin* of higher caste. Power of high caste is based on land-ownership and wealth, and *kamins* do not hold such power. Gould (1987:173) has asserted: "Basically the distinction is between the landowning cultivating castes, on the one hand, who dominate the social order and the landless craft and the menial castes, on the other, who are subordinate to them." Pocock (1963:79) similarly declares: "If *jajmani* relations do not constitute a system, they constitute an organisation. They are organised around one institution, the dominant caste of a given area." There are norms concerning duties, rights, payments and concessions for the *jajmans* and the *kamins*. *Jajman* has to be paternalistic towards his *kamins* and fulfil their demands. *Kamin* has also to behave like a son to his father. He has to support *jajman* in his factional disputes.

The cultural value in the *jajmani* system is that generosity and charity are religious obligations and inequality is God-given. The sacred, semi-sacred and the secular Hindu literature and oral traditions authorise and justify the *jajman-kamin* relationship. The caste council has the power of punishing erring *jajmans* and *kamins*. At the same time, the sanctions permit that the *kamin* may not perform the required services and the *jajman* also may take away land rented or granted to *kamin*.

For example, if one Kumhar (potter) family attempts to take over the *jajmans* of another, then the injured Kumhar family appeals to its caste council to call off the intruders. And, if the Kumhars of the village believe that the *jajman* farmers are unfair to them, they may try to have all Kumhars of the village boycott the *jajman* farmers until they give up their unfair practices.

Jajmani System: An Exploitative System

Is *jajmani* system an exploitative system? Do *jajmans* exploit the *kamins* by paying them meagre quantity of foodgrains or a small amount of money by compensating them or in some other manner? Beidleman (1959) explicitly equates the *jajman* with 'exploiter' and the *kamin* with 'exploited' and characterises the system as 'feudal'. He believes the *jajmani* system to be one of the chief instruments of coercion, control and legitimation wielded by high caste landowning Hindus. Similarly, Lewis and Barnouw (1956) are of the opinion that the vast difference in power between the rich and the influential *jajmans* and the poor and the landless *kamins* leads to the exploitation of the *kamins* and coercing them into sustaining the power of those who have the higher rank and the upper hand. Some intellectuals opine that there is no force or coercion involved in the *jajmani* system. First, *kamins* are not totally dependent upon their *jajmans* for their livelihood. They are free to sell their goods and provide services to other individuals and families who pay them cash. Secondly, when *kamins* feel that injustice has been done to them, they take the help of their caste panchayats which compel the *jajmans* to accept the demands of their *kamins*. Likewise, when the landowner *jajmans* feel convinced that one of their *kamins* (service groups) is derelict in its obligations or threatens or challenges the power and status of the landowners, the *jajman* (patron) families can put collective pressure on them by withholding payment or by some other way. However, collective action on either side does not affect the interests of the caste as a whole. Caste solidarity prevails over loyalties to *jajmani* associates. Thirdly, the *jajmans* treat their *kamins* in a paternalistic way and help them socially in emergencies. Fourthly, the *jajmani* rules are so flexible that these can be interpreted in any way and shift in service arrangements can be made possible. However, minimum standards are maintained at any given time in each *jajmani* relation. Lastly, the members of high caste want to avoid the polluting as well as the specialised work. They have, therefore, to depend on the families which provide them the required services and goods. Considering the *jajmani* exchanges as mutually beneficial, they tolerate the occasional irrelevant demands of their *kamins* just as the *kamins* tolerate the occasional coercion of their *jajmans*. Therefore, to consider the *jajmani* system an exploitative system would be illogical. Rao (1961), Kolenda (1963:21-29), Orenstein (1962) and Gould (1985) have also maintained that condemning *jajmani* arrangements as brutally exploitative is too sweeping and obfuscating a generalisation. Gould (1987:176-177) has said that an analysis of the *jajmani* system which sees it as a component of a feudal order seems unwarranted. The magnitude of the system is small by any measure of economic activity. The system persists not because of any 'rational' economic motivations but because of its importance to the maintenance of the social status and patterns of social interaction that are essential to the successful practice of rural Hinduism. The *jajman* is not primarily an economically and politically homogeneous class but a religio-economic category uniquely adopted to Indian civilisation. The bond between *jajmans* and the servicing castes is enjoyment of a common religio-economic relationship and not enjoyment of a common relationship to the sources of wealth and power in society.

It may thus be asserted that in the *jajmani* system, the *jajman* status neither coincides with a landlord class, a dominant caste or the like nor does it depend upon membership in any particular social group but upon the possession of land, or access to the produce from land by whatever means. Mayer (1960), Mathur (1958) and Pocock (1963) have also maintained that access to farm land has always been 'caste free' in India which means that the modest means needed to maintain at least some semblance of *jajman* status has technically always been available to members of any caste in the hierarchy. Following Gould (1987:177) that *jajman* status refers to a religio-economic category rather than a social stratum, it may be concluded that *jajmans* cannot be perceived as exploiters (as a social class). At most it may be said that amount of money given by *jajmans* to *kamins* is rather low in the present age which compels them to seek cash income from other sources. On the other hand, the *jajman's* status was never confined (even in the old social order) merely to landed aristocracy. People from different castes had the opportunities to become *jajmans*. But being a *jajman* and being part of the currently dominant political order were not automatically coterminous. Membership in the political hierarchy was merely one means of achieving material and power position enabling one to be a *jajman* if one so desired. It was never the exclusive means.

Being a *jajman* means being an orthodox Hindu whose value system made necessary the engagement of certain specialists (of serving castes). Being a landlord meant being a member of the ruling class (Gould, 1987:185). And a *jajman* was not an 'exploiter' of a *kamin* though a landlord could be an exploiter. The desire to become a *jajman* is not a desire to get 'feudal status' or a 'common inclination to exploit the weak' but the wish to practise certain rituals and a way of life necessitating the avoidance of impurity.

Changes in Jajmani System

Jajmani system is related to other systems like caste system, religious system, system of landownership, kinship system, and the political structure of a village. As such, changes in these systems have also affected the functioning of the *jajmani* system in the present times. The more important changes in society that have affected the *jajmani* system in the last five or six decades are: reduction in the powers of village elders' councils, effect of the factory system and industrialisation on the quality of services rendered by *kamins*, changes in the rigidity of the caste system, spread of education, migration of people of intermediate and lower castes to cities in search of jobs and material amenities, abolition of the *jagirdari* system, introduction of land reforms, better employment in urban areas, feasibility of market transactions owing to the availability of modern transport, and so forth. Because of all these factors, the *jajmani* system has been largely supplanted in many villages while in some it has completely disappeared. Artisans prefer to get money for their goods. Cultivators who have money prefer to buy things of quality from the market place by paying in cash. The dominant caste prefers to summon political help rather than depend on their *kamins* for support. No wonder that the *jajmani* system has been very much weakened today. Iravati Karve and Y.B. Damle (1963:151-52) might have found two-third of their respondents (222 out of 326) in a survey conducted in 1962 in five villages in Maharashtra and Bose and Jodha (1965:118-123) might have found 86 per cent (111 out of 129) of their respondents in their survey conducted in 1963 in Barmer district in western Rajasthan, in favour of the *jajmani* system because of economic benefits, availability of ritual services, and dependable support from some of the families and castes to the landowners in their factional struggles, and getting patron's protection in exigencies, yet the fact is that the traditional *jajmani* relations have very much weakened in recent years. Not much of the village economy is now carried on through *jajmani* arrangements. Biedleman (1959) too is of the opinion that it is doubtful if the *jajmani* system will survive in the coming years.

ECONOMIC DEVELOPMENT: ITS DETERMINANTS AND SOCIAL CONSEQUENCES

In the study of sociology of economic development, some important questions of sociological relevance are: What is economic development? How does economic growth begin? What social infrastructure is needed for economic development? What are the preconditions for economic change and how can these be induced? Can factors which accelerate economic development be identified? Can social and cultural barriers to economic development be overcome and its pace increased? What are the social consequences of economic development? How can dysfunctional aspects of economic development be checked? In this section, we will try to find out the answers to these questions.

What is Economic Development

In the broadest sense, economic development might be viewed as "any growth in real income per capita from whatever source" (Robert Faris, 1964:889). Bach (1960:167) has described it as "growth in the total output of goods and services in the economy". Novack (1964:151) has referred to a very old definition of economic growth, according to which it is "continuous substantial increase in per capita consumption of goods and services". The substantial consumption of economic goods is possible only when there is substantial production of economic goods, and substantial production these days depends upon greater use of technologies. In a narrower sense, therefore, it may be said that economic development refers to "the extensive application of inanimate power and other technologies to the production and distribution of economic goods" (Faris, 1964: 889). In this sense, economic development is practically equivalent to industrialisation. But to say that economic development is only industrialisation would not be correct because besides involving the use of power and technology in production, it also involves labour mobility, extensive educational system, and so on.

Jaffe and Stewart (1951), who described economic development as "rationalisation of economic production", have given a dichotomy of developed and underdeveloped countries on the basis of per capita income and factors like high literacy, high expectation of life at birth and low fertility, low proportion of labour force engaged in agriculture, and high production of kilowatts of electricity per capita. Besides these, we may add a third category to this classification, that of a country which is in between the developed and the underdeveloped countries, that is, the developing country. In terms of the per capita income, the United States, Canada, Australia and western Europe (Italy, France, Germany, England) are considered to be developed countries. On the other hand, South Africa, Mexico and most of the southern and eastern European countries are developing countries. India too, in terms of its per capita income, is a developing country.

Jaffe and Stewart have said that economic development entails changes in everything at once to achieve the above characteristics (of developed countries). But, Robert Faris believes that this conclusion (of achieving everything at once for economic development) is not justified. He thinks that though its proximate measurement will be taken as an increase in real income per capita, yet all other changes would depend upon the degree of requiredness.

Determinants of and Barriers to Economic Development

The factors that are generally believed to contribute to economic growth of a society are: natural resources, capital accumulation, technology, sources of power, manpower, labour force, characteristics of population and its economic organisation, and social environment. According to Faris (1964:890), the important prerequisites of economic development are: (i) values or ideology; (ii) institutions or normative complexes, that is, unanimously accepting and following the rules of conduct or normally sanctioned prescriptions for behaviour; (iii) organisation (policies), that is, whether the government wants to promote public sector or private sector or both; and (iv) motives (incentives) pertaining to profit/prestige. Gunnar Myrdal (1968:1942) in his three volumes of *Asian Drama*, in which he has analysed poverty and development of the countries of South Asia, has pointed out six important factors affecting development: output and income, conditions of production, levels of living, attitude towards life and work, institutions, and politics. The first three refer to economic factors, the next two to non-economic factors, and the last one to a mixed category. Myrdal has maintained that the economic factors are significant and decisive.

Novack (1964:156) holds that chief criteria of underdevelopment are scarcity of capital, low industrial population and lack of natural resources. On the other hand, the prerequisites of economic development include capital, quality of technology, and natural resources. He further maintains that the factors which impede economic growth in the underdeveloped areas are: (i) lack of sufficient quantity of innovation, (ii) lack of agrarian reform, (iii) lack of discipline, (iv) population growth, and (v) foreign exchange shortages.

Jacob Viner (see, Jean Meynaud, 1963) has also referred to six barriers to economic development. These are: unfavourable physical environment, low quality of working population, scarcity of technical knowledge, scarcity of capital, rapid growth of population, and defects in agrarian structure.

In Europe, the Protestant Reformation paved the way for the rise of capitalism and growth by changing the outlook of society and its institutions. Along this line developed the 'Protestant Ethic' which was conducive to economic growth. Writing about this European occurrence, Max Weber emphasised the institutions of capitalistic society that have accompanied rapid economic development in the West: (1) private ownership and control of the means of production; (2) barriers and government price-fixing; (3) the reign of calculable law, enabling people to know in advance under what rules they operate in economic life; (4) freedom of individuals to work for wages; (5) 'commercialism' of economic life through a market system of wages and prices to mobilise and allocate productive resources; and (6) speculation and risk taking (which had been largely prevented in the preceding feudal societies). However, some scholars have referred to some holes in this thesis.

Obstacles to Economic Development in India

The above mentioned factors can also help in understanding obstacles to economic development in India. According to Thomas Shea (see, Jean

Meynaud, 1963), the four important barriers to economic development in India an context are caste, pattern of land tenure, population growth, and property laws (which lead to fragmentation of landholdings).

The basic obstacles pointed out by A.R. Desai (1959:130) are: (a) the social and institutional framework and values inherited from the past (i.e., caste system); and (b) persistence of backward types of loyalties.

The caste system though has been theoretically and juridicaly abolished by the Constitution of India, yet its significance in real life, its influence on the economic development, its effect upon the patterns of property relations and patterns of consumption, and its impress upon the configurations of power structure in the economic, political, social and cultural fields are still not properly comprehended and hence gravely underestimated. Caste prevents mobility of people so essential for dynamic economic development. It prevents certain groups from taking to certain vocations, certain patterns of economic behaviour, and certain forms of consumption. It has been found that most of the controlling positions in economy, administration and cultural pursuits are monopolised by a few castes all over India. In fact, a few castes control the destiny of most people of the country, leading to caste and regional tensions and social unrest. This unrest becomes the cause of and keeps alive a bitter competitive struggle among the privileged groups themselves as well as between them and the underprivileged groups. This has a detrimental effect on the development of a healthy national economy.

Besides caste (which inhibits occupational and social mobility), some important barriers in economic development of India have been identified as joint family system, communalism, regionalism and linguism. It has also come to be accepted that changes in the caste system have made development possible. Since Gunnar Myrdal had not given importance to changes in social institutions like caste, family, etc., as also to their functional aspects in the analysis of development, his analysis of economic development has been described as negative, patchy and disjointed.

Another sociological implication is the persistence of backward types of loyalties resulting into factionalism and division of the Indian people into groups with petty egos, to the detriment of the growth of a highly developed national consciousness. Some types of loyalties that very much persist (besides the caste loyalty) in India are kinship loyalties, regional identifications and religious attachment. These divisions tend to inhibit the development of a feeling of unity in the society and of identify among its members. The normative pressure rooted in such an environment profoundly affects the conduct of the individual in external situations and relations.

A. R. Desai (1959: 131-32) further holds that this parochial mentality, together with the old outmoded institutions, obstructs the proper economic development in a number of ways: (i) it leads to nepotism; (ii) it results into the growth of the harmful practices of unproductive investment patterns and wrong consumption patterns; (iii) it generates distorted attitudes to work, efficiency, vocations and allocation of resources; and (iv) it obstructs the growth of those mores and sanctions which are basic to a developing economy in modern times, namely, mores and sanctions founded on law, respect for personality, concept of equal citizenship, etc.

The barriers to economic development in India as given by Yogendra Singh (1973) are: (i) transcendence (according to which legitimation of traditional values cannot be challenged); (ii) holism (according to which the relation between individual and society (or group) is such that individual subordinates his rights and aspirations to that of society's welfare; it also means precedence to collectivity over the individual); (iii) hierarchy (stratification in caste occupation and social status); and (iv) continuity (belief in rebirth and *karma*, etc.).

Stages in Economic Development

Rostow (1960:4) has referred to five stages in the economic development. These are: (i) traditional society, (ii) preconditions for take off, (iii) the take off, (iv) the drive to technological maturity, and (v) age of high mass consumption.

A traditional society is basically agricultural. Its members are fatalistic, superstitious and ignorant of the world outside their community. The units of loyalty in such a society are family, village, caste or ethnic group. Traditional (peasant) communities are not self-sufficient but dependent on towns for markets, and for religion, philosophy and even government, as leadership is poorly developed within the communities. The decisions for the peasants are made from the outside. Often they do not even know how or why these decisions are made. Try though they might, they can have no part in the making of these basic decisions which affect them from the outside. This produces not only a fatalistic outlook towards life but also a suspicion of outsiders and a wariness of new ideas. The distrust of the outside world does not unite them with their neighbours. The extended family draws together to defend itself against the dishonesty of its neighbours. This is one segment of unity with the traditional society. Production in the traditional society is limited due to limited resources, especially land.

Then comes the process of gradual transition. In this stage, the preconditions for take-off are developed. Generally, these pre-conditions arise from external intrusion by an advanced society. These intrusions stimulate new ideas and feelings and people begin to believe that economic progress is good as well as possible. Some people go for education, some leaders emerge, and some new areas of investments like trade and commerce appear. All this happens slowly because conventional social structures and old values are difficult to change. Before the transition in institutions and values take place, certain prerequisites of social change and economic growth must be present. These are: an awareness of purpose, an eye to the future, a sense of urgency, the need for variety of opportunities and roles, an intellectual appreciation of and an emotional preparedness for self-imposed tasks and sacrifices, and the emergence of a dynamic leadership.

In the take-off stage, resistances to steady growth are overcome and growth becomes a normal condition. There is accumulation of capital, technological development in industry and agriculture, and the emergence of a political group which takes up the modernisation of the economy as a serious business. New industries expand rapidly and profits are reinvested to yield more expansion. The number of workers increases and so do their wages.

A long interval of sustained growth follows the take-off. During this interval, there is a drive to spread modern technology through an economic activity. New industries accelerate their rate of expansion and production. An important aspect of the drive to maturity is that goods formerly imported are now produced at home. Maturity is usually reached forty years after the take-off.

In the age of high mass consumption, there is a shift towards durable consumers' goods and services. America has emerged from this stage while western Europe and Japan are beginning to experience its joys. Since no country has developed beyond this stage, it is impossible to say what the next stage will be.

Does Social Change Precede or Follow Economic Development?

One view is that without economic development, change in social system is not possible, while the other view is that it is the change in institutions operating in society which makes economic development feasible. According to Frankel (see, Jean Meynaud, 1963), however, economic development and social change are dependent on each other, that is, each is the cause and effect of the other.

If we are to speak of the effects of technical change, we must be careful to avoid falling into the common error of thinking that changes in "knowing how to do a certain thing" can be separated from changes in "the actual doing of it". The idea that technical change is an exogenous force altering the established day-to-day activities of society springs from this erroneous way of speaking and thinking. It consists in the fallacious belief that society's activities proceed in two separate compartments: the first containing the *process* of knowing, and the other containing the *application* of such knowing. The same thing may be said about economic development and social change, that is, whether the former leads to the latter or the latter leads to the former. As pointed out above, social change neither precedes economic development nor follows it. Both are interrelated. For example, when there is a change from farming to industry (say, cement industry, or sugar industry, or paper industry, or steel industry), this will involve the development of new aptitudes and new habits of work. If we regard the introduction of an industry as a purely mechanical process which will have certain social consequences, we fail to see that what we regard as the result or consequence is but the continuous process of change itself. Thus, if workers in the industry are independently housed, or suffer deficiencies in the standard of nutrition, education or recreation, now necessary in their new environment, these are not the consequence of the process of change in industry, but rather of a failure to complete it. Even the direct activity of increasing the production (say, of cement, sugar, paper or steel, etc.) cannot be brought to optimum efficiency unless all other economic and social activities to which the task must be related, have been developed. Indeed, an industry cannot even begin until some changes in the previous attitudes, habits and patterns of social organisation have taken place.

Let us take another example of what may be regarded merely as a technical change. Let us assume that it is desired to increase the productivity of land and cattle-ownership of a village community which has never engaged in the production of butter or other milk products, either for sale or its own consumption. It is hoped that not only will this community consume these products itself but will also market some of these as to enable it to increase its income by selling the surplus dairy produce. At first, the problem might appear to be merely one of introducing new methods of production and the tools, instruments or machines appropriate thereto. But, what is really involved is a vast change in social beliefs and practices. Here, let us for a moment consider only what far-reaching social changes will have to be made to enable technical change to be introduced at all. The utilisation of cattle (besides possessing land) as a source of income presupposes a basic alteration in social and economic structures of the community. It also implies recasting of the traditional values of the members of the community. Thus, it suggests a change in the traditional beliefs as to how and by whom the land is to be cultivated, whether by men or by women, by individuals working for themselves or for others. This, in turn, presupposes the growth of new attitudes and patterns of behaviour which will regulate their social and mutual relations. There is also an assumption of the parallel emergence of a group of persons concerned not only with dairy production itself but also with transport, distribution, marketing and finance of all that the new producers have to buy and all that they have to sell. This also necessitates the political structure—local, provincial and even national—suited to the establishment of these complementary economic activities. It further implies the willingness of the community to permit the growth of all legal, political and administrative institutions necessary to harmonize the rights and duties of persons engaged in this new interdependent economy.

The purpose of this long list of social adjustments is to show that whatever it be that we may care to designate as technical change, it is but one aspect of mutually determined and determining processes of growth on many fronts of the social structure as a whole. It is idle to endeavour to ascertain which change is the innovation or cause and which is the effect. Frankel has said that when we take one change as cause and other as effect, we are merely examining the process of change itself from different points of observation.

Sociological Problems of Economic Development

Economic development is not possible without structural change. Scholars like H.W. Singer (see, Jean Meynaud, 1963: 157) have submitted that for the economic development of the underdeveloped countries, industrialisation is very necessary. Poor underdeveloped countries have 60 to 80 per cent of their population engaged in agriculture. Their national income and per capita income are very low. As such, for the economic development of these countries, there are two alternatives: (i) by improving the existing predominantly agricultural structure (that is, changing low productivity within the existing structure); and (ii) by changing the entire structure, that is, shifting away from agriculture and taking to industry development. The choice between the above two alternatives depends upon which of the two approaches is more challenging? To our mind, correct approach is to emphasise both.

As this point, the two main questions arised are: (i) How can agricultural improvement be brought about cheaply? (ii) How can the existing industries be improved? Agricultural improvement is possible by changing land tenure system, and by providing more irrigation facilities. Industrial improvement is feasible by extensive re-equipment, and by relocation. Singer (see, Jean Meynaud, 1963: 158) has further suggested that in change from agricultural to industrial structure, the cost of industrilisation can be lowered in three ways: (i) by avoiding urbanisation, which means bringing industry to villages so that there is less demand of transport, water, etc., this will also discourage migration to towns; (ii) by concentrating on industries requiring little capital; and (iii) by applying a technology which uses much labour and little capital. This shows how improving the existing structure as well as attempting structural change is possible. Wilbert Moore (1964) has referred to the impact of industry on social and economic structures in following terms: (i) shift from agriculture to manufacture and services, (ii) occupational specilisation, (iii) division of labour, (iv) coordination of specialised activities, (v) labour mobility, (vi) creation of banks, (vii) extension of market, (viii) change in consumption, and (ix) change in network of social relationships.

A.R. Desai (1959:127) has referred to four sociological problems of economic development in India: (1) replacing the old social organisation and evolving new web of social relations; (2) modifying or discarding old social institutions and developing new types of social institutions; (3) altering or removing old forms of social control and creating new devices of social authority; and (4) revising or liquidating old agencies of social change and determining new instrumentalities and factors of social change.

The British kept India underdeveloped. Whatever industrial development was made, it was predominantly regulated to suit the needs of British capitalism. Heavy industries were not permitted to grow. While the British retarded the development of India's economy, they also made a dent into social organisation, social institutions, and social outlook of the Indian people. The traditional self-sufficient village community which operated through the institutions of panchayat, caste and joint family and was governed by custom, was almost fatally undermined. However, it was not replaced by a new social framework, a new institutional matrix, or a new outlook. In the absence of these, the introduction of the new legal system resulted in disorganising the then prevailing social relations. The old principle of cooperation and coordination was replaced by the principle of competition which set into motion a whirlpool in the social structure. After independence, the government undertook the task of the reconstruction of economy through Five Year Plans. Economic development has created on the one hand sociological problems (i.e., problems of social relations, social institutions, social control, and agencies of social change) of negative character and on the other hand of positive character.

The negative type of sociological problems are the result of the persistence of old social institutions like authoritarian joint family and traditional religious institutions, etc. These problems have also emerged out of old forms of social control like supernatural sanctions, authoritarian norms, and family, caste, tribal, religious and other customary sanctions. Besides, these have arisen out of the old world outlook which was basically religious, fatalistic and anti-democratic in content. Lastly, these have emanated from large-scale illiteracy, unemployment, corruption, casteism and poverty. The positive type of problems are the result of the policies of industrialisation, commercialisation and monetisation (i.e., introducing the money economy). Industrialisation has uprooted the old division of labour, created new occupational patterns demanding new discipline and a new mode of living. Further, modernisation—whether in agriculture or in industry—has separated man from the traditional processes and techniques of his social units and from the skills he learned from his family. Commercialisation has also created numerous problems. It has brought about a shift in power and authority. Not farmers and producers but land and industry owners and administrators have become the new ruling elite. In villages, the centre of political power has shifted from elders of upper castes to usurers (moneylenders), merchants, landlords and officials. Lastly, monetisation is also fraught with numerous sociological problems. It has created dangers of greater fluctuation in land values, greater price-spreads of food articles, greater money illusions, and greater proportion of expenditure on non-food items. Besides these dangers, the introduction of money economy has meant atomisation of individuals within the family and destruction of family relationships. Thus, the three processes (industrialisation, commercialisation and monetisation) have generated numerous sociological problems.

Economic Development, Planning and Social Change in India

The economic development in India after independence can truly be described as a revolutionary change. If we compare the economic development in the British period with the one in the Nehru period of about two decades, Indira Gandhi and Rajiv Gandhi periods of about two decades, the period of more than six years of V.P.Singh, Chandra Shekhar and Narasimha Rao's governments, about two years period of United Front governments, and about one year period of BJP-led government, the truth behind the above statement becomes self-evident. The economic growth in the two centuries of the British colonial rule between 1757 and 1947 remained 1 per cent or even less—a rate of growth so pathetically low that it reduced India to a mere supplier of raw materials and a gaping market for western exports. The industrial sector was overwhelmingly dominated by the British capital. A fragment of the industrial sector owned by Indians was managed by the British agencies. In the agricultural economy, the cultivators were in the clutches of zamindars, jagirdars and local moneylenders (*sahukars*). Savings and investments were very low. Technology was of inferior level. There was no concept of regional balance through enforced backward area development. Foreign capital was not available for building India. Low incomes lead to low savings, which further lead to low investment, low growth, and once again to low incomes. The theory of vicious circle of poverty and never-ending cycle quite fitted the economy of the colonial period.

After independence, the task for the new government was two-fold: dismantling the colonial economy and erecting in its place base for a modern, independent and self-reliant economic order. The blueprint for the country's modern economy and nationhood—the socialist pattern of society—was provided by the Avadi session of Congress in 1955 (during the Nehru era) and by the Bangalore session in 1969 (during the Indira Gandhi era). There is no denying the fact that the Nehru model of socialism did improve our economy in the four decades of the 1950s, 1960s, 1970s and 1980s, though there is a school which decries its (Nehru model's) performance in comparison with the economic growth in South Korea, Singapore, Hong Kong, Thailand and Taiwan. We have now millions of modern industrial enterprises where there were once but a handful; we have a huge reservoir of technical and entrepreneurial skills; we have big public projects like Bhilai and Rourkela as well as big dams like Hirakud; we have the highest rate of savings in the developing world; we have growth rate of 5 per cent per annum (in 1998-99); we have sustained growth in exports, a twenty-fold increase in the deposits of Non-Resident Indians (NRIs); we have unparalleled credibility in international money market; and we have dropped the percentage of population below the poverty-line (from 51 per cent in 1972-73 to 36 per cent in 1997-98, as claimed by the government after accepting Lakdawala Committee's recommendations). In spite of all this development, it is also a fact that we are faced with the problem of inflation and high debt. The balance of trade deficit is very high and the budget deficit is in trillions.

The Narasimha Rao's government discarded the socialist model in 1991-92 and launched a new revamped model based on the philosophy of liberalisation, marketisation and privatisation (what is now called Nehruvian capitalism), which the Congress government claimed gave a big boost to our economic development. The then Congress government maintained that the essence of the new model was that it combined trust in the state as well as the private entrepreneurs, and held unflinching faith in a plural democracy and mixed economy. The United Front government and the BJP-led government also continued this economic policy.

The Tirupati session of the Congress in April 1992 adopted a new ideological paradigm which was a shift from left-of-centre to right-of-centre. It was a technique of discarding Nehru in Nehru's name. It focused on cutting down subsidies to various sectors (including agriculture and public distribution system), discarding licence-permit *raj*, introducing the exit policy, opening the country for multinational corporations, removing import controls, and not treating public sector merely as a job distribution agency characterised by a non-work ethic. Thus, the rhetoric stayed socialist while the content of policies became capitalist with a vengeance.

There are scholars who do not believe that the new economic policy will really rejuvenate the Indian economy. They maintain that our economy can be revived best by imposing curbs on import, promoting exports, widening the tax-net, debureaucratising the public sector, unearthing black money, introducing cuts in defence spending, taking more interest in tapping natural resources, creating a very large market for goods, bringing radical land reforms, and so on. These scholars also believe that country should depend on the internal rather than the external measures.

Sociologically, it may be held that the economic development—both through Nehru and liberal models—has affected our social structures in a direction as we desired it. Whatever sociological model we may use for evaluating our society, viz., evolutionary (assessing evolving of society in series of stages), conflict (emphasising competition and continuous struggle for power), functional (analysing the consequences of each institutional practice for all other elements in the social structure), etc., it will be obvious that change has taken place in the network of social relations, social institutions, social systems and social structures, social norms, etc. People in India are no longer as conservative as half a century ago. They do not cling tenaciously to the moral norms and social values that came down to them from the past. Men individually strive towards individual liberty and collective security. There is also change in their outlook and ideas. They wish for new experiences. They have a curiosity to borrow not only technologies but also cultural elements from other societies. They have a creative urge for innovations. They are not much afraid of the consequences of the acceptance of innovations and social changes. They may protest and agitate against the power elite for failing to mitigate the problems of poverty, unemployment, corruption, inflation, nepotism, terrorism, casteism, regionalism, etc., yet they know that social order in India will never be in a state of disequilibrium. Indian culture, with divergence of interests, will not only survive but develop too. Social change, through economic development, will provide clues and directions to social structures and social behaviour—traditional as well as transitional.

ECONOMIC INEQUALITY

Levels

It has already been pointed out that poverty and inequality are not the same thing. A wealthy business-person and a comfortably-off college/university lecturer are materially unequal but a lecturer is not poor. Social inequality means that certain individuals or groups have more material resources than others. Poverty implies some *insufficiency* in the material resources of an individual or group. There is considerable disagreement about the concept of 'poverty'. Is not being able to afford a scooter poverty? Is not being able to send one's child to a good English-medium school poverty? Some might include such situations in poverty, but others may hold that such situations involve inequality rather than poverty.

The exploitation of the poor by the rich can be contained by reducing the level of inequality between the rich and the poor, which in turn depends upon reducing poverty through economic reforms. If economic reforms bring about steady and sustained growth in the economy (which, in fact, is their main objective), the poor could benefit in two ways. First, experience has shown that growth (particularly the agricultural growth) trickles down to the poor. Second, sustained growth creates an environment which is, on the whole, congenial for empowerment of the poor. The dependence of the poor on the groups dominating them becomes less precarious owing to expansion of opportunities for employment, education, occupational mobility, and for achieving higher social status. The poor would also find it easier to mobilise for political action at the same time as pragmatic considerations induce a mood favouring accommodating the poor among the groups confronting them.

It may be pointed here that the economic reforms undertaken so far have definitely helped achieve some stable and sustained growth. The Economic Survey presented in the parliament in May 1998 had shown that growth was not adequate. But, the figures now show that we did fairly well in the last one decade or so. The growth of GDP is now rising. There is increase in the growth rate in agriculture as well as industry. Agricultural production in 1999-2000 is expected to be more by 6.5 per cent in comparison to 1998-99. There has been little increase in the export growth. Inflation was just 1.7 per cent in first week of August 1999. Thus, though the economic reforms are taking place, yet many support measures are needed to make them work effective. The groups dominating policy-making processes have to stop pursuing narrow interest and have now to work more for the larger society. A major breakthrough on the inequality and poverty fronts would occur only when the poor acquire political voice powerful enough to make up policy-making groups.

Causes

The following few important causes may be pointed out for income inequality in our country:

Government Policy

The top band of income tax was reduced from 50 to 30 per cent. The tax policy shifted from the progressive (taxing the rich relatively more) to the regressive (taxing the less well-off relatively more) level.

Policy Liberalism

A free market increases inequality. The policy of liberalism adopted by Narasimha Rao government since 1991 and thereafter continued by three non-Congress governments has directly contributed to inequality.

Increasing Unemployment

In the last 2-3 decades, there has been little industrial growth in the country. The service sector too experienced massive job losses. It increased unemployment, insecurity and inequality.

Increasing Salary of High-Paid Employees

The increase in the salary (before and after Fifth Pay Commission recommendations) of higher-paid employees in *absolute* terms is more than the lower-paid employees. This has increased inequality.

The Subsidies

Why should government spend so much on subsidies? By cutting subsidies on fertilisers, foodgrains and domestic gas in February 1999, the BJP-led government saved more than Rs. 2,000 crore. Had it not succumbed to the pressures of its coalition partners and partially resorted some subsidies, it would have saved nearly Rs. 4,000 crore. It is estimated that by cutting non-merit subsidies on higher education, sports and arts, reducing subsidies on water supply and sanitation, increasing charges on irrigation (at present, the authorities charge less than Rs. 75 per hectare on irrigation water supplied for *Rabi* and *Kharif* crops), eliminating subsidy of State Electricity Boards, the government can save about Rs. 9,000 crore immediately and Rs. 30,000 crore in four years (*India Today*, February, 15, 1999:39). The objection of some political parties that the 'poor people' will suffer is illogical because people below the poverty line (i.e., 36% of total people in India) do not use cooking gas. The foodgrains supposed to be supplied to the poor at cheap rates through the public distribution system (PDS) reach the poor only in pittance. Five poorest and *BIMARU* states (Bihar, Madhya Pradesh, Assam, Rajasthan and Uttar Pradesh) receive barely 10 per cent of PDS supplies.

It is, therefore, high time that subsidies are cut and Rs. 1,40,000 crore or 14 per cent of the GDP spent on subsidies saved and fiscal deficit reduced. Our political leaders have only to *educate* the people and make them realise what is good and necessary for the country. It is shocking to know of the enormous debt burden of the central and the state governments. While in absolute terms, the total debt has more than doubled from Rs. 314 thousand crore in 1997-98, the interest payments increased from 40 per cent of the revenue to 48 per cent in the same period. The subsidies, the interest payments and the defence expenditure consume as much as 78 per cent of the revenue (*Outlook*, February 15, 1999:40).

In simple terms, 94 paise of every rupee the government borrows go into debt servicing. Why should not the government seriously think over the suggestion of several economists that it must institute a freeze on further borrowings? Unless the government aggressively reduces the fiscal deficit and the burgeoning debt burden, our country cannot check inflation. The political parties only require the necessary will to do this.

OCCUPATIONAL DIVERSIFICATION AND SOCIAL STRUCTURE

Economic development involves occupational diversification, commercialisation of agriculture, and change from primary to secondary and tertiary occupations. Occupation-wise, people in India may be divided in three groups: those engaged in primary occupations (i.e., agriculture, mining and quarrying), in secondary occupations (i.e., trade, commerce, manufacturing and transport), and in tertiary occupation (i.e., service). Age-wise, people belonging to 15-59 years age group are said to be belonging to 'working' age group. About 38 per cent people in India belong to 0-14 years age group, 55 per cent to 15-59 years age group, and 7 per cent are 60+ years. Of the total people belonging to the 'working' age group (about 46 crore), 62.7 per cent are engaged in primary, 14.9 per cent in secondary and 22.4 per cent in tertiary occupations (*Manpower Profile, In-*

dia, 1998:229). Of the total rural population in 1991 (i.e., about 62.8 crore), 79 per cent are engaged in primary, 10.3 per cent in secondary and 13.6 per cent in tertiary occupations (*Ibid*: 236). Of the total urban people (i.e., about 21.7 crore), 14.2 per cent are engaged in primary, 32.3 per cent in secondary and 54.5 per cent in tertiary occupations (*Ibid*: 231). Broadly, about 44 per cent of rural and 34 per cent of urban people are in the workforce. While the male workforce participation rates are only slightly lower in the urban areas than in the rural areas, those for female population are around 32 per cent in the rural areas but only 15 per cent in the urban areas (*Ibid*: 190). During 1951-91, sectoral distribution of employment showed a decline by 8 per cent in the primary sector, the gain being equally shared by the secondary and tertiary sectors. The diversification has been larger in the case of males in the rural areas and in the case of females in the urban areas.

Occupational diversification affects institutions like family, caste, kinship, etc. Bailey (1957) has maintained that the joint family cannot survive divergent interests and disparate income among its members. Epstein, however, does not agree with this view. He contends that conversion from a subsistence to a cash economy rather than the diversification of the economy is responsible for the breakup of the joint family system. M.S.A. Rao (1968) held that joint household organisation is not incompatible with cash incomes and diverse occupations. T.N. Madan (1968) has held that urbanisation and industrialisation do not necessarily lead to the disintegration of the joint family. But M.S. Gore does accept their effect on the joint family. Their effect on caste and kinship has also been accepted by many sociologists like Narmadeshwar Prasad, etc. S.C. Dube has referred to the effect of education on occupational diversification and development of society. Oscar Lewis has offered an analytical account of the development scene in India. He has posed choice between village-centred development and town-centred development, making a plea for a serious examination of the possibilities of the latter. Gunnar Myrdal's *Asian Drama* (1968) describes poverty in South Asia through an *institutional* approach to the problem of economic development and discusses occupational diversification and economy.

Further Readings

Desai, A.R., *Rural Sociology in India*, Vora and Co., Bombay, 1959.

Dube, S.C., "Sociology of Economic Development" in (ICSSR Journal) *Survey of Research in Sociology and Social Anthropology*, Vol. II, 1974.

Gould, Harold, "A Jajmani System of North India: Its Structure, Magnitude and Meaning" in *The Hindu Caste System*, Chanakya Publications, New Delhi, 1987.

Joshi, P.C., "Economic Development and the Indian Elite", *Link*, January 26, 1968.

Myrdal, Gunnar, *Asian Drama*, The Penguin Press, Harmondsworth, 1968.

More, Wilbert, "Social Aspects of Economic Development" in Robert Faris (ed.), *Handbook of Modern Sociology*, Prentice Hall, New Jersey.

Novack, David, "Sociological Approach in Economic Development" in *Development and Society: The Dynamics in Economic Change*, Prentice Hall, New Jersey, 1964.

Pocock, David, "Notes on Jajmani Relationships", *Contributions to Indian Sociology*, No. VI, December, 1962.

Shome, Parthasarthi and Hiranya, Mukhopadhyay, "Economic Liberalisation of the 1990s", *Economic and Political Weekly*, July 18-24, 1998.

6 Political System

POLITICAL SYSTEM: CONCEPT AND TYPES

A 'system' is an integrated whole of various parts. A 'social system' is a set of integrated functioning units, each unit functioning in terms of role assigned to it. A 'political system' is collectivity of political institutions (e.g., government), associations (e.g., political parties) and organisations performing roles based on set norms and goals (like, maintaining internal order, regulating foreign relations, and providing security from external forces). It is also described as 'a collectivity of political institutions and associations which administer the society through power, compelling conformity to the existing system of authority and which works on the basis of some principles and procedures'. Almond and Coleman (1959) have defined it as "a system which performs political functions in a society". Max Weber has explained it as "organisation that successfully claims the monopoly of the legitimate use of physical force within a given territory, i.e., state". Eisenstadt has defined it as "the organisation of a territorial society having the legitimate monopoly over the authorised use and regulation of force in the society".

The political system is characterised by four elements: (1) use of legitimate force, (2) comprehensiveness, (3) interdependency, and (4) existence of boundaries. David Easton (1953) has referred to its three components: (1) It allocates values by means of policies. (2) Its allocations are authoritative. (3) Its authoritative allocations are binding on the society as a whole. Almond and Coleman (1959) have given four common properties of political systems: (1) All political systems have political structures (i.e., patterned social relations, norms, and rights and obligations). (2) Some functions are performed in all political systems, though with different frequencies and different styles. (3) All political systems are multifunctional [e.g., evaluating (government) policies/roles, creating awareness among people, controlling people/groups/systems]. (4) All political systems are *mixed* systems in the cultural sense (i.e., there is no 'all modern' culture or 'all primitive' culture.

Talking of functions of political system, Almond and Coleman have described three functions: (1) To maintain integration of society by determining norms, making them universally applicable, implementing them, and imparting punishment for violating them; (2) To adapt and change elements of social, economic and religious systems necessary for achieving collective (political) goals; (3) To protect the integrity of the political system from outside threats. Almond and Coleman have explained these functions in an other way also. They classify them as output functions and input functions. The 'output' functions are: rule-making, rule application and rule adjudication. The 'input' functions are: political socialisation, interest articulation, interest aggregation, and political communication. Eisentadt has described the political activities of a political system as: legislative (i.e., formulating general rules for maintaining or changing the existing order in the society), decision making (i.e., determining society's primary goals), and administrative (i.e., dealing with the execution of basic rules in different social spheres and providing various services to various groups in the society).

The political systems have been mainly classified by Shills as: (i) *Democratic* system, i.e., rule by the consent of the governed through elected representatives of the citizens. Although democracy is based on majority rule, the protection of minority rights has always been regarded as an essential aspect of the democratic system. Also important in the political democracy are equality before the law, freedom of speech, press and assembly, and protection from arbitrary arrest. (ii) *Totalitarian* system, i.e., a system in which the state controls and regulates all phases of life considered essential for perpetuating its power and for carrying out programmes arbitrarily. Centralised authority is stressed over the autonomy of individuals or subgroups within the society. In practice, the state is represented by a politically powerful ruling class or elite that dominates all other interest groups. (iii) *Oligarchic* system, i.e., a system in which a small group rules and holds supreme power over a larger society.

Eisentadt has classified the political systems as pluralistic, authoritarian, totalitarian and patrimonial. The *pluralistic* systems/regimes are characterised by strong centre, large scope of political freedom, and are capable of absorption of sustained growth. The *patrimonial* regimes have emerged after World War II. It is a 'personal rulership' in which the followers of the ruler do not have belief in his personal qualities but in material rewards and incentives he offers.

DEMOCRATIC POLITICAL SYSTEM AND STRUCTURE IN TRADITIONAL AND MODERN INDIAN SOCIETY

Democracy in its broader sense denotes not only a political concept but also way of life in the society in which each individual is believed to be entitled to equality as regards his participating freely in the structures and institutions of the society is concerned. In a narrower sense, democracy denotes the opportunity of the members of the society to participate freely in decisions in all realms of life which affect their lives individually and collectively. In its most restricted sense, the term (democracy) denotes the opportunity of the citizens of a state to participate freely in *political* decisions. Democracy, thus, seeks to set up an *equalitarian* society.

There are different kinds of democracy—political, social, economic and moral. *Political* democracy is delimited to adult franchise and elections for the choice of political leadership. *Social* democracy aims at creating a classless and casteless society and breaking down the social stratifications and prejudices. *Economic* democracy lays emphasis on a welfare state and revolts against concentration of wealth and economic disparities. *Moral* democracy is directed towards orientation of the popular attitude and thinking with the concepts of right and wrong conduct. The philosophy underlying democracy is fellow-feeling, brotherhood and good conduct.

Democracy in Ancient India

The *Rig Veda* is so committed to democratic principles and ideals that it has made democracy a deity and aptly called it '*Samjnana*'. The term *Samjnana* means the collective consciousness of the people, the national mind to which the individual mind is to pay its homage as the source from which it derives its potency. The hymn addressed to *Samjnana* (in *Rig Veda*) called upon the people to gather in their assembly (*Samgachchaddhvam*) and speak there in one voice (*Samvadaddhvam*), in a union of minds (*Sammanah*), of hearts (*Samachittam*), of policy (*Samanmantrah*), and of hopes and aspirations (*akuti*). Thus, democracy was taken to depend upon the 'inner unity' of its citizens and their emotional integration. The democratic principle was at work in different spheres of the public life—political, social and cultural. The democratic tradition of the Vedic era governed the entire growth of Indian polity through the ages. Even where there was monarchy, it was a limited or constitutional monarchy, so that the pattern of monarchy remained fundamentally democratic. It was based on decentralisation and local autonomy. The people formed the following appropriate associations and groups to excercise their rights in self-government in an ascending order: *kula* (clan), *jati* (caste), *sreni* (guild), *puga* or *pura* (village community) and *janapada* (state). Each group had its own rules and regulations and was working for democracy at its respective stratum of self-government. Some of the *janapadas* in ancient India were republican in form and some had monarchical organisation. But each of them often had an assembly (*samiti*)—the precursor of the modern parliament—which was attended by the high and the low together with a view to taking decisions about the affairs of the state. R.K. Mukherjee (1961:42) has remarked: "Side by side with the monarchy, there also developed the regular republican type of polity of which glimpses are given in different literary texts—Brahmanical, Buddhist and Jain." The *Mahabharata* has also mentioned some republics called *Samghatagana*. Five Republican Unions were called: *Andhakas*, *Vrishnis*, *Yadavas*, *Kukuras* and *Bhojas* which constituted a *Sangha* or Union, with *Sangha Mukhya* as Union President. Similarly, in the *Mahabharata*, there is a reference to *Ganas* (republics) being governed by their councils of leaders called *Gana-Mukhyas*. All these *Ganas* (republics) had an extremely democratic constitution. Each had its own assembly (*parishad*).

The Jain and the Buddhist texts have also referred to many erstwhile republics and some republican confederations like *Vajji* (*Vriji*) consisting of nine *Mallakis*, nine *Lichhavis* and eighteen *Gana Rajyas* of Kashi-Koshal and other states. It has been mentioned that the death of Mahavira was condoled with a funeral illumination arranged by 36 republics of this Vriji Confederation. The *Lichhhavis* were well-known republics of those times and were governed by the council of 7,707 Rajas, who were constitutional monarchs. The Sakha republic was famous for giving the Buddah to the world. Nearly 80,000 households constituted the 'republic' which had a parliament (*parishad*) of 500 members with a President or *Raja*. Some of the famous republics of the Buddhist era were: Vaisali, Pava, Mithila and so on. While the assembly served as a legislative body, there were executive and judicial functionaries of various sorts to implement their decisions. A single chief was elected as office-holder presiding over the assembly/state. He bore the title of Raja.

It is said that in ancient India, the people led a democratic way of living although political democracy did not exist in its full form. Incidentally, monarchy was also popular.

After the sixth century, democratic organisations started declining. Kings and monarchs often remained engaged in wars. Since there was no strong monarch to uphold the solidarity and unity of the country, consequently a large number of principalities sprang up throughout the country. From the eighth century onwards, the Mohammedans launched their invasions till they established their rule in the twelfth century. The Muslim rulers were autocratic.

The British rule also was against democracy. It was the Government of India Act, 1935 that laid the foundation stone of democratic rule in India. The Congress remained in power only for two years—from 1935 to 1937. From 1940 to 1945, the British government was preoccupied with the World War II. The efforts for giving political freedom to India started from 1946 till it became free in August 1947. The Constitution of free India accepted democracy as the basis of ruling the country.

Democracy in Modern India

Democracy in modern India is based on certain principles: (1) that every individual has his potentialities, worth, and dignity; (2) that every one has the capacity to learn and manage his life with others; (3) that an individual must abide by the decisions of the majority; (4) that every individual should have a part in making decisions; (5) that the control and direction of democratic action lies in the situation and not outside it; (6) that the process of living is interactive and that all individuals work towards commonly recognised ends; and (7) that democracy rests on individual opportunity as well as individual responsibility.

After independence, India decided to have democratic political system. This system is characterised by three elements: one, there is a high degree of autonomy; *two*, economic agents and religious organisations are free from political interference; and *three*, competition between various orders does not endanger integration but helps it. Some people maintain that Indira Gandhi's regime of 16 years—between January 1966 and October 1984—(minus three years of Morarji Desai and Charan Singh regimes) was not democratic but an 'authoritarian' regime which had three characteristics: (1) It required obedience to the authority of the main power-holder(s). (2) It suppressed organised opposition and public criticism (by declaring Emergency for two years). (3) It had greater hold on the autonomous organisations.

Democracy and Coalition Governments

In India, the formation of coalition governments at the centre started with Morarji Desai's regime, though at the state level, these had started functioning from 1967. At the centre, coalition ministeries have been formed seven times between 1977 and April 1999. The first coalition ministry of Morarji Desai lasted for 857 days (between March 1977 and June 1979), of Charan Singh for 171 days (between July 1979 and January 1980), of V.P. Singh for 344 days (between December 1989 and November 1990), of Chandra Shekhar for 224 days (between November 1990 and June 1991), of A.B.Vajpayee for 13 days in May 1996, of Deve Gowda for 325 days (between June 1996 and April 1997), of I.K. Gujral for 333 days (between April 1997 and March 1998), and of A.B. Vajpayee for 394 days (between March 1998 and April 1999). Thus, no coalition ministry could complete the whole term of five years. The two National Front ministries formed at the centre between 1996 and 1998, with the support of 13 parties under the prime-ministerships of H.D. Deve Gowda and I.K. Gujral had to face serious problems from the Congress Party which was supporting them from outside. When the Congress withdrew the support to the United Front government, general elections were held in February 1998 and the BJP formed a ministry with the support of 18 regional parties. It was defeated in parliament by one vote on April 17, 1999.

The majority party in the coalition government has to placate difficult allies, even if they have three or four members with them. The BJP-led government after coming into power had to face the blackmailing of some of its allies. At least four regional parties (from Tamil Nadu, West Bengal, Punjab, and Haryana) kept threatening the government about withdrawing support at the drop of a hat. The leader of the regional party from Tamil Nadu in the coalition ministry had no fewer than four dozen cases pending against her in the courts. Since she had a good number of members in her party in the parliament, she encashed her party support for getting many concessions by intermittently holding the government to ransom. Ultimately, she withdrew the support from the government in April 1999, which led to the loss of confidence motion in the Lok Sabha by a single vote on April 17, 1999. The regional party from West Bengal also extracted its pound of flesh for extending support to the government by insisting on a Bengal package and having a particular portfolio in the Union Ministry. The demands of the other regional parties too were ridiculous and the central government had to succumb to their pressure tactics many a time.

How can the majority party in a coalition ministry keep the government stable under threats from its allied partners? How can it plan development of the country and discuss trade, commerce and other relations with the developed countries? Does the withdrawal threat of a coalition partner on even a minor issue not make the government jittery? Then, each political party has the problem of intra-conflicts too. It is not easy to keep all the disgruntled party members happy. The key trouble-makers within the party instigate some of the allies to raise issues which invariably embarrasses the government.

Politics in India may not yet be the last resort of the dishonest and the corrupt, yet it cannot anymore boast of the qualities people associate with public service. Today, it is nothing more than a means to gain and excercise power. The politicians at the time of Independence had raised politics to a high level of moral idealism, setting aside personal and sectarian interests in favour of the common good. They sought power for the people, for the nation, and not for the individual. Today, personal power and personal ambition have become the keywords in political vocabulary of the politicians. The public and the national interests have been replaced by personal and sectarian interests. This has disastrous consequences for the actual conduct of the polity. The parties function not on the basis of ideological basis and programmatic commitments but on regional, communal and caste basis. In recent times, many leaders have left behind their ideological baggage in favour of what they describe as political pragmatism, but in reality these people are political opportunists in pursuit of power. The political maneuveres of some political parties which have made opportunism a virtue, are glaring examples of politics without any commitment to idealism or ideology. The opportunism motivated by personal ambition for power, has made political ideology a matter of convenience rather than of conviction. It reflects a serious pathology of our political life and total lack of idealism, which adversely affects the functioning of coalition governments.

The fourth government being ousted from power in a span of three years since 1996 indicates that coalition governments are not good for the country—economically and politically. In economic terms, about Rs. 900 crore were spent on elections in 1998; now the most conservative estimate is that Rs. 1,000 crore were spent on September 1999 mid-term polls. Besides, frequent elections retard economic growth, increase fiscal deficit, adversely affect business confidence, plummet stocks, and raise the prices of commodities used by the common people. Political uncertainty hampers development and affects foreign relations. Experiments in the last three years in our country have also proved wrong the assumption that coalition ministries are more logical for federal polity. The spectre is of governmental instability, fragmented national politics, and policies on vital issues suffering from interruptions. Out of 12 Lok Sabhas constituted between April 1952 and April 1999, seven could complete their 5-year term (1st, 2nd, 3rd, 5th, 7th, 8th and 10th), the fourth Lok Sabha (constituted in March 1967) could complete 3 years 9 months, sixth (constituted in March 1977) could complete 2 years 6 months, ninth (constituted in December 1989) could complete 1 year 3 months, eleventh (constituted in May 1996) could complete 1 year 7 months, and twelfth (constituted in March 1998) could complete 1 year 1 month. How long the 13th Lok Sabha constituted in October 1999 lasts is yet to be seen.

Some alternatives are suggested for the success of the coalition governments which now seem inevitable for India:

1. Only national parties should be permitted to contest elections for parliament and regional parties should not be given this opportunity. At present, there are six national parties and 48 state recognised parties in our country. The regional parties may best articulate the regional aspirations but at national level, regional aspirations harald disintegration of the country. Allowing only national parties in parliament elections will reduce, if not wipe out, political opportunists. Some parties (like Bahujan Samaj Party) openly say that they want political instability in the country. How can such parties, having no programme of national development, be ever entrusted with the task of ruling at the centre or even in a state? Only that political party may be recognised as a national party which contests elections at least in half of the total states in the country and secures at least 5 per cent votes. At present, the Election Commission declares a party a national party which has achieved the status of state party in at least four states. However, if several regional parties form a National Front and submit a common national programme, such Front may be permitted to contest the parliamentary elections.
2. Second option could be that a no-confidence motion mover against the ruling government should name the successor to the Prime Minister in the motion so that an alternative is already there.
3. Third option in case of a fractured mandate could be directing the House to elect its leader or the Prime Minister.

This indirectly is a suggestion for a National Government. But is National Government practical? My contention is that it is unrealistic. Parliamentary democracy has to function through political parties. After Nehru's death, or say after 1971 general elections, the Congress Party in particular and our political system in general got fragmented and localism and sectional politics came to dominate over the larger issues of national concern. It is doubtful whether the National Government can rectify this malady. I believe, we can focus on national rather than the regional issues by strengthening our political parties. They should make themselves more representative, responsive and accountable. Talking of single individuals as candidates for prime-ministership is to ignore the crucial role which political parties play in sustaining and enriching the entire process of politics. Even an outstanding individual will remain an individual without a good organisation. Participation of large number of people in politics through the political parties is an important ingredient for a successful democracy. Of course, there are the usual criticisms against the political parties. Some of these are: they promote corruption and partisanship, work on the basis of vested interests, are factional and divisive, and often lead to political instability. Assuming that these criticisms are true, it cannot be denied that political parties do perform some important political functions, including one of controlling the policies and programmes of the party in power. The leader of the national party, howsoever charismatic he may be, cannot bridge the wide gap between the ruler and the ruled and redress the genuine grievances of the masses. Only the political parties focusing on national interests can ensure political stability.

Some people suggest that parliamentary democracy is inappropriate for India and it should be replaced by the Presidential form of government. My contention is that it will be wrong to make short-term assessments, particularly on the basis of what has happened in the last three years. The important thing to be noted is that at no point of time did any political party question the ideological underpinnings of the Indian Constitution or the relevance of the institutions of parliamentary democracy. All the eight coalition governments upheld the sanctity of the institutions of governance enshrined in our Constitution. Instead of having highly centralised presidential form of government or government of a one or two-parties, parliamentary democracy is very relevant for our country. As already stated, the three vital spheres of national concern are: foreign relations, defence policy, and economic policy. The last five decades have shown that in spite of some short-period governments and coalition governments, our policies have been characterised by continuity as well as flexibility. Continuity has sustained the credibility of India's position in the international community. Flexibility is necessary to be responsive to internal requirements. Even on nuclear weaponisation and missile development, there has existed (more or less) a national consensus. Only because of some political instability created by some opportunist politicians in coalition governments, how can we hold that parliamentary democracy be discarded? The people of India have now become mature enough to throw out such persons (and also the political parties) from power who, contest elections for their vested interests, blackmail the coalition ministries they join, and affect the arithmetic of the Lok Sabha.

POLITICAL ELITE: RECRUITMENT, ORIENTATIONS AND ROLE IN SOCIAL CHANGE

Concept of Political Elite

Who are the elite? Elite are the most influential and prestigious stratum in a society. The 'elite' are those persons who are recognised as outstanding leaders in a given field. Thus, there are political, religious, scientific, business, and artistic elite. Pareto, Mosca, Wright Mills, Lasswell, Mannheim, Bottomore, etc., have given different definitions. Parry Geriant (1969) has defined elite as "small minorities who play an exceptionally influential part in the affairs of society in specific fields". Bank (1966) has described elite as "decision-makers whose power is not subject to control by any other body in the society". Nadel (1956) maintains that elite are "those who have an influence over the fate of the society because of their superiority". The members of an elite group have important influence in shaping the values and attitudes held by their segment of society. Wright Mills (1956) has described them as "those who make decisions having major consequences, who are able to realise their will even if others resist, and who have---the most of what there is to have-money, power and prestige".

I describe elite as "a *dominant group* which possesses distinctiveness and exclusiveness" (in Sachchidananda and Lal, 1980:124). *Secondly*, the term does not apply to any one person but refers to a plurality, a collectivity of persons, however small it may be. *Thirdly*, this identifiable collectivity has certain attributes and skills which give it not only a certain superiority but also power of decision-making and influencing others. *Lastly*, elite is a relative term. A group is identified as an elite group in a particular field in which it is 'power excerciser' or 'influential' or commands 'excellence', but in other groups, these elite may be considered as 'ordinary' members.

On this basis, the term 'political elite' may be defined as "a group of high stratum decision-makers in political culture or concrete political structure which monopolises political power, influences major political policies and occupies all important posts of political command". If we were to operationalise this term, we could say, political elite include those: (a) who are elected/nominated to central and state legislatures, (b) who occupy important positions in national or state-level political parties, (c) individuals who do not hold any formal positions either in the government or in political parties but are still considered as persons of great political prestige and power because they control power-excercisers (e.g., Gandhi, Jaya Prakash Narayan).

Wright Mills (1956) has used the term 'power elite' for the political elite who monopolise power and rule the country. Pareto (1935) has called them 'governing elite', Marx (see, Bottomore, 1964), referred to them as 'ruling class', Riesman as 'veto group', and Floyd Hunter as 'top leaders'. I have used the term 'oligarchic elite' for them in my own empirical work on political elite in Bihar. I describe the 'oligarchic elite' as those who control the functional groupings within the structure with the minimum consultation of the 'subjacent elite'.

Recruitment and Changing Character of Elite in Post-Independence India

With the above mentioned definition of political elite, we will now examine the recruitment and change in the nature of the elite operating in the political field in India after independence. This change can be analysed by classyfying the political elite in five phases:

(i) Immediately after independence phase (i.e., 1947 to April 1952), in which there was no longer any struggle between the people and the government and in which though the interests of the people and the power elite were one and indivisible (i.e., rebuilding the society), the latter were more preoccupied with the problems of restoration of law and order after partition, refugee resettlement, maintenance of communal peace, and the controversy over the redistribution of territories between various states.

(ii) Consolidation phase (i.e., April 1952 to March 1962 or MPs, MLAs and party office-holders elected in April 1952 and April 1957 elections), in which the political elite worked for the economic uplift and social development through the Five-Year Plans.

(iii) Chaotic phase (i.e., April 1962 to March 1971 or individuals elected in April 1962 and March 1967 elections), in which non-congress and coalition governments came into power in several states affecting the inter-state and state-centre relations.

(iv) Authoritarian phase (i.e., March 1971 to November 1989 or individuals elected in March 1971, March 1977, January 1980, December 1984, and November 1989 elections), in which one person was catapulted to the position of supreme national leadership, first Indira

Gandhi for 16 years (excluding period from March 1977 to January 1980) and then Rajiv Gandhi for five years and the power-holders came to believe in the personality cult, and in which all plans for change and development of society were centralised.

(v) Multiple-party phase (i.e., December 1989 till April 1999) in which except in Narasimha Rao's period of 5 years, in the remaining period, a number of political parties joined hands to rule the country on a common-programme basis (V.P. Singh ministry for 11 months—December 1989 to November 1990), Chandra Shekhar ministry for about eight months—November 1990 to June 1991), Atal Bihari Vajpayee ministry for 13 days—from May 1996 to May 1996), P.V. Narasimha Rao ministry for five years (June 1991 to 1996), United Front governments of Deve Gowda (June 1996 to April 1997) for 11 months and I.K. Gujral (April 1997 to March 1998) for one year and BJP-led government of A.B.Vajpayee (March 1998 to April 1999).

Who were the elite in the first phase? These elite were those who had a stable economic background (though politics was not their profession for earning their livelihood), were highly educated, mostly belonged to the upper castes, and were committed to societal interests. Their socio-political ideology was based on nationalism, liberalism and religio-cultural reforms. This first generation of power-wielders in free India had earned their reputation for courage, vision and action, and acquired their charisma *before* they stepped into office as inheritors of political power and earned it more *through* functioning in office. The elite in the second (consolidation) phase, particularly those elected in the 1952 elections, some of whom had only a part-time interest in politics. They wanted rewards in the form of a political office for participating in the national struggle for independence. These elite caused a certain amount of disequilibrium in the beginning in their party structures but their pressures for active participation in politics were pitched in such a low key that they were soon integrated in their party systems.

Then came the 1957 elections when the long established dominance of the so-called political sufferers was broken and political power was placed in the hands of a new breed of elite who were either petty landholders or traders, businessmen, professional persons, small industrialists or social workers. These elite were not as highly politicised as their older counterparts. They thought that since they could trust the integrity of old professional politicians, they need not concern themselves quite so directly with politics. Over the years, yet newer elite further down the social scale appeared in the 1962 elections representing the intermediate and lower castes, middle-class professions, small farmers, industrial workers, or even obscure religious and social sects, to name a few, seeking entry into the political decision-making processes. Though these elite came to seek a greater role in policy formulation, the older elite still retained their influence. There was thus toleration on the part of the new and accommodation on the part of the old elite. Both old and new elite revised their values to fit situations and establish new relationships. This type of interaction between the old and the new elite implies a dilution of the pure force theory group of elite or that the position of the old elite depended upon some sort of bargain. We can thus say that change in the elite structure up to 1967 was slow and 'peaceful', not involving any 'conflict' in Marxian terminology.

In the 1967, 1971, 1977, 1980, 1984, 1989, 1991, 1996 and 1998 elections,, emerged the elite amongst whom many were found to have politics as their major source of livelihood. They believed more in using the ties of kinship, caste and language to smoothen the way through the corridors of power. They were blind to the practicalities of the plans and believed in seeking cooperation of the masses by coining attractive slogans and speaking half-truths. They posed as democrats; even their slogans were democratic but their actions belied their utterances. Democracy as a way of life was foreign to their nature and nurture.

Ideologically, there were four types of elite functioning in 1967-1971, 1971-1989, and 1989-1999 phases: *traditionalists, rationalists, moderates* and *synthetics*. The second and the third types had two sub-variations: (a) those who reflected secular but vested national ideology, and (b) those who professed a neo-secular and vested parochial ideology. Since these elite with different ideologies functioned within the party, the variation in their ideologies led to segmentation of the party which affected the functioning of both the party and its elite at various levels. The new political elite who were brought into power first in December 1989 elections and then in May 1996 and March 1998 elections got public votes not because of their rationalist liberal ideologies or because their radicalism was greatly appreciated but because people wanted to throw out the government of the day dominated by one political party for about four decades and also the weak political United Front government which was based on factions. Even the BJP-led government of A.B.Vajpayee which came in power in March 1998 proved unstable because of constant threats from 3 or 4 of its constituent parties.

Using this description for comparing the 'new' elite with the 'old' elite and for identifying the present structure of political elite, we could say, the 'intellectual committed politicos' of first phase were replaced by 'mediocre, uncommitted, partisan' elite in the following phases. The last one decade political elite are characterised not only by a plurality of structural background but ideologically also they manifest varied shades. Their political affiliations are guided more by their particularistic loyalty rather than by their ideology commitment. The old elite wielded power independently, i.e., in their own right as intellectuals, whereas the present-day elite are incapable of exercising independent political power. Barring a few activist elite, most of the present elite do not believe in militating against the status quo. As such, the task of social engineering becomes far more difficult for those few activist revolutionary elite who are really committed to modernisation and believe in economic radicalism, political democratisation and social growth.

Referring to changing eliteship in India, Yogendra Singh has averred: "Among the political elite, there existed a high degree of cultural and status homogeneity before Independence. All of them came from upper castes and had an urban, middle-class background of English education. The top group was exposed to foreign culture and was educated there; hence their self-image in terms of expected roles was also that of a generalist rather than a specialist. Following independence, this pattern of elite composition has considerably changed."

Referring to trends of change in the present political leadership, Yogendra Singh holds (1973:137): (i) there is increasing influence of rural-based political leaders; (ii) there is slight decrease in the influence of leaders drawn from various professions; (iii) there is significant increase in the number of persons belonging to the middle class; (iv) there is greater articulation of regional and interest-oriented goals in political cultural ideologies; and (v) there is slight breakdown in the exclusiveness of upper castes to the elite position. And what was stated by Yogendra Singh 25 years ago is true even today.

Typology of Political Elite

We can compare the old and the present elite by developing a typology of elite by referring to their values and ideologies and their differential orientation to the society as a whole, i.e., their 'public' or 'collective' interest and their 'private' or 'individual' interest, considering public interest, as a necessary condition for desire for modernisation. Indicating public interest by 'P' and self interest by 'S', we get four types of elite: (i) P-, S- (ii) P-, S+ (iii) P+,S- and (iv) P+,S+. We can term these four types as *indifferent, manipulative, progressive*, and *rationalist* elite respectively. In this classification, though both the progressive and the rationalist elite work for public interest, the former believe that the course of progress moves on automatically regardless of the interference of men and is not subject to human control while the latter believe that progress rests upon conscious control. Applying this classification, we could say, the present elite are more indifferent (P-,S-) and manipulative (P- ,S+) in comparison to the progressive (P+,S-) and rationalist (P+,S+) elite of the past. We could also maintain that the present elite are 'irrational specifics' in comparison to 'rational-universalists' of the past.

Circulation of Political Elite

The recruitment and the changing character of the elite in India in different phases (after political independence) can also be discussed in terms of Pareto's theory of circulation of elite. If the theory of 'circulation of elite' refers to the process of movement in which individuals *circulate* between the elite and the non-elite, I would submit, on the basis of my own study of political elite, that this theory does not hold good in the context of Indian society. In India, the 'governing' elite at a higher political culture base (say national level) are recruited not from the 'non-governing' elite at the *same* level but from the governing elite functioning as a *lower* political cultural base (say state, district or block levels). These elite of lower political base are found holding important posts in state legislatures or state political parties, etc., before becoming office-holders at the higher political base. Once these elite rise from state or district level, they never go back to the old level but continue to function at the higher political level as long as they remain active in politics. This, however, does not mean that they cease to take interest in politics at the level from which they have moved up in the hierarchy. This means, there is no *circulation* but only an *upward movement* of the elite. However, if Pareto's theory refers to a process in which one member of the elite group is replaced by another within the group of governing elite, we may concede that his theory does explain the political phenomenon of 'movement of the elite' in the context of our society also. Bottomore maintains that both conceptions are to be found in Pareto's work, although the former predominates.

My study (of political elite) revealed two types of movements (not circulations): (i) movement from lower to higher strata of governing elite both functioning at macro-level, and (ii) movement from sub-category functioning at micro-structural level to sub-category functioning at macro-structural level. In the former, I found circulation between 'oligarchic' (dominant) and 'subjacent' (dominated) elite and between 'radical' activists and 'passive' activists. Activists functioning at micro-level ultimately joined the ranks of activists at the macro-level with the result that some of the activists already functioning at this level were deprived of their monopoly of power. This elite mobility may be explained in terms of: (i) the rise of new political interests; and (ii) the rise of new elite with more manipulating qualities. To us, therefore, both individual and structural factors are important in the social ascent or social descent of the elite. Schumpeter also believed that both the individual qualities and the social factors are important in the circulation of elite.

The Marxian approach, which is basically non-elitist, views the relations between the elite (privileged class which commands power and wealth) and the non-elite (classes which do not possess either of these) as based on conflict, in which effort is made to overthrow the 'power elite' to occupy its position. My study revealed that the process of overthrowing the elite in power and succeeding them is not *always* based on conflict, but that it involves manipulation, toleration, accommodation, compromise and bargain too. It could, therefore, be maintained that we can neither draw from Pareto's theory of 'circulation of elite', nor from Karl Marx's theory of 'class struggle' to understand the changing character of political elite in India. We have to use different approach for analysing the recruitment and the changing structure of elite in India.

Political Elite, Social Change and Modernisation

Let us now turn our attention to the role of political elite in the modernisation of society. For analysing this problem, we can divide the elite into two groups (following David Apter's model): (i) 'development system' elite, and (ii) 'maintenance system' elite. The former seek to reconstruct society by attempting to mobilise and tap available resources and political energies. Their attack on economic backwardness, in order to achieve material advancement, is through change in institutions and attitudes. The political party or governmental apparatus serves for them as the central instrument for modernisation. They create new institutions or change old institutions to remove obstacles to economic and social growth. We could say, 'development system' elite are characterised by allegiance to economic and social progress, ideological commitment, and constant policies. The 'maintenance system' elite, by contrast, are those who give high priority to maintaining and preserving the existing political system instead of advocating economic and social change. They believe in compromise among competing political and interest groups. The elite of this system are characterised by multiple loyalties, tactical flexibility, acceptance of compromise and ideological diffuseness. Thus, power elite in the maintenance system have a much more limited scope of action, and a wider variety of constraints operates on their development policies. Borrowing

Apter's formula, we could say, 'development system' elite fight society and 'maintenance system' elite are prisoners of society.

The present political elite in India who have more vested interests to achieve, belong more to 'maintenance system' than to 'development system' with the result that they have failed to reconstruct the nation's social and economic framework or to develop and implement radical economic policies and social programmes. In the Leninist variant of Marxism, they have failed to convert the masses from atomistically separated inchoate individuals into conscious and disciplined agents of total social change.

We in this country can understand this better if we could know first the goals we had set for ourselves in economic, social and political fields after independence and then find out the extent to which our political elite have attempted to achieve these goals and ideals. Our goals in the economic field are: advanced technology, abundant economic production, free trade by curbing industrial monopoly and encouraging competitiveness, freedom of occupation, distributive justice, and ending poverty and destitution; in the political field, our goals are: democracy, decentralisation of power, free public opinion and free elections; in the social field our goals are: equality, mobility, secularism, individualism, a break with traditional customs and rituals, and achieving social status through individual potentialities rather than through birth.

But have we achieved these goals? It cannot be asserted that the political elite alone determine the nature and process of development and modernisation in any society. There are many factors like the structural character of various institutions in society, the competence of the mass of the population, political stability, cultural heritage, and the political pattern, etc., which affect the prosperity of a nation or its development. Yet, the political elite, being the planners and decision-makers, play a very significant role in the country's development. Nobody would deny that we have made progress in different fields. It may even be conceded that much of our development is due to the efforts of the 'activist' elite we had in the last few decades. But this also is a fact that if our country has as yet reached only its half-way point, it is because our political elite have proved to be a barrier in the process of modernisation of our society in several ways. Their discriminatory attitude, blind conformity to tradition, indifference to development, their vested interests, political rivalries, factionalism and corruption have adversely affected the techno-social changes taking place in our society.

Can an average Indian be a beneficiary of programmes and policies which are motivated by monopoly-dominated and by powerful pressure groups? Can a country build a robust viable industry and agriculture on a per capita consumer expenditure of a few rupees a day? Can a society be modernised by the elite whose 'crash' programmes are to appoint committees and commissions for suggesting, initiating and implementing efficient means and mechanisms for solving various socio-economic problems of the society? Words and promises can never raise the standards of living of an impoverished people. The elite have to organise specific campaigns with specific objectives. It should not be a snowballing of public opinion. Campaigns should not be based on advertising gimmicks. The elite are not selling any commodity; they are trying to sell people pipe dreams about their whole life. This requires a different kind of insight.

Barriers for Political Elite

There are some oligarchic activist elite who do possess this insight and who are committed to development, but they too have not been able to do much in our country because of several problems they face in their functioning. The main problems they face are: (i) the problem of split ideologies, namely, the ideologies of passive party officialdom, of party militants, of the disinterested and uncommitted rank and file of party members and party identifiers, and the party's public ideology; (ii) the problem of confusion of cross-cutting issues and alternative preferences; and (iii) the problem of in-fighting among the elite for power-sharing. We know that the important political parties functioning at national level these days are conglomerations of groups and sub-groups with conflicting loyalties. When it becomes difficult to find a solvent to dissolve political and ideological divergencies, some members either become apolitical or start encouraging centrifugal forces in the country or in the state or quit the party and join some other party which may offer them some public office. As an illustration, a reference may be made to office-seeking legislators of whom many changed sides at least twice, some three times and a few four times. This ideological gulf between the office-seeking elite and the ideologically-oriented elite always forces the former to indulge in activities which are usually motivated by extraneous considerations. We could say that the ideologically-oriented elite occupy the political left and right while the office-seeking elite pre-empt the centre. It is these centralists who not only bring the party into disrepute with the public but also hinder the development and modernisation of the country.

Paradoxically, the upper and lower strata elite blame each other for putting the party in the doldrums and for creating barriers in the development of society. The upper-stratum elite accuse lower-stratum elite of casteism, regionalism, linguistic divisions and communalism while the lower-rung elite blame the ruling elite for parochialism, corruption and slow progress of the country. This only shows the nature of the relations that exist between upper and lower stratum elite and their mutual suspicions. Dahrendorf has also maintained that mutual suspicion and differential distribution of authority invariably becomes the determining factor of systematic social conflicts. I have termed the elite nuclei or the upper-stratum elite who monopolise the political power as 'oligarchic' elite and the lower-stratum elite who have an underlying position as the 'subjacent' elite. The concept of 'oligarchic' elite has been developed as an alternative to C. Wright Mills's concept of 'ruling class' in order to pinpoint a number of their unsatisfactory features and to demonstrate the theoretical difficulties in accepting them, though all the three concepts refer to the dominant political positions of the group involved.

The oligarchic elite and the subjacent elite do not find a common set of goals. The aims of the oligarchic elite are either so personal (capturing office) or so general (maintaining status quo) or even so radical (reserving 27% seats for OBCs without rational analysis) that they fail to motivate the subjacent elite. The subjacent elite are also unable to articulate their desire for economic improvement and social development or for getting higher offices, much less to organise themselves to obtain them. The result is that these politically ineffective elite are manipulated by the oligarchic elite, often through promises and slogans that portend economic development, socialism, social justice, end of monopoly, etc., as ends, while at the same time they (the oligarchic elite) themselves operate through largely undemocratic and monopolistic means. On the surface, the oligarchic elite are ideologically motivated, but in practice their ideology seldom remains operative. As long as the subjacent elite remain inarticulate and thus incapable of holding the oligarchic elite responsible for their suppression, both the big as well as small political cultural groups will continue to be dominated by the oligarchic elite and they will continue to deny political legitimacy to the leaders of the lower rung as well as to the new entrants.

To understand modernisation at a macrocosmic level in India, we have to assess the pattern of economic, social and political development at microcosmic level in its constituent states, and have also to examine the relations between the elite functioning at two different levels, viz., national and state levels.

If we take the relationship between degree of participation in political issues of the oligarchic elite at the state level and the level of monopoly of the oligarchic elite at the national level, and consider the national base as the *large political context* and the state base as the *smaller political context*, we may hold that the higher or the lower level of monopolistic tendencies at larger political culture base determines the relative degree of the elite's participation in politics at the smaller political cultural base. The higher the monopoly at the higher political cultural base, the lesser are the elite to participate in public welfare issues at lower political cultural base. This is because the greater monopoly of elite at the national level discourages the oligarchic elite at the state level in expressing their views freely and frankly. Where political power is concentrated more in the hands of the few oligarchic elite at the national level, the desire to participate in local socio-political issues increases dissatisfaction among the non-monopolistic non-activist elite at the state base, leading to their withdrawal of support to the activist elite in their own state. The underlying assumption here is that the active oligarchic elite at the state level are likely to be those who aspire to play a significant role not only in the state political culture but also in the larger national political culture. As such, criticism of the oligarchic elite at the national level decreases among the oligarchic political activists at the state level since they are aware of the fact that compliance with the norms of monopolists at the centre has greater relevance to the political roles they hope to play at the country level. This tendency of the activists creates discontent among the non-activists because of which they refuse to cooperate with the activist elite in the state. As an illustration, we can cite one case. What was the role of elite—both political and non-political—in the emergency period when many leaders of the country were bundled into jails, the press was muzzled, dissenters in all walks of life were harassed and the entire country was enveloped in a fog of fear and uncertainty. I would say that the elite—the politicians, the intellectuals, the bureaucrats and even the elite in the judiciary—instead of exposing the megalomaniac leaders and the monstrous coercion, corruption and unscrupulousness to the public-became victims of their own prejudice and subconsciously saw in one individual leader the protector of its narrow class interests. During 19 months, the elite cheered like a mob and abdicated its responsibility of giving sober counsel to the government and to the nation.

How is it that the decisions of the emergency passed muster with all types of political decision-makers in parliament? Are we to understand that whatever actions were taken by the government during the emergency, the slow and systematic strangulation of the constitution and democracy that took place was really with the consent of all decision-makers in power? Are we to understand that when laws were passed in Parliament in conditions so blatantly malafide, the activist political elite had no remedy? Are we to understand that emergency and the high-handed behaviour of a few monopolisers of power that followed it were perfectly justified in the eyes of *all* committed political elite? These are questions that the political elite had best ask of themselves. The point that is being made is that the activist political elite in power fail to perform their roles in a crisis of vast dimensions and delivery in the interests of the society.

I would as well maintain that even after the historic national and state elections of November 1989 and again in May 1996 and February 1998, though the new political elite got an opportunity to excercise their judgement, yet, unfortunately, they wasted this opportunity. Public expectations were that the new political elite in power would curb industrial monopoly, end destitution in a specific period, not allow price-rise beyond the capacity of the common man to pay, build up a viable public distribution system and establish institutional structure for combating corruption. But so far we have not seen the beginning of the end of a period of economic stagnation and social decline.

We can now reiterate what was said earlier:

(1) The higher level of monopolistic tendencies at a larger political culture base has resulted in a lower degree of elite participation in politics and hampered their interest in modernising the society.

(2) The few high-stratum elite who occupy dominant positions in the political structure and monopolise political power (conceptualised as 'oligarchic elite') are not at all close-knit and lack any coherence as a political force.

(3) The present elite's central concern, including those who came in power in March 1998 but lost it in April 1999, is achieving and preserving power because of which they have failed to establish a close rapport with the people.

(4) The present activist and committed political elite believe neither in conscious rejection of modernisation nor in conscious rejection of traditional order but in the regulation of content, direction and speed of modernisation as well as of certain elements of traditionalism.

To sum up, we maintain that unless the behaviour of the present political elite is motivated more by altruistic values rather than by the mundane or pragmatic considerations, the goals of modernisation will not be achieved and the struggle for social change will continue to be hampered.

POLITICAL PARTIES IN INDIA

A democratic political system cannot be run without political parties. Each political party has its own structural form, ideological orientation, leadership pattern, and operational style. Political parties are supposed to be associations of people who have like-minded ideas and ideologies in regard to the policies that a government should follow and the functions it should discharge. These ideas and programmes are embodied before each election in what is called 'party manifesto' on which the electorate is supposed to vote.

The political parties are expected to perform four main functions: (1) assess the problems facing the country and suggest alternative solutions on the basis of which the party can formulate its policy; (2) educate the electorate in regard to these problems and convince it of the wisdom of the solutions the party advocates; (3) critically evaluate the policies and programmes of other parties, particularly of the one in power and point out deficiencies and short comings in them; and (4) mobilise the people to participate in governmental decision-making.

According to Sirsikar (1964: 31-36), growth of the party system would depend upon the type of the society. He has classified societies in four groups: (1) homogeneous underdeveloped society, (2) homogeneous developed society, (3) heterogeneous underdeveloped society, and (4) heterogeneous developed society. Homogeneous society is one which has one religion, one language and one dominant race, whereas heterogeneous society is one which has plurality of religions, languages, races, castes, etc. An underdeveloped society is one which has low level of economic development, singularity of purpose, and lacks urgency of goal-attainment. Example of the first type of society is Italy, of the second type are Germany, China and Russia, of the third type is the United States and of the fourth type are India and Pakistan. The last type of society has multiple parties with different ideologies.

The political parties can be identified on the basis of six different criteria: (1) on the basis of interest, they can be classified as religious (e.g., Akali Party), cultural (e.g., Dalit, BJP) etc., while on the basis of ideology, they can be described as communist, socialist etc.; (2) on the basis of the type of membership, they can be viewed as mass-based (open to every individual) and cadre-based (open to those who believe in specific ideology); (3) on the basis of the style of operation, they can be described as open (with open forum of discussion) and latent (where decision-making is restricted to elite); (4) on the basis of the recruitment of the activists, these can be classified as elective and cooperative; (5) on the basis of the territorial and functional structuring, the two types of parties can be unitary (where power is concentrated in single source) and federal (where power is distributed; and (6) on the basis of scope of activities the parties may have limited or unlimited scope.

On the basis of level of functioning; in India we have three types of political parties: (a) those which function on national basis (e.g., Congress, CPI, CPI(M), BJP, Janata Dal, and BSP), (b) those which function in a few states (e.g., Samata Party, Samajwadi Party), and (c) those which function in one state (e.g., Shiromani Akali Dal, Telgu Desam Party, Dravida Munnetra Kazhagam (DMK), AIADMK, Tamil Maanila Congress, National Conference, Asom Gana Parishad, Manipur People's Party, Shiv Sena, Indian National Lok Dal, Rashtriya Lok Tantrik Morcha, Sikkim Sangram Parishad, Haryana Vikas Party, Sikkim Democratic Front, Kerala Congress, etc. There are some parties which have been recognised as political parties by the Election Commission but do not hold power in any state (e.g., Muslim League, Janata Party, Jharkhand Mukti Morcha, Tirnamul Congress, etc).

We may describe here the profile and policies and programmes of a few important political parties.

The *Congress Party*, known as Indian National Congress, was formed in 1885. For about 35 years (from 1885 to 1920), it functioned as a pressure group, for about 27 years (from 1920 to 1947) as national movement, and for about 40 years as the ruling party [from 1947 to 1996, with an exception of two years three months (March 1977 to June 1979) of Morarji Desai regime, six months (July 1979 to January 1980) of Charan Singh regime, 11 months (December 1989 to November 1990) of V.P.Singh regime and six and a half months (November 1990 to June 1991) of Chandrashekhar regime].

There has been a coalition of leaders of centrist, leftist and rightist ideologies in this party. Bal Gangadhar Tilak, who dominated the party up to 1920, gave it militantly nationalist fervour, while Gokhale acted as a reformer rather than a militant patriot. Bipin Chandra Pal was a radical, M.M. Malviya, Naoroji, and Ferojshah Mehta were moderates. After 1920, started the Gandhi era which laid emphasis on *Satyagraha*, non-violence, civil disobedience and non-cooperation. Subash Chandra Bose, who believed in armed struggle, left the Congress Party in 1934, while Jayaprakash Narayan, Lohia and Acharya Narendra Dev left Congress in the late 30s and in the early 1940s, and formed the Congress Socialist Party. In 1937 elections, Congress won elections in eight out of 11 provinces and got 70 per cent votes and assumed ministerial responsibilities for two years, but resigned in 1939 during the first world war. In 1942, it launched Quit India Movement and became the first ruling party in 1947. During Nehru's and Indira Gandhi's regimes of 33 years, its parliamentary wing remained more powerful than the organisational wing. It faced crisis in early and mid-1960s, lost hold in several states and split in 1969 as

Congress (I) and Congress (O). In March 1971 parliamentary elections and 1972 state elections, it got massive majority votes but lost in March 1977 elections due to the Emergency declared by Indira Gandhi in 1975 and coercive methods adopted by Sanjay Gandhi for family planning. But it again got the majority of votes and remained in power at the Centre from January 1980 to November 1989 and then from 1991 to 1996.

Its religious policy has been secular, political policy federal, and economic policy a mixed one. The main reason for its remaining in power for a long period was lack of unity in the opposition parties, while the main reasons for its losing power were internal bickerings and factions, corrupt image, leaders remaining cut off from the masses, centralised authority, austentatious living of power-holders, inability to solve social problems like, poverty, unemployment, inflation, communal riots, Kashmir and Punjab problems, centre-state relations, inefficiency in administration, licence rule, and so on.

The *Bharatiya Janata Party* (BJP) was originally the Hindu Maha Sabha which advocated Hindu nation. Vir Savarkar became its president in 1937. After Independence, realising the need for an alternative party, as the tendency in the Congress party for concentrating all power in a few hands was growing, Shyama Prasad Mookherji left Nehru cabinet on the issue of Nehru-Liaqat Pact in April 1950, (according to which Indian government was not to have any say regarding the minorities in Pakistan), and joined Hindu Maha Sabha in 1950. In 1951, the Hindu Maha Sabha came to be known as All India Jan Sangh and in 1952 as Bharatiya Jan Sangh. It contested all Lok Sabha elections and got 3 seats in 1952, 4 in 1957, 14 in 1962, 35 in 1967, and 22 in 1971. It can be said that the Jan Sangh reached its highest watermark in the 1967 general elections contested under the presidentship of Balraj Madhok, in which he had forged alliances with the Swatantra Party and the Akalis and the alliance won about 100 seats in the Lok Sabha. The Jan Sangh also emerged as the main opposition party in Haryana, Uttar Pradesh, Himachal Pradesh, Madhya Pradesh, and Bihar. In Punjab, the Jan Sangh-Akali Dal alliance ousted the Congress while in Rajasthan, the Jan Sangh and the Swatantra Party secured a majority of one. Thus, the Jan Sangh emerged as the potential nationalist democratic alternative to the Congress. Deen Dayal Upadhyaya succeeded Balraj Madhok as President of the Jan Sangh in December 1967 but he was murdered in May 1968. Vajpayee then succeeded him as President of the party. The Party (BJP) became more popular when L.K.Advani became its President and particularly after he (Advani) undertook 35-day Rath Yatra in March-April 1990. In 1951, while the Party had only a few thousand members, in 1999 it has more than 20 lakh members and units in all the states, except in Nagaland, A&N Islands, and Pondichery, though in some states the organisations are in their early stages. In 1996, the BJP won 119 seats in the Lok Sabha which enabled it to form government at the centre in May 1996 and remained in power for 13 days. In February 1998, it won 181 seats in the Lok Sabha and formed the government at the centre in March 1998 with the support of 18 small regional parties, which continued in power till April 1999. In Rajasthan, Uttar Pradesh and Gujarat also, it had its ministries.

The popularity of this party in the 13 months it was in power (March 1998 to April 1999) considerably dwindled and the BJP-led government's image was adversely affected because of the pressures of *Sangh Parivar* hardliners—Vishwa Hindu Parishad, Bajrang Dal, and RSS—which have fanatic, anti-Muslim, anti-Christian Missionaries attitudes and too rigid Hindu ideologies, with emphasis on aggressive *Hindutva*. They are also committed to issues of Ram Mandir, cow slaughter, and a uniform civil code. The result was that the party lost the confidence motion in parliament in April 1999.

The *Communist Party of India* is an old party and has leftist orientation. There were so many ideological, political and organisational conflicts within it that it split into two parties in 1961—the CPI (Marxist) and the CPI. The latter supported the ruling Congress Party and criticised the Chinese aggression of 1962, while the former adopted a pro-China line. The split was formalised in 1964. The CPI(M) formed government in West Bengal which continues to be in power for the last two decades under the chief ministership of Jyoti Basu.

Initially, the Soviet government remained neutral in India-China conflict but subsequently it went full steam against China and gave unreserved support to India. This gave confidence to that unit within the CPSU which was pro-Congress and created resentment in the other group against the CPSU. Thus, the party came to be divided in two groups of pro-ruling party and anti-ruling party, or the 'Right' Communist and the Marxist. The CPI (M) which has now become the major party (with 32 members in parliament in February 1998 elections) claims to be the continuation of the old CPI. The 'Right' Communists were given the name of CPI by the Election Commission. This (CPI) party got nine seats in parliament in February 1998 elections. The basic programme of both the Communist parties is oriented towards struggles of the working people against imperialism, feudalism, and monopoly capital. The CPI and the CPI (M) and two other Leftists groups—Forward Block and Revolutionary Socialist Party (RSP) have now separate election manifestos. Some other parties came into existence but have ceased to exist now. Such parties were Congress Socialist Party (of Acharaya Narendra Dev, Jayaprakash Narayan, Ram Manohar Lohia, Achhyut Patwardhan) which came into existence in 1934, opposing Gandhian policy of non-violence, dropped the word Congress in 1946, merged with Acharya Kriplani's Kisan Mazdoor Praja Party (KMPP) and came to be known as Praja Socialist Party (PSP) and again SSP in 1964 and Socialist Party (SP) in 1971. It ceased to exist after that. So was the case with the Swantantra Party (founded by C. Rajagopalachari in 1959). The Bhartiya Kranti Dal came into existence after the Janata Party, Jan Morcha and Lok Dal combined. The United Front consisted of the Janata Dal, Congress (S), DMK, TDP, and AGP.

Multiplicity of Parties

The main trouble with India is that there are too many political parties since the 1980s. A democracy can be run efficiently only with two parties which present the possibility of government's alternative to each other. The formation of United Front coalition government of 13 parties (by Deve Gowda in June 1996 and Gujral in April 1997) and BJP-led coalition government of 18 parties (in Vajpayee's regime) in March 1998 were found to face pressures of coalition partners contributing to instability and hinderances in progressive measures. The pressures of various parties like AIADMK, Tirnamul Congress, Akali Dal, Indian National Lok Dal (Om Prakash Chautala of Haryana) and Samta Dal (Bihar) during 13 months on Vajpayee's government and threats of withdrawing support on slight issues are well known. Why in a country like the United States, we have only two-party system is that there is no such thing as a party whip which controls the voting pattern of the legislators. There is no such thing as centralised control in the two political parties. Though there are multiplicity of political parties and coalition governments in many European countries yet these do not make government in power ineffective and unstable as in India. This is because a large number of political parties which join coalition ministry at the centre have basically parochial and vested interests. Their leaders are more interested in getting positions of ministers and ministries of their own choice which can help them in getting more money and power, rather than serving the national interests. A weak ministry with several coalition parties fails to pay attention to continuity in the pursuit of policies, both internal and external. Thus, though we are not against having number of political parties in our country and regional parties confined to one particular state, what is important is that after joining the coalition ministry at the centre, the regional parties should separate the regional and the national interests and take national interest seriously. Looking at the growth of the regional parties as a threat to national unity is illogical. Regional parties do not necessarily believe in secessionism; they only want to protect the interests of their regions. The DMK in Tamil Nadu at one stage wanted to separate from India but it soon realised that it would not be in the interests of the state and, therefore, dropped the idea of separation. A regional party is formed only when it is felt that the interests of the region are neglected and ignored by the national party in power at the centre. Focus on the regional interests by the regional parties cannot and should not be considered anti-national.

A unique feature of several political parties in India is that they trace their origin to the Indian National Congress. When the leaders of these break-away parties could not get a place of status in the Congress Party, they separated and formed a separate party. Some leaders, however, separated because of their ideology (like Acharya Narendra Dev, Ram Manohar Lohia and Jayaprakash Narayan). Some of these parties survived but some could not. The tendency among the politicians to give their political loyalties not to ideologies but to particular individuals and leaders is very great. Such political parties which are based on patronage than on ideology fail to survive. The party survives so long the leaders and the active members give favours to its members. If the political workers fail to get favours, they withdraw their support to the leader and join some other party. This degeneration of political parties has caused politics in India to become an incredibly lucrative career for unqualified and incompetent people instead of being a channel of service to the country.

One other characteristic of our political parties is the extreme centralisation of their organisations. Most of them have had no elections for a very long time and the office-bearers are all nominated by the central leader. The most deleterious effect of this highly centralised control is that many states do not have Chief Ministers elected by the MLAs but those who have been imposed on them by the Central party. People who are given party tickets to stand for elections from various constituencies are not the candidates chosen by the people of the constituency but people imposed almost arbitrarily by the outside authority. Though in theory, the names of the candidates to be given party tickets originate from the local communities, yet they are changed at district, state and national levels by the higher authorities. What has developed recently is the corruption that has crept into the selection process. If the main object of any Indian political party is to attain and maintain political power for the benefit of the patronage it can dole out to its members, it follows that the party must ensure that every centre of power is brought under its control.

As a result of this, not only the central government but the state governments also try to have hold on all centres of political power, such as police, universities, student organisations, local bodies, etc. Linked with this desire of controlling power is the idea of giving party tickets even to smugglers and criminals. The criminalisation of politics has thus affected the functioning of the political parties. The desire of the political party to maintain control on potential power has even affected the appointment and functioning of governors in states who do not terminate their connection with their parties but sometimes actively take interest in party controversies. The examples of former governors of Uttar Pradesh, Bihar, Gujarat, etc., can be easily cited.

Yet another characteristic of Indian political parties is that there is no public accountability of the manner in which they collect or spend their funds. Their accounts are never subject to audit. It is a well-known fact that contributions to political parties by the rich people are made from the unaccounted (black) funds. The contributors later pressurise government for return favours. Increase in prices of commodities like sugar, cement, oil, etc., during elections is a common phenomenon in our country.

What greatly affects the political parties today is defection of elected members from one political party to another, particularly at the time of the formation of governments. This has happened at the centre and also in states like Uttar Pradesh, Gujarat, Haryana, Bihar, Rajasthan, etc. The Anti-Defection Act, 1985 has not been able to serve its purpose. In fact, it has helped larger parties to break smaller parties. Forming 'coalition' ministries after manipulating defections sometimes leads to the formation of very big-sized and even 'jumbo cabinets'. This is what happened in Uttar Pradesh in November 1997 when the BJP Ministry was formed after six months' term of Mayawati's government (in coalition with the BJP) was over. The same tactics of defection were tried by the BJP government at the centre in May 1996 but these did not succeed and it had to quit after 13 days.

This analysis of the party system shows how party system in India has degraded our democratic system in providing good and honest governments at national and state levels. We are not suggesting abolition of multi-party system; we are only insisting on introducing the accountability system. If election system is restructured, the working of the political parties can be improved, which would help the country to have a better government. Prohibiting contesting elections to panchayats and local bodies on party basis, introducing audit system for funds of political parties, and ensuring autonomy of institutions and keeping them safe from political interference may be some other measures which could control the functioning of political parties and check deterioration in the standards of our political life.

DECENTRALISATION OF POWER AND POLITICAL PARTICIPATION

What is the type of the power structure we have in the present democratic political system? Is it pluralist or elitist power structure? The *pluralist* power structure is characterised by: (i) decentralised structure (i.e., power is distributed at various levels, and large number of people have a share in decision-making processes); (ii) mutually interdependent actors; (iii) symmetrical relations (i.e., there is reciprocity and mutual interaction among components, i.e., A,B,C... have power over D,E,F... and vice-versa); (iv) many components have causal impact on the system. Against this, the *elitist* power structure has (i) centralised structure (i.e., power of decision-making is monopolised by a few at the top, (ii) comparatively independent actors, (iii) asymmetrical relations (i.e., dominance and one-way action), and (iv) its many components have causal impact on the system.

This enables us to identify the type of power structure we have in India. It is definitely the elitist power structure.

The present political leaders cannot be described as politically committed leaders. If we use two terms of 'role specificity' (i.e., role-performers are interested only in politics) and 'role-diffuseness' (i.e., role-performers are partly interested in politics and partly in business, agriculture, etc.), we could hold that the political ideology of present leaders is not 'specific' but it is 'diffused'. While perceiving one's political role in 'narrow' terms heightens political commitment, the self-image of diffused competence constrains one's commitment to politics.

In my own study of political elite, I analysed the *level* of political commitment of the respondents by correlating it with *role specificity* and *role diffusion*. It was found that the level of commitment among those who saw themselves only in specific role of a politician was high in comparison to those who saw themselves in diffused roles.

If we were to describe the political participation of present political leaders in India, we could say, a large number of them identify themselves with parochial rather than national issues, seek political offices, power and economic benefits, suffer from status anxiety, have limited capacity for empathy and have low desire to serve community. Many important persons in politics have now become synonymous with the country's very corrupt persons. Politics has become a family business. If father loses power, his son, daughter, wife, sister, brother, etc., manipulate to get party tickets and contest elections. The children of our self-serving politicians are studying abroad with the money their parents are laundering from 'public service' here. The examples of former Prime Ministers' sons, Central Ministers' sons, Chief Ministers' sons, State Ministers' sons, Political Party Presidents' sons and even MPs' sons can be found in abundance. The corrupt practices of our politicians are mind-boggling and reprehensible. The Indian political scenario today would have been much different if our political leaders, after 1971, would have been more committed to public life. Centralisation of power has made these non-committed politicians still more power-thirsty. Dozens of scandals, involving thousands of crores of rupees, against national and state political leaders have gone unpunished in this era of judicial activism.

Indian politicians, instead of representing three main interests—caste, communal and regional—should have a development agenda which has totally disappeared from the country's political need. Adding to this lack of vision among politicians is the fact that India's bureaucracy has also increasingly become their handmaiden which constrains their skills to deal with complex issues of development. What then we have is only a pretence to govern but no substance. The people of India require competent, honest, knowledgable and committed political leaders with a vision and strategy for change, who understand the crisis of governance and who can provide impetus for reforms so that India can meet its enormous challenges and becomes a truly dynamic, proud and livable country.

Further Readings

Ahuja, Ram, *Political Elite and Modernisation*, Meenakshi Prakashan, Meerut, 1975.

Bhambhri, C.P., *Bureaucracy and Politics in India*, Vikas Publications, Delhi, 1971.

Geriant, Parry, *Political Elite*, George Allen and Unwin, London, 1969.

Mohanty, Jagannath, *Democracy and Education in India*, Deep and Deep Publications, New Delhi, 1989.

Mukherjee, R.K., *Glimpses of Ancient India*, Bhartiya Vidya Bhawan, Bombay, 1961.

Sachchidananda and Lal, A.K., *Elite and Development*, Concept Publishing Co., New Delhi, 1980.

Singh, Yogendra, *Modernisation of Indian Tradition*, Rawat, Jaipur, 1984.

Singhvi, L.M. (ed.), *Indian Political Parties*, Institute of Constitutional and Parliamentary Studies, Delhi, 1971.

7 Educational System

EDUCATION AND SOCIETY

Much has been written on the relationship between education and society, on education, liberalism, and social change, on under-achievement in education, on the functional view of education, and on the crises in higher education. Education provides necessary knowledge and skills which enable an individual to operate ideally in the society and also contribute to its efficient functioning. Education is inspired by ideological postulates that derive from society; but its function does not end at transmitting cultural heritage and in promoting the ideals and values held by society. Given a purposive orientation, education can be a powerful instrument for reshaping and modernising the society. Educational institutions do not exist in a vacuum. They are an integral and sensitive part of society. No educational system can operate without being influenced by the norms and values of society.

In India, before independence, three schools of thought pertaining to education were visible (Dube, 1990: 282-83): (i) The first had nativistic and revivalistic view which rejected everything that was foreign and not enshrined in the ancient heritage of society. The Hindu revivalists set up a number of schools and institutions of higher learning modelled on the *Gurukula* system of ancient India. These institutions laid emphasis on austere life and concentrated on the teaching of Vedic literature. (ii) The second school of thought was aimed at indigenisation of education. The educational institutions of this character were not consciously set out to reject modern learning of foreign origin. Their principal objective was to make education more relevant to Indian conditions and to impart to it a nationalistic flavour. The Banaras Hindu University, the Aligarh Muslim University, Kashi Vidyapith, the Gujarat Vidyapith and the Jamia Millia Islamia were institutions of this type. (iii) The third school of thought focused on setting up educational institutions on the British model—London and Oxford. This purpose is expressed in Macaulay's statement in 1835: "We must create a class who may be interpreters between us and the millions whom we govern—a class of persons, Indian in blood and colour but English in tastes, in opinions, in morals and in intellect."

Free India experienced a phenomenal growth in education at all levels—primary, higher secondary, and college/university levels. But the quantitative growth affected the quality of education. The pattern, by and large, remained colonial. A number of committees were appointed for suggesting measures to improve the quality of education system but the old pattern continued to persist. The tendency was to maintain the status quo.

Currently, the vision and policy of the government in the field of education aim at universalisation of primary education, vocationalisation of secondary education, and rationalisation of higher education. On the one hand, policies are being framed for stamping out illiteracy and arranging 'Education for all' (EFA) to ensure that all children between the age of six years and fourteen years (i.e., about 24% of the total population of the country) get an opportunity to attend school, and all illiterate adults (estimated at about 40% of the total population in the year 1998) learn to read and write. On the other hand, efforts are being made to improve the quality of education.

OBJECTIVES OF EDUCATION

The three perennial objectives of education have been described as: (1) pursuit of man to know himself and the universe and to relate himself with the social world as effectively as possible; (2) building bridges between the past and the future, i.e., transmission of the accumulated results of the past to the growing generation so as to enable it to carry forward cultural heritage and to build the future; and (3) accelerating, as far as possible, the process of human progress. Apart from these objectives, education is also believed to have three other objectives. These are: integral growth of personality traits, like intelligence, skill, will-power, character, attitudes and so forth; (b) development in terms of man's condition of life, i.e., development of both individual and society—the development of society refers not only to economic growth but also to social, political, and cultural growth. In individual development, education helps in creating 'rationalistic and idealistic mind'; and (c) generating and strengthening harmony and peace. 'Peace' here is not conceived negatively as 'absence of war' but positively as undertaking harmonious activities aimed at pursuit of international understanding and cooperation, It implies respect for all people, their cultures, civilisations, values, and ways of life.

According to the report of the International Commission on the Development of Education, established by the UNESCO in 1971, the central demand of education is 'to know, to possess and to be'. Here, the idea of 'to be' refers to the idea of 'personality and its development'. At simple level of understanding, it may be averred that the objective of education at primary level is learning of the three R's, at secondary level is character building, at higher secondary level is understanding society, and at college/university level is skill-training.

THE TRADITIONAL AND THE MODERN CONTEXTS OF EDUCATION

Education in the Past

Education in early, medieval, and the British periods has to be viewed in (a) the perspective of historical growth, and (b) its philosophic significance. From the latter point of view, in the Vedic period, schools were boarding schools where a child was handed over to the teacher at the age of about eight years, and he was imparted knowledge for developing ideal behaviour and not for its utilitarian end. Knowledge, it was felt, was something that lent meaning, glory, and lusture to life. The teacher took personal interest in the life of his students. Education was all comprehensive. For example, physical education was compulsory. Students were taught to build up a strong and healthy body. Training was given in the art of war, including archery, riding, driving, and in other allied fields. School education began with phonology, including study of grammar. After that, study of logic was taken up which dealt with the laws of reasoning and art of thinking. Then came science of Arts and Crafts. Lastly, came the discipline of life which was concerned with sexual purity and chastity in thought and action, including simplicity in food and dress, emphasis on equality, fraternity and independence, and respect for the teacher. Thus, language, logic, craft, discipline and building up character formed the basics of education in early India (Kanal, 1955: 81-83.)

In the *Brahmanical* period, the Vedic literature formed the chief subject of instruction. The main aim of education was the learning of the *Vedas*. But the Sudras were excluded from the right to education. Education was given on the basis of caste rather than ability and aptitude. Women also were debarred from education (*Ibid*:82). In the *Muslim* period, the objectives of education changed. It was more to teach the three R's and train in religious norms. The higher education was imparted through schools of learning while the vocational and professional training was given within the caste structure. Sanskrit and Arabic or Persian were the mediums of instruction. The teachers' remuneration was paid by the rulers through grant of land, presents from pupils, allowances paid by wealthy citizens, and payment in the form of food, clothes or other articles. The financial position of the schools was not very strong. They did not have special buildings of their own. In many cases, schools were held in local temples or mosques or teachers' houses. The schools were conducted almost exclusively by *Maulvis* (priests) for the Muslim students and by Brahmins for the Hindu students. Vocational training was provided by father, brother, etc. to the child. Thus, the caste system provided vocational training and transmitted skills from generation to generation and also provided gainful employment. There was no emphasis on physical education, developing thinking ability, or teaching some craft. Chastity, equality, simplicity were not the ideals of student life. The specialisation of professional roles had not reached a stage at which a separate class or caste could take up education work as a specialised function. Education was more practical.

In the *British* period, education aimed at producing mainly clerks. Education was student-centred rather than teacher-centred. Unlike today, education in this period never aimed at freedom of individual, excellence of individual, equality amongst all people, individual and group self-reliance, and national cohesion. Christian missionaries engaged in imparting education gave considerable importance to conversion of religion. Education in schools and colleges was not productive which could break down the social, regional and linguistic barriers. It never aimed at making people masters of technology. It also did not focus on fighting injustice, intolerance and superstition.

Education in the Present Period

Education today is oriented to promoting values of an urban, competitive consumer society. Through the existing education system, India has produced in the last five decades number of scientists, professionals and technocrats who have excelled in their fields and made a mark at the national and international levels. The top scientists, doctors, engineers, researchers, professors, etc., are not those who were educated abroad but had got their entire education in India. If these experts and all those people who have reached the highest level have come through our present educational system, how could we deny the positive aspects of the education system as it is found today? Thus, while we cannot totally criticise our present education, there are some issues which need our urgent attention, if we are really concerned with a better future. The question relates not to the past nor to the present but rather to the future. How are we going to prepare the experts in various fields to meet the challenges of the newest and latest technology of the twenty-first century? It is not a question of the extent to which education provides or fails to provide employment to people but it is a question of education providing modern technology for the benefit of the poor and deprived people. It is a question of the quality of education. Instead of merely viewing the growing population as a liability, we should change the population into an asset and strength along with trying to control its growth. This can be done only by education and human development. Merely giving a degree and a certificate to a young person that he is qualified for appointment is not enough. We have to make our younger generation think. The present education system does not encourage a person to think. He is taught a set syllabus which he is expected to reproduce during the examinations. This is deficient system. The youngsters have to be provoked to ask more and more questions which will not only help them to think but will also compel teachers to read and learn more. We have, thus, to change the examination system. We have to compel students to take learning more seriously. We have to wean them away from cutting classes, indulging in strikes, participating in students' politics, seeking admission only for contesting elections and offering courses only as a part-time study course. We have to build their character.

Though it is true that the number of educational institutions and students at all levels has increased but it cannot be contented that the quality of education, the interest of students, and dedication of teachers has also increased simultaneously. The number of pre-primary schools has gone up, during the period from 1961 to 1998, by about 21 times (from 1,909 to 40,553), of primary schools has almost doubled (from 3.3 lakhs to 6.107 lakhs), of middle/senior schools has increased by little more than three and a half times (from 49,663 to 1.85 lakh), of higher secondary schools by about six times (from 17,257 to 107,100) and of universities (including deemed universities) by about five times (from 45 to 228). (*Manpower Profile, India*, 1998:70 and *The Hindustan Times*, May 2, 1999). The number of teachers in primary schools has increased from 1961 to

1997 by about two and a half times (from 7.4 lakh to 17.89 lakh), and in higher secondary schools by about five times (from 2.96 lakh to 15.42 lakh). Lastly, the number of students in primary schools during 1961 to 1997 has increased by about three times (from 336.31 lakh to 1103.94 lakh), in higher secondary schools by about five times (from 34.63 lakh to 178.62 lakh) and in graduate and postgraduate classes by about twelve and a half times (from 4.28 lakh to 53.73 lakh) (*Manpower Profile*, India, 1998:80-81). However, weaknesses and deficiencies in education have been pointed out by almost all Commissions and Committees. The three main deficiencies in the present education system may be described as follows: (1) The present education does not generate or fortify the type of knowledge that is relevant to our changed society. (2) Technology associated with a particular body of knowledge is inappropriate to our stage of development in terms of its employment potential or investment demands. (3) Education has failed to provide value framework which may prepare committed politicians, bureaucrats, technocrats, and professionals on whom our nation can depend for sophisticated system of support services to be useful in taking the country to the highest level.

Education for the Future

Our society is moving towards an unknown future. The crises that the contemporary society is encountering are likely to increase in their frequency and intensity. With rising population and dwindling resources, our country has to face new problems. To meet the challenges of this future, we will need knowledge and skills that may contribute to problem-solving capacity not only in the fields of science and technology but also in the fields of human relations and management. Unfortunately, the education system today is decaying more and more instead of responding creatively to the challenges of contemporary predicament. We need to reset our priorities.

First, we accept the philosophy of 'education for self-reliance'. The emphasis must shift from higher secondary and higher education to primary and adult education.

Second, the content of education at higher secondary and college/ university levels needs serious consideration.

Third, the problem is of management of education. At present, bureaucratic styles persist. Bureaucrats are not sensitive and responsive to the changes in the environment of education. Low budgets, high indiscipline, administrative lapses and interference and political pressures make decision-making in the field of education hazardous. As such, management of education should be made free from bureaucrats' and politicians' interference.

Fourth, the problem is of accountability of teachers, particularly in higher education. Many cases are reported where teachers fail to take classes for months and even years together. They rarely take interest in regularly going to libraries and reading journals and latest books. We have to restore purpose to education and determine suitable techniques of teaching. Then we have to regulate the factors that debase and vulgarise it. Control on teachers is the most important requisite in the educational system.

Fifth, the problem is that we have to create greater seriousness regarding studies among students, for whom acquiring knowledge is the most vital question. Education is believed to be mobility multiplier. It works for the perpetuation of status and privileges. But should higher education be open to all students? Many students seek admission to Law, Arts and Commerce courses only because they have to 'kill time' till they settle in life. Should they not be directed to technical and professional courses? Should education be not brought round to subserving their interest?

Sixth, the issue is that we have to give a push to vocational/professional education which has considerable demand in the open market. We have to assume that every educated person cannot become a specialist or an expert but has to equip himself with a skill which can help him earn his livelihood. We have to think of the coming two or three decades and pay attention to the type of agriculture, type of developing industry, trade and commerce and new fields of service and employment that the future decades will throw up. This will help us in building education system which will give us better cultivators, better skilled workers, better mechanics, or whatever.

Seventh, the issue is of linkages between various departments like Agriculture, Industry, Labour, Electronics, Law, Science and so forth so that universities, IITs and colleges know the type of skilled people required. What is needed is full education in each field which will prepare the individual to find employment of his choice and enable the employer to get a candidate of his liking.

Eighth, the issue is of making all illiterate people literate. According to the available estimated figures for the year 1998, assuming that the literacy rate in India has gone up from 52.21 per cent in 1991 to 60 per cent in 1998, there are about 400 million people to be educated. This is a tremendous task. While it is a well-known fact that all state governments have schemes of raising literacy level, it needs to be emphatically stated that we require more than 25 years to achieve the set goal. Perhaps policies like compelling students to teach the illiterate during two months' vacation period will help in reducing the target period.

Ninth, the point is of reducing the number of drop-outs at the primary level. The available figures show that the percentage of drop-outs in 1996 at different stages of school education among boys and girls was as high as 38 to 41 per cent. In 1997-98, according to the Human Resource Development Ministry, 38.23 per cent of boys and 41.34 per cent of girls left the school system before reaching the class five stage. By the time the survivors of the primary stage reach class eight, more than half (54.14%) drop out. Of them 50.72 per cent are boys and 58.61 per cent are girls. Less than a third clear secondary school (*The Hindustan Times*, May 2, 1999). Measures can be adopted to contain this problem. It is not good enough to keep treading the same path. If we know that we are not making progress, we must change our models and policies and programmes and try new ones.

Tenth, the issue is of the present examination system. In a way, they are becoming more and more a farce. In the present set-up, students consider it easier to read guides and cheap books and pass examinations. They view attending classes a waste of time. Teachers take least pains in preparing lectures, in reading books and journals, and equipping themselves with latest research results. They have little time to read through all the pages in the examination answerbook. Their concern is to get more and more examination scripts from different universities and earn more remuneration. Should we continue to live with the system as it is today? It has to be made flexible and open which lays emphasis on creative thinking.

Lastly, there is the question of regulating higher education. Why should every student who wants admission be admitted? Why should higher education be cheap? Why should 100 to 150 students be admitted to one class? To what extent education should be subsidised? Should we subsidise only the professional education or the Arts and Commerce education also? These are questions which need to be linked with reorganising and restructuring of graduate and post-graduate programmes, better performance of students, more accountability of teachers, and functional use of summer vacations. We have to remove deficiencies and shortcomings in teaching and examination system, if we logically want to plan education for the future.

EDUCATIONAL INEQUALITY AND SOCIAL MOBILITY

Though it is true that human beings are not equal in ability and proficiency and though it would be illogical and not ideal to think of a society which may give equal status and equal rewards to all its members, yet providing equal opportunities to all people for achieving their goals and aspirations is necessary. Here we are not talking of economic inequalities among people but of what Beteille (1977:3) has called inequalities in *conditions of existence*. We are thus talking neither of inequalities based on *nature* (i.e., differences in age, health, bodily strength, or qualities of mind) nor those based on types of societies like, tribal, agrarian, and industrial) but inequality in terms of *qualities* and *performances*, or the factors which enable a person to achieve status and power.

The effort of a society which seeks to equalise opportunity, therefore, largely takes the form of providing services which compensate for the inequality in economic background through socialised community services and through provision of educational facilities. There are, of course, obvious difficulties in the way of providing such facilities adequately and universally. It is almost impossible for a society like India to provide free education to all those desirous of benefiting by it, except at selected stages, say at primary level and to those who are needy and meritorious. This already gives rise to one type of inequality in opportunities. While the children of the needy can have education only if they are meritorious, the children of the well-to-do can go to schools so long as they can pay for it.

Equality of opportunity for improving one's social standing is a recent idea that has been accepted after rejecting the all-importance of the ascribed status and recognising the importance of the achieved status in individual's life. Gore (1994:29) has also said that social mobility has become feasible after individual status has been freed of its hereditary moorings. He holds that acquiring technical expertise, occupying high administrative office, and learning a new profession are some of the avenues for the achievement of monetary success and social esteem in a society. Achieving merit and ability is possible only through education. Though education does not guarantee high status and higher positions to all people, yet without education, an individual is unlikely to achieve social mobility. Gore avers that education plays a role in equalising opportunities in three ways (*Ibid*:30): (1) by making it possible for all those who have the desire to be educated and the ability to benefit by that facility; (2) by developing a content of education which will promote the development of a scientific and objective outlook; and (3) by creating a social environment of mutual tolerance based on religion, language, caste, class, etc. for providing equal opportunities of social mobility to all individuals in society, and for providing equal opportunity to secure good education is crucial. Of course, education is not the only channel to social mobility, and class, cultural background, and parental support, etc. are also important variants which influence opportunities but lack of education is bound to prove a great handicap in mobility. As already stated, society attempting to equalise opportunity provides educational facilities to selected people.

How is education related to equality of opportunity can be perceived on the basis of the findings of one empirical study conducted in eight states in 1967 on the social background of students (age, sex, caste, father's occupation, father's education, etc.) studying at various levels—high school, college and professional colleges. This study presented two possible propositions: (1) education is a priority with those in the white-collar group, and children in this group use educational facilities more than other groups; and (2) education is differentially available to those who do not belong to white-collar group (see Gore, 1994:33). If the first proposition is correct, it probably underlines the irrelevance of education to non-white-collar groups in our society. Their lack of interest in secondary education arises out of the fact that for the occupations they aspire to, secondary education makes no meaningful contribution. Does this throw light on the defective planning of our education or the 'backwardness' of the underprivileged groups of not aspiring for social mobility? The disadvantaged people (i.e., SCs, STs, OBCs, women, and religious minorities) in our society have been terribly exploited because of their illiteracy. Some studies have been conducted on descriptions of inequality in education as evidenced in regional, rural-urban, sex, and caste disparities and imbalances in enrolment and retention at school or college and the consequences of disparities. All these studies have pointed out the impact of education on the status and the identity of the disadvantaged people. Studies on SCs and STs have indicated that so long these people remain educationally backward, they have to be provided protective discrimination in the form of economic support or reserved admissions to institutions of higher education. One such study was sponsored by the ICSSR in 1974 under the coordination of I.P. Desai. It covered 14 states and was concerned with the situation and problems of SC and ST school and college students in the country. This study, pointing out apathy of ST students to education, indicated that illiteracy increases inequality and prevents occupational as well as social mobility. Chitnis (1972) had also probed inequalities in enrolment in higher education among college students in Bombay city and the problems encountered by them. Victor D'Souza (1977) traced the pattern of disparity between the education of the SCs and of others in Punjab and pointed out how the structure of caste system, caste behaviour, economic factors and the form and operation of welfare programmes influence the pattern. M.L.Jha (1973) studied tribal education and disparities. V.P. Shah (1973) pointed out relationship between education and untouchability in Gujarat. Sachchidanand Sinha (1975) has described the situation of SC students of colleges in Uttar Pradesh. All these studies, thus, throw light on education as an instrument of equality for SCs and STs.

Similarly, there have been studies on women too (another important category of those who are educationally disadvantaged and backward) by K.Ahmad (1974) and others in terms of significance of education to their role in a developing society. Baker (1973) studied the aspirations of female students with a view to understanding the problems they encounter in making use of educational facilities. Chitnis (1977) studied the impact of co-education on Muslim women students in Bombay. All these studies point out the consequences of inequalities and the need for change.

EDUCATION, SOCIAL CHANGE AND MODERNISATION

In the analysis of relationship between education and social change, the question is: how does education lead to social change? In association between education and modernisation, the main question is: what kind of education and under what conditions will it generate and strengthen the process of modernisation in a society? Education has been accepted as one major agency of socialisation, and teachers and educational institutions as socialising agents. In describing education as an instrument of social change, three things are important: the agents of change, the content of change, and the social background of those who are sought to be changed, i.e., students. Educational institutions under the control of different cultural groups reflect the values of those groups which support and control education. In this situation, teachers impart specific values, aspirations and attitudes to the children. Thus, for analysing the role of teachers as agents of change, we have to remember the three types of educational institutions which existed in India before independence: one, which wanted to teach Vedic philosophies (*Gurukuls*); two, which focused on Indianisation of education; and three, which, wanted to impart western type of education. The second and third type of institutions believed that English education, particularly at the higher levels, would lead to change of social values. Social reformers, who were educated through English, emphasised values like removal of caste restrictions, equality of women, doing away with evil social customs and practices, voice in the governance of the country, establishing democratic institutions, and so on. They, thus, wanted to teach liberal philosophy through education for changing society. In other words, they regarded education as a flame or light of knowledge which dispelled the darkness of ignorance. However, it is doubtful that the teachers—both in schools and colleges—accepted and taught this liberalism in values. As such, the educational institutions did not impart the message of social equality, political democracy, and rationality, etc. to students. It was only after independence when the concept of popular democracy was accepted that new goals of egalitarianism, secularism, individualism, socialism, humanism, undermining the institution of caste and the supermacy of Brahmins, etc. to be achieved through education came to be emphasised in schools and colleges by changing the content of education.

The use of education for spreading the values of modernisation came to be emphasised from the 1960s and 1970s onwards. Highly productive economies, distributive justice, peoples' participation in decision-making bodies, adoption of scientific technology in industry, agriculture and other occupations and professions were accepted as goals for modernising the Indian society. And these goals were to be achieved through liberal education. Thus, modernisation was not accepted as a philosophy or a movement based on rational value system but as a process that was to characterise our society. Modernisation was, thus, not to be confined only to economic field but was to be achieved in social, political, cultural and religious fields too. Education was sought to be utilised as a channel for the spread of modernity.

The problem is that there is open disagreement among the elite in our society about the socio-political framework and the values of modernisation. As such, the question is: who will impart values of modernisation? Who will educate? If agents of change are themselves traditional and do not incorporate modern values in their own lives, how can they impart such values to students? Even though the Education Commissions and the New Policy of Education of 1986 have spelt out with unusual directness the values and characteristics of a modern society, yet the path of modernisation through education is not likely to be an easy one. Quite a few political leaders of Hindu organisation in power in some states and at the centre are really keen on some traditional cultural elements to be taught through education. With such philosophies and lack of consensus on the validity of particular values of modernisation (like secularism, individualism, socialism, egalitarianism, etc.), how can we expect to achieve goals of modernisation? We may, thus, conclude that use of education as an instrument for the spread of modern influences is an issue which requires serious and fresh thought.

Several sociologists like A.R. Desai (1974), S.C. Dube (1971), M.S. Gore (1971), N. Jayaram (1977), K.Ahmad (1979), and A.B. Shah (1975), etc., have focused upon the issue of education as an instrument for social reconstruction and modernisation. Ahmad (1974) has said that although formal education can play a vital role in 'ideational' change through transformation of knowledge, attitudes and values of the people, its effectiveness in bringing about structural changes in society is extremely limited. This is because of the linkages between the existing practices and procedures in education and vested interests of the status quoists. Chitnis (1978) has also pointed out the uneven functioning of education as an instrument of development. A.R. Desai (1974) too has questioned the validity of education as an instrument of social change. His contention is that after Independence, education has not been purposively geared to obtain the desired changes. He has criticised the policies and funding and financing of education to attain the goals of social mobility and equality. To support Desai, we can give the example of education of SCs, STs, women and the minorities which has failed in uplifting their status. The unemployment and under-employment of uneducated youth is another example of failure of education for achieving the aspirations of youths. The failure to achieve development of the rural areas and alleviating poverty is yet another example. Unless the pattern set by the prevailing distribution of power is broken and there is a tilt in the policies towards the poor, it will be difficult to find resources for the necessary transformation. Change in higher education is also necessary for social change. Gore, (1971) has pointed out the necessity of change in the content and methods of education, in the environment and context in which it is conducted, and in the convictions and the commitment of teachers and administrators responsible for education for the effectiveness of education in achieving the required development. Some empirical studies have been conducted in India on the relationship between education and modernisation. One such study was conducted by the NCERT in Delhi (in the early 1960s) covering eight states. These studies described the extent to which the attitudes, aspirations and outlook of school and college students and teachers in the country have 'modernised'. Modernisation in these studies was measured in terms of an adaptation of a scale developed by Alex Inkles. The results pointed out low effect of education on modernisation. Students continue to be traditional in matters of family life, etc. Yogendra Singh (1979) conducted a study into the implications of attitudes and values of teachers in Rajasthan University, to modernisation. This study measured the levels of aspiration, commitment, morale and authoritarianism among university teachers with a view to understanding how the role structures and value systems of teachers affect their role as agents of modernisation. He found significant relationships between the two and thus held that teachers' values influence the modernisation of students.

Earlier, in 1975, E. Haq had conducted a study on the content of secondary school text books and the process of secondary school education in terms of their effectiveness in political modernisation. He also pointed out a relationship between education and demographic change.

PROBLEMS OF EDUCATION

Students' Unrest

Of the many types of studies made on students, relates to student unrest. We will analyse this problem here in detail. "*Students' indiscipline*" is described as 'disobedience to authority, disrespect to teachers and elders, deviation from norms, refusing to accept control, and rejecting socially sanctioned goals and means'. Three situations create indiscipline among students: (i) students lose interest in the goals of education and educational institution and refuse to follow its norms; (ii) students accept the goals but doubt whether the institution can achieve them. They, therefore, try to 'improve' the institution by deviating from its norms; and (iii) norms of institution fail to achieve goals and students, therefore, want a change in norms. *Students' unrest* is characterised by "collective discontent, dysfunctional conditions in educational institutions and concern (of public and students) for change in existing norms". *Students' agitations*, on the other hand, are characterised by 'action based on the feeling of injustice, identifying source of discontent, frustration and deprivation, emergence of leadership, mobilisation for action, and collective reaction to stimuli'.

Students' unrest leads to protests. The important elements of protests are: (i) action expresses grievance, (ii) it points out conviction of injustice, (iii) protesters are unable to correct the condition directly by their own effort, (iv) action is meant to provoke ameliorative steps by the target group, and (v) protesters bank upon the combination of coercion, persuasion and discussion to move the target group. If the protesters indulge in looting, it is not to acquire property, if they indulge in breaking windows, it is not to seek vengeance, if they shout slogans against a person, it is not to insult him. All these methods are resorted merely to express resentment against their unfulfilled demands and towards the callous attitude adopted by the powers that be in relation to their grievances.

Students' protests sometimes lead to aggression, agitation and movement. *Aggression* is a physical or a verbal behaviour or a hostile act intended to harm, hurt or destroy. *Agitation* is to bring grievance and injustice to the notice of people in power. It is to shake up, to move, to stir up, to cause anxiety, and to disturb the power-holders. *Movement* is the activity of diffused collectivity oriented towards changing the social order. Students' agitation is behaviour of students whose goal is neither injury to a person nor destruction of public property but protest. It is neither the result of innate destructive drive nor it is an inborn reaction to frustrations. Various forms of students' agitations are: demonstrations, shouting, strikes, hunger strikes, road blocks, gheraos, and boycott of examinations. The pre-conditions for students' agitations are: (a) structural strain, (b) identifying the source of strain, (c) precipitating factor in initiative action, and (d) mobilisation of force for action by a leader. The important functions of student agitations are: to create collective consciousness and group solidarity, to organise students to work for new programmes and new plans, and to provide opportunities to students to express their feelings and make some impact on the course of change.

Agitations could be violent or non-violent. For example, about a decade ago there were about 5,000 student agitations in a year in India, of which about 20 per cent were violent. Further, a little more than half of the agitations related to non-academic issues within the campuses (like fixing up statues, changing name of the university, reducing bus-fare, etc.), about 20 per cent to academic issues, and about 25 per cent to some social issues (e.g., reservation issue, etc.).

Student agitations may be classified as: student-oriented agitations and society-oriented agitations. The former include problems at college/university level, while the latter refer to taking interest in state/country's politics and policies and programmes). Student-oriented agitations are generally discontinuous and problem-oriented rather than value-oriented. For example, students will agitate for removal of a particular vice-chancellor of a university but they will never fight for a change in the system of selecting vice-chancellors in universities in India.

Students' agitations grow in stages. These include: (i) the *discontent* stage, which is the stage of dissatisfaction and growing confusion with the existing conditions; (ii) the *initiation* stage, in which a leader emerges, the causes of discontent are identified, excitement increases, and proposals for action are debated; (iii) the *formalisation* stage, in which programmes are developed, alliances are forged, and support is also sought of some crusaders; (iv) the *public support* stage in which students' trouble is viewed as public trouble.

The important students' agitations in India between 1983 and 1990 were: Gujarat agitation in 1985 on reservation issue, anti-reservation agitation by students in Madhya Pradesh in 1985, Assam agitation in 1983-84 on the issue of refugees from East Bengal, and anti-Mandal agitation in

1990 in different states in the country.

Students' agitations may be classified as: (1) *persuasive* agitations, in which students attempt to change the attitude of the powers that be by discussing their problems with them and making them accept their viewpoint. (2) *Resistance* agitations, in which the object is to keep the power-holders in their place. (3) *Revolutionary* agitations, which aim at bringing sudden sweeping changes in the educational or the social systems.

Who are the students who are receptive to agitations? Five types of students have been identified in this context: (1) *socially isolated*, i.e., who feel alienated and cut off from the larger society; (2) *personally maladjusted*, i.e., who have failed to find a satisfying life role, e.g., they do not have an adequate interest in studies; (3) *unattached to family*, i.e., who lack intimate ties with their families; (4) *marginals*, i.e., who are not fully integrated with their caste/religious/linguistic group, and (5) mobile/migrants, i.e., who have little chance of getting integrated into the larger community.

B.V. Shah (1968) conducted a study of university students in Gujarat. He classified students in four groups on the basis of their social status and individual abilities to identify indisciplined students: (1) high status, high ability, (2) low status, low ability, (3) low status, high ability, and (4) high status, low ability. He felt, more unrest is found among students of second and fourth categories.

The causes of students' unrest and agitations, as pointed out by the UGC committee in 1960, are: (1) economic causes, like demands for reducing fees, increasing scholarship; (2) demands for changes in existing norms pertaining to admissions, examinations and teaching; (3) poor functioning of colleges/universities; (4) conflicting relations between students and teachers, e.g., behaviour of teachers with girl students or student leaders, cutting classes and so on; (5) inadequate facilities in the campus, e.g., inadequate hostels, poor food in hostels, lack of canteen facility, etc.; and (6) student leaders being instigated by politicians.

Using theoretical approaches, students' agitations have been explained on the basis of Discontent Theory (agitations are rooted in discontent and feeling of injustice), Personal Maladjustment Theory (agitations are a refuge from personal failure in life), Relative Deprivation Theory and Resources Mobilisation Theory.

The measures suggested for controlling students' agitations are: (1) Proper channelising of students' enthusiasm through guidance. (2) Solving problem not *for* them but *with* them; i.e., associating students with decision-making bodies. (3) Removing minor irritants without unnecessary delay. (4) Prescribing a code of conduct for political parties: refraining from instigating students to agitate on small issues. (5) Framing rules regarding police intervention in educational institutions.

Adult Education Programme

Spread of literacy has been a conscious effort of the government since independence. Between 1951 and 1991, the percentage of literacy improved more than three times—from 16.67 per cent to 52.21 per cent. However, in absolute terms, the number of illiterate persons in 1991 was 328.9 million, including 220.5 million women (*Manpower Profile, India*, 1998:46). According to recent projections of illiteracy situation in the world, India's share of the world's illiterate population in the age group of 15 and above is projected to be one-third of world's illiterates by 2000 A.D. The Education Commission in 1964 highlighted the role of adult education and recommended intensive efforts to spread literacy in the age group of 15-25 and linked it with the development programme. However, nothing much was done till 1975-76. In 1978, the government announced National Adult Education Programme (NAEP) for approximately 100 million illiterate persons in the age group of 15-35. Kothari Commission (1981-82) pointed out a number of shortcomings and inadequacies in the programme: (1) The programme largely remained confined to illiteracy. (2) Linking illiteracy to development was not easy. (3) Object of creating awareness could not be achieved. (4) Little attention was paid to programme in science. (5) A number of states (including Assam, Himachal Pradesh, Madhya Pradesh, and Orissa) remained almost unaffected by NAEP. (6) The programme was not flexible and decentralised. (7) No attention was paid to the diverse needs of men and women. (8) The programme mainly remained the responsibility of the state governments. Media and voluntary agencies were not involved.

Literacy was given importance in the 20-point programme too. In 1986, New NPE also suggested new guidelines for making literacy programme a success. The literacy programme was restructured by introducing flexibility in the project structure, giving importance to spoken language of the learners, laying emphasis on training of functionaries, decentralisation of the supervisory system, increasing the number of women instructors, providing continuity in the duration of the project, strengthening technical resource system, improving management system, and evaluation of management system. In spite of these changes, the literacy programme is yet to be accelerated. New thrust is needed in educational policy for this.

NATIONAL POLICY ON EDUCATION

The Government of India announced its desire in January 1985 to formulate a new Education Policy for the country. After receiving views and suggestions from different quarters, the NPE was announced in 1986. It laid stress on: (1) radical reconstruction of the education system; (2) improving quality of education at all stages; (3) giving greater attention to science and technology; (4) cultivating moral values; (5) strengthening integration; and (6) developing a sense of common citizenship and culture.

The important measures proposed in the policy were:

(1) Initiating funded programmes by the government for providing access to education to all students, irrespective of sex, caste and creed.
(2) Adopting common education structure of 10+2+3 in all parts of the country. The break up of first ten years will be five years for primary, three for middle, and two for high school.
(3) Providing equal opportunity of education to women, SCs, STs and OBCs, minorities and the handicapped.
(4) Assuming responsibility by the nation of providing resource support, reducing disparities, universalisation of elementary education, adult literacy and technological research.
(5) Implementing programme of adult education.
(6) Implementing programme of vocational education.
(7) Taking steps for de-gradating of higher education. Courses to be redesigned to meet the demands of specilisation. Enhanced support to be provided to research in the universities.
(8) Initiating open university system.
(9) Delinking degrees from jobs.
(10) Developing new pattern of rural university.
(11) Strengthening technical and management education, and also system of rural polytechnics.
(12) Giving better deal to teachers with greater accountability.
(13) Focusing on imparting value education.
(14) Providing infrastructure for physical education, sports and games.
(15) Introducing reforms in examination system.

EDUCATION OF WOMEN, SCHEDULED CASTES, SCHEDULED TRIBES AND OTHER BACKWARD CLASSES

Education of Women

Education to women is necessary so that they can attain equality. It is a pre-requisite for value change as without value change, the social objectives cannot be achieved. The social legislations have given them political, economic, social and religious rights but merely giving them rights does not motivate them to avail these rights to their benefit. The law may give them the right to vote in elections, contest elections and hold political posts but it cannot compel them to do so. The law may give them the right to get a share in father's property but women may not compel their brothers to give them their due share. The law may give them the right to select their own life partner and to divorce the husband who humiliates them, tortures them or exploits them, but how many women insist on using this right? This is mainly because illiteracy has made them stick to traditional values. Lack of courage prevents them from taking initiative for a bold step. Education will make them liberal and broadminded and change their attitudes, values and role perceptions.

The literacy rate of women has gone up from about 10 per cent in 1951 to 29.75 per cent in 1981, 39.29 per cent in 1991, and is estimated to have gone up to 39 per cent at the beginning of 1999. Enrolment of girls as a ratio of total enrolment during 1990-91 was only 41.4 per cent at primary stage, 37.4 per cent at middle stage, 33 per cent at secondary and higher secondary stage and 33.3 per cent at higher education stage (*India 1992*, 107). In states, the highest female literacy rate in 1991 was in Kerala (75.65%) followed by Mizoram (68.60%) and Delhi (62.57%), while the lowest rate was in Rajasthan (20.44%), followed by Bihar (22.89%), Uttar Pradesh (25.31%), Madhya Pradesh (28.85%). (*Manpower Profile, India*, 1998:42). Age-wise, 68.4 per cent females are less than 3 years of age and have no education. In 3-6 years age group, 19.3 per cent females have education; in 7-11 years age group, 7.1 per cent have education; in 12-14 years age group, 4.2 per cent have education; and in 15+ years age group, 1 per cent females have education (*Ibid*:48). The literacy rate of females among SCs in India is 23.76 per cent while among STs it is 18.19 per cent.

The empirical study conducted in eight states in 1967 on 11,500 students studying at various levels points out 'gender' as the most pronounced differentiation in educational opportunity. While broadly speaking (as shown by above figures) education of girls has made strides and today in many faculties and departments of universities, more girls than boys are to be seen, the above-mentioned empirical data show that the girls who enter the educational system are largely those from the urban high caste, white-collar families. Rural residence, low caste, and low economic standing definitely tend to deny opportunities of education to a girl. (Gore, 1990:36). The following specific steps have been taken for improving girls'/women's participation in education: (1) Under the scheme of Operation Blackboard, the government has provided assistance since 1987-88 for the creation of about one lakh posts of primary school teachers mainly to be filled by women. In five years (i.e., up to 1992) about 75 per cent of these posts were filled up of which about 60 per cent were women teachers. (2) The number of NFE centres for girls had gone up to about 81,000 by 1991 which received 90 per cent assistance from the government. (3) The 'Mahila Samakhya' (Education for Women's Equality) Project was launched in April 1989 which aimed at mobilising rural women for education through *Mahila Sanghas* in each of the villages concerned. This is a Central scheme where full financial assistance is provided to Mahila Samakhya societies in Uttar Pradesh, Karnataka, and Gujarat. As an Indo-Dutch programme, it receives cent per cent assistance from the government of the Netherlands. The focus of the programme is on generating demand for education and introducing innovative educational inputs for pre-school, non-formal, adult, and continuing education. (4) By conscious action, admission of girls to the extent of 28 per cent in Navodaya Vidyalayas has been ensured. (5) Special attention is given to enrollment of women in adult education centres. (6) Under the rural functional literacy programmes, of the total adult illiterates enrolled by 1995, about 55 per cent were women.

The law cannot compel a woman to educate herself. Nor the parents can be compelled to send their daughters to schools. And without education, women's equality cannot be attained. What is needed is change of attitudes both in men and women towards girls' education.

The National Policy on Education, 1986 also laid emphasis on education for attaining women's equality which will foster the development of new values. The strategies proposed are: encouraging educational institutions to take up active programmes to further women's development, removal of women's illiteracy, removing obstacles inhibiting their access to elementary education, and pursuing policy of non-discrimination to eliminate sex stereotyping in vocational, technical and professional courses.

Education of SCs, STs, and OBCs

Education is directly related to the development of an individual and the community. It is the most important single factor for economic development as well as social emancipation. For the weaker sections of society, education has a special significance because for a number of centuries, their illiteracy and social backwardness have been used for their harassment, humiliation and economic exploitation. The problems of education of the underprivileged groups and the general population are different both quantitatively as well as qualitatively. The literary rate for general population in India (52.21%), according to the 1991 census, was 15 per cent to 23 per cent higher than that of SCs and STs (with SCs having 37.41% and STs having 29.60% literacy rate) (*Manpower Profile, India*, 42-43). We find such difference in the literacy rate of males (64.13%, 49.91% and 40.65% respectively) as well as females (39.29%, 23.76% and 18.19% respectively). Even in states, the literacy rate of SCs, STs is not the same. In India, in comparison to 37.41 per cent literary level among the SCs, in states, it is the highest in Kerala (79.66%), followed by Gujarat (61.07%) and Goa, Delhi, Arunachal Pradesh, Maharashtra, Manipur (varying between 58.73% and 56.46%) and the lowest in Bihar (19.49%) followed by Andhra Pradesh, Madhya Pradesh, Karnataka (varying between 31.59% and 38.06%). Among the STs, in comparison to 29.60 per cent literacy level in the whole of India, in states it is the highest in Kerala (57.22%) and lowest in Andhra Pradesh (17.16%) (*Ibid*: 44). Within the state also, there are some tribes which have a high level of literacy and others which have very low literacy. For example, in Rajasthan Meena tribe has very high literacy in comparison to Bhils, Saharias, Rawats etc. So is the case in Kerala. In comparison to percentage of literacy for all STs in the state (57.22%), tribes like Kathunayakan, Eravellan, Irulan, Mathuwan, Paniyam, etc., have very low literary (less than 10% each). Similar figures for OBCs are not available.

It was in this context of quantitative and qualitative differences that the Central Advisory Board of Education recommended about two decades ago (in July 1976) that: (1) Universalisation of elementary education of SCs and STs is necessary, particularly in selected areas. (2) Since SCs and STs are not homogeneous groups (with high variations in literary levels—tribe-wise and caste-wise in different states), differentiated programmes are necessary for them. (3) Since educational infrastructure is non-existent in many cases in the tribal areas, a network of educational institutions of single-teacher schools and hostel facilities according to the density of school network need to be planned for each micro unit.

Measures Adopted for Educational Development of SCs and STs

(1) Our Constitution has directed the states to promote the educational interests of the weaker sections of the people, particularly of SCs and STs in terms of establishment of and admission to educational institutions and grant from state funds for scholarships, etc. It has thus consciously provided a policy of temporary discrimination for them.

(2) In view of these directions, a provision has been made in all Five Year Plans providing crores of rupees for raising the level of education among the SCs and STs by opening schools, giving pre-matric and post-matric scholarships, constructing hostels particularly for girls,

creating book-banks, mid-day meals, loans to students, coaching centres, houses for teachers and so forth.

(3) Reserving seats in educational institutions including engineering and medical colleges.

(4) Relaxation in age and marks for admission.

(5) Free special coaching to students aspiring for admission to professional courses or preparing for central and state level competitive examinations.

The National Policy on Education, 1986 contemplated the following measures for the education of SCs: (1) Incentives to SC families to send their children to school regularly till they reach the age of 14. (2) Pre-matric scholarship scheme for children of families engaged in low occupations (scavenging, tanning, etc.) from class I onwards. (3) Constant monitoring to ensure enrolment, retention and successful completion of courses. (4) Recruitment of teachers from SCs. (5) Facilities in hostels. (6) Locating schools, *Balwadis* and Education Centres in such a way as to facilitate full participation of SCs. (7) Constant innovation in finding new methods to increase participation. For the STs, besides the above measures, other measures suggested were: (1) Priority to opening primary schools in the tribal areas. (2) Devising instructional materials in tribal languages at the initial stages. (3) Encouraging educated tribals to take up teaching in tribal areas. (4) Establishing residential schools on a large scale.

For the OBCs, the recommendations in NPE, 1986 were: (1) Incentives to all educationally backward sections of society particularly in the rural areas. (2) Providing institutional infrastructure in hill and desert districts and in remote and inaccessible areas.

Success and Failure of Educational Schemes for SCs and STs

Though there has been some progress in the educational schemes meant for the SCs and STs, like increase in educational level among the SCs from 14.67 per cent in 1971 to 37.41 per cent in 1991 and among the STs from 11.30 per cent to 29.60 per cent and also increase in the number of students in graduate, postgraduate and professional courses, yet equalisation of opportunity still remains a distant ideal. Opportunities for entering class I and II services are not yet fully open. Is it because of the defects in the implementation of the educational policies by the government, or is it because the illiterate SCs and STs have not yet understood the importance of education for their children, or is it because of their poverty and inability to spend even a small amount of money on children's education?

We point out the following shortcomings and deficiencies in education programmes for the SCs and STs:

(1) *High percentage of drop-outs*: Though the number of SC/ST children in primary classes has gradually increased in the last five decades yet a large number of students drop out by the time they pass 5th standard. It is estimated that the percentage of wastage in different states both among SC and ST communities vary from 30 (Himachal Pradesh) to 88 (Manipur). However, wastage among the STs is much higher than that among the SCs.

(2) *Ineffective reservations*: All reserved seats are not filled up due to non-availability of the required qualified candidates.

(3) *Meagre scholarship*: Money spent on education is much more than the money received as scholarship.

(4) *Inadequate facilities*: In some tribal areas, schools are located in distant places and children find it difficult to reach school. Similarly, adequate hostel facilities are also not easily available.

(5) *Frequent absence of teachers in remote areas*: Most of schools in tribal as well as non-tribal areas are one-teacher schools. Teachers are either not willing to be posted in these isolated areas or they remain absent so frequently that students' education suffers.

(6) *Medium of instruction*: Tribal children speak their own dialect while teaching in primary classes is through the state language. This language problem makes students disinterested in their studies as they cannot read the text books written in unfamiliar language.

(7) *Cultural and social barriers*: Among many tribals, the custom of marrying daughters at an early age and not permitting daughters-in-law to go for studies acts as a barrier to acquiring education. Moreover, most tribals have a feeling that the educated tribal youths would not respect the traditional norms and values of life.

It may, therefore, be averred that unless tribals are taught both their tribal dialects and state languages, teachers are given incentives for working in isolated areas, single-teacher system is replaced by two or more teacher system, and unless school timings are fixed according to the convenience of the local people, an education will remain inaccessible to the vast majority of SC/ST students. Only especially crafted education policy will fulfil the needs of SCs and STs (see, Prasad, 1986: 908-32).

EDUCATIONAL RECONSTRUCTION

The reconstruction of education aims at five goals: (1) To make education relevant to the country's development needs and expectations of society.

This requires giving employment and vocational orientation to the entire education system. (2) To develop thinking power of students by reorganising the content, the teaching method, and the examination system. (3) To reduce inequality of educational opportunity and to widen access to education. This presupposes organisation of non-formal education programmes for children, youth and adults. (4) To improve educational infrastructure and the quality of education. Even though lot of resources have been invested in creating the required infrastructure, yet it leaves a great deal to be desired. Further, due to insufficient attention by the local community and obsolescence of equipment, the available infrastructure is not fully functional. Lack of motivation to teachers for working as committed teachers is also lacking. (5) To strengthen the content of science and technology in education. (6) To create a national system of education in which a common Indian identity is reinforced.

In spite of the NPE, 1986, educational reforms have failed to materialise. About three decades ago, it was envisaged that the investment in education would increase from 3 per cent to 6 per cent of GNP but we are still in the vicinity of 3 per cent. There is no increase in the share of education in the Five Year Plans. Unless the infrastructures are strengthened (including primary, secondary and tertiary education and education for equality), unless there is reorientation of education (including vocationalisation and value education) and unless there is radical departure from the old system, including change in programme of non-formal education, delinking degrees from jobs, professional management of education, especially higher education, and examination reform, education cannot be improved.

Further Readings

Albatch, P.G. (eds.), "Students, Politics and Higher Education in India", in Albatch (ed.), *Turmoil and Transition: Higher Education and Student Polity in India*, Lalvani Publishing House, Bombay, 1988.

Beteille, Andre, *Inequality Among Men*, 1977.

Chitnis, Suma, "Education for Equality: The Case of Scheduled Castes in Higher Education", *Economic and Political Weakly*, Vol. 7, 1972.

—, "Review and Trend Report on the Sociology of Education", *A Survey of Research in Sociology and Social Anthropology*, ICSSR, Delhi, 1974 (vol. 1) and 1980.

Dube, S.C., *Tradition and Development*, Vikas Publishing House, New Delhi, 1990.

Gore, M.S., *Education and Modernisation in India*, Rawat Publications, Jaipur, 1982.

---, *Indian Education: Structure and Process*, Rawat Publications, Jaipur, 1994.

Iqbal Narain, "Reforming Educational Administration in India", *Indian Journal of Public Administration*, July-September, 1986.

Joshi, P.C., Students, "Youth and National Development", *Yojana*, May 1967.

Kanel, S.P., *Dialogues on Indian Culture*, Panchal Press, Delhi, 1955.

Prasad, L.M., "Educational Policy for SCs and STs and Its Implementation", IJPA, October-November, 1986.

8 Religion

RELIGION: CONCEPT AND ITS SOCIOLOGICAL RELEVANCE

Religion is referred to as a system of beliefs, practices, and values concerned with the *sacred*. It is related to supernatural entities and powers which are considered as the ultimate concern of all mundane existence among human groups (Sinha, 1974:508). Sociologists are not concerned with the competing claims of different religions. They mainly deal with the social effects of religious beliefs and practices. In other words, the sociological analysis of religion is concerned with how religious beliefs and practices are articulated in society, how they affect interaction among persons of different religious faiths, how they lead to conflicts and riots (communalism), and how secularism can contain interreligious biases. The following are the kinds of questions addressed by sociologists of religion: How does religion reinforce the collective unity or social solidarity of a group through religious worship and rituals? (Durkhiem). How does religion block the emotional and intellectual development of people? (Marx). How is a particular type of economic system (say, capitalism) the product of a specific religious ideology (say Protestantism)? (Max Weber). Is one religion (say Hinduism) more tolerant and accommodative than another religion (say Islam)? What is the effect on a person's way of life of being religiously described as an untouchable? Is there something in the belief systems of two sects of the same religion (say, Shias and Sunnis in Islam) which makes conflict between them inevitable? Does religion (say

Islam) oppose family planning measures? But before analysing some of these aspects, let us understand the demographic dimensions and the geographical distribution of different religions in India.

RELIGION: LIVING PATTERNS

Demographic Dimensions and Geographical Distribution of Different Religions in India

If we divide Indian population by religion, according to the 1991 census, 82.41 per cent are Hindus (including SCs and STs), 12.12 per cent Muslims, 2.30 per cent Christians, 1.84 per cent Sikhs, 0.60 per cent Buddhists, 0.44 per cent Jains, and 0.29 per cent others. There are five states in India where Hindus are in minority. These include Jammu and Kashmir, Mizoram, Manipur, Nagaland, and Lakshadweep. The Muslims predominate in Jammu and Kashmir, Assam and West Bengal. The Muslim concentration varies between 8 per cent and 29 per cent in states like Assam (28.4%), West Bengal (23.6%), Kerala (23.3%), Uttar Pradesh (17.3%), Bihar (14.8%), Karnataka (11.6%), Maharashtra (9.7%) and Andhra Pradesh (8.9%) (*The Hindustan Times*, July 8, 1995). Though 12.12 per cent of Indians are Muslims, only about 5 per cent speak Urdu and all those who speak Urdu are not Muslims.

Neighbourhood Living Patterns

Muslims prefer to live in areas in which Muslims predominate. This is because: one, Hindus do not like to take Muslims as tenants; two, Muslims feel secure in such areas; three, they are able to preserve their culture. In areas in which both Hindus and Muslims live, there are clusters, cleavages and polarities. *Polarity* is "sense of affinity, affiliation, belongingness, concern and identity which people share with a particular issue, which may be religious, political, economic, or ideological in nature". *Polarisation* is "the heightened sense of identity and belongingness resulting in emotional, mental or physical mobilisation of individuals or groups to cause cohesion". *Cleavage* is "a phenomenon by which population in a particular place is divided into two different polarities which have conflicting, contrasting or opposite principles or tendencies". *Cluster* refers to "the habitation pattern of the people belonging to one polarity sharing commonness in a given area at a particular time". The living pattern of Muslims is based on polarity, polarisation, cleavages and clusters which help them in interpersonal relationships as well as give them security.

In areas inhabited by Hindus and Muslims, there is hardly any exchange of things or mutual invitations. Hindus and Sikhs, however, living in one neighbourhood exchange things and even attend each others' marriages, etc. It requires liberalism and flexibility so that the individual can spontaneously enter into intimate relationships with others. Love and fraternity are cementing forces. Social relationships are participatory and reciprocate sense of responsibility to regain self-identity without suppressing individuality and freedom.

INTERRELIGIOUS INTERACTION AND CONVERSIONS

Contemporary Indian society as described above has plurality of religions. Our society is in fact, confronted with two kinds of religious traditions: First, religions which emerged in India, viz., Hinduism, Buddhism, Jainism, and Sikhism; second, religions which took birth in other countries but gradually spread in Indian society, such as Islam, Christianity and Zoroastrianism. Plurality of religious beliefs and faiths in Indian society reflects variety of styles of life. The multiplicity of religious traditions has taken a negative stance of exclusiveness. When emphasis is on the external ritualistic aspects of religion, exclusivism tends to dominate. (Singh, in Murty, 1994: 102-106).

The present Indian society has a distinct world-view which is radically distinct from the ancient and the medieval views. Modernity does not mean complete break with traditions. It is a continuum. While traditional Indian society was characterised by predominance of religious values, spirituality, belief in other-worldliness and submission to authority, modern secular Indian society has four important characteristics: freedom of thought, dominance of material culture, discarding other worldliness, and revolting against submission to authority. Thus, modern Hindu society has accepted a view of man which is held by Christianity, Islam and Sikhism. In contemporary India, unity takes precedence over diversity. Earlier, when other cultural groups came in contact with native religious beliefs, they retained their uniqueness but simultaneously adapted to regional cultural conditions. In this socio-cultural milieu, the concept of unity in diversity emerged. But today, it appears that different religions do not want to accommodate each other. Earlier, some Christian missionaries had converted some people, particularly tribals and low-caste Hindus, to Christianity. Today, some Hindu fundamentalists, particularly members of Vishwa Hindu Parishad and Bajrang Dal, want to reconvert Christians and Muslims to Hinduism. The recent attacks on Christians in December 1998 and January 1999 in Gujarat and Orissa is a proof of this attempt of reconverting the converted Hindus.

The problem that we need to understand today is how people of different religious traditions and faiths co-exist in a pluralistic society. Forces of separatism, communalism and narrow dogmatic outlook are disturbing elements. It will not be wrong if we say that the resurgence of religious fanaticism has increased since the 1970s. A few Hindu and Muslim fanatics, to whom religion provides a smoke-screen for their nefarious deeds, hold society to ransom. It is an interesting phenomenon that people of different religions blame one another for communal tensions and riots. Hindus and Muslims blamed each other for killing thousands of persons of different religious faiths in India and Pakistan at the time of partition of the country. During the 1960s, 1970s and the 1980s also, Hindus and Muslims held each other responsible for various communal riots. In 1993, Muslims blamed Hindus for demolishing a 'disputed construction' at Ayodhya in Uttar Pradesh and killing Muslims in Maharashtra riots. After Indira Gandhi's assassination in 1984, Sikhs blamed Hindus for killing hundreds of Sikhs in Delhi, Uttar Pradesh and a few other states. In 1998-99, Christians blamed Hindus for attacking some Christians in Gujarat and Orissa. Religion degenerated into a tool to exploit the situation. The Bhindrawala movement in Punjab and pro-Pakistan attitude of some Muslims in Kashmir are two instances of extreme alienation of religious minorities. The slogan of *Hindutava* raised by a section of the Bharatiya Janata Party provoked anti-Hindu feelings among Muslims and Christians.

Yet, there is unity in diversity as well as toleration. The Britishers tried to divide Hindus, Muslims and Sikhs by exploiting their religious sentiments but they remained united in their struggle for freedom. Today also, there are inter-religious marriages. There is common celebration of festivals. There are common invitations on occasions of Id, Diwali, and on other occasions. Just as some medieval *bhaktas* (saints) like Kabir, Namdev, Ravidas, Nanak, Chaitanaya, etc., tried to transcend religious limitations, and sought a unifying dialect and condemned ritualism, after Independence also there have been some persons like Gandhi, Nehru, etc., (and political parties too) who emphasised unity of man. Today, there is no *official* religion in India. The constitution provides freedom to all religions. It is true that in some states, politicians use religion for the sake of maintaining or capturing political power. People, however, have begun to understand this debased manipulation of religious faiths. Some people, however, hold that there exists no such situation in our country in which different religions tolerate oneanother. They say that there are some religions in India which emphasise the dynamic view of reality while others on static view. There are religions which give priority to personalism (e.g., Islam and Christianity) and others to impersonalism of the

Divine Being. There are religions which do not have divinity as their basic principle (e.g., Jainism, Buddhism) while there are others which have the divinity. But this reflects only diversity and not intoleration.

Religious ideology has, however, now come to be related to politics. There are persons with progressive ideology who want new social structure based on tolerance and accommodation and others with conservative or reactionary ideology who do not want to make any change in the existing social structure. The two dialectical ideologies give birth to protests as well as lead to riots. As such, in the existing situation, it is not easy to reconcile the conflicting religious ideologies. Therefore, free interaction among different religious communities in coming years may not be easy.

COMMUNALISM

The rising trend of communalism and the accompanying violence have created a feeling of insecurity among the religious minorities. Muslims, Sikhs and Christians in particular, fear discrimination and confrontation in the days to come. This may just be a fear, but the nation cannot afford to let about one-fifth of the country's population to fall victim to panic, suspicion and insecurity. The events between 1984 and 1999 in Kashmir, Punjab, Uttar Pradesh, Bihar, Gujarat, Assam, Orissa, Andhra Pradesh and Delhi give ample evidence and taste of the destructive outcome of the communal virus in its varied forms. Religious minorities in India are protected by the Constitution which provides for justice, tolerance, equality and freedom. But in an age in which religious fundamentalism is getting transferred into religious bigotry, intolerance and narrow-mindedness, the notion of 'Ram Rajya', is not infrequently misinterpreted by the minorities, especially Muslims, to mean the rule of Lord Ram, i.e., Hindu rule. The presence of police in and near religious shrines to keep an eye on and check the hide-outs of terrorists (as in Amritsar in 1985 and in Kashmir in November 1993 and May 1995) is viewed as interference in religious faith. Therefore, to prevent damage to the peace and integrity of the nation, there is need to analyse and debate the problem of communalism and communal violence. It has become absolutely important to define 'communalism'. Also, it is equally pertinent to discover who is 'communal'.

Concept of Communalism

Communalism is an ideology which states that society is divided into religious communities whose interests differ and are at times even opposed to each other. The antagonism practised by the people of one community against the people of other community and religion can be termed 'communalism'. This antagonism goes to the extent of falsely accusing, harming, and deliberately insulting a particular community and extends to looting, burning down the homes and shops of the helpless and the weak, dishonouring women, and even killing persons. 'Communal persons' are those who practise politics through religion. Among leaders, those religious leaders are 'communal' who run their religious communities like business enterprises and institutions and raise the cries of "Hinduism, Islam, Sikhism or Christianity in danger", the moment they find that donations into their holy 'corporations' have begun to dwindle, or their leadership has come to be challenged, or their ideology has been questioned. Thus, 'communal' is not one who is 'a man of religion' but 'one who practises politics by linking it with religion'. These power politicians are not good Hindus nor Good Muslims, Sikhs, Christians, Parsis or Buddhists. They can be viewed as dangerous political 'scum'. For them, God and religion are merely instruments to be used to live luxuriously as the 'king parasites' of society and to attain political goals (*Day After*, June, 1990:35-36).

T.K. Oommen (1989) has suggested six dimensions of communalism: assimilationist, welfarist, retreatist, retaliatory, separatist, and secessionist. *Assimilationist* communalism is one in which small religious groups are assimilated/integrated into a big religious group. Such communalism claims that Scheduled Tribes are Hindus, or that Jains, Sikhs and Buddhists are Hindus and they should be covered by the Hindu Marriage Act. *Welfarist* communalism aims at the welfare of a particular community, say, improving living standard and providing for education and health of Christians by the Christian associations, or Parsi associations working for the uplift of the Parsis. Such communal mobilisation aims at working only for members of one's own community. *Retreatist* communalism is one in which a small religious community keeps itself away from politics: for example, Bahai community, which forbids its members from participating in political activities. *Retaliatory* communalism attempts to harm, hurt, injure the members of other religious communities. *Separatist* communalism is one in which one religious or a cultural group wants to maintain its cultural specificity and demands a separate territorial state within the country, for example, the demand of Mizos and Nagas in North-East India or Bodos in Assam, or of Jharkhand tribals in Bihar, or of Gorkhas for Gorakhaland in West Bengal, or of hill people for Uttrakhand in Uttar Pradesh, or of Vidharbha in Maharashtra. Lastly, *secessionist* communalism is one in which a religious community wants a separate political identity and demands an independent state. A very small militant section of Sikh population demanding Khalistan or some Muslim militants demanding independent Kashmir were engaged in practising this type of communalism. Of these six types of communalism, the last three create problems engendering agitations, communal riots, terrorism and insurgency.

Communalism in India

The pluralist society of India is composed of many religious groups; however, these groups are further divided into various sub-groups. Hindus are divided into sects like Arya Samajis, Shivites, Sanatanees, and Vaishnavas, while Muslims are divided into Shias and Sunnis on the one hand, and Ashrafs (aristocrats), Azlafs (weavers, butchers, carpenters, oilmen), and Arzals on the other. Strained relations between Hindus and Muslims have existed for a long time, whereas some Hindus and Sikhs have started viewing each other with suspicion only during the last fifteen years or so. Although in a few states, we now hear of some conflicts between Hindus and Christians and Muslims and Christians too, yet, by and large, Christians in India do not feel deprived or exploited by other communities. Among Muslims, Shias and Sunnis too bear prejudicial attitudes towards each other. Here, we will mainly analyse Hindu-Muslim and briefly Hindu-Sikh relations.

Hindu-Muslim Communalism

Muslim attacks on India started in the tenth century, but early Muslim conquerors were more interested in looting rather than establishing religious dominance. It was when Qutubdin became the first Sultan of Delhi that Islam found a footing in India. Later, it were the Moghuls who consolidated their empire and Islam in the process. Some of the policies, proselytisation efforts, destruction of Hindu temples and construction of mosques over these temples by Moghul rulers aroused communal bickerings between Hindu and Muslim communities. When the British established their dominance in India, they initially adopted the policy of patronising Hindus, but after the First War of Independence in 1857 in which Hindus and Muslims fought shoulder to shoulder, the Britishers adopted the policy of 'divide and rule' which resulted in deliberately fostering communal clashes deliberately for keeping their hegemony intact. The relations between Hindus and Muslims were further strained when during the freedom struggle, power politics came into play. Thus, though antagonism between Hindus and Muslims is an old issue, Hindu-Muslim communalism in India can be described a legacy of the British rule during the freedom struggle. This communalism operates today in a significantly changed social and political milieu. It is the single largest threat to the secular ideals that are enshrined in our Constitution.

Let us examine the genesis and historical roots of Hindu-Muslim communalism after the First World War in order to provide some understanding of this phenomenon in its contemporary context. What were the religious and political ideologies and aspirations of the political parties that participated in the freedom struggle? The nationalist appeal was to address itself to two important factors to unite the diverse groups: first, freedom from the exploitation of colonial rulers, and second, democratic rights for all citizens. But the major political parties such as the Congress, the Muslim League, the Communist Party and the Hindu Maha Sabha did not share these sentiments in the thirties and forties of the twentieth century. The Congress from its very inception adopted a policy of 'unity from the top' in which the effort was to win over the middle-class and upper-class Muslims who were accepted as leaders of the Muslim community, leaving it to them to draw the Muslim masses into the movement. This 'unity from the top' approach could not promote Hindu-Muslim cooperation in fighting imperialism. All serious efforts between 1918 and 1922 at bringing about Hindu-Muslim unity were in the nature of negotiations among the top leaders of Hindu, Muslim and Sikh communities and the Congress. Quite often, the Congress acted as an intermediary among the different communal leaders instead of acting as an active organiser of the forces of secular nationalism. There was, thus, an implicit acceptance within the early nationalist leadership that Hindus, Muslims, and Sikhs were distinct communities which shared only the political and the economic concerns but not the religious, social and cultural practices. This is how seeds of communalism were sown in the first and second quarters of the twentieth century. However, the Muslim League and the Hindu Maha Sabha remained fairly weak organisationally till 1936. In the 1937 elections, the Muslim League won only 22 per cent of the total seats reserved for Muslims (482) in the provincial assemblies. It did not fare well even in the Muslim-majority provinces. It was only after 1942 that the Muslim League emerged as a strong political party and claimed the right to speak for all Muslims. Jinah described Congress party as a 'Hindu' organisation, a claim that the British supported. Within the Congress itself, some leaders like Madan Mohan Malviya, K.M.Munshi and Sardar Patel took up pro-Hindu positions. Thus, the Congress could not purge its ranks of communal elements.

While the slogan of Pakistan was first articulated by the Muslim League in 1940, the Congress leaders accepted partition of the country in 1946 which led to displacement of millions of Hindus, Muslims and Sikhs amid bloodshed and carnage. Even after the partition, the Congress failed to come to grips with communalism. It could, thus, be said that Hindu-Muslim communalism in India had politico-social origins and religion alone was not the cause of the conflict between Hindus and Muslims. Economic interests and the cultural and social mores (such as festivals, social practices and lifestyle) were factors that further divided the two communities.

Sixteen cities in India have been identified as more vulnerable to Hindu-Muslim communal riots. Of these, five (Moradabad, Meerut, Aligarh, Agra and Varanasi) are in Uttar Pradesh; one (Aurangabad) in Maharashtra; one (Ahmedabad) in Gujarat; one (Hyderabad) in Andhra Pradesh, two (Jamshedpur and Patna) in Bihar, two (Silchar and Gauhati) in Assam, one (Calcutta) in West Bengal; one (Bhopal) in Madhya Pradesh; one (Srinagar) in Jammu and Kashmir; and one (Cuttack) in Orrisa. Since eleven cities lie in the northern belt, three in the eastern belt, and two in the southern belt, could it be presumed that the Muslims in South India are culturally better assimilated because of their involvement in trade and commerce which calls for goodwill with all communities? Strangely, this fact applies to the five cities in Uttar Pradesh also. We have, therefore, to search another explanation for this phenomenon.

The Hindu-Muslim antagonism can be ascribed to a complex set of factors: These are: (1) Muslim invasions in which the invaders looted property and constructed mosques over/near Hindu temples. (2) British encouragement of Muslim separatism for their own ends during their imperial rule. (3) The behaviour of some of the Muslims in India after partition, indicating their pro-Pakistan attitude. Such behaviour creates a feeling among the majority community that Muslims are not patriotic. The stereotype image of an Indian Muslim which is entrenched in the Hindu psyche is that of a bigoted, inward-looking outcaste. A Muslim similarly looks upon a Hindu as a conniving, all-powerful opportunist and he views himself as victimised by him and alienated from the mainstream of society. (4) A new aggressiveness on the part of the Muslim political parties in an effort to find a place in the country. Reports are rife about some Muslim extremists obtaining 'foreign money', 'turning into foreign agents', indulging in a well-designed plan to soil the secular ideal of the country, and attempting to incite Indian Muslims. (5) A failure on the part of the Muslim leaders to unite Muslims and resolve their problems is perhaps due to frustration because they have been influenced by the wave of Islamic fundamentalism sweeping West Asia and Pakistan. The leaders have only exploited the numerical strength of the Muslims (especially in Kerala, Kashmir and Uttar Pradesh) to strike barter deals, secure a chunk of Muslim seats in parliament and legislatures, and seek power and pelf for themselves and their friends. (6) The government is also responsible for neglecting Muslims, large sections of whom feel alienated and consequently become willing victims of selfish leaders. The ruling elite merely preach religious amity and have little understanding of the real problems of the Muslims. The Hindu leadership only deals with those Muslim leaders who toe their line.

The Indian Muslims, not surprisingly, tend to consider their future as a question of 'Us' versus 'They'. When they make their demands known, as any segment of society would do to voice their grievances, it more often than not explodes into an orgy of Hindu-Muslim violence which leads to the accusation of foreign incitement. Should the Muslim problem be perceived only as a communal problem? Is it not a fact that the Hindu-Muslim issue is not any different from the anti-Brahmin agitations in Tamil Nadu, or the intercaste conflicts in Uttar Pradesh, Bihar and some other states, or the Bengali-Assamese trouble in Assam, or the Maharashtrian-non-Maharashtrian conflict in Maharashtra? The problem in reality is one of social and economic interests and rigidity and change in values.

The militant Hindus maintain that Muslims in the country are being pampered. The Ramjanam Bhoomi-Babri Masjid issue in 1992-93 further affected the delicate balance of communal harmony. After getting disillusioned with the Congress, Muslims developed faith in the Janata Dal (1990), in the Samajwadi Party (1995), in the Bahujan Samaj Party, and in the United Front (1996). The break-up of the Janata Dal (November 1990) followed by the assassination of Rajiv Gandhi (May 1991), coming to power of Bharatiya Janata Party in November 1993 elections in four states (Rajasthan, Uttar Pradesh, Madhya Pradesh, and Himachal Pradesh), and at the centre in 1998, and Janata Dal in Karnataka and Telgu Desham in Andhra Pradesh in 1994 elections, and Shiv Sena and BJP in Maharashtra and BJP in Gujarat in March 1995 elections, breakdown of coalition Ministry of SP and BSP and of BJP and BSP in Uttar Pradesh, failure of SP and BSP to get majority in Uttar Pradesh elections in October, 1996, and failure of Samajwadi Party to support Sonia Gandhi in forming Minsitry at the centre after Vajpayee's defeat in Parliament in April 1999—all these have created confusion. The Muslims today feel far more concerned about their safety and security than before.

Hindu-Sikh Communalism

The Sikhs constitute less than 2 per cent (1.3 crore) of India's population. Though dispersed widely over the entire country and even abroad, their largest concentration is in Punjab, where they form the majority of the state's population.

The Sikh agitation started in Punjab in the early eighties. The number of killings increased and the Sikh protests became organised, militant and increasingly violent. In 1984, when the military launched Operation Blue Star for seizing weapons and arresting militants from the Golden Temple at Amritsar, the Sikhs reacted violently. In October 1984, when Indira Gandhi was assassinated and thousands of Sikhs were killed in Delhi and other states, and their property was looted, burnt or destroyed, some Sikh militants became so agitated that they killed hundreds of Hindus in trains and buses, destroyed their property and forced many Hindus to leave Punjab. In May 1988, when operation Black Thunder was launched once again by the military to clear militants from the Golden Temple in Amritsar which remained under their control for about ten days, the Sikhs retaliated by exploding bombs, killing Hindus and looting banks. The relations between Sikhs and Hindus thus remained strained for about one and a half decade. However, the militancy of extremist Sikhs in Punjab has now been suppressed and from 1993 onwards, there has been considerable improvement in the relations between the people of the two communities. There is goodwill and respect among them for each other's religious beliefs and places of worship.

Ethnic Violence

Besides the Hindu-Muslim conflicts and Hindu-Sikh skirmishes, how do we perceive relations between different ethnic groups, say between the Assamese and the non-Assamese? In Assam, for nearly 150 years the economic development of the state was fuelled by the labour and enterprise imported from outside the state. Over this period spanning a century and a half, Assam has been home to generations of the so-called 'outsiders', who have known no home, no land other than the soil of Assam itself. Some have indeed grown rich, but most have remained desperately poor. The Assamese have now raised the question of nationality. The All Assam Students Union (AASU) and the All Assam Gana Parishad (AAGP) agitation (which fathered the AGP as a political party) confused 'outsiders' with 'foreigners' (including Bengali refugees from the Bangladesh). Fantastic figures were brandished ranging from five million to seven million as the number of foreigners (*bahiragat*) illegitimately lurking in the state. This issue of ridding Assam of foreigners held the state to ransom for six years—from 1979 till the Assam accord on 15 August, 1985. Hatred was stoked up against the Bodos, the Bengalis, the Marwaris and the non-Assamese Muslims. This secessionist movement was responsible for thousands of innocent deaths. The massacre of 1,383 women and children and some men in ten villages in and around Nellie in Nowgong district was a part of this ethnic violence. The AGSP which remained in power between 1985 and 1990 could not contain the ethnic tension.

The ULFA militants launched a movement which became so strong that President's rule was imposed in the state in November 1990 instead of holding elections due in January 1991. The army and the security forces launched an operation to round up rebels and recover weapons. The President's rule was, however, lifted in June, 1991 when the new Congress government assumed power in the state. But the ULFA militants jolted even the new government by kidnapping some government servants including a few top ONGC officials from different parts of the state on the very first day of the government's tenure. The May 1996 elections also did not prevent reprisals from the Bodos. The militants are yet to realise that Assam is like all other states in India, and it belongs to all the legitimate citizens of India, whatever language they speak, whatever religion they follow and whatever rites and rituals they practise. The Bodos—a tribe which comprised about 49 per cent of Assam's population in 1947 and about 29 per cent in 1991 and which ruled over Assam until around 1825—are now demanding autonomy. Though an accord was signed by the Assam government and the Bodo leadership represented by the All Bodo Students Union (ABSU) and the Bodo People's Action Committee (BPAC) in February 1993 yet the problem still remains unresolved. The Bodo leaders and the state government have failed to arrive at an agreement on the boundary issue and transfer of about 3,000 villages to the Bodoland Autonomous Council. The Bodos also do not want that Assamese language should be thrust upon indigeneous tribals. The Bodo movement in the 1960s, the 1970s, the 1980s, and the 1990s operated in fits and starts, however, it has gathered momentum now. The Bodos now demand a union territory called 'Udayachal'. Violent activities like bomb blasts and blowing up roads and railway bridges by the Bodo militants point out the domestic and 'foreign' aid to the militants and the need for firm action by the government to contain insurgent activities.

Communal Violence

The Concept

Communal violence involves people belonging to two different religious communities mobilised against each other and carrying the feelings of hostility, emotional fury, exploitation, social discrimination and social neglect. The high degree of cohesion in one community against another is built around tension and polarisation. The target of attack are the members of the 'enemy' community. Generally, there is no leadership in communal riots which could effectively control and contain the riot situation. It could thus be said that communal violence is based mainly on hatred, enemity and revenge.

Communal violence has increased quantitatively and qualitatively ever since politics came to be communalised. Gandhi was its first victim followed by the murder of many persons in the 1970s and the 1980s. Following destruction of Babri structure in Ayodhya in December 1992, and bomb blasts in Bombay in early 1993, communal riots in Maharashtra, Tamil Nadu, Bihar, Uttar Pradesh and Kerala have considerably increased. While some political parties tolerate ethno-religious communalism, a few others even encourage it. Recent examples of this tolerance, indifference to and passive acceptance of or even connivance of the activities of religious organisations by certain political leaders and some political parties are found in attacks on Christian missionaries and in violent activities against Christians in Gujarat, Madhya Pradesh, and Allahabad. Emergency of the mid-1970s commenced the trend of criminal elements entering mainstream politics. This phenomenon has now entrenched itself in Indian politics to such an extent that religious fanaticism, casteism and mixing of religion and politics have increased in varied dimensions. Political parties and political leaders adopt 'holier than thou' attitude in relation to each other instead of taking a collective stand against these negative impulses affecting our society.

The Hindu organisations blame Muslims and Christians for forcibly converting Hindus to their religions. Without indulging in the controversy whether prosylitisation or religious conversions were coercive or voluntary, it may only be said that raising this issue today is patently irrational fanaticism. Hinduism has been tolerant and talks about all humanity being one family. Therefore, it has to be accepted that the doctrine of *Hindutva* blighting Indian politics has nothing to do with Hindu thought. It is time secular political leaders and political parties ignore political and electoral considerations and condemn and take action against those religious organisations which disrupt peace and stability through statements and threaten the unity and pluralistic identity of India.

Features of Communal Riots

A probe of the major communal riots in the country in the last five decades has revealed that: (1) Communal riots are more politically motivated than fuelled by religion. Even the Madan Commission which looked into communal disturbances in Maharashtra in May 1970 had emphasised that "the architects and builders of communal tensions are the communalists and a certain class of politicians—those all-India and local leaders out to seize every opportunity to strengthen their political positions, enhance their prestige and enrich their public image by giving a communal colour to every incident and thereby projecting themselves in the public eye as the champions of their religion and the rights of their community". (2) Besides political interests, economic interests too play a vigorous part in fomenting communal clashes. (3) Communal riots seem to be more common in North India than in South and East India. (4) The possibility of recurrence of communal riots in a town where communal riots have already taken place once or twice is stronger than in a town in which riots have never occurred. (5) Most communal riots take place on the occasion of religious festivals. (6) The use of deadly weapons in the riots is on the ascendancy.

Incidence of Communal Riots

In India, communal frenzy reached its peak during 1946-48 whereas the period between 1950 and 1963 may be called the period of communal peace. Political stability and economic development in the country contributed to the improvement of the communal situation. The incidences of rioting shot up after 1963. Serious riots broke out in 1964 in various parts of East India like Calcutta, Jamshedpur, Rourkela and Ranchi. Another wave of communal violence swept across the country between 1968 and 1971 when the political leadership at the centre and in the states was weak.

The communal riots in Uttar Pradesh, Gujarat, and Andhra Pradesh in December, 1990, in Belgaum (Karnataka) in November 1991, in Varanasi and Hapur (Uttar Pradesh) in February 1992, in Seelampur in May 1992, in Samaipur Badli in Delhi, Nasik in Maharashtra, and Munthra near Trivandrum in Kerala in July 1992, and in Sitamarhi in October 1992—all point out the weakening of communal amity in the country.

After the demolition of the disputed shrine in December 1992 at Ayodhya, when communal violence flared up in various states, more than 1,000 people were said to have died in five days, including 236 in Uttar Pradesh, 64 in Karnataka, 76 in Assam, 30 in Rajasthan and 20 in West Bengal. It was after this violence that the government banned Rashtriya Swayam Sewak Sangh (RSS), Vishwa Hindu Parishad (VHP), Bajrang Dal, Islamic Sevak Sangh (ISS) and the Jamait-e-Islami Hind in December 1992. After the bomb blasts in Bombay and later in Calcutta in April 1993, the communal riots in Maharashtra and other states claimed more than 200 lives of both Muslims and Hindus. Soon after the Bombay blasts, a well-known Imam of Delhi stated: "It is basically a matter of survival now. We cannot rule out taking up arms in order to stay alive". The Sangh Pariwar leaders claimed that India is a Hindu Rashtra, that only the Hindu culture is the authentic Indian culture, that Muslims are actually Mohammadi Hindus, and that all Hindustanis are by definition Hindus. It is such aggressive approach of Hindu and Muslim fanatics that leads to communal riots. While 61 districts out of 350 districts in India were identified as sensitive districts in 1961, 216 districts were so identified in 1979, 186 in 1986, 254 in 1987 and 186 in 1989. Apart from the loss in terms of lives, the communal riots cause widespread destruction of property and adversely affect economic activities. For instance, property worth Rs. 14 crore was damaged between 1983 and 1986 (*Times of India*, July 25, 1986). In the 2,086 incidences of communal riots in three years between 1986 and 1988, 1,024 persons were killed and 12,352 injured.

After the communal riots in Maharashtra, Bengal and other states in 1993, no serious riots were reported for about three years; but in May 1996 Calcutta once again witnessed communal riots on an issue of taking a Moharrum procession along a particular route in violation of police permission. It was reported that the trouble was not spontaneous but was planned and had background of political rivalry. Bootleggers and land-builder mafia had also played an important role in spreading communal violence. Thus, recurrence of communal riots in different states from time to time even now points out that so long as the political leaders and religious fanatics continue using communalism as a powerful instrument to achieve their goal or so long as religion remains politicised, our country will remain ever so vulnerable to communal tension.

Causes of Communal Violence

Different scholars have approached the problem of communal violence with different perspectives, attributing different causes and suggesting different measures to counter it. The Marxist school relates communalism to economic deprivation and to the class struggle between the haves and the have-nots to secure a monopoly control of the market forces. Political scientists view it as a power struggle. Sociologists see it as a phenomenon of social tensions and relative deprivations. The religious experts perceive it as a diadem of violent fundamentalists and conformists.

The class analysis of communalism requires some attention. The explanation is that the economic, social and political situations in a society sometimes create such problems and crises for the people that even though they try to come to grips with these crises, they fail to do so. Without attempting to grasp the real causes for this failure, they 'perceive' the other community (numerically much stronger than their own) as the cause of their woes. Communalism is thus a social reality which is generated and reflected in a distorted way.

After independence, though our government claimed to follow "socialistic pattern of economy" yet in practice the economic development was based more on capitalist pattern. In this pattern, on the one hand the development has not occurred at a rate where it could solve the problems of poverty, unemployment and insecurity which could prevent frustration and unhealthy competition for scarce jobs and other economic opportunities, and on the other hand, capitalist development has generated prosperity only for certain social strata leading to sharp and visible inequality and new social strains and social anxieties. Those who have benefitted or have gained, have their expectations soar even higher. They also feel threatened in their newly gained prosperity. Their relative prosperity arouses the social jealousy of those who fail to develop or who decline in power and prestige. The efforts of the government to solve the problems of the religious minorities arouse intense resentment among those prosperous sections of the community who are in numerical majority and who have achieved economic, social and political power through manipulations. They feel that any rise in social scale of the minority community will threaten their social domination. Thus, feelings of suspicion and hostility on the part of both the communities continuously foster the growth of communalism. Particularly, it (communalism) makes a ready appeal to the urban poor and the rural unemployed whose number has grown rapidly as a result of lop-sided economic and social development and large-scale migration to cities. The social anger and frustration of these rootless and impoverished people often find expression in spontaneous violence whenever opportunity arises. A communal riot provides a good opportunity for this. But this economic analysis is not considered objective by many scholars.

Is religion responsible for communalism? There are intellectuals who do not believe that religion has any role to play in it. Bipan Chandra (1984), for example, holds that communalism is neither inspired by religion nor is religion an object of communal politics, even though the communalist bases his politics on religious differences, uses religious identity as an organising principle, and in the mass phases of communalism uses religion to mobilise masses. The religious difference is used to 'mask' non-religious social needs, aspirations and conflicts. However, religiosity, i.e., "too much religion in one's life" or the intrusion of religion into areas other than those of personal belief, tends to create a certain receptivity to communal ideology and politics. Moreover, religious obscurantism, narrow-mindedness and bigotry in the name of going back to fundamentals tends to divide people whom life and history have brought together. In this respect, different religions have different elements in their structure, rituals and ideological practices which relate to communalism in different manners. Their analysis and elimination has to be specific to different religions.

Some scholars have proposed a multiple-factor approach in which they give importance to several factors together. Ten major factors have been identified in the etiology of communalism (Surolia, 1987: 62): These are; social, religious, political, economic, legal, psychological, administrative, historical, local, and international. The *social* factors include social traditions, stereotyped images of religious communities, caste and class ego or inequality and religion-based social stratification; the *religious* factors include decline in religious norms of tolerance and secular values, narrow and dogmatic religious beliefs, use of religion for political gains and communal ideology of religious leaders; the *political* factors include religion-based politics, religion-dominated political organisations, canvassing in elections based on religious considerations, political interference in religious affairs, instigation or support to agitations by politicians for vested interests, political justification of communal violence, and failure of political leadership; to contain religious feelings; the *economic* factors include economic exploitation and discrimination of minority religious communities, their lop-sided economic development, inadequate opportunity in competitive market, non-expanding economy, displacement and non-absorption of workers of minority religious groups, and the influence of gulf money in provoking religious conflicts; the *legal* factors include absence of common civil code, special provisions and concessions for some communities in the Constitution, special status of certain states, reservation policy, and special laws for different communities; the *psychological* factors include social prejudices, stereotype attitudes, distrust, hostility and apathy against another community, rumour, fear psychosis and misinformation/misinterpretation/misrepresentation by mass media; the *administrative* factors include lack of coordination between the police and other administrative units, ill-equipped and ill-trained police personnel, inept functioning of intelligence agencies, biased policemen, and police excesses and inaction; the *historical* factors include alien invasions, damage to religious institutions, proselytisation efforts, divide and rule policy of colonial rulers, partition trauma, past communal riots, old disputes on land, temples and mosques; the *local* factors include religious processions, slogan raising, rumours, land disputes, local anti-social elements and group rivalries; and the *international* factors include training and financial support from other countries, other countries' machinations to disunite and weaken India, and support to communal organisations.

Against these approaches, we need a holistic approach to understand the problem of communalism and communal violence. The emphasis of this approach would be on various factors, distinguishing the major from the minor. We can classify these factors in four sub-groups: most conspicuous, chief cooperating, minor aggravating, and apparently inoperative. Specifically, these factors are: communal politics and politicians' support to religious fanatics, prejudices (which lead to discrimination, avoidance, physical attack and extermination), the growth of communal organisations, and conversions and proselytisation. Broadly speaking, attention may be focused on fanatics, anti-social elements and vested economic interests in creating and fanning violence in the rival communities.

My own thesis is that communal violence is instigated by religious fanatics, initiated by anti-social elements, supported by political activists, financed by vested interests, and spread by the callousness of the police and the administrators. While these factors directly cause communal violence, the factor which aids in spreading violence is the ecological layout of a particular city which enables rioters to escape unapprehended. The case studies of Baroda and Ahmedabad communal riots in Gujarat in Central India, Meerut, Aligarh and Moradabad riots in Uttar Pradesh, Jamshedpur in Bihar, and Srinagar in Kashmir in North India, Hyderabad and Kerala riots in South India, and Assam riots in East India vindicate my thesis.

In the holistic approach to communal violence, a few factors need explanation. One is the illogical feeling of discrimination among the Muslims. Upto 1998, the percentage of Muslims in the IAS was 2.9, in IPS 2.8, in banks 2.2 and in the judiciary 6.2. Muslims, thus, feel that they are discriminated against and denied opportunities in all these fields. The fact is that the number of Muslims who compete for these jobs is very low. The feeling of discrimination among Muslims is ludicrous and irrational.

The other factor is the flow of money from the Gulf and other countries to India. A sizeable number of Muslims migrate to the Gulf countries to earn a handsome income and become affluent. These Muslims and the local Sheikhs send money to India generously for building mosques, opening *madarsas* (schools), and for running charitable Muslim institutions. This money is, thus, believed to help Muslim fundamentalism. Pakistan is one country whose rulers always had a feeling of hostility for India. This country's power elite have been continuously interested in creating instability in India. It has now been established that Pakistan is actively supporting Muslim terrorists (of Jammu and Kashmir and Punjab) by providing training and military weapons. These destabilising efforts of Pakistan and other governments have further created ill-feeling and suspicion among the Hindus against the Muslims. The same can be said about Hindu militants and Hindu organisations in India which whip up antagonistic feelings against the Muslims and Muslim organisations. Issues like the Ram Janambhoomi-Babri Masjid dispute in Ayodhya, the Krishna Janam Bhoomi and nearby Masjid alteration in Mathura, the dispute over Kashi Viswanath temple and its adjoining mosque in Varanasi, and the controversial Masjid in Sambhal claimed to be the temple of Lord Shiva from the days of Prithviraj Chauhan, and incidents like a Muslim leader giving call for non-attendance of Muslims on Republic Day and the observing of January 26, (1987) as a 'black day', have all aggravated the ill-feeling between the two communities.

The mass media also sometimes contribute to communal tensions in their own way. Many a time the news items published in papers are based on hearsay, rumours, or wrong interpretations. Such news items add fuel to the fire and fan communal feelings. This is what happened in Ahmedabad in the 1969 riots when '*Sewak*' reported that several Hindu women were stripped and raped by Muslims. Although this report was contradicted the next day, the damage had been done. It aroused the feelings of Hindus and created a communal riot.

One of the issues which has been agitating both Muslims and Hindus in recent years is the Muslim Personal Law. With the decision of the Supreme Court in favour of Shah Bano, and its advice in April 1995 to the government that it should enact a uniform civil code, the Muslims fear that their personal law is being interfered with. The politicians also exploit the situation to keep themselves in power. The Bharatiya Janata Party, the Vishwa Hindu Parishad, the Shiv Sena and the RSS are the organisations which claim to be the champions of Hinduism. Likewise, the Muslim League, the Jamait-e-Islami, the Jamait-Ulema-a-Hind, the Majlis-e-Ittehadul Musalmeen, and the Majlis-e-Mushawarat use Muslims as their vote banks by championing their religious sentiments. The communal politics in Jammu and Kashmir, Andhra Pradesh, Kerala, Uttar Pradesh, Maharashtra and Bihar are examples of such behaviour. Politicians charge the social atmosphere with communal passion by their inflammatory speeches, writings and propaganda. They plant the seeds of distrust in the minds of the Muslims while the Hindus are convinced that they are unjustly coerced into making extraordinary concessions to the Muslims in the economic, social and cultural fields. They also exploit the deep religious traditions of both the communities and highlight differences in their respective practices and rituals. The leaders also try to use economic arguments to instill fear and suspicion in the minds of people and prepare their followers to start a riot at the least provocation. It has happened in Bhiwandi, Moradabad, Meerut, Ahmedabad, Aligarh and Hyderabad.

Social factors, like large sections of Muslims refusing to use family planning measures, also create suspicion and ill-feeling among the Hindus. A few years ago, leaflets were distributed in Pune and Sholapur in Maharashtra by one Hindu organisation criticising/debunking the Muslims for not accepting family planning programme and practising polygyny with the aim to allegedly increase their population and install a Muslim government in India. All this demonstrates how a combination of political, economic, social, religious and administrative factors aggravates the situation which leads to communal riots.

Theories of Communal Violence

Communal violence is collective violence. When large sections of people in a community fail to achieve their collective goals, or feel that they are being discriminated against and deprived of equal opportunities, they feel frustrated and disillusioned and this collective frustration (or what Feierabends and Nesvold have called 'systematic frustration') leads to collective violence. However, it is not the whole community which launches a violent protest. In fact, the action planned by the discontented people against the ruling group or the power elite (against whose ways they protest) is often non-violent. It is only a small band of protesters who consider non-violence ineffective and violence essential for the success of their struggle, and who snatch every precipitating opportunity to use violence to assert the strength of their ideology. This sub-group indulging in violent behaviour does not represent the whole community or the total group of the discontented people. The behaviour of this sub-group, by and large, is not equivocally supported by the rest of the community. My contention, thus, comes close to the old 'riffraff theory' of violent riot behaviour which holds that the majority of the people disown and oppose the violent/delinquent behaviour of the sub-group by describing it as 'irresponsible' behaviour.

The question is, what causes the 'group of individuals' to be violent. Two of the important theoretical propositions on collective violence are: (i) it is normal response to provocation, and (ii) it is a response that is consistent with norms supporting its use. This calls for analysis of some of the important existing theories.

Excluding the psycho-pathological theories (because they focus on the aggressors' psychological personality characteristics and pathological disorders as the chief determinants of violence, and I consider these important for explaining individual violence but not collective violence), other theories may be classified into two categories: (a) at the level of the socio-psychological analysis, and (b) at the level of the socio-cultural or sociological analysis. In the first group, theories like Frustration-Aggression Theory, Perversion Theory, Motive Attribution Theory and Self-Attitude Theory may be included, while in the second group theories like Social Tension Theory, Anomie Theory, Theory of Subculture of Violence, and Social Learning Theory may be included. My contention is that all these theories fail to explain the phenomenon of collective violence in communal riots. My theoretical approach (called Social Barriers Approach) concentrates on the sociological analysis of social structural conditions.

Social Barriers Theory

The conditions which lead to collective communal violence are: stress, status frustration, and crises of various kind. My thesis is that aggressors use violence because they suffer from insecurity and anxiety. The origin of these feelings and anxieties in an individual can be traced to social barriers created by the oppressive social systems, the power elite, as well as the individual's background and upbringing which have probably put up hurdles for him and which serve to aggravate his tendency to irrational and unrealistic attitudes to social norms and social institutions. My theory also takes into account three factors in aggressors' behaviour, namely, adjustment (in status), attachment (to community) and commitment (to values), as well as the social environment (in which individuals/aggressors live) and the socialised personalities of the individuals (aggressors). My theoretical model, thus, gives importance to the social system, the personality structure of individual aggressors, and sub-cultural patterns of the society in which individuals use violence. In social system, I include strains and frustrations which are the result of functioning of social structures in society; in personality structure, I include adjustment, attachment and commitment of the individual aggressors, and in sub-cultural patterns, I include the values which operate as a means of social control.

My thesis is that maladjustment, non-attachment, and non-commitment of an individual lead to his feeling of relative deprivation. Relative deprivation is the perceived discrepancy between groups' expectations and their capabilities (conditions of life individuals/groups think they are capable of attaining or maintaining, given the proper opportunities and legitimate means).Here the important term is 'perceived' (by the members of the groups); hence different variations in behaviour or relative deprivations do not always lead to violent behaviour.

Relative deprivation (of a group) occurs when (i) expectations increase while capabilities remain the same or decline, or (ii) when expectations remain the same while capabilities decline. Since both expectations and capabilities rest on perception, value orientations of a group have an important bearing on (a) the way the group will perceive deprivation, (b) the target to which it (relative deprivation) will be directed, and (c) the form in which it will be expressed. Since each group/individual is subjected to different forces, each group/individual will respond differently in terms of violence or participation in collective communal violence.

The Social Barriers Theory is not essentially an elitist theory of violence where a small group, ideologically superior, takes the initiative to spread violence and decides to use it 'for the good' of the whole frustrated group on whose behalf it violently vocalises its protest. Further, the small group does not depend upon the widespread collective action of the frustrated masses. In this context, my explanation is opposed to the orthodox Marxist theory because Marx did not envisage this kind of uprising and mass revolution.

Theory of Polarisation and Cluster Effect

Recently, a new conceptual paradigm has been developed to explain the inter and intracommunity violence in India (Singh, 1990). The paradigm is based on three concepts—polarity, cleavage, and cluster. The paradigm has been built up on the basis of the facts in 'pre-riot', 'riot' and 'post-riot' situations and the analysis of group behaviour of individuals belonging to different social groups (polarities) in animosity with each other. Since the communal disturbances involve two antagonistic social groups, it necessitates a careful analysis of animosity (state of mind and psyche), structural conduciveness (physical situation), and prejudices.

The individual in isolation is weak and insecure. The strength lies in assemblies, collectivities and groups. The individual joins them for his gain and security. Various polarities exist in society at all times. To each individual, these polarities are of two types—permanent and temporary. To the former category belong ideology, religion, language, caste, region and sex. These polarities constitute individual's basic identity which lasts with the individual. To the second category belong occupation, profession, functions based on vested interests. Though normally the polarities are not mutually exclusive yet they become exclusive when society undergoes a cleavage phenomenon due to perceived difference and division of population as a consequence of polarisation. When masses in general assign the same closeness to single polarity, it becomes a dominating polarity at that time at that particular place for that particular population.

This dominant polarity sets the pattern of inhibitions of the population (cluster formation), that is, the polarity-based clusters determine the demographic living pattern. Such clusters in old cities and towns are based on religion, caste and sect, but in modern cities these are more class-based. When such clustering takes place because of two different polarities (say, of religion or religious sects), there is a clash. The social dynamics of living in clusters is that these prove highly conducive to the emergence of a riot-prone situation, as interpersonal relationships deteriorate and build irritants which are often perceived as deliberate insult, deprivation and injury by one to the other. The incidents affect most people in the clusters due to physical proximity. This prompts people to build contacts among one's own polarity population and also facilitates the building of mass insurrection.

The communal call given at the level of leadership also accelerates the process of polarisation. For example, Shahi Immam Bukhari's inflammatory speech in Meerut city to the Muslim population in 1982 sparked off a great reaction among Hindus to polarise against Muslims to safeguard their interest which ultimately resulted in communal riots in the city. He gave a similar provocative speech in Anantnag, Kashmir in April 1988, inciting Kashmiri Muslims by claiming that they have been enslaved since the partition. He asserted that the centre had not created better economic conditions for them, they were being deprived of their rights, and their problems were not looked into.

The nature of polarity dominance depends upon five factors: (1) time and space (that is, period, area, location and situation or geographical limits), (2) social structure (that is, caste, community and social group), (3) education (that is awareness of interest), (4) economic interests, and (5) leadership (that is, emotional speeches, promises and policies of the leaders).

On the basis of the above analysis, V.V. Singh describes the riot-prone (communal) structure as follows: (1) bi-polarity population in identifiable clusters; (2) close proximity; (3) common interest and resultant animosity; (4) potency of polarised population. Potency is based on numerical strength, economic prosperity, state of possession of arms, cohesion, type of leadership, and the strength of activity; and (5) administrative expediency and inefficiency of district police and public administration.

Measures to Contain Communal Violence

Measures to meet the challenge of communalism and communal violence can be of two types: long-term and short-term. The long-term remedy lies: *Firstly*, in initiating the process of de-communalising the people at all levels, say, by bringing home to them that communal assumptions are false, by explaining to them the socio-economic and political roots of communalism, and by telling them that what the communalists project as problems are not real problems and what they suggest as remedies are not real remedies. *Secondly*, communalisation of the state and of the political elite in power has to be checked because it leads to inaction against communal violence, and covert or overt political and ideological support to communalism by the state apparatuses, including the media under state control. *Thirdly*, the communalisation of civil society also needs to be checked because it leads to more communal riots and other forms of communal violence. People with communal ideas and ideologies pressurise the government to act in a manner which is always against the principle of secularism. The secular state, the secular party in power and the secular power elite many a time succumb to the pressures of these communal people. It is here that intellectuals, political parties and voluntary organisations can be most effective. *Fourthly*, the role of education, particularly emphasising value-oriented education both in schools and colleges/universities, is important in preventing communal feelings. Education based on new cultural ideologies can protect the young people against philosophies and ideologies of hate. Particularly harmful in the Indian context has been the role of teaching of history. Communal interpretation of history, specially of the medieval period, forms the bedrock of communal ideology in India. Teaching of history along scientific lines in educational institutions has to be a basic element in any ideological struggle against communalism. *Fifthly*, the media can also prove to be significantly useful in preventing communal feelings. Communal press can be banned and legal action can be taken against communal writers. *Sixthly*, the ideology that economic development, industrialisation, growth of capitalism and the growth of the working class would automatically weaken and ultimately eliminate communalism should not be overplayed. This economic reductionist approach of the left parties and organisations like Naxalites only increases communal poison. It is not being suggested that modern economic development is not needed in our society. What is being pointed out is that economic development alone cannot contain communalism. It is not class struggle which increases communalism but communalism surely hampers class unity. Communal violence is more prevalent in developed states like Maharashtra, Punjab and Gujarat and in developed cities like Mumbai, Ahmedabad, Jamshedpur and Kanpur.

Some immediate measures are imperative for containing communalism and communal riots: *Firstly*, Peace Committees can be set up in which individuals belonging to different religious communities can work together to spread goodwill and fellow-feeling and remove feelings of fear and hatred in the riot-affected areas. This will be effective not only in diffusing communal tensions but also in preventing riots from breaking out. *Secondly*, the state has to plan and use new strategies in dealing with communal violence. India's experience in recent years confirms the utility of this step. Whenever strong and secular administrators have used or threatened the use of strong steps, riots either did not occur or were of short duration. For example, strong police and army intervention prevented repetition of riots in Calcutta in November 1984 and in Mumbai in January 1994. When the anti-social elements and religious fanatics and people with vested interests realise that the government is impartial and the police is serious in putting down communal violence with all the force at its command, they immediately cease spreading communal frenzy. This also calls for non-communalising law-enforcement agencies. Experience of riots in Mumbai, Ahmedabad, Bhiwandi and Meerut, and violence in Amritsar, Jullundar and Ludhiana in Punjab shows that communalised officials invariably make the communal situation worse. *Thirdly*, the role of media is immensely heightened during the course of communal violence. Newspapers can pour oil over the troubled waters or extinguish the raging fire. The fear and hatred can be checked if the press, radio and TV report events in a way conducive to soothing the frayed nerves of people instead of inflamming the temper further. The media can contradict rumours in a sober manner. A careful restraint has to be exercised in reporting the number of persons of different religious communities killed or injured. *Lastly*, the government in power has to treat the extremist communal outfits as its immediate targets and cripple their capacity to disrupt law and order. The secessionists in Kashmir, the militants in Punjab, the ISS (now banned) in Kerala and other extremist organisations of Hindu, Muslim and Sikh communalism have to be dealt with by the state through its law and order machinery. The small insecure communities always look to government or move towards communal parties for protection. The Pandits in Kashmir, the innocent victims of communal riots in Mumbai, Uttar Pradesh, Gujarat and other states, and the sufferers of violence by extremists in Bihar, Assam, etc., look towards the secular state of India for security of life and property. The communalism of the 1980s and of the nine years of the 1990s has placed a clear responsibility at the doors of the secular state squarely to confront the communal elements who have emerged as merchants of death. Today, communalism is on the march and secularism is on the retreat, and the state is on the defensive. The state was on the defensive in post-Blue Star Operation phase, on the retreat on Shah Bano case, and under siege on Mandir-Masjid issue in Ayodhya in 1992 and Hazratbal siege in November 1993 and in Charar-e-Shrief shrine siege in May 1995 in Kashmir. In all these situations, Sikh, Muslim and Hindu communalists were on the offensive. The challenge of Hindu, Muslim and Sikh communalism has to be met by the Indian State at political and ideological levels both with short-term and long-term strategies. The government is also facing the problem of the emergence of religion-based politics as a central factor in public affairs and elections, although election results in several states in the last five-six years have proved that the people have rejected such politics.

If the surging tide of communalism is not reversed, it will swamp the country. Before independence, it was easy to argue that communal violence was the result of the British policy of divide and rule. Now the reality is more complex. Religion has come to be politicised and politics has come to be criminalised. Unless all communities consider themselves a part of one nation, the containing of communal disharmony will remain difficult. A country that prides itself on the secular character of its policies has to be wary of politicians who speak only for their own religious community. It has to expose and alienate the bureaucrats who consider secularism only as a theoretical possibility. The police can no longer afford to allow communal issue to foster in the manner that it has. Stopping communally-minded politicians and debarring them from contesting elections, giving deterrent punishment to religious fanatics for arousing anti-religious feelings, adopting corrective measures like keeping the police department free from the politicians' control, strengthening the police intelligence section, restructuring the police force, gearing the police administration to be more sensitive, and reworking the training programme of police officials and enabling them to acquire a secular outlook and making them responsible for their failures could prove to be effective measures in tackling the problem of communal riots. An efficient police organisation, enlightened policemen, well equipped and especially trained police wings are bound to yield positive results.

The government has also to take measures for removing the perceived feeling of discrimination and deprivation which does not actually exist. The Minorities Commission set up in 1978 during Morarji Desai's tenure as Prime Minister, was recognised as a statutory body in May 1992 with a view to enhancing its effectiveness. Before this, it functioned as a toothless tiger because in the absence of legal sanction, it could do little beyond suggesting remedies or advising the government and the administration. The Commission is intended to safeguard the interests of the minorities whether based on religion or language. Its seven-point objectives are as follows:

- Evaluating the working of various safeguards for the minorities in the Constitution and the laws passed by the union and state governments.
- Recommending the most effective way to implement the laws pertaining to the minorities.
- Looking into specific complaints.
- Conducting studies and research on the question of avoidance of discrimination against minorities.
- Reviewing union and state government policies towards minorities.Suggesting appropriate legal and welfare measures to be undertaken by the union and state governments.
- Submitting reports (on minorities) to the government from time to time.
- Serving as a national clearing house for information in respect of the conditions of the minorities.

Its status was such that nobody took the Commission seriously because both the centre and the state governments were not bound to follow its suggestions. Over the years, the Commission's annual reports on the plight of the minorities gathered dust. But, the statutory status will now change the position. Its role will not only be investigative but also a judicial one. It is expected that with more powers, the Commission would now become a truly effective tool in tackling the deteriorating communal situation in the country and ensuring the welfare of the religious minorities which comprise 17 per cent of the total population of the country.

Symbolic gestures will not suffice. It is necessary to look at the real problems of the religious minorities in terms of employment, literacy and getting them a fair share of representation in every field. Efforts are needed for the development of the minority communities and removing their mass illiteracy and unemployment. Secular structures have to be promoted and preserved. Vigorous attacks need to be launched on religious institutions which foster communalism. Suspicions between communities must be rigorously weeded out. A common civil code in the country is the need of the day. There should be no special laws for specific communities and no special status for any state. The reservation policy has to be reconsidered. Political manipulation has to be tackled. Politicians interfering with police functioning and disallowing arrests of trouble makers have to be severely dealt with. Public opinion and mass enlightenment have to be brought about to make secular values functional.

Along with these measures, other measures that should be undertaken by the government to contain communal violence are: (1) Posting of secular-minded police officials in riot-prone areas. (2) Setting up of special courts to try communal offences. (3) Providing immediate relief and adequate financial assistance to victims of communal riots for their rehabilitation. (4) Taking severe action against all those who incite communal tensions or take part in violence.

Thus, multipronged measures are needed to contain communal tensions and bring about communal harmony in the country. We have not only to fight religious communalism but have also to contain political communalism which is more degrading and dangerous. A vast majority of Muslims and Sikhs in India have no appetite for communal violence, and this is also true of the sentiments of most Hindus. The members of the Muslim and Sikh communities are convinced that the growing communal tension can be stopped if politicians are somehow prevented from exploiting people for their narrow ends. The Muslim on the street is slowly recognising the exploitative intentions of politicians. Religious sloganeering does not affect him so much now. He no longer harbours a sneaking desire to seek economic redress across the border. He feels far more secure here.

If Muslims and other minorities are encouraged to consider themselves as a valuable commodity to be traded at election time, rather than being equal citizens of a free India, they can never be motivated enough to participate in the greater endeavour for the national good. Social scientists and intellectuals have to evince serious interest in controlling the national malaise of communalism and in related issues like religious violence, separatism, secessionism, and terrorism.

SECULARISM AND SECULARISATION

'Secularism' is the belief/ideology that religion and religious considerations should be deliberately kept out from temporal affairs. It speaks of neutrality. Secularisation, according to Peter Berger, is the process by which sectors of society and culture are removed from the domination of religious institutions and symbols.

One characteristic of modern life is that it features a process of 'desacuralisation', i.e., the supernatural is now little used to explain events and behaviour. The way the world is seen today is qualitatively different from the ancient and the medieval worlds in which it was believed that "God is all powerful" or that "spirits intervened in everybody's life", or that "what happens in individual's life is predestined". Today, belief in mystery and miracle has receded, although by no means entirely. The trumph of reason has been at the cost of myth and fables. This is the process of secularisation.

Weber considered secularisation as the process of rationalisation. For achieving given ends, the principle used is one which is based on scientific thought, i.e., which is rational. This thought has undermined religion. Darwin, Freud, and Marx were also major contributors to the replacement of religious explanations of human behaviour by scientific ones.

What has been the effect of modernity on religion? Berger is of the opinion that increased social and geographical mobility and the development of modern communications have exposed individuals to plurality of religious influences. They have therefore, learnt to tolerate each others' beliefs. People now feel free to search cultures for new ideas and new perspectives. In India also, we find that educated and modernity-oriented Muslims have started asking for changes in religion-oriented norms like, asking for maintenance allowance to divorced wives (not permitted by religion), adoption of children, more liberal laws permitting women to divorce their husbands, restrictions on polygyny, and so forth. Hindus also no longer accept religious restrictions on women, on intercaste marriages, on divorce, on widows' remarriage, on *sati* and so on. People try to construct meaning out of their experience. Of course, non-religious philosophies too construct a meaningful interpretation of existence.

Let us now turn to secularisation debate about India. The thesis that Indian society has become more secular is easy to grasp but complex to demonstrate. Broadly, the secularisation thesis proposes that many religious values have changed and several practices have declined and that science and rationality have increased in importance (Mike O' Donnell, 1997: 532-33). It is correct, there should be a radical and fundamental change in the cultural and institutional foundation of society. We do find weakening effect of religion on marriage, family, caste, and many institutions, but it is also a fact that there is evidence of the continuing vitality of religion. There may be change in the attitudes of people towards religion, in going to religious places, in visiting places of pilgrimage, in undergoing religious fasts, and celeberating religious festivals; there may be increase in civil marriages, even the number of actively religious people might have declined, but decline in formal religious practices does not necessarily indicate the secularism process among Hindus. Sikhs continue to follow religious restrictions. Religion as a source of personal meaning and fulfillment survives much more widely and with greater vitality than institutional religion. The secularisation thesis is, therefore, less applicable to personal religion than to formal religion. No wonder that scholars like David Martin hold that the term secularisation is so unconvincing that should be abandoned (O'Donnell, 1997: 538). A potential conflict between liberalism and fundamentalism must be referred here. Liberalism is based on mutual toleration of difference between (religious) groups, i.e., it is pluralistic. Fundamentalism is associated with opposition to liberalism and sometimes indicates violent attitude to pluralism. Countries like Pakistan, Saudi Arabia, Iran are described as more fundamentalist. The distinction between liberalism and fundamentalism is relevant to the concept of secularisation applied to the global context. While the western society has been secularised (in terms of loosening of authority of church), in several Muslim countries, the Islamic law governs civil as well as religious life. Recently, Pakistan also has accepted this ideology, because of which it has come to be described as a theocratic state. India, however, has remained a country where we find religious, social, cultural and even political pluralism. Muslims in India who continue to follow Islamic traditions have remained fundamentalists which prevents them from accepting modernity. Liberalism in vast majority of Hindus is compatible with the development of a modern Hindu society.

Secularism in the Indian context has tried to enhance the power of the state by making it a protector of all religious communities and an arbiter in their conflicts. It checks patronising any particular religion by the state.

The concept 'secular' in fact was first used in Europe where the church had complete control over all types of properties and nobody could use property without the consent of the church. Some intellectuals raised their voice against this practice. These people came to be known as 'secular' which meant 'separate from church' or 'against church'. In India, this term was used in a different context after independence. After the Partition of the country, the politicians wanted to assure the minority communities, particularly the Muslims, that they would not be discriminated against in any way. Hence, the new Constitution provided that India would remain 'secular' which meant that: (a) each citizen would be guaranteed full freedom to practise and preach his religion, (b) state will have no religion, and (c) all citizens, irrespective of their religious faith, will be equal. In this way, even the agnostics were given the same rights as believers. This indicates that a secular state or society is not an irreligious society. Religions exist, their followers continue to believe in and practise the religious principles enshrined in their holy books, and no outside agency, including the state, interferes in legitimate religious affairs. In other words, two important ingredients of a secular society are: (a) complete separation of state and religion, and (b) full liberty for the followers of all religions as well as atheists and agnostics to follow their respective faiths.

In a secular society, leaders and followers of various religious communities are expected not to use their religion for political purposes. However, in practice, Hindu, Muslim, Sikh and other religious communities do use religion for political goals. Several political parties are labelled as non-secular. After the demolition of Babri Masjid structure at Ayodhya in December 1992, a case (popularly called S.R. Bommai case) was filed in a court for the dismissal of the state governments run by the Bharatiya Janata Party (BJP). The judges constituting the nine-judge bench dwelt upon the term 'secularism' and averred that though the term was embedded in the Constitution it was wisely left undefined because it was not capable of any precise definition. Secularism in the Constitution guaranteed equal treatment to all religions, and state governments were to regulate the law in order to enforce secularism. As such, on legal consideration the plea for the dismissal of the BJP governments was not accepted. No wonder, some people say that S.R. Bommai's case in the Supreme Court had held that an appeal to *Hindutva* was permissible under the Representation of the People Act. What was banned was the criticism of the other party's religion. It may, thus, be said that secularism for political parties has implied the creation of a vote bank comprising Muslims, the scheduled castes, the scheduled tribes and the OBCs. In the elections for the Lok Sabha in May 1996 and for Uttar Pradesh Vidhan Sabha in October 1996, and again in February 1998 and September 1999 for the Parliament when the BJP emerged as the largest single party at the centre political parties with vested interests joined together in describing the BJP as a communal party. The cry against communalism was raised only to seek votes and attain political power. A coalition of 13 parties at the centre (in June 1996) and joining together of number of political parties in April 1999 to defeat the BJP-led government was based not on any common acceptable minimum programme but only on one programme of preventing the so-called 'Hindu party' from forming a government.

Communalism, thus, is neither a political philosophy nor an ideology nor a principle. It came to be imposed on the Indian society with a political objective. The communal-secular card is now being played for political motives only. The bogey of communalism is being kept alive not for checking national disintegration but with a view that minority vote bank does not dissipate itself into the larger Indian ethos. Even those political leaders who are known to be honest extensively practise casteism and accuse political leaders of opposite parties for being communal. The power seekers thus use secularism as a shield to hide their sins, thereby ensuring that people remain polarised on the basis of religion and India remains communalised.

Nirbhai Singh has maintained (1994: 111) that the present crisis in India is partially due to over-emphasis on secularisation and politicisation of religion by the fundamentalists and politicians. This trend has alienated the ethnic minorities from the mainstream of Indian society. In this sense, the very process of secularism has become a challenge to the religious plurality of India. It has set in process devaluation of religious values. What is needed today is new insights and openess of mind towards other religious faiths. To appreciate other faiths is to guarantee freedom to them. In this sense, freedom of religious conviction can be upheld along with plurality of religions.

RELIGION IN SECULAR SOCIETY

How is religion relevant in secular society? Religion played and continues to play a key role in the affairs of man and society because of its functions. S.C. Dube (1994: 79-80) has identified nine functions of religion: (i) *explanatory* function (explains why, what, etc., relating to the mysterious), (ii) *integrative* function (provides support amid uncertainty and consolation amid failure and frustration), (iii) *identity* function (provides a basis of maintenance of transcendental relationship for security and identity), (iv) *validating* function (provides moral justification and powerful sanctions to all basic institutions), (v) *control* function (holds in check divergent forms of deviance), (vi) *expressive* function (provides for satisfaction of painful drives), (vii) *prophetic* function (expressed in protest against established conditions), (viii) *maturation* function (providing recognition to critical turns in an individual's life history through *rite de passage*), and (ix) *wish-fulfilment* function (covering both latent and manifest wishes).

As the area of scientific knowledge and technology widens, the area of religion shrinks. Some of its functions are taken over by other agencies. Dube (1994:80) holds that the range of its influence is greater in simpler societies which have inadequate empirical knowledge. In technologically less developed societies, rituals and symbolic acts are employed on a wide scale to placate supernatural powers for worldly gains. In modern industrial societies, the hold of religious beliefs declines, although interest in religion persists. It remains a personal concern rather than collective and communal concern. The process of secularisation/rationalisation starts because of which religion loses control over several fields of social activities such as economics, trade, education, medicine, and so on. Many of traditional functions of religion are taken care of by secular institutions. A total religious world view, in which the entire framework of action has a religious orientation, undergoes a thorough modification.

But secularism varies from society to society. India perhaps has failed to develop diversified institutions that may take over the traditional functions of religion. As such, it remains communal, and religious beliefs continue to prevail. Problems are viewed in a narrow and communal rather than a wide national perspective. Religious orientations still shape the attitudes to work and wealth, and hinder the emergence of an ethic that would be conducive to progress. Of course, no society is completely secular, nor are all basic teachings of religion dysfunctional. In India also, though religious values and cultural orientations have been preserved, yet religion is trying to adapt itself to the changing ethos. This is true not only for Hindu religion but also for Muslim, Sikh, Jain, religions. Dube (1941:81) also avers that all religions in India have made situational adjustments and compromises. No religion has been able to preserve its original form but has accepted necessary modifications. On this basis, religion in India is not a barrier to modernisation. A secular and modern society is not against religion. Many people will continue to need faith and support during extreme distress and religion provides faith and support during traumatic experiences. Thus, separate religious identities will be permissible in our country so long they do not question the legitimacy of larger national boundaries. But they cannot be upheld if they inhibit national integration.

Further Readings

Ahuja, Ram, *Social Problems in India*, (revised edition) Fifth chapter on Communalism, Secularism and Regionalisation, Rawat Publications, 1997.

Chandra, Bipin, *Communalism in Modern India*, Vikas Publications, New Delhi, 1984.

Dube, S.C., "*Tradition and Development*", Vikas Publishing House, New Delhi, 1990.

Engineer, Asghar Ali (ed.), *Communal Riots in Post-Independent India*, Sangam Books, Delhi, 1984.

Singh, Nirbhai, "Contemporary Indian Society and the Plurality of Religions" in Murty, Satchidananda K., *The Divine Peacock*, New Age International Publishers, New Delhi, 1994.

Singh, V.V., *Communal Riots*, 1990.

Sinha, Surajit, "Sociology of Religion" in *A Survey of Research in Sociology and Social Anthropology*, Vol. 2, ICSSR, 1974.

9 Tribal Society

TRIBAL COMMUNITIES IN INDIA: STRENGTH AND DISTRIBUTION

The tribal population in India, according to the 1991 census, was 67.76 million. This was almost equall to the population of the United Kingdom. The tribals formed 8.08 per cent of the country's total population (*The Hindustan Times*, July 11, 1995). At present, India has the second largest tribal population in the world, next only to Africa. The tribes in India are spread over the length and breadth of the country. They vary in strength in different states from a few hundreds to several lakhs. The highest number of tribals according to the 1991 census are found in Madhya Pradesh (15.4 million), followed by Maharashtra (7.3 million), Orissa (7 million), Bihar (6.6 million) and Gujarat (6.1 million) (*The Hindustan Times*, July 11, 1995; also see, *Crime in India*, 1994:246). Of the total tribal population of the country, a little more than three-fifths (62.75%) of tribals are found in above-mentioned five states. In Mizoram, the tribal population constitutes 95 per cent of the total population of the state, in Nagaland 89 per cent, in Meghalaya and Arunachal Pradesh 80 per cent each, in Tripura 70 per cent, in Madhya Pradesh and Orissa 23 per cent each, in Gujarat 14 per cent, in Rajasthan 12 per cent, and in Assam and Bihar 10 per cent each. Thus, in four states (Mizoram, Nagaland, Meghalaya and Arunachal Pradesh) tribal population is more than 80 per cent of the total population of the state.

The most numerically high are the *Gonds* (Madhya Pradesh, Maharashtra and Andhra Pradesh)—about 4 million, the *Bhils* (Rajasthan, Gujarat, Maharashtra and Madhya Pradesh)—about 4 million, and *Santhals* (Bihar, Orissa and West Bengal)—more than 3 million. The smallest tribal community is the Andamanese with the strength of only 19. The bulk of the tribal population regard themselves as Hindus. Religion-wise, 89 per cent tribals are Hindus, 5.5 per cent Christians, 0.3 per cent Buddhists, 0.2 per cent Muslims, and 5 per cent others. All those who regard themselves as Hindus do not stand fully incorporated in the Hindu social order. In this context, the tribals can be classified as: (i) those incorporated in the Hindu social order, i.e., who have accepted the caste structure, e.g., Bhils, Bhumij; (ii) positively oriented towards the Hindu social order, i.e., though they have adopted the ethos and symbols and the world-view of Hindus yet they have not included themselves in the caste frame, e.g., Santhals, Oraon, Munda, Gonds; (iii) negatively oriented towards the Hindu social order, e.g., Mizos, Nagas; and (iv) indifferent towards the Hindu social order, e.g., some tribes of Arunachal Pradesh.

From the point of view of geographical distribution, L.P. Vidyarthi (*ICSSR Survey of Research in Sociology and Anthropology*, Vol. III, 1972:32) divided the tribal people into four major zones: (a) The *Himalayan Region*, comprising Jammu and Kashmir, Himachal Pradesh (Bhot, Gujjar, Gaddi), Terai area of Uttar Pradesh (Tharus), Assam (Mizo, Garo, Khasi), Meghalaya, Nagaland (Nagas), Manipur (Mao) and Tripura (Tripuri) and having 11 per cent of the total tribal population of the country; (b) *Middle India*, comprising West Bengal, Bihar (Santhal, Munda, Oraon and Ho), Orissa (Khonds, Gond) and having about 57 per cent of the Indian tribal population; (c) *Western India*, comprising Rajasthan (Bhil, Meena, Garasia), Madhya Pradesh (Bhil, etc.), Gujarat (Bhil, Dubla, Dhodia), and Maharashtra (Bhil, Koli, Mahadeo, Kokna) and containing about 25 per cent of the Indian tribal population; and (d) *Southern India*, comprising Andhra Pradesh (Gond, Koya, Konda, Dova), Karnataka (Naikada, Marati), Tamil Nadu (Irula, Toda), Kerala (Pulayan, Paniyan) and Andaman and Nicobar Islands (Andamanese, Nicobari) and containing about 7 per cent of the Indian tribal population.

The tribals living in different states belong to various *racial* groups (e.g., proto-australoid, which include Santhals, Munda, Oraon and Bhumij, and Mangoloid which include Garo, etc.), *linguistic* groups (austric like Santhals, Munda, Bhumij, Dravidian like Oraon, and Tibeto-Chinese like Garo, Bhutia, etc.), *economic* (food-gatherers, cultivators, labourers), *social* and *religious* categories. There is also a wide range of variation in their level of development and their level of socio-cultural integration. But there are also certain similarities. The tribals as a whole are technologically and educationally backward. Though the majority of the tribals follow patrilineal system of social organisation, yet there are quite a few who have matrilineal systems (like Garo, etc.). A sizeable proportion of Nagas, Mizos, Santhals, Oraon, and Munda, etc., have embraced Christianity. Some (like Bhutia, Lepcha) are largely identified with Buddhism.

DISTINCTIVE FEATURES OF TRIBAL COMMUNITIES

Tribes are relatively isolated from larger cultural influences, have a relative cultural homogeneity and a simple technology. They believe in spirits, magic and witchcraft. They have their own taboos which prohibit certain actions that are punishable by the community, by the supernatural, or by magical consequences. Large number of the tribes believe in animism, according to which all objects—both animate and inanimate—are permanently or temporarily inhabited by spirits or souls. Often, an activity is believed to be caused by these spirits. Some spirits are worshipped and treated with fear and respect. Some scholars have maintained that animism was the earliest form of religion of the tribes. Many tribes believe in ancestor worship too.

Some important features of tribes in India are:

(1) *Common name*: Each caste has a distinct name of its own through which it is distinguished from others.
(2) *Common territory*: Tribes generally occupy common geographical areas.
(3) *Common language*: Members of one tribe speak the same language. Each tribe has its own dialect, if not the script.
(4) *Common culture*: Each tribe has prescribed patterns of behaviour and festivals and deities to worship.
(5) *Endogamy*: Each tribe has the practice of marrying members within their own tribe.
(6) *Political organisation*: All tribes have their own political organisation. They have councils of elders which control members
(7) As against the national average of 43 per cent, 57 per cent of the tribals are economically active.
(8) As regards the nature of work, against 73 per cent national average, 91 per cent tribal workers are engaged in agriculture. About 3 per cent tribals are engaged in manufacturing (against 11% of general population) and 5 per cent in servicing (tertiary) sector (against 16% average of general population). About 1 per cent tribals are engaged in forestry and food-gathering.

Some other features of the tribals are: most of them live in isolated terrains; the main sources of their livelihood are agriculture and gathering of forest produce; they do not cultivate for profit; they still largely rely on barter system; they spend a greater part of their earnings on social and religious ceremonies; and a large number of them are illiterate and are victimised by unscrupulous forest contractors and moneylenders.

TRIBE AND CASTE

There are no specific criteria by which we may distinguish a tribe from a caste. In broad terms, a tribe is defined as "a community occupying a common geographic area and having a similar language and culture or beliefs and practices" (Theodorson, 1969:443). Nadel has described tribe as "a society with a linguistic, cultural and political boundry". But there are many tribal societies which lack government and the centralised authority in the ordinary sense of the term. Likewise, cultural homogeneity in a tribe is also elusive in this age.

Scholars like G.S. Ghurye, T.B. Naik, F.G. Bailey and Verrier Elwin have used different criteria like religion, geographical isolation, language, economic backwardness, and political organisation for distinguishing caste from tribe.

On the basis of *religion*, it is said that the religion of tribals is Animism and that of the people with caste system is Hinduism. Hutton (1963) and Bailey (1960:263) believe that tribals are not Hindus but are animists. The basic characteristics of animism are: the beliefs that all animate and inanimate objects are permanently or temporarily inhabited by spirits; all activities are caused by these spirits; spirits have power over the lives of men; men can be possessed by spirits; and they can be influenced by magic. On the other hand, the chief characteristics of Hinduism are: *dharma*, *bhakti*, *karma* and rebirth. It will be wrong to say that the Hindus, particularly the lower caste Hindus, do not believe in spirits and ghosts or in magic and possession. Similarly, there are many tribals who worship Hindu gods and goddesses, celebrate Hindu festivals and fairs and observe Hindu customs, traditions and rituals. It is, therefore, not easy to distinguish between Animism and Hinduism. Elwin (1943), Risley (1908) and Ahuja (1965) have also maintained that the distinction between Hinduism and Animism is artificial and meaningless. Religion as a single criterion, thus, cannot be used to distinguish between a tribe and a caste. Ghurye, Naik and Bailey have also rejected this criterion.

On *geographical isolation* basis, it is said that tribals live in geographically isolated regions like hills, mountains and jungles but caste Hindus live in the plains. Due to isolation and negligible contacts with their (civilised) neighbours, tribals are comparatively less civilised than the Hindus. Though it is true that at one time some tribals lived away from means of communication yet many caste Hindus also lived in isolated regions, while many tribals lived in plains. In this age, no groups live in isolation. Geographical isolation too, thus, cannot be accepted as a criterion for differentiating tribe from caste.

Using *language* as a criterion for difference between a tribe and a caste, it is said that each tribe has its own language but not a caste. But then there are tribes which do not have their own languages but speak the dialect of one of the main Indian languages, as in South India. Therefore, language also cannot be accepted as a criterion for distinction.

Economic backwardness too is not a correct criterion for distinction. If tribals are backward and primitive, caste Hindus are also almost equally poor. On the other hand, we have economically advanced tribes too. Bailey (1960:9) also rejects this criterion by holding that it is wrong to hold sociologically that 'economic backwardness' refers to a 'standard of living' rather than to 'a type of economic relationship'. He himself used 'economic structure' and 'politico-economic organisation' for differentiating the Konds (tribe) from Oriyas (caste) in Orissa. Bailey (1960) presented a systematic interactional model for considering the position of the tribe vis-a-vis caste as two ideal poles in a linear continuum. He concentrated on two factors: control over land and right to resources of land. He maintained that in both the tribal and caste societies, we find landowners and landless people who are dependants on landowners for their share of land resources. But analysing the economic organisation of a 'village territory' (inhabited by castes) and a 'clan territory' (inhabited by tribes), he found that a village is divided into economically specialised interdependent castes arranged hierarchically whereas though a clan territory is also composed of economically specialised groups, yet these are not hierarchically arranged; nor are they economically interdependent on each other. In other words, in a tribal society, a larger proportion of people has a direct access to land while in the case of caste-based society, a very few people are land-owners and a large number achieve the right to land through a dependent relationship. Thus, according to Bailey, a tribe is organised on a 'segmentary solidarity' while a caste is organised on an 'organic solidarity'. But Bailey avers that at what point of continuum a tribe ceases and a caste begins is difficult to say. In India, the situation is such that there is hardly any tribe which exists as a separate society, having a completely separate political boundary. Economically too, the tribal economy is not different from the regional or national economy. But we do regard some communities as tribal and include them in the recognised list of scheduled tribes.

H.N.Banerjee worked in 1969 on the detailed pattern of tribe-caste continuum among the Kora of Barabhum. N.K. Bose (1949) has held that the tribes are being pulled towards the caste system mainly through the agriculture and craft-based economy of the caste society. M. Orans (1965) has said that while the higher economy of the Hindus pulled the tribes towards emulating the caste pattern, the forces of political solidarity pushed the tribes away from the Hindu caste system. L.P. Vidyarthi (*ICSSR Report*, 1972:33) has maintained that tribal group works as an affix to the caste system and in a few cases as suffix too. From an anthropological point of view, tribes in India appear to be gradually merging with the caste system. Ghurye has opined that some tribes are not isolated from the Hindu castes of the plains in language, economy or religion. He regards them as backward Hindus. Thus, it may be said that tribes and castes are two ends of the same scale.

TRIBAL STUDIES

The analytical tribal studies and monographs on important tribes in India were published after 1950 by scholars like S.C. Roy (Munda, Oraon, Birhor, Kharia), D.N. Majumdar (Khasa), Surjit Sinha (Bhumij), S.C. Dube (Kamars), L.P. Vidyarthi (Manjhi), G.S. Ghurye (Kolis), the Anthropological Survey of India (Gaddis), B.K. Roy Burman (Bhots), B.S. Guha (Abor), Verrier Elwin (Baiga, Maria), T.B. Naik (Maria) and Thurston (tribes in South India), etc. These studies have examined five aspects of tribal society: (1) *social structure*, with particular reference to division of tribe in clans, sub-clans and lineages, family, kinship, marriage, status of women, and the panchayat system; (2) *tribal economy* with emphasis on occupational structure and change in livelihood means from hunting to food-gathering, from forests to agriculture, ownership of land, economic relationship between tribal and non-tribal communities, different patterns of industrialisation in the tribal areas, role of market, social cost of industrialisation, economic role of women, role of moneylenders in tribal life, and economic transformations (3) *religious beliefs* and rituals, magic, witchcraft, religious movements (like Bhagat, etc.), and impact of Christian missionaries; (4) *political organisation* with focus on the concept of law and justice, panchayat leadership, impact of political parties, voting behaviour and political participation; and (5) *cultural life*, which describes folk music, dances, fairs and festivals, etc.

TRIBAL EXPLOITATION AND UNREST

For ages, tribals were considered a primitive segment of Indian society. They lived in forests and hills without having more than a casual contact with the so-called civilised and advanced neighbours. There being no population pressures, there was no attempt to penetrate their areas and impose alien values and beliefs on the tribals. But when the British consolidated their position in the country, their colonial aspirations and administrative needs necessitated 'opening up' the entire country through an effective communication system. The British introduced the system of landownership and revenue. Annual tax was trebled which was beyond the paying capacity of tribal cultivators. Under the increasing pressure of population, many outsiders also started settling in tribal regions. With their money power, they offered credit facilities at the doorstep. Initially, it provided relief to tribals but gradually the system became exploitative. Newly established courts of law helped the exploiters. This economic, and later social and cultural exploitation, aroused the tribal leaders to mobilise fellow tribals and start agitations. With the increasing feelings of deprivation, mass agitations, struggles and movements also increased. Initially, they were against blood suckers and usurpers of their rights but ultimately they turned against the government or the rulers.

Tribal unrest and discontent, thus, may be described as the cumulative of a number of contributory factors. The main factors were:

- Lethargy, indifference, and lack of sympathy from administrators and bureaucrats in dealing with tribal grievances.
- Harshness of forest laws and regulations.
- Lack of legislation to prevent the passing of tribal land into the hands of non-tribals.
- Ineffective government measures to rehabilitate tribal population.
- Lack of interest and dynamism among the political elite to solve tribal problems.
- Delay in implementation of recommendations made by high level bodies.
- Discrimination in implementation of reformatory measures.

In short, the causes of tribal unrest may be described as economic, social and political.

TRIBAL PROBLEMS

The main problems the tribals face are:

- They possess small and uneconomical landholdings because of which their crop yield is less and hence they remain chronically indebted.
- Only a small percentage of the population participates in occupational activities in the secondary and tertiary sectors.
- Literacy rate among tribals is very low. While in 1961, it was 18.53 per cent, in 1991 it increased to 29.60 per cent which compared to general literacy rate of 52.21 per cent in the country is very low, be-

cause while the growth of literacy rate in the past three decades in the country was 28.21 per cent, among the STs it was only 11.7 per cent (*The Hindustan Times,* July 11, 1995). Though tribal literacy rate in Mizoram is 82.71 per cent and in Nagaland, Sikkim and Kerala it is between 57 per cent and 61 per cent, lack of literacy among tribal people has been identified as a major development problem.

- A good portion of the land in tribal areas has been legally transferred to non-tribals. Tribals demand that this land should be returned to them. In fact, tribals had earlier enjoyed considerable freedom to use forests and hunt animals. Forests not only provide them materials to build their homes but also give them fuel, herbal medicines for curing diseases, fruits, wild game, etc. Their religion makes them believe that many of their spirits live in trees and forests. Their folk-tales often speak of the relations of human beings and the spirits. Because of such physical and emotional attachment to forests, tribals have reacted sharply to restrictions imposed by the government on their traditional rights.
- Tribal government programmes have not significantly helped the tribals in raising their economic status. The British policy had led to ruthless exploitation of the tribals in various ways as it favoured the *zamindars*, landlords, moneylenders, forest contractors, and excise, revenue and police officials.
- Banking facilities in the tribal areas are so inadequate that the tribals have to depend mainly on moneylenders. Being miserably bogged down in indebtedness, tribals demand that Agricultural Indebtedness Relief Acts should be enacted so that they may get back their mortgaged land.
- About 90 per cent of the tribals are engaged in cultivation and most of them are landless and practise shifting cultivation. They need to be helped in adopting new methods of cultivation.
- The unemployed and the underemployed want help in finding secondary sources of earning by developing animal husbandry, poultry farming, handloom weaving, and the handicrafts sector. Most of the tribals live in sparsely populated hills and communications in the tribal areas remain tough. The tribals, therefore, need to be protected against leading isolated life, away from towns and cities, through a network of new roads.
- The tribals are exploited by Christian missionaries. In several tribal areas, mass conversion to Christianity had taken place during the British period. While the missionaries have been pioneers in education and opened hospitals in tribal areas, they have also been

responsible for alienating the tribals from their culture. Christian missionaries are said to have many a time instigated the tribals to revolt against the Indian government.

Relations between the tribals and non-tribals thus started worsening and non-tribal residents were increasingly depending for protection on the para-military forces. The demand for separate states for tribals took the shape of insurgency in Mizoram, Nagaland, Meghalaya, Bihar, Manipur, Arunachal Pradesh, and Tripura. Neighbouring countries, unfriendly to India, were active in exploiting these anti-Indian sentiments. Infiltration of foreign nationals, gun-running, trafficking in narcotics and smuggling even today are very serious problems in these states surrounded by tribal belts.

In short, the main problems of the tribals are poverty, indebtedness, illiteracy, bondage, exploitation, disease and unemployment.

After independence, tribal problems and tribal unrest have become politicised. An articulate and effective political elite have emerged in several tribal areas. These elite are conscious of tribal rights and are capable of making calculated moves to gain their acceptance. The tribals of Jharkhand region in Bihar and of Bastar region in Madhya Pradesh are recent examples where tribal political leaders have succeeded in compelling the central government to agree to form separate states. A separate tribal state in Bihar (Vananchal) would comprise 18 districts of South Bihar, with tribal population of 26 per cent. The demand for greater Jharkhand state consists of 26 predominantly tribal districts of Bihar, West Bengal, Orissa and Madhya Pradesh. In areas where tribal leadership does not exist, political parties—national, regional or local—are moving in to fill the vacuum. S.C. Dube (1972:30) has also said that today we find a shift in the political attitudes and strategies of the tribals—from politics of compliance and affirmation to politics of pressure and protest. It may be said that the political culture of the tribes is undergoing a radical transformation. This parochial political culture and 'participant' political culture is oriented more to sub-national tribal identities than to a broader national identity. When interests of the smaller unit (tribe) and the larger unit (nation) clash, the tendency is to ignore or sacrifice the latter. This perspective resulting in exclusive focus on purely tribal interests and on their solution unlinked with broader national interests imparts parochial overtones to the emerging political culture. On the other hand, in participative political culture, the tribals take an active interest in formulating policies, questioning the usefulness of political decisions of the government and suggesting correctives (*Ibid*:31). The key issue, thus, is of harmonising the national and tribal interests. In other words, the tribal problems have to be viewed not in isolation but in the context of strategies operating in national life.

TRIBAL MOVEMENTS

Numerous uprisings of the tribals have taken place beginning with the one in Bihar in 1772, followed by many revolts in Andhra Pradesh, Andaman and Nicobar Islands, Arunachal Pradesh, Assam, Mizoram and Nagaland. The important tribes involved in revolt in the nineteenth century were Mizos (1810), Kols (1795 and 1831), Mundas (1889), Daflas (1875), Khasi and Garo (1829), Kacharis (1839), Santhals (1853), Muria Gonds (1886), Nagas (1844 and 1879), Bhuiyas (1868) and Kondhs (1817).

Before describing tribal movements, the typology of movements needs to be specified. Cameron has classified them in four groups: (1) *Reactionary*, which seek to bring back the good old days. Linton calls them 'revivalistic' movements. (2) *Conservative*, which are organised to obstruct the current changes and seek to maintain status quo. Linton calls them 'perpetuative' movements. (3) *Revisionary*, which desire specific changes by modifying the existing customs, improving or purifying the culture or social order and eliminating some institutions. However, these movements do not attempt to replace the existing structure as a whole. These movements have also been termed as 'social mobility' movements. These movements are found mostly among low castes but not amongst the tribals. (4) *Revolutionary*, which aim at replacing the whole of the culture or social order with another more progressive. This does not mean that everything is to be replaced. This movement is also termed as 'revivalistic' movement.

Most of the social movements among tribals in early India had their origins in religious upheavals like Buddhism and Vaishnavism. Some Vaishnavist movements were found among Meithei tribe in Manipur, Bhumij in West Bengal, Nokte Naga in Assam, Bathudi in Orissa, and tribals in Jharkhand (Bihar), Orissa and south India (Mahapatra 1972: 402). These movements have also been called religious movements. These were also found among Gonds in central India, Kond in Orissa and Bhils in Rajasthan. The Britishers had to face some tribal movements in the nineteenth and the twentieth centuries when they sought to stop head-hunting, human sacrifice, or slavery in north-eastern India. There were also movements against oppressing landlords, moneylenders and harassment by police and forest officials in Bihar, Bengal, Orissa and central Indian states. Bhagat movements were found among Oraon of Chotanagpur, Bhils of Rajasthan, etc. These were revivalist movements for avoiding animal food, liquor and blood sacrifices.

After independence, tribal movements may be classified into three groups: (1) movements due to exploitation of outsiders (like those of the Santhals and the Mundas), (2) movements due to economic deprivation (like those of the Gonds in Madhya Pradesh and the Mahars in Andhra Pradesh), and (3) movements due to separatist tendencies (like those of the Nagas and Mizos).

The tribal movements may also be classified on the basis of their orientation into four types: (1) movements seeking political autonomy and formation of a state (Nagas, Mizos, Jharkhand), (2) agrarian movements, (3) forest-based movements, and (4) socio-religious or socio-cultural movements (the Bhagat movement among Bhils of Rajasthan and Madhya Pradesh, movement among tribals of south Gujarat or Raghunath Murmu's movement among the Santhals).

Such reformative movement was reported among the Mundas too under a powerful charismatic leader Dharti Aba who preached Hindu ideals of ritual purity, morality, and asceticism, and criticised the worship of priests. Among the Gonds in Madhya Pradesh, there were religious and social mobility movements in the 1930s by charismatic leaders, claiming Kshatriya status and seeking to purify religion and social institutions.

Surajit Sinha (1972:410) has referred to five types of tribal movements:

(1) Ethnic rebellious movements during the British rule in the eighteenth and the nineteenth centuries, like Birsa movement among the Mundas, Kol rebellion in 1832, Santhal rebellion in 1857-58 and Naga rebellion in the 1880s.
(2) Reform movements, emulating the pattern of the higher Hindu castes like the Bhagat movement among the Oraon, Vaishnavite movement among the Bhumi and Kehr movement among the Santhals.
(3) Political movements for tribal states within the Indian Union in the post-Independence period like Jharkhand movement in Chotanagpur and Orissa, Hill states movement in Assam and Madhya Pradesh, etc.
(4) Secessionist movements like the Naga and Mizo movements.
(5) Movement relating to agrarian unrest like Naxalbari movement (1967) and Birsadal movement (1968-69).

If we take into consideration all the tribal movements, including the Naga revolution (which began in 1948 and continued up to 1972 when the new elected government came to power and the Naga insurgency was controlled), the Mizo movement (guerrilla warfare which ended with the formation of Meghalaya state in April 1970, created out of Assam and Mizoram in 1972), the Gond Raj movement (of Gonds of Madhya Pradesh and Maharashtra, started in 1941 for a separate state, reaching its peak in

1962-63), the Naxalite movements (of the tribals in Bihar, West Bengal, Andhra Pradesh and Assam), the Agrarian movements (of the Gonds and the Bhils in Madhya Pradesh), and the forest-based movements (of the Gonds for getting customary rights in the forests), it could be said that the tribal unrest and the resultant movements were mainly movements launched for liberation from (i) oppression and discrimination, (ii) neglect and backwardness, and (iii) a government which was callous to the tribals' plight marked by poverty, hunger, unemployment and exploitation. Recently, a growing interest has been shown by scholars and politicians in the tribal movement in Chotanagpur in Bihar. This movement is popularly called the Jharkhand movement. The Oraon, the Munda and the Hos are the major tribal communities in Chotanagpur. Their total population is about 50 lakhs comprising 10 per cent of the total population of the state. This movement was started in 1928 by Chotanagar Unnati Samaj under the leadership of a few educated tribal Christians. Later on, the Samaj was renamed Adibasi Sabha. In 1938, it declared itself a political party fighting for tribal interests, when it took the name of Jharkhand Party. The BJP-led government proposed in late 1998 and early 1999 to create a separate Jharkhand state (called Vananchal state comprising six districts and two divisions, Chotanagpur and Santhal Parganas of Bihar).

Two instances of tribal exploitation are highlighted here to explain the cause of their movements. At the time of independence, there existed a government order in Andhra Pradesh according to which all land transactions had to be in favour of the tribals. In 1974, the then Congress government passed an order which permitted non-tribals to own 15 acres (5 wet and 10 dry) of land in the area. After this order, non-tribals took away a sizeable part of tribal land. Tribals claimed that about 30,000 acres of land had passed into the hands of non-tribals between 1974 and 1984. During this period, about 2,000 cases of land disputes were lodged in courts and about 400 tribals convicted. The Telugu Desam government quashed the Congress government order in 1984 because of which non-tribals took a defensive position. Tribals were organised by extremists against the non-tribal feudal classes. There were series of incidents of violence between Gonds (tribals) and non-tribals. The non-tribals put up a fight. They burned tribal huntments, criminally assaulted women, wounded and killed the tribals and forced them to do bonded labour for them. In another incident, 21 non-tribals who were allegedly stealing firewood from a forest were caught by the tribals and taken to their village and kept imprisoned till the police rescued them.

The second case refers to a tribal convention organised in February, 1984 in Vidarbha region near Nagpur in Maharashtra. The venue was a small village called Kamalpur, with a population of 1,000 persons. The convention was expected to be attended by 20,000 persons. It was to be inaugurated by the President of Nagpur High Court Bar Association and presided over by eminent persons like a playwright, a film director and a cine artist. Two days before the conference, all routes leading to the venue were sealed, about 1,000 persons were arrested, and prohibitory orders banning the assembly of five or more persons were issued. Interestingly, the persons arrested were charged for carrying objectionable literature, felling trees in forests, and theft of forest wealth (*Onlooker*, 7 April, 1984:29). The chairman of the Reception Committee was arrested on the charge of theft of forest wealth. He was released by a magistrate but promptly rearrested on a different charge. Among others arrested included musicians who were to perform at the convention, and representatives of student organisations from Bombay, Hyderabad, and Madras. Thus, what could have passed off as innocuous conference with a few fiery speeches was transformed into a major episode giving the venue a battlefield look.

All this shows that when the law does not help tribals, and the government remains callous, and the police fail to protect them, even harasses them, they take up arms against their exploiters. The above-mentioned movements indicate that the tribals adopted two paths of achieving goals: (a) non-violent path of bargaining and negotiating with the government and using a variety of pressure tactics without resorting to violence/revolts, and (b) militant path of revolts or mass struggles based on developing the fighting power of the exploited/oppressed tribal strata. The consequences of both these paths are different. One indicates struggle oriented to reforms, while the other indicates structural transformation of the community. To conclude, since tribals continue to face problems and also continue to feel discontented and deprived, this fact shows that both the above paths have not helped them to achieve their goals.

TRIBAL LEADERSHIP

Following L.P. Vidyarthi's appraisal of tribal leadership in initiating and promoting movements, we may point out several characteristics of tribal leadership:

(1) The tribal leaders are characterised with the concept of sub-nationalism.
(2) The leaders are generally those who are exposed to modern forces.
(3) The Christian-oriented and western-educated model which was the exclusive model of leadership for several decades in several tribal areas is now breaking its exclusiveness. For example, the Jharkhand

party which had the dominance of Christian adivasis and which was essentially started for the consolidation of Christian converts fast expanded its scope, and the Hindu tribals as well as non-tribal elements got associated with it and it started emphasising the needs and problems of the region. With secularised objectives, political pressures and persuasion, and political convenience, there is a marked turning point in the functioning of the leaders.

(4) While the tribal leadership at the regional and state-level seems to be keeping pace with the modern democratic interests, the village leadership in the interior tribal areas continues to be mostly institutional (say *Mukhiya*), formal (say *Sarpanch*), and hereditary.

(5) Tribal leaders sometimes join hands with political leaders of other political parties in achieving their political goals.

(6) The issues taken up by the leaders are generally those which find expression in tribalism, regionalism, localism and sometimes in religious extremism.

(7) The leaders are rural-based as well as urbanised, tradition-oriented as well as modern in outlook, and are Hindus as well as Christians.

(8) The leaders are not much educated but are those who believe in certain broad ideologies-religious, political, economic and social.

TRIBAL WOMEN

The term 'status' of women refers to (i) the position women occupy as householders, workers, and citizens; (ii) power and prestige attached to these positions; and (iii) rights and duties they are expected to exercise. Mason (1984) points out that the status of women has three dimensions: prestige, power and autonomy (freedom to take decision about education, marriage, employment, health care, etc.).

The status of women is not the same in all tribes; it differs from tribe to tribe. However, by and large, the status of tribal women is very low in the sense that they have no access to knowledge, to economic resources, and to power, and they have the lowest degree of personal autonomy. Though the extent of tribal female labour-force participation is very low, yet most of the tribal women work irrespective of their economic position. They share more or less equal responsibility with men in the economic activities. When men work in other towns and cities, women carry out agricultural work. If we take education as a socio-economic indicator of status, the literacy rate of ST women is low. While the literacy rate among women in general in our country in 1991 was 39.3 per cent among tribal women it was only 18.19 per cent. The highest percentage of ST women are educated up to primary school. The large gender gap may be attributed to non-availability of schools in villages, non-availability of female teachers, feeling shy of sending girls to schools due to prevalent traditional values, using grown-up girls for looking after infants when their mothers go to work, and requiring girls' help in household chores. Tribal women are not allowed to own land. Women are totally unaware of their rights regarding property. Their political awareness is also very low, as they neither read newspapers nor do they listen to the news on the radio and TV. They have also no place in the micro-level village power structure. They are woefully unrepresented in the political structures like tribal councils and village panchayats. However, there are some tribal communities (like Meena, Sema Naga, and Tharus, etc.) in which the status of women cannot be said to be low on every count.

There is no serious widow problem in tribal societies. A widow is free to remarry. There are some tribes where a widow marries her deceased husband's younger brother (levirate marriage). The bride-price custom has not elevated the status of women. It rather degrades them to be treated in the manner of articles of property and a commodity to be bought and sold. Divorce is permitted in many tribal societies. The procedure of divorce is also simple as it consists of mutual consent, a formal ceremony, and paying back of the bride-price.

PROTECTIVE DISCRIMINATION AND TRIBAL WELFARE AND DEVELOPMENT (OR TRIBAL TRANSITION)

'Tribal transition' is tribal welfare and tribal development. The governmental programmes implemented in India for the uplift and rehabilitation of tribals have not been able to achieve their goals and tribal proletarianisation has persisted since independence. No wonder, the problem of tribal welfare engaged the attention of a number of scholars in different parts of the country not only in the 1970s and the 1980s (like L.P. Vidyarthi in Bihar in 1971, A.K. Danda and M.G. Kulkarni in Maharashtra in 1974, and Ranjit Gupta, and M.V.T. Raju in Andhra Pradesh in 1971) but also in the 1990s.

Tribal Welfare

The strategies adopted by the British administrators for solving the problems of the tribals included acquiring tribal land and forests and declaring certain tribal areas as excluded or partially excluded. But, the British government had also established a number of schools and hospitals in the tribal areas with the help of Christian missionaries who converted many tribals to Christianity. Thus, by and large, during the British period, the tribals remained victims of colonial-feudal domination, ethnic prejudices, illiteracy, poverty, and isolation.

After Independence, provisions were made in the Constitution to safeguard tribal interests and promote their developmental and welfare activities. Gandhiji and Thakkar Bapa also did some pioneering work among the tribals. Nehru enunciated the policy of *Panchseel* for tribal transformation, which rested on following five principles:

(1) Avoiding imposing the culture of the majority people on them and encouraging in every way their (tribal) own traditional arts and culture.
(2) Respecting tribal rights on land and forest.
(3) Training tribal leaders for administrative and developmental activities with the help of some technical personnel from outside.
(4) Avoiding over-administering of the tribal areas.
(5) Judging results not on the basis of money spent but the quality of human character evolved.

In 1960, the Scheduled Tribe Commission was set up under the chairmanship of U.N. Dhebar to work for the advancement of the tribals. After the Fifth Five Year Plan, the Tribal Sub-Plan (TSP) strategy was designed in 1980 which consisted of two things: (i) socio-economic development of the STs, and (ii) protection of tribals against exploitation. The funds for TSPs are provided by state governments and the central ministries.

However, TSP results have not been commensurate with the expectations and the investments made so far as heavy emphasis is laid in several states on infrastructural development without corresponding emphasis on the development of the STs. The TSP schemes are supposed to lay emphasis on family-oriented income-generating schemes in sectors like agriculture, animal husbandary, cooperatives, tribal crafts and skills, etc., besides laying emphasis on education, health, and housing.

In the Five Year Plans, the programmes for the welfare of the STs aim at: (1) Raising the productivity levels in agriculture, animal husbandry, forestry, cottage and small-scale industries, etc., to improve the economic conditions, (2) rehabilitation of the bonded labour (3) education and training programmes, and (4) special development programmes for women and children. But various evaluation studies on all these programmes for the integrated development of the tribals have brought out the inadequacies of these programmes.

ACCULTURATION AND CHANGES IN TRIBAL CULTURE

Cultural change is 'change in knowledge, attitudes, ideas, behaviour, religious beliefs, and moral doctrines of individuals who compose the community or the society'. Thus, cultural change is a multifactorial process. Several factors as identified by Raha and Dubash Roy (1997: 149-159) which have brought about changes in the tribal culture are: measures undertaken by the government, communication facilities, spread of education, process of urbanisation, occupational mobility, community development projects, frequent contacts with the neighbouring Hindus in the urban areas, construction of dams in the tribal areas, impact of Christianity, facilities of bank credit, modern medicare, cooperative societies, modern legislation, cash and market economy, and reformist movements.

The tribe-caste interaction and the process of acculturation is found among many tribes in different states. Its best example has been pointed out by Binay Kumar Patnaik's study of Sabaras (tribe) in Ghorabar village in Orissa, who comprise 5 per cent of the total 235 households with 280 people (see Pfeffer, 1997:317-329). The process of undergoing acculturation by this tribe is found in the following changes:

(1) The structural change in the tribe is found in discarding egalitarianism (with least of functional dependency) and accepting caste system and thereby introducing the system of stratification in the community.
(2) The community is hierarchically divided in four segments on the basis of ritual superiority which resembles Hindu *varna* framework. There is functional distribution of occupations among the four divisions like the four *varnas*—hunting and fighting, worshipping, cultivation, and dancing and singing respectively. The difference is that while in the *varna* system, worshipping occupies the highest ritual status, in this tribe it occupies second place in the hierarchy. Secondly, purity and pollution is absent in the Sabaras tribe as it is found in the caste system. Thus, Sabaras are accepted as a separate 'caste' and not as a tribe in the village.
(3) Like the caste system among the Sabaras too, each sub-caste has its own panchayat which acts as a watch-dog of the community customs and taboos.
(4) Each sub-division of the Sabaras claims descent from three Sabaras who figure in Hindu mythologies—Mahabharat and Ramayana.
(5) The imprint of Hindu culture is prominent on the marriage customs of Sabaras, though inter-caste (inter-segment) marriage is absent. Polygamy is a taboo. Bride-price has been replaced by dowry.

Why the adopting of Hindu traits by the Sabaras is termed as a process of 'acculturation' and not 'sanskritisation' is because (a) the benefit of acculturation is 'economic gain' and not achieving higher ritual status. By entering the Hindu-fold as a caste group, they have been assigned the occupation of wood-cutting and basket making permanently. After deforestation, they have become agricultural labourers; and (b) the model adopted for mobility is not Brahmanic but Vaishya, which assures economic superiority to ritual superiority. Since the Sabaras are dependent on Telis for their occupations, they accepted them (Telis) as their reference group.

If we examine change in the culture of tribes in India, we find six main changes. These are as follows:

(1) The lifestyle of tribals, particularly those who live in or near the urban areas or in the midst of the numerically dominant non-tribal population, has changed due to imbibing of a large number of cultural traits of advanced Hindus. Many of their traditional traits have been replaced by alien traits.

(2) The nature of change is such that the tribes are not losing their identity and also their traditional cultural heritage. They are not being 'Hinduised'. However, tribals undergoing the process of Hinduisation have been pointed out by Bose (1953), Dutta Majumdar (1937), Deogaonkar (1990), Raha and Debash Roy (1997:153), referring to the examples of tribes like Pati Rabhas (in Assam), Hos and Juangs (in Orissa), Santhals (in Bihar), Bhumij, Oraon, Munda, and Korkus (in Maharashtra), etc. Our contention is that adopting few cultural traits of Hindus is not undergoing the process of Hinduisation. The fact that these tribes still describe themselves as 'tribes' and not Hindus is important in our argument and contention of rejecting the process of Hinduisation.

(3) In some parts of India, the tribals have adopted some traits of Christianity also. Nagas, Mizo, Santhals, Oraon, Munda, Kharia, etc., are some tribes in North East and North West India on which we find marked imprint of Christianity. The evidence is provided by micro-level studies of tribals made by Dutta Majumdar (1956), Sahay (1976), Sachchidananda (1964) and Bose (1967).

(4) The changes among tribal people from Chotanagpur working as labourers in tea gardens of Assam and North Bengal are more visible in their material life than in their religious beliefs and practices. Those who work in industries have developed individualistic outlook due to the economic security provided to them which in turn has made them indifferent towards their traditional life.

(5) Agro-industrialisation in the tribal areas has affected the socio-cultural life of the tribals to the extent that changes in the family structure, marriage institution, authority structure, interpersonal re-

lationships and weakening of clan panchayat's authority have come to be observed (Kar, 1981). Trade unions also have much impact on the *adibasi* (tribal) labourers. Tribal labourers have organised themselves as a 'class' which has ultimately opened up a wider opportunity for taking part in active politics. The tribals who work in mines and collieries since long fail to retain link with their community because of which they are so compelled to adjust themselves with the rhythm of mining work, that they relinquish many traditional beliefs and social practices and adopt new attitudes and behaviour patterns. Sachchidananda (1964) has referred to such changes among Munda and Oraon tribes of Bihar. R. Chandra (1989) has also referred to similar change in the socio-cultural life of Juangs and Irula tribes in Orissa who traditionally were accustomed to hunting, food-gathering and shifting cultivation but have now become settled cultivators and labourers on plantations. They have attained progressive outlook and have started using modern facilities of schools, banks, cooperative societies, medicare, etc.

(6) Discarding traditional practices and adopting modern beliefs and values due to the impact of modern forces has not always proved functional for the tribals. Many tribes face the problem of maladjustment. Baiga tribe according to R. Joshi (1984) is one such tribe whose members earlier were fun-loving and contented, who spent evenings in dancing and drinking mahua, who owned land but had no demarcated 'pattas', whose women wore gold and silver ornaments without worry and fear but have now become very fearful and have come to be cheated by people with vested interests. Happiness has given place to suffering.

Thus, it is evident that tribals have changed a lot culturally, socially as well as economically due to exposure to various forces which having benefited them in many ways have also brought a number of evils in their communities. Many tribals have come to be deprived of their rights over land and forests and in many cases they are being fleeced by money lenders, big landowners, traders, businessmen and others. In spite of this, we cannot support ideas of scholars like Verrier Elwin who advocated keeping tribals in partial or full isolation and strongly advised that these people should be allowed to maintain their traditional and original tribal life as far as possible. While we do not want tribal culture to be destroyed, at the same time, we do not want that tribes should remain 'backward' and not be benefited by industrial development, occupational mobility, education and benefits of welfare schemes. The isolated and segregated condition of the tribal world which results in their poverty, illiteracy, exploitation, etc., cannot be tolerated in this age. Their exposure to justice, enlightenment, help and cooperation is essential.

DISPLACEMENT AND RESETTLEMENT OF TRIBALS

During recent years, displacement of tribals has drawn the attention of several scholars. It is estimated that development schemes like dams, mines, industries and various projects have resulted in the displacement of about 40 per cent tribals between 1951 and 1991 (Fernandes, 1994:24). The illiterate and powerless tribals have been compelled to leave their resource-rich regions and migrate to other places. This has resulted in the problem of their resettlement. One estimate is that about 20 per cent of the STs have been rehabilitated. In Maharashtra and Gujarat under the 'land for land' scheme, only 15 per cent of about 10,000 eligible tribal families were granted land (*Ibid*:36). This has resulted in impoverishment and marginalisation of tribals. In many areas, tribals have resisted the take-over of their support system and started agitations. Such tribal agitations have been reported from Andhra Pradesh, Bihar, Karnataka, Arunachal Pradesh, Orissa, Madhya Pradesh and so on. Surprisingly, tribals agitate more than the high caste non-tribal farmers, even though they are illiterate and less organised. This can be explained in terms of difference in the extent of dependence on natural resources, exposure to external society, nature of leadership among them and the benefits they expect from the project (Fernandes in George Pfeffer, 1997:82). Tribals resist these projects because much of their food and other daily needs are met by the forests and the shifting cultivation in forests. This dependence on forests develops a symbolic relationship of the tribals with the source of their livelihood. The second reason is inadequacy of benefits. No compensation is paid for the forests because what the tribals consider common property land is in fact government land. Even the compensation for the little individual land they own is very low (say, about Rs. 3,000 per acre). What little amount they get is appropriated by moneylenders and middlemen. They are thus left impoverished. The third reason is that their literacy is so low that they cannot hope to get jobs in the new project. At most they get temporary jobs of unskilled labourers. All these reasons compel them to agitate against new projects and being displaced from their native lands.

Bal Govind Baboo (1997:92-94) avers that the four sections involved with the construction of dams are: (a) government and bureaucrats, (b) scientists and environmentalists, (c) people in the catchment area, and (d) people in the command area. Government supports construction of dams for achieving political and economic ends. Bureaucrats support them because they are the mouthpiece of the government and have to enhance the chances of their promotion. Scientists, technocrats and environmentalists are more objective. But their perspective is technical and limited. While technocrats are concerned with the feasibility of the project, environmentalists are concerned with the ecological dimensions. People in the catchment area do not want to be dislocated, even if they are poor because they are afraid of starting life afresh amid uncertainties. They also do not want to be cut off from their kin and village network. The people in the would-be command area like the idea because of the anticipated agricultural prosperity and year-round employment.

The utility of dams cannot be denied. The question is only of taking up the issue of the rehabilitation of the affected poor, particularly the poor tribals in the tribal areas. The social and cultural upheaval of the oustees is crucial. The questions which need attention are: (1) Do the displaced tribals like to stay in the resettlement colonies (RCs)? (2) Does the government follow any method to choose displaced people to rehabilitate them in the RCs? (3) Is the compensation scheme foolproof and is the compensation money properly utilised? (4) How do the displaced people who do not settle in the RCs get along with regard to their livelihood? (5) Do the displaced people rehabilitated in the RCs maintain their traditional occupations or do they adjust themselves with new occupations? (6) Do the displaced people undergo any traumatic experience during and after shifting?

The success and the utility of the dams in the tribal areas would depend upon taking into consideration the above-mentioned questions seriously and finding logical solutions to them because tribals have distinct cultural and structural traits as compared with caste groups. They are rigid in their cultural practices and less exposed to external factors of change.

INTEGRATION AND ASSIMILATION

The British administrators like Dalton, Risley and others talked of 'Hinduised tribes' and 'Hinduised section of the tribe'. They referred to a number of cultural traits which tribal people have adopted from the neighbouring Hindus. Have the welfare and the development programmes drawn the Adivasis to the fore of the national front? Have they been able to elevate their social position? It has been accepted by many scholars that the gap between tribals and non-tribals is partly the result of political policy of the imperial colonial power and partly because the non-tribals considered the tribals ethically and culturally distinct from the rest of the population. As such, the demands of the Adivasis after Independence for distinctive treatment and even autonomy were valid. Anthropologists sympathetically endorsed this demand. The census officers were emphatic about their religious distinction. They designated them as animists. Ethnologists pointed out their racial background and ethnic traits. But according to Ghurye, on the cultural and linguistic plane, the tribals are not markedly different from the neighbouring non-tribal or Hindu rural communities. This viewpoint has been supported by Majumdar and Aiyappan. Many tribal groups moved out of their semi-isolated habitats and entering plains accepted many norms of the Hindu caste system. The large number of social reform and religious movements among the tribals are evidence of their desire to get absorbed in the Hindu caste system. Some tribes like Mizos, Khasis, Nagas, Mundas, Meenas, Bhils, etc., have become somewhat modernised but some have still remained 'backward'. Their techno-economic backwardness and their sticking to traditional cultural values have remained a barrier to their integration in Hindu society.

The question is: do measures taken by the government aim at total assimilation of the tribals in the main stream of the national life or at social integration by conveying the concern for protecting their interests, customs and institutions, safeguarding their ways of life, and ensuring their development? It appears that various plans and programmes aim at protecting them against social injustice and exploitation and the raising of their general way of life. The creation of tribal areas, reservation of seats in educational institutions and public services, introduction of TMS scheme—all aim at uplift of the tribals and their social and cultural integration in Hindu society. But 'integration' should not be confused with 'homogeneity' through the process of assimilation. We should be clear about three processes of change, viz., acculturation, integration (social and cultural) and assimilation.

Acculturation is acquiring and modifying the culture of a group through contact with one or more other cultures. In the case of tribes, it means that the tribes take over such cultural traits of Hindu society which they find functional for their uplift and progress. *Social integration* is uniting of separate groups (i.e., tribes) into one group (i.e., Hindu society) by removing the previous social and cultural group (tribal) differences. *Cultural integration* is the adjustment of traditional cultural traits by absorbing new cultural traits. Integration of tribes in Hindu society does not involve totally discarding old tribal traits; it implies unity within a system resulting from taking over new traits from the Hindus. *Assimilation* is a (one-way) process in which one group (say a tribe) takes over the culture and identity of another (larger) group (say, Hindu society), and becomes a part of that group. The merging of the group (say, a tribe) thus involves complete elimination of cultural differences of tribals and non-tribals.

Tribes are faced with the problem of preserving their cultural identity and their social existence. Each tribe has three alternatives: (i) to exist side by side with the majority, (ii) to absorb itself in the dominant group, and (iii) to secede and seek political independence on the basis of equality. Different tribes have adopted different processes from amongst the above-mentioned three processes. For example, the Bhils and the Meenas have adopted the first process of co-existence, the Oraon and the Rhond tribes have adopted the second process of absorbing themselves in the Hindu society, while the Nagas and the Mizos have adopted the third process of secession. Our government has not adopted a uniform policy of cultural integration of all tribes because different tribes are at different stages of development and have different goals and aspirations. Naturally we find different levels of integration of different tribes. We can only hold that tribes are gradually being drawn into the wider economic frame-work of the country and they are getting themselves involved in the market economy. Agriculture has come to occupy a central place in the economic activity of many tribes. According to the 1991 census figures, about three-fourth of the tribals in the country work as cultivators and about one-fifth as agricultural labourers and the rest as labourers in mines, forests or are engaged in other services. The fact that the tribal cultivators are responding positively to modern methods of cultivation points out a positive change in tribals' economic system. The economic integration of the tribes, however, does not necessarily mean that all tribes have achieved a high level of income. Many are still living below the poverty line.

Tribals are also being integrated in the political system of the country. The introduction of the Panchayati Raj has offered them opportunity for an increased involvement in the political activities. By contesting elections, they have started acquiring power at Panchayat Samiti and state levels. This has also resulted in educational and social development of tribals. In social life too, because of the reservation policy, they now occupy important social positions. Though clan panchayats have not become altogether irrelevant for them, yet their role is confined more to marital and land conflicts. The tribal councils have thus weakened now. It may be averred that on the one hand, the tribals have maintained their cultural identity and on the other hand, they have integrated themselves in the broader economic., social, political, and religious systems of the country. This integration has enabled the tribals to bridge the social distance that existed between tribals and non-tribals, though they have not succeeded in achieving social equality.

While analysing the tribal integration in larger society, would it be relevant to adopt Ghurye's (1943) model of labelling tribals as 'backward Hindus', or Majumdar's (1944) model of adopting Hindu ideas by tribals through contacts with caste Hindus, or Srinivas' (1952) model of sanskritisation, i.e., tribes emulating high caste practices, or Bailey's (1960) model of postulating a continuum at the two ends of which stand a tribe and a caste? Lutz and Munda (1980) criticising Ghurye and Srinivas's models have suggested 'modernisation model' for understanding tribal change. Seeking to answer the question "how are tribal societies becoming like caste Hindus or Christian society", Lutz and Munda have referred to working together of anthropologists and government to induce change in tribes. Anthropologists have been evaluating the effectiveness of government programmes and pointing out the causes of their failure. In 1966, Roy Burman had observed the strong ethnocentric bias of Indian society, the Indian government, and the social scientists vis-a-vis the tribes. He maintained that these groups were designated as 'tribes' because the mainstream caste Hindu society perceives these tribes as being radically different from itself—in the past as well as in the present. Vidyarthi (1968) asserted to incorporate the tribal viewpoint which is considered significant for the tribal change. Our contention is that tribals themselves must discard their feeling of 'being tribals and thus having limitations'. They must develop self-pride and self-confidence, and must stop thriving on borrowed concessions and government's reservation policy. It is this attitude which will help them achieve social elevation and equality. Government policies alone cannot contribute to their development through 'appeasement' approach. It is not by being rooted in the traditional culture but by seeking opportunities to assert themselves that they can elevate themselves in Indian society.

Further Readings

Bose, N.K., *Cultural Anthropology and Other Essays*, Asia Publishing House, Calcutta, 1953.

Dube, S.C., *Tribal Situation in India*, 1972.

ICSSR, *Survey of Research in Sociology and Social Anthropology* (1969-1979), Satvahan Publications, New Delhi, 1985.

Majumdar, D.N., "Tribal Culture and Acculturation", *Man in India*, 1939.

—, *The Affairs of a Tribe: A Study in Tribal Dynamics*, Universal Publishers, Lucknow, 1950.

Pfeffer, George and Deepak Behera, *Contemporary Society: Tribal Studies* (Vols. I and II), Concept Publishing Co., New Delhi, 1997.

Singh, K. (ed.), *Tribal Situation in India*, Indian Institute of Advanced Study, Simla, 1972.

10 Rural Social System

SOCIO-CULTURAL DIMENSIONS OF RURAL COMMUNITY

Rural people, whose main occupation is agriculture, are more close to nature, have close personal ties of kinship and friendship, and lay stress on tradition, consensus, and informality. The density of population in villages is so low that it not only affects production and distribution but also the total life of the community and peoples' living standard. Both birth rate and death rate are high in villages in comparison to cities which adversely affects the quantitative and the qualitative growth of the rural people. Another aspect of the life of rural people which requires study is their distribution in age and sex groups. About 45 per cent of rural people belong to productive age (15-59) and about 55 per cent are sustained by working people (*Manpower Profile, India*, 1998:135). The preponderance of children (14 –) and the aged (60+) considerably influences the economic and the social life of the working section of the people. Similarly, the fact that the number of females per 1,000 males is higher in the rural areas than in the urban areas and that 33 per cent of rural women belong to the working force (against 56.1% of rural men) affects sex mores, social codes, social rituals, and social institutions. The family structure, caste composition, religious variations, economic life, land relations, poverty, and the standard of life in villages also affect villagers' life. We will describe each of these aspects separately.

The Family

Family and familism play a decisive role in the material and cultural life of villages and in moulding the psychological characteristics of the rural collectivity. While joint family continues to be the predominant form, nuclear family also exists as a result of the growth of market economy in the agrarian areas, migration of youth to cities, and the impact of urban socio-economic forces on the rural society. In spite of this change, in comparison to urban family, rural family is far more homogeneous, integrated, and organically functioning. The ties between parents and children, husband and wife, siblings and siblings and among affinal kin are stronger and last longer than those in an urban family. Another characteristic of the rural family is that it is generally agriculture-oriented, i.e., a very large majority of its members are engaged in the agricultural occupation. Since members of the rural family form a single economic unit, cooperate with one another in agricultural operations, hold property in common usually managed by the oldest member of the family, and since they spend most of their time together, their beliefs, attitudes, aspirations and values are similar. The interdependence of members on each other enables them to develop more collectivist family consciousness and less individualistic emotion. Though the impact of urbanisation, industrialisation, education, etc., has weakened traditional authority structure, created centrifugal tendencies, and reduced economic homogeneity based on a single economic activity, yet the family has not become atomistic, and family as an institution continues to be strong. It will not be illogical to hold that though rural family is undergoing a qualitative change, the dominance of familism is dropping off, family ego is diminishing, and the rule of custom is being replaced by the rule of law, yet family is not disintegrating.

Caste System

There was a time (say, up to the 1940s) when the caste system in rural areas was rigid, caste councils were very powerful, and caste determined the status and opportunities for mobility of individuals. Even land ownership and power structure existed on caste lines. But after the 1950s, spread of means of communication, education, growth of competitive economy, etc., have transformed self-contained castes into mobile classes. Certain castes have been losing previous status and functions and slowly submerging into the lowest class groups of modern society, while on the other hand, many lower castes are gaining economic and political power and emerging as dominant castes. Scholars like A.R. Desai, Andre Beteille, Yogendra Singh, B.R. Chauhan, etc., have pointed out change in the caste system, its decreasing effect on people, and increasing effect of the class system.

There is also change in the economic life including rural indebtedness based on caste system. R.K.Nehru has vividly pointed out in his exploratory study of a few villages what close relation existed earlier and exists today between caste and indebtedness and credit in the rural areas. There used to be castes which were predominantly composed of members who were almost hereditary debtors while some others were those who were mainly creditors. Recent studies have shown change in this aspect. There is also change in the habitat pattern based on caste. While earlier, the areas in which houses were located and the type of the houses built, depended on caste membership, today there is no relation between caste and habitat. Another factor important in the caste system in rural areas was occupational, economic, and social mobility. Now the members of a caste do not necessarily perform caste-determined occupation. As the result, some castes slide down the economic ladder while some castes go up. Earlier, caste determined the attitude of rural men towards education but now even the most backward castes have started giving their children, including girls, education. Religious life of rural people which was rigorously determined by caste is no longer affected by it. Religious practices are slowly changing in villages. Caste, however, influences today political life of the villagers. The choice or rejection of candidates as well as the nature of propoganda in political elections are not fully determined by caste considerations alone. Extra-caste considerations too, to a large extent, influence political prejudices and predilections. Leadership too is not totally based on caste membership in the rural society. Caste leaders are no longer leaders of the social, economic, political, and ideological life of the villagers. The *jajmani* system and inter-caste economic relations have also undergone significant change. New legislative measures too have affected inter-caste relations among the villagers. In short, caste in rural life has undergone crucial changes in varied fields.

Religion

Rural religion can be studied in relationship to three aspects: (i) as providing a specific outlook, say belief in possession by spirits, magic, witchcraft, worship of dead ancestors, and so on (ii) as a body of religious practices including prayers, sacrifices and rituals (iii) as an institutional complex, i.e., as a conglomeration of numerous sub-religious and religious cults, say Vaisvanism, Shivaism, etc.

In period before independence, religion played a significant role in determining the life processes of the rural society. This was because rural people had greater predisposition to religion than what the urban people had. Explaining high and low production in agriculture, dependence on the forces of nature like rains, natural calamities, etc., and pleasure and displeasure of gods also pointed out religiosity among the villagers. Belief in spirits, magic, ghosts, witchcraft and other forms of primitive religion was rampant among the rural people. Further, religious outlook of the rural people overwhelmingly dominated their intellectual, emotional and practical life. It was difficult to locate any aspect of their life which was not permeated with and coloured by religion. Religious beliefs also affected their folk songs, paintings, marriage customs, and social festivals, etc. Rituals are religious means by which purity of an individual and his social life becomes guaranteed. There are eating rituals, birth rituals, marriage rituals, death rituals, occupational rituals, sowing and harvesting rituals, and so on. Rituals dominated the life of the rural people. They prescribed a pattern of behaviour for individuals as well as for various social groups in all spheres of life. Particular sets of rituals were dictated to a particular caste. Social condemnation and even a threat of excommunication provided sanction for the strict enforcement of rituals among their members.

Temples too had and continue to have great significance in rural areas. These are used not only for prayers but also for education, organising cultural activities, social functions, social welfare work, holding political and public meetings, propagating ethical values, dispensing justice, and so on. There are temples with idols of gods and godesses as well as local deities. Some village temples are owned publicly and some privately.

In the new economic and political environment, after independence, new norms, basically non-religious and secular and derived out of a liberal democratic philosophy, have emerged and increasingly began to supersede the authoritarian religious norms. Villagers started picking up democratic and equalitarian ideas. New secular institutions and associations and new secular leadership and social controls began to emerge within the rural society. This also does not mean that religion does not excercise a powerful hold over the mind of the rural people today. In fact, the contemporary rural society has become a battle-ground of struggle between the forces of religious orthodoxy and authoritarian social conceptions on the one hand and those of secular democratic advance on the other.

AGRARIAN CLASS STRUCTURE

If we analyse class structure in rural India in post-independence period, we find four classes: the three classes in the agricultural field are of landowners, tenants, and labourers, while the fourth class is of non-agriculturists. According to A.R. Desai (1959), landowners constitute about 22 per cent, tenants about 27 per cent, agricultural labourers about 31 per cent and non-agriculturalists about 20 per cent. A large majority of the cultivators (60%) are marginal cultivators with less than 2 hectares land, followed by small cultivators (16%) with 2 to 5 hectares land, medium cultivators (6%) with 5 to 10 hectares land, and big cultivators (18%) with more than 10 hectares land (*Ibid*:125). The available land per family in villages is less than one acre (or 0.4 ha). About 75 per cent of the total sown area is under food crops. About 35 per cent of the total produce is sold by cultivators. In about 65 per cent of these sale transactions, commodities are sold to the trader in the village itself. The marketing of agricultural produce in the *mandis* (markets) is largely in the hands of intermediaries who represent private interests and who control both credit as well as disposal of the produce. Thus, a large number of agrarian proletariat, a large number of uneconomic holders of land, and a small number of artisans and self-employed people in villages reveal a miserable economic life lived by these people.

With this background of agrarian structure, let us now analyse agrarian relations. The relations may be classified as (a) those which are defined and enforced by law, (b) which are customary, and (c) which are of fluctuating character. Daniel Thorner (1956 and 1973; also see, Gupta, 1991: 261-270) rejected the often-described classification of cultivators in rural areas in three categories: landlords, tenants, and labourers. This was on the ground that one and the same man can belong simultaneously to all three of these categories. A person can himself cultivate a few acres of land he owns, give some land on rent, and in emergency may work on other's field as labourer. He has analysed agrarian relations by using three specific terms: *Malik* for agricultural landlords, *Kisan* for working peasants (including tenants), and *Mazdoor* for agricultural labourers. The *Malik* derives his agricultural income primarily (although not necessarily solely) from property rights in the soil, i.e., from a share of the produce of lands possessed by him. The share is realised in cash as well as in kind (percentage of produce). He may give his land either to tenant(s) or may cultivate it by hiring labourers. He may manage the hired labourers himself or through a manager. The *Malik* may also have subsidiary income from business, profession, etc. The *Maliks* are of two types: those who are absentee landlords and those who reside in the village in which they own land. *Kisans* are the working peasants, who may be small landowners or tenants. The difference between the *Malik* and the small *Kisan* is the size of the land held. The *Kisan* himself and one or more members of his family actually perform the field labour. Sometimes the income of the *Kisan* is so low that he himself or his family members(s) work as agricultural labourers. *Mazdoors* are those landless villagers who earn their livelihood primarily from working on other people's land. They receive wages in cash and sometimes in kind also. When they are not able to find work in villages, they migrate to other states either for working as agricultural labourers (as Biharis migrating to Punjab) or as construction or industrial labourers.

While Daniel Thorner has analysed agrarian social structure in terms of three classes on the basis of three criteria, viz., (a) income obtained from the soil (i.e., rent, own cultivation, or wages), (b) the nature of rights (i.e., ownership, tenancy, sharecropping and no rights at all), and (c) the extent of fieldwork actually performed (i.e., doing no work, doing partial work, doing total work, and doing work for others). D.N. Dhanagre (in Desai, 1983) has suggested a different model of agrarian classes. He has proposed five classes: *landlords*, who derive income primarily from landownership by collecting rent from tenants, sub-tenants and share croppers; *rich peasants*, i.e., small landowners with sufficient land to support the family and who cultivate land themselves, and rich tenants who have substantial holdings and have to pay a nominal rent to their landlords; *middle peasants*, i.e., landowners of medium size holdings and tenants with substantial holdings and paying higher rent; *poor peasants*, i.e., (a) land-owners with holdings insufficient to maintain a family, and therefore forced to rent others' land, (b) tenants with small holdings, (c) sharecroppers, and (d) *landless labourers* (also see, Gupta, 1991:271-275). The rich peasants and the trader moneylenders exploit the poor tenants and the landless labourers so much that relations amongst them are always sour. The former two classes wield considerable economic, social, and political power. The emergence of cooperative and credit societies in the villages have no doubt affected the power of the *Maliks*, yet they continue to be strong.

Two things are to be noted here: one, cooperative societies have not been much successful in villages, and two, private trader continues to operate successfully. People with vested interests want to maintain the status quo. Even land reforms have not reduced the power of *Maliks* and moneylenders. Unless economic, social and political progress takes place in the countryside, unless a movement is born which leads to more even distribution of productive resources, greater economic strength on the part of the smaller units leading to ability to withstand pressures from either the top cultivators' strata or the moneylender trader classes, no great success can be achieved in improving class relations.

The problems of landless agricultural labourers are more economic than social. We do not deny that their place in the social structure is of great importance but we hold that the problem of employment opportunity to them, and the problem of their wages are more crucial. Employment opportunity is related to the growth of agricultural economy and incentives to artisans in the villages. In the Agricultural Labour Enquiry, an agricultural labourer was described as a person who worked as an agricultural labourer for more than one-half of the total number of days on which he actually worked during the year. On the basis of this definition, about 30 per cent workers were identified as agricultural labourers, one-half of them being without land and the rest being in possession of a little land (say one bigha or so). As many as 85 per cent of agricultural labourers get only casual work during times of harvesting, weeding, preparation of soil, and ploughing. Today, the average wage of an agricultural labourer varies from Rs. 30 to Rs. 60 per day. The extent of employment varies under different conditions in various parts of the country, the average being about 200 days. Thus, there is work for wages for about six months in a year, total unemployment for rather more than three months, and some kind of self-employment for less than three months. In this way, their (agricultural labourers) average income is hardly about Rs. 10,000 a year. They, thus, live below the poverty line.

The Agricultural Labour Enquiry was concerned primarily with certain economic aspects but the social disabilities and low social position of the bulk of agricultural labourers are in themselves no small part of the problem. The vast majority belong to SCs, STs, and OBCs. Some of their social handicaps might have diminished because of the government's discriminatory and reservation policies, yet their economic and social status has not much improved. They are not considered a part of social life in a village.

POWER STRUCTURE: TRADITION AND CHANGE

Who holds power in the villages? What was the traditional power structure and what is the new power structure that has emerged? The power-holders may be classified in four groups: (a) those who have power based on the ownership and control of land, (b) those who have power based on their caste, (c) those who have power based on numerical strength, and (d) those who have power because of the positions they hold, e.g., in panchayats, etc.

In the *traditional* power system, the main dimensions of power system were: the zamindari system, the caste system, and the village panchayat. The villagers referred their social, economic and other problems either to the zamindar or to their caste leader or to the village panchayat. In a state like Rajasthan, traditional power structure was feudalistic. In other states also, zamindari was hereditary. The jagirdari and zamindari systems were in fact land revenue systems. The kings granted lands to their favourite chosen men like ministers, courtiers and military commanders, etc. The jagirs were bigger estates than the zamindaris. The jagirdar was an intermediatry between the tiller of the soil and the state but he behaved practically as the owner of the land in respect of peasants. He collected revenue from peasants for their support and also of the military force which he maintained. The zamindars were big landlords but possessed no title. The jagirdars levied number of taxes and took a great portion of the produce as land revenue. They discouraged reforms and social awakening. The zamindars were those who were assigned land by the feudal chiefs and had to pay tribute to the ruler. They used to give their land to tenants whom they exploited in every respect. Thus, ownership of land and their economic status were the fundamental sources of jagirdars' and zamindars' power in a village.

The caste leaders had social status in a village. Since caste councils were very powerful through severest sanctions, they could even ostracize defaulters from the caste. The leaders enjoyed great power over members.

The village panchayats consisted of village elders from amongst all the major castes in the village. These were informal organisations. The members gathered whenever issues involving the interests of the village were to be decided.

After independence, the jagirdari and zamindari systems were abolished and many land reforms were introduced which weakened the traditional power structure and created a new power structure. In place of hereditary and caste leaders, elected persons with political backing became leaders. Individual merit and not caste or class became an important factor in leadership.

Yogendra Singh (1961) in his study of changing power structure in Uttar Pradesh villages concluded that the power system has a tendency to incline in favour of the groups which fulfill the economic expectations of the people in the village. Some studies in Haryana and Rajasthan villages conducted in the 1970s and the 1980s have also shown that linkages with politicians and officials have strengthened the already priviledged position of the upper classes in rural stratification. Andre Beteille (1965:180) noted in his study that power has become independent of class to a greater extent than in the past. Ownership of land is no longer the decisive factor in acquiring power. A.R. Hiraman (1977) has pointed out that the distribution of power and authority in the village does not show any correlation with landholding or caste. Iqbal Narain and P.C. Mathur's study in Rajasthan (1969) concluded that the upper class continues to have a monopoly of leadership but new leadership of younger age group has also emerged at the village level. Sirsikar (1970), Carrass (1972), Inamdar (1971) Ram Reddy (1970), Ishwaran (1970), and Yogesh Atal (1971) also studied the impact of elections on finding base by the political parties in villages and the introduction of Panchayati Raj Institutions (PRIs) on the nature of change in leadership pattern in the villages. Oommen (1969) also pointed out the influence of decentralised decision-making process on rural leadership and the character of the village community power structure.

RURAL POVERTY AND INDEBTEDNESS

About 74 per cent of India's population lives in villages. The incidence of poverty is much higher in villages—roughly 39 per cent of the rural population are poor. Agriculture is a source of livelihood for 70 per cent of the population but agriculture accounts for less than 40 per cent of the national income. One of the reasons for this is the unequal distribution of land. Ten to 20 per cent of landholders hold 70 per cent of the total land and 50 per cent of landholders are marginal farmers with less than one hectare (2.471 acres) of land. Thus, any agenda for fighting poverty must address itself to the rural sector. No doubt our policy-makers have always been emphasising agricultural and rural development ever since the planning process was initiated in 1952. But how far have we been able to alleviate poverty in villages?

According to the Integrated Rural Development Programme (IRDP) definition, approved by the Ministry of Rural Development, as revised in May 1991, a rural household with an annual income of less than Rs. 11,000 is described as a poor household. These 'poor households' have been further classified into four groups: the *destitutes* (with an income of less than Rs. 4,000 per annum at 1991-92 price level), *extremely poor* (with an income between Rs. 4,001 and Rs. 6,000 per annum), *very poor* (with an income between Rs. 6,001 and Rs. 8,500 per annum), and *poor* (with an income between Rs. 8,501 and Rs. 11,000 per annum).

The National Council of Applied Economic Research (NCAER) after four years of study of 33,000 rural households in 16 states looking at 300 parameters came out with a human development profile of rural India that needs to be taken seriously by the development authorities. The 1994 report, which was released in December 1996 in Bhopal at a UNDP and State Government workshop revealed that 39 per cent of the rural population was living below the poverty line or earning less than Rs. 2,444 per person per year (the Planning Commission in 1993-94 had claimed that the population living below the poverty line was 18.1%). According to the NCAER survey, however, the all-India annual income per family in village India in 1994 was Rs. 4,485. It was Rs. 3,028 in Orissa, Rs. 3,157 in West Bengal, Rs. 3,169 in Bihar, Rs. 4,185 in Uttar Pradesh, Rs. 4,166 in Madhya Pradesh, Rs. 4,229 in Rajasthan, Rs. 6,380 in Punjab, and Rs. 6,368 in Haryana (*The Hindustan Times*, December 4, 1996). The survey showed that 55 per cent of the rural population of Orissa and 51 per cent of West Bengal was living below the poverty line. These poor are insecure and survive without knowing where the next meal will come from. Even affluent states like Punjab and Haryana have pockets of rural poverty. Thirty-two per cent of the rural poor in Punjab and 27 per cent in Haryana live below the poverty line.

Poverty can also be measured by the persons' access to piped water, electricity, *kutcha* or *pucca* houses, and the public distribution system. A staggering 55 per cent of the rural population of the country still live in *kutcha* houses. Further, in most backward states (like West Bengal, Bihar, Orissa, Uttar Pradesh and Madhya Pradesh), 15 to 19 per cent rural homes have electricity, 9 to 11 per cent have piped water and 11 to 16 per cent have access to public distribution system.

Causes of Rural Poverty

On the basis of an empirical study in seven districts in Rajasthan in 1996 sponsored by the World Bank, the following causes of poverty in rural areas were identified:

(1) Inadequate and ineffective implementation of anti-poverty programmes.
(2) Low percentage of population engaged in non-agricultural pursuits.
(3) Non-availability of irrigational facilities and erratic rainfall in several districts.
(4) Low agricultural productivity resulting from dependence on traditional methods of cultivation and inadequate modern skills.
(5) Non-availability of electricity for agricultural as well as industrial use in most of the villages.
(6) Poor quality of livestock.
(7) Imperfect and exploited credit market.Lack of link roads, communication facilities and markets (i.e., infrastructure).
(8) Low level of education. The general literacy level in the rural areas in

the country is low (42.85%) while for females it is very low (24.85%).
(10) Absence of dynamic community leadership.
(11) Failure to seek women's cooperation in developmental activities and associating them with planned programmes.
(12) Intercaste conflicts and rivalries.
(13) Spending a large percentage of annual earnings on social ceremonies like marriage, death feast, etc., and people being unwilling to discard expensive customs.

These causes may be grouped together in four categories and explained through a model.

Model Presenting Causes of Rural Poverty

Resources barriers	*Supportive barriers*	*Social system barriers*	*Market barriers*
• Nature of soil	• Low and erratic rainfall	• Inaccessibility to credit facilities	• Non-feasibility of increase in prices of agricultural products.
• Non-exploration and/or poor quality of minerals	• Inadequate irrigation	• People's illiteracy and unwillingness to deviate from established expensive social practices	• Denial of periodic increase in wages of agricultural labourers
• Inadequate capital for industrial investment	• Poor quality of livestock	• Not ensuring required resources (electricity, raw materials, etc.)to small entrepreneurs.	• Unapproachable roads to reach markets or non-availability of marketing facility for selling products.
• Lack of common property resources	• Absence of industries	• Failure in monitoring poverty alleviation programmes (PAPs) leading to benefit reaching to those who are not really poor	• Non—lucrative profit margin on products • Inadequate credit system

Some Effective Strategies for Alleviating Rural Poverty

For reducing poverty in the rural areas, following strategies may be suggested:

(1) Strengthening credit disbursing agencies.
(2) Providing cheap power supply for agricultural and industrial use.
(3) Activating cooperative societies for selling products of household industries.
(4) Making allocations in poverty alleviation programmes (PAPs) flexible and sanctioning special allocations to districts/blocks/villages showing good results.
(5) Integrating varied PAPs in one or two schemes and making availability of benefits easier.
(6) Developing human resources by focusing on education, health and skill programmes.
(7) Introducing double distributive system for the destitutes and the extremely poor.
(8) Creating social awareness to arrest increasing debt growth among the poor.
(9) Improving animal husbandry and developing dairy and poultry farming.
(10) Activating panchayats to focus on adult education programme, road construction and maintaining tree plantations.
(11) Activating NGOs in role-play like digging of tanks, tree plantations, training of youth, imparting skills to women, creating social awareness among the people, and so forth.

BONDED LABOUR

A man keeping another man in perpetual bondage for his selfish and personal designs is a kind of man's cruelty to man which is not confined to a particular country or a particular region but is found as a global phenomenon for thousands of years, right from the Biblical days to the present era. The nomenclature changed from period to period and place to place: slave, serf, and bonded labour. In India, this type of exploitation of man remained prevalent in the name of *begar* and *ryot* for years. The term 'bonded labour' or *bandhua mazdoor* is of recent origin. Despite the abolition of the *zamindari* system, land reforms, *Bhoodan* movement, enactment of legislation (Bonded Labour Abolition Act, 1976), establishment of *Panchayati Raj*, interest shown by Social Action Groups and spirited individuals from society, lakhs of bonded labourers continue to be exploited and carry the yoke of neglect, suffering and frustration in abject silence. In fact, the system of bonded labour, as prevalent in Indian society, is a relic of feudal hierarchical society. A considerable interest has come to be shown in bonded labour during the past two decades by social workers, social scientists and the government because it is considered incompatible with our social ideal of egalitarianism with our commitment to human rights. The magnitude of bonded labour is just baffling as lakns of adult males and females as well as children are condemned to suffering under its yoke.

The Concept

We have to understand the terms 'bonded labour system' and 'bonded labour'. The 'bonded labour system' refers to "the relationship between a creditor and a debtor who obtains loan owing to economic compulsions confronting his day-to-day life, and agrees to abide by the terms dictated by the creditor". The important term of agreement is that the debtor agrees to mortgage his services or services of any or all the members of his family for a specified or unspecified period. The relationship built on the agreement is on such unequal terms that while for every labour or service, there must be some fair remuneration equivalent to the price of labour in the market, under the bonded labour system, the service is rendered for the debt or in lieu of the interest accruing to the debt. The debtor either works without receiving any remuneration or if at all there is any remuneration, it is much less than the minimum wage (notified under the Minimum Wages Act) or the prevailing rate of market wage.

The 1976 Bonded Labour (Abolition) Act defines 'bonded labour system' as "the system of forced labour under which a debtor enters into an agreement with the creditor that he would render service to him either by himself or through any member of his family or any person dependent on him, for a specified or unspecified period, either without wages or for nominal wages, in consideration of loan or any other economic consideration obtained by him or any of his ascendants, or in pursuance of any social obligation, or in pursuance of any obligation devolving on him by succession". The agreement has other consequences too, such as, forfeiting the debtor the freedom of employment, denial of freedom of movement in any part of the country, and denial of the right to sell at market value any of his property or product of his labour.

The term 'bonded labour' has been defined by the National Commission on Labour as "labour which remains in bondage for a specific period for the debt incurred". The Commissioner for Scheduled Castes and Scheduled Tribes explained the term bonded labour in its 24th report as "persons who are forced to work for the creditors for the loan incurred either without wage or on nominal wage" (Sharma, 1990:52). The 'bonded labour' is different from 'contract labour' employed in industries, mines, plantations and docks, etc. Contract labour includes workers who are not directly recruited by the establishment, whose names do not appear on the pay-roll and who are not paid wages directly by the employer. In theory, contract labourers in India are covered by the Factory Act, 1948, the Mines Act, 1952, the Plantations Labour Act, 1951 and the Dock Workers Act, 1948 so as to give them benefits as are admissible to labour directly employed. However, the advantages of employing both bonded labour and contract labour are the same: (i) labour is engaged at a lower cost, (ii) the employers have not to extend fringe benefits to the workers, and (iii) the employers are not under any obligation of providing welfare and security measures to the workers as stipulated in various Acts. The system of contract labour in our country was abolished in September 1970 by an Act called 'Contract Labour (Regulation and Abolition) Act'.

The two basic features of bonded labour are: indebtedness and forced labour. Forced labour can hereditarily descend from father to son or be passed on for generations together. During the period of bondage, the debtor cannot seek employment with any other person. In economic terms, this means that he cannot 'sell his labour in the market at market value'. The bonded labour system is mostly found among agricultural labourers in villages, though today it has extended to workers working in stone quarries, brick kilns, bidi factories, glass factories and in detergent, carpet, gem stones and many other factories.

Bonded labourers are known by different names in different parts of India. For example, in Andhra Pradesh and Karnataka they are known as '*Jeethams*', in Gujarat and Madhya Pradesh as '*Halis*', in Bastar district in Madhya Pradesh as '*Kabadis*', in Hyderabad as '*Bhagela*', in Rajasthan as '*Saggris*', in Bihar as '*Kamias*' or '*Kamiantis*', in Orissa as '*Gothees*', in Tamil Nadu as '*Pandiyals*', in Kerala as '*Adiyas*', '*Paniyas*', and '*Kattunaikens*', and in Uttar Pradesh as '*Koltas*'.

Causes of Bonded Labour

Though the main causes of origin, growth and perpetuation of bonded labour system are economic, the social and religious factors too support the custom. The *economic* causes include: extreme poverty of people, inability to find work for livelihood, inadequate size of the landholdings to support family, lack of alternative small-scale loans for the rural and urban poor, natural calamities like drought, floods etc., destruction of men and animals, absence of rains, drying away of wells, meagre income from forest produce, and inflation and constant rising prices. The *social* factors include: high expenses on occasions like marriage, death, feast, birth of a child, etc., leading to heavy debts, caste-based discrimination, lack of concrete social welfare schemes to safeguard against hunger and illness, non-compulsory and unequal educational system, and indifference and corruption among government officials. Sometimes, exploitation by some persons in a village also compels people to migrate to some other place and seek not only employment on the employer's conditions but also get protection from influential persons. *Religious* arguments are used to convince the people of low castes that religion enjoins upon them to serve people of high castes. Illiteracy, ignorance, immaturity and lack of skill and professional training sustain such beliefs. Broadly speaking, it may be maintained that bondage originates mainly from economic and social pressures (Sharma, 1990:52).

The Legislation

The pernicious and inhuman, callous, reprehensible practice of bonded labour existed in many states in India. After independence, it could not be allowed to continue to blight national life any longer. As such, when the Constitution of India was framed, Article 23 was enshrined in it which prohibited 'traffic in human beings', '*begar*' and other similar forms of forced labour. However, no serious effort was made to give effect to this Article and stamp out the shocking practice of bonded labour. The Forced Labour (Abolition) Convention adopted by the International Labour Organisation (ILO) in 1919 was ratified by India only in November 1954. Some states in India had also enacted laws for abolishing bonded labour. For example, the Bihar Kamianti Act was passed in 1920, the Madras Agency Debt Bondage Regulation in 1940, Kabadi System Regulation in Bastar in Madhya Pradesh in 1943, Hyderabad Bhagela Agreement Regulation in 1943, Orissa Debt Bonded Abolition Regulation in 1948, Rajasthan Sagri System Abolition Act in 1961 (which was amended in 1975), and Bonded Labour System (Abolition) Act, Kerala in 1975. It was specifically laid down in most of these regulations (like those of Madras, Orissa, Bihar, and Hyderabad) that the agreement between the creditor and the debtor entered into after the commencement of the regulation was to be wholly void if (a) the full terms of the agreement were not expressed in writing and a copy thereof was not filed with the designated authority, (b) the expressed and implied period of labour exceeded one year, (c) the interest provided for was not simple interest over one year, and (d) the interest exceeded 6 25 per cent per annum. But it was after the announcement of the 20-point programme on July 1, 1975 that the legislative excercise at the national level began with some amount of seriousness and urgency. The ordinance was enacted in October 1975 which was later replaced by the Act passed in February 1976, called the Bonded Labour

System (Abolition) Act. All the state laws became inoperative after the enactment of the Act by the union government in 1976.

The Act implies: (i) identification of bonded labourers; (ii) release of bonded labourers; (iii) action against offenders, i.e., creditors who had forced agreement upon the debtors; (iv) holding of regular meetings of vigilance committees at the district and tehsil level; (v) maintenance of the prescribed registers; and (vi) conferring of judicial powers to executive magistrates. The Act also provides for the rehabilitation of bonded labourers who are freed from their creditors. The 1976 Act was amended in 1985 in which it was clarified that the contract workers and inter-state migrant workers, if they fulfil the conditions laid down in the Bonded Labour System (Abolition) Act, will be considered as bonded labour.

The main problem that is faced in the implementation of the 1976 Act is the identification of bonded labourers. Neither the administrators at the district and *tehsil* levels admit the existence of bonded labourers in their areas nor do the creditors accept that any bonded workers are serving them, nor are the workers themselves willing to give statements that they are being forced to work as bonded labourers since long. It is the social workers attached to non-political social action groups and voluntary organisations who identify the bonded labourers. The other handicap which aggravates the problem is the economic rehabilitation of the released labourers. The economic rehabilitation includes: finding jobs for them, getting them minimum wages, giving them training in arts and crafts, allotment of agricultural land, helping them in developing the allotted land, helping them in the processing of forest produce, educating them and their children, arranging for their medical care, etc. All these are Herculean tasks. Besides ensuring economic rehabilitation, the state governments are also expected to arrange for their psychological rehabilition and integration of various schemes of central and state governments. In chalking out plans and strategies of rehabilitation, the freed labourers are to be given the choice between various alternatives (Sharma, 1990:54).

Misery and Suffering in Bondage

One former Chief Justice of the Supreme Court (Justice P.N. Bhagwati) described bonded labourers as 'non-beings, exiles of civilisation living a life worse than that of animals', for the animals are at least free to roam about as they like and they can plunder or garb food whenever they are hungry, but these outcastes of society are held in bondage and robbed of their freedom even. They are consigned to an existence where they have to live either in hovels or under the open sky and be satisfied with whatever unwholesome food they can manage to get, inadequate though it may be to fill their hungry stomachs. Not having any choice, they are driven by poverty and hunger into a life of bondage, a dark bottomless pit from which, in a cruel exploitative society, they cannot hope to be rescued (*Yojana*, May 1-15, 1987:32-33).

It is estimated that there are about 32 lakh bonded labourers in India. Of these, 98 per cent are said to be bonded due to indebtedness and 2 per cent due to customary social obligations. The highest number is believed to exist in three states of Andhra Pradesh, Karnataka and Tamil Nadu, followed by Orissa, Uttar Pradesh, Bihar and Madhya Pradesh. According to the figures released in May 1997 on the basis of a state government-sponsored survey (conducted as per the Supreme Court direction), Tamil Nadu has the maximum number of 24,000 bonded labourers, in the country, engaged in 30 different occupations (*The Hindustan Times*, May 13, 1997). It has been pointed out that the majority of bonded labourers work as agricultural labour in villages and belong to the outcaste or tribal communities. Of the total labour force in the rural areas, about 33 per cent are engaged in non-agricultural activities, 42 per cent work as cultivators, and 25 per cent as agricultural labourers. Of those who work as agricultural labourers, 48 per cent belong to Scheduled Castes and 33 per cent to Scheduled Tribes. Being unskilled and unorganised, agricultural labourers have little for their livelihood other than personal labour. Bonded agricultural labourers occupy the lowest rung of the rural ladder. Social and economic stratification in a village is linked with land and caste which in turn govern economic and social status of the people. Bonded labourers thus live in pitiable and miserable conditions. They are socially exploited because though in theory they are assured food, clothes, free tobacco, etc., in practice they get the food that is left over, and clothes that are discarded by family members. They are made to work for 12 to 14 hours a day and are forced to live with cows and buffaloes in shed. If they fall ill, they may be procured some medicines from the local *Hakim* depending upon the sweet will of the employer.

The total number of bonded labourers identified and freed in India by March 1989 was 2.42 lakhs, of whom 2.18 lakhs (i.e., 90%) were said to be rehabilitated also (*Yojana*, May 1989:23). Thus, hardly 8 per cent of total bonded workers in India have been identified so far, indicating lack of interest of state governments in solving the problem of bonded labour.

At least four reports submitted to the Government of India between 1979 and 1983 pointed out how the disgusting and squeamish practice of bonded labour existed in India and continued to disfigure the social and economic life of the country. These reports were: (a) Report of the Centre for Rural Development to the Ministry of Labour, Government of India, on 'Rehabilitation of Bonded Labour in Monghyr District, Bihar', (b) Report of the Public Policy and Planning Division of the Indian Institute of Public Administration to the Ministry of Labour, Government of India, on 'Evaluation Study of Bonded Labour Rehabilitation Scheme in Tehri Garhwal, Uttar Pradesh', (c) Report of Laxmi Dhar Misra, Director General (Labour Welfare) of Government of India based on the 'Spot Studies Regarding Identification, Release and Rehabilitation of Freed Bonded Labourers in Uttar Pradesh, Madhya Pradesh, Andhra Pradesh, Karnataka, Orissa, Bihar, Rajasthan, Tamil Nadu and Kerala', and (d) Report of the National Seminar on 'Identification and Rehabilitation of Bonded Labour' held from February 7-9, 1983.

Of the 2.42 lakh bonded labourers identified and released up to March 1989, 26 per cent were got released in Karnataka, 20 per cent in Orissa, 16 per cent in Tamil Nadu, 14 per cent in Andhra Pradesh, 11 per cent in Uttar Pradesh, 5 per cent in Bihar, 4 per cent in Madhya Pradesh, 3 per cent in Rajasthan, 0.5 per cent in Maharashtra, 0.3 per cent in Kerala and 0.2 per cent in Haryana (*Yojana*, Ibid:23).

Rehabilitation

Getting bonded labourers identified and freed was the statutory obligation of the state governments only but from November 1987 onwards, voluntary organisations also came to be authorised both for identification and rehabilitation. Of the 2.18 lakh bonded labourers rehabilitated up to March 1989, three-fourths were in four states of Orissa (23.8%), Karnataka (23.3%), Tamil Nadu (17.1%) and Uttar Pradesh (12.1%), one-fifth in three states of Andhra Pradesh (11.1%), Bihar (5.2%) and Madhya Pradesh (3.5%), and the remaining 4 per cent in three states in Rajasthan (3.2%), Maharashtra (0.4%) and Kerala (0.4%) (*Indian Labour Journal*, August 1989:1277). There is also a provision in the 20-point programme (of 1986) regarding the identification and rehabilitation of the bonded labour. Under this programme, the Government of India issued instructions in August 1986 to the Deputy Director General (Labour Welfare) of all the states to take follow-up action. Since then, the Union Ministry of Labour has been monitoring and evaluating the programme of identification, release and rehabilitation of bonded labourers from time to time.

Rehabilitation is both physical and psychological. Physical rehabilitation is essentially economic whereas psychological rehabilitation has to be built up through a process of assurance and reassurance. The two must go side by side. The first prerequisite of psychological rehabilitation is that the freed bonded labourers must be wrenched away from the old habitat and be rehabilitated at a place where they will no longer be subject to the ruinous influence of the erstwhile bonded labour-keepers. Unless they are psychologically assured that after release from bondage, debt will not regulate their destiny any longer, there is every possibility that they may slide back to debt bondage.

Basically, there are three phases of rehabilitation: (i) immediate physical subsistence after release; (ii) short-term measures to help the freed workers to start a new life (for example, allotment of a house site, assistance for construction of a house, allotment of a plot of agricultural land, supplying a pair of bullocks and agricultural implements, or provision of avenues of gainful employment, etc.); and (iii) long-term measures (such as, arranging credit, training in new skills, developing existing skills, providing a remunerative price support, ensuring non-formal literacy of adult members and formal literacy for children, securing medical care, protection of civil rights...). It is thus rehabilitation which will give the freed bonded labourers the status of human beings so that they may be able to identify themselves with the mainstream of a civilised human society and realise the dignity worthy of human existence.

Lacunae in Effective Rehabilitation

Qualitatively reviewing the implementation of the rehabilitative programmes for bonded labourers in different states, we find that while some states, like Orissa, Uttar Pradesh, Kerala and Andhra Pradesh point out the welcome features of identification and rehabilitation, some other states need to introduce innovative changes. The following visible lacunae in the implementation of the programme need to be dealt with immediately:

Firstly, instead of treating the programme in isolation as the programme of a particular ministry/department, there has to be coordination among various ministries/departments concerned like those of agriculture, animal husbandary, irrigation, forest, fishries, etc., so that the programme is dealt with as an integrated national programme. *Secondly*, since the social milieu and the social structures which prompted the bonded labour system in the past continue to dominate the village life and its economy even today, they need to be probed and changed with commitment. *Thirdly*, the development departments are so much burdened with schemes like IRDP, JRY, TRYSEM, etc., that their programmes mostly remain time-bound and target-oriented without taking into account the needs, aptitudes and preferences of the beneficiaries.

The need is, therefore, to design programmes in such a manner that they serve as target-group oriented rather than target-oriented. *Fourthly*, with poor infrastructure and lack of qualified and committed staff and resources, the beneficiaries are not provided protective covers on a long-term basis with the result that very often productive assets turn into liabilities. *Fifthly*, middlemen operate like parasites and take away the limited fruits and benefits of rehabilitation to their advantage. What is required, therefore, is carefully and rationally formulated scheme with varied linkages, keeping an eye on the type of infrastructure already available. *Sixthly*, the freed bonded labourers who come from the lowest strata of the society and represent the extremes of poverty and destitution are unable to exercise choice of a particular scheme which may be most profitable to them. Their dependence on the officials concerned in selecting a particular scheme for them deprives them of the real benefits of rehabilitation. This dependence needs to be reduced. *Lastly*, the attitude of the erstwhile bonded labour keepers, employers at large, and officials in various departments has not changed at all towards the poor bonded labourers. Even when the labourers are assaulted by their erstwhile masters and landlords, their land is forcibly taken away, their children are not permitted to pass through the paddy fields of the landlords to reach schools, their animals are whisked away by their exploiters and they complain to the police, or approach doctors for help, or lodge complaints with the officers of the departments concerned, they (officers, police, doctors, etc.) are not at all moved by their pathetic stories and remain callous, unresponsive, insensitive and ineffective. They hardly ever help them. Without a change in the attitude of people and the officials concerned, the freed labourers cannot withstand the organised onslaughts against them by the more influential sections of the society. Their ignorance, illiteracy and lack of capacity to fight for their rights will always hamper them from enjoying the gains of freedom and development. Changing social systems and social structures as to benefit the poor (who become bonded labourers) is not easy. Let us take two illustrations. A tribal needs money to pay bride-price for his own or his son's marriage. He obtains loan by mortgaging his services and thus becomes a bonded labourer. Similarly, suppose an individual is convicted by the courts for illicit distillation and is heavily fined. Since he has no money to pay fine, he takes a loan from an influential person by pledging his labour and becomes a bonded labourer. Now, is abolishing the custom of bride-price possible? Is imposition of fine by the courts for an illegal action wrong? Many economic needs cannot be gratified by the poor individuals without seeking loans. In such cases, what is needed is careful scrutiny of the agreements for obtaining loans so that pledging labour as security may be prevented and the system of bonded labour be controlled.

The *group-approach* to development will bring the freed bonded labourers together, enable them to pool their resources, get help from various agencies, departments and banks, and integrate themselves for a common purpose for a qualitative and permanent rehabilitation. Such a 'group-effort' can be land-based, craft-based or asset-based for success. This requires proper selection of beneficiaries, the place where they are to be rehabilitated, selection of skills to be taught to them, and building awareness among the beneficiaries themselves and converting them into willing partners in a joint venture for their rehabilitation, progress and advancement.

The crucial problem is that if the freed bonded labourers are not rehabilitated, they will suffer even more. The question before them would be: should they choose hunger or slavery, freedom or security, hard work in serfdom or crime to support family and the resultant fear of imprisonment? While the rehabilitation work was totally assigned to state governments till about a decade ago, in 1983 the central government also sponsored a scheme through the Ministry of Labour. The central government provides for four to five crore rupees a year to the state governments for formulating specific schemes on a matching grant basis. A Planning Commission report says that the progress of rehabilitation work is very slow. The state government officials lack initiative or remain indifferent to identification and rehabilitation programmes. Social workers too face many handicaps in their work. It is hoped that central aid and the involvement of voluntary organisations will make the identification and rehabilitation programmes of the bonded labourers more effective.

In 1982, the Supreme Court declared 'forced labour' as violation of fundamental rights of such labourers, and in 1983 described labour with below the prescribed minimum wages as 'forced labour'. In 1984, it further described the failure of the state governments to implement the provisions of the Bonded Labour (Abolition) Act, 1976 as violation of the Constitution. It also described rehabilitation after release as obligatory so that freed labourers are not driven by poverty, helplessness and despair into serfdom once again (Sharma, 1990:56). Such judicial interpretations are expected to strengthen the efforts of the state governments and voluntary organisations in getting the bonded labourers freed from the clutches of their employers.

Effective Concern

The plight of bonded labourers continues to be a serious social problem and a matter of concern for public, government, judiciary, social scientists and social workers. If about 17 lakh crimes in a year, for which about 26 lakh persons are arrested under the IPC, are considered a serious issue for the Indian society, freeing of three million bonded labourers must be viewed as a very crucial issue. For this purpose, it is necessary that researches be sponsored by different funding agencies to ascertain the extent and the nature of the problem, examine handicaps in identification, utility of various rehabilitation schemes, coordination of activities between central government and voluntary organisations, necessity of amending the 1976 Act, determining responsibilities and accountability of the concerned officers, and introducing after-care programmes for the freed bonded labourers. Unless serious efforts are taken to save bonded labourers from ruthless exploitation by vested interests, the problem will continue to be a social menace. The total abolition of the system of bonded labour through legislation may not be feasible in the forseable future, yet doing away with the legislation may cause further distress to the victims. Removing poverty, unemployment and illiteracy, which are believed to be the three basic causes of bonded labour system, is also not easy. The formulation of future plans, programmes and projects for bonded labourers would require a broad approach and action at various levels.

The problem of bonded labour has, thus, to be fought at various fronts/social, psychological and legal. We have to educate the exploited not to succumb to pressure tactics. We have to tell the exploiters that law cannot be circumvented and has to take its course in democratic India. We have to create committed opinion among the masses. We have to involve not only intellectuals but also the enlightened citizens to carry the message to those who matter. We have to enforce laws rigidly. We have also to impress upon politicians to tackle the issue with concerted interest and missionary zeal. The system based on exploitation by a few socially and economically powerful persons, trading on the misery and suffering of large numbers of men and holding them in bondage constitutes a shameful feature of our national life. The bondage of the economically impoverished segments of society for a small debt is totally incompatible with the egalitarian socio-economic order promised to Indians. Wiping out this system is basic and crucial to human dignity and is in conformity with constitutional values.

LAND REFORMS: NATURE AND SOCIAL CONSEQUENCES

Land Reforms

The important land reforms introduced after independence in our country are: (1) abolition of zamindari system; (2) accepting the fundamental principle that lands belonged to those who do the tilling; (3) enacting Land Ceiling Act; (4) encouraging Bhoodan and Sarvodyay movements; and (5) devising suitable rational basis for obtaining land revenue. The proposal 'land belonging to the tiller' was meant to redistribute rural income to the advantage of those who work in the fields and to the disadvantage of those who do not. Another effect of this proposal was that control of a very considerable amount of land was to pass from rent-receivers to tenants, crop-shares and labourers. What were the possible measures to effect this proposal through legislation? (i) to provide that at the death of non-tilling owners, their rights in land could pass only to those who already are actual tillers, or (ii) the legislation might lay down that no further transfers of agricultural land may occur except to those who are now tillers and who propose to till the land with their own hands, or (iii) to take away forthwith the rights in the land of non-tiller landowners and compensation be provided to them or providing them rehabilitation grants to take up other occupations. But the programme of abolishing proprietary rights was not easy to implement.

Bhoodan Movement

With the disappointing progress of legislative land reform, Acharya Vinoba Bhave's Bhoodan (land-gift) movement offered a promising way forward. The focus was on improving the position of the landless. Assuming that there were 50 million landless peasants in India, Vinobaji set himself the task of collecting land-gifts of 50 million acres so that one acre could be given to each landless peasant. He called upon the landowners to give to the Bhoodan movement one-sixth of their holdings. Since roughly 300 million acres were under cultivation in 1951 in India, the gifts would have totalled up to the required 50 million acres. These gifts were then to be distributed to the landless under the guidance of Bhoodan workers. The movement got off to a good start as within three years (1952 to 1954) more than 3 million acres of land were received as Bhoodan. However, the movement soon slowed down. It was found that much of the land donated was rocky, barren or otherwise agriculturally poor or was under dispute in litigation. Further, distribution of land created more problems. Out of a total of 3.75 million acres of land received by May 1955, about 0.2 million acres (or 5%) could be redistributed. The district and *taluk* leaders were far from enthusiastic. They associated themselves with the Bhoodan only to enlarge or strengthen their following. Vinobaji resisted these efforts. The appeal was to the rich and landed peasants who opposed all types of land reform in their vested interests. Thus, like ceilings, Bhoodan also failed.

The Green Revolution

The green revolution which aimed at increase in agricultural productivity, was brought about in 1966. The introduction of high-yielding varieties of wheat, rice, maize, millet, etc., benefited the larger landholder more than the small landholder. This was because it required a reliable supply of water, costly fertiliser, high quality of seed, and pesticides, and use of machinery. These could be afforded only by the richer farmers. According to P.C. Joshi (1974:33) in Punjab, Haryana and some other regions, the trend that emerged was that small landowners rented their land to big farmers who needed a larger landspread to use their machinery profitably. On the one hand, this enriched the larger landholder, on the other hand, it increased the number of landless labourers most of whom are low caste and untouchables.

Before independence, though about 70 per cent of the rural population was engaged in agriculture yet agricultural production was so low that we were dependent on foreign countries for our food supply. The low agricultural production was the result of British policy of collecting land revenue, lack of use of modern technology in agriculture, lack of credit facilities to small owners of land, exploitation of small cultivators by zamindars and jagirdars, and lack of interest on the part of cultivators to accept new models of cropping. The result of the British policy of land revenue was that many cultivators who were unable to pay taxes had either to sell or mortgage their land or turn for help to money lenders. Because of this, the proportion of landless and land labourers increased from 13 per cent of the rural population in 1891 to 38 per cent in 1951 (Patel, 1952). When population of the country in the early 1950s was growing at the rate of 0.67 per cent, the agricultural output was growing at the rate of 0.5 per cent. The land reforms introduced after independence further led to the concentration of land in the hands of the larger landowners. The principle of land reform was 'land to the tiller'. The large landowners, anticipating this type of legislation, had got evicted long-term tenants prior to the enactment of legislation. Many tenants had voluntarily given up their land rights to the owners out of fear. Thereafter, the large landowner rented out his land to short-term or seasonal tenants, or cultivated it himself with the help of casual labour. By 1953-54, the upper 10 per cent of landowners owned more than half of the land, 47 per cent owned less than 1 acre per household, and 23 per cent were landless. The agricultural production which was growing at the rate of 3 per cent per year in 1951-52 increased to 6 per cent in 1994-95, 10 per cent in 1996-97, but decreased to 6 per cent in 1998-99 (*India Today*, March 8, 1999: 18-19). It is estimated that using high-yield techniques, the upper 10 per cent of landholders could produce enough food to feed urban and other non-agricultural population of India. This means that about 48 million cultivators' families would be pushed off the land. This is a wrong assumption. Commercialisation of agriculture and the green revolution of last three decades would neither affect the cultivators adversely nor spell the demise of patronage system in the villages.

PLANNED RURAL DEVELOPMENT

Two types of policies affect rural life: (i) production-oriented activities targeting production and services, e.g., subsidised fertilisers, providing irrigation, credit, locating village industries, and so on; and (ii) non-production oriented activities targeting living standards. The first type of activities are defined as rural development measures. These activities may affect either the whole community or a particular section of the community. Examples of the former type of activities are: community development projects (1952), Panchayati Raj (1962), land reforms (1950s), poverty alleviation programmes (PAPs) like Integrated Rural Development Programme (1978) etc., while of the latter type of activities are Tribal Development Programme (1959), Drought-prone Area Programme (1979), Desert Development Programme (1977), Food for Work Programme (1977), National Rural Employment Programme (1980), TRYCEM, etc. (Sagar, 1990:251-261). Some programmes aimed at increasing assets (including increasing production) and benefitting people economically, e.g., IRDP, Minimum Agricultural Wage, Rural Employment Programme, etc., while others aimed at social uplift of people, e.g., zamindari abolition, land reforms, Panchayati Raj, TRYSEM, etc. Some programmes indeed aimed at poverty alleviation (e.g., self-employment programmes of NREP, DPAP, training programme of TRYSEM, etc.) while some others were politically motivated, e.g., Garibi Hatao and 20-point programme. However, the basic aims of achieving community participation, removal of social evils, and improving the quality of life have yet to be achieved.

The Strategies

Three distinct strategies for rural development may be identified:

(i) Initially, in the 1950s, policy-makers stressed maximisation of economic growth by stepping up investment assuming that the benefits arising out of it would 'trickle down' and diffuse among all sectors of the rural society. But in the 1970s, it was realised that the benefits of agricultural growth did not percolate to the rural poor.

(ii) This gave birth to the second approach led by structural school which suggested distribution of assets through land reforms, community development programmes and cooperative farming. But this also did not work.

(iii) Then came the idea in the 1980s that suggested attack on poverty through rural development programmes, such as IRDP, TRYSEM, NREP, and RLEGP which later on merged in JRY programme. Before analysing these anti-poverty progranmmes, we shall evaluate the role of Five Year Plans, and 20-Point Programme in poverty alleviation.

The Five Year Plans

The Planning Commission set up in 1950 has been formulating Five Year Plans for India's development taking an overall view of the needs and resources of the country. The First Plan was launched in April 1951 and the Third Plan ended in March 1966. After this, there were three one year plans from April, 1966 to March 1969. The Fourth Plan started in April 1969 and the Ninth Plan started in April 1997 (though it got cabinet approval only in January 1999).

The *First Five Year Plan* (1951-56) aimed at achieving an all-round balanced development and accorded top priority to agriculture and irrigation investing 44.6 per cent of the total plan budget in this sector. This was to reduce the country's dependence on agricultural imports and save foreign exchange. However, the plan did give importance to the development of social welfare programmes. At the end of the plan, the country's national income increased by 18 per cent and per capita income by 11 per cent.

The *Second Five Year Plan* (1956-61) strongly felt that the benefits of development should accrue more to the relatively underprivileged sections of society and that there should be a progressive reduction in the concentration of income. However, the performance of the plan did not justify the hopes that had been placed on it. Achievements in almost all sectors of the economy were lower that the plan targets. Consequently, as against a near 13 per cent fall in price index during the First Plan, the Second Plan witnessed a 12.5 per cent rise in the price level.

The *Third Five Year Plan* (1961-66) aimed at securing a marked advance towards self-sustaining growth. It listed a set of five objectives, namely, increase in annual national income by 5 per cent, self-sufficiency in agriculture, growth of basic industries (like steel, power, chemicals), maximum use of manpower resources, and decentralisation of economic power. Agriculture was once again given top priority and about 35 per cent of the outlay was allocated to this sector. The performance of the Third Plan was also as disheartening as that of the Second Plan. Over the five year period, the national income grew by 2.6 per cent as against the target of 5 per cent. In the agricultural sector also, the production suffered a setback.

The shape of the economy was in fact so bad at the end of the Third Plan that the Fourth Plan, which was to be launched in March 1966 had to be abandoned and was replaced by three Annual Plans. The three year period between 1966 and 1969, sometimes described as a period of 'plan holiday', was devoted to rectifying the ills that had crippled the planning process during the operation of the Third Plan. The main objective of the three Annual Plans was to continue the unfinished tasks of the Third Plan.

The *Fourth Five Year Plan* (1969-74) aimed at increasing national income by 5.5 per cent, creating economic stability, reducing inequalities in income distribution, and achieving social justice with equality. Simultaneous growth of both agricultural and industrial sectors was fully recognised under the Fourth Plan. But this plan could not ensure economic growth. Neither could it achieve self-sufficiency in foodgrains, nor could the generation of employment opportunities make any significant dent in the widespread unemployment problem. The inflationary situation was also aggravated.

The *Fifth Five Year Plan* (1974-79) mainly aimed at removal of poverty and attainment of self-reliance. The plan also aimed at increase in employment opportunities, self-sufficiency, policy of minimum wages, removal of regional imbalances, and encouragement of exports. The plan ended during the Janata regime in 1978 instead of 1979 and the Sixth Plan was started as the 'rolling plan'. But when the Congress once again came to power in 1978, the period of the Fifth Plan, was described as being 1974 to 1979. The Fifth Plan however, could not achieve its targets in any field, except in increase of foodgrains.

The *Sixth Five Year Plan* (1980-85) was formulated after taking into account the achievements and shortcomings of the past three decades of planning. Removal of poverty was the foremost objective of the plan. Stress was laid on economic growth, elimination of unemployment, bringing down of inequality in the distribution of income, self-sufficiency in technology, raising the lifestyles of the weaker sections of society, improving the public distribution system, and control of the increasing population. This plan had a fairly convincing success. According to NSS (National Sample Survey), the proportion of people living below the poverty line declined from 48.3 per cent in 1977-78 to 36.9 per cent in 1984-85.

The *Seventh Five Year Plan* (1985-90) had three priorities of increasing food, work and productivity. With its emphasis on generating substantial productive employment, the Seventh Plan aimed at significant reduction in the incidence of poverty and improvement in the quality of life of the poor. However, this plan also failed totally in achieving its targets. There was a severe setback on the agricultural front, in the manufacturing sector, in creating employment, and in the balance of payments position of the country.

The *Eighth Five Year Plan* (1992-97) which was to be started in 1990 was actually enforced from April 1992. The 1990-91 and 1991-92 years were considered to be yearly plans. The plan was supposed to be oriented towards employment generation. The plan size was nearly double the previous plan but then all plans have been twice the size of the previous plans. The growth rate was also more or less what the previous plans aimed at. The fact that they rarely reached the target except in the First and Sixth Plans is a different matter. The Eighth Plan was thus no different from the earlier plans, and its results also were no different either.

The *Ninth Five Year Plan* (1997-2002) was approved by the Cabinet only in January 1999. It is described as ambitious and growth-oriented. The plan's thrust areas are: agriculture, employment, poverty, and infrastructure. In agriculture, the top priority is to be given to irrigation. The efficiency and productivity of five infrastructure sectors—irrigation, power, mining, railways and communication—is also expected to improve. The plan is described as 'delivery-oriented'.

Assessment of Five Year Plans

If we make an appraisal of all the eight completed plans, we find that in the five decades of planning, all our plans have been oriented towards something, sometimes self-reliance in agricultural production, sometimes employment, sometimes industrial growth, and so on. But poverty and unemployment have always increased.

During this period of 48 years, the average rate of economic growth has been 3 per cent. Though it is not bad in comparison to the world's average of 4 per cent, it is definitely poor in comparison to the average of the developing countries of 7 per cent to 10 per cent. During 1951-1998, our annual national income had increased by about 3.5 per cent, agricultural production by 2.7 per cent, industrial production by 6.1 per cent, and the per capita consumption by 1.1 per cent. While the government claimed that the number of people below the poverty line had come down to 33 per cent by 1998, since the number of unemployed people had increased, we cannot concede that poverty has been contained. No wonder, more people feel frustrated today and the number of agitations is increasing every year.

20-Point Programme

Indira Gandhi announced this programme in July, 1975 for reducing poverty and economic exploitation and for the uplift of the weaker sections of society. The five important goals of this programme were: (a) controlling inflation, (b) giving impetus to production, (c) welfare of the rural population, (d) lending help to the urban middle classes, and (e) controlling social crimes. The programmes included in the 20-point programme were: increase in irrigational facilities, increase in programmes for rural employment, distribution of surplus land, minimum wages to landeless labourers, rehabilitation of bonded labour, uplift of the Scheduled Castes and the Scheduled Tribes, growth of housing facilities, increasing power production, formulating new programmes of family planning, tree plantation, extension of primary health facilities, programmes for the welfare of women and children, making primary education measures more effective, strengthening of public distribution system, simplification of industrial policies, control of black money, betterment of drinking water facilities, and developing internal resources.

The 20-point programme was discontinued with the change of government, when the Janata Party became the ruling party at the centre. However, in January 1982, the programme was again implemented with a revised format. Among other things, the revised programme included an increased tempo of rural development and a direct attack on rural poverty, besides specific schemes for the uplift of the Scheduled Castes and the Scheduled Tribes.

In the light of the experience gained in the Sixth Plan period (1980-85), the 20-point programme was restricted and revised in August 1986. This restructured programme aimed at eradicating poverty, raising productivity, reducing income inequalities, removing social and economic disparities and improving the quality of life. The 20-point programme in the restructured plan of 1986 contains the following commitments: attack on rural poverty, strategy for rainfed agriculture, better use of irrigation water, bigger harvests, enforcement of land reforms, special programmes for rural labour, clean drinking water, health for all, two-child norm, expansion of education, justice to Scheduled Castes and Scheduled Tribes, equality for women, new opportunities for youth, housing for people, improvement of slums, new strategy for forestry, protection of the environment, concern for consumer, energy for villages, and a responsive administration.

The fact that the rural people and the urban poor are more discontended and feel more frustrated today points to the failure of the 20-point programme in fulfilling its commitments.

State Poverty Alleviation Programmes

Several poverty alleviation programmes have been launched by the central government for the rural poor, comprising small and marginal farmers, landless labourers and rural artisans. The important programmes currently functioning are: IRDP (subsidies/loans for self-employment and supportive land-based activities like irrigation, animal husbandry, etc.), TRYSEM (Training Rural Youth in Skills for Self-Employment), Jawahar Rozgar Yojna (generating additional gainful employment for the rural unemployed and underemployed, and providing employment for 50 to 100 days in a year to at least one member in a poor family, NREP (wage employment in slack season), RLEGP (80 to 100 days of wage employment to every landless household), DPAP (area development of drought-prone areas), and DDP (area development of hot and cold deserts).

We will discuss each of these programmes separately.

IRDP

The Integrated Rural Development Programme (IRDP) is a major instrument of the government to alleviate poverty. Its objective is to enable selected families to cross the poverty line by taking up self-employment ventures in a variety of activities like agriculture, horticulture and animal husbandry in the primary sector, weaving and handicrafts in the secondary sector, and service and business activities in the tertiary sector. The aim of the IRDP is to see that a minimum stipulated number of families is enabled to cross the poverty line within the limits of a given investment and in a given time-frame. Thus, the three variables involved are: (a) number of poor households, (b) resources available for investment, and (c) the time-span over which the investment would yield an income which would enable the family to cross the poverty line.

The IRDP was launched by the centre in March 1976 in 20 selected districts, but from October 1982 it was extended to all districts in the country. This programme considers a household as the basic unit of development. The functional aspect of this programme can be gauged from the fact that above 80 lakh households are said to have been assisted within five years—between 1993-94 and 1997-98—in the matter of improving their economic conditions and rising above the poverty line. A number of institutions have undertaken studies with respect to the implementation and working of the IRDP. They point out flaws in the implementation of the programme. None of these studies have, however, questioned the utility of the programme. The main criticisms against this scheme are: (1) There are leakages in the programme and all assets created under IRDP are not with the poor. This is mainly because of three factors: (a) the poor are unable to pay large bribes, fill up complicated forms, influence the village headman and find 'guarantors' for themselves; (b) bank officials are often reluctant to deal with poor borrowers because they believe—rightly or wrongly—that giving loans to the poor is risky since recovery is often used as a major indicator of the performance of a particular branch of a rural bank; and (c) the poor themselves take inadequate interest in the programme because they are afraid of being cheated or of not being able to repay. (2) There is much corruption, misuse and malpractice in the implementation of the loan programme. The loans are often misallocated with little apparent violation of the guidelines of the schemes for (a) the guidelines make it clear that for fair allocation of loans, Gram Sabha (village assembly) meetings should be convened for selecting the beneficiaries but in practice this does not happen because the village headman and the Gram Sevak act as intermediaries between the villagers and the administration; (b) bribing is a *spine qua non* of obtaining a loan; and (c) household surveys on which the list of eligible households are supposed to be based are conducted only once in five years. (3) The programme is household-based and is not integrated with the development needs or resource base of the area. Thus, the IRDP loan neither raises the living standards of the beneficiaries nor does it have any impact on rural poverty by raising the poor people above the poverty line. This has been indicated by studies in several districts in Rajasthan, Gujarat, West Bengal, Uttar Pradesh and Karnataka. The latest study was conducted in seven districts in Rajasthan under a World Bank project on poverty. The reports were separately submitted by each district in April 1997. Similar studies have been planned in three other states also—West Bengal, Andhra Pradesh and Madhya Pradesh.

This does not mean that this particular poverty alleviation programme of the government needs to be dispensed with. The government cannot abdicate its responsibility. It has only to concentrate more on programmes of employment generation and removal of corruption to enable the disadvantaged groups to get benefits of the existing scheme.

TRYSEM

The scheme called Training Rural Youth for Self-Employment was started on August 15, 1979 to provide technical skills to the rural youth to enable them to seek employment in fields of agriculture, industry, services and business activities. Only youth in the age group of 18-35 and belonging to families living below the poverty line are eligible for training. Priority for selection is given to Scheduled Castes and Scheduled Tribe persons, ex-servicemen and those who are ninth pass. One-third seats are reserved for women. Stipend to the trainees ranges from Rs. 75 to Rs. 200 per month. On completion of training, TRYSEM beneficiaries are assisted under the IRDP. In four years between 1992-93 and 1995-96, about two lakh youths were trained every year, of whom about 45 per cent became self-employed and 30 per cent remained employed on wages (*Economic and Political Weekly*, 1995). The main criticisms against this programme are: (i) its coverage is very small in relation to need; (ii) skills provided have not been linked with rural industrialisation process. Training is provided on the basis of ad hoc considerations and skills imparted are of low level; and (iii) amount of stipend is rather inadequate to motivate the youth to go for training.

NREP

The National Rural Employment Programme (NREP) was planned for creating additional employment opportunities in the rural areas with the help of surplus foodgrains. Initially, this programme was called Food for Work Programme (FWP). It was drawn up at the end of 1976-77 but it actually came into effect on April 1, 1977. Under this scheme, millions of mandays of employment were created every year by utilising lakhs of tonnes of foodgrains. The works undertaken were flood protection, maintenance of existing roads, construction of new link roads, improvement of irrigation facilities, construction of *panchayat ghars*, school buildings, medical and health centres and improvement of sanitation conditions in the rural areas. On finding certain shortcomings in the programme, it (FWP) was restructured in October 1980 as part of the Sixth Plan (1980-85) and came to be known as NREP. It took care of those rural poor who largely depended on wage employment and virtually had no source of income in the lean agricultural period. The important points on which stress was laid in the implementation of this programme were: (1) 10 per cent allocation was earmarked exclusively for drinking water wells in harijan colonies and community irrigation schemes in Harijan areas. Likewise, another 10 per cent was earmarked for social forestry and fuel plantations. (2) Only such works were undertaken which had some durability. (3) Allocations were made both at the inter-state and inter-district/block levels. The central government released the state's share of the NREP allocation in cash every quarter.(4) Maintenance of assets created under this programme was the responsibility of the state governments. (5) PRIs were actively involved in this programme. This programme has now been merged in JRY.

RLEGP

The Rural Landless Employment Guarantee Programme (RLEGP) aimed at providing supplemental employment to the poor on public works at a very low wage of Rs. 3 per day. Maharashtra was one state which had used the Employment Guarantee Scheme (EGS) for the unemployed in rural areas by levying EGS surcharge or collections on land revenue, sales tax, motor vehicles, irrigated holdings, and on professionals. The amounts so collected, with matching contributions from the state government, were credited to an EGS fund for taking up employment works. This programme too has now been merged (along with NREP) into the JRY.

Jawahar Rozgar Yojna

This programme was announced in April 1989. Under the scheme, it is expected that at least one member of each poor family would be provided with employment for 50 to 100 days in a year at a work place near his/her residence. About 30 per cent of the jobs under this scheme are reserved for women. Both the rural wage employment programmes (i.e., the REP and the RLEGP) were merged in this scheme. Central assistance to the scheme is 80 per cent. The scheme is implemented through village panchayats. The central government claims that 3121.33 million mandays of employment were generated in various states between 1992-93 and 1995-96 under JRY at an outlay of Rs. 13,248 crore (*Rajasthan Patrika*, June 16, 1966). The scheme covers 46 per cent of our population.

Antyodaya Programme

'Antyodaya' means development (*udaya*) of the people at the lowest level (*ant*), that is, the poorest of the poor. This programme was initiated by the Government of Rajasthan on October 2, 1977 for special assistance to the people below the poverty line. The idea was to select five of the poorest families from each village (out of 27,000 inhabited villages) every year and to help them in their economic betterment. Initially, a random survey was undertaken in 25 villages situated in different ecological regions of the state and information about individual families with regard to indebtedness, dependency ratio, physical assets of land, cattle, occupation, educational level, income and size of the family was collected. Thereafter, a detailed scheme of Antyodaya was drawn up. The economic criterion, in order of priority, for the selection of the poor families was laid down as: (1) families under severe destitution without any productive assets and with no member in the age-group of 15-59 years capable of any economic activity; (2) families without any productive assets of land or cattle but having one or more persons capable of working and with a per capita income up to Rs. 20 per month; (3) families having some productive assets with per capita income up to Rs. 30 per month; and (4) families having per capita income up to Rs. 40 per month.

The task of identification of the families was entrusted to the village assembly (Gram Sabha). Under this scheme, help was given in the form of allotting land for cultivation, monthly pension, bank loan or help in getting employment. Each selected family was given a pension of Rs. 30-40 per month. A bank loan was sanctioned for purchasing bullocks, carts, animal husbandry (purchasing buffaloes, cows, goats and pigs), basket making, purchasing carpentry tools, opening a tailor's shop or a tea shop or a barber's shop or a grocer's shop and for manufacturing activities like soap-making and niwar-making.

The administration of the Antyodaya scheme was entrusted to collectors at the district level, and to the Agriculture Department at the state level. The Government of Rajasthan had planned to help about six lakh families in five years (from 1978 to 1982) under this scheme. Of the sanctioned amount, one-third was to be given as pensions, about two-third as loans, and 4 per cent as help (subsidy and loan) through the Khadi Boards. Under this scheme, during 3 years (1978 to 1980), out of about two and a half lakh families identified, 83 per cent were assisted. Of the selected families, 29 per cent were allotted land, 40 per cent were given loans, 22 per cent were given social security benefits, and 9 per cent were provided employment and other benefits (Mehta, 1983:347). The Government of Rajasthan, however, revived the programme in 1981. It selected 1,800 families below the poverty line in every block for benefiting them during a period of three years. Social security benefits and allotment were taken out of the assistance package.

Following in the footsteps of the Government of Rajasthan, Uttar Pradesh and Himachal Pradesh also launched the programme on the same model in 1980. But political changes in the states affected the programme. It may now be said that by and large this scheme was a total failure. The main reasons for the failure were: partiality in selecting families, lack of cooperation on the part of officials, delay in the payment of loans, and neglect of after-care aspect of the programme. The Government of Rajasthan, however, has reintroduced the scheme since September 1990 in the state, though it does not seem to be much operative at present (1999).

Garibi Hatao and Bekari Hatao Programmes

The *Garibi Hatao* slogan was given by Indira Gandhi in March 1971 at the time of the national elections while the *Bekari Hatao* slogan was given by the All India Congress Committee (AICC) at its annual session in April 1988. In fact, the Congress has been talking of 'socialism' since the 1950s. It declared 'socialism' as its main goal in its Avadi session in 1955, Bhubaneshwar session in 1964 and Kamraj Nagar session in April 1988. But the extent to which the Congress has succeeded in achieving this goal is indicated by the fact that more than 10 lakh people in our country live by begging and about half a lakh people survive on donated blood.

Critical Evaluation of the Anti-Poverty Programmes

Various studies carried out by experts and academicians have shown that no programme has been able to make a dent in the poverty level of the rural people. A large mass of villagers languish without basic needs. The underlying flaws in the way various programmes have been carried out remain unaddressed. *First,* policies are guided by ideologies (for convenience) of politicians and bureaucrats' whims rather than by compulsions of the ground realities and requirements of the rural people, with the result that the dimensions of rural economy are ignored. *Secondly*, since every programme is launched often with an eye to the next election, the programme is carried out in a piecemeal fashion and many programmes thus wither away after some time. *Thirdly*, programmes are designed in such a way that they are in fact foisted on the rural economy without taking into account their unique vocational patterns and local requirements. Consequently, the assets created are not durable. *Fourthly*, programmes focus more on the agricultural sector. Rural industrilisation seems to be getting nowhere near the attention that it deserves. *Fifthly*, despite the fact that the government has given top priority to agricultural production and productivity, removal of social and economic disparities and reduction in income inequalities, the fruits of these schemes, have not reached the poorest in all parts of the country. Water resources, credit, subsidy and other facilities have been usurped by a handful of big farmers and the medium and poor farmers have to buy these things at a much higher price. *Sixthly*, there is no coordination among various programmes. After the merger of various employment programmes into the Jawahar Rozgar Yojna, the government is even now not able to pass on funds to the panchayats on time. *Seventhly*, officials associated with these programmes do not appear to have much faith in the goals set by the government, with the result they lack commitment to the roles assigned to them. As such, they take least pains either in creating necessary awareness among people for the success of these programmes or in getting their cooperation and confidence. No wonder, the government has not been able to use even the available resources in the most effective manner. *Lastly*, central funds in schemes like Jawahar Rozgar Yojna are diverted for party purposes by the states. For example, one study has revealed that Rs. 30,000 sanctioned by the central government for new irrigation wells in Nalgonda district in Andhra Pradesh were swindled and not a single well was sunk. Planning by itself is not enough. What really matters is sincere and honest efforts on the part of the implementing agencies to make anti-poverty drive a big success.

Community Development Projects

The integrated scheme of community projects initiated by the state in 1952 for transformation of social and economic life of villages proposed the establishment of a network of extension workers throughout the country over a period of ten years. The community project area, consisting of about 100 villages and a population of about 60,000 to 70,000, was divided into three Development Blocks. The Development Block, in turn, was divided into groups of five villages each, each group being the field of operation for a village level worker (VLW).The initial programme was started with approximately 55 projects covering about 18,500 villages with a total population of about 15.2 million. Agricultural production was the most urgent objective in the selection of the initial projects. Irrigation facilities and assured water supply were given importance in the selection of the project areas. The activities in a community project were divided into agriculture, irrigation, communications, education, health, employment, housing, training, and social welfare. The organisational structure consisted of a Central Committee in the Planning Commission, or at the central level with an administrator of the community projects, a Development Committee at the state level, a commissioner as secretary at the district level, a Development Officer at the project level, and an Executive Officer with 125 supervisors and village level officers (VLOs) at village level. The essence of the programme was to ensure people's participation right from the start. Bharat Sevak Samaj, which was the non-official counterpart of the organisation, was to perform the role of mobilisation of voluntary effort on part of the villagers. The villagers were to contribute through labour or in cash.

But the programme could not succeed in bringing about social and economic transformation of the villages. Those who benefited were already somewhat better off. The evaluation of the community development projects (CDPs) was done by scholars like A.R. Desai, S.C. Dube, Oscar Lewis, Mandelbaum, Opler, Carl Taylor, Wilson, and many others. All these evaluators had assumed that the CDPs were desirable and appropriate as a technique of reconstructing agrarian economy and rural society. Assessing the impact of the CDPs on the life of the rural people, almost all of them concluded that rural people could not be mobilised and they did not actively participate in any of the stages of implementation. Taylor's view was that the government machinery failed to assimilate the true spirit underlying the entire programme. A.R.Desai was of the opinion that sociological assumptions on which the CDPs were based, viz., that all individuals, groups, sections and strata forming the village community had common interests to bind them together, that common interests will create enthusiasm, that interests of different sections of the community were not irreconcilably conflicting, were not correct. S.C.Dube held that planning was from the top down. Oscar Lewis maintained that there was considerable confusion and conflict with regard to powers and duties among the staff of different departments and there was absence of social service mentality. In short, the CDPs failed in achieving their goals.

What was lacking in rural development programmes was unified planning and integrated functioning. In order to execute all multi-sectoral development programmes like IRDP, NREP, RLEGP, MNP, DPAP, DDP, etc., the establishment of a *combined agency* at the district level was suggested. This agency was to be headed by an officer of a rank higher than BDO but below that of the Collector. It was to have adequate number of multi-disciplinary supporting staff and full-time specialists from relevant disciplines. Some persons were to be associated as part-time members. Besides the integrated planning, an integrated administrative structure too was suggested for the implementation of the planned programmes. It was to cover banks also. However, these suggestions were not fully implemented.

PANCHAYATI RAJ

The failure of the community development programmes in involving people with the development of the rural communities led to the establishment of Panchayati Raj on the recommendations of Balwantrai Mehta

Committee. The objects of the Panchayati Raj were democratisation, decentralisation and modernisation. The panchayats were expected to tackle village problems at the grassroots level and mobilise local manpower resources for purposes of economic and social progress. In fact, Panchayati Raj in India has come into existence through a long process of evolution. Its expansion may be analysed in five phases: from 1950 to 1960, from 1961 to 1964, from 1965 to 1985, from 1986 to 1992 and from 1993 to 1999.

A provision was made in the Constitution of India promulgated in January 1950 about organising village panchayats as local self-governing units. The First Five Year Plan also emphasised in 1951-52 promoting people's participation in the management of rural development through local representative institutions. Balwantrai Mehta Committee reviewing the CDPs also recommended in 1956 the establishment of PRIs to ensure continuity in the process of improving economic and social conditions in rural areas. The Planning Commission had already forcefully opined that village panchayats should be strengthened and this new democratic set-up should gradually be given the responsibility for taking over development administration. The B.R. Mehta Committee had this plea in view while recommending organisation of three-tiered Panchayati Raj system.

The Panchayati Raj system was initially set up by three states in 1959. After 1959, a network of PRIs went on being built up by most of the state governments. By 1964-65, the PRIs began to function in 12 out of the then 15 states in India. Among the six union territories, only one set up Panchayati Raj. The structure, however, differed in these states. During 1965-85, the Panchayati Raj began to stagnate and even declined in efficacy of its role in the management of development processes. Its credibility began to suffer a setback. Its powers and functions were reduced by the executive orders of the government on grounds of inefficiency, corruption and factionalism in many states. The Janata Party government in 1977 appointed Ashok Mehta Committee to inquire into the causes of decline in the working of Panchayati Raj and suggest measures to strengthen the PRIs. In 1978, this Committee made a number of recommendations for revitalisation of PRIs. These included: assigning more powers to PRIs, making Zilla Parishad primary unit in PR system, political parties taking part in Zila PR elections, and imparting training to panchayat members.

The Santhanam Committee was appointed to study the problems of resources and finances of PRIs. It recommended measures like: (i) giving powers to panchayats to levy special taxes based on land revenue, house-tax, etc., (ii) sanctioning of grants to panchayats by state governments,

(iii) handing over sources of revenue to PRIs, (iv) evolving mutual financial relations between different levels of PRIs, (v) augmenting financial resources through gifts and donations, and (vi) setting up Panchayati Raj Financial Corporation to provide loans and financial assistance to panchayats and help them in providing basic amenities in villages.

However, revival and renovation of panchayats came in 1985, when earlier in 1984, the then Prime Minister wrote to Chief Ministers to hold overdue elections to PRIs as well as to revitalise their functioning. Two Committees were also appointed in 1985 (G.V. K. Rao Committee) and in 1986 (L.M. Singhvi Committee). The G.V.K. Rao Committee recommended that (1) PRIs have to be activated and provided with all the required support to become effective organisations, (2) PRIs at district and block levels should be assigned the work of planning, implementation, and monitoring of rural development programmes, and (3) Block Development office should be the spinal chord of the rural development process. The L.M. Singhvi Committee found that PRIs were not functioning properly owing to lack of political will, lack of evaluation and feedback, and indifference to corrective measures. The Committee suggested locating means to ensure availability of adequate financial resources for PRIs. The Committee found that PRIs were often reluctant to raise revenue resources through exercising their taxing powers. It, therefore, suggested some compulsory and optional levies.

Taking the views of these committees, the government decided to amend the Constitution. This amendment was made by the Lok Sabha in December 1992, by the Rajya Sabha in December 1993, and after being ratified by 17 State Assemblies, it came to be known as Constitution Amendment Act, 1993. It came into force from 1994. Today, PRIs are functioning in 22 out of 25 states and in six out of seven union territories. In 15 states, it is a three-tiered system, in four it is 2-tiered and in three, it is one tier system.

The functions assigned to panchayats may be classified as obligatory, discretionary and transferred functions. These functions include: providing civic amenities, infrastructural facilities and developmental activities. Broadly, the functions may be described as: health and sanitation (control of epidemic, construction and maintenance of lavatories, maintenance of burial grounds, cleaning of roads, tanks, ponds and drains), public works (construction and maintenance of roads, drinking water pumps, wells, street lights), agriculture and animal husbandry (distribution of improved seeds and pesticides, planning for increasing agricultural production, arranging cattle fairs, improving cattle breeding, development of poultry and fishing), uplifting the weaker sections (arranging for their education, cultural activities and residential houses), and some miscellaneous works (meeting calamities, encouraging and strengthening cottage industries, strengthening cooperative societies, development of forests, welfare of women and children, adult education programmes).

Since their inception, roles of panchayats have been gradually changed and the scope of their functioning has been enlarged. Even the assumptions have undergone a change. Not only the representatives of the people (i.e., panchayats) have been assigned the responsibility of administering local public affairs but also of raising the required finances and locating man-power resources.

The main problems faced by the panchayats before the 1993 Constitutional Amendment were: (1) Functions and powers given to panchayats were limited. (2) Panchayats were ill-equipped in terms of manpower to undertake planning. (3) Panchayats had no power to generate their own resources through taxation, etc. (4) Elections were not held on regular basis. (5) Women and weaker sections had no representation. Thus, the high hopes with regard to the panchayats were not fulfilled. The main obstacles in the successful functioning of PRIs were described as: non-legalistic status of PRIs, irregular elections, frequent suppressions and suspensions, inadequate representation of weaker sections, insufficient powers given to panchayats, lack of financial resources, non-cooperation on the part of bureaucracy, lack of people's participation and lack of political will. Barnabas (1998:450) has identified five causes of failure of the Panchayati Raj: confusion about functions, absence of autonomy, confusion in administrative arrangement, abs ce of coordination and fragmented and overlapping structure.

Confusion about functions refers to non-delineation of functions between the three tiers. What functions are to be performed at each level is not clear. There is also variation of functions in different states. The role of planning assigned to Gram Sabhas does not exist in reality because they do not have the required capacity of formulating objectives, identifying priorities, and formulating strategies. Ashok Mehta Working Group and Rao Committee had suggested Zila Parishads as appropriate forum for the planning function. The Gram Panchayats and the Panchayat Samitis can indicate their needs to the Zila Parishads. The 74th amendment has provided for the constitution of District Planning Committee for planning but the composition of this committee has been criticised.

Absence of autonomy refers to lack of autonomy at district level as state and national plans have to be accommodated. Many schemes (like

IRDP, ICDS, drinking water supply, etc.) are centrally funded and their targets and norms are more or less defined. How can district plan, therefore, be meaningful? In the hierarchical administrative system in our country, there is little scope for culture of decentralisation. More than 95 per cent of panchayat budgets are committed. In the absence of functional and financial autonomy, how can panchayats be expected to be free in working?

Confusion in administrative arrangement refers to loyalty of the extension officers to their departments (agriculture, animal husbandry, cooperatives, etc.) and independent functioning as opposed to integration. Even the District Rural Development Agency (DRDA) which shared a major share of rural development budget was not within the panchayat set-up; though now it has been brought under the purview of the Zila Parishad.

Absence of coordination refers to fragmentation of the administrative structure at the district and the block levels. There is no coordination between various units. The VLW (now designated as Village Development Officer-VDO) is assigned varied functions. He has to cover a number of villages and a number of schemes. He has to collect taxes levied by the village panchayats, mobilise people's participation in development programmes and undertake several activities for helping the poor.

Fragmented and overlapping structure means that all development programmes have not been assigned to panchayats. Varied programmes, therefore, create confusion in the absence of clearly defined responsibilities. Analysing the performance of the PRI in the early 1990s, it was decided by the central government to amend the Constitution and make panchayats more powerful and effective. As already mentioned, the 73rd Constitutional amendment made in 1993 came into being in April 1994. After this amendment, the main changes introduced in Panchayati Raj were: (1) Establishment of panchayats at three or two levels and a gram sabha in each village was made mandatory. (2) Tenure of PRIs was fixed as five years, i.e., every five years, direct election of all members at three panchayat levels was made mandatory. (3) While election of chairman at the intermediate and district levels was to be indirect, election of the chairman at the village level was left to the state governments to decide. (4) A list of 29 functions was provided to panchayats. These relate to rural development, infrastructure, social welfare, public distribution system, maintenance of community assets, etc. (5) Seats were reserved for SCs, STs, and women at all three levels of panchayats. (6) Finance Commission was set up to devolve funds and suggest ways of financing panchayats. (7)

PRIs were given power to impose taxes, duties and fees and were assigned their share in taxes collected by the state government. The grants-in-aid were also released to them. (8) Election Commission was empowered to conduct panchayat elections. (9) State legislatures have been given discretion to provide for the reservation of OBCs and association of MPs/MLAs in panchayats. (10) While before the amendment, the Sarpanchs of gram panchayats were made members of the Panchayat Samitis and Pradhans of Panchayat Samitis were made members of Zila Parishads, after the amendment, this provision of becoming ex-officio members of panchayats at higher level was withdrawn. However, the state governments were given the discretion of associating Sarpanchs with Panchayat Samitis and Pradhans with Zila Parishads.

The positive consequences of these changes after making the Amendment (in 1993) are supposed to be: (1) Structural change regarding direct elections at all three levels will improve the working of the panchayats. Earlier, there were no direct elections to Panchayat Samitis and Zila Parishads. All Sarpanchas constituted members of the Panchayat Samiti and all Pradhans of the Panchayat Samitis became members of the Zila Parishads. The role and the responsibilities of the directly elected members will now widen. (2) Increasing powers of panchayats and financial resources will improve the position of panchayats. (3) Reservation for SCs, STs and women will enable weaker sections to participate more actively in the panchayat system. (4) The new structure will enable panchayats to contribute to planning from below, mobilise local resources, evoke large scale community participation, reduce corruption, and improve the quality of development effort.

The negative effect could be: (i) direct elections may check vertical interaction among panchayats at three levels; and (ii) rotation of reserved seats might reduce the commitment of the representatives to carry on long-term development work.

Hooja and Hooja (1998:474-75) have pointed out several issues which need to be studied for successful functioning of the panchayats. These are: (1) What should be the level of decentralised planning? (2) Since District Planning Committee would now become very large, what should be the organisational set-up to operationalise decentralised planning and implementation? (3) What functions would be most appropriate at which level in the multi-level framework? (4) What changes would be required at the state government level? (5) What safeguards are necessary and feasible to keep local elite or vested interests from capturing panchayats or from distorting the decentralised planning process? (6) When planning and implementing bodies are the same (i.e., village panchayats and panchayat samitis), how can it be ensured that the planner would not fix targets for himself which are easy to achieve rather than more ambitious ones? (7) How can possible conflicts between different panchayat levels and the state level be avoided?

The Progress After the Constitutional Amendment

How serious are the state government officials in making Panchayati Raj functional? Their non-seriousness is indicated in the following manner: (1) Bureaucrats are unwilling to transfer power to panchayats. (2) They are always reluctant to release funds. (3) Officers do not show any faith in elected representatives. (4) Some states have not yet even conducted elections, though panchayats were supposed to have come into existence within one year after the enforcement of the 73rd Constitutional Amendment in 1993. Though Zila Pramukhs are to be Chairmen of the District Rural Development Agencies, (DRDAs) which run all poverty alleviation programmes, yet in practice they will only preside over the meetings of the Governing Councils of the DRDAs; the financial powers would rest with the Collector who would continue to be the chairman of the Executive Committee of the DRDA. Thus, relationship between panchayats and DRDAs needs to be clearly specified. One fails to understand why the elected bodies should not have fully independent charge of development plans and allowed to take initiative so that people at large participate fully in the development process.

It may be concluded that the pragmatic philosophy of miniaturised participative democracy, where every man matters, is the cornerstone of developmental dynamics. The growing consensus is that rural development can be accelerated if people's resources are mobilised and they are prompted to take part in making the decisions that affect their lives and livelihoods (*The Third World: Tomorrow*, 36). At present, there is deep factionalism in our villages. Misuse of funds, oppression of the powerful, denying opportunities to women, terror against dalits, and subversion of elections are pathologically pervasive in the countryside. To overcome these problems is a tough proposition. No valid reason exists to reject grassroots self-government. Justice Krishna Iyer (*Yojana*, January 23, 1989, 20) assuming that there will be favouritism, casteism, ill-will, bureaucrats' apathy and non-cooperation, even so Panchayati Raj experiments will eventually open the political eyes of the populace. It is fashionable to exaggerate villagers' weaknesses and urbanites' abilities, but our rural geniuses are sure to measure up to the challenge of participative roles.

Further Readings

Barnabas, A.P., "Good Governance at Local Level", *IJPA*, July-September, 1998.

Beteille, Andre, *Caste, Class and Power; Changing Patterns of Stratification in a Tanjore Village*, University of California Press, Berkeley, 1965.

Desai, A.R., *Peasant Movements in India*, Oxford University Press, Delhi, 1983.

Desai, A.R., *Rural Sociology in India* (Rev. ed.), The Indian Society of Agricultural Economics, Bombay, 1959.

Dhanagare, D.N., "The Model of Agrarian Classes in India" in Desai, A.R., *Peasant Movements in India*, Oxford University Press, Delhi, 1983.

Gupta, Dipankar, *Social Stratification*, Oxford University Press, Delhi, 1991.

Hooja, Meenakshi and Hooja, Rakesh, "Panchayati Raj in Rajasthan", *The Indian Journal of Public Administration*, July-September, 1998, Vol. XLIV, No. 3.

Khanna, B.S., *Panchayati Raj in India*, Deep and Deep Publications, New Delhi, 1994.

Mathew, George, *Panchayati Raj From Legislation to Movement*, Concept Publishing Co., 1994.

Mishra, Sweta, *Democratic Decentralisation in India*, Mittal Publications, New Delhi, 1994.

Mishra, S.N., Kumar, Lokesh and Pal, Chaitali, *New Panchyati Raj in Action*, Mittal Publications, New Delhi, 1996.

Marriott, McKim, *Village India: Studies in Little Community* (ed.) University of Chicago Press, Chicago, 1955.

Lewis, Oscar, *Village Life in Northern India: Studies in a Delhi Village*, University of Illinois Press, Urbana, 1958.

Sagar, Deep, "Rural Development Policies of India", *IJPA*, April-June, 1990.

Singh. S.S. and Misra, Suresh, *Legislative Framework of Panchayati Raj in India*, Intellectual Publishing House, Bombay, 1993.

Sharma, A.N., "Bonded Labour", Tata Institute of Social Sciences, Bombay 1990.

Taylor, C.C., *A Critical Analysis of India's Community*, University of Chicago Press, Chicago, 1955.

Thorner, Daniel, *Agrarian Structure*, Allied Publishers, Delhi, 1956.

Yojana, Special Issue on "Could we break their shackles", Vol. 31, No.8, May 1-5, 1987.

11 Urban Social Organisation

With urban growth and urbanisation process in India after 1951, sociologists' interest in urban themes has changed. They not only analyse change in urban organisation but also study stratification and mobility in urban communities and examine new emerging urban problems. The change from 1951 till today (1999) indicates that the rate of urbanisation (movement of population from rural to urban areas and the resultant increasing proportion of population that resides in urban rather than rural areas) is low but the rate of urban growth (percentage increase in absolute size of the urban population) is high. Whereas the percentage of urban population has increased by 1.5 times from 1951 to 1991 (from 17.3 to 25.73%), absolute size of the total population has increased by 2.6 times (from 356.9 million to about 940 million) during the same period. The urban growth has far-reaching implications. Not only rural urban development cannot take place in a balanced manner but also the problems of socio-economic adjustment would accentuate.

CONCEPTS OF URBAN, URBANISATION AND URBANISM

If the future of India is linked with rural development, it is equally linked with the growth of cities and metropolitan areas. Though increasing urbanisation has led to problems like pollution, overcrowding and slums, unemployment and poverty, crime and juvenile delinquency, communication and traffic control, violence and sexual harassment of women, tensions and strains, yet cities are centres of civilisation and culture. Before analysing rural-urban interactions, changes in urban social organisation, mobility, integration of ethnic communities, etc., it is necessary to understand the concepts of urban, urbanisation, and urbanism.

The term *urban* is used demographically and sociologically. In the former sense, it lays emphasis on the size of the population, density of population and nature of work of residents, while in the latter sense it focuses on heterogeneity, impersonality, interdependence, and the quality of life. Thus, population of not less than 5,000, density of not less than 1,000 persons per square mile, and 75 per cent or more of working population engaged in non-agricultural activities (like manufacturing, trade and commerce, service, etc.) are said to be important characteristics of town/city or 'urban' (Ramchandran, 1998: 101-103). The 1991 census has defined urban place as any place with a minimum population of 5,000, 75 per cent of the male population being non-agricultural, population density of at least 400 persons per square km (or 1,000 persons per square mile) and with a municipality/corporation/cantonment/notified area. These criteria have, however, been described as vague and conservative on several bases: (1) Though the number of places with more than 5,000 population is defined as 'urban' and there are 12,000 such places in India but the census recognises only 3,245 places as urban. (2) The density of population that qualifies a place as urban is unrealistically low. (3) A place with more than 75 per cent of male working population engaged in non-agricultural activities is to be recognised as urban but according to 1981 and 1991 censuses, at least 25 per cent towns have agriculture as the dominant activity. (4) Female workers are excluded from working population (*Ibid*: 106-107). On this basis, 'urban community' is defined as 'a community characterised by a large heterogeneous population, predominance of nonagricultural occupations, complex division of labour, a high degree of specilisation in work, dependence on formal social controls, and a formalised system of local government'.

Urbanisation is the movement of population from rural to urban areas. Anderson (1953:11) holds that urbanisation involves not only movement of population to cities but also change in the migrants' attitudes, beliefs, values, and behaviour patterns.

Urbanism is a way of life, characterised by *transiency* (short-time relations), *superficiality* (impersonal and formal relations with limited number of people), *anonymity* (not knowing names and lacking intimacy), and *individualism* (people giving more importance to one's vested interests). Louis Wirth (1938:124) has given four characteristics of ***urban system*** or urbanism: heterogeneity of population, specialisation of function, anonymity and impersonality, and standardisation of behaviour.

RURAL-URBAN DIFFERENCES: DEMOGRAPHIC AND SOCIO-CULTURAL CHARACTERISTICS

The term 'community' is used by sociologists to describe a *quality of relationship* which produces a strong sense of shared identity among persons living in a fixed geographical area. They describe 'rural' as a community and 'urban' as a society. When sociologists hold that a society moves from traditional to modern, they in fact contrast pre-industrial, largely rural, traditional society with industrial, largely urban, modern society. While American sociologist Louis Wirth had used the terms 'rural and urban' for contrasting communities, German sociologist Ferdinand Toennies used the terms 'gemeinschaft and gessellschaft', M. Durkheim 'mechanical and organic' solidarity, and Talcott Parsons 'traditional and modern' societies. Wirth (1938) distinguishing urban from rural society, defined city in terms of three fundamental features: population size, density, and heterogeneity. These characteristics meant that though the city-dweller would experience more human contacts than the rural inhabitant, he would also feel more isolated because of their (contacts) 'emotionally empty' nature. According to Wirth, social interactions, typical of city, are impersonal, segmental (narrow in scope), superficial, transitory, and usually of a purely practical or 'instrumental' kind. He describes these as 'secondary' contacts which are totally different from 'primary' contacts in rural areas. According to Max Weber, the most fundamental feature of a city is that it functions as a market-place and it displays a relative predominance of trading-commercial relations.

Rural and urban communities may be distinguished from each other on the basis of several criteria like occupation, size, and density of population, environment, homogeneity-heterogeneity, social stratification, mobility and system of interaction: (1) The main occupation of people in rural community is agriculture though a few people are engaged in non-agricultural pursuits also. People in urban community are mainly engaged in non-agricultural pursuits like manufacturing, trade and commerce, service and professions. (2) Rural communities are of small size while urban communities are of larger size. In India, according to the 1991 census figures, of the 74.27 per cent population living in villages, 36.57 per cent villages have population of less than 2,000, 21.37 per cent between 2,000 and 5,000, and 13.33 per cent more than 5,000. On the other hand, of the 25.73 per cent population in urban areas, 0.72 per cent urban areas have less than 10,000 population, 5.27 per cent between 10,000 and 50,000, 2.75

per cent between 50,000 and one lakh, and 16.4 per cent above 1 lakh (These figures exclude population of Assam and Jammu and Kashmir). (*Manpower Profile*, India, 1998: 23-24). The average size of a household in rural areas in 1991 was 4.9 and in urban areas it was 4.4 members. (3) Density of population in rural community is low (200 to 1,000 persons per square mile) while in urban community, it is high (more than 1,000 persons per square mile). (4) People in rural areas are close to nature while people in urban areas are surrounded more by man-made environment and are isolated from nature. (5) Rural communities are more homogeneous while urban communities are more heterogeneous. (6) While rural communities are stratified more on caste and less on class basis, urban communities are stratified more on class basis. (7) Mobility in rural areas is more from villages to villages and villages to cities, while mobility in urban areas is more from one city to an other city. In 1991, of the 225 million migrants in the country, 17.7 per cent had migrated from rural to urban areas, 11.8 per cent from urban to urban areas, 64.5 per cent from rural to rural areas, and 6 per cent from urban to rural areas (*Manpower Profile, India*, 1998:26). (8) Relations amongst people in rural areas are predominantly personal and relatively durable while in urban areas, relations are more secondary, impersonal, casual and short-lived. (9) The infant mortality rate in rural areas is one and a half time more than the rate found in urban areas (80:49) ratio. (10) Labour force participation rate in rural areas is more than three times than that found in urban areas. In 1993-94, it was 294 million in rural areas against 85.7 million in urban areas. Among males, it is little less than three times (189.3:67.3 million ratio). While among females it is more than five times (104.7:18.4 million) *Manpower Profile, India*, 1998:129). (11) The number of working children in the rural areas is 10 times more than in the urban areas (In 1991, it was 10.26 to 1.03 million).

If we follow Toennies' terms gemeinschaft and gesellschaft (1887), it may be said that gemeinschaft relationships are typical of rural life and gesellschaft relationships of urban life. The gemenschaft type rural community is characterised by predominance of intimate primary relationships and by emphasis upon tradition, consensus and informality. Social bonds are based on close personal ties of kinship and friendship. On the other hand, in the gesellschaft type urban society, social relationships are formal, contractual, expedient and specialised. Urban society has weak family organisation and lays stress on utilitarian goals and impersonal and competitive nature of social relationships.

Following Durkheim's (1933) concepts of mechanical and organic solidarity, it may be said that solidarity in rural community is mechanical and in urban community is organic. The rural community based on mechanical solidarity is characterised by homogeneity of values and behaviour (i.e., everybody sharing same religiously inspired beliefs and habits), strong social constraint and loyalty to tradition and kinship. It is further characterised by simple division of labour, very little specialisation of functions, only a few social roles, and very little tolerance of individuality. The urban community, based on organic solidarity, is characterised by unity based on the interdependence of a very large number of highly specialised roles, and complex division of labour that requires co-operation of almost all groups and individuals of the society.

RURAL-URBAN INTERACTION

Rural-urban interaction is an important aspect of urbanisation. It is expected that urbanisation and urban growth would have their impact on rural areas and activities in rural areas would have their effect on the nearby towns and cities. A few studies have been made on this rural-urban interaction which have shown that: (1) Urbanisation has impact on the economy of the surrounding villages. There is increase in farm productivity (due to the availability of fertilisers, better seeds, tractors, etc., in nearby cities), increase in commercialisation of crops and decline in the density of farm population. (2) Level and pattern of migration has been affected. (3) Villagers have imbibed several urban characteristics.

Social science literature has often exaggerated contrasts and dichotomies of rural and urban social organisations and ways of life. This type of perspective tends to ignore difference in the size of urban areas ranging anywhere between 5,000 and 15 million. The dichotomous perspective further neglects the existence of continuous interdependent, complimentary and overlapping relationships of rural and urban sectors which are reflected through mutual exchange system of goods and services. The ruralites are dependent on the urbanites for their banking and credit needs, for the purchase of agricultural equipment and other supplies, for marketing of farm products, and even for commercial recreation. The urban sector is dependent on the rural sector for food supply, for cheap labour, and for vast market of its manufactured goods. The urban professionals like doctors, lawyers, etc., draw a large number of their patients/clients from rural masses because hospitals and courts are concentrated in the urban centres (Nagpaul, 1996:155-156).

Yet other double dimensional phenomenon which affects rural-urban relationships is migration. Most rural migrants who move to urban areas are young males who take up unskilled and semi-skilled occupations.

Even those ruralites who receive higher education prefer to settle in cities. This migration from rural to urban areas exerts pressures on urban public services and creates problems of social disorganisation.

Migration from rural to urban areas is of different types. One is to settle down permanently in the urban area of one's choice. This is called *translocatory* migration. Other is one in which migrants hang on to their rural base and migrate repeatedly and for varying durations, either to the same urban area or to different ones. This is termed *circulatory* migration. Yet others migrate in graded steps from a smaller to a larger settlement. This is known as *step-migration*. Mary Chatterjee (1971) has shown that the stability of migration is a function of distance from the native place, as well as of occupational status. The longer the distance from the native place, the greater the number of migrants who regard their stay in city as temporary. Relatively, more migrants from lower-prestige occupations than those from higher occupations regard their stay in city as temporary.

Migration from rural to urban areas also follows certain patterns. One, it depends upon the 'pull' factors at the urban and 'push' factors at the rural end. Thus, migration of agricultural labourers from Bihar to Punjab during the harvest season is of this type. Then there is migration which is caused by rural poverty and urban opportunity of getting work. Migration of young children as well as of adults from Uttar Pradesh and Bihar to other states for the lure of a job is of this 'pull' type.

Along with cooperative relationships and functional dependence, there are cleavages and conflicts also between rural and urban sectors. The conflicts have been classified as primary or secondary, manifest or latent, and episodic or continuous. However, rural-urban conflicts are not clear-cut and do not erupt in open violence. It is difficult to fix their beginning or ending. The three factors identified by (Nagpaul, 1996:158-160) which promote/foster cleavages and conflicts among the rural people for the urban people are: contrasting environmental subcultures, modernisation, and urban bias.

Natural environment of the ruralites is different from artificial environment of the urbanites. Rural work is determined by seasons and weather while urban work is carried out indoors in predictable conditions. Both sectors, therefore, develop somewhat distinctive subcultures of their own which further shape their social institutions and personalities. Although ruralites outnumber urbanites numerically, urbanites usually come to dominate in most facets of life. In economic field also, urbanites enjoy a better living standard. Urbanites, therefore, dominate the rural people both economically and politically.

Modernisation is another factor that fosters conflict. As part of modernisation programme, the Government of India has introduced several schemes and plans in the last five decades in the form of Five Year Plans, social legislation, agrarian reforms, abolition of untouchability, population control, and distributive justice, etc. The four important consequences of these modernisation programmes have been: (1) increasing pace of urbanisation and concentration of power in the urban sector (2) political democratisation (3) weakening of traditional institutional structure based upon caste and religion and (4) widespread emergence of revolution of rising expectations (Nagpaul, 1996:160-161). More and more people are moving from rural to urban areas, draining off young males from the rural sector, feminising the rural household, increasing rural-urban contacts, and diffusing urban ways of life far and wide in the villages. Ruralites feel envious of the material comforts enjoyed by city people. The increasing contacts promote more and more cleavages and conflicts between the villagers and the city-dwellers. Political democratisation has brought new tensions because the traditional patterns of leadership derived from landownership, caste, etc., are giving way to new types of leadership based on elections and formalism. The increasing involvement of women has produced some conflicts and stresses and strains. Though the rigidity of the caste system has declined yet caste has become a major factor affecting politics. The introduction of modernisation programmes has weakened traditional institutions (of caste, family and religion) relatively more in the urban sector/centres as compared to the rural sector. The lower caste associations have become pressure groups in political life. The rising expectations of people have also led to the emergence of agitations and movements.

Lastly, *urban bias* also acts as a source of conflict between rural and urban sectors. Inequalities in income, and better opportunities for occupational mobility and for raising living standards create biases among the villagers for the city people. Though the government has laid emphasis on agricultural development, rural reconstruction and poverty alleviation programmes, in practice, the villagers' lot has not improved much. The rural people also feel strongly about the diversion of rural funds to urban infrastructure of education, health, housing and transport facilities, etc. Some people describe the urban bias as a state of mind, yet the fact is that it creates stresses and conflicts.

Generally, researchers study adjustments which villages have to make due to changes taking place in towns and cities. But Victor S. D'Souza examined how changes taking place in the rural areas produce their impact on the urban centres. He found large-scale transformation in urban functions and increasing trade and commerce predominating most of the towns and cities because of the rural impact.

On the other hand, scholars like B.R. Chauhan (1970) and N.R. Seth (1969) found lack of meaningful and intimate interaction between people in the towns and those of the villages. N.R. Seth has even pointed out social, political and economic differences dividing urban and rural communities in India. Notwithstanding this disjunction, intimate and complementary relationship between the two segments is considered to be normal and desirable state of affairs. A town and a city, by and large, act as service centres for their surrounding village community. L.K. Sen (1971) has shown that like a town and a city, a large village also performs central-place functions for the city as well as surrounding smaller villages.

IS INDIAN SOCIETY MOVING FROM 'RURAL' TO 'URBAN'

If instead of using the terms rural and urban we use Parsons' terms of traditional and modern societies, it would enable us to use his pattern variables and distinguish between the two societies. The characteristics of traditional society are: *Ascription* (status given by birth), *role diffuseness* (broad relationship), *particularism* (each person treating others in a personal way), *affectivity* (satisfaction of emotions), and *collective orientation* (shared interests). The modern society is characterised by *achievement* (status acquired through one's own efforts), role *specificity* (relationships developed for specific purposes), *universalism* (same rules applying to everybody equally), *affective neutrality* (controlled emotions) and *self-orientation* (individual interest being important). It makes sense to think in terms of a graded rural-urban continuum of which above-mentioned pattern variables are the extremes. In India, these characteristics appear together in various 'mixes' both in rural and urban areas. Since the rural communities have urban characteristics too and urban societies have rural characteristics also, it will be illogical to hold that Indian society is moving from rural to urban.

URBAN SOCIAL ORGANISATION: CONTINUITY AND CHANGE

The urban social organisation needs to be analysed at two levels: (i) level of change which family, caste, and kinship systems and religious values are undergoing, and (ii) its comparison and contrast with rural social organisation. If we take the second aspect first, it could be said that while rural social organisation is caste-based, urban social organisation is class-based. D'Souza (1985) (*ICSSR Report*, 1974, Vol.1:161) too has said urban social organisation is class-based and secularoriented. However, some other scholars like William L. Rowe (1973), David S. Daykin, and Bradley R. Hertal (1978) hold that caste. kinship, and religion still have their traditional hold over urban communities in India. The change in rural and urban communities on this level is not because of the place of residence but because of the difference in the socio-economic status. S.P. Jain (1971) holds, on the basis of his study in Uttar Pradesh towns, that Hindus and Muslims continue to have traditional caste hierarchy. Sylvia Vatuk (1973) too on the basis of a study of migrants in a North Indian town held that kinship continues to assume importance among the migrants. Mary Chatterjee (1974) and M.F. Khan (1976) have said that kinship is the primary principle of social organisation. The traditional features of social organisation in towns and cities are brought out in a clear focus especially during religious occasions. Milton Singer (1968) has pointed out the prevalence of traditional Indian joint family in urban and industrial settings. Several studies on relationship between caste and politics in urban areas have indicated the use of caste by Rajputs, Nadars, Jats, Reddys, Brahmins, Yadavs, etc., for seeking votes. On the other hand, some castes have used politics in cities for social mobility. Thus, there is doubtless continuity in the traditional principles of social organisation, i.e., functioning of caste and kinship systems and the importance of religious values.

However, there is some change also in the functioning of caste and kinship systems in urban areas. In the day-to-day interaction among people in urban areas, neither caste nor kinship nor religious values are given any importance. For economic and social help on different occasions, people depend more on neighbours and acquaintances and office colleagues than on caste and kin.

Urbanisation and Family

The effect of urbanisation on family structure has been pointed out by scholars like M.S. Gore, Aileen Ross, K.M. Kapadia, and I.P.Desai. Urbanisation affects not only the family structure but also intra and inter-family relations as well as the functions the family performs. I.P.Desai (1964) in his study of family in a small town in Gujarat found that traditional joint families; (i.e., joint in residence, authority, property and with members of more than three generations) are being replaced by functionally joint families, the size of the family is shrinking; and kinship relationship is confined to two or three generations only. Kapadia (1959) in his comparative study of rural and urban families in Gujarat found that in the rural community, the proportion of joint families is almost the same as that of nuclear families (49.7:50.3); in the urban community, there are more joint families than nuclear families, the proportion being two nuclear families for every three joint families. Ross in her study of middle and upper class Hindu families in Bangalore in 1957 found change in structure and size of families as well as weakening or breaking of relations with distant kin. Gore (1968), however, found little change in family due to urbanisation.

Urbanisation and Caste

As regards effect of urbanisation on *caste*, scholars like Ramu (1975), Hemlata Acharya (1976), and D.A. Chekki (1974) have pointed out both change as well as continuity in caste and kinship networks. A person in a city derives his status not only from caste but also from other considerations. Broadly speaking, it will not be wrong to say that caste identity tends to diminish with urbanisation. Urbanites participate in networks which include persons of several castes. According to Rajni Kothari, the structure of particularistic loyalties has been overlaid by a more sophisticated system of social and political participation with crosscutting allegiances. Andre Beteille (1966:209-10) has pointed out that among the westernised elite, class ties are much more important than caste ties.

The educated members of some castes with modern occupations sometimes organise themselves as a pressure group. As such, a caste association competes as a corporate body with other pressure groups for political and economic resources. This type of organisation represents a new kind of solidarity. These competing units function more as social classes than as caste structures.

Yet another change we find today is the fusion of sub-castes and fusion of castes. Kolenda (1984:150-51) has identified three kinds of fusion: (i) persons of different castes and sub-castes meet in their work-places and in newer neighbourhoods in the city. They are usually of approximately equal rank. Neighbourhood or office group solidarity develops. This has been generally found in government housing colonies in big cities; (ii) intersub caste marriages take place, promoting fusion of subcastes. This is because many a time it is difficult to find a sufficiently educated groom for an educated daughter within one's own sub-caste, but one may find it in neighbouring sub-caste; and (iii) democratic politics fosters fusion of sub-castes and of adjacent castes. For example, the Dravida Munnetra Kazagam (DMK) and the Anna Dravida Munnetra Kazagam (ADMK) parties of Tamil Nadu composed of members of higher non-Brahmin castes.

Urban-dwellers do not strictly conform to caste norms. There is a change in commensal relations, marital relations, social relations, as well as in occupational relations. A study of caste system in Bihar (Narmadeshwar Prasad) revealed that urbanisation does affect all characteristics of the caste system uniformly. On the basis of a study in Bihar of 200 persons belonging to five different castes (Brahmins, Rajputs, Dhobis, Ahirs and Chamars), it was found that all respondents had married in their own castes, though 20 per cent of the respondents living in cities (against 5% in rural areas) were in favour of intercaste marriages. As regards occupation, not a single respondent in the city was engaged in his traditional caste occupation, though 81 per cent respondents in rural areas were still engaged in their traditional occupations. Likewise, caste solidarity was not as strong in urban areas as in rural areas. Caste panchayats were very weak in cities. G.S. Ghurye, K.M. Kapadia, A.P. Barnabas, Yogendra Singh, R.K. Mukerjee, M.N. Srinivas, Yogesh Atal and S.C. Dube have also referred to change in the caste system and in inter-caste relations due to the impact of urbanisation.

Urbanisation and Status of Women

Status of women in urban areas is higher than that of women in rural areas. Urban women are comparatively more educated and liberal. Against 25.1 per cent literate women in rural areas, there are 54 per cent literate women in urban areas according to the census of 1991. Some of them are working too. (16.5% urban women belonged to the labour force in 1993-94; *Manpower Profile, India,* 1998:129) As such, they are not only aware of their economic, social and political rights but they also use these rights to save themselves from being humiliated and exploited. The average age of girls at marriage in cities is also higher than the corresponding age in villages.

However, in the labour market, women are still in a disadvantaged situation. The labour market discriminates against women and is opposed to equality of opportunity—understood in a comprehensive sense to include equality of employment, training and promotional opportunities. In this sense, change is not possible in the sex segregated labour market whose structures ensure that the career patterns of women will normally be marked by discontinuity, unlike the normal male career patterns which assume continuity. Because of the constraints of the sex segregated labour market, women tend to cluster in a limited range of occupations, which have low status and are poorly paid. Women normally prefer teaching, nursing, social work, secretarial and clerical jobs—all of which have low status and low remuneration. Even those women who have surmounted the hurdles to professional education are disadvantaged as they find it difficult to harmonise competing demands of a professional career and home.

Generally speaking, it is difficult for a woman to remain single or to combine marriage with career. Apart from the general expectation that all wives must be housewives, it has been noted that women are called upon to sacrifice their career when the need arises, thereby subordinating their own career to that of their husbands. This often creates frustration among women, leading even to psychotic illness in a few cases. Rural women, however, do not have to face such problems.

It has been further found that in the cities of India, high level education among girls is significantly associated with smaller family size. Though education of women has raised the age of marriage and lowered birth rate, it has not brought about any radical change in the traditional pattern of arranged marriages with dowry. Margaret Cormack (1961:109) found in her study of 500 university students that girls were ready to go to college and mix with boys but they wanted their parents to arrange their marriage. Women want new opportunities but demand old securities as well. They enjoy their newly found freedom but at the same time wish to carry on with old values.

Divorce and remarriage are new phenomena we find among urban women. Today, women take more initiative to break their marriages legally if they find adjustment after marriage impossible. In Delhi alone, 20 couples file cases every week seeking divorce from their spouses. About 2,000 divorce cases were filed in Delhi courts in five months between January and May, 1999 (*The Hindustan Times*, June 12, 1999). Surprisingly, a large number of divorces are sought by women on the grounds of incompatibility and mental torture.

Politically also, urban women are more active today. The number of women contesting elections has increased at every level. They hold important political positions and also possess independent political ideologies. It may, thus, be concluded that while rural women continue to be dependent on men both economically and socially, urban women are comparatively independent and enjoy greater freedom.

Thus, it may be said that though we may accept the views of scholars like Ashis Nandy (1975) who have talked about new aspects of urban social organisation which have replaced traditional ties, yet we cannot reject the prevalence of traditional aspects in the functioning of family, caste, kinship, and religion in urban settings.

STRATIFICATION AND SOCIAL MOBILITY IN URBAN COMMUNITIES

Indian social stratification is characterised by caste and class. Urbanisation and industrialisation have induced mobility in the stratification system. D'Souza (1978), however, has maintained that the role of industrialisation in bringing change in caste and social mobility has been overemphasised. Urban areas do provide more opportunities for social mobility, but do castes in towns and cities succeed in raising their social status? James Freeman in his study of an urbanised Hindu village in 1974 and Shyamlal in his study of Bhangis near Jodhpur in Rajasthan in 1975 did not perceive mobility in caste system. On the contrary, lower castes in urban areas showed strong inclination to maintain their traditional privileges and obligations. The other view is that in this age, one's occupational prestige is by and large dependent upon one's education. The higher the education, the higher the possibility of attaining higher occupational status. Since urban communities offer better educational facilities, the chances of status mobility are higher here. However, Rajendra Pandey (1974) in a comparative study of differences in occupational aspirations of rural and urban college youth concluded that the structural background of the rural and urban societies does make a difference to the aspirations, urges, and values of the youth and accordingly the rural and the urban youth aspire for different kinds of jobs.

The caste system, however, does admit mobility; but it is the group as a whole which changes its position in the caste hierarchy. Scholars like Lynch (1969), Hardgrave (1970) and Ashis Nandy (1978) have pointed out many instances, including those of Jatavs, Nadars and Mahishyas where urbanisation and industrilisation have supported caste mobility. Satish Saberwal (1976) has discussed the process of upward mobility among the Ramgariahs, a carpenter caste of Punjab.

ETHNIC DIVERSITY AND COMMUNITY INTEGRATION

Since selective type of people migrate to urban areas, urban communities often have some ethnic minorities. This poses the problem of their integration in urban social structures. D'Souza has referred to the studies of two scholars in this context—one by K.S. Nair in Poona in 1978 and other by Andrea Menefee Singh. Both these scholars studied the integration of Brahmin south Indians, following their white-collar occupations, in urban social structures. In both studies, it was found that the migrants had not imbibed the mode of life of the local members, but, on the contrary, they had recreated in the localities of their segregation the conditions of their home communities by establishing south Indian services, institutions and associations. We find the same pattern of integration among Bengalis, Punjabis, Keralites, Tamils, Maharashtrians, Kashmiris, etc. who migrate from their cities of origin to cities in other states. Not only do they create their associations but they meet each other on specific occasions where they continue to follow their traditional social practices. B. Punekar (1974) also found the same process of integration among north Indian migrants in Bangalore city. Punekar, Singh, and Nair analysing the relationships between different ethnic groups living in a city, found mutual indifference and non-interference. In rare cases, they noticed hostility. M.S.Gore (1970) noted hostility in his study of neighbourhood relations in Bombay where the Maharashtrians expressed negative attitude against neighbours who hailed from other regions. However, Maharashtrians are so much affected by the ideology of Shiv Sena Sainiks (Maharashtra for Maharashtrians) that it cannot be said that similar ideology determines relations among different ethnic groups in other parts of the country. The pattern of adjustment of different ethnic groups in cities is one of accommodation and toleration.

URBAN NEIGHBOURHOODS

Neighbours, as described by sociologists, are the member of a primary group who have close and intimate relationships with one another. But urbanisation has of late affected neighbourhood relations to the extent that the neighbours do not even know each other, not to talk of having social interaction or close relations. Besides M.S. Gore's study on neighbourhood relations mentioned above, Subhash Chandra's study in 1977 examined the level of social participation in neighbourhoods in Kanpur in Uttar Pradesh. He found that neighbourhood interaction is marked by a high degree of informality. Harish Doshi in his study of neighbourhoods in Ahmedabad in 1974 found persistence of traditional neighbourhoods as well as some adaptation to the changing circumstances. Niranjan Pant in his study in 1978 found that persons of higher socio-economic status in neighbourhoods are more active in community affairs and in articulating the needs and demands of neighbours.

An analysis of the occupants of the inner city shows that in terms of factors like income, education and occupation, people in the same neighbourhood lead radically different lives. Residents in a neighbourhood can be divided into various groups: immigrants, professionals, students, intellectuals, businessmen, service class, less educated, highly educated and members of middle and rich classes. These varied social classes, though they live in close physical proximity, yet socially they live in different 'worlds'. A member of an upper class may live at a stone's throw from a person belonging to a poor or a lower middle-class community but is sealed off from its occupants by wealth, privileges and power. We find similar social differences among people of different classes who come to live in newly developed colonies in big cities. Their residences may not be secluded but socially they live distinct lives. The rich people living there do not consider themselves to be 'part of the local community'. Members of upper class know each other but others only know of them. Sometime, middle class people buy property in previously working class areas in the city. This process is referred to as 'gentrification'. It affects the quality of the social patterns of residents.

PROBLEMS OF URBAN SOCIETY

Urban problems are endless. To name the more important among them are: pollution, corruption, unemployment, crime and juvenile delinquency, overcrowding and slums, drug addiction and alcoholism, and begging. We analyse here some of the more crucial problems.

Housing and Slums

Housing people in a city or abolishing 'houselessness' is a serious problem. Government, industrialists, capitalists, enterpreneurs, contractors, and landlords have been unable to keep pace with the housing needs of the poor and the middle class people. According to the 1988 UNI report (*The Hindustan Times*, 9 May, 1988), between one-fourth and half of the urban population in India's largest cities lives in makeshift shelters and slums. Millions of people are required to pay excessive rent, that is, one which is beyond their means. In our profit-oriented economy, private landlords and colonizers find little profit in building houses in cities for the poor and the lower middle-class people; rather they consider it gainful to concentrate instead on meeting the housing needs of the rich and the upper-middle class. The result has been higher rents and a scramble for the few available houses. Almost half of the population are either ill-housed or pay more than 20 per cent of their income on rent. In some states, Housing Boards and City Development Authorities have tried to remedy the city housing problem with active financial support from the Life Insurance Corporation, HUDCO and such other agencies. They even charge the total housing cost in monthly instalments on interest varying between 9 per cent and 11 per cent. Thus, housing in cities even today continues to be a gigantic problem next only to food and clothing. The estimated shortage of houses at the beginning of the Eighth Plan was about 30 million units, out of which about 8 million were required for urban areas. By 1998, the shortage was expected to grow to 13 million units in urban areas. In Delhi alone, which has seen a population increase from

6.2 to 9.3 million between 1981 and 1991, there is an addition of 60,000 people each year who need to be provided with new housing. Almost 70 per cent of Delhi's population, according to a UNI report, lives in sub-standard conditions. With the country's slum population of 1991 standing at nearly 40 million, slum dwellers form 44 per cent of population in Delhi, 45 per cent in Mumbai, 42 per cent in Calcutta, and 39 per cent in Chennai. The situation is no better in eight other metropolises of Banglore, Hyderabad, Ahmedabad, Kanpur, Pune, Nagpur, Lucknow and Jaipur. Slum population, governmental efforts notwithstanding, is expected to show a sizable increase by 2010 aggravating the housing existing problem and squalor conditions. Living conditions in slum areas are characterised by overcrowding, poor environmental conditions, scarcity of health and family welfare services, and total absence of minimum level of residential accommodation. As a result, conditions of people living in slums is far more pathetic than in rural areas.

Crowding and Depersonalisation

Crowding (density of population) and people's apathy to other persons' problems (including their neighbours' problems) is another problem growing out of city life. Some homes are so overcrowded that five to six persons live in one room. Some city neighbourhoods are extremely overcrowded. Overcrowding has very deleterious effects. It encourages deviant behaviour, spreads diseases, and creates conditions for mental illness, alcoholism, and riots. One effect of dense urban living is people's apathy and indifference. City-dwellers do not want to 'get involved' in other people's affairs. Some people do take interest in accidents and in cases of molestations, assaults and even murders but most people choose to be mere onlookers.

Water Supply and Drainage

We have reached a stage where no city has round the clock water supply. Intermittent supply results in a vaccum being created in empty water lines which often suck in pollutants through leaking joints. Cities like Chennai, Hyderabad, Rajkot, Ajmer, and Udaipur get water from municipal sources for less than an hour a day. Many small towns have little water rain supply and are dependent on tubewells. Even a relatively planned and serviced city like Delhi has now to reach as far as 180 km to the Ramganga for augmentation of water supply. Banglore pumps water from far off distance with a lift of about 700 metres. Most towns and cities which normally get good rain every year, have been undergoing the agony of acute water shortage in the last eight-nine years. What seems to be sadly lacking is a national water policy which would assess the total water resources and then allocate water. This in spite of the State Chief Ministers' meeting at Delhi in September 1987 which approved National Water Policy which aimed at giving priority to drinking water requirements.

When we look on the other side of the water problem, that is, drainage, we find the situation equally bad. One of the less known facts about India is that there is not a single city which is fully sewered. Not even Chandigarh can claim this distinction because unauthorised constructions in and around it lie outside the purview of the main system. Because of the non-existence of the drainage system, large pools of stagnant water can be seen in every city even in summer months. Just as we need a national water policy, we also need a national and regional drainage policy.

Transportation and Traffic

The transportation and traffic picture in all Indian cities is extremely unsatisfactory. A majority of people use buses and tempos, while a few use rail as transit system. The increasing number of scooters, motorcycles, mopeds and cars make traffic problem worse. For example, in Mumbai, automobiles have trebled (from 3.1 lakh to 8.73 lakh) between 1986 and 1996 (*The Hindustan Times*, November 29, 1996). They pollute the air with smoke. In Mumbai alone, daily pollutants let out into the air are about 3,000 tons, of which 52 per cent come from automobiles, 2 per cent from domestic fuels, and the remaining 46 per cent from industries.

The number of buses plying in metropolitan cities like Delhi, Mumbai, Chennai and Calcutta is not adequate and commuters have to spend about one to two hours to get into a bus, which means leaving home two hours in advance in the morning to reach their place of work and reaching home two hours late in the evening. The main reason for this messy condition is that the low income of commuters forces them to live in areas with cheap accommodation which necessitates extensive travel. Further, since city residents cannot afford to pay high fares for using public transport system, fares have to be kept very low which results in all city bus services sustaining such annual losses as hamper their expansion or maintenance of a fleet adequate to meet city needs.

Power Shortage

Closely linked with transportation is the question of power shortage. The use of electrical gadgets has considerably increased in cities; on the other hand, the establishment of new industries and the expansion of the old ones has also increased dependence on electricity. Most states are not in a position to generate the power that they need with the result that they remain dependent on the neighbouring states. Conflict over distribution and supply of power among states often leads to severe power crises in cities.

Sanitation

Municipalities and municipal corporations in Indian cities are so riddled with maladministration that they have time for sanitation of their cities, particularly with regard to removing garbage, cleaning drains, and unclogging sewers. Sweepers rarely and reluctantly perform their assigned duties and every few months threaten to go on strike on the issue of wages, etc. Garbage disposal fleets operate to a third or half of their capacity. If removing garbage work is assigned to private contractors, they always complain of non-payment of money and stop working on slight pretexts. There is, thus, total lack of motivation to tackle the basic sanitation needs of the cities. The spread of unauthorised slums in congested urban areas and lack of civic sense among the settlers in these slums further adds to the growing mound of filth and diseases.

Various forms of racketeering in municipal work exist in our cities. For instance: (a) since payment for garbage removal is made on the basis of trips and not the weight of the garbage picked up, a large number of trips are shown on records and money is split between the contractor and the municipal employees; (b) a large number of vehicles used for garbage-collecting operations are actually used for unauthorised work; (c) debris is diverted and sold to private parties for filling up building sites while payment for debris disposal is taken from the municipality; and (d) drivers of trucks and dumpers sell diesel meant for sanitation trucks.

Obviously, the basic problem is excessive urbanisation and the resultant slumming of cities. Since our politicians use migrants as vote-banks, they remain unconcerned with taking necessary civic action. Lack of understanding at the planning level, lack of coordination between the agencies concerned, mismanagement of municipalities, and lack of necessary funds to be provided by state governments will always remain barriers to putting sanitation maintenance cycle in proper shape. If cities continue to treat sanitation and sewage as low-priority areas, overcoming health crisis in urban areas will be an insurmountable task in years to come. As a long-term remedy, what is needed is using new techniques of refuse collection, new technology for the disposal of garbage, and a fundamental change in the municipal infrastructure and land use planning.

Pollution

Our cities and towns are major polluters of the environment. Several cities discharge 40 per cent to 60 per cent of their entire sewage and industrial effluents untreated into the nearby rivers. The smallest town contributes its share of garbage and excreta to the nearest waterway through its open drains. Urban industry pollutes the atmosphere with smoke and toxic gases from its chimneys. Areas recording higher levels of air pollution abound with many ailments which particularly affect children below five years and people above fifty years of age. The high synergistic effect of sulphur dioxide, nitrogen dioxide, etc. causes many diseases. The ambient air quality in Delhi gives it the dubious distinction of being the fourth most polluted city in the world. The issue of environmental pollution in urban areas is considered so significant that even the Supreme Court in July 1995 had to ask for strict enforcement of environmental laws leading to closure or relocation of about 146 hazardous industries in Delhi by November-December 1996. The orders led to even agitations by the affected workers in December 1996, but the Apex Court stuck to its decision of not allowing industries within the National Capital Region (NCR), and shifting them to neighbouring states. The vehicular emissions in Delhi account for 64 per cent of Delhi's air pollutant load, power plants are responsible for 16 per cent and industries account for 12 per cent.

Similar significant role was played by the Supreme Court in yet another judgement on environment protection in Andhra Pradesh in October 1996. The judgement banned shrimp (small marine fish) culture within 500 metres of the high tide line along the 6,000 km coastline and the dismantling of all structures within the restricted zone by March 1997. The country earns more than Rs.600 crore in foreign exchange through export of shrimp from Andhra Pradesh and Tamil Nadu alone. According to an estimate by the Central Pollution Control Board, the effluent generation from acquaculture farms on the east coast alone was about 2.37 million cubic metres (*The Hindustan Times*, January 6, 1997). The poison we put in the environment comes right back to us through our air, water and food, slowly seeping into our bodies and showing up as cancer, immune disorders or as hormonal system disorders. No wonder, the doctors claim that the worsening environmental condition in India has increased the chances of catching cancer dramatically in the four metros—Delhi, Mumbai, Bangalore and Chennai—the chances of having cancer are as high as 7 to 11 per cent during a lifetime. A conservative estimate of cancer patients in India by the year 2001 stands at eight lakhs. Of course, the poor suffer more than the rich from environmental degrada-

Causes of Urban Problems

Following McVeigh and Shostak (1978:198-205) who have linked urban problems in the United States to four factors, we can identify following five major causes of problems of urban life in India:

Migration

As already indicated, people migrate to towns/cities because of the relatively better employment opportunities available there. In India, rural to urban and urban to rural migration is crucial. The 1991 census figures pointed out that in 17.7 per cent cases, migration was from rural to urban, and in 11.8 per cent cases it was from urban to urban (*Manpower Profile India*, 1998:26). The analysis of intra-dsitrict migration (short distance migration), inter-district or intra-state migration (medium distance migration) and inter-state migration (long distance migration) shows that about 68 per cent migrations are short distance, 21 per cent are medium distance and 11 per cent are long distance migrations (Bose, 1979:187).

Entry of the rural poor into a city depletes sources of revenue. On the other hand, the rich people today prefer to live in suburban areas. This movement of the rich causes financial loss to the city. This migration to the city and away from the city aggravates problems.

Industrial Growth

While the urban population growth is 4 per cent in India, the industrial growth rate is about 6 per cent per annum. The ninth Five Year Plan postulated an industrial growth rate of 8 per cent per annum. This growth was expected to take care of additional job requirements in the cities. The tertiary sector also provides refuge to migrants, though their earnings remain at low level.

Apathy of the Government

The administrative mismanagement of our cities is also responsible for the mess in which city-dwellers find themselves. Municipal authorities have not kept pace with city growth, either spatially or in terms of management infrastructure. There is neither the will nor the capacity to plan for the future. There is also no skill and capability to manage what exists. Until we improve the capacity of our cities to govern themselves, we cannot emerge from the urban mess. On the other hand, state governments also put many restrictions on local governments in raising necessary funds for dealing with particular urban problems.

Defective Town Planning

A more alarming factor in the general deterioration in the standard of civic services is the growing sense of helplessness of our planners and administrators.. From the Planning Commission downwards, there seems to be a fatalistic acceptance of uncontrolled growth of our metropolitan cities. In fact, a member of the National Commission on Urbanisation had expressed a feeling that very little is being done in our country to plan the growth of the cities in a proper way.

Vested-interest Forces

The last cause of urban problems is the vested interest forces that work against people but enhance private commercial interests and profits. The city residents are usually powerless to affect decisions that the elite make to further their own interests, power and profit. When these powerful elite can make more money, they adopt plans and programmes no matter how many people are hurt in the process. The best example of the role of the vested interests was the transfer of one Municipal Commissioner in Maharashtra for 25 times in 25 years who refused to toe the line of politicians, burreaucrats and petty officials for their motivated interests and got demolished many unauthorised constructions.

Solutions to Urban Problems

Some measures have to be adopted if we want to remedy urban problems. The measures suggested are as follows:

Systematic Development of Urban Centres and Creation of Job Opportunities

One important solution to our urban problems is the systematic development of the fast growing urban centres and planning an investment programme, which over the next 20 years or so, could give rise to a large number of well distributed, viable urban centres throughout the country. So far we have been focusing attention on programmes for providing wage employment in rural areas through IRDP, NREP and JRY to hold people back in villages. While there is ample justification for providing rural employment, this by itself is not enough. It is not possible to provide gainful employment in the agricultural sector beyond a certain point. For this purpose, we have to lay emphasis on programmes which can permit multifunctional activities to sustain people in cities.

Regional Planning along with City Planning

Urban planning is almost city-centred. We have always been talking of town and city planning but never of the planned development of the whole region so that population is logically dispersed and activities are properly distributed. City planning is an ad hoc solution but regional planning could be a more lasting one. For example, instead of providing houses to slumd-wellers in cities through city development authorities, if through regional planning migrants could be diverted to other areas which may provide attractive employment, the pace of growth of existing cities could be checked. It is to be appreciated that at least beginning from the Ninth Five Year Plan (1997), the Government of India has started helping states in setting up regional planning organisations and evolving meaningful regional settlement plans.

Encouraging Industries to Move to Backward Areas

Land pricing policy which gives land in large chunks at throwaway prices has to be replanned to encourage industries to move to backward areas/districts. This will also take care of linear development of metropolitan and big cities. A policy of the state taking over potential high value land in and around large cities with a view to exploiting its full cost at a later date also needs serious consideration.

Municipalities to Find Own Financial Resources

People do not mind paying taxes to the municipality if their money is properly utilised to maintain roads, provide sewage system, reduce water shortage and provide electricity. It is a well known fact that cities suffer from crippling resource constraints. If deterrent punishment is given to the corrupt municipality officials, there is no reason why the municipal corporations should find it difficult collecting money from the residents of a city. A city must bear the cost of its own development. High financial support from state government is becoming difficult. By revising property, water and electricity taxes, money can be collected and more money per head per annum can be made available for providing necessary amenities. When any new industry or business is located in a city or on its periphery, it could be moderately taxed so that additional money becomes available to the local body.

Encouraging Private Transport

Why should city transport be a public monopoly? When transport is handled by state employees, it has been noticed that they tend to behave extremely rudely and callously. Backing of the trade unions encourages them to go on strikes frequently. It is necessary then that private transportation be encouraged. Privately operated mini bus and tempo services will charge a little more fare and commuters would not mind paying this in view of better services.

Amendment of Rent Control Acts

Laws which inhibit the construction of new houses or giving of houses on rent must be amended. Which landlord would like to spend Rs. 3 or 4 lakh on a two-three room house and give it on rent for Rs. 1,000-1,500 a month for the next 10 to 20 years without having the authority to increase the rent or get the house vacated on appropriate grounds. Maharashtra has taken a lead in amending Rent Control Act which has made thousands of houses available for rent. A similar step in other states would be welcome.

Adopting Pragmatic Housing Policy

In May 1988, the central government presented National Housing Policy (NHP) to the parliament which aimed at abolishing 'homelessness' by the turn of the century and upgrading the quality of accommodation to a fixed minimum standard. Such policy sounds too ambitious and utopian. It is a dream impossible to accomplish in a span of remaining one year or so by which time the twentieth century will have ended. The government policy and planning has to be more down to earth. This is not to say that the concept of NHP is irrational. The NHP strategy is broadbased. It seeks to provide easy access to finance as well as land and materials for building houses at reasonable rates. It also seeks to encourage manufacturers to use new type of building materials. Moreover, it seeks to review the entire gamut of laws relating to land tenure, land acquisition and ceiling to apartment ownership, municipal regulations and rental laws. But these are all thorny issues. The NHP is oriented towards rich developers, landlords and contractors. The NHP has to discourage luxury housing and promote cooperative and group housing societies. It has to develop special schemes for the poor and low-income people. It has also to provide incentives to employers to build houses for the employees.. It has to increase its authorised capital of Rs. 100 crore which cannot go anywhere near meeting its financial needs. Unless a more pragmatic NHP is adopted, it will be impossible to achieve the set goals.

Structural Decentralisation

One proposal by innovative planners and some radicals envisions a structural decentralisation of local self-government itself. This could entail the creation of 'neighbourhood-action groups', to be called 'community centres' consisting of representatives of residents and municipality officials.

These centres will identify and act upon neighbourhood needs. For example, many new colonies have come to be established in many cities in which as many as 10,000 to 50,000 people reside. Thus, these colonies are small towns by themselves. Some taxes like house tax, road tax, light tax, etc., could be passed on directly to these community-centres instead of giving them to municipalities. The centres would direct the affairs of the neighbourhood without reference to the city municipal corporation and use the collected money for maintaining roads, lights and so forth. The argument for this kind of decentralised structure within the city is that the same system that allows lakhs of people a substantial control over their civic destiny denies them an effective role in shaping the institutions that shape their lives. Community centres will allow them to create their own exclusive environment.

To conclude, it may be pointed out that the effects of urbanisation and urbanism and the problems of cities can never be solved until urban planning is modified and radical measures are taken. These should not be based on profit motive which would benefit a few vested interests. The use of land, technology, and taxes should be for the benefit of the people and not for the benefit of a few powerful interests. City dwellers have to become active and organise themselves and agitate to change the existing economic and social systems in the cities.

DE-URBANISATION OF CITIES AND URBANISATION OF VILLAGES

If we analyse city not as a physical entity but as a focal point of activity of groups of people, the most powerful of whom are businessmen, politicians and civil servants, we find that sometimes these groups act in concert and sometimes in conflict but their major decisions affect the lives of the rest of the people. Further, in cities (as in Ludhiana, Calcutta, Mumbai, Indore, Bhilwara, etc.) the area around the business centre is inhabited by low income groups and beset by social problems. In addition, advanced technology and large scale industry make craft industries and other small-scale production units obsolete and uncompetitive. Much new economic development, notably in the service sector occurs outside the old, inner urban industrial areas. People, therefore, migrate to other areas. Those who remain in the inner city are drawn disproportionately from the old, socially disadvantaged, unskilled and semi-skilled workers. They are joined by immigrants who are prepared to do unskilled and semi-skilled work in the inner city. This process of economic decline of urban areas and of population movement out of them are referred to collectively as 'de-urbanisation'. On the other hand, 'urbanisation' of many suburban rural areas also occurs. Of course, not all urban areas decline. It is mainly the 'old' industrial cities that experience de-urbanisation. Many industrial towns undergo a parallel increase in population. Nor is the process of de-urbanisation irreversible.

In Delhi, when the High Court ordered the shifting of heavy industries from Delhi to other areas for preventing pollution, thousands of persons working in these industries had to leave Delhi and settle near the new place of industry. Many government offices were also shifted from Delhi to Ghaziabad and nearby Gurgaon town which also compelled the affected people to leave Delhi. The suburban areas where these industries and offices are opened gradually become urbanised. Thus, de-urbanisation process affects the urbanites and the urbanisation process affects the villagers.

On Rural-Urban Fringe

One change witnessed after independence is the occurance of rural-urban fringe around cities. The cities have penetrated into rural areas to a distance of 14-15 km. Much of this development has occured in unplanned, haphazard and spontaneous manner. As one moves out of the city, one observes new residential colonies, a few factories, commercial squatters on either side of the road, cold storage plants, warehouses, timber yards, etc. These features symbolise the physical expansion of the city. The term rural-urban fringe has been used to designate such areas. The fringe area is, thus, defined as "an area of mixed urban and rural landusers between the point where city services cease to be available and the point where agricultural landuses predominate".

These areas not only affect the social life of the people living there but they have also generated jobs for the rural population. Even those who continue with farming, get an expanding market for vegetables, fruits, milk, etc. This affects the traditional attitudes and values as well as the lifestyle of ordinary rural people.

Structurally, rural-urban fringe comprises urban fringe plus rural fringe. The former consists of municipal or non-municipal town and urbanised villages contiguous to town/city. The latter consists of municipal or non-municipal town, partially urbanised villages away from the main city and wholly rural villages. Thus, urban-rural fringe includes urban corridors and suburbs but not satellites and green belts. The 'corridor' sometimes extends to a distance of over 30 km from the city centres while the 'suburb' implies a location near the periphery of a city. Most suburbs are purely residential in character. People in the suburbs identify themselves with the city and claim to be living within the city. The difference between the suburb and satellite is merely one of distance from the city centre. Suburbs are closer to the city while satellites are located farther away.

The villages in the fringe area undergo a process of change in three ways: (a) changes in land uses within the village, (b) occupation changes, (c) changes in the social and economic life styles of the people of the village.

It may be concluded that cities in India are now developing unevenly. Pollution, inequality, absence of transport facilities to cover distance from home to work-place and back—all these and other similar factors require that policies of settlement and providing amenities in different areas in the city should not be left only to state governments and local bodies but the local residents must also be effectively and beneficially involved in any revitalisation of their localities. Louis Wirth's model of rural-urban, and the Gemeinschaft-Gesellschaft framework of Toennies, now seem inadequate as conceptual frameworks to deal with contemporary urban issues. Unemployment, poverty, caste and communal conflicts, public disorder and pollution, have increased the urgency of the debate on urban policy.

Further Readings

Durkheim, E., *The Division of Labour in Society*, Macmillan, New York, 1993.

Fox, R.G. (ed.), *Urban India: Society, Space and Image*, Duke University, Duke, 1970.

Gore, M.S., *Immigrants and Neighbourhoods: Two Aspects of Life in a Metropolitan City*, Tata Institute of Social Sciences, Bombay, 1970.

Jain, S.P., "Religion and Caste Ranking in a North Indian Town", *Sociological Bulletin*, 1971, 20 (2): 134-144.

Khan, M.E., "Muslim Society Structure in an Urban Setting", *Indian Anthropologist*, 1976, 6(1):28-39.

Mary, Chatterjee, *Sociological Bulletin*, 1971, 20 (2) : 145-158.

Nagpaul, Hans, *Modernisation and Urbanisation in India: Problems and Issues*, Rawat Publications, Jaipur, 1996.

Ramchandran, R., *Urbanisation and Urban Systems in India*, Oxford University Press, Delhi, 1998.

Singer, Milton, in Singer M. and Cohn B.S., *Structure and Change in Indian Society*, Aldine Publishing Company, Chicago, 1968.

Sylvia, Vatuk, *Kinship and Urbanisation: White-Collar Migrants in North India*, University of California Press, Los Angeles, 1973.

William, L. Rowe, "Caste, Kinship and Association in Urban India" in A. Santhall (ed.), *Urban Anthropology*, Oxford University Press, New York, 1973: 211-249.

Wirth, Louis, *The Ghetto*, University of Chicago Press, Chicago, 1938.

12 Population Dynamics

DEMOGRAPHIC ANALYSIS

The study of population focuses attention on its size, structure, distribution, growth and effects of its growth on social, economic and cultural aspects of society. It may be said that the two broad areas within the scope of population are: (a) demographic analysis (i.e., size, distribution, composition, fertility, mortality, migration and mobility), and (b) population analysis (i.e., relationship between population changes and economic, social and cultural variables like poverty, illiteracy, ill-health, family structure, business activity, etc., using concepts and principles of various social sciences. We will briefly analyse both the aspects here.

Age Composition

The age composition of people in a country is functionally related to components of population change like fertility, mortality, marriage age, migration, etc. Its distribution also has its important socio-economic effects. Participation in productive work, income, participation in reproduction process, level of consumption, and services needed are all affected by age. In India, according to the 1991 census, 37.8 per cent population belongs to 0-14 age group, 55.5 per cent to 15-59 age group and 6.7 per cent to 60+ age group (*Manpower Profile, India*, 1998: 19). On sex basis, among males, 37.73 per cent belong to 0-14 age group, 55.60 per cent to 15-59 age group, and 6.67 per cent are above 60 years; while among females, 37.79 per cent belong to 0-14 age group, 55.55 per cent to 15-59 age group, and 6.66 per cent are 60+ years of age (*Ibid*:16). It is estimated that by 2,000 A.D., about 32 per cent of total population will be below 14 years, 8 per cent above 60 years and 60 per cent will belong to 15-59 years age group (*India, 1992*:19). Since 1951, proportion of population in age group below 15 years has increased owing to decrease in the mortality rate. The effects of this age structure are: (1) more allocation of funds to provide for health, medical and educational needs for children; (2) rapid population increase in a year; (3) more dependants on working people; and (4) low productivity of labour.

Sex Composition

Sex ratio in a population is important because it has bearing upon the marriage rate, death rate, birth rate, and even migration rate. According to the 1991 census figures, there are 927 females per 1,000 males in India. The reasons for sex imbalance are: female infanticide, neglect of female infants, early marriage, death consequent on child birth, and bad treatment and hard work of women. The sex ratio has been continuously declining from the level of 972 in 1901 to 950 in 1931, 946 in 1951, 930 in 1971, and 927 in 1991 (*Census of India*, 1991 and *Manpower Profile, India*, 1998:10). Invariably sex ratio is higher in the urban areas than in the rural areas because of migration of single males from rural to urban areas for education, work and other reasons.

There is also variation in the sex ratio in the states. There are 13 states with sex ratio above the national level and 12 states with sex ratio lower than the national level (*Manpower Profile, India*, 1998:15).

Marital Composition

The mean age at marriage in 1994 was 19.4 for females and 24.7 for males. (*Ibid*:462). Urban women marry more in 20-24 age group than in 24-27 age group. Marriage age is considerably higher in urban areas than in rural areas. It is also higher among more educated women. Both among males and females, there is significant change in marriage age from 1951 onwards (from 15.4 to 19.4 among females and from 19.9 to 24.7 among males). In terms of marital status, in 1994, 50.4 per cent people were unmarried, 44.6 per cent were married and 5 per cent were widowed/divorced/separated. On sex basis, 45.6 per cent females and 54.9 per cent males are never married, 46.6 per cent females and 42.7 per cent males are married, and 7.8 per cent females and 2.4 per cent males are widowed/divorced/separated (*Ibid*:464). In general, though age at marriage in India shows continuously an upward trend yet in comparison to the developed countries, it is quite low. Low marriage age adversely affects the social status and health of women. The social effect is particularly on decrease in educational level, increase in higher proportion of widows, increase in number of children and higher dependence on men. Child birth at immature age has physical effects on the health of mothers and infants.

Rural-Urban Composition

Of the total population, 25.73 per cent is urban and 74.27 per cent is rural according to the 1991 census. In 1998, urban population was estimated to be 28.3 per cent (*Ibid*:14). Even though there has been a considerable increase in the percentage of urban population (from 10.8 per cent in 1901 to 17.3 per cent in 1951, and 23.7 per cent in 1981), yet 26 per cent population in 1991 cannot be considered a high level of urbanisation. Of the 224.9 million people (or 26.6% of the total population of India) who had migrated from their place of last residence to some other place in 1991, 64.5 per cent were rural to rural migrants, 17.7 per cent were rural to urban migrants, 11.8 per cent were urban to urban migrants, and 6 per cent were urban to rural migrants (*Ibid*:26). In the West, the migratory movement which accompanies urbanisation is considered desirable since it provides employment opportunities and other facilities, but in India, it represents a transfer of rural poverty to the urban areas and increase in the number of slum-dwellers. However, despite a sluggish growth of urbanisation in India, the scale of population pressure on the existing cities and towns is accelerating rather sharply. The increase in migration from rural to urban areas is expected to supply cheap labour to industrial and commercial sectors, but at the same time, it is expected to create more social problems in towns and cities. Though the rural population of India has also increased yet of the total rural population (i.e., 74.2%), about 18.44 per cent live in small villages of less than 1000 persons and 36.57 per cent in small villages of less than 2000 population (*Ibid*:23).

Occupational Structure

The number of dependants (persons below 14 years or above 60 years) on economically active persons (of 15 to 59 years age) is very high. In 1993-94, about 45 per cent (exactly 44.86%) people in India (in 15-59 age group) were estimated to be economically active or were in work-force and about 55 per cent were economically inactive (*Ibid*:128). In 1993-94, 44.9 per cent people in the rural areas and 36.3 per cent in the urban areas were engaged in labour force (*Ibid*:49). In terms of sex, 67.6 per cent of males (in 15-59 age group) and 32.4 per cent of females are engaged in productive work. In the working age of 15-59, the activity rate of males in urban and rural areas is 26.2 per cent and 73.8 per cent respectively, while of females in urban and rural areas is 14.9 per cent and 85 per cent respectively

(*Ibid*:129). In 1993-94, 64.6 per cent people were engaged in primary sector (agriculture), 14.2 per cent in secondary sector (manufacturing) and 21.2 per cent in tertiary sector (service) (*Ibid*: 229). The largest number of male non-workers are full-time students and largest number of female non-workers are engaged in household work. This occupational structure has its repercussions at social level, influencing the status of women.

Urban participation rates in labour force are invariably lower than those in the rural areas for both the sexes. The age-specific activity rate of age group 0-14 indicates the practice of child labour of both males and females in the rural as well as the urban areas. In rural areas in 1993-94, it was 1.1 per cent in 5-9 age group and 13.8 per cent in 10-14 age group among males and 1.4 per cent in 5-9 age group and 14.1 per cent in 10-14 age group among females. In the urban areas, it was 0.5 per cent among males and 0.5 per cent among males and 4.5 per cent among females in 10-14 age group (*Ibid*:218).

Literacy Structure

In the 1991 census, the literary level was calculated for population aged 7 years and above, unlike earlier censuses which took into account population of five years and above for this purpose. The results showed increase in literary levels. Of the total population, 52.21 per cent were found literate (64.13% males, and 39.29% females) (*Ibid*:42). The NSS has estimated that by the end of 1997, the literacy level among males has increased to 72 per cent and among females to 49 per cent (*The Hindustan Times*, December 8, 1998). The highest literacy rate is found in Kerala (89.81%) and lowest in Bihar (38.48%). In terms of educational composition, the data shows some important characteristics: (1) The overwhelming majority of the literates has only a few years of schooling and the extent of school drop-outs is very high. Of the total literate people in India in 1991 (846.3 million), 56.7 per cent had less than 3 years education, 23.8 per cent 3-6 years education, 11 per cent 7-11 years education, 6.8 per cent 12-14 years education and 1.7 per cent more than 14 years education (*Ibid*:48). (2) On the one hand, there is low supply of highly educated people, and, on the other hand, we encounter a mass of educated unemployed.

Language Composition

Of the 15 major languages specified in our Constitution, the highest percentage (in round numbers) speak Hindi (43%), followed by those who speak Bengali, Telugu and Marathi (8% each), Tamil and Urdu (6% each), Gujarati (5%), Malayalam, Kannada and Oriya (4% each), Punjabi (3%), and other languages (including Assamese, Kashmiri, Sindhi, Sanskrit, etc.) (1%).

Religious Composition

Though India has been described as a secular country in the Constitution, yet there is a blend of several religions. Of the total population, Hindus comprise 82.6 per cent, Muslims 11.4 per cent, Christians 2.4 per cent, Sikhs 2.0 per cent, Buddhists 0.7 per cent, Jains 0.5 per cent and others 0.4 per cent. While Jains are more urbanite (with 60%) followed by Muslims (29%), Hindus are the most rural (with 76% of urban and 84% of rural population).

Scheduled Castes and Scheduled Tribes

The scheduled castes belong mostly to Hindu religion. According to the 1991 census, 16.49 per cent of the population was enumerated as SCs and 8.08 per cent as STs (*Ibid*:34). Thus, roughly one in every 4 persons in India belongs to SCs and STs. There are great variations in the state wise distribution of these groups. Of the total SCs, the highest number are found in Uttar Pradesh, followed by West Bengal, Bihar, Tamil Nadu and Andhra Pradesh, while Nagaland, Mizoram, Arunachal Pradesh have no SCs at all. Nagaland and Meghalaya have more than 80 per cent of ST population, and Haryana, Jammu and Kashmir, Punjab, Sikkim, and Goa have no STs. The highest number of tribals are found in Madhya Pradesh, followed by Maharashtra, Orissa, Bihar and Gujarat. Of the total tribal population, three fifths (62.75%) are found in the above mentioned five states (*Ibid*:34).

POPULATION EXPLOSION

The post-World War II period (i.e., period after 1945) is generally referred to as a period of population explosion in demographic parlance. It is a period in which the world population including population in India, experienced unprecedented and accelerated growth. For example, while India's population was estimated to be 100 million in 1600 A.D., it was 120 million in 1800, 238.4 million in 1901, 361.1 million in 1951, 846.3 million in 1991, and estimated to be 100 million in August 1999 (*Ibid*: 10 and *The Hindustan Times*, August 28, 1999). This means that while it increased by 20 per cent in 200 years between 1600 and 1800 A.D and by about 100 per cent (exactly 98.66%) in next 100 years between 1800 and 1901, it increased by 319 per cent in the following 99 years (or say about 100 years between 1901 and 1999). If the growth of population is sub-divided into three distinct periods, say (a) from 1901 to 1931, (b) 1931-1961, and (c) 1961-1999, we find that the first period of 30 years witnessed an addition of only 17 per cent, the next 30 years saw an increase of 57.4 per cent, and in the following 38 years (or about four decades), India experienced an explosive growth of 127.4 per cent. Thus, population growth prior to 1921 was *sporadic*, between 1921 and 1951 it was *rapid*, and after 1951 it can be called *explosive*.

Increase in Population

According to the National Population Policy draft prepared in 1997 by the Ministry of Health and Family Welfare, the goal of total fertility rate (TFR) of 2.1 will be achieved by the year 2010. But, according to the projections made by the Registrar General, the TFR of 2.1 would not be reached before the year 2026, if the existing demographic trends continued. This shows how lackadaisical the government and the nation have been in controlling the population growth.

The phenomenon of galloping population in India has the following aspects:

- Every sixth person on the globe today is an Indian, and by the turn of the century, every fifth living person will be an Indian.
- India adds 46,500 persons to its population every day.
- Addition to India's population is an equivalent of a Chandigarh (with 6,40,725 population) in nine days, two Bhopals a month, and an Australia (with 18.52 million population) every eight months. During 1981-91, addition to the population was to the tune of 163 million, equalling to little less than the combined population of France (58.683 million), Britain (58.649 million) and Italy (57.369 million).
- By 2035, India would overtake China as the world's most populous nation. While the rate of annual population growth in India is 3.5 per cent, in China it is 2.1 per cent. Thus, while China's population would double in 60 years, India's population would double in 34 years.
- Around 49 per cent of the increase in India's population in one decade is in the five states of Bihar, Madhya Pradesh, Assam, Rajasthan and Uttar Pradesh (known as *BIMARU* states).
- More than three times as many couples enter the reproductive span than those leaving it, with the fertility rate of the younger group being three times higher than that of those passing out of the reproductive range.
- At the present rate of growth, life for most Indians would be unbearable—medical facilities would be difficult to provide, expenses on education, housing, etc., would be exorbitant, technical and profes-

sional education would become the exclusive prerogative of the elite, and the scarcity of food would once again plunge more than half of the nation below the poverty line.

In analysing the growth of population or demographic transition, it may be averred that a country goes through three different phases, having different tendency in each stage. These three phases show a sequence of high birth -- high death, high birth – low death, and low birth – low death. In the first 'stationary' phase, both fertility and mortality rates are high and uncontrolled, so that the growth of population is low. The second phase is 'expansion' phase because birth-rate is considerably high and death-rate keeps declining. The third phase is of 'decline type'. India is still going through the second phase, where fertility remains above mortality. Fertility will be lowered only when economic and social conditions are improved to a certain level. Some indices of economic and social change are urbanisation, industrialisation (both of which reduce the importance of the family and kinship ties for achieving goals), literacy, and infant mortality.

Causes of Population Growth

After 1951, the growth of population is explained by a decline in mortality due to availability of curative and preventive medicines, control of famines and epidemics, reduction of wars, and a large base population.

We may identify the following important causes for population explosion:

Widening Gap Between Birth and Death Rates

The average annual birth rate in India which was 42 per thousand population in 1951-61 came down to 28.1 per thousand in 1996. The death rate also came down from over 27 per thousand population in 1951-61 to 9.1 in 1996 (*Manpower Profile*,1998:37). Thus, since birth rate has shown negilible decline and death rate has gone down rather sharply, the widening gap has increased our population rapidly. The total fertility rate (average number of children born per woman) came down from about six in the fifties to 4.4 in 1993-94 (*Ibid*:33). If we add the annual figures of abortions (between 10 and 11 million, including 4 million spontaneous and 6.7 million induced) to the annual number of births (17 million) that take place in the country, we come to the shocking conclusion that in this age of family planning, one out of every five Indian women in the reproductive age group of 15-45 years is pregnant at any time.

Low Age at Marriage

Child marriages have been very common in our country. According to the 1931 census, 72 per cent marriages in India were performed before 15 years of age and 34 per cent before ten years of age. Since then, there has been a continuous increase in the mean age of marriage among both males and females. Though the mean age of marriage is estimated to be continuously increasing, yet a large number of girls even today marry at an age at which they are not ready for marriage either socially and emotionally, or psychologically and chronologically.

The infant mortality rate is directly related to the age of women at marriage. The average infant mortality rate in India was 74 per 1,000 live-births in 1995—in rural areas it was 80 and in urban areas it was 49. If we divide women in three groups in terms of age at marriage, namely, below 18, 18-20, and 21 and above, the infant mortality rate in each of these three groups in rural areas (in 1978) was 141, 112, and 85 respectively while in the urban areas, it was 78,66 and 46 respectively. If we relate fertility rates (average number of children born per woman) with age groups, we find that as the age group increases, the fertility rate decreases. If population growth is to be controlled, marriage of females (in rural and urban areas) is to be preferred in 21-23 or 23-25 age groups rather than in 15-18 or 18-21 age groups.

High Illiteracy

Family planning has a direct link with female education, and female education is directly associated with age at marriage, general status of women, their fertility and infant mortality rate, and so forth. According to the latest 1999 figures given by NSS, the overall literacy percentage in India was 61 as compared to 52.21 in 1991 and 43.56 in 1981. The male literacy percentage in 1991 was 64.13 while the female literacy percentage is 39.29 (*Ibid*:42). In 1999, it is estimated to be 73 per cent and 49 per cent respectively. Education makes a person liberal, broad-minded, open to new ideas, and rational. If both men and women are educated, they will easily understand the logic of planning their family, but if either of them or both of them are illiterate, they would be more orthodox, illogical and religious-minded. This is evident from the fact that Kerala which has the overall literacy rate of 89.81 per cent and female literacy rate of 86.91 per cent (in 1991) has the lowest birth rate (17.8 per thousand) while Rajasthan's appallingly low female literacy rate of 20.44 per cent (*Ibid*:37 & 42) gives rise to the third highest birth rate in the country (34.6 per thousand), the highest having been registered in Uttar Pradesh (36 per thousand), followed by Madhya Pradesh (34.7 per one thousand). These statistical figures hold good for most of the other states too.

Religious Attitude Towards Family Planning

The religiously orthodox and conservative people are against the use of family planning measures. There are women who disfavour family planning on the plea that they cannot go against the wishes of God. There are some women who argue that the purpose of a woman's life is to bear children. Other women adopt a passive attitude: "If I am destined to have many children, I will have them. If not, I will not have them. Why should I bother about it".

Indian Muslims have a higher birth rate as well as fertility rate than the Hindus (Muslim women having fertility rate of 4.4 as compared to 3.3 among Hindu women). According to a survey conducted among the Muslims by the Operations Research Group in 1978, although a majority of both male and female respondents were aware of modern family planning methods, they were either not using them on religious grounds or they lacked clear adequate knowledge about them.

The survey conducted by the Population Research Centre, Udaipur in 1992 showed that out of 218 Muslim male interviewees, 43.1 per cent approved family planning, 26.6 per cent disapproved it, and 30.3 per cent did not give specific response (*Ibid*:110). In comparison to this, out of 2748 Hindu male interviewees, 61.7 per cent approved it, 14.5 per cent disapproved it and 23.8 per cent were unsure (*Ibid*:110). This indicates that Muslims are more conservative towards family planning than the Hindus.

Other Causes

Some of the other causes responsible for the increase in population are: joint family system and lack of responsibility of young couples in these families to bring up their children, lack of recreational facilities, and lack of information or wrong information about the adverse effects of vasectomy, tubectomy and the loop.

Many poor parents produce children not because they are ignorant but because they need them. This is evident from that fact that there are some 35 million child workers in our country. If families stop those children from working, their family incomes will be terribly diminished.

Producing more children by the poor people illustrates the paradox of population-poverty interrelationship. Poverty is both the cause and effect of the population growth. Having produced many children (sons) to combat one's family's growing needs, the parents are forced to keep them out of school to supplement their household income. In turn, unlettered and ignorant children will inherit their father's lot and like him, opt to have as many sons as are needed to work for sustenance. Ironically, a huge family size is the poor man's only way to combat poverty caused by the population boom.

Effects of Population Explosion

The growth of population has a direct effect on the living standards of people. This is why, despite our spectacular progress in the agricultural and industrial spheres since independence, our per capita income has not risen appreciably.

How has the population growth affected India? It is estimated that 25 million people (out of 1000 million people, i.e., 2.5%) are homeless, 171 million people (i.e., 17%) have no access to safe drinking water, 328.9 million adults (i.e., 33%) are illiterate, 53 per cent children below five years are underweight, and country as a whole has 135th position in the World Human Development Index. The appalling overcrowding of our cities (which like cancerous growths are mushrooming unchecked with slums proliferating) has brought about a virtual breakdown of transportation, electricity and other services. It has also led to the rise of crime and an increase in violence in the urban and the semi-urban areas. All this has been directly fuelled by the addition of about 17 million people every year or an annual population growth rate of 2.14 (*Ibid*:11). If the population continues to increase at this rate, in a few years from now, we will have an army of unemployed, hungry and desperate people who will threaten the very foundations of the social, economic and political systems and institutions of the country. All sectoral demands have a numerical dimension. Whether it is education, employment, health, housing, water supply or any other sector, the perennial question is for how many? Even for the present population of 100 crore (in August 1999), it is futile to think of jobs for all or shelter for all or health protection programmes for all by 2000 A.D. especially when another 1.7 crore people will have been added and, hence need to be accommodated.

It has been calculated that for every addition of about 165 lakh people every year in our country, we will require every year 1.5 lakh primary and middle schools, 10 thousand higher secondary schools, 50 lakh primary and middle school teachers, 1.5 lakh higher secondary school teachers, 5,000 hospitals and dispensaries, 2,000 primary health centres, two lakh hospital beds, 50 thousand doctors, 25 thousand nurses, 5 lakh tonnes cereals, 25,000 metres of cloth and 2.5 million houses and 30 lakh new jobs (*The Hindustan Times*, July 4, 1997).

The impact of the population boom on the quality of life is now being examined in terms of Household Misery Index (HMI), i.e., in terms of peoples' deprivations and basic needs (see, Bose, 1996). The HMI index has five parameters: *pakka* housing, safe drinking water, electricity, sanitation (toilets), and fuel for cooking. Some scholars have examined it (population boom) in terms of effect on human resources (literacy, health, etc.).

At present, 49.1 per cent people in India have no electricity in their households, 69.7 per cent have no toilets (flush or others), 51.5 per cent have no *pakka* houses, and 19 per cent have no safe drinking water (*Outlook*, August 21, 1996:53). If we compare Human Development Index (HDI) on certain selected items in India with some other countries in 1990, we notice the serious effects of increasing population on the quality of our life.

According to 1996 UNDP report (*Ibid*:51), India invests only 14 dollars (about Rs. 500) per person annually on health and education unlike other developing countries like South Korea and Malaysia which spend 150 to 160 dollars. The impact of this insufficient sum on the 36 per cent population of our country living below the poverty line (i.e., about 34 crore people) can easily be imagined.

What do these figures predict? The countdown for India's great leap into the twenty-first century has begun. In the beginning of the 1970s, there was light and hope. Then came darkness in a Biblical reversal in the 1980s. Population explosion, militancy and separatism gathered momentum. Matters touched rock-bottom as the 1980s staggered to a close and we entered and then crossed the middle of the 1990s. What do the remaining fifteen months of the 1990s have in store for us? Our country has to come to terms with the highly competitive world economy. India will be looking for a leader who can be bold enough to take up the issue of controlling population explosion seriously. Unless India can find such a leader, its future cannot be bright.

THEORETICAL EXPLANATIONS OF POPULATION GROWTH AND CONTROL

Development and Control over Population

The relationship between population and development was explained by the Population Research Office of the Princeton University in the 1940s on the basis that development reduces fertility rate. Now it is said that development lowers the death rate faster than the birth rate resulting in population growth. However, birth rates too inevitably fall, perhaps after a time, causing population growth rates to slow down once again. But the theory does not answer the crucial question as to when decline in birth rates would set in as development progresses. It also does not tell us the level to which fertility would decline and the time-span over which the decline would occur. The questions of threshold and speed of fertility declines inevitably bring up the question of identification of factors which cause fertility declines. For estimating the threshold of demographic transition, a United Nations study examined 12 variables including per capita income, urnbanisation, female literacy, etc. The results proved futile.

Theory of Economy of Households

According to this theoretical approach, a household weighs the cost of a large family with its benefits. As long as the cost of rearing children remains low, compared to the benefits they bring in terms of additional income, birth rates would remain high. The transition would occur when as a result of socio-economic changes like urbanisation, compulsory schooling, market penetration, etc., the cost of bringing up children becomes higher than the benefits. John Caldwell's Theory of Fertility Decline (1982) also postulated that fertility declines begin when there is a reversal of net flow of resources towards children rather than parents and this reversal is, in turn, associated with broader socio-economic changes.

Theory of Diffusion of Ideas Regarding Access to Contraception

The above theory which bases itself on economic and social determinants of fertility has been powerfully challenged by another theory which stresses the role of diffusion of ideas regarding fertility control and access to contraception. Ansley Coale (1973) supported this theory through his study of fall in fertility rate in Europe between 1850 and 1930. Availability of contraceptives reduces fertility rate and vice versa.

Studies in India have supported all these theories and pointed out other factors too which affect the course of fertility, like higher age at marriage, or what act as impediments in the use of contraception like female literacy, importance of sons, poverty, female participation in economic activities, and so on. Some empirical studies in this context have also been conducted with Indian data by K.G. Jolly, Anirudh Jain, etc. Jolly (1986) found positive relationship between contraceptive prevalence rate and level of urbanisation, female literacy, female participation in economic activities and negatively related to the degree of economic inequality and per cent of non-Hindu population. Jain (1985), working with inter-state data, found infant mortality rate as most important variable while factors like female literacy, urbanisation, etc., were indirectly related. Another study has found female literacy the most important factor in contraceptive prevalence rate (see Pranab Banerji, 1992:250-256).

POPULATION POLICY

'Population policy' in its narrower sense, according to the UNEP (1973:632) is "an effort to affect the size, structure and distribution or characteristics of population". In its broader range, it includes "efforts to regulate economic and social conditions which are likely to have demographic consequences". Nortman (1975:20) describes the narrower meaning as 'explicit policy' which affects directly the population characteristics, and the broader meaning as 'implicit policy' which affects the characteristics indirectly, sometimes without any explicit intention.

Two types of population policies have been suggested: (a) the antenatal policy which aims at discouraging the growth of population, and (b) the distributional policy which deals with distributional imbalances of population. The National Academy of Sciences has discerned population policy as one (a) which influences the demographic processes according to a pre-set objective (for example, encouraging people to move from urban to suburban areas), and (b) which will cope with the demands created by the demographic processes (for example, providing basic facilities to people in suburban areas).

The population policy of a developing country like India has to aim at: (i) decreasing birth rate, (ii) limiting the number of children in family to two, (iii) decreasing mortality, (iv) creating awareness among the masses regarding the consequences of galloping population, (v) procuring necessary contraceptives, (vi) enacting laws like legalising abortion, and (vii) giving incentives as well as disincentives. On the other hand, it also has to aim at: (a) checking concentration of people in congested areas, (b) providing necessary public services for effective settlement in new areas, and (c) relocation of offices to less populated areas.

Once the need for population control is realised, policy has to be framed by appointing various committees and commissions for studying and advising and consulting experts. It has then to be implemented through various programmes and also evaluated from time to time.

India's population policy is the direct result of: (a) the total size of the population, (b) a high growth rate, and (c) the problem of uneven distribution in rural and urban areas. Since our policy needs to aim at 'enhancing the quality of life', and 'increasing individual happiness', it has to act as a means to attaining a broader objective of achieving individual fulfilment and social progress. Initially, the policy framed in 1952 was adhoc in nature, flexible, and based on a trial and error approach. Gradually, it was replaced by more scientific planning.

The sub-committee on population appointed in 1940 under the chairmanship of Radha Kamal Mukherjee by the National Planning Committee (appointed by Indian National Congress in 1938) laid emphasis on self-control, spreading knowledge of cheap and safe methods of birth control and establishing birth control clinics. It also recommended raising the marriage age, discouragement of polygamy, and an eugenic programme of sterilising persons suffering from transmissible diseases. The Bhore Committee of 1943 appointed by the government criticised self-control approach and advocated 'deliberate limitation of families'.

After independence, a Population Policy Committee was created in 1952 and a Family Planning Research and Programmes Committee in 1953. A Central Family Planning Board was created in 1956 which emphasised sterilisation. During the 1960s, a more vigorous family planning programme was advocated for stablising the growth of population over a reasonable period. While earlier, it was assumed by the government that the family planning programme had created enough motivation among the people and the government was only to provide facilities for contraception, it was later realised that people needed motivation and masses had to be educated.

In April 1976, the Minsiter of Health and Family Planning, Karan Singh, presented before the parliament the National Population Policy framed after prolonged and intensive consultations with governmental and non-official organisations, academic institutions, as well as eminent demographers and economists. This policy covered a wide spectrum of programmes including raising the statutory age of marriage, introducing fiscal incentives to states which perform well in the field of family planning, paying special attention to improving female literacy, public education through all available media (radio, television, press, films), introducing direct monetary incentives for adoption of vasectomy and tubectomy operations, and a new thrust towards research in reproductive biology and contraception. Though this policy was endorsed by the parliament, it was planned at a time when the Emergency was in operation. There were so many excesses in the sterilisation campaign under the leadership of Sanjay Gandhi, the president of Indian Youth Congress, that it came to be regarded with hostility by people. The programme was so overzealously and insensitively implemented in some of the North Indian states that during the election in 1977 after the Emergency, these excesses became an important election issue and the Congress lost the elections at the Centre. When in 1980, Indira Gandhi returned to power, she became extremely cautious and unenthusiastic about reviving her commitment to the family planning programmes. Since then the policy of almost all governments in the states and at the centre has been so lopsided that the growth rate of population which was expected to have fallen below the 2 per cent mark, is still around 2.35 per cent.

The Working Group on Population Policy in 1979 recommended adoption of a long-term demographic goal of reducing the Net Reproductive Rate to 1. The implications of this long-term goal were spelt out as follows: (1) the average size of the family would be reduced from 4.3 children to 2.3 children, (2) the birth rate per 1,000 population would be reduced from 33 to 21, (3) The death rate per 1,000 population would be reduced from 14 to 9 and the infant mortality rate from 129 to 60, (4) As against 22 per cent of eligible couples protected with family planning, 60 per cent would be protected, and (5) the population of India will stabilise at 1,200 crore by the year 2050 A.D.

In 1993, the Swaminathan Committee was appointed for proposing a National Population Policy which submitted a policy draft report in May 1994.

FAMILY PLANNING

India was the first country to evolve a government-backed family planning programme in the 1950s when the rest of the world was not aware of the problem. Today, after 49 years, India is trailing behind in population control. During the notorious Emergency regime between 1975 and 1977, the political leaders, the government officials and policemen shouted themselves hoarse advocating sterlisation. They devised ambitious programmes and carried them out against popular wishes, and even used such harsh and coercive methods for sterilisation that today one is reluctant to talk of family planning to the populace. The concerned officials in family welfare/planning departments have been scared away from it. The experts have jettisoned hopes of reaching targets. In fact, for all practical purposes, the country is without an effective programme or an effective target. Political parties studiously skirt the subject, and election campaigns are conducted without a word about it. What was once a highly dramatic political issue has suddenly become taboo.

In 1977, 'family planning' was rechristened 'family welfare', and tasks beyond its competence embracing all aspects of family welfare, including improvement of women's educational level, were included in it. In its family planning awareness drive, the Government of India adopted the UNEP guideline of delaying the first child and spacing the subsequent birth(s).

The methods in family planning are: sterlisation, loop, pill, withdrawal, rhythm, sheath, and diaphragm. The condom and the pill seem most popular among the high socio-economic groups; so are the withdrawal method and the condoms among the middle socio-economic groups and sterilisation is preferred by people belonging to the low social strata. Operations for family planning are not very popular among the socially well-placed, as this group is exposed to other methods of birth control. A good number of women use more than one method, depending on circumstances, availability and mood of the moment.

Measures Adopted

Officially mobilised in 1951, about 150 family planning clinics were established during the First Five Year Plan period (1951-56). Since then, a network of Community Health Centres (CHCs), Primary Health Centres (PHCs) and Sub-Centres (SCs) have been created for implementing family planning programme through state governments with a hundred per cent assistance. A large number of centres and sub-centres are created in rural areas in each Five Year Plan. In 1998 there were about 1.5 lakh SCs, 25,000 PHCs and 2500 CHCs in the country.

Of the various methods of family planning, the government till recently depended more on the 'camp approach' which relied implicitly on the district authorities applying pressure on their officials to intensify the sterilisation campaign (mostly male sterilisation). The government set targets for different states and districts and adopted persuasive, monetary, as well as coercive measures to achieve targets. The highest rate of target achievement (200%) was in 1976-77, while the achievement rate of sterilisation targets in different years has normally varied between 40 per cent and 65 per cent. The highest rate of achievement in 1976-77 has been described as 'Sanjay effect' which was the result of coercion, cruelty, corruption, and inflated achievement figures. The worst victims of cruelty and brutality were the Harijans, peons, clerical staff, school teachers, innocent rural people, hospital patients, jail inmates and pavement-dwellers. This brutality through family planning (sterilisation) method ultimately led to the fall of the government in 1977.

The Primary Health Centres in villages, engaged in family planning programmes, perform two specific functions: providing services to people and disseminating information about these services in an effective manner in order to motivate people to accept family planning. Nearly half a million medical and para-medical persons are engaged in the programme, besides half a million part-time village health guides.

Progress Achieved

After the First Five Year Plan, the following Five Year Plans gave increasing priority to the programme but it was only in 1968-69 that the decline in the birth rate became noticeable. The birth rate which stood at 41.7 per thousand in 1961 came down to 28.7 in 1994 and 25.2 in 1995. Between 1956 and 1996, about 13 crore births—equal to the current population of Japan—were averted (*The Hindustan Times*, February 11, 1997).

The achievement of the targets has not been disastrous in all fields though the number of sterilisations has fallen. According to the National Family Health Survey (NFHS, 1992-93) which was launched by the Minsitry of Health and Family Welfare, only 6 per cent of Indian women between the ages of 13 and 49 years use any modern contraceptive. Yet another report says that half of the couples do not practise family planning though over 90 per cent are aware of it (*The Hindustan Times*, February 11, 1997). The use of condom in India is as insignificant as a mere six per couple per year. The data dished out by the survey about sterilisation rate (30%)—the mainstay of the family planning programme's achievement—is unreliable as most of the sterilisations are undertaken only after having had three or more children. The total fertility rate (TFR) in India is still as high as 3.5 and it is well known that bringing down TFR from 3 to 2.1 is a real difficult task and that phase has not even begun in India (Sahay, 1997). Today, the effort has altogether slackened to the extent that Ashish Bose, a noted demographer of our country, in his talk on 'Indian Population in the 1990s' on February 8, 1991 at Delhi said that "family planning programme has completely failed in the country and entirely a new approach is needed for its success".

The progress in containing population growth has been extremely slow as is evident when we compare it with China which has avoided the birth of 200 million children since 1970 through a vigorous family planning programme and brought the fertility rate down to 2.5 from 5.82 among eligible mothers (the average number of children a woman will have during her child bearing years of 15 to 49) (*The Hindustan Times*, July 11, 1994). China adopted the norm of one child per couple in the urban centres and a ceiling of two children per couple in the rural areas, with several incentives for the planned child as also the parents. Those who violated these norms were penalised. The planned child was given special allowances till the age of 14 for education and upbringing, and the couple was provided with land for building a house or for farm machinery. A major component of the programme in China is encouraging late marriage and late childbirth.

The available facts pertaining to reproductive health in India (*Outlook*, August 21, 1996:58) point out that:

- Of the total conceptions that take place annually, about 78 per cent are unplanned and about 25 per cent are definitely unwanted.About 30 million women in India desire better family planning services since they are not satisfied with the available facilities/programmes.
- Out of about 11 million abortions every year, 69 per cent are induced and 31 per cent are spontaneous.
- Over one lakh women die every year during pregnancy and childbirth.
- About three-fourth babies are delivered at home and only one-third deliveries are assisted by a doctor, a nurse or a midwife.
- One in every 13 children dies within the first year of life and one in every nine dies before reaching the age of five. Infant mortality is as high as 52 per cent in rural areas.

Attitudes Towards Family Planning

The idea of family planning has been successfully brought to the notice of an average Indian woman. The attitude of a woman towards family planning is influenced by her education, age, income background, husband's occupation, and her (working) status among other factors. In terms of age, it has been found that the percentage of women approving family planning decreases as the age group increases. But the acceptance is about two-third even among the older age groups. This clearly shows that the great majority of Indian women approve of family planning, irrespective of age.

In a survey conducted in Rajasthan in 1988 by Kothari and Gulati (1989:71), it was found that out of total persons studied, 88.1 per cent were in favour of family planning and 11.9 per cent were against it. Kothari (1994) also noted that according to the findings of the National Family Welfare Survey, conducted in Rajasthan in 1993, of the women married in the 13-49 years age group, 90 per cent knew some method of family planning, and 76.2 per cent were aware of some sources of getting the required contraceptives, though only 31.8 per cent were actually using the contraceptives.

A survey was conducted on attitude towards family planning in Velore city of Tamil Nadu and its surrounding villages by Rao and Inbaraj. In all, 2,426 persons were interviewed with the intention of finding out whether they considered it within the power of the couple to control the number of children. Around 37 per cent replied in the affirmative and 41 per cent replied in the negative (*The Journal of Family Welfare*, 2-22). Of those 899 persons who considered it possible, 46.6 per cent considered it possible through family planning measures, 37.5 per cent through control on self, while 15.9 per cent did not point to any specific method. When they were asked whether they themselves were in favour of family planning, 64.6 per cent said 'Yes' and 25.4 per cent said 'No'. The reasons given for hostility to family planning measures were: it was harmful to women, it went against family economy, it was against God's will, and it constituted unnatural behaviour. However, since seven out of every ten persons were in favour of family planning, it points to the fact that people today have ceased to be very traditional in their beliefs and values.

A study made by the National Institute of Community Development covering 365 villages in 16 states and 43 districts and 7,224 respondents also revealed that 51.6 per cent were in favour of family planning and 23.7 per cent were against it.

Since illiteracy is found more among the poorer section of our society, it is seen that women with low education in the lower strata are more reluctant to accept family planning methods. Their contention is that since they have no money to fall back upon, their only hope of survival is their children's income. An average poor Indian couple is not satisfied with fewer than two or three children. Time and again, studies in various parts of the country have revealed this fact. About a decade ago, a large-scale survey covering some 32,000 respondents sponsored by the Ministry of Health and Family Welfare came to the conclusion that most couples wanted not only three or more children but they also wanted that two of them should be sons (*The Hindustan Times*, November 5, 1987).

A survey was conducted in 1991 on 'Socialisation of Indian Youth About Population' by the Family Planning Foundation, Delhi in collaboration with Operation Research Group, Delhi. This survey studied the attitudes of 17,185 male and female children selected from 251 schools from urban and rural areas of 22 districts of Uttar Pradesh, Rajasthan, Haryana and Delhi. A large number of the respondents were in favour of two-children family. While about 90 per cent subjects preferred one son and one daughter, 73 per cent were not very keen about giving undue importance to the sex of the children. A majority of the respondents did not consider the age of marriage of both boys and girls below 22 years as the correct marriage age. A good number of them had slight knowledge of contraceptives but they were not very well informed about the subject. A large number had acquired this knowledge from watching the TV (*The Hindustan Times*, March 15, 1992).

A survey was conducted by Population Research Centre of Udaipur University in Rajasthan in 1992 in which 5,211 women (1,019 from urban areas and 4,192 from rural areas) from 27 districts in 13-49 years age group were interviewed. The survey revealed that among the currently married women (i.e., 5058), 99 per cent in urban areas and 84 per cent in rural areas had knowledge of at least one modern method of family planning (i.e., sterilisation, condom, pill, IUD and injection) as different from the traditional method of periodic abstinence, withdrawal, etc.) (*Ibid*:82). As regards their husbands, amongst 2,433 rural husbands, 57.1 per cent approved family planning, 16.8 per cent disapproved it, and 26.1 per cent were unsure. Amongst urban husbands, 74.9 per cent approved it, 9.4 per cent disapproved it, and 15.7 per cent were unsure.

Of the women studied, 27.7 per cent (women or wives of sterilised men) had undergone sterilisation. The reasons given by 2035 (39%) women for not using any method of family planning were (Ibid: 103): wanted children (39.7%), wanted son or daughter (22.9%), worry about the side-effects (1.3%), lack of knowledge (3.7%), fear of sterilisation (4.3%), against religion (1.4%), opposed to family planning (0.8%), opposition by husband (3.7%) or in-laws (0.7%), health did not permit (2%), inconvenient (0.4%) and menopausal (10.7%).

Out of 3,027 women (2,433 rural and 594 urban) interviewed (i.e., excluding those who either themselves or their husbands were sterilised), 75.5 per cent were in favour of family planning, while 23.4 per cent did not express specific attitude (*Ibid*:110). Of these, 50.5 per cent currently married women were actually using some contraceptive method (*Ibid*:86).

Evaluation of the Programme

Broadly speaking, bureaucrats are hoodwinking people in India by arguing that since our crude birth rate (CBR) has declined from 42 per thousand in 1960 to 25 per thousand in 1996, family planning has been quite successful. But this claim is fallacious. It is not enough for a developing country that its CBR is declining. What is important and critical is the rate of decline. Thailand brought down its CBR from 44 per 1,000 in 1960 to 17 per 1,000 in 1996, whereas in India the CBR has declined from 42 to 25 in the same period. Thailand has achieved a contraceptive prevalence rate (CPR) of over 75 per cent whereas it is only 43 per cent in India, and here again most of the family planning programme (30% out of 43% of our CPR) is undertaken only after having three or more children. Only 6 per cent of Indian women in the age group of 13-49 years use any modern contraceptive.

Population control is a hundred per cent centrally sponsored programme since its inception in 1951. Expenditure on population control has been increasing over the years. From a budget of Rs. 14 lakh during the First Plan period (1951-56), it increased to Rs. 6,500 crore in the Eighth Plan period (1992-97). In terms of percentage, however, this allocation is only 1.5 per cent of the total public sector outplay. The question is: Why should population control be the sole responsibility of the central government? Why should states not share the expenditure? Will they not benefit from control over population growth? However, states spend more money on programmes like elementary education, health centres, etc., which indirectly contribute to checking population growth. But how do states actually spend money even on these schemes (of health and education, etc.)? An illustration will help us understand it. A sub-health centre in a village is supposed to have male (MPW-M) as well as female workers (MPW-F or ANM). Expenditure on the salary of ANMs is met out of the central government's grant under the family welfare programme, whereas on the male workers, it is met by the state governments from their health budgets. As a result, states fill up all posts of female health workers (ANMs) but keep all posts of male health workers vacant on the pretext of economy measures. For example, Uttar Pradesh and Assam do not have even a single post of male worker though as per norms, Uttar Pradesh should have 20,000 male workers and Assam 5,000 male workers. Not even a single post of ANM is vacant in these two states (*The Hindustan Times*, February 27, 1996). While PHCs and CHCs in the rural areas are supposed to be run from the state budget, they are actually run out of a grant of about Rs. 300 crore from the central government under the Family Welfare Centres Programme. Why should the central government not revamp and revitalise the family planning programme with an active partnership of financial commitment of the state governments on equal cost-sharing basis? It is time that states changed their attitude from 'get as much as you can' to 'do as much as you can', if family planning programme is really to be made a success.

Family planning in India has come to a standstill. In fact, the programme is moving backward as today (in 1999) we are producing 52 children every minute in comparison to 21 children per minute in 1971 and eight children per minute in 1941. This stagnation is bound to wipe out all the effort that has been made since 1952. While it is true that the couple protection percentage has gone up steadily from 10.4 in 1971 to 43.96 in 1995, it should be asked: who are these couples who are supposed to have obtained protection? It is none other than those who have had three or more children and who have already done their part of the damage to the two-children family norm.

The question that is being asked is: If it took 28 years for the country's birth rate to dip by 11.6 points (from 36.8 in 1970 to 25.2 in 1998), how many years will it take to bring about a drop of 7.7 points so as to realise the birth rate target of 21 per thousand set for the turn of the century?

The official calculations of the Health Ministry point out that it is the four larger states of Uttar Pradesh, Bihar, Madhya Pradesh, and Rajasthan with high fertility levels which have to bear the cross. These four states together hold 40 per cent of the country's population. The birth rate in these states was much above the national average of 25.2 per thousand population for 1995 (the birth rate was 35.4 in Uttar Pradesh, 32.8 in Madhya Pradesh, 33.7 in Rajasthan and 32.5 in Bihar) (*Outlook*, August 21, 1996:56). While the growth rate of population in these four states is 23.1 per thousand (in 1995), the growth rate in four states of Andhra Pradesh, Tamil Nadu, Kerala and Karnataka in South India is only 13.6. Surprisingly, the targets of sterilisations set for these four states are much lower than what their population size should warrant. Unless these four states improve their performance level, containing population may continue to remain a big problem for the country.

Various studies have highlighted the fact that the services of Primary Health Centres (PHCs) in the rural areas are grossly underutilised. In states like Uttar Pradesh, Bihar, Rajasthan and Madhya Pradesh, where the need is more pronounced, utilisation is less than 15 per cent. Countless studies have pointed out that in villages only the media which answers people's questions instantaneously can help in family planning. The Block Extension and the Health Assistants have been assigned only this role. But significantly, interpersonal communication is very insignificant.

What should be our objectives and methods of family planning propoganda? One important suggestion made is that our slogans should be: 'Third child should not be born and no child after 35 years of age'. These are two options which are entirely within the control of the couple. This type of propoganda linked with improving the standard of living, provision of better education, and health guarantee of (two) children and improved services for the health of women/mothers will put the couples in a frame of mind where they would themselves be anxious to work for this objective. Money incentives cannot be a motivating factor. The money may be incentive for the campaigner to motivate the couple but not for the person undergoing sterilisation.

Some scholars present optimistic blueprints for checking population explosion in the coming years. One point usually made is that our country has many untapped resources which, if properly developed, will sustain even three times the present population. The second point urged is that industrial growth, economic development and increase in exports will take care of poverty, unemployment and the increasing population.

Both these views are rather naive and unsound. What is useful and important for any country is the goods and services actually available and not likely to be available to meet the needs of the population. With the present political instability in the country both at the centre and in the states, with the political parties laying focus on achieving and retaining power rather than on 'community development', and with increasing casteism, parochialism, regionalism, and linguism, how can we expect our power elite to take interest in development and modernisation and/or tapping the untapped resources?

Swaminathan Committee

The policy draft submitted by the Swaminathan Committee suggested a holistic approach to health and some structural changes to implement the policy. The important measures suggested by this Committee were: (1) Stabilising population by achieving a total fertility rate of 2.1 by 2010 A.D. (2) Implementing a speedy and effective minimum needs programme. (3) Replacing the present vertically structured family welfare programme with decentralised, democratic planning through panchayats, *nagar palikas* and state legislatures. (4) Abandoning the idea of fixing targets for the use of specific contraceptive methods by the central and state governments, except the goal of achieving the national average of fertility rate. (6) Discontinuing incentives in cash or kind to contraceptive users and motivators. Instead, a Population and Social Development Fund may be set up out of the funds available from government and international donor agencies. This fund will be utilised for filling the gaps in the effective implementation of the village, town, district and state level socio-demographic charters. (7) Appointing a State Population and Social Development Commission to plan, implement and monitor the population policy of the country. The sub-committees of PSDC will also be set up at the state, district and panchayat levels comprising elected representatives of people from different political parties, professionals, representatives of NGOs and womens' and youths' organisations. (8) Sadly, Family Planning has become a responsibility of women alone. As such, there is a clear need for checking this trend of putting the entire responsibility for family limitation on women.

Some socio-economic and medical goals set by the Committee in the field of population welfare for forming a necessary part of the national population policy were: (i) reducing the incidence of marriage of girls below the age of 18 years to zero; (ii) increasing the percentage of deliveries conducted by trained personnel to 100 per cent; (iii) reducing the infant and maternal mortality rates; (iv) universal immunisation of children against tuberculosis, polio, diptheria, whooping cough, tetanus and measles; (v) provision for primary health care for all; (vi) providing information to individuals on birth limitation methods so that they have the fullest choice in planning their families; (vii) making available and accessible quality contraceptive services on a universal basis; and (vii) universalisation of primary education.

However, many experts have criticised the recommendations of this committee and have suggested that they should be rejected outright. Their main arguments are: (1) The report lacks in-depth analysis, justification and urgency. The approach suggested is purely managerial and the strategies pointed out are at best a reiteration of the failed aphorism that 'development is the best contraception'. (2) Minimum needs have no relationship with population control. How could all the goals, which could not be achieved in the past over four decades in spite of nine Five Year Plans and thirteen general elections with all the political promises, be achieved by 2010 A.D. and more so when our population has already crossed the 100 crore (in 1999) mark with about 32 crore still below the poverty line? (3) A politically-oriented population commission will be ineffective. (4) The committee has not recommended any disincentive for those who violated family planning norms. The Karunakaran Committee had proposed the introduction of disincentives—even if unpopular—to make family planning programmes more effective and fast-acting. One such programme was introduced by the Government of Rajasthan according to which no individual could contest any election if he had more than three children. However, this programme exists only on paper. It is yet to be put in practice. (5) The report does not spell out why we failed in controlling our rapid population growth, though population programmes have been going on in India uninterrupted since 1951. Is this failure because of the drawbacks in the administrative set up or because of wrong policies or faulty or tardy implementation? This is the fundamental issue which is ignored by the report. Without this analysis, the structural changes as proposed in the report may be quite irrelevant. (6) The biggest hurdle in the success of population control in India is political apathy, but the Committee did not give any importance to this aspect. Political leaders have to be bold regarding enacting legislative measures which may focus on the urgency of the issue. Denying promotions, debarring from holding any elected office, not giving reservation benefits, refusing bank loans, etc., to those who do not observe small family norm of two children could be some of the disincentives brought about through legislation.

MEASURES SUGGESTED TO CONTROL POPULATION EXPLOSION

The continuing population explosion in our country calls for some soul searching. The government is aware of the magnitude of the problem and considers the alarming population growth as the biggest challenge facing the nation as well as the government. But the 1976-77 experience of the government in adopting serious measures to achieve the set targets in the field of family planning has made all the following governments very cautious. There is, however, still time to act. The following programmes may be suggested to check population growth:

Incentives vs Disincentives

Some of the incentives required to induce couples to adhere to a two-child family norm have been identified as: cash awards, promotion/increment in pay and special allowances, extension of retirement age, educational allowance for two children, preferential treatment in housing loans, purchase of transport, etc., and free medical treatment/reimbursement of medical expenses up to two children. The denial of these incentives to those who transgress the two-child family norm would amount to disincentives. An important question has now been raised by some thinkers pertaining to population policy—that of cooperation vs coercion, or incentives vs disincentives, or Kerala model vs Chinese model? There are some thinkers who support cooperation while there are others who support coercion. An Indian professor (Amartya Sen, Nobel Laureate now settled in the USA) in a prestigious JRD Tata Memorial Lecture in Delhi in August 1995 on 'Population Stabilisation Programme' favoured 'cooperation' approach and denounced the use of 'coercion' to bring down the lines of two famous theories of Condorcet (of France) and Malthus (of Britain). He supported Condorcet's approach to the problem of population which talked of the emergence of new norms of small family size based on 'the progress of reason'. Condorcet believed that female education would lead people to choose voluntarily smaller families and lower fertility rates. Malthus, however, was sceptical about this view of 'voluntary acceptance of family planning'. In his opinion 'positive checks' such as economic penury or rise in mortality rate would eventually coerce people to reduce population growth rate. Sen described Condorcet's path of cooperation as unequivocally right and Malthus' path of coercion as undesirable and even counter-productive in checking population growth. He gave the example of Kerala in support of his viewpoint (same argument is given also in his book *India: Economic Development and Social Opportunity*) and developed a hypothesis called 'Kerala hypothesis of demographic transition'. In this hypothesis, increase in literacy and better primary health care are described as two important factors in population control. But while supporting his hypothesis, Sen it seems, has ignored some figures pertaining to Kerala. During 1941-1971, there was an increase in the literacy rate in Kerala yet the population growth rate (PGR) also increased during this period (from 2.08% to 2.3% per year). It was only in 1971-81 and 1981-91 decades that the state's PGR registered a decline. How can Kerala hypothesis, therefore, be accepted as valid? Yet another lacuna in Kerala hypothesis is that while according to the 1991 census report, Kerala's total literacy was 94 per cent and female literacy was 90 per cent, yet in spite of this 'near total literacy', the population growth rate of Muslims (who constitute one-fourth of Kerala's population) is as high as 2.3 per cent per year which is more than even the national PGR of 2.11 per cent per annum and almost double the PGR of Hindus in Kerala itself. Ignoring such facts only renders the hypothesis untenable.

Opposed to the 'Kerala model' is the 'Chinese model' of coercion in population control. Looking at the near catastrophic state of our population scenario, thinkers support this 'coercive model' as the only effective solution of the population problem. These thinkers also point out the vested political interests that are promoting population growth rates of various vote banks to the detriment of the nation. Some thinkers, however, talk of a combination of cooperation and coercion or incentives and disincentives to check India's population growth, but the nature of disincentives has not been identified so far. Would denying the 'benefit of reservation' to people with more than two children prove a disincentive? Can denying promotion or admission or voting right or right to contest election be disincentives? Will such denials not be the violations of fundamental rights? Laying down mechanisms to implement disincentives in the prevailing socio-political situation in India, particularly when thirteen to twenty political parties with different ideologies on 'social justice and reservation issue' join together to form a coalition government at the centre, will not be easy.

Division into Zones and Regions

A study conducted in February 1990 by two population experts of the Operation Research Group at Baroda has shown how the problem could be tackled. On the basis of the fertility pattern, they have divided the country's 350 districts into 16 zones and four regions. They have identified districts and zones which reflect the positive impact of family planning on fertility rates, the areas where fertility rates have remained low despite hardly any family planning efforts, and those regions which are the hard core areas where the maximum effort is needed. The 1990 survey had pointed out that the areas of high fertility are Arunachal Pradesh, Bihar, Haryana, Madhya Pradesh, Uttar Pradesh, and Rajasthan (birth rate varying between 34% and 37.7% in 1990 and between 32% and 35% in 1995). This region-wise approach is expected to help in correcting the lacuna in the implementation of the family planning programme.

Searching for New Contraceptives

The search for a new, inexpensive, easy-to-use and harmless contraceptive has not met with dramatic success so far. Though pills have come to be accepted in a big way and this method is catching on in Haryana, Madhya Pradesh, Punjab, West Bengal, Gujarat and Orissa, it is necessary that Indian herbs also be thoroughly investigated for their medicinal effects. Pursuing vigorous investigation of the health status and dietary habits of some of the tribals in Andaman and Nicobar Islands, among some of whom fertility rate is found to be extremely low, might provide the needed solution. It may be said that scientists and pharmaceutical companies do not appear to be much interested to make a breakthrough in contraceptive technology. We are still dependent very largely on condoms and operative techniques when our need is non-invasive techniques like an anti-pregnancy vaccine or a pill, which do not impinge physically and psychologically upon the human anatomy.

Increase in Marriage Age

There is a direct relationship between age of marriage, size of family and attitude towards family planning. A study in Kerala revealed that the average age of marriage went up in mid-1970s. In 1969, the number of married women in the age group 15-19 years was 30 per cent whereas in 1974 it dropped to 14 per cent. For those in the 20-24 age group, the decline was from 73 per cent in 1969 to 56 per cent in 1974 (*India Today*, March 1-15, 1980). Sociologically, this is an important reason for the dramatic decline in birth rate in Kerala. Raising the marriage age is, thus, bound to reduce the family size in other states too. This calls for serious and whole-hearted efforts for creating the necessary public awareness.

Educating Females

Education is the most important factor in reducing fertility rate. It has direct, indirect as well as joint effects. Direct effect is in changing attitudes and beliefs towards a small family. Indirect effect is in following respects: (i) it delays entry into marriage, (ii) it facilitates acquisition of information related to family planning, (iii) it enhances exposure to family planning propoganda, (iv) it creates aspiration for upward social mobility, (v) it enhances possibilities of outdoor female employment, (vi) it reduces the perceived economic utility of children, (vii) it helps husband and wife to accept birth control measures, (viii) it reduces infant mortality, and (ix) it increases rationality. The joint effects (of education) are industrialisation, urbanisation and modernisation. Modernisation influences fertility jointly with education.

J.C. Pant (*IJPA*, July-September, 1992, 333-340) studied 486 rural and urban families of Punjab from April 1985 to June 1986 to analyse relationship between level of education and number of children in family. He found that in the case of illiterate women, the average number of children in rural, urban and total sample were 3.61, 3.30 and 3.52 respectively; in the case of women educated from first to eighth class were 2.27, 3.30 and 2.50 respectively; for women educated from ninth to eleventh class were 2.42, 2.48 and 2.45 respectively; for women educated from matric to intermediate class were 1.87, 1.53 and 1.63 respectively; and for women who were graduates were 1.57, 1.62 and 1.60 respectively (*Ibid*: 338). This shows that fertility is inversely related to the levels of education, and that graduate and postgraduate women follow the small family norm.

Economic Development

Economic development may prove to be the best contraceptive. We have to go for quick population control at any cost on sheer economic principles of supply and demand. To balance any economic equation, we can either increase the supply which depends on both financial and material resources, or reduce the demand which depends on the number of people asking for varied services and commodities. For example, on the supply side, in housing alone, an annual outlay of Rs.3,000 crore would be required to build three million houses for the 17 million people added to country's population every year, assuming that we require only Rs. 10,000 to build one small house. But if we tackle the same problem from the demand side and prevent the annual addition of 17 million to the population through an effective population control strategy, the demand for three million houses or Rs. 3,000 crore required per year for constructing the houses will disappear (Ahluwalia, 1987). Thus, preventing the demand is as good as working for the supply. This is balancing the supply and demand at no cost. And it is the no-cost solution we are looking for. What applies to housing also holds good for education, jobs, transport and health sectors. Tackling each problem from the demand side will have an enormous pay off.

This approach has another important dimension. If we tackle the problem from the supply side, it will increase the demand *per se* in other sectors. For example, if we increase the number of houses, it would increase demand for cement, bricks, wood material and electrical goods. But if we approach the problem from the demand side and reduce the number of houses needed, the pressure in all sectors will be relieved. With 52 births every minute or about 17 million births every year, the demand for money and materials in sectors like education, transport and welfare, will so enormously increase that in ten years' time the situation will have crossed the point of no return and incalculable and irretrievable damage will have been done to the country and its economy.

The declared core theme of the Third International Conference on Population and Development held at Cairo from 5-13 September, 1994 was linkage between population issues, economic growth and sustainable development. However, for six out of ten days, the Conference was bogged down on the question of the legitimacy and efficacy of 'abortion' as a tool of population control. There was no discussion or debate on such vital issues as poverty eradication, illiteracy, employment, rural uplift, or free market access to Third World exports. In the first two International Conferences on Population held in 1974 and 1984, it was argued that large families were the result of poverty rather than the cause of it. The stress was, therefore, on eliminating poverty. Eliminate poverty and you eliminate the need for large families. However, the Third Conference did not give much importance to this issue. The experience of the developed countries has been that higher family incomes and improved services meant that fewer children were born. They, therefore, suggest that Third World also should be allowed to follow the same path. The Brand Report while commending an expanded family planning programme also noted that family planning programmes are effective only when they go hand in hand with economic and social progress. It is thus held that development alone will provide the most propitious environment for stabilising the country's population.

While the linkage between population and development is well taken, the nature or mode of 'development' has itself been a somewhat debatable question. There are leading Third World analysts who contend that 'development' (through high technology, mass production, and induced consumerism) as projected by the affluent nations and sold to the Third World tends to aggravate the population problem. Hence, to continue to talk and apply this technology indicates how little people have thought about this problem. What this viewpoint implies is that modern technology generates a largely profit-motivated elite in an industry which is concerned only with its own interests and is indifferent to the poverty and misery of workers. The result is an economic and demographic scenario that is becoming explosive both at the top (due to growing wealth) and at the bottom (due to increasing poverty of the masses). Thus, the feeling is that population problem should not be viewed out of social context. Development which aims at distribution and equality alone can remove poverty and contain population growth.

Role of NGOs

Success of any programme depends on its acceptance by people. Unless the community is fully involved in the programme and it considers it to be its own programme, it may not be possible to achieve the desired results. This can be achieved in a better way by the non-government organisations as these have very intimate relations with people. Their role in removing deep-rooted beliefs favouring large families and male children, improving female literacy, raising age at marriage of girls, essential new-born care, birth spacing, etc., can be very significant. Such organisations not only have the capacity to reach the remote areas but their activities are cost-effective also. The Department of Family Welfare has launched several schemes in the last five to six years to ensure better participation of the NGOs in the family welfare programme. Some of these schemes are: (1) Helping NGOs to the extent of 90 per cent of the cost of the project on promotion of small family norm and population control schemes. (2) Wide publicity of the government for informing voluntary organisations to come forward to undertake these schemes. (3) Holding of a number of regional conferences in last four to five years to increase the involvement of the NGOs. (4) Recognising six larger organisations (in Delhi, Mumbai, Calcutta, Chennai and Lucknow) as Mother Units for identifying small NGOs in their areas and giving them grants for approval schemes. (5) Setting up State Standing Committees on Voluntary Action set up under the chairmanship of the Family Welfare Secretary with power to sanction up to Rs. 10 lakh per project. (6) Asking states to identify one institution in the NGO sector for the purpose of providing training to health workers. (7) Arranging study tours for NGOs from states with poor community participation to better performing states. The NGOs can perform the following functions: (1) make advice and services more easily accessible particularly in under-served areas; (2) coordinate with hospitals and health guides; (3) train functionaries, particularly low-level functionaries; (4) help in continuous supply of contraceptives; (5) provide follow-up services to the acceptors; and (6) contribute to making educational activities more effective.

Why the NGOs have not proved to be effective in family planning programme is due to following reasons: (1) Many NGOs are not familiar with government grant-in-aid schemes. (2) The application procedure for grants is very lengthy and cumbersome. (3) NGOs working in small towns have low accessibility to granting agencies. (4) Government officers' attitude to NGOs is non-supportive. (5) NGOs are short of funds and trainer manpower.

Conclusion

It may be concluded that earlier we committed the mistake of believing that our rising population was an asset and now we are making the blunder of thinking that India's rapid population growth will be checked through the process of development, i.e., literacy, healthcare, employment, etc. If the nation wants to save itself from an increase of 1.7 crore people per year, the only way left is to administer a bitter dose of disincentives and compulsory family planning. This requires a suitable population policy. The new economic policy has no chance of succeeding unless it is supplemented with a compatible population policy.

The population policy of our government should aim not only at controlling the unregulated human growth of numerical strength (population explosion) but also at checking the unregulated movement of population and the increasing concentration of people in the urbanised areas (population implosion), and providing adequate living space and attractive environment to heterogeneous mixture of people (population displosion). These goals have to be jointly linked with the formulation and implementation of policies aimed at population regulation and planning for harnessing both natural and human resources. Thus, only population growth *per se* may not be perceived as a problem but its relation with the availability of resources may be viewed with great concern (Mishra, 1980:272-73).

Family planning needs to be salvaged from the morass into which it has drifted. For this, the programme has to look inwards and treat itself as a development input in its own right. In fact, development is the best method of controlling population growth though the reverse is also true: high population growth is a sure recipe for slow, if not negative, development. A variety of measures will have to be introduced to put the family campaign back on its feet. Along with some compulsion, persuasion will also be necessary. Legal measures may help, but what is urgently required is social awareness and involvement to create responsible parenthood.

What is to be stressed most in achieving a commensurate demographic effect is promoting spacing method instead of overemphasising sterlisation in the family planning programme. About three-fifth (57.1%) of married women in our country are of low age (under the age of 30 years) and already mothers of two or more children. We have to check the phenomenon of 'children producing children'. This could be achieved only by promoting spacing methods and marrying girls after 21 years of age.

In addition to its important role in checking population explosion, family planning will help to improve the general status of women. A woman who has a large number of children to support and who goes through repeated deliveries spends more time as a mother and a wife and is confined to the four walls of her home. She cannot play any role in the community and the society, unless she is able to limit her family to a reasonable size. Family planning will improve not only family welfare but will also contribute to social prosperity and individual happiness.

Further Readings

Agarwal, S.N., India's Population, Institute of Economic Growth, Asia Publications, Bombay, 1960.

Banerji, Pranab, "Development and Population Policy", *Indian Journal of Public Administration*, July-September 1992.

Barnabas, A.P., *Population Control in India: Policy Administration*, IIPA, 1977.

Bose, Ashish, *From Population to People*, Delhi, B.R., 1988.

---, *Meeting India's Basic Needs*, 1996.

Chandrasekhar, S., *India's Population Fact and Policy*, Meenakshi Prakashan, Meerut, 1967.

Ganguli, B.N., *Population and Development*, S. Chand, New Delhi, 1973.

Indian Journal of Public Administration, IIPA, Delhi, July-September 1992, Vol. XXXVIII, No. 3.

International Institute for Population Studies, Bombay, *Dynamics of Population and Family Welfare in India*, Popular Prakashan, Bombay, 1979.

Jolly, K.G., *Family Planning in India*, Hindusthan Publishing House, Delhi, 1986.

Kothari, Devendra and Anuja, Gulati, "Family Welfare Programme in India: A Proposal for Structural Change", *Administrative Change*, Jaipur, July 1990-June 1991.

Malgavkar, P.D., *Population and Development*, Centre for Policy Research, Delhi, 1980.

Sahay, K.B., *The Hindustan Times*, January 16, 1997.

13 Corruption

Corruption in India has become deep-rooted and is galloping unchecked and unhindered. Very often, we hear the top politicians at the centre and in the states talking of 'waging war against corruption', 'fighting the evil of corruption', 'no compromise on corruption', 'not to spare any corrupt person, howsoever high', yet it is well known how our country appears to be sinking deeper and deeper in corruption. A minister manages to purchase government land for personal use at one-fourth its real worth. A senior bureaucrat arranges to get free marble, wood and other material for constructing his house. A newly elected independent MLA is offered Rs. 40 to 75 lakhs and a ministership for supporting the ruling party. A peon in a government office asks for Rs. 50 to locate a file. A railway ticket-examiner who allots vacant berths in a compartment earns Rs. 100-150 every day. Raiding the residence of an Income Tax Commissioner, the CBI officers recover undeclared assets worth lakhs of rupees. Many politicians, bureaucrats, engineers and officers are arrested on corruption charges, cases are filed against them in the courts but how many are found in 'C' and 'D' classes in the central prisons? We have yet to come across high-level politicians, ministers and high-status government functionaries convicted and imprisoned for accepting huge bribes and kickbacks and working as carpenters, durry-makers, niwar-makers or cooks in jails like ordinary prisoners.

CONCEPT

Corruption in simple terms may be described as "an act of bribery". It has also been described as "the use of public power for private profits in a way that constitutes a breach of law or a deviation from the norms of society". D.H. Bailey (in Doughlas and Jhonson, 1971) has explained it as "misuse of authority as a result of consideration of personal gain which need not be monetary". Andriski (in Machael, 1983) considers it as "the use of public power for private advantage in ways which transgress some formal rule or law". Szeftel (in Machael, 1983) has observed that "corruption is behaviour which is deviance from norms and duties governing the exercise of public role or office for private gains". This private gain is achieved by ignoring prohibitions against certain acts, by exercising legitimate discretion to act, or by fulfilling obligations to act. J. Nye (1967:410) states that "corruption denotes the abuse or misuse of public offices for personal gains". Corruption is also described as "deviation from formal duties of public role for pecuniary or status gains".

Corruption is spread over in the society in several forms. Of these, the major ones are: bribe (money offered in cash or kind or gift as inducement to procure illegal or dishonest action in favour of the giver), nepotism (undue favour from holder of patronage to relatives), misappropriation (using other's money for one's own use), patronage (wrong support/encouragement given by patron and thus misusing the position), and favouritism (unduly preferring one to other).

Nepotism

Sociological analysis indicates that social bonds and kinship play an important role in corruption. The modernisation ideals upheld and practised by administrators today run counter to the values and standards of public behaviour of the traditional society. Today, kinship ties and caste and parochial loyalties get precedence in a public servant's mind. The first obligation of a modern administrator is to his family members, followed by close kin, lineage, or ethnic group. Such ties are more compelling than administrative rules and procedures. Kinship and caste groups do not consider that behaviour which deviates from the formal duties of a public role as 'deviation' or 'corruption' but view it as a 'family obligation'. This explains corrupt actions of many a public servant both at the lower as well as the higher levels.

CORRUPTION: A HISTORICAL PERSPECTIVE

Corruption is a global phenomenon. It is found almost in every society in one or the other form since time immemorial. In ancient times, the judges received bribes in Egyptian, Babilonian and Hebrew societies. In Rome, bribe was a common feature in elections to public offices. In France, judicial offices were sold during the fifteenth century. England was described a 'sink-hole' of corruption in the seventeenth and the eighteenth centuries. In the nineteenth century also, corruption was so rampant in Britain that Gibbon described it as the most infallible symptom of constitutional liberty (*Seminar*, No. 421, September, 1994).

In India, Kautilya has referred in his *Arthasastra* (Samasastry, 1967:15-17) to embezzlement by government servants out of the state revenue. He has mentioned about forty types of embezzlement and corrupt practices adopted by government servants. During Ashoka's regime, corruption prevailed on a lower scale (Majumdar, 1960:113). In medieval society, scope for corruption was minimum because only few authorities existed for the collection of taxes. So long they amassed taxes for the ruler, they were praised rather than censured. During the British rule, bribes were accepted not only by the Indian officials but by the highly-placed British officials too. Clive and Warran Hastings were found corrupt to the extent that they were tried by a parliamentary committee after their return to England. The expansion of the economic activities during the first and the second world wars opened new vistas of corruption in the country (Hallaya, 1948:13-51). War-time controls, restrictions and scarcities provided ample opportunities for bribery, corruption and favouritism. After independence, though top political elite at the national level remained very honest for about one and a half decade yet after the third and the fourth general elections in the 1960s, the new political elite lost peoples' faith in their honesty. The government employees in all public concerns at all leveis started accepting huge bribes even for small favours. Today, both at the central and the state levels, the number of ministers with an honest image can be counted on finger-tips. In the 1970s, the 1980s, and the 1990s, several union ministers and chief ministers who were top-level politicians were publicly accused of adopting corrupt practices during their political tenure. Since then, the prime minister, a large number of chief ministers, ministers and top level bureaucrats in almost all states have been accused of enriching themselves illegitimately and practising nepotism. The licensing system of the government, control regulations, and the expansion of the public sector spread corruption in all walks of life.

At present, India is viewed as the seventh most corrupt country in the world according to a non-government German organisation called 'Transparency International' (*The Hindustan Times*, May 5, 1996). This organisation ranks countries for honesty or corruption in their transactions according to the perceptions of businessmen dealing with those countries and of financial journalists. In a study conducted in 1995, this organisation found New Zealand, Denmark and Singapore as honest countries (getting more than 9 marks out of 10) and Indonesia, China, Pakistan, Venezuela, Brazil, Philippines, India, Thailand, Italy, and Mexico as corrupt countries (getting between 2 and 3 marks out of 10).

CORRUPTION AMONG PUBLIC SERVANTS

Corruption among public servants has always existed in one form or the other although its shape, dimensions, textures and shades have been changing from time to time and place to place. At one time, bribe was paid for getting wrong things done but now bribe is paid for getting right things done at the right time.

In public service, what are the acts which have been labelled 'corrupt'? Though the term 'corruption' has wide connotations, the following patterns of behaviour among public servants can be described as 'corrupt' within the provisions of law (Malhotra, 1992:254-256): (i) acceptance of gratification as reward for work done in official capacity, (ii) obtaining any object or pecuniary advantage illegally, (iii) fraudulent misappropriation of public property, (iv) being in possession of financial resources or property disproportionate to one's known sources of income, (v) misuse or abuse of official position, (vi) 'borrowing' money for purchasing a costly article from a person with whom one has official dealings with a 'known' understanding that the 'borrowed money' will not be returned, (vii) accepting gifts by 'persons of position' from persons with whom they have 'positional' relations, (viii) disregard of neglect of rules purposely to help citizen in avoiding dues/tax/duty due to be paid to government, and (ix) refusal to do duty on some plea which may benefit the other party (e.g., police officer not registering a case to protect a criminal).

There are at least four ministries in the union government which are regarded as gold mines for making money These are Defence, Petroleum, Power and Communication. The Defence Ministry spends between Rs. 30,000 and Rs. 40,000 crore on defence purchases every year and it is said the commissions between 15 and 40 per cent are not uncommon on purchase of weapons, ammunition, spare parts, and overhaul of mirages etc. The Petroleum Ministry spends about Rs. 30,000 crore on import of oil and natural gas every year and barrels of oil imported yield a kickback to somebody. Lot of money is also involved in giving drilling rights, fixing pipelines, opening of petrol pumps, and so forth. The Power Ministry spends about Rs. 4,000 crore every year which provides many opportunities to its officials to accept kickbacks. The budget of the Communication Ministry also runs in thousands of crores every year and kickbacks are common in the ministry.

Four other departments where corruption is rampant are: Public Works, Police, Excise and Revenue. The Public Works Department gets a huge portion of budget and plan provision for civil engineering works like construction of buildings, maintenance of roads, digging drains, construction of dams, and so on. Corruption in this department flows from top to bottom—at all stages, like accepting tenders, purchase of materials, execution of work, payment of bills, and settlement of disputes. It is said that out of the total cost sanctioned for a project, about 70 per cent is invested in the work, 20 per cent on contractor's profit, and 10 per cent goes into various officers' pockets.

The Police Department is said to be the most corrupt department where bribes are taken by constables upwards to high status officers. What is surprising is that the police takes money both from the accused and the complainants. The powers enjoyed by the police are so wide that they can accuse, arrest, and harass even an honest person. Cases of beating poor people (e.g., rickshaw-pullers, labourers, shopkeepers, vendors, etc.) on small pretexts and taking away all the money in their pockets, accepting money from truck-drivers, taking 'hafta' (weekly fixed amount) from shopkeepers and the like are very common cases of corruption.

The scope of corruption is greater where substantial decisions are taken, e.g., assessment and collection of taxes, sanctioning contracts, passing bills, issuing cheques, approving supplies, and so forth. A predetermined percentage is paid to the officials and this money is shared by all in the establishment. On the railways, money is paid for allotment of wagons, booking parcels of perishable goods, passing damage claims, and so on. In many establishments, while awarding contracts, a fixed percentage is taken as a norm. Similarly, failure to pay commission results in delay in getting bills passed and receiving cheques. Often, dishonest contractors and suppliers wanting to deliver inferior goods or getting approval of sub-standard work, spend a portion of their ill-earned profits for getting their work done. Tax evasion, sub-standard construction, supplying goods in small quantities, and charging heavily for the repair of government vehicles, are other examples of corruption.

Corruption is noticeable not only at the top—it percolates all the way down. Assistant and junior engineers, middle and low rank officials in government departments like telephones, state electricity boards and waterworks, cops in police, inspectors in revenue and excise departments, clerks in secretaraits, and junior staff on the railways accept bribes in return for big and small favours. In many establishments, junior officials have a fixed rate of kickbacks. For example, in the engineering department, a junior engineer asks for 5 per cent of the total amount of the transaction, an assistant engineer for 3 per cent, while an executive engineer will have to be content with a paltry 2 per cent. In the income tax department, the rate varies from Rs. 10,000 for the inspector to Rs. 5 lakh or more for the Commissioner, depending upon the amount of tax involved. In police department, the rate varies for a constable from Rs. 100 to Rs. 2,000, for a sub-inspector and inspector from Rs. 1,000 to Rs. 10,000, and for deputy superintendent and superintendent from Rs. 10,000 to Rs. 20,000 or more. A clerk in the secretariat accepts Rs. 100 to Rs. 2,000 for issuing the required papers. In government offices, even after the permission has been granted for something, the concerned clerk will refuse to type the sanction letter or to post it unless he is paid bribe amounting to 1 to 2 per cent of transaction. At the lowest level, even the peons want a tip of Rs. 10 to Rs. 20 to inform the officials of a visitor wishing to see them. Corruption is so pervasive in government departments that even a former Prime Minister had to state at a public meeting that out of every Rs. 100 sanctioned by the government for any public programme, the people actually get the benefit worth only Rs. 20. No wonder that an attitude of weary resignation among the people has allowed an astonishing complacency to develop over the magnitude of corruption in the country.

'Gift-giving' is a major form of corruption in cities. When a contractor gives boxes of dry-fruits and sweets and silver glasses to the engineer or the Accounts Officer for passing his bills, or a doctor or even a police officer gives 'gift' to the Minister for getting him transfered to the place of his choice, or a businessman who has been successful in getting a favourable assessment of income tax gives a fridge or a car or some costly electric gadget or a gold-chain on his son's birthday or daughter's marriage, a pattern of 'gift-giving' and along with it certain 'cultural values' are clearly involved.

'Speed money' is a common type of corrupt practice, particularly in matters relating to grants and sanctions. This practice is the result of 'administrative delay' in public offices. Once a file comes to an office, it needs a tremendous effort to get a 'decision' on it. To get the delay avoided, dishonest practice like one of 'speed money' is used. Sometimes, even when an order is passed on the file, communicating it to the applicant concerned is delayed till he pays 'appropriate' money to the subordinate officials concerned.

Share of kickbacks keeps on shooting up every few years. The Preparatory Committee for Alternative Economic Policies—a group of largely left-wing economists—has done some research in kickbacks. It estimates that the kickbacks shot up from Rs. 3,036 crore in 1980-81 to an astonishing Rs. 19,414 crore in 1990-91, i.e., the amount involved increased by more than six times in one decade.

Registered number of cases of corruption in India under the Prevention of Corruption Act, 1947 varied from 300 to 500 between 1981 and 1987 but after the enforcement of 1988 Act, the number now varies between 1,700 and 2,100 per year. Whereas 1,295 corruption cases were registered in 1988, the number registered in 1995 was 2,104 and in 1996 it was 2,664. Of the registered cases, persons in 70 to 75 per cent cases are charge-sheeted (*Crime in India*, 1996:338). The highest number of cases were reported from Maharashtra, followed by Gujarat, Karnataka, Rajasthan, Andhra Pradesh and Punjab. Out of 2,664 persons tried in 1996, only 13.9 per cent were convicted (*Crime in India*, 1996:346).

POLITICAL CORRUPTION AND SCANDALS

It is well known that a large number of politicians, not only in India but almost in all countries, are corrupt. People never feel shocked when politicians' corruption is divulged. Honest politicians are a rare breed today. Corrupt politicians not only go scot-free, unharmed and unpunished but they also manage to strut on the political stage as honourable leaders. Examples of ministers like Lal Bahadur Shastri and Sardar Vallabh Bhai Patel are rare who had very little bank balance at the time of death. In this land of ours, while a thief who commits theft for feeding his hungry children after remaining unemployed for a long time is promptly put behind bars, those who plunder the country masquerade as honourable citizens with all the paraphernalia merely because they happen to be big-wigs in politics or close to centres of power.

In the last two decades or so, several scandals and financial irregularities, including paying of massive commissions, pay-offs and kickbacks, have been reported in our country. Mostly, it is the chief ministers, ministers, leaders holding important political positions, bureaucrats and big businessmen who are reported to be involved in these scams. But nothing tangible has been done in uncovering, tracing, apprehending, prosecuting and punishing the culprits on the plea of 'inadequate evidence'. Some of the most notorious scandals were: the Bofors Payoff Scandal (1986) involving kickback of Rs. 64 crore, the Havala Scandal (1991) involving 115 senior politicians and bureaucrats, the Animal Husbandry Scam (1990) against the former Bihar chief minister and many others involving a kickback of Rs. 133 crore, the Telecommunication Department Scam (1996) in which Rs. 3.5 crore were found in cash in the house of a Central Minister besides jewellery, NSCs, FDRs etc., worth millions of rupees when he was in London for medical treatment, Bitumen Scam in Bihar (1996) involving Rs. 100 crore, JMM Scandal (1993) involving four MPs of Jharkhand Mukti Morcha and three MPs of the Janata Party for receiving Rs. 40 lakh each, the Indian Bank Scam (1991-95) resulting in a loss of Rs. 2,358 crore to the public sector bank, the Cement Scandal (1982) involving the chief minister of Maharashtra, the Plot Scandal (1988-89) involving another chief minister of Maharashtra, the Securities Scandal in Maharashtra (1992) involving a former Prime Minister for receiving Rs. one crore, the Sugar Scandal (1994) involving a Union Minister, which cost the country about Rs. 650 crore, the Treasury Fraud Scandal in Assam (1995) involving Rs. 200 crore, and more than three dozen scams against a former chief minister of Tamil Nadu including the land scandal. Incidently, this leader successfully blackmailed the BJP-led government in Delhi during 1998-99.

Corruption is very common in civil services. When complaints are received against highly placed officials, enquiries are held, vigilance agencies are set in motion to pacify the people and the media, but rarely the accused officials are punished. The Santhanam Committee has pointed out that there is a belief that "while governments were against corruption, they were not against corrupt individuals, if such individuals had the requisite amount of power, influence and protection". A central communication minister, in whose house a huge amount of money was found while he was in London for medical treatment and who was accused of being involved in several cases, and former chief ministers of Bihar and Tamil Nadu who were even sent to jail for a short period and whose cases are pending in the courts, (October 1999), are yet to be convicted and punished.

CAUSES OF CORRUPTION

Number of factors have been pointed out as causes of corruption or public dishonesty. *First* cause is the emergence of political elite who believe in interest-oriented rather than nation-oriented programmes and policies. In fact, the post-British *raj* (rule) has been described as the "*Raj* of ministers and bureaucrats". The political elite in the first two decades after independence was honest, dedicated and nation-oriented to the extent that they always worked for the country's progress. From the fourth general elections in 1967 onwards, such persons came to hold political power both at the centre and in the states about whom it was said that they worked only on the basis of some vested interest, say, interest of self, family, caste, region, party, and so forth. Their policies and programmes incidentally might have been nation-oriented but essentially they were 'interest-based'. They also encouraged the bureaucrats to follow suit. A majority of bureaucrats in our country are described as 'ritualists' who do not take much interest in the 'development-oriented' policies for the betterment of society. The politicians and bureaucrats thus have started using their power and position for illegal benefits. The emergence of the new business leaders who wanted profits even by sharing them with the people in power became equally responsible for the mushroom growth of corrupt practices among the public servants. Corruption also emerges from the power of the government officials of taking decisions, say, issuing licences, assessing income tax, giving extensions and so on. It is not the rules but the interpretation of the rules which enables officers to receive kickbacks and pocket the bribe. Many officers pay lakhs and thousand of rupees to get themselves posted in particular positions only because those positions enable them to earn thousands and lakhs of rupees every month as illegal gratification. The *second* cause is the economic policy of the government. Most of the recent scandals have been in areas where either purchase policies or prices are controlled by the government. Sugar, fertilisers, oil, military weapons, electronic equipment are some examples. One NRI businessman claimed in the courts that he had to pay twenty lakhs of rupees to Chandraswami, with verbal assurances from a former prime minister, to get a contract for selling pulp to India. Similar kickbacks were paid in Bofors, telecom and many other scams. The real issue is freeing the economy from the clutches of misguided government regulations. But a slap-dash approach to privatisation will also not do. Clear and transparent rules are needed. Arbitrary decision-making by certain individuals (like minister, or director-general or secretary) is an invitation to corruption. The Enron project in Maharashtra in 1995 ran into trouble because negotiations and terms of the deal were shrouded in secrecy. *Thirdly*, corruption is caused by scarcity. When things required are in short supply, people in power demand 'consideration' to ensure their regular supply or increase their cost. This happens whenever there is high demand but low supply of commodity of daily use like cement, sugar, oil, etc. *Fourthly*, corruption is caused as well as increased because of the change in the value system and ethical qualities of men who administer. The old ideals of morality, service, honesty and sacrifice are regarded as non-utilitarian and accepting 'favours' as a 'need' than a folly or aberrant behaviour. *Fifthly*, corruption can be traced to ineffective administrative organisation. Lack of vigilance, enormous powers to the ministerial staff, unaccountability, defective information system, etc., give scope to officials not only to be corrupt but also remain unaffected even after following corrupt practices.

Causes of corruption can also be categorised as economic, social, political, legislative and judicial. The *economic* causes include: craze for higher living standards, inflation, licence system, profiteering tendencies, and lack of morality in business community. The *social* causes include: materialistic outlook of life, erosion in social values, illiteracy, acquisitive cultural traits, feudalistic hangover, peoples' toleration, public indifference, and exploitative social structure. The *political* causes include: political patronage, ineffective political leadership, political apathy, political immorality, election funding, nexus of criminals with politicians, and political subculture. The *legislative* factors are: inadequate legislation, loopholes in law, and callousness in implementation of laws. The *judicial* causes include: expensive judicial system, judicial indifference, lack of commitment among judges, and frequent acquittal of the accused on technical grounds.

Some factors promoting corruption could be described as: *One*, concentration of power in one officer for whom autocratic decision-making is possible and the 'aggrieved' citizen is not in a position to obtain effective redress. Power and discretion are vested in the executive, police and judiciary, all members of which do not possess strength of character. *Second* factor which allows administrative corruption to thrive is the economic and social backwardness. The gulf in the status of the civil servant and his clientele compels the former to forget civil servant's obligations to society and the latter to tolerate insulting language of the former. *Third* factor is the attitude of the public of unquestioning subjugation to power bred by colonial and feudal forces. *Fourth* factor is the unaccountability of officers and the administrative delay. *Fifth* factor is the clumsy handling of corruption cases. Those in the hierachy vested with disciplinary powers shirk accountability and show unwillingness to use these powers against a corrupt subordinate. This is common in police, secretariat, PWD, customs, and many other such departments. *Lastly*, lack of public outcry and lack of strong public forum to oppose corruption also promote it. Our social system is so 'soft' that people remain mute witnesses and passive onlookers against even most corrupt persons, tolerate their anti-social behaviour, and fail to channelise their resentment into strong public propaganda against it.

IMPACT OF CORRUPTION

While talking of corruption, should we be concerned only with big financial deals and scams, or types of corruption called political, bureaucratic, industrial, institutional, etc., or should we also be concerned with those corruption cases which remain invisible but pervade our daily life and corrode the very fibre of our moral fabric? Some people feel that we should filter corruption into various grades. While according to one view, 'amount' should be the criterion of corrupt act, according to the other, 'need' should be the focus. A few rupees spent to gain a major benefit is not worth bothering about. Yet another view is that 'price' paid for the required 'service' is in order. Corruption comes in only when the price is paid but for which no service has been done. But what about adulteration in food or spurious drugs sold to us and things like that? Generally, such cases in our daily life are not regarded as 'corruption'. Is cheating in an examination corruption? Is increasing marks in an answer-book by an examiner on getting 'recommendation' from a colleague or a friend or a kin (but not by accepting money) corruption? In their defence, examiners say that they only 'oblige' and how can 'obliging' be corruption? Many clerks go to their offices and sign attendance registers but are never found on their seats. They become 'available' only when they are offered money for the file they move. This is corruption.

Some people say that while corruption is found even in most developed countries like the United States, Japan, England, France, Canada, and Germany, why should we unnecessarily get perturbed about it in India? These people forget that nature of corruption in the developed countries is different from the one we find in our own country. Corruption in these countries exists only among the highest echelons of business giants, while in India we have to pay for railway reservation, for getting admission not only in a professional institution but also in a good primary school, for buying a cinema ticket, for purchasing a gas cylinder, for driving the scooter without a helmet, for getting the arrear-bill passed, for getting tax-refund, and so on. Thus, while in other countries, money is paid for getting illegal things, in India it is paid for getting legal and authorised things. All these affect the day to day living of the common man. As such, we have got to be concerned with corruption and various corrupt acts.

We should not forget that corruption has affected our society in several ways: (1) It has retarted economic development of the country. (2) It has created violence and lawlessness in the society since the corrupt man has the money power to influence the executors of law to serve him. (3) It has given rise to casteism, linguism and communalism. (4) It has diminished morality and destroyed individual character. (5) It has heightened inefficiency, nepotism, and lethargy and has created indiscipline in all fields of administration, making the life of a common man miserable. (6) It has reduced the credibility of officials in the eyes of the masses. (7) It has increased black money in the country. (8) It has led to adulteration of eatables, spurious drugs and shortage of many consumer items. (9) It has destabilised governments both at the centre and in the states. We have, therefore, to focus on both types of visible and hidden corruption cases which stir up our conscience.

THE LEGISLATION

The Prevention of Corruption Act came into force in September 1988. It consolidated the provisions of the Prevention of Corruption Act, 1947, some sections of the Indian Penal Code, the Criminal Procedure Code, and the Criminal Law Act, 1952. The sole idea was to bring all relevant provisions in a single Act. Finding that bribery and corruption among public servants had considerably increased during and after the Second World War and many unscrupulous officers had amassed huge wealth, and the existing provisions of the IPC and the CrPC were inadequate to tackle this problem, the Prevention of Corruption Act, 1947 was passed.

In the Criminal Procedure Code, offences relating to public servants are not cognisable, but the 1947 Act made it obligatory for the court to make *certain presumptions of guilt* against the accused. The 1947 Act shifted the burden of proof from the prosecution to the accused. The investigation against the accused was to be made by an officer not below the rank of Deputy Superintendent of Police. The 1947 Act declared such corrupt acts offences as taking bribe, misappropriation, obtaining a pecuniary advantage, possessing assets disappropriate to income, and abusing official position. However, the authority for prosecution was vested only in the department authorities and not in the Central Bureau of Investigation (CBI).

The 1988 Act enlarged the scope of the term 'public servant' and included a large number of employees within its ambit. Besides the employees of the central government and the union territories, the employees of public undertakings, nationalised banks, office-bearers of cooperative societies of the central and the state government receiving financial aid, employees of the University Grants Commission (UGC), vice-chancellors, professors, and scientists in institutions receiving financial aid from the central or state governments or even from the local authorities have all been declared as public servants. However, MPs and MLAs, even though performing 'public duties', have been kept out of the ambit of the Act. The Act covers all the 'corrupt' acts as covered by the 1947 Act, (bribe, misappropriation, obtaining pecuniary advantage, possessing assets disproportionate to income, etc.). The Act extends to whole of India except Jammu and Kashmir and applies to all Indian citizens, whether living in the country or outside it.

If the offence against the public servant is proved in the courts, it is punishable with imprisonment of not less than six months but extending to a maximum period of five years. Six months imprisonment is thus *mandatory* and the courts have no discretion in this regard. If public servant is found committing offence habitually, he is to be punished with imprisonment of not less than two years but not more than seven years, and also a fine.

MEASURES TAKEN TO CONTAIN CORRUPTION

The existing CBI and the anti-corruption police have proved helpless in investigating, initiating action and penalising corrupt ministers and high political persons. No wonder, in recent times people have come to talk about 'judicial activism'. It is a well known fact that the CBI could investigate the case of former Bihar chief minister more speedily only under the protective wings of the High Court. The CBI being a government agency cannot report to the judicial courts directly on a long-term basis bypassing the government, and without government supervision over its functioning. The CBI officials have confessed to political pressures on them. It, therefore, appears that the CBI will have the limited role of exercising vigilance on the lower and middle categories of public servants. The Lokpal and Lokayukts will have to prosecute ministers and highly-placed politicians. The society cannot depend on the police for surveillance as it does not enjoy the reputation of being honest. Allegations of police fabricating evidence, foisting false cases and manipulating evidence against corrupt officials have been routinely and repeatedly made in our country. A committee on Prevention of Corruption was appointed by the Government of India in 1962 under the chairmanship of K. Santhanam. This Committee gave its report in 1964. The recommendations pertained to various aspects of corruption. The measures suggested by the Santhanam Committee for efficient working of the department were: (1) Independence to vigilance officers to investigate complaints of corruption and malpractices. (2) Assurance to vigilance officers of promotion for efficient work. (3) Protection to vigilance officers against sending them back to their parent cadre for investigating the cases of highly placed officials. (4) Giving representation to Central Civil Services and technical services in the Central Vigilance Commission. (This recommendation was implemented by reconstituting the Vigilance Commission in the last few months of 1998). (5) Intensive training to non-gazetted inspectorial staff of the Vigilance Department in departmental rules and procedures since about 80 per cent of the vigilance cases are enquired at the lower level. (6) Cutting down the number of stages by the government to check delay in processing cases.

It was on the basis of the recommendations of this Committee that the Central Vigilance Commission was set up in 1964 for looking into cases of corruption against the central government and other employees.

The central government has set up the following four departments as anti-corruption measures: (i) Administrative Vigilance Division (AVD) in the Department of Personnel and Training (ii) Central Bureau of Investigation (CBI), (iii) Domestic Vigilance Units in the Ministries/Departments/Public Undertakings/Nationalised Banks, and (iv) Central Vigilance Commission (CVC). Some suggestions given by the former Chief Vigilance Commissioner for effectively tackling corruption are worth consideration (See, *The Indian Journal of Public Administration*, July-September, 1997:438): (1) Establishing the Lokpal institutions to deal with political corruption with powers of initiating action against central ministers and MPs (2) The Lokpal should have its own independent investigating and prosecuting agency without having to depend on the CBI. (3) The Lokpal should have legal powers to prosecute an accused minister in specially designated courts after a prima facie case is established against him by the Lokpal's own inquiry. (4) The charged minister must compulsorily resign after the filing of the charge-sheet in the court. (5) The Chief Vigilance Commissioner should be redesignated as the Central Lokayukta. (6) The Central Lokayukta should be appropriately linked to the Lokpal through common officers and staff and investigating and prosecuting agencies.

The main functions of the CVC are: (1) to undertake an inquiry into any complaint of corruption against a public servant; (2) to advise the disciplinary authority about the type of proceedings to be initiated against accused person involved in corruption; (3) to direct the CBI to register a regular case; and (4) to exercise general check and supervision over the vigilance and anti-corruption work in ministries/department/banks/public undertakings.

VARIOUS COMMISSIONS ON CORRUPTION OF POLITICIANS AND PUBLIC COMPANIES

In the last four and a half decades (i.e., between 1955 and 1999), more than two dozen commissions have been appointed by the Government of India to inquire into the charges of corruption against politicians and public companies. Of these, nine commissions were appointed during the period 1963 to 1983 against the Chief Ministers of different states. These were: Das Commission against Sardar Pratap Singh Kairon, Chief Minister of Punjab (1963), Ayyangar Commission against Bakshi Gulam Mohmad, Chief Minister of Jammu and Kashmir (1965), Khanna Commission against Biju Patnaik, Chief Minister of Orissa (1967), Kapur Commission against Dayanand Bandodkar, Chief Minister of Goa (1968), Mudholkar Commission against V.K. Mahtab, Chief Minister of Assam (1968) Sarkaria Commission against M. Karunanidhi, Chief Minister of Tamil Nadu (1976), Grover Commission against Dev Raj Urs, Chief Minister of Karnataka (1977), Vimada Lal Commission against Vengala Rao, Chief Minister of Andhra Pradesh (1977), and Gurudev Singh Commission against Zail Singh, Chief Minister of Punjab (1979).

Five commissions appointed against ministers were: Chagla Commission (1956) against Union Finance Minister T.T. Krishnamachari (and also Finance Secretary and Chairman of Life Insurance Corporation), Aiyer Commission (1967) against five ministers of Bihar, Madholkar Commission (1968) against thirteen ministers of Bihar, a commission (1969) against R.K. Kunju, minister in Kerala, and Reddy Commission (1977) against contracts entered by Union Defence Minister, Bansilal.

Five other commissions appointed to investigate corruption were: Vaidyalingam Commission (1979) on charges of corruption and wielding extra-constitutional authority to interfere in government affairs against Kanti Desai, son of Morarji Desai, and Gyatri Devi, wife of Charan Singh, Prime Minister of India, Kailasam Sadasivan and Ray Commissions (1981) against spirit scandals in Kerala and Tamil Nadu, Shankeranand Committee (1990) on corruption charges in Bofors deal, and Jankiraman Committee (1992) on Security Scam. Corruption charges were recently levelled against two Chief Ministers of Tamil Nadu and West Bangal (1995). The Governor of Tamil Nadu even permitted the Janata Party President in April 1995 to prosecute the then Tamil Nadu Chief Minister for two out of 38 charges against her under the Prevention of Corruption Act. Of these two charges, one involved Rs. 365 crore coal-import deal in August 1993 and the other related to the purchase of a large plot of land from the state government for Rs. 1.82 crore when its estimated market value was Rs. 4.27 crore. This Chief Minister had also been accused of spending Rs. 50 to Rs. 100 crore on the wedding of her foster son in September, 1995. The cases against this former Chief Minister, whose AIADMK party was a constituent of BJP-led Ministry at the Centre in 1998-99, were transferred to special courts in Tamil Nadu but were retransferred to ordinary courts in February 1999 to placate her because she had been threatening to withdraw support to the government every now and then. Yet another Chief Minister who was charged in April 1995 for corrupt practices is a person who has been the Chief Minister of West Bengal for more than 18 years. The charges were levelled by the former Tripura Chief Minister and a veteran Marxist leader. This case has now been dropped.

The Vohra Committee was set up in July 1993 to study corruption in India by taking stock of the links between government functionaries and political personalities and crime syndicates and mafia organisations. The Committee submitted its report in October 1993. The government had shelved the report for 18 months but under pressure from the opposition parties in the parliament, the report was tabled in the two houses of parliament in August 1995. The report has made a scathing commentary on the nexus between politicians and criminals. It has stated that the "network of the mafia is virtually running a parallel government pushing the state apparatus into irrelevance". The Committee has even stated that some parliamentarians and State Assembly members have come into political power through the leadership of gangs and armed senas. The Committee has recommended the setting up of an agency to collate information from all agencies and take immediate, effective and deterrent action against the crime syndicates, smuggling gangs and economic lobbies in the country which have over the years developed an extensive network of contacts with government functionaries and bureaucrats at the local levels and politicians and media persons at the state and the central levels.

Eleven states in India (including Bihar, Himachal Pradesh, Karnataka, Madhya Pradesh, Rajasthan and Uttar Pradesh) have set up Lok Ayuktas for investigating charges of corruption against ministers, MLAs and other public functionaries. There is no such institution as yet at the national level which may act as a watchdog body on ministers' probity, though in 1992 and again in 1994, the then Prime Minister had promised that an institution like Ombudsman in Sweden and a few other European countries will be established by law at the central level. Lok Pal Bills were introduced in the Lok Sabha five times in 29 years (1968, 1971, 1977, 1985 and 1989) for appointing Lok Pals but these bills were never passed. The United Front Government introduced the Lok Pal Bill in the parliament in September 1996, which could not be passed even by the BJP-led government upto April 1999 when it lost confidence vote in the parliament. The real hurdle in passage of the bill was the lack of political will. There is no substitute for Lok Pal whose jurisdiction is to be confined to investigation of the corruption charges against those holding high offices, including the Prime Minister. Prosecution under the Prevention of Corruption Act is possible only if the complainant gets government permission which is seldom given for obvious reasons. No citizen can invoke the Special Courts Act as long as the government does not agree that a *prima facie* case calling for action exists. Both these handicaps will be absent in the Lok Pal which can be moved by anyone to start a case by filing an affidavit. Only the new government constituted in October 1999 can take a fresh initiative for getting the Lok Pal bill passed.

COMBATING CORRUPTION

Is it possible to contain corruption in our society? Many leaders when come to power for the first time declare their determination to eradicate corruption but soon they themselves become corrupt and start amassing huge wealth. When the Communist government came to power in West Bengal in 1977, it said it would eradicate corruption in a few years. Today, most of the leaders in power are themselves accused of corruption to the extent that one politburo member, who was at one time the Tripura Chief Minister, was expelled from the party in mid-April 1995 only because he had accused the highly placed politician of the party being personally corrupt and indulging in nepotism. When Rajiv Gandhi became Prime Minister in 1984, he too declared war against corruption but soon he himself became the victim of Bofors payoff scandal. Corruption today has thus come to be institutionalised.

There are many myths about corruption which have to be exploded if we really want to combat it. Some of these myths are: corruption has become a way of life and nothing can be done about it; or that corruption is a post-independence phenomenon and it is the result of too much freedom and licence to people in a democracy; or that the poor people of underdeveloped countries are generally dishonest and untrustworthy by nature and easily tempted, while people of the developed countries are less prone to corruption; or that corruption exists only at the lower and the subordinate levels; or that corruption is found more among the illiterate than the educated people; or that corruption spreads mainly because of politicians. All these fallacies are too crude and we have to guard against them while planning measures to contain corruption.

Some methods have been suggested for reducing corruption. These are: *One*, for controlling corruption, we have to focus on law, procedure and administration. Laws and rules pertaining to the organisation and behaviour of persons in specific situations with specific status are essential. 'Bad' laws/rules have to be changed or repealed. If the law/rule is too harsh, complicated, and ambiguous, it leads to corruption. Laws should not be such that they leave too much scope for discretion. Discretion will have to be commensurate with the status of the officer and the type of the role assigned to him. 'Administrative' factors include both structural and functional aspects. How an organisation is structured will determine the lacunae for corruption. 'Functioning' refers to the 'ongoing' process of working which refers both to the quantity and the quality of work, supervision, magnitude of lapses permitted, and so on. *Two*, artificial shortages and scarcities which facilitate illegal gratification have to be controlled. *Three*, vigilance should be increased. It is a myth that vigilance hampers efficiency; on the contrary, it improves it. Suspect officials of doubtful integrity should be kept away from sensitive posts. Surprise checks should be carried out at vulnerable points of corruption. *Four*, liberalisation policy should be introduced very cautiously. Eventually, liberalisation and free market may reduce corruption but at present 'liberal sanctions' are granted in return for a 'consideration'. Capitalist countries like the United States, Japan, South Korea, Indonesia, Thailand, Malaysia are considered to be enormously corrupt societies. In Japan, we frequently hear of corruption scandals, pointing out the institutionalisation of hypocrisy and dishonesty. *Five*, expenses in elections have to be strictly controlled. *Lastly*, cooperation of the people has to be obtained for successfully containing corruption. We will elaborate the last two measures.

Why are cases of corruption not reported by the people to the police? It is because they are afraid (that the corrupt will harm them), indifferent (that it is not their duty to reform the society) and pessimists (that the corrupt are influential and powerful people and no action will be taken against them). Yet, there are people who do try to bring corrupt cases to the notice of the concerned authorities. These are the people who have a feeling of uneasiness, who have a sense of guilt and who get comfort of mind for doing something good for the community. Corruption is a hydraheaded monster which can be vanquished only by the collective efforts of the people. If they make sure that the dishonest politicians do not get elected to legislatures, half the battle is won. But the big question is: will it ever happen?

In a democratic country like India, will people ever realise that they have to play a crucial role in combating evils like corruption? In fact, much of the corruption exists because of people's tolerance or complete lack of public outcry against it, as well as the absence of a strong public forum to oppose it. While many intellectual, educated, well-informed and articulate citizens remain worried about this monstrous problem in the country, they fail to channelise their resentment into strong public opinion against it. A concerted effort by responsible and enlightened citizens can surely make a serious dent in the corruption level. Even our university youths can take up such society-oriented goals and organise movements for curbing the evil.

Yet another effective method of containing corruption could be to introduce method which will enable political parties to secure electoral funds in a bonafide manner, or the central government may finance elections through an election fund. This system is being followed in Germany, Norway and Sweden and some other advanced countries of Europe. The political parties may be funded by the state in accordance with the votes polled by them in the previous general elections. The money may be fixed according to the percentage of votes secured. The idea of State funding of elections has been discussed in our parliament more than once in the recent years. All earlier governments including the las BJP-led government felt that the government is strapped for cash. This does not appear to be true. At the present level of inflation, about Rs. 1,000 crore are required for the parliamentary and Rs. 2,000 crore for the assembly elections. Since elections are held after every five years, this would mean an allocation of merely Rs. 600 crore in the annual central government budget. Since our present annual budget is more than Rs. 50,000 crore, it would mean that election expenses would be about 1.2 per cent of the annual budget every year. If the government thinks that even this paltry sum cannot be set aside, an election cess on the voters may be imposed. This state funding of elections will reduce corruption to a large extent.

State funding of elections will not only eliminate contributions from corrupt businessmen and interest groups but will also contribute to free and fair elections, drawing men of integrity in assemblies, equalising the amount spent by various political parties, and so forth.

Besides the above measure, appointing Lok Pals to look into the charges of corruption at the highest echelons of power, as stated earlier, could prove to be an effective measure in containing corruption. At present, Lok Ayuktas in eleven states have been rendered impotent because of numerous disabilities. Learning from their experience, the powers of the Lok Pal should be widened. His recommendations should have a statutory force. These should be tabled in parliament and duly publicised in the media. The Lok Pal could comprise a single retired judge of the Supreme Court or two or three judges. He/they should be selected not by the executive but by a committee of four persons consisting of the Prime Minister, Chief Justice of India, Speaker of the Lok Sabha, and the Leader of the Opposition. The Lok Pal should have an independent investigative machinery at his disposal.

In may be concluded that corruption today has ceased to shock people. Even when malpractices are detected, ministers and officers go scot-free. At the most, officers are transferred. So long corruption fails to attract legal, moral and social censure, there is no hope of eliminating or even reducing it. It may not be possible to root out corruption completely at all levels but it is certainly possible to roll down or to contain it within tolerable limits. Corruption is a cancer which every Indian must strive to obliterate. Honest and dedicated persons in public life known for their honesty and integrity, reduced government control in the economy, popularly called liberalisation policy, and control over electoral expenses could be three most important prescriptions for corruption. People have tolerated corrupt persons for long. It is now time containing corruption is taken up by dedicated political rulers.

Further Readings

Agarwal, U.C., "Galloping Corruption: Need for Effective Vigilance", *The Indian Journal of Public Administration*, New Delhi, July-September 1997.

Choudhary, P.C., "Corruption" in *Seminar*, No. 421, September, 1994.

Doughlas and Johnson, *Deviance*, Lippincott Co., Philadelphia, 1971.

Gopinath, P. Krishna, "Corruption in Political and Public Offices" in *The Indian Journal of Public Administration*, New Delhi, October-December 1982.

Halayya, M., *Corruption in India*, 1948 (quoted by Choudhry, P.C. in *Seminar*, *op.cit.*).

Kohli, Suresh, *Corruption in India*, 1975 (quoted by Choudhry, P.C. in *Seminar*, *op. cit).*

Levine, Victor T., *Political Corruption: The Guana Case*, 1957.

Machael, Clarke (ed.), *Corruption: Causes and Consequences*, Francecis Publishers, London, 1983.

Malhotra, K.L., *Facets of Vigilance*, Malhotra Publications, Delhi, 1988 and 1992.

Mathur, K.M., "Corruption in Administration", Working Paper for DIG Police Seminar held at Internal Security Academy, Mount Abu, from October 12 to October 17, 1992.

Monterio, J.B., *Corruption*, Manaktalas, Bombay, 1966.

Nye, J., "Corruption and Political Development: A Cost-Benefit Analysis", *American Political Review*, 1967.

Samassastry, R., *Arthasastra* (translated), Mysore Printing House, Mysore, 1967.

Santhanam Committee Report on "Prevention of Corruption", Government of India, 1964, *Sunday*, Calcutta, 27 November-3 December, 1994.

Szeftel, Morris, "Corruption and the Spoil System in Zambia", in Machael Clarke (ed.), *Corruption: Causes and Consequences, op. cit.*, 1983.

Writh, Ronald and Simpkins, Edgar, *Corruption in Developing Countries*, London, 1963.

14 Black Money

Black money is both an economic and a social problem. In the latter context, it is perceived as a problem with adverse sociological effects on society, like social inequalities, social deprivations, etc.; in the former context, it is perceived as a parallel economy, an underground economy or an unofficial economy that is the consequence of the economic policies of the government and has damaging effects on country's economy and nation's planning development. While a problem like poverty affects those who are poor, unemployment affects those who are unemployed, alcoholism and drug abuse affect those who consume them, black money is a problem which does not affect those who have black money but it affects the common man in society. No wonder, it has been described as a problem with a difference.

THE CONCEPT

Black money is tax-evaded income. It can be earned both through legal and illegal means. Its legitimate source is that the income-earners do not reveal their whole income for tax purposes. For example, government doctors earning money by private practice even when they get non-practising allowance; teachers earning money through tuitions, examinations and book royalty and not including it in income-tax returns; advocates charging much higher fee than shown in their account books, and so forth. Its illegitimate source is bribe, smuggling, black-marketing, selling commodities at prices higher than the controlled prices, taking *pugree* for house, shop, etc., selling house at a high premium price but showing it at much lower price in the account books, and so on.

It is possible to convert black money into white money and vice versa. For example, when a person manages to get the receipt from the shopkeeper by paying sales-tax for a commodity but does not purchase it actually, he generates black money as reimbursement is made to him against the receipt. The money not actually paid is the black money in this case. In such case, the shopkeeper sells the same commodity to another person without giving him any receipt for it. On the other hand, if a person purchases second-hand car and pays Rs. 90,000 for it out of white money but gets a receipt of only Rs. 60,000, the balance of Rs. 30,000 becomes black money for the seller. In this case, white money becomes black money.

MAGNITUDE OF PREVALENCE

It is not easy to calculate the magnitude of black money in any society. The economists in the United States, the United Kingdom, Norway, Sweden and Italy adopted different measures but could not estimate the amount involved in black money. Norway and Sweden used questionnaire method for eliciting answers from persons whether they had participated in illegal activities as buyers or sellers. Italy attempted to estimate the underground economy by finding out the difference between the size of the labour-force officially reported and actually employed. This enabled the authorities to determine productivity in the underground sector. The United Kingdom tried to assess parallel economy by comparing the official estimates of the Gross National Product (GNP) made from the consumption side with those made from the income side. In the United States, Guttman assumed that only cash is used in illegal transactions. He tried to find out the difference between currency required for economic transactions in a fixed period and actual currency held outside banks in the same period.

In spite of the varied methods used, it is not possible to estimate the magnitude of black money in a society, even though it is described as a world-wide phenomenon. It is said to be in operation not only in the developing countries but also in the developed countries like the United States, the United Kingdom, Russia, Japan, Canada, France, Germany, etc.

A study conducted by the IMF about a decade and a half back (Vito Tangani, 1983:13) showed that in regard to the size of the underground money, India holds the first rank followed by the United States and Canada having the second and the third ranks.

In India, black money or unaccounted wealth estimated by Prof. Kaldor in 1953-54 as Rs. 600 crore was estimated by Wanchoo Committee as

Rs. 1,000 crore in 1965-66 and Rs. 1,400 crore in 1969-70. Rangnekar placed the figures of black money at Rs. 1,150 crore for 1961-62, Rs. 2,350 crore for 1964-65, Rs. 2,833 crore for 1968-69, and Rs. 3,080 crore for 1969-70. Chopra's estimate (*Economic and Political Weekly*, Vol. XVII, Nos. 17 & 18, April, 24 and May 1, 1982) showed that black money in 1960-61 was Rs. 916 crore which increased to Rs. 8,098 crore in 1976-77. According to Gupta (*Economic and Political Weekly*, January 16, 1982:73), the amount of black money in our country was Rs. 3,034 crore in 1967-68 and Rs, 40,867 crore in 1978-79. According to his estimate, black money which constituted 9.5 per cent of the GNP in 1967-68 swelled to nearly 49 per cent in 1978-79. In 1981, black money was estimated by one source at Rs. 7,500 crore (6.8% of the national income at 1981 prices) and by an other source at Rs. 25,000 crore (22.7% of the national income at 1981 prices). The National Institute of Public Finance and Policy estimated the quantum of black money in economy in 1985 at around Rs. 1,00,000 crore or about 20 per cent of the national income. The Planning Commission study, however, estimated it to be in the range of Rs. 70,000 crore. Further, it is generated at the rate of Rs. 50,000 crore per year (*The Hindustan Times*, 2 August, 1991:11). The flight of capital has resulted in an overseas stash which government officials conservatively place at $50 million (about Rs. 1,30,000 crore). In 1996, the estimated black money in our country was believed to be more than Rs, 4,00,000 crore (*The Hindustan Times*, January, 20, 1997). Recently, Prof. Arun Kumar of Centre for Economic Studies, Jawaharlal Nehru University, Delhi has authored a book on black money in India (1999). He holds that black economy is equivalent to 40 per cent of the GDP, out of which 32 per cent is in the legal sectors (business and professionals like doctors, filmstars, etc.) and 8 per cent in the illegal sector (narcotics, etc.) (*The Hindustan Times*, September 12, 1999).

Some scholars have pointed out that of the total black money in our society, about one-fourth (26%) is from the tax-evaded income. In the United States, black money is expected to be about 8 per cent of its Gross National Product (GNP). While in India, black money is more from legal sources (about 80%), in the United States too it is more from legal sources (about 75%).

CAUSES OF GENERATING BLACK MONEY

Unrealistic Tax Laws and Tax Frauds

The increase in taxes and duties compels some people to evade them. The present rules (September 1999) prescribe the limit of Rs. 50,000 (excluding standard deduction of Rs. 20,000) as free income for levying income tax.

Can a middle-class person survive within the limit in this age of inflation? A mason or a carpenter earns about Rs. 150 per day in a city and Rs. 150 to Rs. 200 per day in the metropolitan areas. Even a good '*gol-gappa*' seller or a *pan* shopkeeper earns more than Rs. 300 a day. Assuming that these people work for 300 days in a year, their income will exceed the prescribed income tax limit. And how many of these workers pay income tax? A film actor getting Rs. 30 or 40 lakh per film had to pay 40 per cent of his income as income tax up to March 1997 which has now (in 1999) been reduced to 30 per cent with no standard deduction. Instead of paying such a high tax, he maintains 'double' accounts and evades paying tax and amasses more and more black money. A doctor with a private practice of more than Rs. 500 per day, a surgeon charging a fee of Rs. 5,000 to 10,000 per operation and doing at least ten operations a month, an advocate charging Rs, 2,000 per hearing, a shop-keeper doing a business of more than Rs. 5,000 per day, a contractor with a turnover business of Rs. 10 crore per year, an industrialist with a profit of millions of rupees per year—all these people are bound to hide their real income to escape paying income tax of 30 per cent of the total income. Indirect taxes, like excise duty, customs duty, sales tax and octroi, etc., also encourage evasion of taxes and increase in black money.

Tax evasion by big companies and corporations is suspected to be around Rs. 400 crore a year in the form of excise duty and Rs. 3,500 crore in the form of customs duty. The excise duty evasion detected in five years, from 1991 to 1996, by the Directorate General of Anti-Evasion increased from Rs. 562 crore in 1991-92 to Rs. 1,236 crore in 1995-96, while the amounts involved in FERA violations increased from Rs. 663 crore in 1994-95 to Rs. 1,447 crore in 1995-96 (*India Today*, November, 30, 1996: 97-103). Overall estimate of excise and customs duty evasion (i.e., combining the two duties) ranges at anywhere between Rs. 7,500 crore and Rs. 10,000 crore or slightly over a tenth of the total collections from these two duties.

The FERA violations of around Rs. 300 crore by a top company (ITC) came to light in the last quarter of 1996. If this could happen in the case of one reputable firm, can others lag behind? The cases of a few ministers in Narasimha Rao's government (like Petroleum and Communication Ministers) being involved in corruption cases of more than Rs. 25 crore each point out the nexus between politicians and big business and the emergence of black money in the country.

In a survey in 1996 conducted by the World Economic Forum of 200 business executives from 49 countries in the world on specified index of corruption in tax evasion, India was ranked 40 (i.e., as dishonest) and corporates ensuring honesty were ranked 46 (*India Today*, November 30, 1996:97).

If income taxes are further reduced, there is more likelihood of hiding less and thereby increasing the revenue. This was demonstrated in 1993-94 when the maximum rate of income tax was lowered to 40 per cent. Besides, fixing a reasonable tax amount for shopkeepers and other self-employed persons also resulted in greater tax collection as more people entered into the tax net.

Different Rates of Excise Duty

Within similar products, there are different rates of excise duty. For instance, in textiles and cigarettes, this leads to tax evasion through misclassification of output. In textiles, separate rates of excise are charged for cloth of different varieties. Manufacturers regularly downgrade a product to pay lower rates of excise. This alone generates Rs. 1,000 crore a year in black money. For the entire manufacturing sector, including steel, evasion in excise, custom and sales taxes accounts for over Rs. 50,000 crore in black money every year.

Control Policy

Another cause of black money is the price control policy of the government. In selecting commodities for control and in determining their prices, the government fails to take into account the elasticities involved in demand and supply. For example, according to the report of the National Council of Applied Economic Research (NCAER) for the year 1981, black money worth Rs. 840 crore was created in the Indian economy over the period of nine years from 1965-66 to 1974-75 as a result of the operation of price controls in six commodities, viz., cement, steel, paper, vanaspati, automobile tyres and fertilisers. Similarly, as result of control on sugar, about Rs. 400 crore of black money were generated in the year 1991-92. Regulation of foreign exchange also leads to over-invoicing of imports and under-invoicing of exports and black-marketing of currency. Thus, the more stringent the measures of control and the more regulated an economy, the greater will be the effort to violate it which will increase hoarding, fraud, artificial scarcity and the resultant black money.

Quota System

Yet another source of black money is the quota system. The import quota, the export quota and the foreign exchange quota are generally misused by selling them at a premium. Unrealistic controls spawn a culture which encourage corporates to break the tax laws, particularly FERA laws. When the government came out with a scheme a few years ago (1992-93) to allow exporters to import goods without paying any customs duty, ingenious ways were devised to make money even out of this scheme, i.e., through over-invoicing exports to get more import benefits as well as avail of the tax setoffs given to exports. During 1992-96, the Directorate of Revenue Intelligence (DRI) and the Customs authorities detected 605 such cases. One export house (Ganpati Exports) benefited as much as Rs. 85 crore (*India Today,* November 30, 1996).

Scarcity

Black money is also caused by scarcity and defective public distribution system. When essential goods become scarce, people have to pay higher than the controlled price, which generates black money. The scarcity of cooking gas, cement, kerosene, sugar, refined oil, etc., has always resulted in illegitimate transactions and black money.

Inflation

The increase in prices of commodities like petrol, etc., in international market, increase in prices of commodities due to high increase in duties and taxes imposed by the government, conspicuous consumption indulged in by people with unaccounted money, diverting resources from production to speculation—all these cause inflation which in turn creates black money.

Elections in a Democratic System and Political Funding

Each election in the country involves an expenditure of thousands of crores of rupees. For contesting Lok Sabha election, a candidate normally spends more than one million rupees and for contesting Vidhan Sabha election, one spends more than Rs. 5 lakh in the present times. It is estimated that a single Lok Sabha election alone could see political parties spend around Rs. 1,000 crore to pay for poll expenses. Politicians also need to draw on business resources to nurse their constituencies. Given the mind-boggling numbers, black money naturally is built into the system. For funding politicians, even honest corporate houses have no option but to find ways to generate unaccounted-for money. Since the expenditure allowed by law for a candidate is limited and the companies are allowed to give up to 5 per cent of their profits as donations to political parties for elections, elections are generally financed by black money holders. These people expect political patronage and economic concessions which are obtained with the consent and the connivance of political elite in power in the form of artificial controls on commodities, laxity in the means of distribution, etc. All these methods create black money.

Real Estate Transactions

Estate transaction is an important source of generating black money. In these days, purchasing a house and/or land is considered to be very profitable. There is a growing tendency to transform rural agricultural land into urban residential land due to paucity of building sites in the urban areas. Establishing unapproved colonies on agricultural land is illegal. The transaction value shown by the colonisers in registration deeds is much less than the actual amount of the market value. This enables the seller of the land to evade capital gain tax. According to an estimate, illegal transaction of property alone generates about Rs. 2,000 crore of black money in a year, assuming that there are about 50 lakh transactions in urban property every year.

The high rates of stamp duty—ranging between 15.4 per cent and 28 per cent in different states—are a major cause of under-valuation of property and unreported deals, or both. The suggestion is that if duties are reduced to 2 per cent to 3 per cent, it will prevent evasion. Another hurdle is the Urban Land Ceiling Act, which reduces the supply of land and creates a flourishing black market. Roughly over Rs. 13,000 crore a year are generated through the real estate route.

Privatisation

Privatisation has opened up a new area to the private sector as well as to ministers and bureaucrats for making black money. Take the example of the Ministry of Communication in 1996 in which the minister concerned (in Narasimha Rao's government) had the authority of sanctioning contracts and licences worth Rs. 1,50,000 crore. The minister rode roughshod over departmental colleagues to give contracts to favoured companies. While the case is still pending (in October 1999) against the former minister in the courts, the Income Tax Department alone was said to be thinking (in November 1996) of realising from him a fine of Rs. 20 crore for violating the income tax rules. However, it could not do so. The former Union Steel Minister (in Narasimha Rao's government) was another powerful person who had been accused of having made huge black money of Rs. 16 crore by clearing the privatisation of a mine at a very low price to one concern in September 1995. A public outcry finally saw the deal getting shelved, though the minister managed to get away. The Petroleum Ministry also was involved in a scam relating to privatisation. The ministry threw open select oil fields in 1992. In one deal, a particular concern was awarded a contract for an oil field and the former Petroleum Minister is alleged to have received Rs. 7 crore for helping the group in getting the contract. It is expected that many scams will come to light for making black money through privatisation.

Agricultural Income

The unwillingness of the rulers on political grounds to bring agricultural income in the ambit of income tax has also contributed to generation of black money. Big industrial houses, over the past few decades, have entered the agriculture sector in a big way by acquiring large farms, growing and producing nothing. The black money accrued from other sources is sought to be converted into white by showing it on the agricultural income account. Taxing agricultural income may help contain this phenomenon.

ECONOMIC IMPACT

Black money causes irreparable damage to the economy of the country and its impact is felt down to the common man in the street. Some of the major economic impacts are: increase in inflationary pressure, distortion of developmental work, uneven distortion of resources, marginalisation of tax base, and creation of a parallel economy. Country's economic equilibrium is at stake, normal business activities are affected, and resources of financial institutions and commercial institutions are diverted and distorted (see *Crime in India*, 1995:339).

SOCIAL EFFECTS

Besides the economic effects, there are also many social consequences of black money. While economically, black money robs the exchequer of its due share, increases economic inequality and hampers programmes of economic development, socially it increases social inequality, acts as a breeding ground for corruption, creates frustrations among honest people, increases crimes like smuggling, bribery, etc., and adversely affects social service programmes for the uplift of the poor and the weaker sections of society. It also distorts the measurement of true rates like growth rate, inflationary rate, unemployment rate, poverty, etc., which in turn affects the government policies for containing these problems.

MEASURES OF CONTROL

Over the past 50 years, the government has at various times announced several schemes offering opportunities to bring black money overboard. Some of these schemes are: introducing the scheme of special Bearer Bonds, demonetising high denomination currency notes, stringent raids, and scheme of voluntary disclosures. In July 1991, the Union Finance Minister proposed a new scheme—National Housing Bank Scheme—to woo black money back into the legitimate operations of the national economy. The scheme offered possessors of unaccounted money an opportunity to deposit any amount of money (with a minimum limit of Rs.

10,000) with NHB without disclosing the source of funds. The offer remained open for seven months and closed on January 31, 1992. It permitted the account holders facility to withdraw 60 per cent of their deposits from the account while the remaining 40 per cent were impounded to be used for projects such as slum clearance and housing for the poor. The withdrawals were to be made after stating the purpose for which the money was proposed to be used. These people were taxed at the rate of 40 per cent while the balance amount was channelled back into the open economy. In 1997-98 budget, amnesty was proposed for legitimising black money by payment of 30 per cent as tax.

Some scholars have maintained that all these measures have touched only the tip of the iceberg. All the schemes have hardly fetched Rs. 5,000 crore over a period of fifty years. The main drawback in these schemes is that they touch the problem of black money already created but they do not go into the root cause of generation of black money and that is why a person is prepared to take the risk of keeping black money despite so many problems. Unless this problem is tackled, the menace of black money will continue to increase. It has been suggested that the problem of black money and parallel economy can be contained by reducing taxes in some areas, giving incentives for voluntary disclosure of income, overhauling the economic intelligence unit, curbing administrative corruption at various levels, exempting tax on money spent on house construction, doing away with control policies, and so forth. Isolated attempts may not yield much but a package of mutually reinforcing measures, along with a strong political will and the commitment of political elite, may prove to be successful to a large extent.

Further Readings

Chopra, O.P., "Unaccounted Income: Some Estimates", *Economic and Political Weekly*, Vol. XVII, Nos 17 & 18, April 24 and May 1, 1982.

Gupta, P. and S. Gupta, "Estimates of the Unreported Economy in India", *Economic and Political Weekly*, Bombay, Vol. XVII, No. 13, January 16, 1982.

Mahajan, V.S., *Recent Developments in Indian Economy*, Deep and Deep Publications, New Delhi, 1984, pp. 56-60.

Pendse, D.R., "Black Money: Its Nature and Causes", *The Economic Times*, March 19,1982.

Varghese, K.V., *Economic Problems of Modern India*, Ashish Publishing House, New Delhi, 1985, pp.242-254.

15 Smuggling

CONCEPT AND NATURE

Smuggling is an economic offence that is qualitatively different from the traditionally known white-collar crime. Economic advantage is the main motive behind this offence. The commodities which are mostly smuggled are drugs (heroin, etc.), gold and silver, diamonds, arms and explosives, wristwatches, electronic goods, synthetic fibres, etc. Globalisation has made possible vast increase in trade, more mobility and fast means of communication—all of which have made smuggling easier. This illicit activity is committed either all alone or in an organised manner with or without associates. Gangs are mainly engaged in smuggling with an intent to earn wealth through illegal means. Qualitatively, these offences are different from other offences in as much as that they differ in *modus operandi* by taking advantage of the deficiencies in laws, rules and regulations. The authorities empowered to act on getting information of commission of this crime are: Directorate of Revenue Intelligence, Directorate of Enforcement, Narcotic Control Bureau, and Directorate General of Foreign Trade.

THE MAGNITUDE

The number of seizures of commodities confiscated by the customs officials varies from 50,000 to 60,000 every year, while the value of the seized commodities in a year varies from Rs. 400 crore to Rs. 1,000 crore. For example, commodities seized by the customs officials in 1995 were worth

Rs. 1,062 crore. On an average, around 153 seizures were made in a day in 1995, and the average value of the goods seized in such seizure amounted to around Rs. 2.9 crore. In 1995, commodities seized were drugs worth Rs. 85.7 crore, electronic goods worth Rs. 63.3 crore, gold worth Rs. 58.3 crore, silver worth Rs. 0.5 crore, and other goods worth Rs. 854 crore. The number of persons arrested for smuggling all these commodities was 1,270 (*Crime in India*, 1995: 342-343). This indicates the gravity of the operations and trade in the contraband goods.

Narcotic drugs are found to be in the priority list of smuggling. Drug trafficking is in fact a money spinner in the under-world market, in spite of the Narcotic Drugs Act, 1985 and PITNDPS Act, 1988. Among drugs, those which are mostly smuggled are ganja, heroin, hashish and opium. During 1995, 14,673 persons were arrested which included 148 foreigners (*Crime in India*, 1995: 344- 45.) This points out that drug smuggling has a thriving market. It has also created a number of neorich class of people who control real estates, film production, airlines, corporate houses, etc. Their role in anti-national and terrorist activities and in clandestine trading in arms and ammunition has been thoroughly exposed in the recent past.

ORGANISED SMUGGLING

Many a time, smuggling is based on a cooperative effort like an organised business, i.e., it involves association of a small group of persons, chalking out plans by which detection may be avoided, development of a fund for successfully smuggling the commodity and providing protection to members, and maintaining political connections by means of which immunity may be secured in case of detection.

Characteristics

Smuggling based on cooperation of several persons and done in an organised way on a long-term basis has the following characteristics:

- Team-work, i.e., association of a group of persons which may last for a long term.
- Hierarchical structure, i.e., structure with grades of authority from the lowest to the highest, involving a system of specifically defined relationships with mutual obligations and privileges.
- Planning, i.e., making advance arrangements for successful smuggling, minimising risks and ensuring safety and protection.
- Centralised authority, i.e., functioning on the basis of centralised control which is vested either in the hands of one individual or a few members.

- Specialisation, i.e., specialising in smuggling just one commodity, say heroin or gold or arms, etc. Some groups, however, are engaged in smuggling more than one commodity.
- Division of labour, i.e., delegating duties and responsibilities.
- Protective measures, i.e., arranging protection against interference from law-enforcement authorities. The protective measures include contacts with policemen, lawyers, doctors, politicians, judges and influential persons in society. Giving money in cash or in gifts, providing help in elections, marriages etc., arranging foreign trips are some of the methods used by the organised smugglers to secure protection and avoid arrest and conviction.
- Conduct norms, i.e., framing rules of conduct and methods of operation for members. This helps in maintaining discipline, efficiency, loyalty, obedience, and mutual confidence.

Organisational Structure

Organised smuggling has a hierarchical structure of positions. If we explain it in the form of a pyramid, at the top are 'lords', powerful leaders who take important decisions and run the organisation. These leaders maintain a master-subordinate relationship with members at middle and lower levels. A middle echelon consists of 'lieutenants' who carry out commands of the 'leaders'. At the bottom of the structure are the 'carriers' who carry the smuggled goods by aeroplanes, trains, cars, buses, etc.

The hierarchical structure is held together by personal loyalties, a code of conduct and a chain of command. The hierarchial structure affects the career of smugglers, particularly those lower in the hierarchy. These bottom smugglers include girls also who carry the smuggled item. These bottom smugglers are either on the payroll of the organisation or get a fixed amount or a cut from the profits. The smugglers at the middle level are sometimes pulled up from the lower levels and sometimes directly recruited, having a record of smuggling. Leaders in the crime of smuggling live segmented lives, retiring to the seclusion of respectability. Their commitment, nevertheless, remains with the world of crime, where in detachment from the values of the larger society, they receive their prestige, power and a lifestyle of luxury.

The smugglers many a time operate through 'syndicates' which usually operate from established headquarters and create their own procedures. They avoid using violence which differentiates them from organised criminal gangs, who frequently use violence or threat of violence. Society knows the members of these syndicates as respectable citizens living in posh residential areas, freely associating with high-status persons and engaged in lawful earning pursuits. The smugglers' syndicates generally operate in big metropolitan areas and cities which happen to be big centres of communication, transportation and distribution of goods.

States in the North-East, Kashmir, Punjab, Bihar, and Tamil Nadu are some of the areas where terrorists, militants, naxalities, insurgents are engaged in fighting the police and the military for achieving their goals. They get the required weapons from the organised smugglers of arms and ammunition. The arrest of six crew members of an aircraft owned by a London-based company run by a New Zealander who dropped a large cache of sophisticated weapons in Puralia district of West Bengal in December 1995 is an example of oraganised smugglers engaged in systematic gun-running operations. Amongst the main accused Indians, one was from Bihar while the other held a Singaporean passport.

The Conduct Code

There is no evidence that various smugglers' organisations follow one particular code of conduct. But generally a smuggler works on the basis of the following directions: do not be an informer, work as a team member be loyal to the organisation, do not interfere with other's interests, do the assigned work quietly and safely and keep your eyes and ears open and mouth shut. The conduct code of the smugglers is, thus, similar to the codes adopted by professional criminals whose activities and conditions of existence bring them into confrontation with official authority. Among the unwritten rules are: maintain secrecy, put the organisation before self, reveal nothing to your close kin and friends, and do not disobey orders.

Survival Mechanisms

What is it that makes organised smuggling survive? Four factors appear to be important in this context: structural organisation, code of conduct, immunity measures, and loopholes in law. Here, structural organisation needs a little explanation. The survival of the organised smugglers depends upon the 'fix'. To put the 'fix' in and maintain important connections with those in government, law, and police, organised smugglers typically have one or more members assigned to corrupt officials to maintain 'good relations with them'. These members may be called: 'corrupters'. A corrupter's job is to bribe, buy, intimidate, negotiate and persuade policemen, politicians, judges, bureaucrats and all those who might help the organised smugglers to maintain immunity from arrest, prosecution and punishment. This may be termed as 'nullification of authority'. Nullification is sought both at the lower and at the higher levels. At the lower level are the individuals in the law-enforcement organisations, i.e., policeman, a prosecutor, a magistrate and so on. By giving 'gifts' to these people, the 'corrupter' nullifies the law enforcement process. At the upper level are ministers, MPs, MLAs, etc.

It could be said that immunity to organised smugglers is achieved in several ways: (i) the leaders are usually not arrested because they stay behind the scenes of operation; (ii) persons lower in the hierarchy, if arrested, are likely to be released by action taken by their supervisors. Such release is assured through 'the fix'; (iii) protection is secured by gaining political power through contributions to political parties or leaders themselves contesting elections for assemblies or parliament or municipal corporations, etc.; (iv) regular pay-offs to law-enforcement officials; and (v) immunity is also provided by loopholes in the law. Lawyers manage to save their clients from legal action because of these loopholes.

Further Readings

Ahuja, Ram, *Sociological Criminology* (Chapter 6 on 'Organised Crime'), New Age International Publishers, Delhi, 1996.

Crime in India, 1995 and 1996, National Crime Records Bureau, Delhi.

16 Social Change and Modernisation

SOCIAL CHANGE IN INDIA: CONCEPT, GOALS, DIRECTION, AND RESISTANCES

The Concept of Social Change

Social change is change in established patterns of social relations, or change in social values, or change in structures and subsystems operating in society. Social change may be partial or total, though mostly it is partial. Just as change in the examination system is partial change in the education system, enacting a law which prescribes punishment for refusing entry to untouchables in Hindu temples, or a law which legally permits divorce in society, or a law which does not permit marriage below a specific age, might be called partial changes in society. Nationalisation of banks, coal mines, etc., are examples of partial change in the economic system of society because these co-exist with private property ownership in other spheres. Total change hardly ever happens. A few aspects of family system, or marriage system or banking system or caste system, or factory system, etc., may change but we never find a total change in any of these social systems. Social change is thus always or mostly partial.

Percy Cohen (1979:176) has said that one might also distinguish between minor changes and major or fundamental changes in a society. Change in the core or strategic features of a society or a social system may be defined as a major change. If we take the example of prison as a social system, its important features are: giving training to prisoners, arranging food, recreation and medical facilities for the inmates, giving punishment to criminals for violating prison norms, permitting offenders to maintain social contacts with their family and friends, making security arrangements to prevent escape from prison, and so forth. Now suppose the entire security force is withdrawn and prisoners are given freedom to go to market at their will during the day time but spend nights compulsorily in jail, it will be an example of change in that feature of the prison system which will affect other features too. As such, it will be termed as a major or fundamental change in the prison system. Similarly, withdrawing social and commensal restrictions in intercaste relations will be termed as major change in the caste system. Isolating core features in a social system may not be difficult. For example, electoral system is an important feature of the democratic political system. If election results do not change the electoral system but changes in the electoral system have an effect on election results, it would be said that the electoral system is a *core* feature of the political system.

Concept and Indicators of Social Development

Social development is the process of planned institutional change to bring about better adjustment between human needs and aspirations on the one hand and social policies and programmes on the other. It is declaring war on poverty, illiteracy, ignorance, inequality, irrationality and oppression prevalent in society. It aims not merely at the uplift of the weak, the under-privileged and the disadvantaged people but also at improving the quality of life of all citizens. If a prerequisite for social development is participation of all people in building their society, it is the privilege of all people to enjoy the benefits of this participation in common efforts. The designing of social development involves four things: (i) assessing needs of people in society; (ii) introducing some structural changes in society which includes discarding some old institutions, creating some new institutions, or changing some existing institutions; (iii) making institutions responsive to people so that these really serve people; and (iv) associating people with decision-making processes, that is, taking planning to grass-roots level.

The methodology involved in designing social development includes: (i) *policy planning*, that is, determining goals, priorities, and strategies; (ii) *programming*, that is, allocating resources; (iii) *administering*, that is, seeking participation of individuals and groups in decision-making; (iv) *organising*, that is, preparing people to gain maximum benefit from services and resources and also (preparing people) to change the system, if necessary; and (v) *evaluation*, that is, measuring gaps in goals and performance and providing feedwork for further planning.

The important indicators of social development are: (i) change in levels of living, (ii) elimination of poverty, (iii) expansion in education, (iv) increase in level of employment, (v) social justice, that is, equal distribution of opportunities, (vi) uplift of the weaker groups, (vii) providing security against various exigencies of life, (viii) improvement in social welfare amenities, (ix) reducing disparities—regional, sectoral and social, (x) protection and improvement of health, (xi) safeguarding environment, and (xii) popular participation in expansion programmes involving both qualitative and structural changes.

Goals of Social Change in India

At the time of political independence of the country, many intellectuals felt that India had failed to modernise itself not because it lacked the wherewithal to develop but because it had been a victim of capitalist imperialism. The socio-cultural transformation we initiated five decades ago and the one which we want to plan for the coming decades in the twenty-first century aims at structural changes which could meet the emerging needs and aspirations of people. The collective goals we had planned to achieve in the very first decade of the republic were: social, economic, political and cultural. The *social* goals were: equality, justice, freedom, rationality, and individualism. The *economic* goals included: distributive justice and economic rationalism in place of economic theology. The *political* goals were: establishing a political system where the ruler is accountable to the ruled, decentralisation of political power, and associating more and more people with the decision-making processes. Our *cultural* goal was a change from sacred to secular ideology.

The goals set by our power elite were:

- To create a strong central government: This was necessary because historically, political authority in India has been fragmented. After independence, it was feared that the religious, linguistic, caste, tribal, class, etc., forces may further attempt to fragment authority. Strong federal government with some authority to state governments alone would thwart attempts at such fragmentation.
- To modernise economy: This was necessary for raising the low per capita income, for making the country self-reliant, and for having an indigenous capital goods sector which is not dependent on foreign private capital.
- To create a socialist pattern of society: This was necessary to restrict, but not eliminate, the role of private capitalists and emphasise public

ownership of major industries. However, since last one decade, economic liberalism has been accepted as our goal.

- To reduce inequalities among castes, regions, and classes.
- To preserve fundamental human rights, such as right of free speech, right of free religious expression, right of political participation, and so forth.
- To establish a society where individuals would be motivated by spirit of selflessness, sacrifice, co-operation and idealism.

Approaches to the Study of Social Change

Yogendra Singh in his early writings on social change (1969:11) talked of three approaches to the study of nature and process of social change in India: philosophico-historical and metaphysical approach, historical and political approach, and social anthropological and sociological approach.

The source for the philosophico-historical approach was described as the Indian and the western philosophies. Indian philosophy and religion have proposed a philosophical theory of change characterised by cyclical rhythm in society. The foundation of this theory was belief in *karma*, *dharma*, and *moksha*. At one time, this theory was much accepted but now it has almost waned because systematic analysis is not possible. Social change by the historico-political approach is studied through records of Indian history. For example, change in the caste system or change in the status of women is studied by systematic analysis of historical records pertaining to different periods. The limitation of this approach lies in the fact that all historical records may not be available or the evidence may not be reliable. Consequently, reliance on this approach for sociological generalisations would be fallacious. The socio-anthropological approach was considered more systematic than the other two (metaphysical and historical) approaches. The method in this approach is intensive fieldwork or participant observation. The theoretical propositions in this approach refer to a body of ethnographic data, either the result of one's own or another's fieldwork. The limitation of socio-anthropological approach lies in the effort to generalise about the macrocosm on the basis of the microcosm. This is on the implicit assumption of 'homogeneity' and 'universality'. But, in India, we find such heterogeneity and diversity. As such, by studying change between two time-periods in a certain institution (say family, caste, etc.) in one village., we cannot generalise that similar change takes place in other villages, or in the whole Indian society as well. The weaknesses in the socio-anthropological approach are eliminated in the sociological approach. In sociological approach, the focus is on systematic empirical inquiries at macrocosmic level and generalisations are developed.

In his later writings on social change, Yogendra Singh (1977) has talked of five approaches in studying social change in India. These are: evolutionary approach, cultural approach (sanskritisation and westernisation, little and great traditions, and parochialisation and universalisation), structural approach (based on functional and dialectical models), ideological approach, and integration approach.

Evolutionary Approach

In the evolutionary approach, gradual development is studied from simple to complex form through a long series of small changes. Each change results in a minor modification of the system, but the cumulative effect of many changes over a long period of time is the emergence of new complex form. Within the evolutionary approach, the four sub-approaches used by different scholars are: unilinear, universal, cyclical, and multilinear.

Conflict Approach

According to this approach, economic change produces other changes through the mechanism of conflict between different parts of the social system. The reasoning behind viewing conflict as the cause of social change is that if there is consensus in society and if various sectors are integrated, there is little pressure for change.

Cultural Approach

In the cultural approach, change is studied by analysing changing cultural elements of society. Within this approach, M.N. Srinivas studied change through sanskritisation and westernisation processes; Robert Redfield through change in little and great traditions; and McKim Marriott through the process of parochialisation and universalisation.

Structural Approach

This approach analyses change in the network of social relationships and in social structures (like castes, kinship, factory, administrative structures, etc.) These social relationships and structures are compared intra-culturally as well as cross-culturally. According to Yogendra Singh (1977:17), a structural analysis of change consists of demonstrating the qualitative nature of new adaptations in the patterned relationships.

Integrated Approach

Yogendra Singh (1973:22-27) feels that none of the above approaches provides a comprehensive perspective on social change in India. He has, therefore, integrated a series of concepts relating to social change and developed a new approach or paradigm, what he calls an 'integrated approach'. In this approach, he integrates (a) direction of change (that is, linear or cyclical), (b) context of change (that is, through macro or micro levels of structures), (c) source of change (that is, through external contacts or internal sources), and (d) substantive domain of phenomena undergoing change (that is culture and social structure).

Nature and Direction of Social Change in India

Have we realised our collective goals? Indian society has been described as traditional society till the first quarter of the twentieth century. Though the British Government did industrialise our country and introduced several economic and social changes, yet it was not interested in raising the quality of life of the mass of people. Have we succeeded in modernising our society after political independence? If yes, what has been the pattern of social change or modernisation? This question can be answered first by trying to understand what is a traditional society and what is a modern society.

A *traditional* society is one in which (i) the status of a person is determined by birth and is fixed, that is, individuals do not strive for social mobility; (ii) individual's behaviour is governed by custom, and ways of behaviour of people vary only slightly from generation to generation; (iii) social organisation is based on hierarchy; (iv) individual identifies himself with primary groups, and kinship relations predominate in interaction; (v) individual is given more importance in social relations than his position; (vi) people are conservative; (vii) economy is simple and economic productivity above subsistence is relatively low; and (viii) mythical thought predominates society.

Does this mean that traditionalism and modernity are two extremes and the two cannot co-exist? Scholars like S.C. Dube, and Yogendra Singh are of the opinion that the two can co-exist. Accepting traditionalism does not mean completely rejecting modernisation. It may simply mean regulating the forces of modernisation. Similarly, accepting modernisation does not mean complete rejection of traditionalism. It may mean retaining only those elements of traditionalism which are considered by the society as functional for it, in view of the set (collective) goals.

Accepting this viewpoint, we have to find out, to what extent Indian society continues to be traditional and to what extent it has become modern.

It will not be wrong to say that the nature of social change in India is such that we find synthesis of tradition and modernity. On the one hand, we have discarded those traditional beliefs, practices and institutions which we believed were more dysfunctional and on the other hand, we have imbibed those modern values and have created those modern institutions which we thought will help us in achieving our basic goal of "change in quality of life of the people".

In comparison to the British period, today we enjoy more individual freedom; we have more opportunities to rise in social scale; we have become more rational in discarding traditional social practices or creating new institutional structures; the number of people living below the poverty line has decreased; our per capita income in real terms has increased in five decades since we became a republic; and active higher social status and position of privilege and rank is no longer an illusion for the backward and the low caste people.

But with all this, have we achieved communal harmony? Have we been able to bring women on par with men? Have we been able to ameliorate the conditions of untouchables? Have we been able to remove the feelings of deprivation among different classes like cultivators, industrial workers, daily wage-earners? Have we been able to alter property relations in favour of the less privileged? Can we claim to have an egalitarian society? The answer to all these questions is the increasing agitations and widespread social unrest in our country.

The existing widespread unrest is the result of increasing contradictions in our social system. Some important contradictions are: our roles have become modern but our values continue to be traditional; we project egalitarianism but we practise discrimination; our aspirations have become very high but the means for achieving these aspirations are either not available or not accessible; we talk of nationalism but we encourage parochialism; we claim that our republic is dedicated to equality but in fact it is mired in an archaic system of caste; we claim to have become rationalists but we endure injustice and unfairness with fatalistic resignation; we proclaim the policy of liberalisation but we still impose too many controls; we support individualism but we reinforce collectivism; we aim at ideational culture but we hanker after sensate culture; many new laws have been enacted and old ones modified but these laws are either not implemented or are full of loopholes and benefit none except the legal profession. There are too many laws and too little justice, too many public servants and too little public service, too many programmes and plans and too little welfare, too much government and too little administration.

The result of these contradictions is that social unrest has increased in our society. Development has encountered formidable opposition from the corrupt and non-committed political elite and sub-elite who are much more interested in their personal prosperity than in the future of the country, from the special interest groups and the economic monopolisers who prefer to flourish in the non-competitive environment, and from the fanatic communal and religious leaders and the uninterested bureaucrats who are reluctant to shed their enormous powers.

Resistances to Social Change

It is true that Indian society is changing and certain directions of social change and development are clearly apparent, yet it is a fact that we have not been able to achieve all those goals which we wanted to achieve. What have been the hinderances in achieving our goals? Some western scholars like Gunnar Mydral suggest that the main cause of India's economic weakness is not lack of technical skills among the people but rather lack of initiative, of interest in improving their status, and of respect for labour. Such views are illogical, biased, and vigorously challenged by Indian and some western scholars like Morris (1967), Milton Singer (1966, 1969), T.N. Madan (1968), Yogendra Singh (1973), and S.C. Dube (1982). A good number of studies in rural India have shown keen desire on the part of the villagers for improvement. They are willing to work hard, change their harmful customs, eschew temptations, and rise above human fallibilities. The impediments to developmental efforts are not human factors but political environment, social structures, and economic handicaps.

Forces of Tradition

Change in a society is possible only by fostering attitudes of receptivity towards new ways of doing things. Sticking to one's traditions and refusing to accept new ideas act as a barrier to social change. The degree of cultural accumulation and the amount of contact with other societies determine the nature and extent of social change within a society. The possibility of invention and the introduction of new traits from other cultures is limited by the degree of cultural accumulation, which in turn depends upon the willingness to discard traditions—if not all, at least non-utilitarian and dysfunctional ones. What transpires through contacts with other cultures is diffusion, the source of most social change. Relatively isolated societies experience little change, whereas societies which are meeting grounds of people from many cultures experience rapid social change. In a society which does not change, one finds people refusing to intermingle freely and declining to share others' customs, knowledge, technology and ideologies. This refusal is born of people's belief that their traditions are sacred. They allege that the merit of traditions derives from transmission from a sacred orientation.

Traditionally transmitted norms are accepted not because they exist, but because they fill the need to have rules in a given situation. They perform a stabilising function in society. So, the role which traditional norms are likely to play in an economically and technically changing society depends, at least in part, on the place which tradition-oriented behaviour holds in society. And here we can draw a division on the continuum of tradition and modernity. For, in traditional society, traditional values are given importance because they have been transmitted from the past. But in modern society, the conditions for change are welcomed because they offer solutions to present problems.

Caste System

Caste system has been a great obstacle in achieving both justice and prosperity. Kingsley Davis (1951:216) was correct when he said that the conception of hereditary occupation is exactly the opposite of the idea of open opportunities, free competition, increasing specialisation and individual mobility associated with dynamic industrial economy. Factionalism is an important factor in the failure of development projects, particularly in rural areas. Caste and sub-caste membership is one basis of the formation of factions. In many areas where farmers belong to one caste amongst many, other castes do not wish to cooperate as it will be of no direct benefit to them. In areas where farmers are the ruling group, the development programme likewise fails to gain widespread acceptance. Any project that apparently aids one caste is opposed by all others castes who are jealous of their position in society or eager to defend their own position at every one else's expense. Like caste factions, the intra-caste factions also act as a barrier to social change.

Earlier, restrictions of caste system on interaction with people of other castes did not permit mobility and industrialisation, and today its use in politics has prevented rulers to function in constructive ways. William Kapp (1963:64) has also pointed out that Hindu culture and Hindu social organisation are determining factors in India's low rate of development. Milton Singer (1966:505), however, does not accept this viewpoint. His contention is that there is no considerable evidence to indicate that Hindu culture and caste system have had any dampening effect on India's development. He describes Kapp's conclusions as largely speculative extrapolations derived from misunderstood scriptual concepts.

Illiteracy, Ignorance and Fear

Ignorance caused by illiteracy creates fear which resists social change. Customary ways of doing things are considered safe because they have been tried. Opinion about trial in villages or in simple societies is not so rationalistic. New is unknown and therefore must be avoided. If inventions, which are in part determined by the existing material culture are frequent, people become accustomed to change and hostility to change tends to break down. Conversely, if material culture inventions are not frequent, change may be rare and feared. When illiteracy promotes hierarchy, education insists on the idea of equality. It encourages rationality too. Educated people generate all kinds of new desires, inventions, etc., and also develop means for achieving them.

The Values

The role played by values in social change is a subject of much controversy. For example, Hegel felt that social change was a result of the unfolding of ideas. Marx felt that values had no effect on long-term social change. He felt that social change was exclusively a result of the interplay of economic forces and was manifested in class struggle. Most of the Indian sociologists agree that values do influence both individual and collective behaviour, thereby influencing social processes. Many also feel that values are the result of change and therefore should not always be considered as primary factors in social change. The values of caste system (hierarchy, pollution, endogamy, etc.) were a great barrier in changing Indian society. It was only when technology and industrialisation were accepted by common people that geographical mobility and consequently social mobility became possible. Fatalism also prevented hard work and social change. Famines, floods, earthquakes, poverty, unemployment were all considered to be the result of God's wrath. In industrial societies, people have proved that control over nature is possible and undesirable situation is not a hopeless block but a challenge to man's ingenuity.

Ethnocentrism (belief in the superiority of one's culture) also prevents people from accepting things/innovations from other cultures. Ethnocentrism is so deeply engrained in the minds of Indians that even when they are sensitive to the philosophy of cultural relativism, they easily fall victim to evaluating others in terms of their own views. Pride and dignity too prevent people from accepting things suggested by others. They think that they are so mature and learned that others' suggestions need to be discarded.

The Power Elite

It has been recognised almost by all scholars in our country that government has been a principal agency of social change and a good part of social change has been stimulated and directed by government agencies. In government, the innovative and reformist functions rest with 'power elite', or what Pareto has called the 'governing elite'. All elite are not committed to community's welfare or society's development; many elite function on the basis of vested interests. In terms of their interest in self (S) and in public (P), I classify them in four groups (Ahuja, 1975:65-66): indifferent (-S,-P), manipulative (S+,P-), progressive (S-,P+), and rationalist (S+,P+). The development of a society depends upon the type of political elite who predominate. My contention is that in the first two decades of independence, our elite were nationalist-rational while in the last three decades, they have been parochialist-irrational. Since indifferent and manipulative elite have dominated over progressive and rationalist elite, our bureaucrats are more ritualist than innovative, our judiciary is more traditional than liberal, our police is committed more to politicians in power than to law. Thus, since our policy-makers and law-enforcers do not share the necessity of social change conducive to people's welfare, development has been tardy.

Population Explosion

The nation's potential for achieving the set goals is handicapped by explosion in our population. About 46,500 persons are added to our existing population every day, or 17 million persons every year, or 170 million people in a decade. It has been calculated, as stated earlier, that for every addition of about 165 lakh people in our country, we will require every year 5 lakh tons cereals, 2.5 million houses, 1.5 lakh primary and secondary schools, 5,000 hospitals and dispensaries, 2,000 primary health centres, 2 lakh hospital beds, and 50 thousand doctors. The large population thus checks our efforts to contain poverty and bring about rapid development.

It may be concluded that as regards direction of social change in India is concerned, there has been considerable cultural continuity along with change based on imbibing modern values, practices and institutions. Traditional patterns have not been held static and modern behaviour is commonly fitted into long-standing pattern of action.

PLANNING AND SOCIAL CHANGE

Planning is commitment to concentrated action. It is adjustment of social institutions to new social, economic, and political conditions. It is not necessarily rational because it is not always guided by reliable scientific information. For example, in India, if for eliminating poverty, emphasis is laid only on increase in production and the issue of control over population explosion is completely neglected, how could it be called rational planning? Social planning aims at: (i) change in social organisation, and (ii) community welfare (like improving educational facilities, increasing employment opportunities, doing away with evil social practices, etc.). According to Riemer, three important characteristics of planning are: (a) prior determination of objectives and proclamation of values; (b) concreteness, that is, laying down concrete details of its subject-matter; and (c) co-ordination of diversified skills and diversified professional training. For the success of a plan, we have to bear in mind a few things: (i) plan must stem from the people themselves, (ii) people's participation is extremely necessary, (iii) initiative for implementing the plan is to be taken not by the planners but by the activists in different walks of life, (iv) priorities have to be decided in advance, and (v) arbitration in decision-making must be by a person who has technical knowledge and is a trained professional because he has the capability of visualising alternative solutions.

In India, economic planning was advocated by M. Visveswaraya in the 1940s. The Indian National Congress appointed a National Planning Committee on the eve of the Second World War (1938-39) to frame an all-India plan. But it was the Bombay Plan (known as Tata Birla Plan) which made people planning-conscious in India. The Government of India set up in 1943 a committee of the Viceroy's Council, known as Reconstruction Committee of Council (RCC), which was assisted by Provincial Policy Committees to chalk out plans for reconstruction. In 1944, the Department of Planning and Development was also created. However, at this stage, government plans were not concerned with definite economic targets. They were mainly concerned with issues like raising standard of living, increasing purchasing power of people, stabilising agricultural prices, developing industries, removing wealth disparities, and raising the level of backward classes. Different provinces were asked to prepare their own plans. There was no resource budget and no priorities. Thus, it could be pointed out that induced social change could not be possible in India till independence because: (i) no priorities for development were determined through adequate planning, (ii) no adequate statistics were prepared regarding the need of production, national income, etc., (iii) limited foreign exchange was available for development purposes, (iv) private enterpreneurs were reluctant to invest huge amounts in industrial development because of the government's policies (v) there was no facility for getting raw materials, machineries and capital goods from abroad, (vi) no serious efforts were made to check the growth of population, (vii) planning mechanism was not possible in the absence of proper co-ordination among the provincial and the central committees, (viii) inflation had increased owing to world wars, and (ix) administrative machinery was developed mainly with a view to discharging policing function of the state. Bureaucrats were not trained to take interest in development schemes.

After independence, the Government of India appointed a Planning Commission in 1950 to coordinate all state and capital plans. The Commission was to: (i) determine priorities, (ii) plan balanced utilisation of the country's resources, (iii) make an assessment of the material, capital and human resources of the country, (iv) assess the progress achieved from time to time and recommend readjustment, and (v) identify factors which retard economic development.

Since its inception, Planning Commission has so far prepared nine Five Year Plans, each focusing on different objectives, say, family planning, increasing employment opportunities, increasing annual national income by 5 per cent to 7 per cent, growth of basic industries (like, steel, power, chemicals), maximum use of manpower resources, decentralisation of economic power, reducing inequalities in income distribution, achieving social justice with equality, and so on. It could be said that the central objective of planning in India has been to raise the standard of living of the people and to open out to them opportunities for a richer and more varied life.

But has planning in India achieved the objectives of planned change? During the period of fifty years of planning, the average rate of economic growth has been 3.5 per cent. Though it is not bad in comparison to the world's average of 4 per cent, it is definitely poor in comparison to the average of 7 per cent to 10 per cent of the developing countries.

Following Ronald Lippit (1958:96-99), it may be pointed out that certain principles have to be put into practice if a development programme has to be successful. Some of the important principles are: (i) development proposals and procedures should be mutually consistent, (ii) goals of development must be stated in terms that have positive value to the community, (iii) planners must have a thorough knowledge of the beliefs and values of the community's culture, (iv) development must take the whole community into account, (v) community must be an active partner in the development process, and (vi) communication and coordination between various agencies of development is essential. The countries, including Japan and Germany, which have done better are those which have no planning commissions and have no plans. Should India follow the same path?

FACTORS OF PLANNED CHANGE

Five Year Plans

The Planning Commission set up in 1950 has been formulating Five Year Plans for India's development taking an overall view of the needs and resources of the country. We have discussed all the nine plans in Chapter Ten.

If we make an appraisal of all the eight completed plans, we find that all our plans have been oriented towards something, sometimes self-reliance in agricultural production, sometimes employment; sometimes industrial growth, and so on. But poverty and unemployment have invariably increased. During the period of 48 years, the average rate of economic growth has been 3.5 per cent. During 1951-1998, our annual national income had increased by about 3.5 per cent, agricultural production by 2.7 per cent, industrial production by 6.1 per cent, and the per capita consumption by 1.1 per cent. Though the government claimed that the number of people below the poverty line came down to 33 per cent in 1998 yet we cannot concede that poverty has been contained since the number of unemployed people has increased. No wonder, more people feel frustrated today and the number of agitations is increasing every year.

Legislative Measures

A number of social legislations and executive measures have been taken in India for the benefit of various categories of population, viz., women, dalits, tribals, labourers, peasants, backward castes and classes, and so on. Important legislative measures are: Child Marriage Restraint Act, 1929 amended in 1974 which restricts marriage for girls below 18 years and for boys below 21 years; the Special Marriage Act, 1954 which permits marriage without the consent of parents, inter-caste marriages and divorce; the Hindu Marriage Act, 1955, which invalidates marriage of girls below 18 years and of boys below 21 years and permits divorce; the Widow Remarriage Act of 1856 which permits remarriage of widows; the Anti-Dowry Act, 1961 which restricts giving and taking of dowry in marriages; the Untouchability Act of 1955 which prescribes punishment for practising untouchability; the Hindu Adoption and Maintenance Act, 1956 which gives right to women to adopt a child; Medical Termination of Pregnancy Act, 1971 permitting abortion; the Hindu Succession Act, 1956 giving right to women as a daughter, wife and mother in property; and Equal Remuneration Act 1976 which restricts discrimination in wages between male and female working conditions during employment.

The executive measures were abolition of zamindari system, implementing Mandal Commissions' recommendations reserving 27 per cent seats for OBCs in services, etc., introducing bill in parliament for reservation of 33 per cent seats for women in parliament and state legislatures, and reservation of 15 per cent seats for SCs and 7 per cent for STs in jobs.

URBANISATION AND INDUSTRIALISATION

The urban population of India is expanding much more rapidly after independence. For the teeming millions, the city is where they come looking for jobs. In the 1901 census, only 10.8 per cent of the total population (or 25.6 million out of 238 million) lived in cities. In 1991, this had gone up to 25.73 per cent; and by 2001, nearly 35 per cent (or about 350 million of the estimated one billion population) will be urban residents. This means that in coming two years, there will be 37 cities with a population between one and ten million. Mumbai, Delhi and Calcutta will have more than 14 million people each (*The Hindustan Times*, January 24, 1999). One factor which has contributed relatively much to the increase in urban population is industrialisation. This is similar to what occurred in the developing West, where accelerated urbanisation was largely the result of industrialisation. Push as well as pull factors account for the movement from villages to cities. Of the push factors, first, population increase means fewer jobs to go round in the traditional agricultural sector. Second, where agriculture is becoming modernised, an absolute reduction in jobs takes place. Of the pull factors, the strongest one is the prospect of making a better living than as a rural peasant. Cities have large economies in which determined or inventive people can survive and in some cases even prosper. Even begging is likely to produce better income in the city. Second, facilities such as electricity, clean water, and educational, communication and recreational are more likely to be available in a city. Third factor is the cultural attraction of a city, and the glamour of the 'modern' way of life. What appeals most to the young villagers—boys and girls—is the urban wealth and lifestyle; but, perhaps, there is a deeper desire to 'become' urbanised—to think and feel like urban youth. Modernisation theorists regard this process as 'liberating'. It is in a city that individualism takes birth and blossoms and it is here that individual gets opportunity to break traditional boundaries and achieve those goals and aspirations that give him an identity of his own.

But the increasing population of cities conceals more than it reveals. All people flooding into a city cannot get a house, either because they cannot afford rent or because it is too far away from the work-place. This compels them to live in slums. In Mumbai, nearly half of the population—6.5 million people—lives in squatter settlements or on pavements. The city's population has increased three times since 1964 but the squatters have grown fifteen-fold. The number of slum-dwellers in metropolitan areas of Delhi, Calcutta and Chennai runs in millions, while their number in big cities like Jaipur, Ahmedabad, Bangalore, Lucknow, etc., is in lakhs.

Besides increase in slum areas, urbanisation also has affected family relations, inter-caste and inter-community relations, status of women, rate of crime and juvenile delinquency, and so forth.

Urban planning has been skewed because it has traditionally reflected the interests of the powerful and the middle-class. The needs of the masses are never taken into consideration. For example, in Bombay while the planned ratio in reclaimed land of commercial to residential use was 20:80 till the 1970s, in 1992, the actual ratio was 80:20, leading to congestion, overcrowding, and enormous pressure on road and suburban rail transport and on water-supply, electricity, sewerage, etc.

The main factors which have created the urban mess are: defective planning, alien designs, lack of understanding and investment in public transport, over-regulation, and not involving private agencies in planning and building.

The solution for reducing the growth of cities lies in developing ring towns. Public transport facilities should also be strengthened with stress on reducing private vehicles but speeding up public transport. In Mumbai, the suburban trains have managed to extend the city's suburbs till 120 kms away.

Urbanisation brings changes in work-force structure too (i.e., people engaged in primary (agriculture), secondary (manufacturing) and tertiary occupation (trade, transport, public administration, banking and other services) and in rural-urban productivity gap. For example, if we take the case of West Bengal, the rate of urbanisation in the state between 1951 and 1991 was slow in comparison to Maharashtra, Gujarat, Tamil Nadu as well as All India level. This affected the distribution of workforce in all the three sectors (primary, secondary and tertiary) in the state. In the urban areas of this state, the percentage of work-force between 1951 and

1991 in the primary sector varied between 3.37 and 8.22, in the secondary sector between 34.78 and 41.06, in the tertiary sector between 52.25 and 60.73 (*Economic and Political Weekly*, November 21-27/December 4, 1998:3035).

Industrialisation has not only promoted urbanisation but has also affected social structure and social institutions. Its one impact is seen on increasing the importance of specialised education, which in turn, has affected the age for marriage. Mature and grown up youths postpone their marriages till they complete their education and settle in life. Post-puberty marriages then affect marital as well as intra-family relations. Individuals become more conscious of their individual interests and aspirations. Further, industrialisation has given impetus to mobility also. Mobility involved is essentially lateral rather than a marked change of social status. But as the worker in the industry achieves skill, his social status also changes, though the change is based more on horizontal than vertical basis.

Industrialisation has affected the means of control too. Informal means have given place to formal means. Loomis too has said that industrialisation has given rise to market economy which does not accept the traditional oral means of social control but lays emphasis on written control measures. Industrialisation has led to the growth of trade unions too, which, in turn, have affected the employer-employee relations. The unions have also focused on protecting the interests and social welfare and social security of the workers. This has forced the government to enact social legislation. Lastly, talking of the impact of industrialisation, sociologists have also pointed out its effect on development of means of communication which has reduced self-dependence of villages, increased longevity of life, and promoted commercialised recreation. In short, industrialisation has affected the interests and the values of society to such an extent that individuals' identity, status, commitment, and behaviour have come to be reshaped and reoriented.

SOCIAL (REFORM) MOVEMENTS

Social movements in India have not only been protest and dissent movements but also reform and reactionary as well as socio-religious and freedom movements. These movements defined as "collective effort to promote/resist change" came into origin only after uniformity in intellectual orientations, social structures, ideological preferences, and perceptions of truth came into existence. It is a well-known fact that characteristics of society shape the styles of movements. Therefore, the elements of social structure and the future vision of society provide the focal point of analysis of social movements.

Till the British period, the orientation of social movements in our country was religious, though national liberation movement also emerged after the 1930s which was overtly against the forces of imperialism and colonialism. But, after independence, the new situation that emerged led to divergence in the targets of attack, say political authority, economic exploitation, cultural domination, male domination and humiliation of women, and so forth. This led to proliferation of diverse movements.

Social movements are often labelled on the basis of the *identity of particular participants*, e.g., tribal movement, Harijan movement, women's movement, peasant movement, student movement, industrial workers' movement, and so on. Similarly, movements are also labelled on the basis of the *nature of collectivities* against whom they are led, e.g., anti-Brahminism, anti-leftist, anti-dalits and so on. Yet an other basis of classification is their *territorial anchorage*, i.e., locality in which they originate and operate, e.g., Vidharbha movement, Telengana movement, Chhatisgarh movement, Jharkhand or Vananchal movement, Uttaranchal movement, and so on. Such names indirectly point out the goals pursued. Movements are also named after the *issues they pursue*, e.g., Anti-Hindi movement. Movements are named after their *initial or top leadership* too, e.g., Gandhian movement, Ramakrishna movement, J.P. (Jayaprakash) movement, etc. M.S.A. Rao (1978) has talked of three types of movements—reformist, transformative, and revolutionary.

We will confine our analysis here to one type, viz., reformist. Reform movements bring about partial changes in value system. They do not affect structural changes (as transformative movements do) nor do they bring about radical changes in the totality of social and cultural systems (as revolutionary movements do). Here we will discuss five reform movements relating to specific social collectivities, viz., peasant or agrarian movements, tribal movements, dalit movements, backward caste/class movements, and women's movements. All these movements are characterised by five elements: (i) collective goal (ii) common ideology of widely accepted programme (iii) collective action (iv) minimal degree of organisation and (v) leadership. Thus, a 'social movement' with above characteristics is different from 'agitation' as the latter has no ideology and no organisation.

Ghanshyam Shah (1998:19) holds that some collective actions termed by some scholars as 'agitations' are considered by others as movements; e.g., demand for the formation of linguistic states. Shah himself considers them as 'movements' or a part of a social movement of a particular stra tum of society. Thus, demand for Vananchal in Bihar, Utranchal in Uttar Pradesh, and Chhatisgarh in Madhya Pradesh can be described as social movements according to him (*Ibid*:19).

Generally two approaches are used in the analysis of social movements: Marxist and non-Marxist. The Marxist approach views a social movement as: (i) collective action to bring about revolutionary change in society; (ii) its cause is located in the economic structure of society or in the antagonistic interests between two opposite classes; (iii) the 'powerful' class uses the coercive power of the state to impose its ideology and to control the exploited classes, while the 'powerless' class resists, protests and revolts against the dominance of the dominant class; (iv) members of the same class not only have common interests vis-à-vis other classes but also share a common consciousness regarding their position in society. (*Ibid*:21). The non-Marxist approach criticises this approach on the ground that (a) it ignores cultural factors and over-emphasises structural factors, (b) it over-determines economic factors, (c) it is 'reductionist' approach. In the approach of non-Marxist scholars, there is a great variation in the analysis of social movements. Some do not inquire into causes while others differ in their emphasis on the causes responsible for the movements. Some lay stress on cultural factors, some on individual traits, some on manipulation by elite, and some on conflict between tradition and modernity.

Our approach in the analysis of above five movements is mainly based on A.R. Desai's, Rajni Kothari's, Gurr's and M.S.A. Rao's approaches. Desai (1986) held that some movements are caused by the inability of our Constitution to protect the civil and the democratic rights of people. Rajni Kothari (1984, 1986) is of the opinion that failure of the state in 'social transformation' of society in which repression and intimidation of large masses of people has become common, compels people to assert their rights through various struggles. Gurr (1970) and M.S.A. Rao (1979) have explained social movements in terms of 'relative deprivation'. Rao focuses on the 'possibility of doing something by the sufferer' along with relative deprivation. Ghanshyam Shah (1979) and T.K. Oommen (1977) do not accept Relative Deprivation Approach in explaining social movements. Oommen's argument is that deprivation theorists do not view movements as 'ongoing process of change'. They also do not deal with the sources of deprivation. Shah holds that deprivation theorists ignore the importance of consciousness and the ideological aspects of the participants.

Tribal Movements

Numerous uprisings of tribals have taken place beginning with one in Bihar in 1772, followed by many revolts in Andhra Pradesh, Andaman and Nicobar Islands, Arunachal Pradesh, Assam, Mizoram and Nagaland. The important tribes involved in revolt in the nineteenth century were Mizos (1810), Kols (1795 and 1831), Mundas (1889), Daflas (1875), Khasi and Garo (1829), Kacharis (1839), Santhals (1853), Muria Gonds (1886), Nagas (1844 and 1879), Bhuiyas (1868) and Kondhas (1817).

Some scholars like Desai (1979), Gough (1974) and Guha (1983) have treated tribal movements after independence as peasant movements, but K.S. Singh (1985) has criticised such approach because of the nature of tribals' social and political organisation, their relative social isolation from the mainstream, their leadership pattern and the *modus operandi* of their political mobilisation. Tribals' community consciousness is strong. Tribal movements were not only agrarian but also forest-based. Some revolts were ethnic in nature as these were directed against zamindars, moneylenders and petty government officials who were not only their exploiters but aliens too (see Shah, 1998:86).

When tribals were unable to pay their loan or the interest thereon, money-lenders and landlords usurped their lands. The tribals thus became tenants on their own land and sometimes even bonded labourers. The police and the revenue officers never helped them. On the contrary, they also used the tribals for personal and government work without any payment. The courts were not only ignorant of the tribal agrarian system and customs but also were unaware of the plight of the tribals. All these factors of land alienation, usurpation, forced labour, minimum wages, and land grabbing compelled many tribes like Munda, Santhals, Kol, Bhils, Warli, etc., in many regions like Assam, Orissa, Rajasthan, Madhya Pradesh, Andhra Pradesh, Bihar, and Maharashtra to revolt.

The management of forests also led some tribes to revolt, as forests in some regions are the main sources of their livelihood. The British government had introduced certain legislations permitting merchants and contractors to cut the forests. These rules not only deprived the tribals of several forest products but also made them victims of harassment by the forest officials. This led tribes in Andhra Pradesh and some other areas to launch movements.

Raghavaiah in his analysis in 1971 of tribal revolts from 1778 to 1970 listed 70 revolts and gave their chronology. The Anthropological Survey of India in their survey in 1976 of tribal movements identified 36 on-going tribal movements in India. It was said that though these revolts were neither numerous nor gravely frequent, yet there was scarcely any major tribe in middle or eastern India which at some time in the last 150 years had not resorted to launching movements to register their protest and despair. Some studies on tribal movements have been conducted and reported in North-East and Central India. However, there was an insignificant number of movements or none at all among the tribals of the southern states. This is so because the tribes down south are too primitive, too small in numbers, and too isolated in their habitat to organise movements, in spite of their exploitation and the resultant discontent (K.S. Singh, 1983:XVI). L.K.Mahapatra (1972:408) also has observed that we do not find any significant social, religious, status-mobility, or political movement among the numerically small and migratory tribes.

After independence, the tribal movements may be classified into three groups: (1) movements due to exploitation by outsiders (like those of the Santhals and Mundas), (2) movements due to economic deprivation (like those of the Gonds in Madhya Pradesh and the Mahars in Andhra Pradesh), and (3) movements due to separatist tendencies (like those of the Nagas and Mizos).

The tribal movements may also be classified on the basis of their orientation into four types: (1) movements seeking political autonomy and formation of a state (Nagas, Mizos, Jharkhand), (2) agrarian movements, (3) forest-based movements, and (4) socio-religious or socio-cultural movements (the Bhagat movement among Bhils of Rajasthan and Madhya Pradesh, movement among tribals of south Gujarat or Raghunath Murmu's movement among the Santhals).

Mahapatra (1972) has classified tribal movements in three groups: reactionary, conservative and revolutionary. The reactionary movement tries to bring back 'the good old days', whereas the conservative movement tries to maintain the status quo. The revolutionary or the revisionary movements are those which are organised for 'improvement' or 'purification' of the cultural or social order by eliminating evil customs, beliefs or institutions.

Surajit Sinha (1968) has classified movements into five groups: (i) ethnic rebellion (ii) reform movements (iii) political autonomy movements within the Indian Union, (iv) secessionist movements, and (v) agrarian unrest. K.S. Singh (1983) has also classified them in more or less the same way, except that he has used the word 'sanskritisation' instead of reform movement and 'cultural' instead of 'ethnic'. S.M. Dubey (1982) has classified them in four categories: (a) religious and social reform movements (b) movements for separate statehood (c) insurgent movements and (d) cultural rights movements. Ghanshyam Shah (1998:88-89) has classified them in three groups: (1) ethnic (2) agrarian, and (3) political.

If we take into consideration all the tribal movements, including the Naga revolution (which started in 1948 and continued up to 1972 when the new elected government came to power and the Naga insurgency was controlled), the Mizo movement (guerrilla warfare which ended with the formation of Meghalaya state in April 1970, created out of Assam and Mizoram in 1972), the Gond Raj movement (of Gonds of Madhya Pradesh and Maharashtra, started in 1941 for a separate state and reaching its peak in 1962-63), the Naxalite movements (of the tribals in Bihar, West Bengal, Andhra Pradesh and Assam), the agrarian movements (of the Gonds and the Bhils in Madhya Pradesh), and the forest-based movements (of the Gonds for getting customary rights in the forests), it could be said that the tribal unrest and the resultant movements were mainly movements launched for liberation from (i) oppression and discrimination, (ii) neglect and backwardness, and (iii) a government which was callous to the tribals' plight of poverty, hunger, unemployment and exploitation. K.S. Singh (1985) analysing tribal movements before independence has divided them into three phases: the first phase between 1795 and 1860, the second between 1861 and 1920, and the third between 1921 and 1947. The first phase coincided with the establishment of the British Empire, the second with intensive colonialism during which merchant capital penetrated into tribal economy, and the third with participation in the nationalist movement and also launching of agrarian as well as some separatist movements. As already stated earlier, tribal movements after independence have been classified by K.S. Singh in four categories: agrarian, sanskritisation, cultural and political. In the first two phases before independence, K.S. Singh holds that in their effort to introduce British administration in the tribal areas, the British came in conflict with the tribal chiefs. The rebellious tribal leaders revolted against the British and exhorted their followers to drive out the outsiders. Such movements were launched by Oraon, Mundas, Maikda, etc., in Madhya Pradesh, Gujarat and North-East India. After independence, the tribal movements were launched either for maintaining cultural identity or for demanding a separate state or for asserting their status as caste Hindus through sanskritisation process or on economic issues.

Stephen Fuchs (1965) has dealt with a large number of first type of tribal movements. He has called them messianic movements led by rebellious persons gifted with abilities for assuming the role of a Messiah, or these gifted people (Messiahs) are given this messianic role by the community when it faces economic distress, social strain or political oppression.

Fuchs has suggested that success of such a movement would depend upon the individual ability of charismatic leaders, thereby ignoring the relevance of system characteristics. Fuchs' analysis of movements is mostly descriptive which lists host of factors for the success or failure of these movements. None of them propose a theoretical framework.

Not many studies have been conducted on the political-separatist dimension in Nagaland, Mizoram, Chotanagpur and Madhya Pradesh. The Jharkhand movement in Bihar is a movement of tribal communities consisting of settled agriculturalists which are sensitised to *Vaishnavism*. Further, Chotanagpur was the most advanced of the tribal regions in terms of literacy, political consciousness and industrial progress. Christian Missions influenced the lives of tribes here substantially. These Missions promoted education, planted the notion of private rights in land, and emphasised a sense of separateness from the rest. The Jharkhand movement after 1950 developed in phases—from ethnicity to regionalism (Singh, 1977). Of these, the phase (1963-1975) after the fourth general elections is characterised by fragmentation of the Jharkhand party and factionalisation of tribal politics. The BJP-led government at the Centre announced in 1998 the creation of two tribal states—one in Bihar and another in Madhya Pradesh.

B.K. Roy Burman (1971 and 1979) has distinguished between proto-national and substantial movements among tribes. Proto-national movements emerge when tribes experience a transformation from tribalism to nationalism. It is a search for identity at a higher level of integration. In contrast, sub-national movements are a product of social disorganisation pioneered by acculturated elite engaged in the contraction of relationship and not exclusion of it with the outside world. While proto-nationalism results from expansion of the orbit of development, sub-nationalism is the result of disparities of development. Sub-nationalism is based on the coercive power of the community, while proto-nationalism is based on the moral consensus of the community (see Oommen, 1985:104).

L.K. Mahapatra (1968) in his study of tribal movements based on a time-sequence and the nature of stimulus in their existence noted certain general tendencies: (1) Most reformist tribal movements, although initiated by charismatic leaders, gradually led to rationalisation and institutionalisation, affecting structure but not always affecting basic changes. (2) Tribal movements, irrespective of their goal orientation, invariably appeared among the numerically strong, usually settled agriculturalists and economically well-off tribes. (3) Primitive and small tribes directly took to large-scale conversion and separatist tendencies are marked amongst them. (4) Given the geographical distribution, a pan-Indian tribal movement is unlikely to emerge. (5) Democratic politics among tribes is fragmentary which in turn blocks the emergence of civil collectivism. (see, Oommen, 105-106).

Surajit Sinha (1972) has proposed several propositions regarding tribal solidarity movements: (1) The nature and degree of involvement of tribes in solidarity movements will depend on several factors like location, size of population, exposure to outside communities, level of economy and the historical experience. (2) The intensity of tribal solidarity will not be strong. (3) Isolated and scattered tribes with a primitive economic base would rarely be involved in solidarity movements.

An instance of tribal exploitation may be taken to explain the cause of origin of a movement.This incident took place in June 1999 among Bettada tribals in Nagarhole forests near Hunsur town in Kodagu district in Karanataka state. About 29,000 Bettada tribals have been evicted from the Nagarhole forest ranges since 1972. These tribals were promised rehabilitation by the Government. In 1998 some land became available in the area and the Bettada Gram Sabha authorised 70 families to take over the land. This was legal because the Centre had empowered gram sabhas to disburse land under their control. But about 200 forest department officials and the police burnt down huts of these 70 tribal families. The local tribal organisation first organised protest dharnas and then a movement calling for severe action against the officials concerned and the rehabilitation of the tribals.

All this depicts that when the law does not help tribals, when the government remains callous, and the police fails to protect them, even harasses them, they take to arms against their exploiters. These movements indicate that tribals adopted two paths of achieving goals: (a) non-violent path of bargaining and negotiating with the government and using a variety of pressure tactics without resorting to violence/revolts, and (b) militant path of revolts or mass struggles based on developing the fighting power of the exploited/oppressed tribal strata. The consequences of both these paths are different. One indicates struggle oriented to reforms, while the other indicates structural transformation of the community. The fact that tribals continue to be faced with problems and also continue to feel discontented and deprived, brings to the fore the conclusion that both paths have not helped them to achieve their goals.

Peasant or Agrarian Movements

There are two views on peasant movements: one, that these movements originated only after independence and that these are purely social and cultural in nature; two, these movements existed long before independence and were against colonial rulers as well as zamindars and money-lenders, i.e., they were political and cultural. Moore Jr (quoted by Ghanshyam Shah, 1998:34-35), writing about the peasant movements in India (in 1967) has not accepted the revolutionary potential of the Indian peasantry. According to him, Indian peasants are traditionally docile and passive because of which cultivation remained lackadaisical and inefficient during the Mughal and the British periods. Hence, there were no widespread peasant movements. But Moore's contention has been challenged by A.R. Desai, Kathleen Gough and D.N. Dhanagare. They argue that a number of peasant revolts have been overlooked by historians. Gough has talked of 77 revolts in the last two centuries, the smallest of which engaged several thousand peasants in active support. A.R.Desai (1979, xii) has also observed that the Indian rural scene during the entire British period and thereafter had been bristling with protests, revolts, and even large scale militant struggles involving hundreds of villages and lasting for years. Ranajit Guha (1983) has said that agrarian disturbances of different forms and scales were endemic until the end of the nineteenth century. There were no fewer than 110 known revolts during 117 years of the British rule. Dhanagare (1983:5) has argued that Moore's generalisations are questionable because there were various peasant resistance movements and revolts in India.

Peasant movements in India, according to A.R. Desai (1986) and Ghanshyam Shah (1998: 31-38), have been classified on the basis of time-periods—into pre-British and post-independence. The post-independence period is classified into pre-Naxalite and post-Naxalite periods or pre and post-green revolution periods. The latter period is further divided into pre and post-Emergency periods. A.R. Desai is also of the opinion that the nature of peasant movements varies according to the agrarian structures which have undergone changes during different periods. He (1986) has classified colonial India into ryotwari areas under British territory, zamindari areas under princely authority, and the tribal zones. The peasant struggles in these areas had different characteristics, raised different issues, and involved different strata of the peasantry. He further divides post-independence agrarian struggles into two categories: struggles launched by rich farmers and by poor farmers. The agrarian structure has thus not evolved a unified pattern throughout the country.

Kathleen Gough (1974) has classified peasant revolts on the basis of their goals, ideology and methods of organisation into five types: (i) restorative rebellions to drive out the Britishers and restore earlier rulers, (ii) religious movements, (iii) social banditry, (iv) terrorist vengeance for collective justice, and (v) mass insurrections for the redress of particular grievances. As regards the issues involved in peasant uprisings, some were related to conflicts between tenants and landlords, some were because of the oppression by zamindars of majority religious community (Hindus), and some were because of the factors like communal outburst, provocation by government officials and police etc., for improving economic conditions, demand for higher wages, forced labour (begar) and so on. It is held by some writers that Gandhiji mobilised the peasantry for the cause of national freedom and not for fighting against zamindars and money lenders. There are other writers who suggest that the relationship between peasant movements and the national movement was one of reciprocity, i.e., give and take. The task of taking up peasants' class demands as well as fighting against imperialists were dealt with simultaneously. In any case peasants' specific needs and interests of security of tenure, debt relief and cheap credit etc., could not be emphasised strongly by the nationalist leaders. After independence, however, the leaders tried to mobilise peasantry against zamindars and landlords. The exploited peasantry was not a united group as they were vertically alligned with the masters through factional ties. Initially, the poor peasants were least militant but as the anti-landlord and anti-rich peasant sentiment was built up by the middle peasant, the revolutionary energy of the poor peasant was transformed into a revolutionary force. But peasants taking up revolutionary action were not on all-India basis. It was only in some regions that peasant movements were organised.

The more important peasant movements in different regions were: Tebhaga, Telengana and Naxalite. The Bhoodan and Sarvodaya movements also took up peasants' interests but they were taken up not by the peasants themselves but by Vinoba Bhave and Jayaprakash Narayan.

Tebhaga movement (1946-47) was caused and facilitated by a large number of factors—the 1943 famine, drive against jotedars, hoarders and black-marketeers, social solidarity of the tribals involved in the movement, and the increased bargaining capacity of sharecroppers. Since this movement was limited in its spread, it failed. The wedge between Hindus and Muslims—the participant groups—i.e., communal politics, lack of harmony between caste and class and the upper class manipulation of loyalties within the peasantry also contributed to its (movement's) failure (Dhanagare).

The *Telengana* movement (1946-51) in south India was initially a success but ultimately a failure because of communist support to the Muslim Razakars against the Indian army, which ran counter to the nationalist sentiment and movement. Dhanagare has referred to this movement as a broad class-base movement as it involved middle, poor and landless peasants against landlords.

The Naxalbari Movement

When the United Front government with CPI participation came into power in West Bengal in February 1967, some active and vocal groups emerged. One of them under the leadership of Charu Majumdar and Kanu Sanyal, insisted on developing militancy on the peasant front, and preparing peasants for an armed struggle. Initially, the leaders preached massive participation of peasants for forcible occupation of *benami* land but later on they emphasised liquidation of class enemies through the use of guerrilla tactics. Thus, mass movements were replaced by underground small group squads. This guerrilla activity of Naxalbari movement struck most in West Bengal and Andhra Pradesh and later on in Bihar also.

The peasant revolt in Naxalbari started in 1972 in three areas in Darjeeling district of West Bengal. Rajbansis (originally a tribe), Oraons, Mundas and Santhals constituted a large proportion of the population in this region. The members of the last three tribes were those who had migrated from Chotanagpur (Bihar) to work in tea-gardens in Darjeeling district. Landowners were called *Jotedars* and tenants were called *adhiari*. The status of *adhiari* was precarious. They were so much exploited and treated like bonded labour that it led to peasant revolt in the 1950s and the 1960s. Kanu Sanyal and others made their first entry amongst the exploited peasants in the 1960s, demanding abolition of zamindari, land to the tiller, prevention of tenant eviction, etc. The call given by the Kisan Sabha to peasants in the late 1950s and the early 1960s for regaining possession of *benami* land was: reap and store the harvest at your own place, ask jotedars to furnish proof of their landownership before the peasant committee, arm yourself to protect the crop and save your crop from the police. In the second phase of Naxalbari peasant uprising in the late 60s and early 1970s, secret combat groups were formed and peasants were urged to seize the lands of *jotedars* and of the plantation workers who had purchased land from poor peasants, cultivate the seized land and retain all the produce from lands, ask landlord for food and if he refused, take it by force, deprive *jotedar* of his firearms. The 1967 Naxalbari uprising in Naxalbari area was suppressed through police action, but the revolt was renewed by August-September 1968 and continued up to 1972.

The important characteristics of Naxalbari peasant uprising in West Bengal were: one, mobilisation to protect the interests of the peasant and the labouring classes and covering all ethnic (including tribes) and caste groups; two, the means adopted were non-institutionlised and violence was encouraged; three, leadership was provided by communist party leaders; four, it aimed at downward mobility of *jotedars* and upward mobility of marginal peasants in bondage. Thus, the difference between Gandhian Sarvodaya movement and Naxalbari movement was that the former aimed at replacing individual ownership of land with communal ownership while the latter aimed at individual ownership.

The factors which had contributed to the failure of this movement were: its anti-national slant as manifested in the Chinese support for it, its vocal denunciation of the Indian national leadership and acceptance of Chinese leadership as source of its aspiration, its declared intention to capture state power, its open support to violence and factionalism among the leftists. R.K. Mukherjee (1978:73-74) has analysed this movement in terms of relationship between social structure and social change. He argues that although the declared intention of the movement was capturing state power, in reality, the revolt was not directed against the *system* but against its *excesses*. It was the exchange of goods between the peasant and the owner landlord that was sought to be properly regulated.

The agrarian movements in India have also been studied by scholars from six different viewpoints: (1) in terms of their functioning as associations at micro and macro levels; (2) relationship between politics and agrarian movements, i.e., mobilising peasants by political parties like Congress, Communists, etc.; (3) relationship between social structure (caste, class and power) and agrarian movements; (4) relationship between the green revolution and agrarian movements (The green revolution not only affected the traditional agrarian relations but it also accentuated economic disparities and accelerated social aspirations of villagers); (5) relationship between agrarian legislation and movements (i.e., movements causing legislation and legislation causing movements); and (6) relationship between mobilisation and organisation of movements.

Some movements for the welfare of peasants were organised on Gandhian principles. Two such movements were Bhoodan movement of Vinoba Bhave and Sarvodaya movement of Jayaprakash Narayan. The immediate object of the Bhoodan movement was collecting land from the rich and its distribution to the poor. However, this movement failed in achieving its goal.

Religious Movements

Religious movements in India have mainly been anti-orthodox Hindu ideology, anti-Brahmin, pro-Muslim, pro-Christian, or pro-Sikh movements. These movements were either protest movements or movements focusing on separate identity or for justifying changes in the existing order of social relationship. Some movements protested against the orthodox ideology of leaders of their faith, some against Brahminical Hinduism and the caste system, some were attacks on the notions of purity and pollution and the corrupt practices of the Brahmins, and so on.

Oommen (1985:87) has classified religious movements in three groups: (1) movements which started essentially as *protest against Hinduism* and came to be established as independent religions, such as Jainism, Buddhism and Sikhism; (2) Bhakti movements which attempted to *purify Hinduism* of its evils and fought against the tyranny of the caste system but subsequently crystalised as sects, such as Arya Samaj; and (3) movements oriented to opting out of the Hindu fold, conversion to other religions.

The first religious protest movements in India were Jainism and Buddhism. Jainism denied the authority of the *Vedas* and revolted against sacrifices. Buddhism also denounced Vedic sacrifices and Brahminic supremacy. *Vaishnavism* and *Shaivaism* movements, and those initiated by Kabir, Chaitanya and Nanak sought to abolish the intermediary between man and God, i.e., Brahmin.

Veerasaivism movement in Karnataka was against the practices of rigid caste system, idol worship, untouchability, etc., but it ended in religious bureaucracy and hierarchial organisation and emerged as a sect.

The Arya Samaj movement originated in Punjab mainly to counter the proselytisation attempts of Christians and Muslims. It also focused on Vedic philosophy, besides emphasising *shuddhi* (purification). Today (1999) this reconversion aspect has been taken up by RSS and *Bajrang Dal*.

Conversion movements lay stress on the following points (Oommen, 1985:91-92):

(1) Conversions, particularly to Islam and Christianity at particular historical periods, were motivated by economic and political gains.
(2) Conversions were group phenomena.
(3) Individual or family conversions, as against mass conversions, were usually confined to upper or intermediate castes.
(4) If in a region, the lower castes got converted first and experienced distinct socio-economic improvement and gained definite political advantage, this demonstrative effect, often prompted non-Brahmin castes also to get converted.
(5) Conversion of a section of a caste generated tensions among the converts and the non-converts.
(6) The strategy of conversions followed by different religious groups, differed. Muslims converted the elite first while Christian missionaries first converted the low caste people.

(7) The converted people were not treated on absolute social equality basis.
(8) Over a period of time, the intensity of conversion movements declined. Today, the emphasis is on reconversion to Hindu faith.

Backward Caste/Class Movements

These movements emerged among depressed castes and deprived sections of society in different parts of India with the spread of the national movement. The difference between the religious and the caste movement is that while the former attacked evils of Hinduism, the latter exhorted its followers to seek solutions to their problems within the framework of Hinduism, i.e., without rejecting their religion.

The backward caste/class movements can be described as: (a) protests against discrimination of various kinds, (b) to gain self-respect, honour and status, (c) status mobility movements, (d) caste unity movements and (e) caste welfare movements. The status mobility movements can be further sub-classified as adaptive movements, movements oriented to cultural revolts, and counter-cultural movements.

The backward castes suffered from relative deprivation in the fields of religion, education, economics and politics. They accepted their lot till certain external influences provided favourable conditions to create an awakening among them. One such exposition was organising of programme by Christian Missionaries for the SCs who were then referred to as the 'depressed classes'. Other condition was the national movement which provided an ideology of egalitarianism and supported social movements which revolted against discrimination of any kind. Third condition was that of reform movements organised by the upper castes which initiated programmes of education and welfare for the backward or the depressed classes. These movements were against many orthodox Brahminical practices. Finally, the egalitarian system of law introduced by the British also provided an opportunity to the backward castes to protest against discrimination. The backward caste movements for higher status were based on three ideologies (Rao, 1953:197-98) First, many castes claimed a higher varna status, e.g., the Ahirs in North India, the Gopas in West Bengal, the Gaulis in Maharashtra, the Gollas in Andhra Pradesh and Karnataka and the Konars in Tamil Nadu claimed descent from the Yadu (Kshatriya) dynasty. This also included adopting the lifestyle of higher castes in their regions, what M.N. Srinivas has described the process of sanskritisation. Imtiaz Ahmad (1971) has said that this process of mobility should be viewed as an initiative process or as protest-oriented movement or as counter-mobilisation. The upper class invariably opposed such attempts. Besides, the desire to claim high status prompted many backward castes to form associations so that by acting as pressure groups, they could collectively impress upon the census officers to describe them as castes with higher ritual status. This mechanism of mobilising caste collectivities became significant by 1931. Other method was reinterpreting Hindu religion in search of self-determination, e.g., Sri Narayana Dharma Paripalana Movement among the Ezhavas (toddy tappers) of Kerala. Ezhavas of Kerala took an overt anti-Brahmin slant and resorted to mass mobilisation and protest to acquire their rights. Second variety of protest ideology was the rejection of Brahminical Aryan religion and culture, e.g., Dravida Kazhagam Movement in Tamil Nadu. Third ideology was abandoning Hinduism and embracing another religion, e.g., Mahars in Maharashtra.

Nadars of Tamil Nadu used political process of influence to achieve high status, while Malis of Maharashtra used cultural revolt process. According to Oommen, what is important to note is that (a) ritually castes were not at the rock bottom, (b) economically they were well off by local standards, (c) their numerical strength was substantial, and (d) they had the support of rulers in their regions, like Maharaja of Kolhapur in Maharashtra. Occupational diversification, exposure to education, urbanisation, outstanding and charismatic leadership were other factors which helped them in their mobility movements. Of course, many castes did not succeed in achieving higher status within the Hindu fold which prompted them to embrace Buddhism.

The counter-cultural movements referred to (a) developing a counter-culture against caste Hindus, particularly Brahminical supremacy, but remaining within the Hindu fold. This process was adopted by *Dravidian movement* of Tamil Nadu, and (b) building a new parallel culture of their own rather than getting themselves absorbed in the 'mainstream' culture, or merely protesting against it. The Dalit Panther movement of Maharashtra exemplified this trend. The Dravidian movement in the South developed in two phases: anti-Brahmin (caste) phase and anti-north (region) phase. In the first phase, the Dravidians identified Brahmins as aliens (Aryans) and intruders into Dravidnad. They also ridiculed the Brahmin-created *puranas* and *varnashram dharma* as irrational. They created a counter-culture which was Dravidian in nature, by denouncing Brahmanicial practices of idol worship, child marriage and enforced widowhood. Gradually, this (Dravidian) movement shifted its goal from anti-Brahminism to North Indian domination with the goal of estabilishing a sovereign Dravidian State.

While the Dravidian movement was confined to Tamil Nadu, Dalit

Panthers movement spread from urban Maharashtra to other states. Its main emphasis was on intellectual awakening and creating consciousness among the oppressed.

The movement of Mahars in Maharashtra is also worth mentioning here. First, they used counter-cultural strategy of abandoning Hinduism altogether, but, later on, they adopted new political strategy for their up-lift.

Though the movements of backward castes succeeded in achieving their goals only partially, yet they provided a model to higher castes of forming associations for their mobilisational activities. But the associations of forward castes were mainly reform-oriented, opposing child marriage, encouraging widow remarriage, women's education, occupational diversification, education, and breaking social barriers between numerous castes.

Government's policy of protective discrimination for the backward castes prompted them to fight for their interests and welfare by organising themselves politically instead of issuing census appeals, sanskritisation, cultural revolts, or the building of counter-cultures. This political strategy aimed at getting themselves enlisted as SCs and OBCs, getting the time-period of reservation extended and insisting on faithful implementation of government policies and programmes. After the implementation of Mandal Commission's recommendations in August 1990 and the establishment of the Minority Commissions in various states, large number of castes are trying for recognition as OBCs and getting the reserved quota (15% for SCs and 27% for OBCs) seats filled up fully in all A, B, C, and D categories of government jobs.

Women's Movements

The status of women has been the central concern of many reform movements before and after independence. Leaders of the Brahmo Samaj and the Arya Samaj were concerned with issues like *sati*, remarriage, divorce, female education, *purdah* system, polygamy, and dowry. Justice Ranade criticised child marriages, polygyny, restrictions on remarriage of widows, and non-access to education. Raja Ram Mohan Roy played an important role in getting the *sati* system abolished. Ishwar Chandra Vidyasagar and Maharishi Karve pleaded for remarriage of widows. Gandhiji took interest in collective mobilisation of women to fight for political freedom as well as for their social and political rights.

Some scholars have examined the role of women in political independence movements at micro level, i.e., on regional basis. For example, Aparna Basu (1984) and Pravin Sheth (1979) studied it in Gujarat,

Raghavendra Rao (1983) in Karnataka, and Uma Rao (1984) in Uttar Pradesh. According to Govind Kelkar (1984), women's role in the freedom movement was that of the 'helpers' rather than that of comrades.

Ghanshyam Shah (*Ibid* 1998:136) has referred to some scholars who have pointed out women's role in tribal, peasant and other movements in Bihar and Maharashtra. For example, Manoshi Mitra (1984) and Indra Munshi Saldanha (1986) have analysed women's militant role in tribal movements when women confronted authorities, wielding traditional weapons and maintaining lines of supplies to the rebels in their hidden places. Sunil Sen (1984), Peter Custers (1987), etc., have analysed their role in peasants' movements in Telengana, West Bengal and Maharashtra. Meera Velayudhan (1984) has analysed their role in communist-led movement of coir workers in Kerala. Sen has pointed out women's participation in struggles launched by trade unions in iron ore mines in Madhya Pradesh.

It may be said that women's participation in movements has been in four major forms: (i) for social, economic and political rights of specific categories of people like tribals, peasants and industrial workers, (ii) for improvement in conditions of work and autonomy to women, (iii) for equal remuneration for work, (iv) in general social movements on issues affecting men and children like abortions, adoption of children, sexual exploitation, etc.

The liberal egalitarian ideology under the British Raj created conditions for a social awakening among Indian women. Several women's associations came into existence both at regional and national levels. Banga Mahila Samaj and the Ladies Theosophical Society functioned at local levels to promote modern ideals for women. The important national organisations were: Bharat Mahila Parishad (1904), Bharat Stri Mahamandal (1909), Women's Indian Association (1917), National Council of Women in India (1925) and All India Women's Conference (1927) and Kasturba Gandhi National Memorial Trust. These organisations took up issues like women's education, abolition of evil social customs (*purdah*, child marriage) equality of rights and opportunities and women's sufferage. Some women leaders with the support of the Congress party, demanded right of franchise and representation in legislatures. It could be said that Indian women's movements worked for two goals: one, liberation or uplift of women, i.e., reforming social practices so as to enable women to play a more important and constructive role in society; and two, equal rights for men and women, i.e., extension of civil rights enjoyed by men in the political, economic and familial spheres to women also. Jana Everett (1979) calls the former as 'corporate feminism' and the latter as 'liberal feminism'. The strategies used by women's bodies were: making demands by organising public meetings, presenting views to government officials, forming committees to investigate conditions and holding conferences to mobilise women.

The factors that provided the required incentive to women's movements were: effect of western education on the male domination on women and on the concept of complementary sex roles, leadership provided by educated elite women, interest of male social reformers in changing social practices sanctioned by religion, changing socio-religious attitudes and philosophies, and decreasing social hostility and opposition of males to women's associations engaged in self-help activities, and benevolent attitude of political national leaders towards fledgling women's movements and their enthusiastic support to women campaigns. The declaring of 1975-85 decade as the International Women's decade also gave impetus to women's movements for removing the notion of inferiority of women and giving them a sense of identity. The Central Social Welfare Board (CSWB) established by the Government of India in 1953, also promotes and strengthens voluntary efforts for the welfare of women. The Ministry of Welfare, Government of India, too gives grants to voluntary organisations for activities like construction/expansion of hostels for working women in cities.

We may now conclude our discussion on social movements by stating that social movements in India mainly focused either (a) on achieving system stability by arresting the onsluaght of rapid social change and reinforcing the existing values and norms and (b) attempting system change through the destruction and replacement of the old and induction of new structures. It can be averred that social movements were either change-resisting or change-promoting, i.e., those which aimed at the participants' deprivation and concerned with their welfare and uplift. We concentrated on those reform movements which pursued their goals through institutionalised means, without unleashing violence and were initiated by some ideological groups through mobilisation process. The analysis of six types of movements suggests that movements are generally initiated and spread by charismatic leaders or by political parties and religious organisations. In the former case, the ideologies are transmitted *downwards* while in the latter case, these are transmitted *upwards*. Once any movement based on certain ideology changes, it is not necessary that it will spread in course of time. It can gain in strength and it can also lose its vitality either because it is considered irrelevant or because it is suppressed by the government. Other thing which emereges from the analysis is that (i) social movements are products of a social structure and emerge out of certain conditions in the social structure, (ii) social movements themselves have a structure which makes them functional relative to their goals, and (iii) social movements have consequences for the social structure of which they are the products (Mukherji in Rao, 1978:18).

PROCESSES OF SOCIAL CHANGE

The Concept of Sanskritisation

The concepts of sanskritisation and westernisation were developed by M.N. Srinivas in 1952. Srinivas had defined 'sanskritisation' as a process by which low castes take over the beliefs, rituals, lifestyle, and other cultural traits of those of the upper castes, especially the Brahmins. In fact, Srinivas had broadened his definition of sanskritisation from time to time. Initially, he had described it as "the process of mobility of lower castes by adopting vegetarianism and teetotalism to move in the caste hierarchy in a generation or two (1962:42). Later on, he redefined it as "a process by which a low caste or a tribe or other groups change their customs, rituals, ideology, and way of life in the direction of a high twice-born caste" (1966:6). The second connotation of sanskritisation is thus much broader because first Srinivas talked of imitation of mere food habits, rituals and religious practices but later on he talked of imitation of ideologies too (which include ideas of *karma, dharma, pap, punya, moksha*, etc.)

In the process of imitation of customs and habits of high castes or Brahmins by the low castes, sometimes even when the low castes followed some such practices which according to the present rational standards are considered to be good and functional, they discard such customs and in their place adopt those ideas and values of Brahmins which according to the present standards are considered degrading and dysfunctional. Srinivas has given some such examples from his study in Mysore. Low castes are liberal in the spheres of marriage, sex, and attitudes towards women. They permit divorce, widow remarriage and insist on post-puberty marriage. But Brahmins practise pre-puberty marriage, regard marriage indissoluble, prevent widow from remarrying and expect her to shave her head and shed all jewellery and ostentation in clothes. They prefer virginity in brides, chastity in wives, and continence and self-restraint in widows. But as a low caste rises in hierarchy and its ways become more sanskritised, it adopts the sex and marriage code of Brahmins. Sanskritisation results in harshness towards women. Let us take a few other examples of irrational practice adopted on sanskritisation: A high caste Hindu wife is expected to treat her husband as a deity. She is expected to take her meal only after the husband has taken it and perform a number of *vratas* (religious fasts) to secure long life for her husband, regard the importance of having sons a religious necessity, and so forth. Sanskritisation involved taking up all such beliefs and practices by the lower castes. These examples thus point out that sanskritisation is nothing but a blind and irrational imitation of the customs, practices, habits and values of higher castes, especially Brahmins.

Could it be said that the process of de-sanskritisation is also possible? Srinivas has said that "it is not inconceivable that occasionally the de-sanskritisation of the imitating castes may take place" (1985:62).

Features of Sanskritisation

A few facts are worth noting in the process of sanskritisation:

(1) The concept of sanskritsation has been integrated with economic and political domination, that is, the role of local 'dominant caste' in the process of cultural transmission has been stressed. Though for some time, the lower castes imitated Brahmins but soon the local dominant caste came to be imitated. And the locally dominant caste was often a non-Brahmin caste.

(2) Sanskritisation occurred sooner or later in those castes which enjoyed political and economic power but were not rated high in ritual ranking, that is, there was a gap between their ritual and politico-economic positions.

(3) Economic betterment is not a necessary pre-condition to sanskritisation, nor economic development must necessarily lead to sanskritisation. However, sometimes a group (caste, tribe) may start by acquiring political power and this may lead to economic betterment and sanskritsation.

(4) Sanskritisation is a two-way process. Not only a caste 'took' from the caste higher to it but in turn it 'gave' something to the caste. We find Brahmins worshipping local deities which preside over epidemics, cattle, children's lives, and crops, besides the great gods of all India Hinduism.

(5) Unit of mobility is group and not individual or family.

(6) The British rule provided impetus to the process of sanskritisation but political independence has weakened the trend towards this change. The emphasis is now on vertical mobility and not on horizontal mobility.

(7) Describing social change in India in terms of sanskritisation and westernisation is to describe it primarily in cultural and not in structural

terms. Srinivas himself has conceded (1989:55) that sanskritisation involves 'positional change' in the caste system without any structural change.

(8) Sanskritisation does not automatically result in the achievement of a higher status for the group. The group must be content to wait for an indefinite period and during this period it must maintain continuous pressure regarding its claim. A generation or two must pass usually before a claim begins to be accepted. In many cases, the claim of the caste may not be accepted even after a long time. Further, it is likely that a claim which may not succeed in a particular area or period of time may succeed in another.

The fact that sanskritisation may not help a lower caste to move up does not prevent it from discarding the consumption of beef, changing polluting occupation, stopping drinking alcohol, and adopting some sanskritic customs, beliefs and deities. Thus, the process of sanskritisation may remain popular without achieving the goal of mobility.

Factors Promoting Sanskritisation

Factors that have made sanskritisation possible are industrialisation, occupational mobility, developed communication, spread of literacy, and western technology. The development of communications carried sanskritisation to areas previously inaccessible and the spread of literacy carried it to groups very low in the caste hierarchy. M.N. Srinivas has specifically referred to one factor which has helped the spread of sanskritisation among the low castes. It is the separation of ritual acts from the accompanying *mantras* (citations) which facilitated the spread of Brahminical rituals among all Hindu castes, including the untouchables. The restrictions imposed by Brahmins on the non-twice-born castes banned only the chanting of *mantras* from the Vedas. Thus, the low caste people could adopt social practices of the Brahmins. This made sanskritisation feasible.

The political institution of parliamentary democracy has also contributed to the increased sanskritisation, according to Srinivas (1985:49). Prohibition, a sanskritic value, has been mentioned in the Constitution of India. Some states have introduced it wholly or partially.

The Concept of Westernisation

This concept refers to 'the changes in technology, institutions, ideology and values of a non-western society as a result of cultural contact with the western society for a long period' (Srinivas, 1962:55). Let us take the example of Indian society: technological changes, establishment of educational institutions, rise of nationalism and new political culture, etc., may all be described as the bye-products of westernisation or of the British rule of two hundred years in India. Thus, by westernisation, Srinivas primarily meant the British impact.

The important features of westernisation are: (1) Emphasis on technology and rationalism. (2) This process (of westernisation) is not retarded by the process of sanskritisation, but to some extent it is accelerated by it. Srinivas had earlier maintained that sanskritisation is a prelude to westernisation. However, later on, he changed his view and maintained that it is not necessary for sanskritisation occurring prior to westernisation (1985:60). But the two processes are linked with each other. It may not be possible to understand one without the other. Harold Gould has also said that for Brahmins and other higher castes, sanskritising is an attempt to maintain distance between them and the lower castes who are sanskritising. Thus, Brahmins are, in a sense, running away from the lower groups who are trying to catch up with them.

The form and pace of westernisation of India varied from region to region and from one section of population to another (Srinivas, 1985:51). For instance, one group of people became westernised in their dress, diet, manners, speech, sports, and in the gadgets they used while another absorbed western science, knowledge and literature, remaining relatively free from westernisation in externals. For example, Brahmins accepted the dress and appearance (tuff giving way to cropped hair), sending their children to westernised schools, using gadgets like radio, car, etc., but they did not accept the British diet, dancing, hunting, and freedom from pollution. This distinction is, however, only of relative emphasis. It is not a clear-cut distinction.

Srinivas prefers the term 'westernisation' to 'modernisation' (whereas Daniel Lerner, Harold Gould, Milton Singer, and Yogendra Singh prefer 'modernisation' to 'westernisation'). He considers the latter term as subjective and the former term as more objective (*Seminar*, 88, 1986:2). The so-called 'rationality of goals' in modernisation could not be taken for granted because human goals are based on value preferences. As such, rationality could only be predicted of the means and not of the ends of social action.

Scholars' Support to the Concepts

Scholars like Bernard Cohn and Milton Singer have supported the validity of the concept of sanskritisation on the basis of their empirical studies. Cohn studied a village in eastern Uttar Pradesh in the 1950s. This village consisted of two main castes—a dominant caste of Thakurs and a large untouchable caste of Chamars. The landless Chamars tended to become sanskritised by adopting their landlord's (Thakur's) rituals at times of marriage and birth through education obtained in the local schools and through rise in their income. On the other hand, many Thakurs migrated to cities and became industrial workers, clerks and teachers, taking on in their dress and manner and in their religious outlook, what may be called a more westernised form of Hinduism. Thus, while upper caste was westernising its style of life and religious beliefs, the lower caste was sanskritising and assuming more traditional forms of ritual, practice and belief.

Singer (1967:66) on the basis of his study of leading industry in the city of Madras found a different process of change (what he calls 'compartmentalisation') in the style of life and religious beliefs of lower and upper castes (as different from Srinivas's process of sanskritisation and westernisation). He found that there was a decline of fear of ritual pollution both in the office and factory. For example, different castes mixed freely in the factories, they ate at the same cafeterias, travelled in the same buses, and attended political rallies freely with one another. Brahmins and upper castes had even taken to work considered highly polluting, for example, the tanning of skins and hides. Singer called it the process of 'compartmentalisation'. There was no conflict in the work of upper castes in industry and their obligations as good Hindus. The two (factory situation and home situation) were separate spheres and had different standards of conduct and behaviour. For example, they used western dress, spoke English, and followed western customs in the factory, while at home they used Indian dress, spoke the local language and conducted themselves as good Hindus. This is what Singer called 'compartmentalisation'.

But Singer's view does not give any new explanation. That individual's behaviour varies from situation to situation is a known fact. This does not mean that there is compartmentalisation. In fact, there is a continuity. Even Cohn feels that compartmentalisation in Indian society is not different from continuity in society. However, it can be conceded that in the Indian continuity, there is conservative persistence of tradition. It is an active, dynamic continuity. And Singer accepts this fact (1967:68). People adapt to new conditions.

Perception of the Concepts

The process of sanskritisation indicates:

(a) a process of change;

(b) upward mobility or aspirations of lower castes to move upward in hierarchy; and

(c) attack on hierarchy and levelling of culture.

As regards attack on hierarchy, it is not only the lower castes but even the tribes and castes in the middle regions of the hierarchy which try to take over the customs and way of life of the higher castes. Thus, Brahminical customs and way of life spread among all Hindus. Could this be called attack on hierarchy and levelling of culture? Gould (1961:965) has described it not as a process of cultural imitation *per se* but an expression of challenge and revolt against the socio-economic deprivations. Some scholars hold that it was an attack on hierarchy but it did not succeed in levelling of culture.

As regards upward mobility, Yogendra Singh calls it 'contextual specific' connotation of sanskritisation. This is because it explains the process of cultural imitation by lower castes of upper castes, which could be Rajputs, Jats, Brahmins, etc. In some places, tribes are reported to imitate the customs of caste Hindus.

Lastly, as regards merely 'the process of change', Yogendra Singh calls it 'historical specific' connotation of sanskritisation. In this sense, it refers to the process in the Indian history which led to changes in the status of various castes or their cultural patterns in different periods of history. It is also indicative of an endogenous source of social change.

Usefulness of the Concepts in Understanding Social Change

The usefulness of the concept of sanskritisation as a tool in the analysis of Indian society has been described by Srinivas himself as "greatly limited because of the complexity of the concept as well as its looseness" (1985:44). We may also point out certain deficiencies in the concept:

(1) Since the reference group is not always a Brahmin caste but in many cases it is the local 'dominant caste' (which could be Rajput, Bania, Jat, etc.), the context of sanskritisation varies not only in each model (that is Brahmin model, Rajput model, Bania model, etc.) but also within the same model from region to region. According to Yogendra Singh (1973:8), this introduces contradictions in various 'contextual specific' connotations of sanskritisation.

(2) Power and dominance have been integrated by Srinivas with the process of sanskritisation. This introduces structural element in the sanskritisation model of social change. Srinivas has not made this explicit. He has maintained that many lower castes in the past ascended to higher positions and became dominant castes either through royal decrees or through usurping power. This means that without going through the process of sanskritisation too, lower castes can rise in the

social scale through structural changes, that is, through conflicts and war, through rise and fall of power, or through political stratagems.

(3) The concepts of sanskritisation and westernisation primarily analyse social change in cultural and not in structural terms. Sanskritisation involves 'positional change' in the caste system without any structural modification.

(4) Zetterberg (1965:40) is of the opinion that Srinivas's two concepts are 'truth asserting' concepts. This connotation is often vague. Srinivas himself has said that sanskritisation is an extremely complex and heterogeneous concept. It would be more profitable to treat it as a bundle of concepts than as a single concept. It is only a name for a widespread cultural process.

(5) Srinivas's model explains the process of social change only in India which is based on the caste system. It is not useful for other societies.

(6) These concepts do not lead to a consistent theory of cultural change. Even their nominal definitions are devoid of theory. Zetterberg (1965:40) has said that these two concepts can be appropriate or inappropriate, effective or worthless, but never false or true.

(7) Harper treats this concept as a functional concept distinct from a *historical* concept of change.

(8) Yogendra Singh maintains (1973:11) that sanskritisation fails to account for many aspects of cultural changes in the past and contemporary India as it neglects the non-sanskritic traditions, which often are a localised form of sanskritic tradition. McKim Marriott (1955:196-97) also found similar phenomenon in his study of a village community in India.

(9) In some parts of the country (like Punjab and former Sind), what was imitated by castes was not sanskritic tradition but Islamic tradition. In Punjab, Sikkhism emerged as synthesis of the Hindu tradition with the Islamic movements of Sufism and mysticism.

All this points out that the two concepts developed by Srinivas indicate only limited and not complete change in India.

Impact of West on Social Change

The impact of the West on India, following Alatas (1972:121), can be discussed in five phases. The first phase is that of hostile contact with the conquest of Alexander, etc., followed by contact of peaceful interchange as the result of trade and commerce of successive centuries. The second phase began by the end of the fifteenth century when Vasco de Gama arrived with his ships at Calicut in 1498 A.D. Within a few years, the Portuguese occupied Goa. But the effect of these westerners was relatively restricted. The third phase began when East India Company established its rule in the beginning of the eighteenth century and later on the British rule was established in the country by the middle of the eighteenth century. This was the most important step in the expansion of western culture in India. The fourth phase commenced with the beginning of the nineteenth century following the industrial revolution. With the economic exploitation of India by the British as source of raw materials, began the spread and dominance of western culture in social and cultural fields too. The fifth and the last phase began after the political independence of the country in 1947.

What has been the impact of the western culture on our society in terms of effect on our culture and our social system? The impact may be briefly described as follows:

(1) Western institutions like banking system, public administration, military organisation, modern medicine, law, etc., were introduced in our country.
(2) Western education broadened the outlook of people who started talking of their rights and freedom. The introduction of the new values, the rational and secular spirit, and the ideologies of individualism, equality and justice assumed great importance.
(3) Acceptance of scientific innovations increased the aspirations of people for a higher standard of living and for providing them material welfare.
(4) Many reform movements came into being. Several traditional beliefs and practices dysfunctional to society were discarded and many new behaviour patterns were imbibed.
(5) Our technology, agriculture, entrepreneurship and industry were modernised leading to the economic well-being of our country.
(6) The hierarchy of political values has been restricted. Accepting the democratic form of government, all native states which had been under a monarchic form of government have been merged into the Indian State and the authority and domination of feudals and zamindars have been abolished.
(7) There have been structural changes in social institutions like marriage, family and caste, creating new forms of relations in social life, religion, etc.
(8) The introduction of the modern means of communication, such as the railways, bus travel, postal services, air and sea travel, the press, and the radio and television have affected man's life in various respects.
(9) There is rise in the feeling of nationalism.

(10) The emergence of a vibrant middle class has changed the dominant values of society.

The impact of western culture has also been described in terms of four types of changes in our culture and social system: eliminative changes, additive changes, supportive changes and synthetic changes. The *eliminative* changes are those which cause the disappearance of culture traits, behaviour patterns, values, beliefs, institutions, etc. As an illustration, we can cite the example of total change in weapons used in fighting wars, abolition of *sati*, and so forth. The *additive* changes refer to the adoption of new culture traits, institutions, behaviour patterns and belief systems covering diverse aspects of life. These additions were not present earlier in the culture of people. Introducing divorce in the Hindu society, giving share to daughters in father's property, introducing election system in panchayats, etc., are a few examples of this type of change., The *supportive* changes are those which strengthen the values, beliefs or behaviour patterns present in society before contact with the West. A simple example of this change is the use of 'Hundi' system in loan transactions. The *synthetic* changes result in the creation of new forms from existing elements plus adopted ones. The most simple instance is the creation of residentially nuclear but functionally joint family which continues to fulfill social obligations to parents and siblings. Continuing dowry system but putting restrictions on amount to be given or taken, and associating children along with parents in mate selection are two other examples of synthetic change.

This categorisation of changes due to western impact is only for analytical purposes. In practice, it is not possible to isolate them from each other. Within one type of change, we may find elements of other types of changes too. For example, the introduction of the textile industry within itself contains a supportive element in the sense that it facilitates the production of cloth. But at the same time, as it pushed back the traditional handloom and weaving industry, it may be said to have an element of eliminative change. The opening of wall-less prisons in the prison system is another example having elements of three different types. So are the changes in the education system, banking system, family system, marriage system, and so forth.

The main question now is: Where has India reached after contact with the West? Has India progressed? Has it contributed to the welfare of the people? Is it possible to answer this question objectively? Can subjectivism and philosophical partiality be avoided in such analysis? Some intellectuals feel that India faced a number of problems at the end of the Second World War, like the problems of economic backwardness and a large number of people living below the poverty line, unemployment, predominance of religion in all walks of life, rural indebtedness, caste conflicts, communal disharmony, shortage of capital, lack of trained personnel with technical skills, imperfect means for mobilising human and material resources, and so forth. The western impact has provided alternative solutions to handle these problems. But other scholars hold that western impact has not helped India much in facing the problems. If some problems have been solved, many other new problems have been created. And India is not trying to meet them through western models. It is using its indigeneous elements in its approach. It was only after the independence of the country that there was a rise in industrial development, dissemination of education, rural development, control over population, and so forth. It was thus independence from western rule rather than contact with the West that made modernisation possible.

The fact is that in certain areas of life, we may be justified in acclaiming the positive impact of the West. Modern medical science, modern technology, modern methods of combating natural catastrophies, modern methods of providing security against external dangers to the country receptiveness to modern ideas of secularism and individualism, and freedom from superstition, religious rites and evil social practices, etc., will go down in Indian history as the incontestable contributions of the West. But India is using at the same time its traditional institutions, beliefs and practices for the uplift of the masses. Thus, even after India's contact with the West, and after the modernisation of various systems, India will remain India. Indian culture will subsist and survive in the years to come.

MODERNISATION: CONCEPT, INDICATORS, NATURE AND PROBLEMS

Concepts of Modernity and Postmodernity

Tradition is a set of social practices which seek to inculcate certain behavioural norms and values implying continuity with the past, and usually associated with widely accepted rituals and other forms of symbolic behaviour. *Modernity* represents substantial break with traditional society. Stuart (1997:40) has referred to five distinctive characteristics of modernity: emphasis on reason, belief in progress, control over nature and environment, (intellectual characteristic), dominance of secular authority and the marginalisation of religious influence from state/political matters (political characteristic), economy in which money system provided the medium for exchange (economic characteristic), decline of religion and the rise of a secular materialist culture (religious characteristic) and decline of traditional social order and the development of new division of labour and the emergence of new classes (social characteristic). Thus, modernity refers to cluster of new social, economic, political, religious and intellectual system, which is totally different from traditional system. However, though transformation from tradition to modernity is powerful, yet it is not complete, i.e., traditional attitudes and behaviour survive. According to Anthony Giddens, three important characteristics of modernity are: industrialisation, capitalism (production of commodities, using wage labour for the competitive market) and surveillance (capacity of state and other organisations to control individuals and groups) (see O'Donnel, 1997:41).

It may be averred that modernity emphasises: rise of science, reason, and belief in progress. Those dealing with modernity perceive scientists as objective experts, science as seeking to discover the laws of the universe, human beings as capable of acquiring great control over nature and the environment, and reason as ability to improve the human condition, i.e., to achieve progress.

The term *postmodernity* or late modernity came to be used when modern society became critically aware of the consequences of modernity, particularly the negative ones. Anthony Giddens prefers to call 'postmodernity' as 'reflexivity' (greater critical awareness or 'reflexive modernisation) as it (new stage) stresses the *unintended* destructive or damaging consequences of modernity (e.g., of industry on environment). Pollution, proliferation of nuclear weapons of 'mass destruction' are examples of unintended high risk consequences of modernity. The difference between modernity and postmodernity is that (i) the former is concerned with belief in science/reason while the latter is concerned about highly damaging effects of applied science on environment, humanity and nature, (ii) the former believes in social progress but the latter focuses on growing awareness of the risks and destructive consequences of the pursuit of progress (e.g., car pollution, accidents), (iii) the former perceives nation state as the boundary of 'society' but the latter refers to the process of globalisation, (iv) the former emphasises economic development but the latter increasing importance of cultural development and, (v) the former tends to see the world in terms of dualisms or opposites (e.g., males/females, objective/subjective) but the latter tends to see similarities and unities in seeming opposites (e.g., subjective and objective) (O' Donnell, 1997: 43).

Characteristics of Modernisation

Karl Deutsch (see Donnell, *Ibid*: 494-95) referring to one aspect of modernisation (that is, socio-demographic aspect, or what he calls 'social mobilisation') has indicated some of its indices: exposure to modern life through machinery, response to mass media, urbanisation, change from agricultural occupations, literacy, and growth of per capita income. According to Eisenstadt (1969:32), some of the indices pertaining to the structural aspects of social organisation (or modernisation) are: specialised roles are 'free-floating' (that is, admission to them is not determined by ascribed properties of the individual), and wealth and power are not ascriptively allocated (as in traditional societies).This is associated with institutions like markets (In economic life) and voting and party activities in politics.

Moore (1961:57-82) has suggested that a modern society has specific economic, political and cultural characteristics. In the economic sphere, modern society is characterised by: (a) the development of a very high level of technology, fostered by the systematic application of knowledge, the pursuit of which became the province of the secondary (industrial, commercial) and tertiary (service) occupations, as against the primary (agricultural) ones; (b) growing specialisation of economic roles; and (c) the growth of the scope and complexity of the major markets, the markets for goods, labour, and money.

In the political sphere, a modern society is in some sense democratic or at least populistic. It is characterised by: (a) the decline of traditional legitimation of the rulers with reference to powers outside their own society; (b) the establishment of some sort of ideological accountability of the rulers to the ruled, who are alleged to be the holders of potential political power; (c) growing extension of the territorial scope of power of the central, legal, administrative and political agencies of the society; (d) continual spread of potential power to wider groups in the society—ultimately to all adult citizens and to moral orders; and (e) total disappearance or weakening of ascriptive political commitment to any given ruler or group.

In the cultural sphere, a modern society is characterised by: (a) growing differentiation of the major elements of the major cultural and value systems, that is, religion, philosophy, and science; (b) the spread of literacy and secular education; (c) a more complex institutional system for the advancement of specialised roles based on intellectual disciplines; (d) expansion of the media of communication; and (e) development of a new cultural outlook, characterised by an emphasis on progress and improvement, on happiness and expression of abilities, on individuality as moral value and stress on dignity of the individual and on efficiency.

Broadly speaking, modernisation has following important characteristics: a temper of science, reason and rationalism, secularism, high aspirations and achievement orientation, overall transformation of attitudes, norms and values, investment in human resources, a growth-oriented economy, a national interest rather than kin, caste, religion, region or language-oriented interests, an open society, and a mobile personality.

Measures of Modernisation

Talking of the measures of modernisation, Rustow and Ward (1964:4) have included in modernisation such specific aspects of change as: (i) industrialisation of economy and adopting a scientific technology in industry, agriculture, dairy farming, etc., to make them highly productive; (ii) secularisation of ideas; (iii) marked increase in geographical and social mobility; (iv) spread of scientific and technical education; (v) transition from ascribed to achieved status; (vi) increase in material standards of living; (vii) high ratio of inanimate to animate energy used in the economy; (viii) high proportion of working force employed in secondary and tertiary rather than primary production (that is, manufacturing and services as opposed to agriculture and fishing); (ix) high degree of urbanisation; (x) high level of literacy; (xi) high national product per capita; (xii) free circulation of mass media; and (xiii) high expectancy of life at birth.

Prerequisites of Modernisation

Before transition from traditionalism to modernisation is made, certain prerequisites of social change and modernisation must be present in the society. These are: (i) an awareness of purpose and an eye on the future; (ii) an awareness of existence, beyond one's own world, of many other societies, (iii) a sense of urgency; (iv) availability of variety of opportunities and roles; (v) an emotional preparedness for self-imposed tasks and sacrifices; and (vi) emergence of devoted, dynamic and committed leadership (Narmadeshwar Prasad, 1970:19).

Modernisation is critical because it requires not only a relatively stable new structure but also one capable of adapting to continuously changing conditions and problems. Its success depends on the society's capacity for internal transformation.

Eisenstadt (1965:659) has maintained that modernisation requires three structural characteristics of a society: (i) (a high level of) structural differentiation, (ii) (a high level of) social mobilisation, and (iii) a relatively centralised and autonomous institutional framework.

All societies do not accept the process of modernisation uniformly. Following Herbert Blumer (1964:129), five different ways may be pointed out in which a traditional society can respond to the process of modernisation. These are:

Rejective Response

A traditional society may reject modernisation. This may occur at different points in different ways. Powerful groups, landed aristocracy, a government oligarchy, a union of workers, and religious fanatics may discourage modernisation to protect their vested interests. Social prejudices, special interests and firm attachment to given forms of traditional life, beliefs and customs may lead certain sets of people to reject the process of modernisation and maintain the traditional order.

Disjunctive Response

This response of conjunction between the old and the new or the co-existence of traditionalism and modernity occurs when the modernisation process operates as detached development, without affecting much the traditionbal life. In this way, there is no conflict between modernisation and the traditional order, because the older system is not threatened.Features of modernisation exist alongside the traditional life.

Assimilative Response

This response consists of absorption of modernisation process by the traditional order without disruption of its own organisation and pattern of life. An example is the acceptance of computer ideology by employees in the banking system, or use of fertilisers and tractors by the peasants in villages. In both cases, modernisation process comes to be woven into the traditional order without endangering or affecting the basic characteristics of the traditional order.

Supportive Response

This response takes the form of accepting new and modern things because they strengthen or reinforce the traditional order. For example, accepting modernisation process in the police or military systems because it increases the efficiency of the police or the power of the military. Different traditional groups and institutions use an opportunity presented by modernisation to pursue more effectively traditional interests and to maintain traditional positions more firmly. Modernisation may provide resources and facilities to further traditional interest.

Disruptive Response

In this response, the traditional order is undermined at many points by the adjustments which are made to the situation introduced by modernisation.

Usually, all five of these responses take place at different points of the traditional order and in different combinations. The responses are governed by preferences, interests, and values.

According to Myron Weiner (1966:8), the main instruments which make modernisation possible are:

Education

It inculcates a sense of national loyalty and creates skills and attitudes essential for technological innovation. Shils has also emphasised the role of education in the process of modernisation. Arnold Anderson, however, maintains that formal education is not adequate for teaching skills. Sometimes, university education may be a waste, for it increases the number of students with degrees without an increase in the number of people with modern skills and attitudes.

Communication

The development of mass communications (including telephone, TV, radio. movies, etc.) is an important means of spreading modern ideas at a faster rate. The only danger is that if these are controlled by the government, they will spread only one type of ideological thought. In democracies, however, the press is often independent to express its views.

Ideology Based on Nationalism

Nationalist ideologies serve as unifying influence in bridging social cleavages within plural societies. They also help the political elite in changing the behaviour of masses of people. Binder, however, has pointed out that the elite may have modern ideology but it is not necessary that it may facilitate development also.

Charismatic Leadership

A charismatic leader is in a better position to persuade people to adopt modern beliefs, practices and behaviour patterns because of the respect and loyalty he commands. The danger is that the charismatic leader might use modern values and attitudes as an instrument for personal glorification rather than national development.

Coercive Governmental Authority

If the government authority is weak, it may not succeed in implementing policies aimed at the modernisation process, but if the government is strong, it may even adopt coercive measures to compel people to accept attitudes and behaviour patterns which aim at development. Myron Weiner is, however, of the opinion that nationalism, under the aegis of an authoritarian regime, may lead a country into suicidal expansion abroad rather than development at home. In this connection, the example has been cited of the policies of the Bush regime (in America) and political elite in countries like Iraq, etc. After Russia lost its supremacy, America's governmental authority has started coercing nations in the name of the process of modernising the under-developed and the developing countries. The most recent example is of America pressurising India on many issues.

Myron Weiner (1966:9-10) has also talked of opportunities and incentives along with value and attitude changes for the modernisation of a society. Many economists have supported this viewpoint. They point to the existence of institutional impediments to productive activities that retard the rate of investment. A few examples of such institutional impediments are land tenure systems that deny peasants the gain from increasing productivity, taxes that slow the flow of goods from one part of the country to another, and elaborate bureaucratic regulations.

Problems of Modernisation

The following are some of the problems of modernisation:

(1) The first paradox of modernisation is that a modern society must change in all ways at once but such a regular, coordinated pattern of growth cannot be conceivably planned. A certain amount of social unrest is, therefore, inevitably created. For example, mass educational system demands that trained individuals must be absorbed in occupational roles commensurate with their training and knowledge. But it is not always possible to provide jobs to all the educated people. This leads to unrest among the educated unemployed.

(2) The social problem is that structural change is uneven during periods of modernisation. For instance, industries may be modernised but family system, religious system, etc., remain conservative. These discontinuities and patterns of change affect the established social and other structures and produce lags and bottlenecks. Another example of this in India is that decreasing the age of voting from twenty-one to eighteen years might have been a step of entering into the modern era but it has created a crisis since a mass electorate rests on the assumption of a mature and literate electorate with a sense of citizenship and an ability to participate in the policy making processes.

(3) The third problem is that modernisation of social and economic insti-

tutions creates conflicts with the traditional ways of life. For example, trained doctors pose a threat to traditional medicine men. Similarly, items produced by machinery deprive traditional workers of their means of livelihood. At the same time, many people in society with traditional and conservative values and attitudes become hostile to people who accept modern way of life. Thus, the conflict between the traditional and modern ways becomes a source of unrest.

(4) The fourth problem is that most often roles adopted by people are modern but values continue to be traditional. For example, even after taking training in medicine and surgery, a doctor tells his patient, "I treat, He cures". This indicates that he has no confidence in himself to diagnose the disease properly. But instead of blaming himself, he blames the way he is socialised to develop values in life.

(5) The fifth problem is that there is lack of co-operation among agencies which modernise, and among institutions and systems which are modernised. This many a time leads to cultural lag as well as institutional conflicts.

(6) The last problem is that modernisation raises the aspirations of people but social systems fail to provide opportunities to them to achieve their aspirations. This creates frustrations, deprivations and social unrest.

Further Readings

Asthana, Pratima, *Women's Movements in India*, Vikas, Delhi, 1974.

Beteille, Andre, *Studies in Agrarian Social Structure*, Oxford University Press, Delhi, 1974.

Desai, A.R. (ed.), *Peasant Struggles in India*, Oxford University Press, Delhi, 1983.

Dhanagare, D.N., "The Politics of Survival: Peasant Organisation and Left-Wing in India", *Sociological Bulletin*, 1975.

Dhanagare. D.N., "The Model of Agrarian Classes in India" in A.R. Desai (ed.) *Peasant Movements in India*, Oxford University Press, Delhi, 1983.

Donnell, Mike O', *Sociology*, (4th ed), Thomas Nelson, U.K., 1997.

Gurr, T.R., *Why Men Rebel*, Princeton University Press, N.J., 1970.

Hall, Stuart, *Questions of Cultural Identity*, Sage Publications, 1996.

Kothari, Rajni, "Masses, Classes and the State", *Economic and Political Weekly*, February 1, 1986.

Mukherjee, Partha, "Social Movement and Social Change: To a Conceptual Classification and Theoretical Framework", *Sociological Bulletin*, 26(1), 1977.

Mahapatra, L.K., "Social Movements Among Tribes in India", in Singh S.K. (ed.), *Tribal Situation in India*, Indian Institute of Advanced Study, Simla, 1972.

Oommen, T.K., "Social Movements" in *ICSSR Journal Sociology and Social Anthropology* (1969-1979), Satvaham Publications, New Delhi, 1985.

—, "Sociological Issues in the Analysis of Social Movements in Independent India" *Sociological Bulletin*, 26 (1), 1977.

—, *A Survey of Research on Sociology and Social Anthropology* (1969-1979), ICSSR, Vol.2, 1985.

Rao, M.S.A., *Social Movements in India* Vol I & II, Manohar Publications, New Delhi, 1978.

Shah, Ghanshyam, *Social Movements in India*, Sage Publications, Delhi, 1998.

Bibliography

Abbi, B.L., 'Urban Family in India', in *Contributions to Indian Sociology*, No. 3, 1969.

Agarwal, S.N., *India's Population*, Institute of Economic Growth, Asia Publications, Bombay, 1960.

Agarwal, U.C., 'Galloping Corruption: Need for Effective Vigilance', *The Indian Journal of Public Administration*, New Delhi, July-September, 1997.

Ahmad, Imtiaz, (ed.), *Caste and Social Stratification Among the Muslims*, Manohar Book Service, Delhi, 1973.

Ahuja, Ram, *Indian Social System*, Rawat Publications, Jaipur, 1993.

Ahuja, Ram, *Social Problems in India* (2nd ed), Rawat Publications, Jaipur, 1997.

Ahuja, Ram, *Sociological Criminology*, New Age International Publishers, Delhi, 1996.

Albatch, P.G., (eds.) *Turmoil and Transition: Higher Education and Student Politics in India*, Lalvani Publishing House, Bombay, 1968.

Almond, Gabrial and Coleman (eds.), *The Politics of Developing Areas*, Princeton University Press, Princeton, 1960.

Altekar, A.S., *The Position of Women in Hindu Civilisation*, Motilal Banarsidas, Varanasi, 1956 (first published in 1938).

Ansari, Ghans, *Muslim Castes in Uttar Pradesh: A Study of Culture Contact*, National Publishing House, Lucknow, 1960.

Asthana, Pratima, *Women's Movements in India*, Vikas Publications, Delhi, 1974.

Atal, Yogesh, *The Changing Frontiers of Caste*, National Publishing House, Delhi, 1968.

Bailey, F.G., *Caste and the Economic Frontier*, University Press, Manchester, 1957.

Bailey, F.G., *Tribe, Caste and Nation*, Oxford University Press, Bombay, 1960.

Barnabas, A.P., *Population Control in India: Policy Administration*, Indian Institute of Public Administration, Delhi, 1977.

Barnabas, A.P., 'Good Governance at Local Level', *Indian Journal of Public Administration*, July-September, Vol. XLIV, No.3, 1998.

Berreman, Gerald, D., *Caste in the Modern World*, General Learning Press, Morristown, N.Y., 1973.

Beteille, Andre, *Caste, Class and Power: Changing Patterns of Stratification in a Tanjore Village*, University of California Press, Berkeley, 1965.

Beteille, Andre, *Studies in Agrarian Social Structure*, Oxford University Press, Delhi, 1974.

Beteille, Andre, *Inequality Among Men*, Oxford University Press, Delhi, 1977.

Bose, Ashish, *From Population to People*, B.R. Publications, Delhi, 1988.

Bose, N.K., *Cultural Anthropology and Other Essays*, Asia Publishing House, Calcutta, 1953.

Chandra, Bipin, *Communalism in Modern India*, Vikas Publications, New Delhi, 1984.

Chandrasekhar, S., *India's Population: Fact and Policy*, Meenakshi Prakashan, Meerut, 1967.

Chauhan, Brij Raj, *A Rajasthan Village*, Associated Publishing House, New Delhi, 1967.

Chitnis, Suma, 'Education for Equality: The Case of Scheduled Castes in Higher Education', *Economic and Political Weekly*, Bombay,Vol. 7, 1972.

Chitnis, Suma, 'Review and Trend Report of the Sociology of Education', *A Survey of Research in Sociology and Social Anthropology, ICSSR*, Delhi, 1974 (Vol. 1) and 1980 (Vol. 1).

Chopra, O.P., 'Unaccounted Income: Some Estimates', *Economic and Political Weekly*, Vol. XVII, Nos 17 and 18, April 24 and May 1, 1982.

Choudhry, P.C., 'Corruption' in *Seminar*, No. 421, Delhi, September 1994.

Cormack, M., *She Who Rides a Peacock: Indian Students and Social Change*, Asia Publishing House, Bombay, 1961.

Dasgupta, S.N., *History of Indian Philosophy*, Kitab Mahal, Allahabad, 1969.

Davis, Kingsley, *The Population of India and Pakistan*, Princeton University Press, 1951.

Desai, I.P., *High School Students in Poona*, Decan College, Poona, 1953.

Desai, I.P., 'Joint Family in India: An Analysis', *Sociological Bulletin*, No. 5 (2), 1956.

Desai, I.P., *Some Aspects of Family in Mahuva,* Asia Publishing House, Bombay, 1964.

Desai, A.R., *Rural Sociology in India*, (Rev.ed.) The Indian Society of Agricultural Economics, Bombay, 1959.

Desai, A.R., *Peasant Struggles in India*, Oxford University Press, Delhi, 1983.

Dhanagare, D.N., 'The Politics of Survival: Peasant Organisation and Left Wing in India', *Sociological Bulletin*, 1975.

Dhanagare, D.N., 'The Model of Agrarian Classes in India' in Desai, A.R., *Peasant Movements in India*, Oxford University Press, Delhi, 1983.

Donnell, Mike O'., *Sociology* (4th ed.), Thomas Nelson, UK, 1997.

Dowse, Robert E. and Hughes, John A., *Political Sociology*, John Wiley and Sons, London, 1972.

Dube, S.C., *Tradition and Development*, Vikas Publishing House, New Delhi, 1990.

D'Souza, Victor, 'Education in Social Structure and Democracy in India', in S.P. Ruhela (ed.) *Social Determinants of Educability in India*, Jain Publications, New Delhi, 1969.

Dumont, Louis, *Homo Hierarchicus*, Chicago University Press, Chicago, 1970.

Easton, David, *The Political System*, Elfred, New York, 1953.

Eisentadt, S.N., *The Political System of Empires*, Free Press, New York, 1963.

Engineer, Asghar Ali (ed.), *Communal Riots in Post-Independent India*, Sangam Book, Delhi, 1984.

Fernandes, Walter, 'Displacement of Tribals' in George Pfeffer, *Contemporary Society: Tribal Studies*, 1997.

Fox, R.G., (ed.), *Urban India: Society, Space and Image*, Duke University, Duke, 1970.

Ganguli, B.N., *Population and Development*, S.Chand, New Delhi, 1973.

Geriant, Parry, *Political Elite*, George Allen and Unwin, London, 1969.

Gerth, H.H., and Mills, C.W., (eds.), *From Max Weber: Essays in Sociology*, Routledge and Kegan Paul, London, 1948.

Ghurye, G.S., *Caste, Class and Occupation*, Popular Book Depot., Bombay, 1961.

Gopinath, P. Krishna, 'Corruption in Political and Public Offices' in *The Indian Journal of Public Administration*, New Delhi, October-December, 1982.

Gore, M.S., *Immigrants and Neighbourhoods: Two Aspects of Life in a Metropolitan City*, Tata Institute of Social Sciences, Bombay, 1970.

Gore, M.S., *Education and Modernisation in India*, Rawat Publications, Jaipur, 1982.

Gould, Harold, *The Hindu Caste System*, Chanakya Publications, New Delhi, 1987.

Gould, Harold, *Caste Adaptation in Modernising Indian Society*, Chanakya Publications, New Delhi, 1988.

Gough, E.K., 'Caste in a Tanjore Village' in Leach (ed.), *Aspects of Caste in South India, Ceylon and North-West Pakistan*, Cambridge University Press, Cambridge, 1960.

Gupta, Dipankar, *Social Stratification*, Oxford University Press, Delhi, 1991.

Gupta, P. and Gupta, S., 'Estimates of the Unreported Economy in India', *Economic and Political Weekly*, Bombay, Vol. XVII, No. 13, January 16, 1982.

Gupta, Raghuraj, 'Caste Ranking and Inter-Caste Relations among the Muslims of the village in North-Western Uttar Pradesh, *Eastern Anthropologist*, Lucknow, 1956.

Hall, Stuart and Gay, *Questions of Cultural Identity*, Sage Publications, 1996.

Hooja, Meenakshi and Hooja Rakesh, 'Panchayati Raj in Rajasthan' *The Indian Journal of Public Administration*, Delhi, Vol. XLIV, No. 3, 1998.

Hutton, J.H., *Caste in India*, Cambridge University Press, Cambridge, 1946.

ICSSR: *A Survey of Research in Sociology and Social Anthropology*, Vols. I and II, 1974 and 1984.

Iqbal Narain, 'Reforming Educational Administration in India, *Indian Journal of Public Administration*, July-September, 1986.

Isaacs, Harold R., *India's Ex-Untouchables*, John Day, New York, 1965.

Jain, S.P., Religion and Caste Ranking in a North Indian Town, *Sociological Bulletin*, 20 (2), 1971.

Joshi, P.C., 'Students, Youths and National Development', *Yojana*, May 1967.

Kali Prasad, *Social Integration Research: A Study in Inter-Caste Relationship*, Lucknow University, Lucknow, 1954.

Kanal, S.P., *Dialogues on Indian Culture*, Panchal Press Publications, Delhi, 1955.

Kapadia, K.M., 'The Family in Transition', *Sociological Bulletin*, 8/27, 1959.

Kapadia, K.M., 'Caste in Transition', *Sociological Bulletin*, September, 1962.

Kapadia, K.M., *Marriage and Family in India*, Oxford University Press, Bombay, 1966 (first published in 1955).

Karve, Irawati, *Kinship Organisation in India*, Asia Publishing House, Bombay, 1953.

Khanna, B.S., *Panchayati Raj in India*, Deep and Deep Publications, New Delhi, 1994.

Khan, M.E., 'Muslim Society Structure in an Urban Setting', *Indian Anthropologist*, 6(1), 1976.

Kolenda Pauline, *Caste in Contemporary India*, Rawat Publications, Jaipur, 1997 (originally published in 1968).

Kothari, Devendra and Gulati, Anuja, 'Family Welfare Programme in India: A Proposal for Structural Change', *Administrative Change*, Jaipur, July 1990-June 1991.

Kothari, Rajni (ed.), *Caste in Indian Politics*, Orient Longman, Delhi, 1970 (reprinted 1973).

Leach, E.R., (ed.), *Aspects of Caste in South India, Ceylon and North-West Pakistan*, Cambridge University Press, Cambridge, 1960.

Machael, Clarke (ed.), *Corruption: Causes and Consequences*, Francecis Publishers, London, 1983.

Madan, T.N., 'On the Nature of Caste in India' in *Contributions to Indian Sociology*, Delhi, No. 5, 1971.

Mahapatra, L.K., 'Social Movements Among Tribes in India' in Singh, S.K., (ed.) *Tribal Situation in India*, Indian Institute of Advanced Study, Simla, 1972.

Mahar, J. Michael, *The Untouchables in Contemporary India*, Rawat Publications, Jaipur, 1998.

Mahajan, V.S., *Recent Developments in Indian Economy*, Deep and Deep Publications, New Delhi, 1984.

Majumdar, D.N., *The Affairs of a Tribe: A Study in Tribal Dynamics,* Universal Publishers, Lucknow, 1950.

Majumdar, D.N., *Caste and Communication in an Indian Village*, Asia Publishing House, Bombay, 1958.

Malgavkar, P.D., *Population and Development*, Centre for Policy Research, Delhi, 1980.

Malhotra, K.L., *Facets of Vigilance*, Malhotra Publications, Delhi, 1988 (and 1992).

Mandelbaum, David G., *Society in India*, (2 Vol.), University of California Press, Berkley, 1970.

Manpower Profile, India, 1998, Institute of Applied Manpower Research, 1988 (6th ed.).

Marriott, McKim, 'Social Structure and Change in a UP village' in M.N. Srinivas (ed.), *India's Villages*, Asia Publishing House, Bombay, 1955.

Marriott, McKim, *Village India: Studies in Little Community*, (ed.), University of Chicago Press, Chicago, 1955.

Mathew, George, *Panchayati Raj From Legislation to Movement*, Concept Publishing Co., 1994.

Mayer, A.C., *Caste and Kinship in Central India*, Routledge and Kegan Paul, London, 1960.

Mills, C. Wright, *The Power Elite*, Oxford University Press, N.Y.1956.

Mukherjee, Partha, 'Social Movement and Social Change: To a Conceptual Classification and Theoretical Framework', *Sociological Bulletin*, 26(1), 1977.

Mishra, S.N., Kumar Lokesh, and Pal Chaitali, *New Panchayati Raj in Action*, Mital Publications, New Delhi, 1996.

Mishra, Sweta, *Democratic Decentralisation in India*, Mittal Publications, New Delhi, 1994.

Monteria, J.B., *Corruption*, Manaktalas, Bombay, 1966.

Mukherjee, Ramkrishna, *The Dynamics of a Rural Society*, Berlin, 1957.

Mukherjee, R.K., *Glimpses of Ancient India*, Bhartiya Vidya Bhawan, Bombay, 1961.

Mukherjee, Ramkrishna, *The Sociologist and Social Change in India Today*, Prentice Hall of India, Delhi, 1965.

Muller, Max, *Vedanta Philosophy*, Calcutta, 1955.

Murty, Satchidananda K., *The Divine Peacock*, New Age International Publishers, New Delhi, 1994.

Nagpaul, Hans, *Modernisation and Urbanisation in India: Problems and Issues,* Rawat Publications, Jaipur, 1996.

Narmadeshwar, Prasad, *The Myth of the Caste System*, Patna, 1956.

Oommen, T.K., 'Social Movements' in *Survey of Research* in *Sociology and Social Anthropology, ICSSR,* (1969-1979), Satvaham Publications, New Delhi, 1985.

Oscar, Lewis, *Village Life in Northern India: Studies in a Delhi Village*, University of Illinois Press, Urbana, 1958.

Pande, Raj Bali, *The Hindu Sanskaras*, Asia Publications, Bombay, 1949.

Parvathamma, C., *The Case for Untouchables*, United Asia, 1968.

Pendse, D.R., 'Black Money: Its Nature and Causes', *The Economic Times,* March 19, 1982.

Pfeffer, George, and Behera, Deepak, *Contemporary Society: Tribal Studies*, (Vol. 1 and 2), Concept Publishing Co., New Delhi, 1997.

Prabhu, P.N., *Hindu Social Organisation*, The Popular Book Depot., Bombay, 1954.

Ramchandran, R., *Urbanisation and Urban Systems in India*, Oxford University Press, Delhi, 1998 (7th Impression).

Rao, MSA, *Social Movements in India*, (Vol. I and II), Manohar Publications, New Delhi, 1978.

Ross, Aileen, *Hindu Family in its Urban Setting*, Oxford University Press, Toronto, 1961.

Sachchidananda, *The Harijan Elite*, Thomson Press, Faridabad, 1977.

Sachchidananda, *Elite and Development*, Concept Publishing Company, New Delhi, 1980.

Santhanam Committee Report on 'Prevention of Corruption', Govt. of India, 1964.

Shah, A.M., *The Household Dimension of the Family in India*, Orient Longmans Ltd., Delhi, 1956.

Shah, B.V., *Social Change and College Students of Gujarat*, M.S. University, Baroda, 1964.

Shah, Ghanshyam, *Social Movements in India*, (4th print) Sage Publications, Delhi, 1998.

Sharma, A.N., *Bonded Labour*, Tata Institute of Social Sciences, Bombay, 1990.

Sharma, K.L., *Social Stratification in India*, Sage Publications, New Delhi, 1997.

Silverberg, James (ed.), *Social Mobility in the Caste System in India*, Monton, Hague, 1968.

Singer, Milton and Cohn, B.S., (eds.) *Structure and Change in Indian Society*, Aldine Publishing Company, Chicago, 1968.

Singh, K.S. (ed.), *Tribal Situation in India*, Indian Institute of Advanced Study, Simla, 1972.

Singh, S.S., and Misra, Suresh, *Legislative Framework of Panchayati Raj in India*, Intellectual Publishing House, Delhi, 1993.

Singh, Yogendra, *Modernisation of Indian Tradition*, Thomson Press, New Delhi, 1973.

Singh, Yogendra, *Social Stratification and Change in India*, Manohar Book Service, New Delhi, 1977.

Sinha, Surajeet, 'Caste in India' in ICSSR Report on *A Survey of Research in Sociology and Social Anthropology*, New Delhi, 1974.

Srinivas, M.N., *Religion and Society Among the Coorgs of South India*, Oxford University Press, Bombay, 1952.

Srinivas, M.N., *Caste in Modern India*, Asia Publishing House, Bombay, 1962.

Sylvia, Vatuk, *Kinship and Urbanisation: White-Collar Migrants in North India*, University of California Press, Los Angeles, 1973.

Taylor, C.C., *A Critical Analysis of India's Community*, University of Chicago Press, Chicago, 1955.

Thapar, Romila, *Seminar*, No. 313, Delhi, September, 1985.

Thorner, Daniel, *Agrarian Structure*, Allied Publishers, Delhi, 1956.

Toennies, Fardinand, *Fundamental Concepts of Sociology*, American Book Co, New York, 1940.

Varghese, K.V., *Economic Problems of Modern India*, Ashish Publishing House, New Delhi, 1985.

Wirth, Louis, *The Ghetto*, University of Chicago Press, Chicago, 1938.

Wiser, W.H., *The Hindu Jajmani System*, Lucknow Publishing House, Lucknow, 1936.

Writh, Ronald and Simpkins, Edgar, *Corruption in Developing Countries*, London, 1963.

Yojana, Special Issue on 'Could We Break Their Schackles', Vol. 31, No. 8, May 1-5, 1987.

Index